Biological Nitrogen Fixation Technology for Tropical Agriculture

Based on papers presented at a workshop held at the Centro Internacional de Agricultura Tropical March 9-13, 1981

Edited by

Peter H. Graham
Centro Internacional de Agricultura Tropical
Cali, Colombia

and

Susan C. Harris
University of Hawaii NifTAL Project
Maui, Hawaii, USA

Centro Internacional de Agricultura Tropical
AA 67-13, Cali, Colombia

Correct citation: Graham, P.H. & Harris, S.C. (Eds.) 1982. Biological Nitrogen Fixation Technology for Tropical Agriculture: Papers Presented at a Workshop Held at CIAT, March 9-13, 1981. Cali, Colombia, Centro Internacional de Agricultura Tropical, 768p.

Production: CIAT Graphic Arts
Design: Piedad Jiménez O.
Printed in the USA
Print order: 2000 copies

Centro Internacional de Agricultura Tropical, CIAT
Apartado Aéreo 6713
Cali, COLOMBIA

ISBN: 84-89206-22-8
CIAT Series No. 03E-5(82)

Keywords:

Biological nitrogen fixation; technology transfer; nitrogen; nitrogen economy; inoculant technology; nodulation; *Arachis hypogaea;* plant breeding; *Vigna unguiculata; Vicia faba; Phaseolus vulgaris; Rhizobium* spp.; salinity; water stress; micronutrients; macronutrients; soil fertility; pH values; *Vigna mungo; Cajanus cajan; Leucaena leucocephala;* antibiotic resistance; savanna; lectin recognition; ureides; ^{15}N labeling; acetylene reduction; *Azospirillum* sp.; *Glycine max; Vigna radiata; Lens esculenta;* intercropping; inoculation trials; cover crops; *Calopogonium* spp.; *Centrosema pubescens; Pueraria phaseoloides; Aeschynomene* spp.; pasture associations; *Stylosanthes* spp.; *Frankia* spp.; *Casuarina* spp.; *Sesbania rostrata;* associative nitrogen fixation; nitrogenase activity; *Paspalum notatum; Saccharum officinarum; Azolla* spp.; economic analysis; technological assessment; mycorrhiza; *Beijerinkia; Pseudomonas; Bacillus; Azotobacter.*

FOREWORD

In recent years there has been a great surge of interest and activity in the field of biological nitrogen fixation. Rightly so, since the increased cost of energy and the growing demand for nitrogen fertilizer is expected to cause dramatic increases in the price of this commodity in the years ahead. As we struggle to feed a growing and hungry world, the need for a better understanding and a fuller application of the mechanism of biological nitrogen fixation is, however, of perhaps even greater importance than is apparent from the problems of cost and supply mentioned above. Most of the food in the tropical developing countries is produced by subsistence farmers, whose resource base is so small, and whose physical access to supply markets so limited, that they cannot take full advantage of new technologies that are overly dependent on purchased inputs. Biological nitrogen fixation, used appropriately, could reduce the production constraints facing these farmers in the many nitrogen-deficient soils of the world.

The importance of this subject was illustrated by the attendance at this meeting: 178 participants from 33 countries. But this was not just another international conference on biological nitrogen fixation. As its title indicates this was a workshop — not just a presentation of formal papers, but a series of discussions on what to do with this knowledge, and how to work together in its development and application. Indeed, one of the stated objectives of the workshop was to develop cooperative links, and in this I believe it has been highly successful. Also important was the applied nature of the workshop, which has been involved with seeking technology for tropical agriculture — a task relevant to the many hungry regions of the world.

All of CIAT's programs adhere to the common philosophy of relevance, complementarity, and minimum inputs. *Relevance*, because CIAT is an institute dedicated to the generation of technology that will enhance agricultural production and productivity. *Complementarity*, because CIAT recognizes that it is only one link in the cooperative network of national programs and institutions working in the field of scientific research and agricultural development, and that it will play its part effectively only if it works in close collaboration with other institutes. *Minimum inputs* to keep the production costs of all new technology within the reach of the small and less advantaged farmers. Since these three elements of CIAT's philosophy were all central to the biological nitrogen fixation workshop, CIAT was delighted to share with the University of Hawaii NifTAL Project and ICRISAT the co-sponsorship of the workshop, and to host it.

I would like to thank the co-sponsors for this very successful cooperative effort and to record their gratitude for the cooperation received from ADAB, the Boyce Thompson Institute, Cornell University, the East-West Center, ICARDA, INTSOY, IRRI, North Carolina State University, UNESCO, University of Puerto Rico, USAID and USDA. I am sure I speak for all the cosponsors, cooperators and participants, in expressing the hope that these proceedings will stimulate greater cooperation in the application of our knowledge of nitrogen fixation to the benefit of farmers and consumers in the tropics.

JOHN L. NICKEL
Director General
CENTRO INTERNACIONAL DE AGRICULTURA TROPICAL

ACKNOWLEDGEMENTS

The workshop on which these proceedings are based was the idea of Jake Halliday, of the University of Hawaii NifTAL Project, Maui, HI 96779, USA. The organizing committee for the workshop comprised:

Jake Halliday, University of Hawaii NifTAL project, Maui, HI 96779, USA.

Peter H. Graham, Centro Internacional de Agricultura Tropical, Cali, Colombia.

Peter J. Dart, International Crops Research Institute for the Semi-Arid Tropics, Patancheru, AP 502 324, India.

in consultation with:

E.J. Da Silva, UNESCO, Paris, France
J. Döbereiner, EMBRAPA, Rio de Janeiro, Brazil
Y. Dommergues, ORSTOM, Dakar, Senegal
L.R. Frederick, USAID, Washington, D.C., USA
J.R. Jardim Freire, UFRGS/IPAGRO, Porto Alegre, Brazil
R.H. Miller, USDA, Washington, D.C., USA
E.L. Pulver, IITA, Ibadan, Nigeria
F. Riveros, FAO, Rome, Italy
T. Rosswall, SCOPE/UNEP, Stockholm, Sweden
R.J. Summerfield, University of Reading, Reading, England
I. Watanabe, IRRI, Los Baños, Philippines

SPONSORSHIP

Major financial responsibility for this workshop was borne by CIAT, NifTAL and ICRISAT.

In addition, the Australian Development Assistance Bureau (ADAB), the United Nations Educational Scientific and Cultural Organization (UNESCO), the United States Department of Agriculture (USDA), and the United States Agency for International Development (USAID) each provided substantial sponsorship.

CIAT Publication

Editing: *Peter H. Graham*
Susan C. Harris
Design: *Piedad Jiménez O.*
Production: *CIAT's Graphic Arts. Section*

TABLE OF CONTENTS

Section 10: The *Azolla/Anabaena* association

Section 11: Critique of methodologies

Section 12: General considerations

KEYNOTE ADDRESSES

BIOLOGICAL NITROGEN FIXATION—PROBLEMS AND POTENTIAL

A. App and A. Eaglesham[1]

The ultimate goal of this Workshop on Biological Nitrogen Fixation Technology for Tropical Agriculture is to increase yields in farmers' fields. We are specifically interested in increasing the supply of nitrogen (N) available for crop production in the tropics. There are three principle sources involved: N fertilizers, organic wastes and green manures, and biological N_2 fixation (BNF). How effective is each of these agents in the LDC's (less developed countries)?

Figure 1 shows the relationship between cereal production and fertilizer usage over the period from 1950-1974 and clearly indicates the value of fertilizer N for increasing crop yields (Hardy, 1975). Estimates vary as to the relative importance of N fertilizers in stimulating world cereal yields, but perhaps one-third to one-half of the increase in yields during the past thirty years can be attributed to the use of N fertilizers (Engibous, 1975; Hardy, 1975; Herdt & Barker, 1975). Roughly 20 million tons of N fertilizer, a third of the world's total consumption, is currently being utilized in the LDC's (Stangel, 1979).

Figure 2 gives a summary of world prices for fertilizer N over the past fifteen years. Note the serious increase in prices experienced during the energy crisis of 1974-1975. No one knew what the future would bring as far as N fertilizer prices were concerned, and there was genuine fear that farmers employing modern technology would soon find fertilizer prices too expensive relative to the risk and potential benefits. We now see that prices have receded, but no one knows how long this situation will exist.

It is much more difficult to document the importance of nitrogenous wastes and green manures for crop production in the LDC's. These sources have been employed in traditional agriculture for centuries, and currently are very important in the People's Republic of China. It is estimated that approximately two-thirds of the N applied to rice in the People's Republic of China is from organic wastes, green manures, composts, etc. (IRRI, 1980).

---

[1] Boyce Thompson Institute at Cornell University, Ithaca, N.Y., USA.

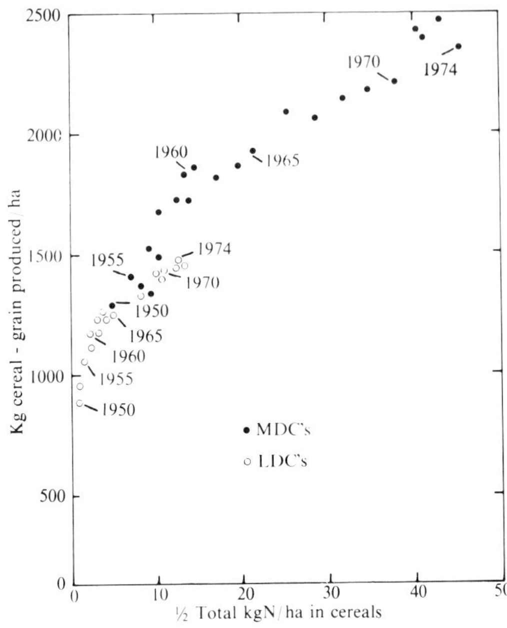

Figure 1.
Relationship between cereal grain yield and N fertilizer use rate for LDC's and MDC's during the past 25 years. Note that one-half of total N fertilizer is included since this is the approximate amount used on cereal grains (Hardy. 1975).

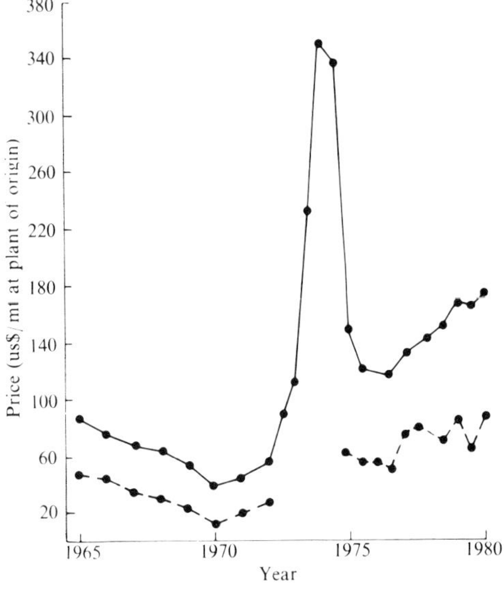

Figure 2.
International spot prices for urea (—) and $(NH_4)_2SO_4$ (- - -) in the period 1965-1980.

Sources:
1965-72 - H.R. Von Uexkull. "The present fertilizer situation in rice," paper presented at IRRI, April 1975.
1973- World Bank Fertilizer Unit as quoted in USDA, ERS.
1976- Foreign Agricultural Economics Report No. 115, February 1976, Fig. 1, p. 5.
1977-1979- FAO Food Outlook, various issues.

Table 1 contains some estimates of the amounts and types of waste available (or employed) in the People's Republic of China and in the LDC's (Stangel, 1979). The total quantity of N contained in these materials appears to be more than three times the quantity of N fertilizer used in these regions during 1980. However, it would be a serious mistake to attempt to employ these sources of N in other regions of the world without recognizing the social, cultural, and economic setting in which they are now utilized.

TABLE 1: Total annual production of N through organic wastes in developing countries (1971-1980) and used in the People's Republic of China (1976) (Stangel, 1979).

Source	People's Republic of China			Developing world[1]	
	Quantity (10^6 t)	N content (%)	Total N (10^3 t)	Total N (10^3 t)	
				1971	1980
Human waste					
Night soil (60% available N)	127	0.60	762	12,250	15,260
Animal waste					
Cattle manure (70% available N)	411	0.60	2,460	17,800	22,250
Pig manure	571	0.50	2,855		
Goat manure	65	0.60	390		
Poultry manure	23	1.46	366		
Farm compost				9,540	11,930
Plant residues	273	0.30	819		
Green manure	48	0.40	192		
Mud silt	144	0.25	360		
Urban compost				480	600
City garbage	13	0.60	78		
Urban sewage				1,430	1,790
Oil seedcakes	4	7.00	28		
Others (bonemeal, bagasse, etc.)	10	0.40	40	6,620	8,290
Total	1,689		8,320	48,120	60,120

[1]Excludes Central America and Oceania, but includes socialist Asia.

We now come to BNF, the topic of immediate concern to this workshop. We have seen that both N fertilizers and organic wastes do make an impact on crop yields, and especially on cereal yields. But the situation with BNF is not so clear. For example, can we demonstrate that BNF is the most limiting factor for grain legume yields in the tropics? Will rhizobia inoculants increase yields? Drought, pests, soil problems, and topography are frequently more serious problems than N deficiency, and may explain why farmers' yields of grain legumes are roughly one-third to one-half those obtained on experimental plots (App *et al.,* 1980). This is not to say that a reasonable degree of nodulation and N_2 fixation is not needed in order to realize the best yields that are currently being obtained on farmers' fields. For example, there are reports of N fertilizer responses by tropical legumes which are not nodulated or are poorly nodulated (App *et al.,* 1980). This fertilizer response can be eliminated if those grain legumes are properly inoculated with an effective strain of rhizobia.

Perhaps the failure to obtain larger yields of grain legumes with inoculants or N fertilizers is partially due to a "yield barrier." Soybean yields in the USA have increased only 14 to 21% in the past twenty-five years, while cereal grain yields have increased approximately 50 to 75% during this same period of time (Summerfield *et al.,* 1978). Tropical legume breeders are more interested in increasing yields, and in developing pest tolerance, than in developing varieties with increased potential for BNF (Kawano & Jennings 1980). High rates of BNF are not a primary selection factor. However, if the yield barrier can be broken, greater inputs of N and other nutrients may be necessary to exploit this enhanced yield potential.

There are problems in attempting to assign a high priority to BNF research in the developing areas of the tropics. Research on BNF is often long-term and expensive. It is not always possible to evaluate the benefits of BNF on crop production in a single season. A better estimation of the impact is usually possible if the N economy and productivity of the complete cropping cycle is examined. Higher priority is often given to other areas of research where direct impact on yield is more obvious in the short term.

For forage legumes, the estimation of productivity is even more difficult since livestock must be included in order to efficiently utilize the forages. The type of research suggested here requires a coordinated effort by crop physiologists, agronomists, economists, livestock specialists, microbiologists, and plant breeders. BNF is only one component of a larger research package for crop improvement.

It is also not clear who the primary users of the BNF technology in the LDC's will be. Many suggest that the "subsistance" or less-advantaged farmer in remote regions, on poorer soil, limited in capital or on a small farm, will utilize this technology. Since he is currently using "traditional" cultural practices, improved systems of BNF should be attractive and appropriate for his agricultural operation. Unfortunately, BNF systems do require inputs for optimum performance: good seed and inoculants, proper soil amendments, some water control, available livestock, and management by the farmer is often needed. In addition, crop selection by the farmer may be based on yield or yield stability, the economic value and desirability of the product as a food/fiber source, suitability to a particular soil. or how well it fits into a crop rotation. BNF is not envisioned as a primary selection factor and would certainly require other modifications to his traditional practices. Farmers who are currently using modern technology, who are located on productive soils, and who are properly financed and served by an adequate infrastructure, are another possible user group. However, they usually use N fertilizer. The yearly quantity of fertilizer employed in the developing tropical world is still increasing.

What would happen if we should suddenly find that N fertilizers were no longer a feasible source of N in the developing areas of the tropics? A recent study compared farms in the U.S. corn belt that used "organic" methods of farming (no fertilizer N, pesticides, etc.) with their neighbors who used conventional practices that included N fertilizers (Lockeretz, Shearer & Kohl, 1981). Selected data from this report are contained in Table 2. With the exception of the hay and oat crops, which usually receive little or no fertilizer, all yields were lower. Wheat was down 25%, but the authors note that this was a minor crop on all the farms studied, and usually received complete fertilization on conventional farms. Livestock numbers were higher on the organic farms in order to utilize the forage that was produced as a result of inclusion of legumes in the crop rotations. Profits were approximately equal since lower costs for off-farm inputs roughly equaled the economic loss resulting from reduced yields. The authors of this study suggested that neither of the situations examined in their study may be the best option. In particular, they suggest that usage of a modest amount of fertilizer N by the organic farmers would likely have a substantial impact on their yields. In other words,

TABLE 2: Yields, livestock numbers, and profitability of organic farmers relative to conventional farmers. (Lockeretz, Shearer & Kohl, 1981).

Crop		Organic Farmer
Maize	(yield)	- 10 %
Wheat	"	- 25 %
Soybeans	"	- 5 %
Hay	"	0
Oats	"	0
Livestock		Greater numbers
Profits		Approx. equal

the combined use of both BNF and moderate amounts of fertilizers may be the optimum choice. This balanced approach may be worth more consideration in the developing areas of the tropics. Research on increasing the efficiency of utilization of fertilizer N should also be included.

In summary, it is time to do the field research necessary to prove that BNF can make a measurable impact on crop production in the tropics. This kind of research will also help us define who the logical users of the improved BNF technology may be. Finally, added research emphasis on the optimum use of both BNF and N fertilizers in cropping systems is suggested.

Several new research projects and programs on BNF were initiated during the 1974 energy crisis and shortly thereafter. Prior to the energy crisis, very few laboratories were doing research in BNF. We have had sufficient time to establish our programs, and it is now time to demonstrate that BNF can effectively increase yields in farmers' fields.

REFERENCES

App, A., Bouldin. D.R., Dart, P.J., & Watanabe, I. (1980) Constraints to biological nitrogen fixation in soils of the tropics. *In:* Priorities for alleviating soil related constraints to food production in the tropics. Inter. Rice Res. Inst., Los Baños, Philippines. Pp. 19-38.

Engibous, J.C. (1975) Possible effects of fertilizer shortages on food grain production. *In:* Impact of fertilizer shortage: Focus on Asia. Asian Productivity Org., Tokyo, Japan. Pp. 193-203.

Hardy, R.W.F. (1975) Fertilizer research with emphasis on nitrogen fixation. *In:* Proceedings of 24th annual meeting of Agricultural Research Institute. Nat. Acad. of Sci., Washington, D.C., USA.

Herdt, R.W. & Barker, R. (1975) Possible effects of fertilizer shortages on rice production in Asian countries. *In:* Impact of fertilizer shortage: Focus on Asia. Asian Productivity Org., Tokyo, Japan. Pp. 205-240.

International Rice Research Institute. (1980) Trip report to the People's Republic of China. Inter. Rice Res. Inst., Los Baños, Philippines.

Kawano, K. & Jennings, P.R. (1980) Tropical crop breeding achievements and challenges. *In:* Potential productivity of field crops under different environments. Inter. Rice Res. Inst., Los Baños, Philippines.

Lockeretz. W., Shearer, G. & Kohl, D.H. (1981) Organic farming in the corn belt. *Science* 211, 540-546.

Stangel, P.J. (1979) Nitrogen requirement and adequacy of supply for rice production. *In*: Nitrogen and rice. Inter. Rice Res. Inst., Los Baños, Philippines. Pp. 45-69.

Summerfield. R.J., Minchin, F.R. & Roberts, E.H. (1978) Realization of yield potential in soybeans (*Glycine max.* (L.) Merr.) and cowpea (*Vigna unguiculata* (L.) Walp). *In*: Proceedings BCPC/BPGRG Symposium-Opportunities for chemical plant growth production. Pp. 215-233.

A ROLE FOR LEGUMES IN TROPICAL AGRICULTURE

M.J.T. Norman[1]

Summary

This paper reviews the economic, nutritive, and biological role for both grain and pasture legumes in tropical agriculture. Particular attention is paid to the importance of legumes in multiple cropping systems and to the role of forage legumes in cropping systems.

INTRODUCTION

In this introductory paper I shall interpret the role of legumes in three ways: economic, nutritive, and biological. By the economic role of legumes I mean their place in the tropical world's agriculture: the areas where they are grown (and we know these with some degree of accuracy only for crop legumes), how the area sown to legumes in a particular region varies over time, and the degree to which crop legumes enter the world trade. I shall then deal with the place of legumes in the diet of both humans and stock, though with an emphasis on pasture legumes as a component of ruminant nutrition. Last, by the biological role of legumes I mean their place in tropical farming systems. With respect to crops this includes temporal and spatial relationships between legumes and nonlegumes in cropping systems and the consequences of their inclusion in, or exclusion from, crop patterns. For pastures the biological role includes the capacity of legumes to raise the productivity levels of tropical grasslands and the constraints to full realization of that capacity.

THE ECONOMIC ROLE OF LEGUMES

Grain legumes

Tables 1, 2, and 3 illustrate significant features of the production and trade of grain legumes in the developing world and China. The tables are deficient in

[1] Dept. of Agronomy and Horticultural Science, Univ. of Sydney, Sydney, 2006 Australia.

TABLE 1: Harvested areas of crop legumes and cereals in the developing world and China: averages for 1969-71 and 1977-9 (1000 ha). Source: FAO (1980a)

Crop	Developing countries								China	
	Africa		Latin America		Near East		Far East			
	69-71	77-79	69-71	77-79	69-71	77-79	69-71	77-79	69-71	77-79
LEGUMES:										
Soybeans	176	224	1568	9252	15	94	1015	1385	13859	14328
Groundnuts	6206	5068	1127	868	546	1072	8531	8594	2165	2390
Dry beans[1]	1813	2045	6419	7265	246	219	8407	9330	3381	4116
Other grain legumes[2]	8878	9295	942	959	1174	1378	16842	17792	8440	9717
Total	17073	16632	10056	18344	1981	2763	34795	37101	27845	30551
Change in Total (%)		-2.6		+82.4		+39.5		+6.6		+9.7
CEREALS:										
Wheat	6213	5532	8555	9547	19999	20863	23617	28746	28336	37001
Barley	4042	4474	1235	1189	6106	6653	3633	2769	12834	14568
Rice	3518	4185	6394	7700	1217	1145	76564	81916	34622	37735
Maize	12349	14111	25852	25844	1824	2079	12933	14432	10521	11707
Sorghum	10657	11136	3525	4779	3256	3942	18167	16667	8571	8570
Millets	14401	15105	160	246	1211	1606	20747	19053	13072	14170
Total	51180	54543	45721	49305	33613	36288	155661	163583	107956	123751
Change in Total (%)		+6.6		+7.8		+8.0		+5.1		+14.6

[1] Largely *Phaseolus* and *Vigna* (except cowpeas).

[2] All grain legumes except dry beans: e.g. peas, lentils, chickpeas, pigeon peas, cowpeas.

that it is only possible to present data for four crop legume groups from the Food and Agriculture Organization's (FAO) statistics; furthermore, the FAO regional grouping obscures the boundaries between tropical and temperate zones. However, a reasonably clear global picture emerges.

In Table 1, changes in crop area over the past eight years for the four crop legume groups and the six major cereals are contrasted. It is said that, in times of food shortage, farmers of the developing world tend to substitute cereals for legumes: if subsistence farmers, in order to secure their food energy base; if cash crop farmers, in order to take advantage of higher cereal prices. While this may occur regionally and over a short-term stress period, Table 1 does not suggest any general shift in the recent past. In the Far East and China the rate of increase in total crop legume area over eight years is of the same order as that of cereals; in the Near East it is about four times as great, and in Latin America ten times as great as in cereals. The main focus of crop legume expansion in the Near East, as defined by FAO, has been in groundnuts in the Sudan, while in Latin America it has been in soybeans, particularly in Brazil but also in Argentina and Paraguay. Only in Africa has a decline in crop legume area been registered; a decline due largely to a fall in Nigerian groundnut production. For grain legumes, both dry beans and others, rates of increase in crop area have been broadly similar to those of cereals in all regions.

Table 2 gives yield and production data for the same legume groups, regions, and time periods. While I appreciate that even three-year averages may be insufficient to iron out seasonal variation for rainfed crops, the table shows one or two interesting changes that may be regarded as real. In Africa, the yield of groundnuts has declined while that of other crops has remained static: this translates the 2.6% fall in total crop legume area to a 7.0% fall in production. In the Near East and China the general yield trend has been upward; percentage increases in production are, therefore, somewhat greater than the increases in area given in Table 1. In Latin America, substantial yield increases in soybeans, and, to a lesser extent in groundnuts, have reinforced the expansion in area to the point where total production of crop legumes has increased by over 150% in eight years.

Looking to the future, it is virtually impossible to predict changes in the area sown to crop legumes relative to other crops. However, it is appropriate at this point to update Khan's (1977) view of the yield potential for legumes and to look briefly at global trends in yield. For the developing countries the average annual rate of change in yield over the past eight years (1969-71 means cf. 1977-79 means) for soybeans is +5.19%, for groundnuts +0.59%, for dry beans – 0.14%, for all grain legumes – 0.16%, and for cereals +1.90% (FAO, 1980a). Since the major contributor to the substantial increase in soybean yield has been the sub-tropical region in Latin America, there is certainly no cause yet for rejoicing among tropical crop legume breeders and agronomists.

TABLE 2: Yield and production of crop legumes in the developing world and China: averages for 1969-71 and 1977-79.

Crop	Developing countries								China	
	Africa		Latin America		Near East		Far East			
	69-71	77-79	69-71	77-79	69-71	77-79	69-71	77-79	69-71	77-79
YIELD (kg/ha):										
Soybeans	396	411	1278	1561	1124	2074	754	885	822	887
Groundnuts[1]	778	765	1225	1350	883	1025	824	875	1216	1110
Dry beans	573	573	604	554	1174	1345	313	339	728	894
Other grain legumes	358	360	672	737	11111	1107	627	610	1015	1033
PRODUCTION (1000t):										
Soybeans	70	92	2003	14347	17	197	766	1226	11398	12714
Groundnuts	4827	3870	1381	1169	483	1098	7027	7519	2634	2654
Dry beans	1039	1172	3876	4023	289	294	2632	3163	2460	3684
Other grain legumes	3176	3343	633	707	1304	1525	10566	10851	8567	10033
Total	9112	8477	7893	20246	2093	3114	20991	22759	25059	29085
Change in Total (%)		-7.0		+156.5		+48.8		+8.4		+16.1

[1]In shell.
(Source: FAO, 1980a).

Table 3 is concerned with current exports of crop legumes and their products from the developing countries and China. (Since trade volumes change so rapidly there seemed to be little point in comparing the 1977-9 figures with those of another arbitrarily chosen three-year period). The table illustrates the dominant position of Latin America as an exporter of soybeans, soybean products and grain legumes, and the no-longer-dominant position of Africa, excluding the Sudan, as an exporter of groundnuts and groundnut products.

TABLE 3: Exports of crop legumes and crop legume products from the developing world and China: average for 1977-79 (1000t).

Crop or crop product	Developing countries				China
	Africa	Latin America	Near East	Far East	
Groundnuts[1]	116.7	71.4	114.1	40.6	22.7
Groundnut meal	299.7	229.5	103.4	618.3	-
Groundnut oil	170.6	171.8	31.5	9.4	12.0
Soybeans	1	3360.1	0	34.6	190.9
Soybean meal	1.4	5684.3	8.3	137.2	8.7
Soybean oil	1	537.9	1	5.6	3.8
Grain legumes	208.4	418.0	241.0	223.9	74.7

[1]Raw nuts both in shell and shelled, expressed as shelled.
(Source: FAO, 1980b).

Pasture legumes

Comparable data on pasture and forage legume production are not available. Even where countries report "sown pasture" areas, it is rarely known whether legumes have been sown. Furthermore, whereas an arable crop is definable, there are all levels of pasture improvement from a full replacement of the native vegetation by sown species to a hopeful scattering of a limited amount of seed with little or no cultivation or fertilizer. However, the most important contrast is between the roles of crop and pasture legumes: the former are established components of developing country cropping systems and have been so for centuries, whereas the improvement of tropical and subtropical lands with sown pasture legumes is still very much a pioneer activity.

Thus, in Australia, where tropical and subtropical pasture improvement has proceeded fastest and furthest, the area sown increased from 0.85 million ha in 1945 to 1.2 million ha in 1960, an annual growth rate of 2.5%, and then increased to 3.8 million ha by 1975, an annual growth rate of over 8%. However, the 1975 area represented only about 4% of the available land with more than 800 mm rainfall, and less than 30% of the pastures contained legumes (Pulsford, 1980). From 1973 to 1975 beef prices fell by 70%, and between 1974 and 1976 phosphatic fertilizer costs increased 2½-fold. These catastrophic changes in input-output balance brought pasture improvement in Australia virtually to a standstill, a situation from which it is only now beginning to recover.

Mannetje (1978) has been brave enough, not to predict the rate at which sown tropical pastureland is likely to increase (a task beyond any scientist or economist), but to predict what a given expansion is likely to mean in terms of animal production. He estimates that within the tropics with more than 4½ months of wet season, plus subtropical regions with year-round or summer rainfall, there are 4.5 billion ha, of which 23% are grazing lands. The number of cattle is 566 million and beef production 7.7 million tons - only about 7 kg/ha of grazing land. Using data from Stobbs (1976), Mannetje calculates that the improvement of 25% of the existing grazing lands of Africa and Latin America would increase their combined output of beef from 6.1 to 13.6 million tons.

At the workshop where Khan (1977) presented his paper on crop legume yield, Jones (1977) made a comparable analysis of pasture legume yield potential. Jones recalled that Colman (1971) had found the yield of pasture legumes to be about half that of nitrogen (N) fertilized grass in various regions of tropical Australia. Ludlow & Wilson (1972) quote transpiration ratios of 305-340 for N fertilized grass and 700 for legumes, and on this basis one might expect potential legume yields of 7-28 t/ha, according to location. In actual practice yields seldom exceed 10 t/ha. On the other hand, management (the defoliation regime) is a major determinant of yield and one that does not apply to crop legumes. Jones was of the opinion that in the wet tropics and wet subtropics inadequate nutrition and poor management, rather than genotype, were currently the dominant yield constraints. However, for the wet-and-dry tropics and, to a lesser extent, for the drier subtropics, native genetic resources are still essentially unexplored, and yield improvement, even if confined to selection within naturally occurring genotypes, is readily feasible.

NUTRITIVE ROLE

Grain legumes

This section draws heavily on recent excellent reviews by Rachie (1977) and Bressani & Elias (1980).

Estimating the daily energy requirement of tropical peoples at about 2100 calories per capita, a reasonable figure for daily protein need is 60 g. Over the world in general, plants contribute about 70% and animals 30% to protein consumption, but in developing tropical countries the average proportion of animal protein consumed may be as low as 10%. In the tropics as a whole, cereals account for 68% of total plant protein consumption, legume grains 18.5% and roots, tubers, nuts, fruit, and vegetables 13.5% (legumes as vegetables contribute substantially to the last figure).

There is, however, wide variation among tropical countries, according to the spectrum of crops grown, the importance of animals in the rural economy, and the contribution of the main categories of crop and animal product to human energy and protein intake. This is evident in Table 4 for India and Uganda.

TABLE 4: Contribution of crop and animal products to human energy and protein intake[1].

Product	% of energy intake by country		% of protein intake by country	
	India	Uganda	India	Uganda
Cereals	68.6	23.2	59.3	22.3
Legumes, nuts, oilseeds	16.1	15.9	27.1	36.6
Other plant sources	8.7	54.8	1.0	18.0
Animal sources	6.6	6.1	12.6	23.1

[1]Summarized from Rachie (1977).

Thus, in India, where root and tuber crops contribute little to diet, cereals account for over two-thirds of the energy intake and nearly 60% of the protein intake, whereas in Uganda, where large quantities of roots, tubers, and plantains are consumed, the contribution of cereals to both energy and protein intake is only about one-third that in India. Because of the low protein content of roots and tubers relative to cereals, the proportion of total protein intake from legumes and oilseeds (and from animal products) is substantially higher in Uganda than in India, even though the legume contribution to energy intake is about the same. Rachie also presents data from Nigeria, where the legume contribution to both energy and protein intake is significantly lower than for India or Uganda: 7.3 and 14.1% respectively.

In discussing briefly the nutritive value of legume seeds for humans and stock, limitations of time and space preclude a consideration of legume oilseed meals, important as they are in stock-feed mixes.

The protein content of grain legumes ranges from 17 to 40%, though for the important species the span is smaller — from 21 to 35%. They are all rich in iron, fairly high in phosphorus, but deficient in calcium. In general, protein content is genetically modifiable, but in *Phaseolus* and possibly other legumes, the percentage of protein is often, but not always, negatively correlated with grain yield. Phosphate amelioration can have positive effects on protein content, but other agronomic influences appear to be small (Bressani & Elias, 1980).

The major nutritional limitation in legume seeds is, of course, their deficiency of sulfur amino acids; the compensation is a relatively high lysine content. Our knowledge of genetic factors determining the make-up of grain legume protein is steadily increasing, and it is also now clear that the amino-acid spectrum within a genotype is little affected by environmental factors. However, we are just beginning to establish genetic control of protein quality, though Boulter (1980) and Bliss (1980) are hopeful of the prospects of breeding for higher quality protein.

Apart from amino-acid deficiencies — and all legume foods are improved by methionine supplementation — legume protein is also relatively indigestible; in cooked material, at least, this seems to be related to tannin content. However, one important nutritional advantage, both for humans and stock, is the complementarity of legume seeds and cereals, largely an effect of balancing out methionine and lysine content. Thus the maximum protein efficiency ratio of rice/bean mixtures (both *Phaseolus vulgaris* and *Vigna mungo*) is reached when 80% of the total protein comes from rice and 20% from beans. Similar results have been obtained with maize and *Phaseolus*, soybeans, and cowpeas (Bressani & Elias, 1980).

Pasture legumes

There is no need to underline the role of legumes in determining the nutritive value of tropical and subtropical grassland. With few exceptions, the annual rate of soil N mineralization in the world's tropical grazing lands, which in the absence of widespread and effective native legumes governs the protein available to the grazing animal, is extremely low. While we must bear in mind free-living bacteria (Odu, 1977) and N_2-fixing associations between bacteria and grasses (Day, 1977; Neyra & Döbereiner, 1977), we are still some way from making accurate estimates of their contribution to the production of N in unimproved grazing lands. On the other hand, the direct and indirect contribution of the legume component to sown pasture protein yield is documented for a number of cases (Henzell, 1968; Henzell & Vallis, 1977; Whitney, 1977; Vallis, 1978) and may be inferred from numerous others. Norman (1970) and Evans (1970) have demonstrated, under widely differing conditions, direct relationships between animal gain and pasture legume content.

A discussion of the total role of the legume in the pasture/soil/animal system is appropriately reserved for the final section of this paper. What concerns us here is the legume as a component of ruminant diet.

Minson (1977) summarized published data on the dry matter digestibility of tropical pasture legumes: the range is from 36 to 69% and the mean 54%, values that are similar to those for the much wider range of tropical grasses that have been studied (Minson & McLeod, 1970). The decline in digestibility with age that occurs in grasses also occurs in legumes, though the rate of decline is generally less. The relationships established by Minson between voluntary intake and dry matter digestibility did not show clear-cut differences between tropical grasses and legumes, but, in mature feed, intake of legume is likely to be higher because the digestibility of the legume is likely to have fallen less with plant age.

A summary of published crude protein values for tropical legumes reveals a range from 5.6% for mature *Stylosanthes humilis* to 35.8% for leafy *Leucaena leucocephala,* with an overall mean of 17.2% (Skerman, 1977). This may be compared with an overall mean of 7.7% from published data on tropical grasses (Butterworth, 1967).

The most useful measure of protein digestibility is the quantity of protein apparently digested per 100 units of feed (DCP). From published data, Minson (1977) established the following relationship between DCP and crude protein percentage (CP) for tropical legumes, which is compared here with the corresponding equation for tropical grasses:

$$\text{Legumes: } DCP = 0.93\ CP - 3.99\ (r = 0.96)$$

$$\text{Grasses : } DCP = 0.90\ CP - 3.25\ (r = 0.98)$$

The similarity of these equations implies that the protein in legumes is digested with approximately the same efficiency as that in grasses having a similar crude protein content. However, as we have seen, the general level of crude protein content is much higher in legumes. Hence the mean quantity of digestible crude protein in legumes is 12.0 g per 100 g of feed, whereas the comparable value for grasses is 3.7 g per 100 g of feed (Butterworth, 1967). In crude terms, a "global average mouthful" of tropical legume will provide the cow with more than three times the digestible crude protein provided by a "global average mouthful" of tropical grass.

BIOLOGICAL ROLE

Legumes in annual cropping systems

Recent literature, both research papers and reviews, on tropical cropping systems and the place of legumes in them is voluminous. Region-orientated reviews include Okigbo & Greenland (1976) and Okigbo (1977a) on Africa; Pinchinat, Soria & Bazan (1976) and Pinchinat (1977) on Latin America; Harwood & Price (1976) and Moomaw, Park & Shanmugasundaram (1977) on Asia; Okigbo (1977b) on the humid tropics; Dart & Krantz (1977) on the semi-arid tropics; and Gomez & Zandstra (1977) and Norman (1979) in general. Important reviews devoted to individual crops include Shanmugasundaram, Kuo & Nalampang (1980) on soybeans, Steele & Mehra (1980) on cowpeas, Gibbons (1980) on groundnuts, and Francis, Flor & Temple (1976) largely on *Phaseolus*.

Excluding legumes as shade or cover crops, there are four main situations to consider; the first two are far more important in global terms than the others:

> Seed (grain and oilseed) legumes intercropped with nonlegumes;
> Seed legumes in sequence with nonlegumes;
> Green-manure legumes in sequence with nonlegumes; and
> Forage legumes in sequence with nonlegumes.

It should be noted that the intercrop situation is listed first, since in developing tropical countries it is the norm rather than the exception. Gutierrez, Infante & Pinchinat (1975) reported that in Colombia 90% of the *Phaseolus* is intercropped, largely with maize, while Pinchinat (1977), summarizing data from six Latin American countries, recorded that in five of the six the proportion of *Phaseolus* intercropped was over 50%. In West Africa perhaps 90% of cowpeas are interplanted with sorghum and pearl millet (Okigbo & Greenland, 1976; Steele & Mehra, 1980), and the same pattern is common for cowpeas in semi-arid India, though less so in higher rainfall regions or under irrigation (Steele & Mehra, 1980). In Nigeria and Uganda 95% and 56%, respectively, of groundnuts are intercropped (Okigbo & Greenland, 1976). Pigeonpea in India is largely sown in combination with sorghum, pearl millet or cotton (Dart & Krantz, 1977), and in Southeast Asia soybeans are commonly intercropped with maize (Shanmugasundaram *et al.*, 1980).

There are a number of reasons why farmers intercrop, but the important one in the context of this paper is that low-growing or climbing legumes may be integrated into the architecture of tall, erect cereals — maize, sorghum or pearl millet — without a major reduction in cereal yield and, in many circumstances, with an increase in total yield compared with sole cropping (Willey, 1979) and a significant increase in protein per ha. The tall-growing pigeonpea is an exception: its main role as an intercrop component in wet-and-dry climates is to utilize stored soil water after the rains have ended and short-season cereals harvested (Dart & Krantz, 1977). Examples of the biological advantages of legume intercropping include the weed-smothering effect of cowpeas in millet, sorghum and maize in West Africa (Steele & Mehra, 1980); reduction in insect attack relative to pure stands in maize/bean polycultures (Altieri *et al.*, 1978); and beneficial residual effects. Residual effects have received little attention, but recently Searle *et al.* (1981) have shown (admittedly in Sydney and not in the tropics) that N uptake by wheat following maize/soybean and maize/groundnut intercrops without N fertilizer was about twice as great as that following maize alone without N, and equivalent to that following maize alone with 100 kg/ha N.

The mention of residual effects naturally leads us on to consider the central problem of crop legumes grown in sequence with nonlegumes. Experiments too numerous to mention have demonstrated that tropical nonlegumes (usually cereals) yield better when they follow nodulated annual crop legumes than when following nonlegumes (often the same nonlegume crops), but surprisingly little is known of the N balance of the sequence, or even of the legume component in it. Wetselaar's work at Katherine, Northern Australia (1967) remains a model for the latter type of study. He not only demonstrated major differences between annual legume crops in post-crop soil N status, but also explained them in terms of plant material removed from, or retained on, the field and the consequent changes in total and available N. To give one example of contrast: Bunting & Anderson (1960) long ago showed that 60-70% of plant N is removed when only the nuts of groundnut crops are harvested, and that 90% is removed when the whole crop is taken; on the other hand, only 30% of the above-ground N of guar (*Cyamopsis tetragonoloba*) is removed in the seed, and most of the remainder returns naturally to the soil as leaf fall (Wetselaar & Norman, 1960).

Most of the experiments have compared nonlegume after legume with two successive nonlegume crops. The latter, however, is not a true control since we rarely know anything of the negative effects of a preceding nonlegume; for example the temporary immobilization of N may follow the incorporation of low-N crop residue. Furthermore, the role of naturally mineralized soil N — the annual amount of which may be of the same order as the amount of N_2 fixed by a short-season crop legume — is rarely taken into account. Finally, how often do we know how much of the legume crop's N is derived from fixation and how much from soil N uptake? Until we get better answers to these questions we shall not properly understand the true role of legumes in tropical cropping systems, either in sequence or as intercrops.

On the subject of annual legumes as green manure crops within arable cropping I shall say little. Green manures have always loomed larger in the agronomist's mind than in the farmers', except in parts of China, and with increasing pressure on the tropical world's cultivated land for food production, I cannot see them becoming any more significant. Their role in increasing soil organic matter has in the past been grossly exaggerated: one might hazard a guess that in the tropics the physical effect of a ploughed-in green manure is not likely to last much longer than the duration of the crop itself. The important consequence of green manure is the addition of N, and, in the vernacular, there must be a better way: for example, greater fixation efficiency, better inoculation, or more attention to residue return of crop legumes grown for food or cash.

Finally, the question of forage legumes in cropping systems. There are two distinct aspects to this: intensive and extensive. In India, for example (Indian

Council of Agricultural Research, 1968; Ruthenberg, 1976), small-scale dairy production is combined with annual irrigated cropping, and legume forages such as berseem clover (*Trifolium alexandrinum*) are grown in the dry season. Where this combination of circumstances — available irrigation water or extended rainfall regimes and the demand for high priced ruminant products — occurs in the tropics, such patterns will presumably be maintained. In general, however, I cannot see any major expansion of this type of cropping in the face of increasing pressure on arable land.

The second aspect of integrated crop and forage legume systems is quite different. At the back of the minds of many agronomists concerned with rainfed shifting cultivation or semi-intensive cropping systems has always been the possibility of improving the restorative value of the fallow break (and providing better nutrition for ruminants) by the deliberate sowing of pasture legumes at the end of the cropping period. At present it is little more than a concept, and to popularize it, a greater incentive than higher fertility and better fed cattle and sheep is perhaps needed — seed production. (I have myself been associated with a project in the North Thailand hills, which, as one of its components, included an attempt to interest opium-growing shifting cultivators in growing greenleaf desmodium for seed as a fallow break.) As a feasible future pattern it deserves far more attention than it is receiving at present.

Legumes in pasture systems

In this concluding section I want to draw attention to the two primary ecological constraints to pasture legume growth in the tropics; to the range of forage utilization systems; and to the central problem of the pasture legume as supplier of N to the soil/plant/animal complex.

I believe that the two most important ecological limitations, on a global scale, are acid soils and long dry seasons. The former topic was thoroughly explored at a recent seminar (Sánchez & Tergas, 1978), and I need scarcely remind you that tropical America alone has 850 million ha of acid infertile Oxisols and Ultisols (Centro Internacional de Agricultura Tropical (CIAT), 1978) with their attendant problems of aluminum toxicity and deficiencies of phosphorus, potassium, sulphur, calcium, magnesium, zinc, molybdenum, boron, and copper. The relevant research priorities have been summarized by Sánchez (1978): the selection and, later, breeding of tolerant genotypes, a clearer definition of mineral nutrient requirements, etc.

Australia, the nation with the largest proportion of the semi-arid tropics (19%) within its boundaries (Dart & Krantz, 1977), has pioneered the improvement of native grasslands through the introduction of pasture legumes, particularly *Stylosanthes humilis* (Norman & Begg, 1973; Gillard & Fisher, 1978), *Macroptilium atropurpureum* (Jones & Jones, 1978) and, lately, other *Stylosanthes* species (Edye *et al.*, 1975; Gillard, Edye & Hall,

1980). The challenge of a long dry season can only be met through a continued search for drought-tolerant (or drought-evading) genotypes that provide green forage for as long a period as possible and maximum nutritive value in standover dry forage, and that have agronomic characteristics that will permit forage to be accumulated for dry season use without losing the legume from the pasture.

Turning now to the place of legumes in forage utilization systems, many pasture agronomists working in the tropics have in their subconscious an ideal pasture community ideotype: a well-managed green denseness of legume and grass, neatly fenced. While tropical pastures in well-watered, closely settled regions with an advanced economy, the output of which is high quality beef or milk, may approximate such an ideotype, there are other patterns more generally relevant to the more than 1 billion ha of tropical and subtropical grazing land climatically capable of supporting pasture legumes (the figure is from Mannetje, 1978).

The first important difference from what might be termed the "ryegrass/white clover" ideotype is related to scale and input/output balance. We are, over a wide range of tropical conditions, developing somewhat comparable intimate grass/legume mixtures, but in comparison with temperate pastures the minimum management unit, the fenced paddock, is usually much larger and the prices obtained for the output, which govern the level of input, are lower. Hence the need for emphasis on cheap seed, ease of establishment under rough conditions, economy in the utilization of mineral nutrients, particularly phosphate, and capacity to withstand gross mismanagement (the last of these being particularly difficult to achieve).

There are other patterns. The system most neglected by research workers, but common over much of South and Southeast Asia, is that of the small-scale crop farmer supporting ruminants (perhaps only a pair of draft animals) in a heavily populated region where he cannot afford to allocate scarce cropland to growing forage and where free grazing and crop residues are limited in quantity and/or quality. Here the need is for shrub or tree legumes that can be grown in odd corners to provide hand-lopped feed or controlled browse. Current research in Hawaii (Whitney, 1977) and Australia (see CSIRO Division of Tropical Crops and Pastures, Annual Reports) on *Leucaena leucocephala* is relevant, but a great deal more work on its utilization, and on the potential of other species, is required.

Finally, there are the special problems associated with very extensive pastoral systems in the semi-arid tropics and subtropics, where fencing and pasture management can only be minimal and inputs per ha will be extremely low. Such conditions are found in developed (Australia) and developing countries (East and West Africa). Under these circumstances the adapted pasture legume could well be a shrubby, deep-rooted perennial, highly economical in its use of mineral nutrients, and preferably unpalatable during the wet season growth period. It would not be regarded as a component of a grass/legume mixture so much as a fall-back protein supplement to native forage. *Stylosanthes scabra* approaches to some degree the genotype required; there may be others within this polymorphic genus or elsewhere.

The two primary functions of the legume in grassland are to provide high quality forage for ruminant consumption and to add N to the soil/plant/animal system. At the most general level the first function, which was discussed in the middle section of the paper, may be subsumed within the second. It is, therefore, appropriate in the concluding section of this paper to concentrate on the N-supplying power of the legume.

The state of the art of understanding the N economy of grass/legume pastures has been ably reviewed by Henzell & Vallis (1977) and Vallis (1978). Henzell (1968) estimated the average N yield of pasture legumes in tropical and subtropical Australia to lie between 40 and 210 kg/ha per yr, with a maximum of the order of 340 kg/ha per yr; similar values have been reported from other countries. The proportion of this derived from fixation in grass/legume pastures on inherently low-N soil is estimated by Henzell & Vallis to be as high as 80-90%.

The situation of the herbaceous legume in an intimate grass/legume mixture, competing directly with grass for light, water, and mineral nutrients, clearly sets limits to N production; limits that apply less to shrub or tree legumes such as *Leucaena*. Whitney (1977) reports N yields from this species of 450 to 550 kg/ha per yr. Whereas in the data compilation by Jones (1977) the highest dry matter yield from herbaceous legumes is 12.6 t/ha (*Macroptilium* and *Centrosema brazilianum*), Whitney (1977) estimates 23 t/ha from recent *Leucaena* selections. To generalize, perhaps dangerously, the concept of legumes whose photosynthetic surface is well above the grass, and whose root system may extend well below that of the grass to absorb water and mineral nutrients, is worth very serious attention.

The careful analysis by Vallis (1978) of the effect of mineral N status on fixation by legumes within a grass/legume pasture led him to conclude that significant advances could be made through a symbiosis more tolerant of high levels of mineral N, if this is physiologically possible. This would seem to be a suitable point at which to conclude, since if mineral N status is important within the highly N-competitive grass/legume pasture, then it must be even more important for crop legumes growing in cultivated soil, where the rate of mineralization is likely to be higher. I return to an earlier theme: that we can only comprehend the biological role of legumes within the context of an understanding of soil N transformations.

REFERENCES

Altieri, M.A., Francis, C.A., Schoonhoven, A. van, & Doll, J.D. (1978) *Field Crops Res.* 1, 33-49.

Bliss, F.A. (1980) Breeding legumes for nutritional quality. *In:* Advances in legume science. R.J. Summerfield & A.H. Bunting (Eds.) Royal Botanic Gardens, Kew, England. Pp. 179-185.

Boulter, D. (1980) Ontogeny and development of biochemical and nutritional attributes in legume seeds. *In:* Advances in legume science, R.J. Summerfield & A.H. Bunting (Eds.) Royal Botanic Gardens, Kew, England. Pp. 127-134.

Bressani, R. & Elias, L.G. (1980) Nutritional value of legume crops for humans and animals. *In:* Advances in legume science, R.J. Summerfield & A.H. Bunting (Eds.). Royal Botanic Gardens, Kew, England. pp. 135-155.

Bunting, A.H. & Anderson, B. (1960) *J. Agric. Sci* (Camb.) 55, 35-46.

Butterworth, M.H. (1967) *Nutr. Abst. and Rev.* 37, 349-368.

Centro Internacional de Agricultura Tropical (1978) Annual Report, 1977. CIAT, Cali, Colombia.

Colman, R.L. (1971) *Trop. Grassl.* 5, 181-194.

Dart, P.J. & Kranz, B.A. (1977) Legumes in the semi-arid tropics. *In:* Exploiting the legume-*Rhizobium* symbiosis in tropical agriculture, J.M. Vincent, A.S. Whitney & J. Bose (Eds.). Univ. Hawaii College Trop. Agric. *Misc. Publ.* 145. Pp. 119-154.

Day, J.M. (1977) Nitrogen-fixing associations between bacteria and tropical grass roots. *In:* Biological nitrogen fixation in farming systems of the tropics, A. Ayanaba & P.J. Dart (Eds.). Wiley, New York, NY, USA. Pp. 273-288.

Edye, L.A., Williams, W.T., Anning, P., Holm, A. McR., Miller, C.P., Page, M.C., & Winter, W.H. (1975) *Aust. J. Agric. Res.* 26. 481-496.

Evans, T.R. (1970) *Proc. XI International Grassland Congress.* Brisbane, Australia. Pp. 803-807.

Food and Agriculture Organization (1980a) Production yearbook, 1979, Vol. 33. FAO, Rome, Italy.

Food and Agriculture Organization (1980b) Trade yearbook, 1979, Vol. 33. FAO, Rome, Italy.

Francis, C.A., Flor, C.A. & Temple, S.R. (1976) Adapting varieties for intercropping systems in the tropics. *In:* Multiple cropping. American Society of Agronomy Spec. Publ. 27. Pp. 235-253.

Gibbons, R.W. (1980) Adaptation and utilization of groundnuts in different environments and farming systems. *In:* Advances in legume science, R.J.

Summerfield & A.H. Bunting (Eds.). Royal Botanic Gardens, Kew, England. Pp. 483-493.

Gillard, P., Edye. L.A. & Hall, R.L. (1980) *Aust. J. Agric.* Res. 31, 205-220.

Gillard, P. & Fisher. M.J. (1978) The ecology of Townsville stylo-based pastures in northern Australia. *In:* Plant relations in pastures, J.R. Wilson (Ed.). CSIRO, Melbourne. Australia. Pp. 340-352.

Gomez, A.A. & Zandstra, H.G. (1977) An analysis of the role of legumes in multiple cropping systems. *In:* Exploiting the legume-*Rhizobium* symbiosis in tropical agriculture. J.M. Vincent, A.S. Whitney & J. Bose (Eds.). Univ. Hawaii Coll. Trop. Agric. *Misc. Publ.* 145. Pp. 81-95.

Gutierrez, W., Infante. M. & Pinchinat, A. (1975) Situación del cultivo de fríjol en América Latina. CIAT, Colombia, *Boletín Informe.* 36 pp.

Harwood, R.R. & Price. E.C. (1976) Multiple cropping in tropical Asia. *In:* Multiple cropping. American Society of Agronomy Spec. Publ. 27. Pp. 11-40.

Henzell. E.F. (1968) *Trop. Grassl.* 2, 1-17.

Henzell, E.F. & Vallis. I. (1977) Transfer of nitrogen between legumes. *In:* Biological nitrogen fixation in farming systems of the tropics, A. Ayanaba & P.J. Dart (Eds.). Wiley, New York, NY, USA. Pp. 73-88.

Indian Council of Agricultural Research (1968) Proc. Symposium on cropping patterns in India. ICAR, New Delhi, India. 639 pp.

Jones, R.J. (1977) Yield potential for tropical pasture legumes. *In:* Exploiting the legume-*Rhizobium* symbiosis in tropical agriculture, J.M. Vincent, A.S. Whitney, & J. Bose (Eds.). Univ. Hawaii Coll. Trop. Agric. *Misc. Publ.* 145. Pp. 39-65.

Jones, R.J. & Jones, R.M. (1968) The ecology of siratro-based pastures. *In:* Plant relations in pastures, J.R. Wilson (Ed.). CSIRO, Melbourne, Australia. Pp. 353-367.

Khan, T.V. (1977) Yield potential for tropical legumes from a geneticist's point of view. *In:* Exploiting the legume-*Rhizobium* symbiosis in tropical agriculture, J.M. Vincent. A.S. Whitney, & J. Bose (Eds.). Univ. Hawaii Coll. Trop. Agric. *Misc. Publ.* 145. Pp. 21-37.

Ludlow, M.M. & Wilson, G.L. (1972) *Aust. J. Biol. Sci.* 25, 1133-1145.

Mannetje, L.T' (1978) *Trop. Grassl.* 12, 1-9.

Minson, D.J. (1977) The chemical composition and nutritive value of tropical legumes. *In:* Tropical forage legumes, P.J. Skerman (Ed.). FAO, Rome, Italy. Pp. 186-194.

Minson, D.J. & McLeod, M.N. (1970) *Proc. XI Intern. Grassl. Cong.* Brisbane, Australia. Pp. 719-722.

Moomaw, J.C., Park, H.G. & Shanmugasundaram, S. (1977) The role of legumes in South and Southeast Asia. *In:* Exploiting the legume-*Rhizobium* symbiosis in tropical agriculture., J.M. Vincent, A.S. Whitney, & J. Bose (Eds.). Univ. Hawaii Coll. Trop. Agric. *Misc. Publ.* 145. Pp. 155-166.

Neyra, C.A. & Döbereiner, J. (1977) *Adv. in Agron.* 29, 1-38.

Norman, M.J.T. (1970) *Proc. XI Intern. Grassl. Cong.* Brisbane, Australia. Pp. 829-832.

Norman, M.J.T. (1979) Annual cropping systems in the tropics. University Presses of Florida. Gainesville, FLA., USA. 276 pp.

Norman, M.J.T. & Begg, J.E. (1973) CSIRO Div. Land Res. *Tech. Paper* 33.

Odu, C.T.I. (1977) Contribution of free-living bacteria to the nitrogen status of humid tropical soils. *In:* Biological nitrogen fixation in farming systems of the humid tropics. A. Ayanaba & P.J. Dart (Eds.). Wiley, New York, NY, USA. Pp. 257-266.

Okigbo, B.N. (1977a) Role of legumes in small holdings of the humid tropics in Africa. *In:* Exploiting the legume-*Rhizobium* symbiosis in tropical agriculture, J.M. Vincent. A.S. Whitney, & J. Bose (Eds.). Univ. Hawaii Coll. Trop. Agric. *Misc. Publ.* 145. Pp. 119-154.

Okigbo, B.N. (1977b) Legumes in farming systems of the humid tropics. *In:* Biological nitrogen fixation in farming systems of the humid tropics, A. Ayanaba & P.J. Dart (Eds.). Wiley, New York, NY, USA.

Okigbo, B.N. & Greenland, D.J. (1976) Intercropping systems in tropical Africa. *In:* Multiple cropping. American Society of Agronomy Spec. Publ. 27. Pp. 63-101.

Pinchinat, A.M. (1977) The role of legumes in tropical America. *In:* Exploiting the legume-*Rhizobium* symbiosis in tropical agriculture, J.M. Vincent, A.S. Whitney, & J. Bose (Eds.). Univ. Hawaii Coll. Trop. Agric. *Misc. Publ.* 145. Pp. 171-182.

Pinchinat, A.M., Soria, J. & Bazan, R. (1976) Multiple cropping in tropical America. *In:* Multiple cropping. American Society of Agronomy Spec. Publ. 27, Pp. 51-61.

Pulsford, J.S. (1980) Trends in fertilizer costs and usage on pastures in tropical and subtropical Australia. *Trop. Grassl.* 14, 188-193.

Rachie, K.O. (1977) The nutritional role of grain legumes in the lowland humid tropics. *In:* Biological nitrogen fixation in farming systems in the tropics, A. Ayanaba & P.J. Dart (Eds.). Wiley, New York, NY, USA. Pp. 45-60.

Ruthenberg, H. (1976) Farming systems in the tropics. 2nd edition. Clarendon Press, Oxford, England. 366 pp.

Sánchez, P.A. (1978) Tropical pasture research in acid infertile soils of Latin America. *In:* Pasture production in acid soils of the tropics, P.A. Sánchez & L.E. Tergas (Eds.). CIAT, Cali, Colombia. 488 pp.

Sánchez, P.A. & Tergas, L.E. (Eds.) (1978) Pasture production in acid soils of the tropics. CIAT, Cali, Colombia. 488 pp.

Searle, P.G.E., Comundom, Y., Shedden, D.C., & Nance, R.A. (1981) *Field Crops Res.* 4, 133-145.

Shanmugasundaram, S., Kuo, G.C. & Nalampang, A. (1980) Adaptation and utilization of soybeans in different environments and agricultural systems. *In:* Advances in legume science, R.J. Summerfield & A.H. Bunting (Eds.). Royal Botanic Gardens, Kew, England. Pp. 265-277.

Skerman, P.J. (Ed.) (1977) Tropical forage legumes. FAO, Rome, Italy. 609 pp.

Steele, W.M. & Mehra, K.L. (1980) Structure, evolution and adaptation to farming systems and environments in *Vigna. In:* Advances in legume science, R.J. Summerfield & A.H. Bunting (Eds.). Royal Botanic Gardens, Kew, England. Pp. 393-404.

Stobbs, T.H. (1976) Beef production from sown and planted pastures in the tropics. *In:* Beef cattle production in developing countries, A.J. Smith (Ed.). Univ. of Edinburgh. Edinburgh, Scotland. Pp. 164-183.

Vallis, I. (1978) Nitrogen relations in grass/legume mixtures. *In:* Plant relations in pastures, J.R. Wilson (Ed.). CSIRO, Melbourne, Australia. Pp. 190-201.

Wetselaar, R. (1967) *Aust. J. Expl. Agric. Animal Husb.* 7, 518-522.

Wetselaar, R. & Norman, M.J.T. (1960) CSIRO Div. Land Res. *Tech. Paper* 10.

Whitney, A.S. (1977) Contribution of forage legumes to the nitrogen economy of mixed swards. A review of relevant Hawaiian research. *In:* Biological nitrogen fixation in farming systems in the tropics, A. Ayanaba & P.J. Dart (Eds.). Wiley, New York, NY, USA. Pp. 89-96.

Willey, R.W. (1979) *Field Crop Abst.* 32, 1-10.

PLANT FACTORS AFFECTING SYMBIOTIC N_2 FIXATION

PLANT FACTORS AFFECTING SYMBIOTIC NITROGEN FIXATION IN LEGUMES

P.H. Graham[1]

Summary

Host-determined traits influence nodule initiation, development, and function, and can be of major importance to the proper functioning of the legume/*Rhizobium* symbiosis under field conditions. This paper reviews such traits and considers their implications for practically oriented breeding programs aimed at enhanced N_2 fixation.

INTRODUCTION

While symbiotic nitrogen (N_2) fixation in legumes is the culmination of a complex interaction between host, *Rhizobium,* and environment, it is the host which currently appears to play the more important role in controlling the symbiosis. Additional host-determined characters continue to be reported (see Tables 1, 3 & 4), justifying the contention of Holl & La Rue (1975) that genetic manipulation of the host legume offers the greatest potential to improve upon current levels of N_2 fixation.

This review emphasizes those host-controlled aspects of the symbiosis which affect nodulation and N_2 fixation under field conditions. It recognizes, but does not dwell on, those traits which are important for nodule function but are normally detectable only as loss mutations or in biochemical or cytological studies. For convenience, three groups of host-controlled factors are considered affecting respectively nodule initiation, development, and function.

NODULE INITIATION

Table 1 lists host-controlled traits regulating *Rhizobium* recognition and the initiation of infection. There have been several recent reviews in this area

1 Centro Internacional de Agricultura Tropical (CIAT), A.A. 6713, Cali, Colombia.

TABLE 1: Some host-controlled factors affecting nodule initiation in legumes.

FACTOR	LEGUME	REFERENCE
Homoserine in root exudate	*P. sativum*	Van Egerat (1972)
Lectins and recognition	*T. repens*	Dazzo (1980)
No nodulation	various	various
Specificity in nodulation	*T. ambiguum*	Hely (1957)
	Lupinus sp.	Lange (1961)
	G. max	Nangju (1980)
Strain selection	*G. max*	Caldwell & Vest (1968)
		Materon & Vincent (1980)
	T. repens	Gareth Jones & Hardarson (1979)
Temperature effects	*P. sativum*	Lie *et al.* (1976)
Toxic seed substances	*T. subterraneum*	Thompson (1960)
	C. pubescens	Bowen (1961)

(Broughton, 1978; Dazzo, 1980); I will only consider some unusual cases of legume/*Rhizobium* specificity and strain competition.

Lupinus and *Ornithopus* spp. nodulate with strains of *R. lupini* (Lange & Parker, 1961; Dilworth, 1969). By contrast Lange (1961) found *Lupinus cosentini, L. albus* and *L. pilosus* readily nodulated by rhizobia from indigenous Australian legumes, whereas *L. luteus, L. angustifolius* and *O. sativus* were rarely nodulated. Similarly Hely (1957) found *Trifolium ambiguum* to be a polyploid series, many accessions of which were not nodulated by isolates from other *T. ambiguum* lines. When *T. repens* was grafted as stock or scion onto *T. ambiguum,* nodulation was normal (Hely, Bonnier & Manil, 1953). In each of these cases the legume with problems in nodulation experienced establishment difficulties in its new environment.

The situation with *Glycine max* is even more complex. On the one hand scientists at the International Institute of Tropical Agriculture (IITA) in Africa have identified cultivars such as 'Mandarin' and 'Orba' that nodulate freely with native (and presumably cowpea-type) rhizobia (Nangju, 1980), and they are breeding for host promiscuity with these strains. On the other, in the USA the difficulty in establishing inoculant strains in soils having large indigenous populations of *R. japonicum* has prompted the idea that the rj_1 non-nodulating gene be incorporated into cultivars to heighten specificity (Devine & Weber, 1977).

The ability of legumes to select particular *Rhizobium* strains from the rhizosphere population is well documented, but poorly understood. A number of examples involve soybean. Thus, Caldwell & Vest (1968) planted the variety 'Peking' in soils where strain 110 constituted as much as 60% of the soil population but recovered this strain in only 1% of nodules. Materon & Vincent (1980) compared the competitive ability of strains of *R. japonicum* on lines of soybean derived from the rj_2 carrier 'Hardee'. While CB1809 clearly outcompeted CC709 and NU 50 on lines not having the rj_2 gene, it formed only 5-25% of nodules in paired tests with them when the host carried this gene (see Table 2). In similar experiments with white clover Gareth Jones & Hardarson (1979) identified some clover lines in which almost 100% of nodules were formed by the strain 75. Inheritance of this trait was additive and without dominance (Hardarson & Gareth Jones, 1979).

TABLE 2: Relative competitiveness of strains of *R. japonicum* as influenced by host plant (from Materon & Vincent, 1980).

	Competing strains	
	CB1809 vs CC709	CB1809 vs NU50
Relative proportion on root	1.12	0.95
Competitive index with:		
'Lee'	1.70	1.10
'Lee' x 'Hardy 36'	3.70	1.70
'Hardee' (rj_2)	0.25	0.08
'Lee' x 31 (rj_2)	0.05	0.07

NODULE DEVELOPMENT

Table 3 lists some host-controlled factors affecting nodule development. I will mention only nodule type, number, and time to nodule formation.

Dart (1975) distinguished three basic nodule types:

Elongate and cylindrical, with apical merismatic activity, as in clover and medic;

Spherical, with several discrete meristematic foci, as occur in soybean and bean, and

Collar nodules, as in lupin, where the nodule extends about the root.

Nutman (1967) found the tendency to high nodule number per plant in subterranean clover dominant over sparse nodulation but probably of complex inheritance. Nodule number was positively correlated with lateral root number and inversely related to nodule size, making it a somewhat unreliable criterion on which to evaluate inoculation success.

TABLE 3: Some host-controlled factors affecting nodule development in legumes.

FACTOR	LEGUME	REFERENCE
Bacteroid development	*T. pratense*	Nutman (1954)
Bacteroid number/ envelope	*Lupinus, Ornithopus*	Kidby & Goodchild (1966)
Nodule form	various	Dart (1975)
Nodule number	*T. subterraneum*	Nutman (1967)
	P. vulgaris	Graham (1973)
Pattern of nodulation	*Lupinus* sp.	Lange & Parker (1961)
Time of first nodule	*T. subterraneum*	Nutman (1967)
	Stylosanthes sp.	Graham & Hubbell (1975)
Not specified	*G. max*	Caldwell (1966), Vest (1970) Vest & Caldwell (1972)

Host-controlled differences in time to first nodule formation have been found in a number of legumes including *T. subterraneum* and *Stylosanthes* spp., and are also commonly strain dependent. Use of cultivar/strain combinations that nodulate rapidly might be an additional way to limit competition from native soil rhizobia. Thus, Gibson (1968) reported that 50% of the native soil rhizobia were slow to nodulate with the sub-clover cultivar Woogenellup. In pot trials with soils having up to 10^4 rhizobia/g, some inoculant strains still produced more than 80% of the nodules, but the slower-to-nodulate TA1 strain was seriously disadvantaged.

NODULE FUNCTION

Table 4 lists some host-mediated traits affecting nodule function. Several of these, each controlled by a single recessive gene, are probably the result of loss mutations at specific loci. Thus, Viands *et al.* (1979) described an ineffective trait in *Medicago sativa* in which nodule development was normal or even enhanced, but carbohydrate accumulated in the root, and there was no bacteroid development. While similar, often strain-specific, defects are relatively common in the literature, I will emphasize in this section effectiveness subgroups and those factors which collectively lead to natural variation between cultivars in ability to fix N_2.

Effectiveness subgroups

Subgroups that vary in their ability to fix N_2 with particular *Rhizobium* strains exist in many of the so-called cross-inoculation groups. Burton (1967)

TABLE 4: Some host-controlled factors affecting nodule function in legumes.

FACTOR	LEGUME	REFERENCE
Bacteroid function	*P. sativum*	Holl (1973)
	M. sativa	Viands *et. al.* (1979)
Delayed senescence	*G. max*	Abu Shakra *et al.* (1978)
Effectiveness subgroups	various	Burton (1967)
		Date & Norris (1979)
Energy partitioning	various	Graham & Halliday (1977)
Energy requirement for fixation	*Lupinus, Vigna*	Layzell *et al.* (1980)
Form of N exported	various	Pate (1980)
Hydrogenase regulation	*P. sativum*	Dixon (1972)
Leghemoglobin synthesis	*Lupinus, Ornithopus*	Dilworth (1969)
Maturity characteristics	*G. max*	Hardy *et al.* (1973)
Not specified	*T. subterraneum*	Gibson (1964)
	T. pratense	Nutman (1968)

found *Vigna unguiculata* and *Arachis hypogaea* to vary in response to a range of cowpea group rhizobia. In the same paper he established six effectiveness subgroups within the genus *Trifolium*. The inability of sub-clover lines to fix N_2 when nodulated with *Rhizobium* from white clover has been a major problem in Australia (Vincent, 1954).

The situation in the genus *Stylosanthes* is even more complex. Date & Norris (1979) reported that 103 of 318 *Stylosanthes* accessions were ineffectively nodulated by the inoculant strain CB 756. These included 67 of 142 accessions of *S. guianensis* and 31 of 41 accessions of *S. hamata*. Nine *S. guianensis* and four other accessions were consistently ineffective in N_2 fixation when tested with 22 rhizobia from a range of *Stylosanthes* spp. (see Table 5). Effective response patterns in *Stylosanthes* have been related to cultivar habitat (Date, Burt & Williams, 1979) and, in *S. guianensis,* to seed isoenzymes (Robinson, Date & Megarrity, 1976).

Cultivar and species variation in N_2 fixation

Variation in ability to fix N_2 occurs both between and within species. At the former level, Layzell *et al.* (1979) found cowpeas to expend less energy in nodule maintenance and respiration than did lupin, while Sen & Weaver (1980) found that the specific nodule activity of *Arachis hypogaea* nodules was greater than that of cowpea nodules.

Differences between cultivars of the same species in ability to fix N_2 in symbiosis with *Rhizobium* have now been demonstrated in a range of legumes

TABLE 5: Response of accessions of *Stylosanthes* spp. to inoculation with *Rhizobium* isolated from that genus (from Date & Norris, 1979).

Species of *Stylosanthes*	Accessions giving ineffective response with CB756	Response of accessions ineffective with CB756 to inoculation with 22 other strains		
		No. accessions tested	Effective with various strains	Effective with no strain
S. fruticosa	0	0		
S. guianensis	47	8	24	9
S. hamata	75	7	22	5
S. humilis	5	2	2	
S. scabra	4	0		
S. subsericea	0	0		
S. viscosa	9	1	0	1
S. spp.	50	4	1	3

including clover (Gibson & Brockwell, 1968; Mytton, 1975), soybean (Hardy, Burns & Holsten, 1973), beans (Graham & Halliday, 1977; Graham, 1981; Rennie & Kemp, 1981), *Medicago* (Gibson, 1962; Seetin & Barnes, 1977) cowpea (Zary *et al.,* 1978), *Vicia* (El-Sherbeeny, Lawes & Mytton 1977), *Pisum* (Holl & La Rue, 1975) and *Desmodium* (Hutton & Coote, 1972; Imrie, 1975). While these differences can be compounded by host/strain interactions (Mytton, El-Sherbeeny & Lawes, 1977; Minchin, Summerfield & Eaglesham, 1978) and climate differences (Graham, 1981; Rennie & Kemp, 1981) they appear to stem mainly from differences in the supply of carbohydrate. Studies undertaken in recent years and using techniques such as leaf and pod removal, grafting, supplemental light, shading, and $^{14}CO_2$ fertilization leave little doubt that photosynthate supply to nodules is the primary factor limiting N_2 fixation in legumes (Lawrie & Wheeler, 1973; Lawn & Brun, 1974; Minchin & Pate, 1974; Hardy & Havelka, 1976; Herridge & Pate, 1977; Mahon, 1977).

A number of host traits interact to regulate carbohydrate supply to nodules. Best documented among these is the time varieties take to flower and mature. Hardy *et al.* (1973) demonstrated that early-flowering soybean cultivars tended to fix less N_2 than those of the later-maturity groups, while N_2 fixation in beans was almost doubled by a photoperiod-induced delay in flowering (J. Day & P.H. Graham, unpublished data). Such results presumably reflect a delay in the onset of competition for energy and other nutrients between developing pods and nodules. Unfortunately, extending the growth cycle of cultivars in the tropics, where many grain legumes are already subject to water stress at flowering, could be difficult.

Source of the photosynthate for nodules is another important factor. Waters *et al.* (1980), using *P. vulgaris,* showed that 85% of the $^{14}CO_2$ absorbed by the leaf at node 4 passed to root and nodules, but that, fed to leaves on higher nodes, it tended to remain in the above-ground parts. Leaves at the lower nodes are subject to shading and tend to decline in efficiency after canopy closure (Tanaka & Fujita, 1979). Differences also exist between legumes in leaf area duration, with *P. acutifolius* and *P. vulgaris* on the low, and *G. max* and *Cajanus cajan* at the high end of the range (CIAT, 1981).

Adequate partitioning of carbohydrate between root and nodules must also be critical to nodule function. Accumulation of carbohydrate in roots is a characteristic of several of the ineffective conditions listed in Table 4; the sym 3 condition detailed by Holl & La Rue (1975) is actually capable of N_2 fixation when supplied succinate as an energy source. Male sterile soybeans have been shown to accumulate up to five times normal carbohydrate levels in the root with little benefit to fixation (Wilson *et al.,* 1978). Among commercial bean cultivars Graham & Halliday (1977) identified some lines that were essentially similar in total root system carbohydrate but differed by 5-100 fold in the carbohydrate recovered from nodules.

IMPLICATIONS FOR BREEDING

Holl & La Rue (1975) suggested a minimum of ten host genes controlling nodulation and N_2 fixation in legumes. From points made in this presentation, and as they themselves suggested, this number is likely to be extremely conservative. With so many genes involved, it is not really surprising that we continue to identify cultivars that are defective in some trait limiting nodulation or N_2 fixation. What is important is that plant breeders and microbiologists cooperate to control this problem, with no lines distributed before they have been evaluated for symbiotic potential. Some breeding programs are likely to be more subject to problems than others; thus, we have preliminary results from which it appears that cultivars selected for low phosphorus (P) tolerance achieve plant growth at low P at the expense of nodule development.

On the positive side, it is becoming evident that the host-controlled differences reported in this paper can be used to overcome current problems in N_2 fixation. Breeding programs underway in several laboratories aim to produce cultivars that bypass the natural *Rhizobium* population in soil but nodulate readily with highly effective inoculant strains. Breeding for enhanced N_2 fixation also does not appear as difficult as originally considered (see also p. 39). With that said, there are still many methodological problems to be faced: for example, what nondestructive criteria could be used to evaluate fixation; under what climatic and fertility conditions should fixation be measured; should we breed for N_2 fixation with a single and highly competitive isolate or with a mixture of strains simulating natural populations; and how do we most effectively combine enhanced fixation rates with other needed agronomic and disease resistance traits.

In pathology circles these days there is much talk of the "gene for gene" relationship: essentially that, in a plant/pathogen interaction, each gene for virulence in the pathogen is paralleled by a corresponding gene for susceptibility in the host species. This concept appears to apply well, in a positive direction, to the legume/*Rhizobium* symbiosis. It could mean that for many of the problems in N_2 fixation today, there is both a host and a *Rhizobium* solution. It is exciting that the host side of things appears to be opening up, and I look forward to both rapid progress and many challenges in the future.

REFERENCES

Abu-Shakra, S.S., Phillips, D.A. & Huffaker, R.C. (1978) *Science* 199, 973-975.

Bowen, G.D. (1961) *Plant Soil* 15, 155-165.

Broughton, W.J. (1978) *J. Appl. Bacter.* 45, 165-194.

Burton, J.C. (1967) *Rhizobium* culture and use. *In:* Microbial technology, H.J. Peppler (Ed.). Van Nostrand Reinhold, New York, NY, USA. Pp. 1-33.

Caldwell, B.E. (1966) *Crop Sci.* 6, 427-428.

Caldwell, B.E. & Vest, G. (1968) *Crop Sci.* 8, 680-682.

Centro Internacional de Agricultura Tropical (CIAT) (1981) Annual report, 1980.

Dart, P.J. (1975) Legume root nodule initiation and development. *In:* The development and function of roots. J.G. Torrey & D.T. Clarkson (Eds.). Academic Press, London, England. Pp. 467-506.

Date, R.A., Burt, R.L. & Williams, W.T. (1979) *Agro-Ecosystems* 5, 57-67.

Date, R.A. & Norris, D.O. (1979) *Aust. J. Agric. Res.* 30, 85-104.

Dazzo, F.B. (1980) Infection processes in the *Rhizobium*-legume symbiosis. *In:* Advances in legume science, R.J. Summerfield & A.H. Bunting (Eds.). Royal Botanic Gardens, Kew, England. Pp. 49-59.

Devine, T.E. & Weber, D.F. (1977) *Euphytica* 26, 527-535.

Dilworth, M.J. (1969). *Biochim. Biophys. Acta* 184, 432-441.

Dixon, R.O. (1972) *Archiv. Mikrobiol.* 84, 193-201.

El-Sherbeeny, M.H., Lawes, D.A. & Mytton, L.R. (1977) *Euphytica* 26, 377-383.

Gareth Jones, D. & Hardarson, G. (1979) *Ann. Appl. Biol.* 92, 221-228.

Gibson, A.H. (1962) *Aust. J. Agric. Res.* 13, 388-399.

Gibson, A.H. (1964) *Aust. J. Agric. Res.* 15, 37-49.

Gibson, A.H. (1968) *Aust. J. Agric. Res.* 19, 907-918.

Gibson, A.H. & Brockwell, J. (1968) *Aust. J. Agric. Res.* 19, 891-905.

Graham, P.H. (1973) Plant-*Rhizobium* interaction and its importance to agriculture. *In:* Genes, enzymes and populations, A.M. Srb (Ed.). Plenum Press, New York, NY, USA. Pp. 321-330.

Graham, P.H. (1981) *Field Crops Res.* 4, 93-112.

Graham, P.H. & Halliday, J. (1977) Inoculation and nitrogen fixation in the genus *Phaseolus*. *In:* Exploiting the legume-*Rhizobium* symbiosis in tropical agriculture, J.M. Vincent, A.S. Whitney & J. Bose (Eds.). Univ. Hawaii Coll. Trop. Agric. *Misc. Publ.* 145. Pp. 313-334.

Graham, P.H. & Hubbell D.H. (1975) Florida Agric. Exp. Sta. *J. Ser.* 5439, 9-21.

Hardarson, G. & Gareth Jones, D. (1979) *Ann. Appl. Biol.* 92, 329-333.

Hardy, R.W.F., Burns, R.C. & Holsten, R.D. (1973) *Soil Biol. Biochem.* 4, 47-82.

Hardy, R.W.F. & Havelka, U.D. (1976) Photosynthate as a major factor limiting nitrogen fixation by field grown legumes, with emphasis on soybeans. *In:* Symbiotic nitrogen fixation in plants, P.S. Nutman (Ed.). Cambridge Univ. Press, Cambridge, England. Pp. 421-439.

Hely, F.W. (1957) *Aust. J. Biol. Sci.* 10, 1-6.

Hely, F.W., Bonnier, C. & Manil, P. (1953) *Nature* (Lond.) 171, 884-885.

Herridge, D.F. & Pate, J.S. (1977) *Plant Physiol.* 60, 759-764.

Holl, F.B. (1973) *Can. J. Genet. Cytol.* 15, 659 (cited by Holl & La Rue, 1975).

Holl, F.B. & La Rue, T.A. (1975) Proc. 1st. Int. Symp. on N_2 Fixation. Washington State Univ. Press, Pullman, WA, USA. Vol. 2, Pp. 391-399.

Hutton, E.M. & Coote, J.N. (1972) *J. Aust. Inst. Agric. Sci.* 38, 68-69.

Imrie, B.C. (1975) *Euphytica* 24, 625-631.

Kidby, D.K. & Goochild, F.J. (1966) *J. Gen. Microbiol.* 45, 147-157.

Lange, R.T. (1961) *J. Gen. Microbiol.* 26, 351-359.

Lange, R.T. & Parker, C.A. (1960) *Plant Soil* 13, 137-146.

Lange, R.T. & Parker, C.A. (1961) *Nature* (Lond.) 186, 178-179.

Lawn, R.J. & Brun, W.A. (1974) *Crop Sci.* 14, 11-16.

Lawrie, A.C. & Wheeler, C.T. (1973) *New Phytol.* 72, 1341-1348.

Layzell, D.B., Rainbird, R.M., Atkins, C.A., & Pate, J.S. (1979) *Plant Physiol.* 64, 888-891.

Lie, T.A., Hille, D., Lambers, R., & Houers, A. (1976) Symbiotic specialization in the pea plant. Some environmental effects on nodulation and nitrogen fixation. *In:* Symbiotic nitrogen fixation in plants, P.S. Nutman (Ed.). Cambridge Univ. Press. Cambridge, England. Pp. 319-333.

Mahon, J.D. (1977) *Plant Physiol.* 60, 817-82.

Materon, L.A. & Vincent, J.M. (1980) *Field Crops Res.* 3, 215-224.

Minchin, F.R. & Pate, J.S. (1974) *J. Expl. Bot.* 24, 259-271.

Minchin, F.R., Summerfield, R.J., & Eaglesham, A.R.J. (1978) *Trop. Agric.* (Trin.) 55, 107-115.

Mytton, L.R. (1975) *Ann. Appl. Biol.* 80, 103-107.

Mytton, L.R., El-Sherbeeny, M.H. & Lawes, D.A. (1977) *Euphytica* 26, 785-791.

Nangju, D. (1980) *Agron. J.* 72, 403-406.

Nutman, P.S. (1954) *Heredity* 8, 47-60.

Nutman, P.S. (1967) *Aust. J. Agric. Res.* 18, 381-425.

Nutman, P.S. (1968) *Heredity* 23, 537-551.

Pate, J.S. (1980) *Ann. Rev. Plant Physiol.* 3, 313-340.

Rennie, R.J. & Kemp, G.A. (1981) *Euphytica* 30, 87-95.

Robinson, P.J., Date, R.A., & Megarrity, R.G. (1976) *Aust. J. Agric. Res.* 27, 381-389.

Seetin, M.W. & Barnes, D.K. (1977) *Crop Sci.* 17, 783-787.

Sen, D. & Weaver, R.W. (1980) *Plant Sci. Letters* 18, 315-318.

Tanaka, A. & Fujita, K. (1979) *J. Fac. Agric. Hokkaido Univ.* 59, 145-238.

Thompson. J.A. (1960) *Nature* (Lond.) 187, 619-620.

Van Egerat. A.W.S.M. (1972) *Medelelingen Landbou Whogescool Wageningen* 72-27, 90 pp.

Vest, G. (1970) *Crop Sci.* 10, 34-35.

Vest, G. & Caldwell, B.E. (1972) *Crop Sci.* 12, 692-693.

Viands, D.R.. Vance. C.P., Heichel, G.H., & Barnes, D.K. (1979) *Crop Sci.* 19, 905-908.

Vincent, J.M. (1954) *Aust. J. Agric. Res.* 5, 55-60.

Waters, L.. Breen. P.J., Mack, H.J., & Graham, P.H. (1980) *J. Amer. Soc. Hort. Sci.* 105. 424-427.

Wilson, R.J.. Burton, J.W., Buck, J.A., & Brim, C.A. (1978) *Plant Physiol.* 61, 838-841.

Zary, K.W., Miller, J.C., Weaver, R.W., & Barnes, L.W. (1978) *J. Amer. Soc. Hort. Sci.* 103, 806-808.

SELECTION FOR ENHANCED NITROGEN FIXATION IN COMMON BEANS, *PHASEOLUS VULGARIS*

J. McFerson, F.A. Bliss, and J.C. Rosas[1]

Summary

A backcross/inbred method of population development in which 'Puebla 152' was the donor parent and 'Jamapa', 'Porrillo Sintético', 'ICA Pijao', 'Ex Rico 23', and 'Sanilac' were the recurrent parents, was used to develop a number of nearly homozygous lines, similar in most traits to the recurrent parent. When these materials were evaluated for nitrogen(C_2H_2) fixation and yield under field conditions, considerable variation in both traits was found, with transgressive segregation evident. In population 24, most families proved better than the recurrent parent, 'Sanilac', in both yield and N_2 (C_2H_2) fixation.

INTRODUCTION

Selection for increased potential for nitrogen (N_2) fixation in a legume must be approached with the host/*Rhizobium* symbiotic relationship clearly in mind. Rhizobial strain improvement must occur with respect to a specified set of host-plant genotypes, while host improvement pertains to a set of rhizobial strains. Under field conditions this set of rhizobial strains may either be initially defined by inoculation with specific strains, or left undefined if native soil rhizobia are relied upon. Clearly, the potential of the symbiotic relationship will be modified further by such factors as the competitiveness and efficiency of the infective rhizobial strains, the prevailing environment, and the cultural practices peculiar to the cropping system.

In common bean (*Phaseolus vulgaris* L.) considerable variability exists among genotypes for N_2 fixation potential. Several studies under both controlled environment and field conditions show large and consistent

[1] Dept. of Horticulture, University of Wisconsin, Madison, WI. 53706 USA.

differences for nodule number, nodule mass, plant specific activity (measured by the acetylene reduction (AR) technique in μmol C_2H_4/plant. unit time), specific nodule activity, and accumulated N (Graham & Halliday, 1977; Westerman & Kolar, 1978; Graham, 1979). However, these important differences are confounded with other plant characteristics that may affect N_2 fixation potential either directly or indirectly. For example, beans with a determinate bush growth habit (Type 1) ordinarily fix less N than Type 2 (indeterminate bush) or Type 3 (indeterminate prostrate) lines, while the highest fixers are usually in the Type 4 (climbing) category (Graham & Rosas, 1977). Late-maturing lines also appear to be better fixers than early-maturing lines. It should be stressed that commercial bean cultivars have shown poor response to inoculation (Graham & Halliday, 1977) and generally exhibit levels of plant specific activity considerably lower than other grain legumes such as soybean (*Glycine max* (L.) Merrill) (Hardy *et al.*, 1968) and cowpea (*Vigna unguiculata* (L.) Walp.) (Zary *et al.*, 1978).

Using superior plant materials identified at the Centro Internacional de Agricultura Tropical (CIAT) by Graham and colleagues, we have undertaken genetic and breeding studies addressing the following questions:

Are host plant differences for N_2 fixation in the common bean heritable?

Can high N_2 fixation potential be transferred into Type 1 and Type 2 plants?

What host factors are associated with high N_2 fixation potential?

MATERIALS AND METHODS

Six bean cultivars were chosen as parents for the breeding and genetic studies: 'Puebla 152', 'Jamapa', 'Porrillo Sintético', 'ICA Pijao', 'Ex Rico 23', and 'Sanilac'. In order to develop populations with a family structure suitable for replicated field trials, we employed a scheme which we call the backcross/inbred method (see Figure 1), a procedure patterned after the one described by Wehrhahn and Allard (1965) for investigating the inheritance of quantitative traits. 'Puebla 152', a high-fixing, high-yielding, Type 3 line, served as the donor parent in each of five crosses to the other five lines. These five lines were selected as recurrent parents since they are well-adapted, commercially acceptable cultivars and represent a range of N_2 fixation levels, yield potentials, plant types, seed colors and other pertinent traits. Development of the backcross/inbred populations involved backcrossing each F_1 to the specified recurrent parent to obtain approximately 60 seeds. Each of the 60 resulting BC_1 plants was again backcrossed to the recurrent parent to produce 60 unique BC_2 seeds. Each BC_2 plant was advanced through three generations of selfing using single seed descent to generate a population of 60 near-homozygous lines (coefficient of inbreeding, 0.98). At this point, sufficient seed of the backcross/inbred families, each incorporating

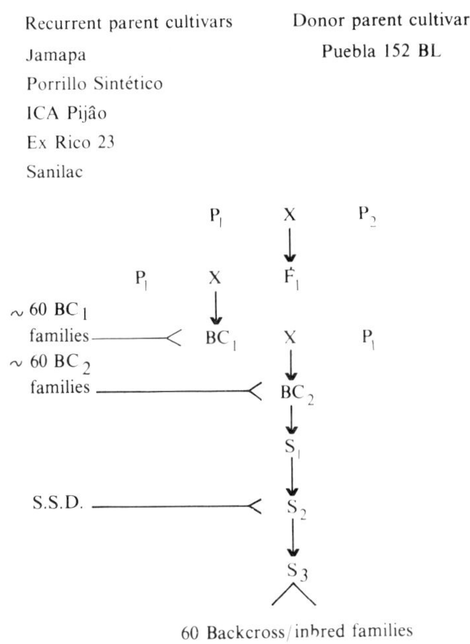

Figure 1. The backcross/inbred method of population development.

different traits of the donor parent into the genetic background of the recurrent parent, was available for replicated field trials.

Three populations having as recurrent parents the cultivars Jamapa (population 20), Porrillo Sintetico (population 21), and Sanilac (population 24), were planted June 3 - 4, 1980, in a completely random design with unequal replications at the Hancock Experiment Station, Hancock, WI, USA. Soil type at the station is a Plainfield sandy loam. Fertilizer 0-0-60 at 150 kg/ha was applied preplant. Rows were 1 m apart with 10 cm between plants. Seed was treated immediately prior to sowing with a fungicide (Thiram) and insecticide (Diazinon). Inoculum composited from four regionally adapted strains was supplied by the Nitragin Co., Milwaukee, WI, USA, and applied by hand at planting. A complete stand was assured by overplanting and thinning seedlings two weeks after planting.

When each entry reached the 50% bloom stage, or R3 stage as defined by Lebaron (1974), a five-plant sample was used to determine acetylene reduction (AR) value, following the general procedure outlined by Graham & Rosas (1977). Previous experiments had shown that AR values peak near this physiological stage. A 469 ml incubation container was used and ethylene gas samples stored in 10 ml vacutainers (Becton-Dickinson, New Jersey, Cat. No. 4710) until gas chromatographic analysis. At maturity a ten-plant sample was taken to determine yield.

RESULTS AND DISCUSSION

The distributions of mean values for AR value and yield of backcross/inbred families for the three populations are shown in Figures 2-4. Parental AR values were lower than had been found in previous studies, due probably to environmental effects. However, rankings and relative differences were similar to earlier results. Parental seed yields were higher than previously, but again, rankings and relative differences were similar to previous results. In all cases we found wide ranges for both AR value and yield, with several families surpassing their respective donor and recurrent parents in both high and low directions. This is particularly striking in population 24 (see Figure 4), where most families were higher than the recurrent parent 'Sanilac' for both AR value and yield. Although the correlation between yield and AR value was highly significant (r = 0.25), the relatively low magnitude indicated the association between yield and AR value was not extremely close. This was

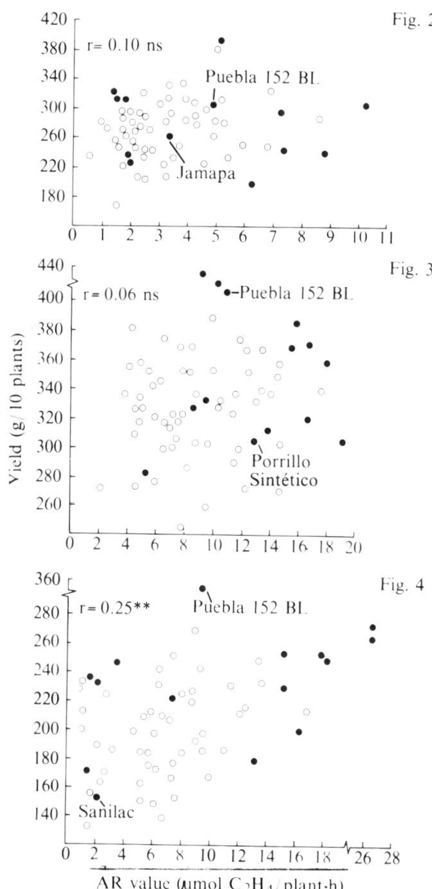

Figures 2-4.
Mean values for yield and acetylene reduction (AR) value of backcross/inbred families. Solid circles represent families selected for further study. Fig. 2 =popn. 20, Fig. 3 = popn. 21, Fig. 4 = popn. 24.

evident in populations 20 and 21 (Figures 3 & 4), where correlations were low and nonsignificant (r=0.10 and r=0.06, respectively). Recombinant families not only differed for AR value and yield, but they also showed comparable variability for other traits such as date to flower, 50% bloom, and harvest; plant type; seed color and size; and percentage of seed protein.

This was the expected result of our backcross breeding procedure, where the goal was to improve an otherwise acceptable recurrent parent by transferring a specific trait from the donor parent. The particular utility of the approach is the rapid development of a large number of recombinant families similar to the recurrent parent but differing *inter se* for an assortment of both qualitative and quantitative traits. The magnitude of these differences should be related to the contrast between the parents for the specific trait. For example, in population 24, where the parents differed widely for AR value; yield; date to flower, 50% bloom and harvest; and plant type, we recovered families exhibiting various combinations of these characters. Thus, we identified high-fixing, high-yielding families that had the 'Sanilac' seed type but differed for the other traits mentioned. The level of variation in populations 20 and 21 where the parents contrasted less was not as great; yet it was sufficient for us to select families that possessed combinations of characteristics of interest in further breeding and physiological studies.

The solid circles in Figures 2-4 represent families we have selected both for field studies in Wisconsin and Colombia and for controlled environment studies in Wisconsin. We hope to characterize more fully the performance of selected families under different environments; particularly high-fixing, high-yielding, recombinant families. At the same time, investigations focusing on some of the physiological differences among families showing different levels of AR value should help us identify more precisely the host factors associated with high N_2 fixation potential. In conclusion, the backcross/inbred method was effective in transferring quantitative traits into agronomically acceptable cultivars and in developing populations of recombinant families useful in genetic and physiological studies.

REFERENCES

Graham, P.H. (1979) Influence of temperature on growth and nitrogen fixation in cultivars of *Phaseolus vulgaris* L. inoculated with *Rhizobium*. *J. Agric. Sci.* (Camb.) 93. 365-370

Graham, P.H. & Halliday, J. (1977) Inoculation and nitrogen fixation in the genus *Phaseolus*. *In:* Exploiting the legume-*Rhizobium* symbiosis in tropical agriculture. J.M.Vincent, A.S.Whitney & J. Bose, (Eds.). Univ. Hawaii College Trop. Agric. *Misc. Publ.* 145. Pp. 313-334.

Graham, P.H. & Rosas, J.C. (1977) Growth and development of indeterminate bush and climbing cultivars of *Phaseolus vulgaris* L. inoculated with *Rhizobium*. *J. Agric. Sci.*, (Camb.) 88, 503-508.

Hardy, R.W.F., Holsten, P.D., Jackson, E.K., & Burns, R.C. (1968) The acetylene-ethylene assay for N_2 fixation: laboratory and field evaluation. *Plant Physiol.* 43, 1185-1205.

Lebaron, M.J. (1974) Developmental stages of the common bean. Univ. Idaho Coll. Agric. *Curr. Info. Series* No. 228.

Wehrhahn, C. & Allard, R.W. (1965) The detection and measurement of the effects of individual genes involved in the inheritance of a quantitative character in wheat. *Genetics* 51, 109-119.

Westerman, D.T. & Kolar, J.J. (1978) Symbiotic N_2 (C_2H_2) fixation by bean. *Crop Sci.* 18, 986-990.

Zary, K.W., Miller, J.C., Weaver, R.W., & Barnes, L.W. (1978) Intraspecific variability for nitrogen fixation in southernpea (*Vigna unguiculata* (L.) Walp). *J. Amer. Soc. Hort. Sci.* 103, 806-808.

BIOLOGICAL NITROGEN FIXATION AS A CRITERION FOR SOYBEAN BREEDING: PRELIMINARY RESULTS

M.S. Chowdhury and A.L. Doto[1]

Summary

While breeding of soybeans in Tanzania has been conducted since 1955. little attention has been paid to the biological nitrogen fixation (BNF) of selected cultivars. In this preliminary study the USA cultivar Bossier was crossed with a local cultivar, IH 192, and F_3 lines were evaluated for both N_2 fixation and desirable agronomic traits. F_3 lines showed transgressive segregation, with some showing better yield and nodulation parameters than either parent.

INTRODUCTION

Soybean (*Glycine max*) was introduced into Tanzania around 1907 and was grown commercially in Bukoba from 1939-1947. A breeding program for soybean was initiated at Nachingwea in 1955 (Auckland, 1970) and has produced several high-yielding, yellow-seeded soybean varieties for the low, medium, and high altitudes (Mmbaga, 1975). Their agronomic properties have also been studied at a number of locations and recommended cultivars have been released for commercial production. Exotic cultivars from a number of sources are still being tested, but some (e.g., 'Bossier') have already proved superior to local cultivars 3H/1 and 1H192. The latter cultivars are tall, bushy, and branched and require 70 and 120 days, respectively, to flower and mature. They perform well in areas or years with good rainfall, but often fail in seasons of uneven or limited rainfall. While effectively nodulated by native roil rhizobia (Chowdhury, 1977), the nodulation and ability to fix nitrogen (N_2) of these cultivars has not been studied in detail. By contrast, 'Bossier' is a short-duration cultivar, short in stature and with less branching. Its yield is comparable to that of IH 192, and it can be successfully grown in

[1] Faculty of Agriculture, Forestry and Veterinary Science, Univ. of Dar es Salaam, P.O. Box 643, Morogoro. Tanzania.

areas with rainfall of short duration. 'Bossier' and other exotic cultivars like 'Improved Pelican' are sparsely or are not nodulated by native soil rhizobia, and they respond favorably to rhizobial inoculation (Chowdhury, 1977; Sachansky, 1977).

Legume improvement through selection and breeding for enhanced N_2 fixation has recently been recommended in order to minimize N fertilizer usage (LaRue, 1978). N_2 fixation has not been a priority in Tanzanian work with soybean improvement and, to the best of our knowledge, has not been considered in other programs of the region, save perhaps for work undertaken at the International Institute of Tropical Agriculture (IITA). As inoculant technology in Tanzania —particularly in regard to the supply and storage of high-quality inoculants— is limited, we have initiated studies to produce agronomically superior, short-duration cultivars able to symbiose effectively with native soil rhizobia.

MATERIALS AND METHODS

Soybean cultivars IH 192 (local) and Bossier (exotic) were used as parents. These varieties were stagger sown in the field as well as in pots so that the flowering of both varieties could be synchronized for crossing. Crosses were made by emasculation and pollination between 6:00 and 7:00 A.M. as well as between 6:00 and 7:00 P.M. Reciprocal crosses were attempted. The pollinated flowers were covered with small plastic bags to avoid excessive dehydration.

Two seeds from a successful cross were planted in Leonard jars using N-free Thornton's medium and inoculated with 1:10 soil:water suspension. One of the plants was grown to maturity, when 16 good seeds from 6 pods were obtained; the other was examined for nodulation at flowering. The 16 F_2 seeds were planted in 5 l plastic buckets containing a mixture of 50% river sand and 50% local soil. F_3 seeds from each plant were collected separately and designated lines 1-16. Twelve seeds from each F_3 line, as well as the parents, were grown in the field with irrigation during the 1980-1981 dry season. Nodulation, $N_2(C_2H_2)$ fixation, plant height, degree of branching, pod number, and seed weight/plant were evaluated.

RESULTS AND DISCUSSION

The one F_1 plant examined for nodulation appeared effectively nodulated by the native soil rhizobia. The other plant completed its life cycle in N-free sand culture and formed 6 pods, indicating some ability to symbiose with the native rhizobia. The sixteen F_2 seeds obtained were all viable, producing plants that grew well in 50:50 soil:sand mixture and showed no sign of deficiency. Again this indicates some ability to symbiose with the native strains, although some plants grew better than others.

TABLE 1: Characteristics of promising segregates and their parents.

Materials		Dry nodule mass/plant (mg)	N_2-ase activity μ mol C_2H_4/ plant · h	Days to flower	Plant height (cm)	No branches/ plant	No pods/ plant	Seed wt/ plant
Parents	'Bossier'	2	1.90	40	47.2	4.9	48.6	5.15
	IH 192	67	6.80	68	50.0	6.6	74.6	4.88
High yielding segregates	Line 3	38	10.30	38	58.7	6.5	103.4	6.83
with high BNF	Line 16	42	10.30	38	57.4	5.4	104.0	11.16
High yielding segregates with	Line 1	14	2.60	38	54.3	4.9	80.1	8.35
low BNF	Line 10	15	1.24	38	55.0	5.3	101.3	9.04
Range of 16 F_3 families		2-191	1.15-10.30	38-40	30.5-58.7	4.1-6.5	24-104	2.2-11.2

The figures in the table are the mean values of 3 to 9 plants.

Transgressive segregation was observed for all the characteristics studied among the 16 lines of F_3 plants grown in the field. The ranges in values of the characters studied for the parents and the F plants are shown in Table 1. Most of the segregates flowered 2 days earlier than their parents except line 9, which took 40 days to flower, as did 'Bossier'. Lines 4, 6, 9, and 11 were shorter in stature than 'Bossier', and all of them had lower seed yields than their parents. Among them, lines 9 and 11 had less nodulation (nodule mass between 2 and 3 mg/plant) and low nitrogenase activity (2.2 μ mol C_2H_4 produced/plant per h), while line 6 showed extensive nodulation (191 mg nodule tissue/plant) and moderate to high nitrogenase activity (7.32 μ mol C_2H_4 produced/plant per h). Two lines (Nos. 3 and 16) showed both high yield and good N_2fixation (see Table 1).

Given the promising nature of these results additional crosses between cvs. Bossier and IH 92 have been made and are being advanced to the F_3 generation for detailed testing of both agronomic traits and ability to fix N_2. With the high cost of fertilizer N to countries such as Tanzania, it is imperative that future soybean breeding programs consider BNF as a prime criterion in the development and selection of new cultivars.

REFERENCES

Auckland, A.K. (1970) Soya bean improvement in East Africa. *In*: Crop improvement in East Africa, C.L.A. Leakey (Ed.). Commonwealth Agricultural Bureaux, England. Pp. 129-156.

Chowdhury, M.S. (1977) Response of soybean to *Rhizobium* inoculation at Morogoro, Tanzania. *In*: Biological nitrogen fixation in farming systems of the tropics. Ayanaba and P.J. Dart (Eds.). Wiley, New York, NY, USA. Pp. 245-253.

LaRue, T.A. (Ed.) (1978) Selecting and breeding legumes for enhanced nitrogen fixation. Proc. Workshop, Boyce Thompson Institute, Cornell Univ., Ithaca, NY, USA.

Mmbaga, E.T. (1975) Highlights of soybean production in Tanzania. *In*: Soybean production, protection and utilization, D.K. Whigham (Ed.). INTSOY Series, No. 6. Univ. of Illinois, Urbana, IL, USA. Pp. 252-255.

Sachansky, S. (1977) *Trop. Grain Legume Bull.* 7, 15-17.

GENETIC MANIPULATION OF NODULATION IN GROUNDNUT

P.T.C. Nambiar, P.J. Dart, S.N. Nigam and R.W. Gibbons[1]

Summary

There is large variation among cultivars of groundnut in ability to nodulate and fix nitrogen (N), and in seasonal and diurnal patterns of nitrogenase activity. Total N uptake, or total dry matter production, may be a useful index in ranking cultivars for N_2-fixing ability.

Certain cultivars of *Arachis hypogaea* ssp. *hypogaea* var. *hypogaea* formed up to 13% of their total nodule number on the hypocotyl, and some cultivars even nodulated on the stem above the crown of the plant. In contrast, cultivars from *A. hypogaea* ssp. *fastigiata* var. *fastigiata* and var. *vulgaris* formed few nodules on the hypocotyl. Non-nodulating plants have been observed in 13 crosses. Genetic analysis indicates that two independent recessive genes are involved. Some progeny of these crosses also form a few big nodules, a trait which seems to be controlled by the host plant.

INTRODUCTION

The number of nodules formed by legumes, and their effectiveness, is governed by both plant and *Rhizobium* genes, with large differences in nodulation and nitrogen (N_2) fixation already reported for cultivars of soybean (Vorhees, 1915), peas (Holl & LaRue, 1976) cowpea (Zary, *et al.*, 1978) and groundnut (Wynne, Elkan & Schneeweis, 1980; Nambiar & Dart, 1980). It may be possible to increase N_2 fixation in legumes by genetic manipulation. This paper summarizes our efforts to establish genotypic differences in N_2 fixation among groundnut cultivars and understand the genetics of non-nodulation in groundnut.

---

[1] CP No. 57. ICRISAT Patancheru, P.O. Andra Pradesh 502 324, India

BOTANICAL VARIATION IN *ARACHIS HYPOGAEA* L.

The genus *Arachis* belongs to the tribe Aeschynomeneae (Leguminosae, subtribe, Papilionoideae) with 22 described and possibly 40 undescribed species (Gregory, Krapovickas & Gregory, 1980). There is a great diversity within the genus. For example plant type varies from upright forms to prostrate types with runners, and the growing period required extends from short-duration annual to perennial. The cultivated groundnut, *A. hypogaea,* is an annual tetraploid (4n = 40). Based on morphology, the species is subdivided into subspecies *hypogaea,* which includes var. *hypogaea,* and var. *hirsuta,* and subspecies *fastigiata* which includes var. *fastigiata* and var. *vulgaris* (Krapovickas, 1973). The *hypogaea* ssp. includes long-duration, alternately branched "Virginia types," mostly with runner and spreading bunch growth habits while the *fastigiata* ssp. includes short-duration, sequentially branched types mainly with an upright branch habit, the "Spanish" and "Valencia types."

The cultivated groundnut is grown throughout the tropics and subtropics between latitudes 40° N and 40° S, where rainfall during the growing season exceeds 500 mm. The crop grows best in well-drained, sandy loams, and tolerates air temperatures between 20° C and 40° C. The crop duration varies with the location and season of cultivation — the Spanish and Valencia types normally mature 90 to 110 days after planting, while the Virginia types mature 130 to 150 days after planting.

VARIATION IN N_2 FIXATION AMONG GROUNDNUT CULTIVARS

N_2 fixation in groundnut is closely related to photosynthesis (Nambiar & Dart, 1980). Figure 1 shows seasonal variation in N_2 fixation among nine groundnut cultivars. In general, the Virginia types ('Florunner', MK 374, 'Florigiant', M 13, and 'Kadiri 71-1') formed more nodules and fixed more N_2 than the Valencia ('Ganpapuri', MH 2, and PI 59747) and Spanish (Ah 8189) types. A similar trend was observed in field experiments in North Carolina by Wynne *et al.* (1980). In all the cultivars, N_2 fixation started at around 25-30 days after planting with significant genotypic differences apparent by 30 days, and with no interaction between sampling date and cultivar ranking until after 50 days, a time that generally corresponds to early pod filling. Cultivar differences in pod filling and partitioning also become evident at this growth stage (McCloud *et al.*, 1980), and in turn affect energy supply to the nodules. This may explain the cultivar x sampling-time interaction for nitrogenase activity per plant that could be observed from the fourth sampling on. In most cultivars nodule senescence started during this stage of plant growth, along with a decline in N_2 fixation per plant.

Fifty-two selected germplasm lines were screened over three seasons (1977-1979) for nodulation and N_2 fixation using the acetylene reduction assay

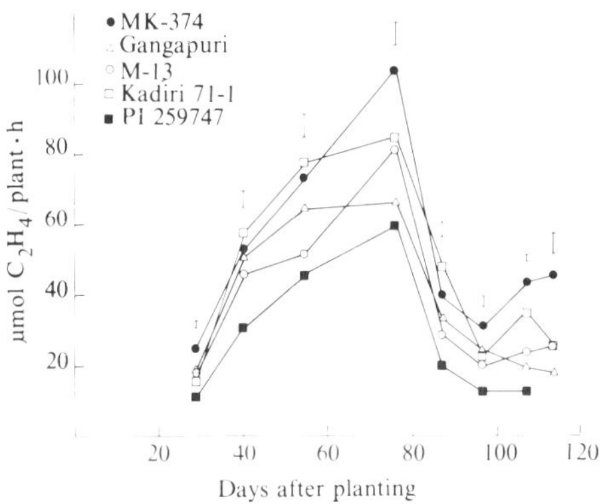

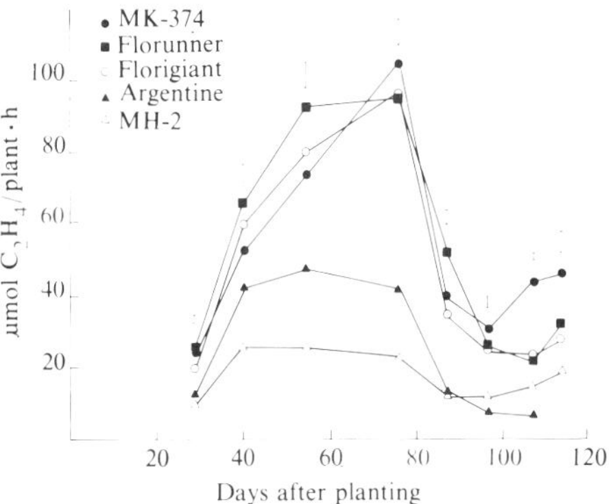

Figure 1.
Nitrogenase activity per plant of selected groundnut cultivars during the post-rainy season, 1980. Virginia cv. MK 374 is presented in both figures for comparison.

(Dart, Day & Harris, 1972). Plants were sampled 20-25 days after flowering. The data was analyzed by the Scott-Knot method (Gates & Bilbro, 1978) and the clusters formed were grouped as high, medium, or low in BNF traits (see Table 1). Three- to five-fold differences in nodulation and N_2 (C_2H_2) reduction were observed among these groundnut genotypes. A Virginia type, NC Ac 2821, ranked high over three tests and a Valencia type, NC Ac 2654, ranked high during two tests, while a Spanish type Ah 3275, was clustered as low during four tests. Crosses have been made between the cultivars of the high and low groups in order to estimate the heritability of N_2 fixation in groundnuts. Wyne *et al.* (1980) reported high heritability for such traits in 30 F_4 lines derived from a cross between cv. 922 (Spanish) and cv. NC 6 (Virginia) in fields at Raleigh. However they observed that correlations between parental and general combining ability effects for N_2 fixation were nonsignificant for progenies of a diallel cross grown in the glasshouse, indicating that simple evaluation of lines for capacity to fix N_2 may not identify superior parents for use in breeding programs (Isleib *et al.*, 1980).

TABLE 1: Variation in the nodulation and N_2 (C_2H_2) fixation of groundnut cultivars over three seasons of testing.

Cultivar	ICG No	Botanical type	1977-1978				1978		1978-1979[1]	
			1st sampling		2nd sampling					
			Nodu-lation	N_2ase	Nodu-lation	N_2ase	Nodu-lation	N_2ase	Nodu-lation	N_2ase
Ah 3277	1218	Spanish	L[2]	L	L	L	L	L	M	M
Ah 3275	1216	Spanish	L	L	L	L	L	L	L	L
No. 421	3158	Valencia	L	L	L	L	–	–	–	–
Ah 39	1161	Spanish	L	L	M	H	L	L	–	–
Ah 5144	1235	Spanish	L	L	M	M	M	–	M	M
NC Ac 888	359	Spanish	L	L	L	L	M	L	L	L
Ah 61	1173	Spanish	L	L	L	M	L	M	–	–
Ah 3272	1213	Spanish	L	L	L	M	L	M	–	–
No. 3527	1524	Spanish	L	–	L	M	L	–	–	–
Faizpur-1-5	1102	Spanish	L	M	L	L	M	M	–	–
No. 418	1500,2202	Spanish	L	L	L	M	–	–	–	–
NC Ac 1337	358	Valencia	L	L	M	M	M	L	–	–
NC Ac 516	279	Valencia	L	–	M	M	L	–	L	L
NC Ac 945	366	Valencia	L	L	M	M	M	–	–	–
NC Ac 699	1630	Spanish	L	L	L	M	L	M	–	–
148-7-4-3-12-B	1573	Spanish	L	–	L	M	–	–	–	–
No. 1780	1508	Spanish	L	L	M	L	–	–	–	–
NC Ac 738	331	Valencia	L	–	M	M	M	–	–	–
TG 17	2976	Spanish	L	L	L	M	L	L	L	L
No. 3270	1489	Spanish	L	L	L	L	–	–	L	M
NC Ac 51	263	Valencia	L	M	L	L	L	–	–	–
TG 8	95	Valencia	L	L	M	M	L	L	–	–
Ah 42	1163	Valencia	L	–	M	L	M	–	–	–
NC Ac 2651	402	Spanish	L	L	L	M	M	–	–	–
NC Ac 1002	380	Valencia	L	–	M	M	M	–	–	–
NC Ac 524	283	Valencia	L	M	M	M	M	M	–	–
GAUG 1	–	Spanish	L	–	M	M	L	L	–	–
NC Ac 2734	420	Valencia	L	L	M	M	M	L	–	–
NC Ac 495	1623	Spanish	M	M	L	M	L	L	L	L
Spancross	3472	Spanish	M	–	M	M	M	L	–	–
NC Ac 1286	389	Valencia	M	L	M	M	M	L	–	–
NC Ac 17149	475	Valencia	M	L	M	M	M	M	–	–
Ah 1069	1196	Spanish	M	M	M	M	L	L	–	–
Kadiri 71-1		Virginia	M	M	M	M	L	L	–	–
Ah 6279	2983	Spanish	M	–	M	M	–	–	–	–
NC Ac 2600	400	Virginia	M	L	M	M	L	M	L	L
POL 2	154	Spanish	M	M	M	M	L	L	–	–
JH 171	3375	Spanish	M	M	M	M	L	L	L	M
NC Ac 1303	393	Spanish	M	L	M	M	M	M	M	L
NC Ac 975	376	Valencia	M	M	M	M	M	M	–	–
Sm-5	2956	Spanish	M	M	M	M	L	L	–	–
Argentina	3150	Spanish	M	M	M	L	L	L	L	L
Tifspan	3495	Spanish	M	M	M	L	L	L	–	–
Robut 33-1	799	Virginia	M	M	M	M	M	–	L	M
Pollachi 1	127	Spanish	M	L	M	M	M	M	L	M
NC Ac 17113	1699	Spanish	M	M	M	M	M	M	–	–
Ah 8254	2962	Spanish	M	M	M	M	M	L	M	M
Ah 7436	1547	Spanish	M	M	M	M	M	–	–	–
NC Ac 490	274	Valencia	M	M	M	M	M	M	H	M
X-14-4-B-19-B	1561	Spanish	H	M	M	M	M	–	–	–
NC Ac 2821	2405	Virginia	H	M	H	M	M	M	H	H
NC Ac 2654	404	Valencia	H	M	M	H	M	–	M	M

[1]The three seasons for testing were post-rainy season, 1977-1978; rainy season 1978, and post-rainy season, 1978-1979.
[2]L = low; M = medium; and H = high.

Groundnut shows a marked diurnal periodicity in C_2H_2 reduction (Nambiar & Dart, 1980). A preliminary survey of nitrogenase activity in 14 groundnut lines selected for differences in foliage production, showed a significant interaction between lines and time of measurement of nitrogenase activity. This suggests that, if cultivars with less diurnal variability in N_2 fixation can be found, they may have larger overall daily fixation.

There are difficulties in relating the nodulation and N_2 fixation scores of groundnut lines obtained from sampling at a particular stage of the growth cycle to their overall seasonal activity. Moreover, such methods are destructive and, hence, not useful for examining early generation populations in a breeding program. An alternate method is to use the total N uptake of the crop at harvest as an indication of N_2 fixation. Nitrogenase activity through the season and total N_2 uptake by two cultivars grown at ICRISAT are shown in Figure 2 and Table 2. Cv. Kadiri 71-1, a Virginia runner, nodulated better and fixed more N_2 than the dwarf Valencia-type cv. MH 2. The differences in N_2 fixation rates are not reflected in the pod yield, but are evident in the total dry matter produced, and total N harvested.

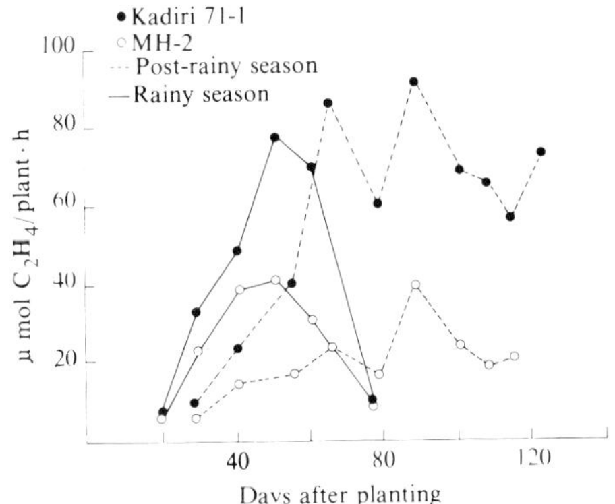

Figure 2. Nitrogenase activity per plant of the cv. Kadiri 71-1 and cv. MH 2 during the post-rainy and the 1980 rainy seasons.

TABLE 2: Dry matter production by cvs. Kadiri 71-1 and MH 2 during post-rainy season.

Cultivars	Pod weight (kg/ha)	Top weight (kg/ha)	Total dry matter (kg/ha·day)	Harvest N index (kg seed/kg tops)
Kadiri 71-1	2426	4103	43	0.37
MH 2	1833	1041	24	0.64

HYPOCOTYL AND STEM NODULATION

Host genotype and *Rhizobium* strain have been shown to influence the distribution of nodules in legumes (Caldwell, 1966). In groundnut, cultivars belonging to the botanical variety *hypogaea* form more nodules in the hypocotyl region than do those from var. *fastigiata* and var. *vulgaris*. Nodules on the hypocotyl of var. *hypogaea* accounted for 13.4% of the total number of nodules per plant while in the other botanical groups they only accounted for 0.5-1.0%. These hypocotyl nodules form 40-60 days after planting and only develop when the soil around the hypocotyl is moist. Some cultivars such as cv. MK 374 (var. *hypogaea*) also nodulate on the stem. During the pod filling stage the nodules on the hypocotyl and stem remained pink while many nodules on the roots turned green, indicating senescence. Selecting for these traits in breeding material might increase N_2 fixation during the pod filling and maturation stages.

GENETICS OF NODULATION

Host plants unable to form nodules have been observed in soybeans and peas (Williams & Lynch, 1954; Holl & LaRue, 1976). Recently Gorbert & Burton (1979) reported non-nodulating lines of *Arachis hypogaea* in the progenies of a cross 487A-1-1-2 x PI 262090. Non-nodulating groundnut lines have also been reported from Georgia (R.O. Hammons, personal communication). During the 1978 rainy season, F_2 progenies from three crosses in the rust screening nursery at ICRISAT segregated for non-nodulation. All the parents of the crosses nodulated normally. Later, during the rainy season 1979, non-nodulating lines were found in 10 additional crosses (see Table 3).

Genetic analysis for nodulation vs. non-nodulation showed that a pair of independent, recessive genes control non-nodulation (Nigam *et al.,* 1980). It is interesting to note that one of the parents in most of the crosses is a rust-resistant Valencia cultivar — either cv. PI 259747, cv. NC Ac 17090, or cv. EC 76446 (292). Any of these parents crossed with cultivars NC 17, Shantung Ku No. 203, or NC Ac 2731, always segregated for non-nodulation, but cv. PI 259747 crossed with cv. NC Ac 17090 or cv. EC 76446 (292) did not produce non-nodulating plants in the F_2 generation, nor did cv. NC Ac 2731 when crossed with cv. Shantung Ku No. 203. This indicates that one set of genes for non-nodulation is present in cvs. PI 259747, NC Ac 17090, and EC 76447 (292) and another set in cvs. NC 17, Santung Ku No. 203 and NC Ac 2731.

Some nodulating segregants formed only a few nodules, which were much larger than those formed by either parents or the normally nodulating F_2 plants. This character is not stable genetically. For example, a plant with three big nodules in the F_5 generation segregated in the F_6 generation into normal nodulating, non-nodulating and "big nodule" types. *Rhizobium* isolates from

TABLE 3: Crosses producing progeny that fail to nodulate.

1.	Shantung Ku No. 203 x NC Ac 17142
2.	NC Ac 2731 x NC Ac 17090
3.	NC Ac 2731 x EC 76446 (292)
4.	NC Ac 2768 x NC Ac 17090
5.	NC 17 x NC Ac 17090
6.	Shantung Ku No. 203 x NC Ac 17090
7.	Shantung Ku No. 203 x EC 76446 (292)
8.	Shantung Ku No. 203 x PI 259747
9.	NC 17 x EC 76446 (292)
10.	NC-Fla-14 x NC Ac 17090
11.	RS-114 x NC Ac 17090
12.	NC 17 x PI 259747
13.	NC Ac 2731 x PI 259747

the big nodule type formed normal nodules on the parent plants under sterile conditions. Moreover, big nodule segregants were observed in F_2 populations grown in controlled conditions and inoculated with a single strain that forms normal nodules on the parents. These observations indicate that the big nodule trait is essentially a plant character.

We are using the non-nodulating groundnut lines in experiments to measure N fixation by groundnut, with the N uptake by the non-nodulated plants providing an estimate of the mineral N uptake by the nodulated plants.

REFERENCES

Caldwell, B.E. (1966) *Crop Sci.* 6, 427-428.

Dart, P.J., Day, J.M. & Harris, D. (1972) Assay of nitrogenase activity by acetylene reduction. Internat. Atomic Energy Agency (IAEA). Pub. no. 149. Pp. 85-100.

Daggar, J.E. (1935) *J. Amer. Soc. Agron.* 27, 286-288.

Gates. C.E. & Bilbro, J.D. (1978) *Agron. J.* 70, 462-465.

Gorbert, D.W. & Burton, J.C. (1979) *Crop Sci.* 19, 727-728.

Gregory, W.C., Krapovickas, A. & Gregory, M.P. (1980) Structure, variation evolution, and classification in *Arachis. In:* Advances in legume science, R.J. Summerfield & A.H. Bunting (Eds.) Royal Botanical Gardens, Kew, England. Pp. 469-493.

Holl, F.B. & LaRue, T.A. (1976) Host genetics and nitrogen fixation. *In:* World soybean research, L.D. Hill (Ed.). Interstate Printers & Publishers, Inc. Chicago, IL, USA. Pp. 156-163.

Isleib, T.G., Wynne, J.C., Elkan, G.H., & Schneeweis, T.J. (1980) *Peanut Sci.* 7, 101-105.

Krapovickas, A. (1973) The origin, variability and spread of the groundnut (*Arachis hypogaea*). *In:* Agricultural genetics: Selected topics. R. Moav (Ed.). National Council for Res. and Devel. Jersusalem, Israel. Pp. 135-151.

McCloud, D.E., Duncan, W.G., McGraw, R.L., Sibale, P.K., Ingram, K.T., Dreyer, J., & Campbell, I.S. (1980) Physiological basis for increased yield potential in peanuts. *In:* Proc. Internat. Workshop on Groundnuts, R.W. Gibbons (Ed.). ICRISAT, Patancheru, A.P., India. Pp. 125-132.

Nambiar, P.T.C. & Dart, P.J. (1980) Studies on nitrogen fixation by groundnut at ICRISAT. *In:* Proc. Internat. Workshop on Groundnuts, R.W. Gibbons (Ed.). ICRISAT, Patancheru, A.P., India. Pp. 110-124.

Nigam, S.N., Arunachalam, V., Gibbons, R.W., Bandyopadhyay, A. & Nambiar, P.T.C. (1980) *Oleagineux* 35, 453-455.

Nutman, P.S. (1969) *Proc. Roy. Soc.* B. 172, 417-437.

Voorhees, J.H. (1915) *J. Amer. Soc. Agron.* 7, 139-140.

Williams, L.F. & Lynch, D.L. (1954) *Agron. J.* 46, 28-29.

Wynne, J.C., Elkan, G.H. & Schneeweis, T.J. (1980) Increasing nitrogen fixation of the groundnut by strain and host selection. *In:* Proc. Internat. Workshop on Groundnuts, R.W. Gibbons (Ed.). ICRISAT, Patancheru, A.P., India. Pp. 95-109.

Zary, K.W., Miller, J.C., Weaver, R.W., & Barnes, L.W. (1978) *J. Amer. Soc. Hort. Sci.* 103, 806-808.

SCREENING FOR NODULATION CHARACTERISTICS IN CHICKPEA AND SUBSEQUENT GENERATION OF SEEDS

O.P. Rupela and P.J. Dart[1]

Summary

Chickpea (*Cicer arietinum*) is a self-pollinating species, the cultivars of which differ widely in nodule number, weight, and nitrogenase activity. Studies at ICRISAT have shown a close correlation between these fixation parameters in 61-day-old plants, and have permitted development of a nodulation score highly correlated with both nodule weight and number. This scoring system permits more rapid germplasm evaluation, and should be adjustable to an absolute rating for field-grown plants.

Field-grown plants can be assayed as intact plants for nitrogenase activity, the nodules removed and weighed, and the plant repotted with 90% survival for plants examined 48 days after planting. This permits seed production from plants of which the genetic potential for nitrogen fixation has already been established, and the use of such plants for hybridization in breeding programs. Chickpeas can also be propagated vegetatively by inducing root development from wounded branches.

INTRODUCTION

Differences in numbers, size and distribution of nodules among cultivars was first observed for soybeans by Voorhees (1915). Since then many reports have appeared on varietal differences in nodulation for various legumes Johnson & Means, 1960; Nutman, 1961; Gibson, 1962; Döbereiner & Arruda, 1967). More recently the interaction between *Rhizobium* strains and cultivars has been examined in detail (Nutman, 1969; Mytton, El-Sherbeeny & Lawes, 1977; Minchin *et al.*, 1978; Mytton, 1978).

Chickpea is a self-pollinating, herbaceous plant that is normally bushy and semispreading. It has been well described botanically (van der Maesen, 1972).

---

[1] CP No. 42. ICRISAT, Patancheru P.O., Andra Pradesh 502 324, India.

In India two types of chickpea are commonly recognized: desi (small, brown seeds that are wrinkled, with a beak at the end) and Kabuli (relatively larger, white, smooth seeds). It is a subtropical crop that is grown mainly on residual moisture in the post-rainy season in India. The *Rhizobium* isolated from chickpea is very specific but will sometimes nodulate *Sesbania bispinosa* and *S. sesban* (Gaur & Sen, 1979).

SCREENING FOR NODULATION

At ICRISAT, nodulation parameters were found to correlate strongly with grain yield under field conditions (Table 1) and to vary widely among 251 germplasm lines examined in the field (see Table 2). We have made crosses between high- and low-nodulating lines to examine the heritability of the parameters. prior to embarking on a breeding program to increase nitrogen (N_2) fixation by chickpea. Unfortunately, observations on nodule number and weight are extremely laborious, and difficult to apply to large-scale germplasm holdings such as those at ICRISAT. Because of this we have developed a visual scoring system, more suitable for evaluating numerous lines. This has proved at least 10 times faster than actual measurement and correlates strongly with nodulation parameters (see Table 3).

TABLE 1: Correlations between N_2-fixing parameters for 61-day-old chickpea plants and final yield.[1]

	Nodule weight	N_2-ase activity/ plant	Grain yield
Nodule number	788***	.778***	.761***
Nodule weight		.763***	.813***
N_2-ase activity/plant			.668**

[1] n = 20, based on means for 5 cultivars grown on a Vertisol with 4 reps and a 25-plant sample at 61 days and 12.6 m^2/plot net final harvest area.
**Significant at 1% ***Significant at 0.1% .

SALVAGING FIELD-GROWN PLANTS

To make observations on nodule number and weight it is usually necessary to harvest destructively. Nondestructive acetylene reduction assays can be used only on a limited scale. For breeding purposes it is important that seed be

TABLE 2: Range of symbiotic parameters and yield of chickpea cultivars.[1]

Parameter	Harvest (days after planting)	Yield	
		1976-77	1977-78
Nodule no/ plant	25-30	4-48	2-18
	45-50	10-75	1-20
	70-75	1-20	4-28
Nodule dry wt (mg/plant)	25-30	0.3-55	1-13
	45-50	2-105	2-34
	70-75	1-195	3-82
Top wt (g/plant)	25-30	ND[2]	0.2-1.7
	45-50	0.7-6.2	1.1-9.2
	70-75	1.8-39.2	10.5-36.5

[1]Two-hundred and fifty-one cultivars were grown in the post-rainy season (1976-77) at ICRISAT, without inoculation and replication. Nodulation was observed 25-30, 45-50, and 70-75 days after planting. Thirty plants per cultivar were scored at each harvest date. In the 1977-78 post-rainy season the same cultivars were again planted at ICRISAT. Seeds were inoculated throughout with *Rhizobium* strain CC-1192. Observations are means for 30 plants from 3 replicates.

[2]ND - No data.

TABLE 3: Correlation between N_2 fixation parameters and visual scoring.[1]

	Nodule weight	Top weight	N_2-ase activity/plant	Specific N_2-ase activity of nodules	Visual scoring
Nodule number	.69***	.64***	.65***	.34**	.79***
Nodule weight		.63***	.84***	.39**	.85***
Top weight			.48***	.28*	.63***
N_2-ase activity/ plant				.73***	.80***

[1]Sixteen cultivars and a check (cultivar K-850, twice) in three replications were assayed for nitrogenase activity by acetylene reduction at 126 days after planting at Hissar. Two bottles containing two plants each were assayed per replication. After assay, individual plants were scored visually and nodule number and nodule weight then measured.

*Significant at 5 %; **Significant at 1 %; ***Significant at 0.1 %.

produced from selected plants already scored for nodulation. The technique we have developed for this is detailed below. Uprooted field-grown plants are brought from the field under wet gunny (hessian) sacks and are kept as cool as possible until scored. After scoring they are transplanted into pots containing sand:vermiculite:grit (1:2:2), covered with polythene bags (see Figure 1); then kept in the glasshouse at temperatures of approximately 25° C and with 70% relative humidity (RH). One can observe, record, and transplant one plant every two minutes. After four to five days the polythene bags can be removed, but pots must always be kept moist. The success rate for establishing field-grown plants 45-50 days old in pots is about 90%. Plants can subsequently be transferred back into the field with almost 100% success.

Glasshouse-grown plants can generally be scored and repotted more easily than those from the field. In one experiment 270 of 291 plants repotted after nodule scoring survived. In another trial with 20 cultivars, 97% of 200 plants potted survived. When ambient conditions are favorable (ambient temperature less than 30° C, and with high RH) scored plants can even be returned directly to the field.

Figure 1. Potted chickpea plants covered with polythene bags (left). After four to five days the covers are removed (right) when the plants establish.

RAPID MULTIPLICATION OF MATERIALS

We developed a method for taking cuttings of chickpea in order to obtain more seeds of a given genetic stock within a short period. Rooting is induced

by wounding a branch by making a transverse cut halfway through at the fourth or fifth internode. The branch is allowed to grow on in the glasshouse at about 25-28° and about 70% RH. After about seven days, 20-50% of the wounds form rootlets on the wound surface closest to the growing point of the branch, while the others swell at the wounds. Wounded branches, with or without roots, are detached from the plant below the wound and potted in sand plus vermiculite. Root growth is hastened if the original wound is dipped in root hormone powder (Seradex B No. 2, May and Baker, India) while potting up the branch. Pots containing these branches should be kept shaded in the glasshouse for about a week. Almost all branches that have aerial roots, and more than 70% of the branches with swelling at the wound, form roots and grow into plants. Removal of reproductive structures after transplanting stimulates plant growth. When the cuttings are growing vegetatively they can also be transplanted to the field for faster seed production with almost 100% success.

REFERENCES

Döbereiner, J. & Arruda, N.B. (1967) *Pesq. Agropec. Bras.* 2, 475-487.

Gaur, Y.D. & Sen, A.N. (1979) *New Phytol.* 83, 745-754.

Gibson, A.H. (1962) *Aust. J. Agric. Res.* 13, 388-399.

Johnson, H.W. & Means, U.M. (1960) *Agron. J.* 52, 651-654.

Maesen, L.J.G. van der (1972) *Medelingen Landbou Whogescool* (Wageningen). 342 pp.

Minchin, F.R., Summerfield, R.J. & Eaglesham, A.R.J. (1978) *Trop. Agric.* (Trin.) 55, 107-115.

Mytton, L.R. (1978) *Ann. Appl. Biol.* 88, 445-448.

Mytton, L.R., El-Sherbeeny, M.H. & Lawes, D.A. (1977) *Euphytica* 26, 785-791.

Nutman, P.S. (1961) *Aust. J. Agric. Res.* 12, 212-226.

Nutman, P.S. (1969) *Proc. Roy. Soc. B.* 172, 417-437.

Vorhees, J.H. (1915) *J. Amer. Soc. Agron.* 7, 139-140.

INFLUENCE OF PLANT GENOTYPE ON SOME PARAMETERS OF NITROGEN FIXATION IN *PHASEOLUS VULGARIS*

F.F Duque, L.T.G. Salles, J.C. Pereira, and J. Döbereiner[1]

Summary

The influence of plant genotype on symbiotic nitrogen (N_2) fixation in cultivars of *Phaseolus vulgaris* was evaluated in a red yellow podzolic soil, low in mineral N. Maximum N_2 (C_2H_2) fixation was found 44 days after planting and correlated well with nodule weight and percentage of pink nodules. Nitrate reductase activity was least at the 44-day harvest and, in general, showed a pattern opposite to that of N_2 fixation. Bean harvest index and N-use efficiency (kg grain produced/kg N in tops) were positively correlated with yield.

INTRODUCTION

Biological nitrogen (N_2) fixation in soybean can provide the N necessary for high yields. In Brazil, as in most countries, soybeans are grown without N fertilization, an economy estimated at US$800 million/year (Döbereiner & Duque, 1980). By contrast, dry beans have proved weak in N_2 fixation and are generally supplied with fertilizer N. Integrated plant physiology, microbiology, and soil science teams are now working in Brazil to enhance levels of N_2 fixation in *Phaseolus vulgaris*. In this paper we summarize results from experiments on plant genotype effects on nodulation and N_2 fixation in this species.

MATERIALS AND METHODS

The field experiments were conducted at the experimental farm, Km 47, Rio de Janeiro, on a red yellow podzolic soil low in mineral N. Dry beans

[1] Programa Fixação Biologico de Nitrogenio, EMBRAPA-UFRRJ, CNP Km 47 23460, Seropedica, Rio de Janeiro, Brazil.

were planted both in the rainy (October) and dry (March) seasons. Sixteen bean genotypes were planted in a randomized complete block design having 4 replicates. Plots were of 5 lines, 4 m long, with 0.5 m distance between rows, and 30 seeds per row. Fertilization included 1.5 t of dolomitic limestone, 160 kg P_2O_5, 160 kg K_2O and 40 kg FTE-Br15 (trace element mixture) per hectare. At the second planting, fertilization was complemented with 80 kg P_2O_5 and 40 kg K_2O/ha applied in the seed row. The seeds were inoculated with a mixture of three strains of *Rhizobium phaseoli*, and lime pelleted. Methods for the assay of N_2 (C_2H_2) fixation and nitrate reductase activity were similar to those used by Franco, Pereira & Neyra (1979). Nodule dry weight was determined at flowering; yield, and N in the grain and aboveground parts were determined at maturity. Harvest index (ratio of weight of seed harvested to weight of tops) and N-use efficiency (ratio of weight of grain harvested to weight of N in tops) parameters were calculated from this data.

RESULTS AND DISCUSSION

Figures 1 and 2 show the seasonal variation in the percentage of pink, healthy nodules and N_2 (C_2H_2) fixation of eight *P. vulgaris* cultivars following wet season plantings. The one cultivar of Type I growth habit ('Goiano Precoce') included in this study showed very poor N_2 (C_2H_2) fixation as confirmed by apparent N deficiency in the field. This cultivar

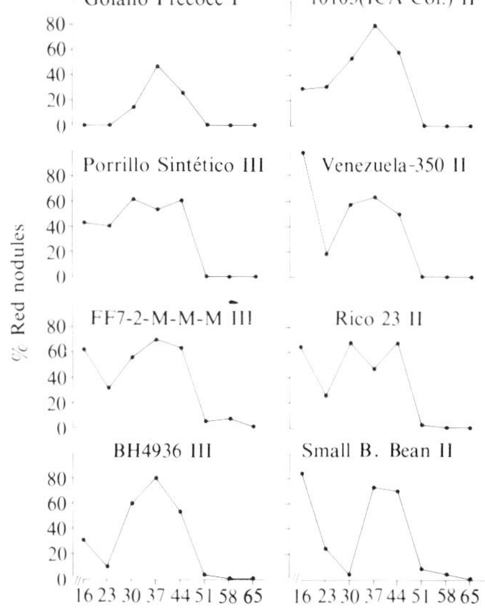

Figure 1.
Percentage of red nodules in dry beans grown during the rainy season. The fresh nodules were taken from the superior third of the roots of five plants/plot, counted, and the internal coloration (red, green or white) recorded.

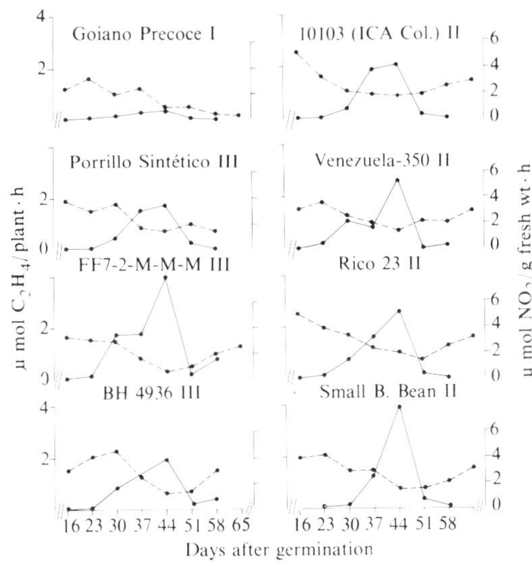

Figure 2.
Relationship between N_2 fixation and nitrate assimilation of field grown dry bean plants. ——: nitrogenase activity (in intact roots systems with nodules). ---: NRA in fresh leaves (*in vitro*).

showed a relatively high proportion of red nodules, but nodule weight was particularly low (see Table 1). The low N_2 (C_2H_2) fixation of cv. BH4936 might be a consequence of heavy infection with rust (*Uromyces phaseoli*). In the other cultivars the proportion of pink nodules peaked one week before maximum N_2 (C_2H_2) fixation was obtained. This occurred in all cultivars at 44 days. One week later rapid decomposition of nodules began, and nitrogenase activity stopped almost completely. This sudden loss of nodules has been reported before and also occurred in irrigated fields, so it cannot be due to water stress. We consider this a major cause of the low N_2 fixation found in field plantings of *Phaseolus vulgaris*.

As Franco *et al.* (1979) observed, nitrate reductase activity was lowest during peak N_2 (C_2H_2) fixation but increased again following the decline in fixation (see Figure 2). The results obtained in the dry season planting (data not included) also showed parallel development during the growth cycle of nodule weight, percentage of pink nodules, and nitrogenase activity. However, all three parameters declined much more rapidly, due, probably, to water stress.

Table 1 shows nodule dry weight, yield, harvest index, and N-use efficiency parameters for all 16 cultivars of *Phaseolus vulgaris*. Each parameter shows marked variation between cultivars, with the poor correlation between nodule dry weight and yield surprising. By contrast there was a highly significant correlation between harvest index or N-use efficiency and yield, with cultivars of Type II growth habit (10103 (ICA, Colombia), FF 1282 -CB-CM-M, 'Small Black Bean' and 'Rico 23') prominent. These correlations were confirmed in the experiment planted during the dry season (data not shown), where the correlation coefficients of grain yields with harvest indices were

TABLE 1: Harvest index and yield of 16 dry bean cultivars grown during the rainy season.

Cultivar	Growth habit[1]	Nodule wt[2]	Yield (kg/ha)	Harvest index[3]	N-use efficiency[4]
10103 (ICA-Col.)	II	48.2	1083	601	24
FF1282-CB-CM-M	II	70.2	857	562	24
Small Black Bean	II	57.5	827	311	19
Rico 23	II	65.4	798	469	19
Porrillo Sintético	III	31.4	788	485	20
Goiano Precoce	I	3.4	556	404	21
FF-46-3-M-M-M	III	51.6	535	389	15
FF-72-M-M-M	III	104.6	497	320	13
FFSST-CB-CM-M	II	49.0	497	355	15
Iguacú	II	42.6	492	226	10
Venezuela 350	II	58.4	492	302	14
FF2-6-3-CM-M	III	28.4	451	346	14
FF-104-CB-CM-M	II	45.4	405	279	11
ICA Pijao	III	76.6	398	252	11
Rio Tibaji	II	41.3	361	253	10
BH 4936	III	45.2	221	129	5

[1]Growth habit defined as Type I–determinate; Types II and III–indeterminate; with short and long guide, respectively (CIAT, 1977).
[2]mg/plant. Determined on 5 plants in each of 4 replicates at flowering.
[3]kg grain-/kg dry wt of aboveground material. r (yield x harvest index) = 0.88. $P > 0.01$.
[4]kg grain/kg total N in crop. r (yield x N-use efficiency) = 0.91. $P > 0.01$.

$r = 0.80$ and 0.89 ($p > 0.01$) for top dry weights and plant N, respectively. The best genotypes were again of Type II growth habit, although they were not the same cultivars ('Porrillo Sintético', 'ICA Pijao', and FFSST-CB-CM-M). The results emphasize that while absolute levels of carbohydrate accumulation and N_2 (C_2H_2) fixation are important, it is the efficiency with which plants utilize accumulated carbohydrate and N that determines grain yield. Breeding programs that emphasize this aspect of plant growth and N_2 fixation are currently underway.

REFERENCES

Döbereiner, J. & Duque, F.F. (1980) *R. Econ. Rural Brasilia* 18, 447-460.

Franco, A.A., Pereira, J.C. & Neyra, C.A. (1970) *Plant Physiol.* 63, 421-424.

HOST-PLANT FACTORS AFFECTING NITROGEN FIXATION OF THE PEANUT

J.C. Wynne, S.T. Ball, G.H. Elkan, T.G. Isleib, and T.J. Schneeweis[1]

Summary

Eight peanut (*Arachis hypogaea* L.) cultivars were evaluated for growth analysis traits to determine the host factors that most affect nitrogen (N_2) fixation. The cultivars differed significantly for fruit yield, nodulation, and N_2 (C_2H_2) fixation and in most of the growth traits analyzed.

In a regression analysis, leaf area duration accounted for 70-75% of the variability in nodulation and N_2 (C_2H_2) fixation. Simple measurements of leaf dry weight accounted for almost 75% of the variability in both nodulation and N_2 (C_2H_2) fixed. These relationships again demonstrate the importance of the photosynthetic assimilatory apparatus to fixation in peanuts.

Leaf dry weight is relatively simple to measure and should be amenable to selection in a breeding program.

INTRODUCTION

The host plant plays a major role in symbiotic nitrogen (N_2) fixation. Host genes involved in nodule initiation, development, and function have been reviewed already in this volume (see p. 27), other genetic studies with peanut (*Arachis hypogaea* L.) are detailed on p. 49. Much research is now in progress to manipulate the leguminous host plant genetically to improve the efficiency of the plant/*Rhizobium* symbiosis.

Evidence is accumulating that the quantitative variation in nodulation and N_2 fixation is sufficient in most leguminous crops to attempt to increase N_2 fixation through breeding and selection (Seetin & Barnes, 1977; Zary *et al.*,

---

[1] North Carolina State University, Raleigh, NC 27650, USA.

[2] The financial support of USAID under project AG/TAB 610-9-76 is gratefully acknowledged.

1978; Isleib *et al.*, 1980; Nambiar & Dart, 1980; Sinclair, Lugg & Spaeth, 1980; Wynne, Elkan & Schneeweis, 1980).

However, in efforts to increase N_2 fixation, it is not necessary to restrict selection to genetic factors that affect nodulation, increase nitrogenase activity or generate larger amounts of accumulated N. Much recent work suggests that the supply of carbohydrates to the nodules may be a major limiting factor in N_2 fixation. Certain cultivars may be superior to others in their allocation of assimilatory resources to the various plant parts (Ham, Lawn & Brun, 1976; Hardy & Havelka, 1976; Pate, 1977). In order to determine which plant factors are responsible for the variation observed in nodulation and N_2 fixation, and to identify other traits that are useful for N_2 fixation selection programs, we must study the functional economy of whole plants and the interactions of their organs during growth.

The peanut is promiscuously nodulated by rhizobia of the cowpea cross-inoculation group and, under many field conditions, can fix most of the N_2 required for growth and high yield (Reid & Cox, 1973). In fields new to peanuts substantial responses to inoculation can be obtained (Barksdale, 1977; Nambiar & Dart, 1980).

Significant variation in nodulation and nitrogenase activity has been found among peanut cultivars. (Duggar, 1935a; 1935b; 1935c; Burton, 1975; Nambiar & Dart, 1980, Wynne *et al.*, 1980). Generally peanut cultivars of the "Virginia type" (ssp. *hypogaea* var. *hypogaea*) are better nodulated, fix more N_2, and yield more than either the "Valencia type" (ssp. *fastigiata* var. *fastigiata*) or the "Spanish type" (spp. *fastigiata* var. *vulgaris*), although variation among cultivars of each type for each trait has been demonstrated (Nambiar & Dart, 1980; Wynne *et al.*, 1980).

The objective of this paper is to describe host-plant factors that account for differences in nodulation and N_2 fixation observed for peanut cultivars grown in soils containing native rhizobia.

MATERIALS AND METHODS

Eight peanut cultivars representing the three major botanical varieties were grown at the Peanut Belt Research Station, Lewiston, NC, USA (see Table 1). The test was planted in a split plot design in a randomized complete block with five replications. Cultivars were assigned to whole plots and sampling dates to subplots. Sampling was initiated two weeks after emergence with samples taken at two-week intervals throughout the growing season. Three-plant samples were taken from each plot until midseason when the sample size was reduced to two plants per plot.

After drying, individual plants were separated into component parts and weighed. The leaf area of the harvested plants was estimated from the dry weight of 10 leaf disks of known area per plant. These data were used to generate 12 growth analysis traits for each cultivar as described by Kvet,

TABLE 1: Peanut cultivars evaluated for N_2 fixation and growth.

Cultivar	Botanical classification	Maturity
Tennessee Red	ssp. *fastigiata* var. *fastigiata*	Very early
Spanhoma	ssp. *fastigiata* var. *vulgaris*	Very early
Florunner	ssp. *hypogaea* var. *hypogaea*	Medium
PI 262090	ssp. *hypogaea* var. *hypogaea*	Late
Florigiant	ssp. *hypogaea* var. *hypogaea*	Medium
NC 4	ssp. *hypogaea* var. *hypogaea*	Medium
NC 6	ssp. *hypogaea* var. *hypogaea*	Medium
Early Bunch	ssp. *hypogaea* var. *hypogaea*	Early

Ondok & Jarvis (1971) (see Table 2). Nodule number, nodule dry weight per plant, and N_2 fixation (as measured by an acetylene reduction methodology similar to that of Hardy, Burns & Holsten (1973)) were determined for each cultivar.

Multiple regression techniques for best model selection were used to determine the relationship of the 12 growth analysis traits to nodulation and N_2 (C_2H_2) fixation. Similar techniques were used to determine the relationship of nodulation and N_2 (C_2H_2) fixation to fruit yield.

RESULTS

The cultivars were significantly different in mean weight of leaf, stem, petiole, peg, and fruit (see Table 3). The Virginia type cultivars generally had greater weights than the Valencia or Spanish type cultivars for all plant parts except fruit.

When the mean weight data from each sampling date and the leaf area data were used to analyze growth traits, cultivars were found to be significantly different for all traits except for relative growth rate, net assimilation rate and unit shoot rate (see Table 4). The Virginia-type cultivars generally had greater means than cultivars of the *fastigiata* subspecies for all traits except leaf weight ratio and specific leaf area. 'Florigiant' had the greatest absolute growth rate, crop growth rate, leaf area index, leaf area ratio and specific leaf area. This indicates that 'Florigiant' had the fastest growth rate because it had the largest assimilatory apparatus. NC 6 had the highest biomass duration and leaf area duration, indicating an ability to maintain photosynthetic capacity longer.

N_2 fixation

The eight cultivars were significantly different for nodulation and N_2 (C_2H_2) fixation (see Table 5). The Virginia-type cultivars had higher means

TABLE 2: Synopsis of growth analysis symbols and formulas.

Derived quantity	Instant value	Mean value
Absolute growth rate	$\frac{dW}{dT}$	$\overline{G}_{1\text{-}2} = \frac{W_2 - W_1}{T_2 - T_1}$
Biomass duration	None	$\overline{Z}_{1\text{-}2} = \frac{(W_1 + W_2)(T_2 - T_1)}{2}$
Crop growth rate	$\frac{1}{P} \cdot \frac{dW}{dT}$	$\overline{C}_{1\text{-}2} = \frac{1}{P} \cdot \frac{W_2 - W_1}{T_2 - T_1}$
Leaf area duration (L_A basis)	None	$\overline{D}_{1\text{-}2} = \frac{(L_{A_1} + L_{A_2})(T_2 - T_1)}{2}$
Leaf area duration (L_A basis)	None	$\overline{D}_{1\text{-}2} = \frac{(L_1 + L_2)(T_2 - T_1)}{2}$
Leaf area index	$\frac{L_A}{P}$	$\overline{L}_{1\text{-}2} = \frac{L_{A_2} - L_{A_1}}{P}$
Leaf area ratio	$\frac{L_A}{W}$	$\overline{F}_{1\text{-}2} = \frac{(L_{A_1}/W_1) + (L_{A_2}/W_2)}{2}$
Leaf weight ratio	$\frac{L_W}{W}$	$\overline{LWR}_{1\text{-}2} = \frac{(L_{W_1}/W_2) + (L_{W_2}/W_2)}{2}$
Relative growth rate	$\frac{1}{W} \cdot \frac{dW}{dT}$	$\overline{R}_{1\text{-}2} = \frac{\log_e W_2 - \log_e W_1}{T_2 - T_1}$
Specific leaf area	$\frac{L_A}{L_W}$	$\overline{SLA}_{1\text{-}2} = \frac{(L_{A_1}/L_{W_1}) + (L_{A_2}/L_{W_2})}{2}$
Net assimilation rate	$\frac{1}{L_A} \cdot \frac{dW}{dT}$	$\overline{E}_{1\text{-}2} = \frac{W_2 - W_1}{T_2 - T_1} \cdot \frac{\log_e L_{A_2} - \log_e L_{A_1}}{L_{A_2} - L_{A_1}}$
Unit shoot rate	$\frac{1}{S_W} \cdot \frac{dW}{dT}$	$\overline{B}_{1\text{-}2} = \frac{W_2 - W_1}{T_2 - T_1} \cdot \frac{\log_e S_{W_2} - \log_e S_{W_1}}{S_{W_2} - S_{W_1}}$

L_A = total leaf area: L_W = leaf dry wt.; P = ground area; S_W = shoot dry wt.; T = time; W = total dry wt.

TABLE 3: Cultivar means for growth components averaged over sampling dates.[1]

Cultivar	Leaf weight	Stem weight	Petiole weight	Peg weight	Fruit weight
			(g/plant)		
Tennessee Red	20.8 d	24.8 c	4.6 d	4.0 e	33.2 c
Spanhoma	22.7 cd	25.9 c	5.4 c	4.7 de	34.6 c
Florunner	27.4 b	30.4 ab	5.2 cd	5.9 bc	33.9 c
PI 262090	24.1 c	33.2 a	5.2 cd	2.6 f	14.6 d
Florigiant	30.6 a	34.8 a	6.2 b	6.9 a	44.9 b
NC 4	29.0 ab	30.9 ab	8.1 a	6.1 abc	30.6 c
NC 6	30.1 ab	36.1 a	5.8 bc	6.8 ab	43.9 b
Early Bunch	27.5 b	25.1 c	6.1 b	5.3 cd	52.4 a

[1]Means within columns followed by the same letter are not significantly different ($P = 0.05$).

for nodulation and N_2 (C_2H_2) fixation than the two *fastigiata* subspecies cultivars. The latter cultivars were similar to the Virginia-type cultivars during the early part of the growing season but showed substantially lower nodulation and N_2 (C_2H_2) fixation during early pod fill. The highest yielding cultivars, NC 6 and Florigiant, showed the greatest nodulation and N_2 (C_2H_2) fixation.

Relationship of host factors to N_2 fixation

When the 12 growth analysis traits were used as independent variables and regressed on the dependent variable, N_2 (C_2H_2) fixation, leaf area duration accounted for more than 70% of the variation in N_2 (C_2H_2) fixation, after adjustment for replicate and cultivar effects. The only other trait that accounted for a significant amount of variability in N_2 (C_2H_2) fixation was leaf area index. Over 90% of the variability in N_2 (C_2H_2) fixation for the cultivar Florigiant, which had the highest N_2 fixation values, was accounted for by leaf area duration.

Leaf area duration expresses how long a plant maintains its active assimilatory surface. Obviously, peanut plants that have the capacity to maintain active photosynthesis are best able to fix N_2. The results are not surprising, since several peanut experiments have indicated a close relationship between N_2 fixation and photosynthesis (Hardy & Havelka, 1976; Dart, 1978; Wynne *et al.*, 1980).

TABLE 4: Cultivar means for growth analysis traits.[1]

Cultivar	Absolute growth rate	Biomass duration	Crop growth rate	Leaf area				Leaf weight ratio (10^{-1})	Specific leaf area (10^{-3})
				Duration (LA)	Duration (LAI)	Index (10^{-3})	Ratio (10^{-4})		
Tennessee Red	2.11 b	1008 d	1.41 b	.33 d	.22 d	3.8 b	3.81 de	3.77 e	1.03 bc
Spanhoma	2.49 ab	1083 cd	1.63 ab	.37 cd	.25 c	5.3 ab	3.96 cd	3.90 cd	1.02 bc
Florunner	2.75 ab	1208 b	1.83 ab	.45 b	.30 b	6.4 ab	4.22 a	4.05 a	1.05 ab
PI 262090	1.93 b	1045 d	1.28 b	.38 c	.25 c	5.2 ab	4.05 bc	4.01 abc	1.02 c
Florigiant	3.41 a	1311 b	2.27 a	.47 b	.31 b	9.1 a	4.22 ab	3.91 bcd	1.08 a
NC 4	2.88 ab	1204 bc	1.92 ab	.44 b	.29 b	7.0 ab	4.16 ab	4.10 a	1.02 c
NC 6	3.28 a	1423 a	2.20 ab	.51 a	.34 a	7.8 ab	4.14 abc	3.86 de	1.08 a
Early Bunch	2.56 ab	1253 b	1.70 ab	.38 c	.25 c	5.2 ab	3.70 e	4.03 ab	0.94 d

[1]Means within columns followed by the same letter are not significantly different (P = 0.05).

TABLE 5: Cultivar means over sampling dates for nodulation and N_2 fixation.[1]

Cultivar	Nodule Number	Nodule Weight (g/plant)	N_2 fixation (μ mol C_2H_4/plant·h)
Tennessee Red	662 bc	.80 de	15.4 bc
Spanhoma	440 c	.64 e	13.1 c
Florunner	855 ab	1.33 bc	22.2 a
PI 262090	718 ab	.96 cde	16.1 bc
Florigiant	959 a	1.75 a	23.5 a
NC 4	934 a	1.47 ab	21.4 a
NC 6	926 a	1.47 ab	23.1 a
Early Bunch	938 a	1.13 bcd	19.1 ab

[1]Means within columns followed by the same letter are not different (P = 0.05).

Differences in leaf area duration accounted for almost 70% of the variability in nodulation. Variability in crop growth rate also accounted for a significant amount of variability in nodulation, but the multiple regression model that contained both crop growth rate and leaf area duration accounted for only 2% more variability than was accounted for when only leaf area duration alone was considered. An examination of regressions for individual cultivars indicated that leaf weight ratio accounted for a significant portion of the variation for nodulation. Leaf weight ratio is the ratio of leaf dry weight to total plant dry weight and should also describe the size of the assimilatory apparatus.

Since leaf area duration and leaf weight ratio were found to account for much of the variability for both nodulation and N_2 (C_2H_2) fixation, the relationship of leaf weight *per se* to the N_2 fixation parameters was determined using multiple regression. Leaf weight accounted for almost 75% of the variation in both nodulation and N_2(C_2H_2) fixation.

Relationship of N_2 fixation to fruit yield

In grain legumes such as peanuts, increases in N_2 fixation do not necessarily lead to increases in fruit yield. In this study about 28% of the variation in yield can be accounted for by differences in nodulation. About 22% of the difference in yield can be accounted for by N_2 (C_2H_2) fixed. The model containing both traits only accounted for 29% of the variation in yield since the two traits are correlated. Since increases in dry matter must be partitioned into the fruit. N_2 fixation is making an important contribution to yield.

Peanut plants with high N_2 fixation have greater leaf weights and leaf area duration. These traits can be easily measured and should be amendable through selection processes in breeding programs.

REFERENCES

Burton. J.C. (1975) Pragmatic aspects of the *Rhizobium*/leguminous plant association. *In:* Proc. First Internat. Symp. Nitrogen Fixation, Vol. 2. W.E. Newton and C.J. Nyman (Eds.). Washington State Univ. Press, Pullman, WA, USA.

Barksdale. W.E. (1977) *Peanut Farmer* 13(4) 42, 44.

Dart, P.J. (1978) Groundnut microbiology program at ICRISAT. Report: Quinquennial Review. ICRISAT Hyderabad, India.

Duggar. J.F. (1935a) *J. Amer. Soc. Agron.* 27, 32-37.

Duggar. J.F. (1935b) *J. Amer. Soc. Agron.* 27, 128-133.

Duggar. J.F. (1935c) *J. Amer. Soc. Agron.* 27, 286-288.

Ham. G.E.. Lawn. R.J. & Brun, W.A. (1976) Influence of inoculation, nitrogen fertilizers and photosynthetic source-sink manipulations on field grown soybeans. *In:* Symbiotic nitrogen fixation in plants, P.S. Nutman (Ed.). Cambridge Univ. Press, Cambridge, England. Pp. 239-253.

Hardy. R.W.F.. Burns. R.C. & Holsten, R.D. (1973) *Soil Biol. Biochem.* 5 47-81.

Hardy, R.W.F. & Havelka, U.D. (1976) Photosynthate as a major factor limiting nitrogen fixation by field-grown legumes with emphasis on soybeans. *In:* Symbiotic nitrogen fixation in plants, P.S. Nutman (Ed.). Cambridge Univ. Press. Cambridge, England. Pp. 421-439.

Isleib, T.G., Wynne, J.C., Elkan, G.H., & Schneeweis, T.J. (1980) *Peanut Sci.* 7, 101-105.

Kvet. J.. Ondok. J.N. & Jarvis, P.G. (1971) Methods of growth analysis. *In:* Plant photosynthetic production: Manual of methods. Z. Sestak, J. Catsky & P.G. Jarvis (Eds.). Dr. W. Junk N.V. Publishers, The Hague, Netherlands. Pp. 343-391.

Nambiar P.T.C. & Dart, P.J. (1980) Studies on nitrogen fixation by groundnut at ICRISAT. *In:* Proceedings of International Peanut Workshop. ICRISAT, Patancheru. India. Pp. 110-124.

Pate, J.S. (1977) Functional biology of dinitrogen fixation by legumes. *In:* A treatise on dinitrogen fixation. III. Biology. R.W.F. Hardy & W.S. Silver (Eds.). Wiley-Interscience, New York, NY, USA. Pp. 473-517.

Reid, P.H. & Cox, F.R. (1973) Soil properties, mineral nutrition, and fertilization practices. *In:* Peanuts: Culture and uses. C.T. Wilson (Ed.). Amer. Peanut Res. and Educ. Assoc., Inc., Stillwater, OK, USA. Pp. 271-297.

Seetin, M.V. & Barnes, D.K. (1977) *Crop Sci.* 17, 783-787.

Sinclair, T.R., Lugg, D.G. & Spaeth, S.C. (1980). Comparative fixation and utilization of carbon and nitrogen among soybean genotypes. *In:* Advances in legume science. R.J. Summerfield & A.H. Bunting (Eds.). Royal Botanic Gardens, Kew, England. Pp. 313-322.

Wynne, J.C., Elkan, G.H. & Schneeweiss, T.J. (1980) Increasing nitrogen fixation of the groundnut by strain and host selection. *In:* Proceedings of International Peanut Workshop. ICRISAT, Patancheru, India. Pp. 95-109.

Zary, K.W., Miller, J.C., Weaver, R.W., & Barnes, L.W. (1978) *J. Amer. Soc. Hort. Sci.* 103, 806-808.

ENERGY COST OF BIOLOGICAL NITROGEN FIXATION

M.C.P. Neves[1]

Summary

Biological nitrogen (N_2) fixation in both free-living and symbiotic organisms is an energy-requiring process dependent upon a supply of carbon and energy. In this paper the energy costs for N_2 fixation and nodule respiration in symbiotic systems are compared with those of free-living N_2-fixing systems, with the theoretical energy requirement for N_2 fixation, and with the cost of utilization of combined N.

INTRODUCTION

Nitrogen (N_2) fixation is an expensive process in terms of energy requirement, whether carried out by the petrochemical industry or by living organisms. Chemical fixation of N_2 uses expensive nonrenewable fossil energy; in the USA, for example, ammonia production consumes about 2% of the nation's natural gas output (Harre, Livingston & Shields, 1974), and additional energy is used in fertilizer transport. Biological N_2 fixation uses solar energy collected through photosynthesis and produces reduced N_2 at the site where it is needed, in the soil. In the case of rhizosphere and symbiotic N_2-fixing micro-organisms, carbon substrates are provided directly by the host plant. Some free-living N_2 fixers depend on soil organic matter, whereas others produce their own carbohydrates, and so are fully autotrophic for both C and N.

Because biological N_2 fixation requires so much energy, it is often limited by a shortage of photosynthate. As attempts to enhance the photosynthetic capacity of plants have met little success, concern has mounted about the energy efficiency of biological N_2 fixation, and about how it might be enhanced.

---

[1] Universidade Federal Rural do Rio de Janeiro, Km 47, Seropedica, 23460, Rio de Janeiro, Brazil.

This paper compares the energy costs for N_2 fixation and nodule respiration in symbiotic systems with those of free-living, N_2-fixing organisms, with the theoretical energy requirement for N_2 fixation, and with the cost of utilization of combined N.

ENERGETICS OF BIOLOGICAL N_2 FIXATION

Thermodynamic considerations

Using glucose as a source of reducing power Bergersen (1971a) estimated a net energy requirement for N_2 fixation of 276 KJ/mol NH_4^+ produced under thermodynamically stable conditions. For cell-free systems Bergersen (1971a) reported the consumption of 355 KJ/mol NH_4^+ produced, a figure probably very close to the *in vivo* cost of fixation. As oxidation of glucose yields 2.813 KJ/mol, and considering perfect energy transfer, the maximum efficiency with which N_2 can be reduced in a biological system is 0.26 moles glucose/mol NH_4^+ produced or 0.67 g C/g fixed N. Using other calculations, Gutschick (1978; 1980) estimated a thermodynamic energy cost of 0.22 moles of glucose/mol NH_4^+ produced or 0.58 g C/g fixed N.

ATP requirements for *in vitro* N_2 fixation

Nitrogenase preparations use much more energy than the predicted thermodynamic cost. Under optimal conditions four to five moles of ATP are required for each pair of electrons transferred by nitrogenase during N_2 fixation (Steifel, 1977). All nitrogenase preparations also reduce protons to H_2 (Dixon, 1976), and if no other reducible substrate is present, all electrons are transferred to protrons and the system wastes energy (Winter & Burris, 1968; Schubert & Evans, 1976). H_2 evolution complicates the estimation of the direct energy needs for N_2 fixation (Schubert & Ryle, 1980) as the exact relationship between proton and N_2 reduction by nitrogenase may vary. Some theoretical analyses of nitrogenase activity suggest that H_2 production with N_2 as substrate at physiological levels may account for 25% of the total electrons transferred (Steifel, 1977). Measurements on intact root nodules indicate that in legumes 25-34% of the electron flux may be allocated to protons (Evans *et al.,* 1980).

The exact nature of the reductant used in N_2 fixation is not firmly established; it varies between different organisms and depends on growth conditions (Rawsthorne *et al.*, 1980). Assuming NADH as the reductant and a ratio of 1 H_2:2 NH_4^+ as proposed by Dixon (1978), then the equation for N_2 fixation can be expressed as:

$$N_2 + n\ ATP + 4\ NADH + 6\ H^+ \rightarrow 2NH_4^+ + H_2 + 4\ NAD^+ + n\ ADP + n\ Pi$$

where n equals 16-20. The drainage of reductants from oxidative phosphorylation results in less ATP production. Each reductant could yield from 1 to 3 ATP, but the ratio of ATP produced per 2e- transferred (P/2 e-) is variable, even for a given organism (La Rue, 1977). Thus, an assessment of the ATP requirements will depend on accurate data for the P/2 e- ratio of the various systems. If a tightly coupled pathway with a P/2 e- ratio of 3 is assumed, then the minimum theoretical cost of N_2 fixation in reaction (1) is 28 ATP equivalents.

Energy can be partially recovered by H_2 recapture coupled with oxidative phosphorylation yielding 2-3 ATP/mol of H_2 (Dixon, 1978), and this decreases the ATP consumption of reaction 1 to 25 ATP. However, if H_2 production accounts for 34% of the total electron flux (1.6 H_2:2 NH_4^+) and there is no H_2 recycling system, the cost increases to 31.7 ATP/mol N_2 fixed. Under optimum conditions values of 35 to 40 ATP equivalents/mol N_2 fixed were obtained with *Klebsiella* mutants blocked in ammonia assimilation and derepressed for nitrogenase biosynthesis (Andersen, Shanmugan & Valentine, 1978).

Assuming that oxidation proceeds via the Embden-Meyerhof pathway followed by the tricarboxylic acid cycle, complete oxidation of glucose would yield 38 ATP/mol glucose (P/2 e-=3). Thus, the glucose needs for N_2 fixation can be estimated as ranging from 0.70 to 0.86 moles of glucose/mol N_2 fixed (or 1.79 to 2.21 g C/g fixed N).

In intact, living systems N_2 fixation is not an isolated process but is coupled with reactions of ammonia assimilation. If asparagine is the major organic nitrogenous compound formed, another 6-7 ATP/mol N_2 fixed will be expended (Boland, Farnden & Robertson, 1980). However, for the majority of tropical legumes, the ureides allantoin and allantoic acid are the major nitrogenous compounds exported from nodules (Sprent, 1980; Goi & Neves, 1981). Despite the complex pathway by which they are synthesized (Triplett, Blevins & Randall, 1980) only 1-4 extra ATP/mol of ureide are required (Minchin *et al.*, 1981). Thus, if we consider ammonia assimilation as an inherent part of N_2 fixation, the theoretical cost will be 0.71 moles of glucose/mol N_2 fixed (or 1.82 g C/g N) if ammonia is assimilated as ureides, or 1.05 moles of glucose/mol N_2 fixed (or 2.70 g C/g N) for assimilation as asparagine.

Estimates of the theoretical cost are likely to change as metabolism related with N_2 fixation becomes more fully understood in each N_2-fixing system.

ENERGY COST OF BIOLOGICAL N_2 FIXATION IN FREE-LIVING ORGANISMS

Free-living N_2-fixing micro-organisms occur in virtually all metabolic categories (Bergersen, 1980). The great majority, however, are heterotrophic and either aerobic or facultative or obligatory anaerobes.

Energy cost for heterotrophic, free-living N_2 fixers can be easily obtained in pure culture by relating the amount of carbon compound consumed per unit of fixed N. The energy cost will depend, not only on the metabolic pathways involved and the energy produced from available substrates, but also on the growth conditions, type and amount of substrate present, etc.

Oxidative phosphorylation provides aerobes with a much greater energy yield than can be achieved by anaerobes. Hill (1978) listed the reported costs of N_2 fixation by free-living bacteria. Carbon consumption by aerobic bacteria was as high as 190 g C/g N, while anaerobes and facultative anaerobes consumed up to 300 g C/g N. While the concentrations of carbon and oxygen to which the organisms are exposed influence the efficiency with which carbon is utilized for N_2 fixation, only minor contribution to the N balance of agricultural systems can be expected from organisms with such high carbon requirements.

Carbon usage by aerobic bacteria is markedly influenced by O_2 concentration around the cells. Up to 80-90% of the utilized substrate may be respired in order to protect the nitrogenase system, with the carbon cost considerably decreased by lowering O_2 concentration (Mulder & Brotonegoro, 1974). Conversely, carbon usage by facultative anaerobes decreases when cultures are supplied with O_2 (at low concentrations) because ATP production is switched from fermentation to the more efficient oxidative phosphorylation pathway (Hill, 1978).

Hydrogen evolution and recapture is another factor influencing substrate utilization in free-living N_2 fixers (Hill, 1978). Although *Azotobacter* has been shown to evolve H_2 (Smith, Hill & Yates, 1976) this gas is not normally detected. *Azospirillum* also has an active uptake hydrogenase system (Volpon, De-Polli & Döbereiner, 1981).

Efficiencies calculated from pure cultures in laboratory conditions may not necessarily mirror the performance of the organisms under field conditions. O'Toole & Knowles (1973) estimated efficiency in soil populations and observed that is was higher in anaerobic than in aerobic soil and reached maximum values of 28.2 and 35.8 g C/g N for mannitol and glucose, respectively. Soils have limited supplies of carbon and energy (Jensen, 1965), especially under tropical conditions where soil organic matter content tends to be low (Nye & Greenland, 1960). This can limit N_2 fixation by heterotrophs.

Dramatic increases in rates of acetylene reduction occur following soil amendment with carbon compounds (Knowles, 1977). Heterotrophic N_2-fixing organisms are frequently found in the rhizosphere where root exudates provide them with a renewable supply of carbon compounds (Döbereiner, 1974), but competition with nonfixing rhizosphere organisms will probably also limit their share of this source of carbon (Vincent, 1974).

Low carbon concentrations are likely to increase the efficiency of N_2 fixation. In fact, efficiency of *Azospirillum lipoferum* increases from 20 to 8.2 g C/g fixed N as cultures approach the stationary phase (Volpon *et al.*, 1981; see Table 1), whereas that of *A. brasilense* goes from 24.2 to 4.1 g C/g N fixed

TABLE 1: Carbon consumption in N_2 fixation of various free-living bacteria.

Organisms	Growth conditions	$g\,C_G/g\,N$[1]	Carbon source	References
Azotobacter vinelandii	batch	18	sucrose	Parker, 1954
Azotobacter chroococcum	N_2 limited chemostat	12	mannitol	Dalton & Postgate, 1969
Azospirillum lipoferum	batch	21	malate	Okon *et al.*, 1977
Azospirillum lipoferum	batch	20-8.2	glucose	Volpon *et al.*, 1981
Azospirillum brasilense	batch	24.2-4.1	lactate	Stephan *et al.*, 1981
Corynebacterium autotroficum	batch	19-6.5	sucrose	Berndt *et al.*, 1976

[1]Calculated as gram of carbon equivalent to the energy state of a glucose carbon atom by the equation:

$$g\,C_G = g\,C_{substrate} \times \frac{Kcal/mol\ substrate}{g\,C_{substrate}} \times \frac{g\,C\ glucose}{Kcal/mol\ glucose}$$

following depletion of substrates (Stephan, Pedrosa & Döbereiner, 1981).

The list of free-living N_2 fixers has been enlarged considerably in the recent years, mainly in terms of autotrophic organisms: cyanobacteria (Stewart, Rowell & Rai, 1980), photosynthetic (Gallon, 1980), and chemosynthetic bacteria (Dalton, 1980). The physiology of all but the cyanobacteria is largely unknown, and the efficiency with which they utilize the energy they capture to fix N_2 has not as yet been measured.

THE ENERGY COST OF N_2 FIXATION IN SYMBIOTIC SYSTEMS

The energy cost of N_2 fixation in the legume/*Rhizobium* symbiosis has been extensively studied. Now that N_2 fixation by pure cultures of *Rhizobium* has been demonstrated, it will be interesting to compare *Rhizobium* efficiency in N_2 fixation in pure culture with that achieved by the nodule system. Major changes in metabolism, including changes in the electron transport systems, occur when *Rhizobium* cells attain the form of bacteroids (Appleby, 1969). Further, conditions inside the nodule are different from those of pure cultures, as carbon flux from plant cells to bacteroids may be under hormonal control (Minchin *et al.*, 1981) with the microenvironment inside the nodule close to that required for the optimum functioning of the nitrogenase (Vincent, 1980).

In vivo energy costs of N_2 fixation may be obtained by relating nodule respiration to nitrogen assimilation by the plant. Since the earliest attempt made by Bond (1941), several values for the respiratory cost of N_2 fixation have been reported (see Table 2). The complexity of estimating the respiration of intact nodules, without confounding this with the respiration of subtending roots has led to the use of a wide range of techniques. Minchin *et al* (1981) have made a comprehensive review of these but have concluded that it is impossible even to speculate which are more correct, especially when some reported values for the respiratory cost of N_2 fixation are smaller than those calculated for ideal *in vitro* systems. Furthermore, methods of plant culture and husbandry in these studies have varied considerably and the importance of this toward nodule efficiency cannot be overlooked.

Comparisons between plant species are, therefore difficult to make, with reported efficiencies ranging from 1.1-7.6 g C consumed/g N_2 fixed. The value of 19.4 g C consumed/g N_2 fixed for soybean, as reported by Bergersen (1971b) and derived from short-term measurements of $^{15}N_2$ fixation and CO_2 evolution of detached nodules, refers to instantaneous efficiency and could be expected to be highly variable. Since the C/N relationship can change considerably with plant age (Minchin, Summerfield & Neves, 1980; Neves, Minchin & Summerfield, 1981) and also show a diurnal fluctuation (Herridge, 1977) estimates are best made from studies throughout plant ontogeny (Herridge & Pate, 1977: Pate & Herridge, 1978; Ryle, Powell & Gordon, 1979a; Neves *et al.*, 1981).

Vigna unguiculata has been the best studied tropical legume. Its efficiency, as measured by two different techniques, is outstandingly high (even higher than the theoretical maximum). However, when plants are grown under adverse environmental conditions favoring wastage of carbon in respiration (Minchin *et al.*, 1980), the cost of N_2 fixation may show a two- to three-fold increase and may affect the carbon economy of the whole plant. The presence of an active uptake hydrogenase in *V. unguiculata* bacteroids (Schubert & Evans, 1976) may contribute to the high efficiency, but the importance of the carboxylation process in the nodules can not be excluded as an explanation of the low CO_2 output. Phosphoenol pyruvate (PEP) carboxylase has been found in nodules of many legumes, including *V. unguiculata* (Layzell *et al.*, 1979). The importance of the system is, as yet, uncertain as the rates of activities reported vary from 0.02 to 4.65 mg C/g fresh weight per h, a 233-fold variation (Minchin *et al.*, 1981).

TABLE 2: Respiratory cost of N_2 fixation by legume and actinorhizal nodules.

Species	g C respired/ g fixed N	References
Tropical and sub-tropical legumes		
Vigna unguiculata	1.1	Herridge & Pate, 1977; Neves *et al.*, 1981
	1.5	Layzell *et al.*, 1979
	3-4	Ryle *et al.*, 1979a
	3.4	Minchin *et al.*, 1980
Desmodium sp.	4.5	Tjepkema & Winship, 1980
Phaseolus vulgaris	6.1	Mahon, 1979
	5.1	Tjepkema & Winship, 1980
Glycine max	7.6	Bond, 1941
	19.4	Bergersen, 1971b
	3-4	Heytler & Hardy, 1979
	2.1	Tjepkema, 1971
	6.7	Mahon, 1979
	3-5	Schubert & Ryle, 1980
Temperate legumes		
Melilotus sp.	7.2	Tjepkema & Winship, 1980
Lupinus albus	1.7	Pate & Herridge, 1978
	3.6	Layzell *et al.*, 1979
Vicia faba	6.7	Mahon, 1979
	4.4	Tjepkema & Winship, 1980
Pisum sativum	1.5	Minchin & Pate, 1973
	6.9	Mahon, 1977
	1.9	Houwaard, 1980
Trifolium pratense	5.4	Tjepkema & Winship, 1980
Non-legumes		
Alnus rugosa	4.4-4.9	Tjepkema & Winship, 1980
Ceanothus americanus	4.9-11.2	Tjepkema & Winship, 1980
Comptonia peregrina	3.9	Tjepkema & Winship, 1980
Eleagnus umbellata	3.6	Tjepkema & Winship, 1980
Myrica gale	4.5-9.8	Tjepkema & Winship, 1980

Presence of an active PEP carboxylase complicates the estimation of the respiratory cost of N_2 fixation and the comparisons between species, cultivars, treatments, or even plant age, as it is not possible to determine whether differences are due to production of CO_2, recapture, or both.

Energy requirements for N_2 fixation of actinorhizal nodules have been estimated recently by Tjepkema & Winship (1980) and were found to be similar to those of legume nodules (see Table 2). However, comparisons involving other symbiotic or associative systems have yet to be performed.

C and N balance studies

As stated earlier, the process of N_2 fixation in legume nodules is coupled with ammonia assimilation and transport. Thus, besides energy and reductants, nodule requirements also include carbon for nodule growth and transport of fixed N, which is, however, recycled back to the shoot. Whole plant carbon and N balances give a more complete view of the carbon expenditure of the nodulated legume, but to date these have only been reported for three legume species (see review by Minchin *et al.*, 1981).

Nodules have a daily intake of 11.6 - 95.3 mg C from the host plant (see Table 3) which represents 13 to 28% of the net daily gain of the plant shoot. Most of the carbon available to nodules is expended in respiration and in export of fixed N to the plant shoot.

N can be exported mainly as ureides (C:N ratio of 1) or amides (C:N ratio of 2 and 2.5 for asparagine and glutamine, respectively). Ureides, thus, represent a saving of about 50% in terms of carbon for plants such as *V. unguiculata* (Herridge *et al.*, 1978; Minchin *et al.*, 1980) *Phaseolus vulgaris* (Cookson, Hughes & Coombs, 1980) and *Glycine max* (Kushizaki, Ishizuka & Akamatsa, 1964) when compared with those using amides, e.g., *Pisum sativum* (Minchin & Pate, 1973) and *Lupinus* (Pate & Herridge, 1978). Although this high percentage of economy may represent a minor carbon saving for plants of low N requirements (Sinclair & de Wit, 1975) it could be a vital saving for a plant such as *V. unguiculata*, that has a high N requirement and pumps N upwards at a rate of 22.6 mg N/plant per day (Neves *et al.*, 1981).

In some systems the CO_2 lost in respiration can account for 50% or more of the nodule carbon income. This is most common under adverse temperature conditions where too much carbon is used in respiration (Halliday, 1975; Layzell *et al.*, 1979; Minchin *et al.*, 1980).

Carbon investment in nodule dry matter is the smallest component of nodule carbon budget varying from 9 - 22% of the total carbon imported from shoot (see Table 3). However, the better comparison is of carbon investment in nodule dry matter with N_2 fixed (C dry matter:fixed N ratio). For the plant species shown in Table 3 a range of 0.38 to 1.20 can be calculated. The *Lupinus* varieties studied represent the extreme values for efficiency (a ratio of 0.38)

TABLE 3: Partitioning of translocated carbon in nodules during the period of increasing N_2 fixation.

System	Total N_2 fixed (mg/plant·day)	Total C imported (mg/plant·day)	% daily C intake to nodules		
			Respiration	N export	Dry matter
P. sativum					
cv. Meteor[1]	3.0	12.4(28)[6]	36	48	16
L. albus					
cv. unnamed[2]	10.6	46.7(13)	40	52	9
cv. Ultra (strain Wu425)[3]	2.8	18.4	55	27	18
V. unguiculata					
cv. Caloona[4]	8.4	25.0(13)	36	43	21
cv. Caloona (strain CB756)[5]	3.7	11.6	49	29	22
cv. TVu1503 (strain CB1024)[5]	22.6	72.5(17)	35	45	20
cv. K2809 (strain CB756)[5]	20.0	95.3(20)	63	21	16

[1]Minchin & Pate (1973)
[2]Pate & Herridge (1978)
[3]Layzell et al., (1979)
[4]Herridge & Pate (1977)
[5]Neves (1978)
[6]Figures in parentheses are % of net daily C gain/plant.

and inefficiency (a ratio of 1.20), which probably reflects not only the cultivar and strain interactions but also the different plant culture and husbandry used in the experiments. All other plant species have similar ratios, averaging 0.67.

ENERGY COST OF BIOLOGICAL N_2 FIXATION VERSUS ASSIMILATION OF MINERAL N BY LEGUMES

The high energy cost of N_2 fixation leading to a diversion of photosynthates that otherwise could be used for plant growth has motivated various comparative studies between the energy needs for N_2 fixation and nitrate assimilation (Schubert & Ryle, 1980). Thermodynamic considerations suggest similar energetic requirements for both systems (Bergersen, 1971a). Furthermore, the ATP consumption as estimated by F.R. Minchin (personal communication) is also similar. For plants supplied nitrate, 12 ATP equivalents are needed for nitrate reduction to ammonia (P/2 e- of 3) and 1 ATP for nitrate uptake by the roots (Penning de Vries, 1975). Assuming ammonia assimilation mainly into asparagine, a major organic nitrogenous compound in most non-nodulated legumes (Pate, 1973), the minimal cost can be calculated as 31 ATP, equivalent to a requirement of 0.84 moles glucose/mol asparagine produced (or 2.16 g C/g N), similar to the aforementioned carbon requirement for N_2 fixation.

Whole-plant studies provide conflicting results. At high N levels (200 ppm NO_3-N) plants of *V. unguiculata* and *G. max* assimilate nitrates mainly in the leaves (Ryle, Powell & Gordon, 1979b; Minchin *et al.*, 1980). Under such a nutritional regime, the ratio of carbon respired by belowground organs per unit of N assimilated is smaller for non-nodulated plants than for their nodulated counterparts (Ryle *et al.*, 1979b; Minchin *et al.*, 1980; Neves *et al.*, 1981). This is because nodule activity increases the specific respiration of nodulated plants (Bond, 1941; Ryle, Powell & Gordon, 1978; 1979b; Minchin *et al.*, 1980; Neves *et al.*, 1981). Furthermore, as no compensatory differences in photosynthesis and shoot respiration have been observed (Ryle *et al.*, 1978; 1979b) it has been suggested that nitrate assimilation in the shoot benefits from an excess of ATP and reductants produced during photosynthesis and proceeds "cost free" for the plants. Energy will, however, be required for synthesis and maintenance of the enzymes that have a high turnover rate (Woolhouse, 1967) and for nitrate uptake by the roots.

At lower N levels nitrate assimilation proceeds mainly in the roots (Oghoghorie & Pate, 1971; Atkins, Pate & Layzell, 1979; Pate, Layzell & Atkins, 1979) requiring energy and reductants derived from respiration. Under such conditions, conflicting results have been obtained. Whereas relative growth rate studies show similar energy requirements for N_2 fixation and nitrate assimilation of *Trifolium subterraneum* (Gibson, 1966), *V. unguiculata,* or *G. max* (Broughton, 1979, cited by Minchin *et al.,* 1981), gas exchange measurements suggest substantially greater energy requirements for

N_2 fixation by *T. subterraneum* (Silsbury, 1977). Even more surprising, root respiration rates of nitrate fed *Pisum sativum* are 8% greater than those of nodulated plants (Minchin & Pate, 1973) while for *Lupinus* the rates are 25% less (Pate *et al.*, 1979). As a result, the respiratory cost for *P. sativum* of nitrate-assimilation root is higher (6.2 g C/g N) than for plants dependent on fixed N (5.8 g C/v N), whereas for *Lupinus* nitrate-fed roots have a smaller ratio (8.1 g C/g N) than nodulated ones (10.2 g C/g N).

As plants assimilating nitrates have a reduced cost for nodule production and root respiration, more carbon will become available for growth. This, however seems more to benefit the vegetative than the reproductive growth of *V. unguiculata* (Minchin *et al.*, 1980; Neves *et al.*, 1981).

The accelerated leaf senescence of N-fed plants and their reduced nitrate assimilation during early reproductive development (Neves, 1978) further reduces the relative superiority of nitrate-fed plants in terms of seed yield.

In contrast with N_2 fixation and nitrate reduction, ammonia assimilation does not have the cost of reduction, but the carbon economy of plants under this nutritional regime has not yet been determined. Additionally, many agricultural plants are not adapted to use N in this form.

CONCLUSIONS

The energy cost of the various N_2-fixing systems depends on the efficiency with which energy is transferred from the energy-yielding reactions to N_2 fixation. Under conditions of limited carbon supply and optimum oxygen concentration for nitrogenase function, some free-living bacteria such as *Azospirillum*, when approaching stationary phase of growth, may attain values of carbon usage for N_2 fixation that are not greatly different from those reported for legume nodules where nongrowing *Rhizobium* cells experience physiological and environmental conditions that favor an efficient N_2 fixation. Since *Azospirillum* spp. are very frequently found associated with grasses, where they infect the inner parts of the roots (Dobereiner & De-Polli, 1980) the reported efficiencies are very encouraging with regard to the potential of such associations.

Evidence also suggests a similar cost for N_2-fixation in actinorhizal and legume nodules, but the correct assessment of *in vivo* energy costs of each N_2-fixing system will depend on improved techniques for accurate measurement of the carbohydrate usage in N_2 fixation, since measurements can be affected by other energy-yielding pathways such as H_2 oxidation. Furthermore, data based on the amount of respiratory CO_2 output in N_2-fixing organs may underestimate cost if an active PEP-carboxylase system is present.

N_2 fixation, as indicated by present knowledge, may have a higher energy requirement than utilization of combined N in the form of nitrates, but this seems to depend largely on the site of nitrate assimilation, although the importance of environmental factors can not be overlooked.

Under conditions prevailing in the field, efficiently nodulated legumes utilize both N_2 and combined N for growth and probably benefit from advantages of both processes, as seed yields under these conditions are very seldom increased by large applications of N fertilizer (Summerfield *et al.*, 1977). The energy cost of such systems has not yet been determined.

If yields are not reduced by the high energy demand of N_2 fixation, then the use of solar energy instead of fossil fuel for supplying plants with reduced N becomes a major saving. For the 1980 soybean crop of Brazil alone this was estimated at 800 million dollars or 80 dollars/ha (Döbereiner & Duque, 1980).

REFERENCES

Andersen K., Shanmugam, K.T. & Valentine, R.C. (1978) *Devel. in Industrial Microbiol.* 19, 279-283.

Appleby, C.A. (1969) *Biochim. Biophys. Acta* 172, 71-87.

Atkins, C.A., Pate, J.S. & Layzell, D.B. (1979) *Plant Physiol.* 64, 1078-1082.

Bergersen, F.J. (1971a) *Plant Soil*, Special Vol. Pp. 511-524.

Bergersen, F.J. (1971b) *Ann. Rev. Plant Physiol.* 22, 121-140.

Bergersen, F.J. (1980) Index of diazotrophic microorganisms. *In*: Methods of evaluating biological nitrogen fixation, F.J. Bergersen (Ed.). Wiley, Chichester, England. Pp. 695-697.

Berndt, H., Ostwal, K.R., Lalucat, J., Schumann, C., Mayer, F., & Schlegel, H.G. (1976) *Arch. Microbiol.* 108, 17-26.

Boland, M.J., Farnden, K.J.F. & Robertson, J.G. (1980) Ammonia assimilation in nitrogen fixing legume nodules. *In*: Nitrogen fixation, Vol. II. W.E. Newton & W.H. Orme-Johnson (Eds.). University Park Press, Baltimore, MD, USA. Pp. 33-52.

Bond, G. (1941) *Ann. Bot.* 5, 313-337.

Cookson, C., Hughes, H. & Coombs, J. (1980) *Planta* 148, 338-345.

Dalton, H. (1980) Chemoautotrophic nitrogen fixation. *In*: Nitrogen fixation, W.D.P. Stewart & J.R. Gallon (Eds.). Academic Press, London, England. Pp. 177-195.

Dalton, H. & Postgate, J.R. (1969) *J. Gen. Microbiol.* 56, 307-319.

Dixon, R.O.D. (1976) *Nature (Lond.)* 262, 173.

Dixon, R.O.D. (1978) *Biochemie* 60, 233-236.

Döbereiner, J. (1974) Nitrogen fixation in the rhizosphere. *In*: The biology of nitrogen fixation, A. Quispel (Ed.). North-Holland, Amsterdam, The Netherlands. Pp. 86-120.

Döbereiner, J. & De-Polli, H. (1980) Diazotrophic rhizocoenosis. *In*: International Symposium in Root-Soil Systems. Londrina, Brazil.

Döbereiner, J. & Duque, F.F. (1980) *R. Econ. Rural* 18, 447-460.

Evans, H.J., Emerich, D.W., Lepo, J.E., Maier, R.J., Carter, K.R., Hanus, F.J., & Russell, S.A. (1980) The role of hydrogenase in nodule bacterioids and free-living rhizobia. *In*: Nitrogen fixation, W.D.P. Stewart & J.R. Gallon (Eds.). Academic Press, London, England. Pp. 55-81.

Gallon, J.R. (1980) Nitrogen fixation by photoautotrophs. *In*: Nitrogen fixation, W.D.P. Stewart & J.R. Gallon (Eds.). Academic Press, London, England. Pp. 197-238.

Gibson, A.H. (1966) *Aust. J. Biol. Sci.* 19, 499-515.

Goi, S.R. & Neves, M.C.P. (1981) *Pesq. Agropec. Bras.* (In press.)

Gutschick, V.P. (1978) *BioScience* 28, 571-575.

Gutschick, V.P. (1980) Energy flows in the nitrogen cycle, especially in fixation. *In*: Nitrogen fixation, Vol. I. W.E. Newton & W.H. Orme-Johnson (Eds.). University Park Press, Baltimore, MD, USA. Pp. 17-27.

Halliday, J. (1975) An interpretation of seasonal and short-term fluctuations in nitrogen fixation. PhD Thesis, University of Western Australia, Nedlands, Australia.

Harre, E.A., Livingstone, O.W. E. & Shields, J.T. (1974) *National Fertilizer Development Center Bull.* Y-70, 68p.

Herridge, D.F. (1977) Carbon and nitrogen nutrition of two annual legumes. PhD Thesis, University of Western Australia, Nedlands, Australia.

Herridge, D.F., Atkins, C.A., Pate, J.S., & Rainbird, R.M. (1978) *Plant Physiol.* 62, 495-498.

Herridge, D.F. & Pate, J.S. (1977) *Plant Physiol.* 60, 759-764.

Heytler, P.G. & Hardy, R.W.F. (1979) *Plant Physiol.* Supplement 63, 84 Abstract No. 468.

Hill, S. (1978) Environmental role of nitrogen-fixing blue-green algae and asymbiotic bacteria. *Ecol. Bull* (Stockholm) 26, 130-136.

Houwaard, F. (1980) *Plant Soil* 54, 51-63.

Jensen, H.L. (1965) Non-symbiotic nitrogen fixation. *In*: Soil nitrogen, W.V. Bartholomew & F.E. Clark (Eds.). Amer. Soc. Agron., Madison, WI, USA. Pp. 436-480.

Knowles, R. (1977) The significance of asymbiotic dinitrogen fixation by bacteria. *In*: A treatise on dinitrogen fixation. Section IV. R.W.F. Hardy & A.H. Gibson (Eds.). Wiley, New York, NY, USA. Pp. 33-38.

Kushizaki, M., Ishizuka, J. & Akamatsa, F. (1964) *J. Sci. Soil Manure* 35, 323-327.

La Rue, T.A. (1977) The bacteria. *In*: A treatise on dinitrogen fixation. Section III. R.W.F. Hardy & W.S. Silver (Eds.). Wiley, New York, NY USA. Pp. 19-62.

Layzell, D.B., Rainbird, R.M., Atkins, C.A., & Pate, J.S. (1979) *Plant Physiol.* 64, 888-891.

Mahon, J.D. (1977) *Plant Physiol.* 60, 817-821.

Mahon, J.D. (1979) *Plant Physiol.* 63, 892-899.

Minchin, F.R. & Pate, J.S. (1973) *J. Expl. Bot.* 24, 259-271.

Minchin, F.R., Summerfield, R.J. & Neves, M.C.P. (1980) *J. Expl. Bot.* 31, 1327-1345.

Minchin, F.R., Summerfield, R.J., Hadley, P., Roberts, E.H., & Rawsthorne, S. (1981) *Pl. Cell. Environ.* 4. (In press.).

Mulder, E.G. & Brotonegoro, S. (1974) Free-living heterotrophic nitrogen-fixing bacteria. *In*: The biology of nitrogen fixation, A. Quispel (Ed.). North-Holland, Amsterdam, The Netherlands. Pp. 37-85.

Neves, M.C.P. (1978). Carbon and nitrogen nutrition of cowpea (*Vigna unguiculata* (L.) Walp). PhD Thesis, University of Reading, England.

Neves, M.C.P., Minchin, F.R. & Summerfield, R.J. (1981) *Trop. Agric.* (Trinidad). (In press.)

Nye, P.H. & Greenland, D.J. (1960) The soil under shifting cultivation. Commonwealth Agricultural Bureaux, Farnham Royal, Bucks, England.

Oghoghorie, C.G.O. & Pate, J.S. (1971) *Plant Soil*, Special Vol. Pp. 185-202.

Okon, Y., Houchins, J.P., Albrecht, S.L., & Burris, R.H. (1977) *J. Gen. Microbiol.* 98, 87-93.

O'Toole, P. & Knowles, R. (1973) *Soil Biol. Biochem.* 5, 789-797.

Pate, J.S. (1973). *Soil Biol. Biochem.* 5, 109-119.

Pate, J.S. & Herridge, D.F. (1978) *J. Expl. Bot.* 29, 401-412.

Pate, J.S., Layzell, D.B. & Atkins, C.A. (1979) *Plant Physiol.* 64, 1083-1088.

Parker, C.A. (1954) *Nature (Lond.)* 173, 780-781.

Penning de Vries, F.W.T. (1975) *Ann. Bot.* 39, 77-92.

Rawsthorne, S., Minchin F.R., Summerfield, R.J., Cookson, C., & Coombs, J. (1980) *Phytochemistry* 19, 341-355.

Ryle, G.J.A., Powell, C.E. & Gordon, A.J. (1978) *Ann. Bot.* 42, 637-648.

Ryle, G.J.A., Powell, C.E. & Gordon, A.J. (1979a) *J. Expl. Bot.* 30, 135-144.

Ryle, G.J.A., Powell, C.E. & Gordon, A.J. (1979b) *J. Expl. Bot.* 30, 145-153.

Schubert, K.R. & Evans, H.J. (1976) *Proc. Natl. Acad. Sci.* (USA) 73, 1207-1211.

Schubert. K.R. & Ryle, G.J.A. (1980) The energy requirements for nitrogen fixation in nodulated legumes. *In*: Advances in legume science, R.J. Summerfield & A.H. Bunting (Eds.). Royal Botanic Gardens, Kew, England. Pp. 85-96.

Silsbury, J.H. (1977) *Nature* 267, 149-150.

Sinclair, T.R. & de Wit, C.T. (1975) *Science* 189, 565-567.

Smith, L.A., Hill, S. & Yates, M.G. (1976) *Nature* 262, 209-210.

Sprent, J. (1980) *Pl. Cell Environ.* 3, 35-43.

Steifel, E.I. (1977) The mechanisms of nitrogen fixation. *In*: Recent developments in nitrogen fixation, W.E. Newton, J.R. Postgate & C. Rodríguez-Barrueco (Eds.). Academic Press, London, England. Pp. 69-108.

Stephan, M.P., Pedrosa, F.O. de & Döbereiner, J. (1981) Physiology studies of *Azospirillum* spp., *In*: Associative N_2 fixation, P.B. Vose and A.P. Ruschel (Eds.). CRC Press, Palm Beach FL USA.

Stewart, W.D.P., Rowell, P. & Rai, A.N. (1980) Symbiotic nitrogen-fixing cyanobacteria. *In*: Nitrogen fixation, W.D.P. Stewart & J.R Gallon (Eds.). Academic Press London, England. Pp. 239-277.

Summerfield, R.J., Dart, P.J., Huxley, P.A., Eaglesham, A.R.J., Minchin, F.R., & Day, J.M. (1977) *Expl. Agric.* 13, 129-142.

Tjepkema, J.D. (1971) Oxygen transport in the soybean nodule and the function of leghaemoglogin. PhD Thesis, University of Michigan, Lansing, MI, USA.

Tjepkema, J.D. & Winship, L.J. (1980) *Science* 209, 279-281.

Triplett, E.W., Blevins, D.G. & Randall, D.D. (1980) *Plant Physiol.* 65, 1203-1206.

Vincent, J.M. (1974) Root-nodule symbiosis with *Rhizobium*. *In*: The biology of nitrogen fixation, A. Quispel (Ed.). North-Holland, Amsterdam, The Netherlands. Pp. 265-341.

Vincent, J.M. (1980) Factors controlling the legume-*Rhizobium* symbiosis. *In*: Nitrogen fixation, Vol. II. W.E. Newton & W.H. Orme-Johnson (Eds.) University Park Press, Baltimore, MD, USA, Pp. 103-129.

Volpon, A.G.T., De-Polli, H., & Döbereiner, J. (1981) *Arch. Microbiol.* (In press.)

Winter, H.C. & Burris, R.H. (1968) *J. Biol. Chem.* 243, 940-944.

Woolhouse, H.W. (1967) The nature of senescence in plants. *In*: Aspects of the biology of ageing, H.W. Woolhouse (Ed.). *Symp. Soc. Exp. Biol.* 21, 179-214. (Cambridge University Press, London, England.)

THE MECHANISM OF RECOGNITION BETWEEN LEGUME ROOTS AND RHIZOBIA: SOME IMPLICATIONS FOR BIOLOGICAL NITROGEN FIXATION IN THE TROPICS

F.B. Dazzo[1]

Summary

This paper reviews the experimental basis for the lectin-recognition hypothesis and considers ways in which the host/*Rhizobium* interaction might be manipulated to enhance the benefits of symbiotic nitrogen fixation in the tropics.

INTRODUCTION

The discrimination that host legume and rhizobia display during nodule initiation suggests that cellular recognition is important to the development of this symbiosis. An understanding of the mechanisms involved might indicate ways in which host plant and *Rhizobium* could be genetically manipulated to increase the range of agricultural crops that enter efficient nitrogen (N_2) fixing symbioses. In addition, it might explain anomalous infections and unusual specificities among tropical legumes, and lead to solutions for problems as diverse as interstrain competition for nodule sites and the inhibitory effects of combined N on root nodulation.

In this paper, I review the experimental evidence for the recognition concept, consider possible models describing the underlying mechanism(s), and examine the effects of specific soil stresses on the recognition process.

THE LECTIN-RECOGNITION HYPOTHESIS

The lectin-recognition hypothesis suggests that recognition at infection sites involves the binding of specific legume lectins to carbohydrates found on the surface of the appropriate rhizobial symbiont.

---

[1] Dept. of Microbiology and Public Health, Michigan State University, East Lansing, MI 48824, USA. Publication no. 9861 of the Michigan Agricultural Experiment Station. Research support under NSF grant PCM 78-22922, 80-21906 and USDA grant 78-59-2261-0-1-050-2 is gratefully acknowledged.

An important test of the lectin-recognition hypothesis is to determine whether the legume has a lectin that binds to specific receptors present on the surface of the rhizobial symbiont. Considerable evidence of this process and the factors controlling it has now been assembled. Initial work using seed lectins from soybean and clover has demonstrated specificity in the binding of these substances to strains of *Rhizobium*. This correlates well with the ability of strains to nodulate particular hosts (Bohlool & Schmidt, 1974; Wolpert & Albersheim, 1976; Bhuvaneswari *et al,* 1977; Dazzo *et al.,* 1978). However, some anomalous lectin-binding interactions have been found and are reviewed by Dazzo (1980a; b; c; d). One suggestion to explain these is that the legume in question may contain several different lectins, some of which may be on root hairs and recognize unusual saccharides on the *Rhizobium* that are not present on erythrocytes.

The presence of lectins at the infection site on the legume root has also been demonstrated. Indirect evidence for the presence of lectins on bean roots was first provided by Hamblin & Kent (1973). Later, we demonstrated receptor sites on the tips of clover root hairs that specifically bound FITC-labeled capsular polysaccharide (Dazzo & Brill, 1977) encapsulated cells of *R. trifolii* (Dazzo & Brill, 1979, see Fig. 1), and antibody to seed-trifoliin A, a white clover lectin (Dazzo *et al.,* 1978). Undifferentiated epidermal cells did not bind the bacterial polysaccharide, and quantitative immunocytofluorimetry using antitrifoliin A antibody showed that trifoliin A accumulated in greatest quantity on young seedlings where the epidermis differentiates into root hairs (Dazzo *et al.,* 1978). The specificity of these receptor sites was demonstrated by the ability of unlabeled capsular polysaccharide from *R. trifolii,* but not

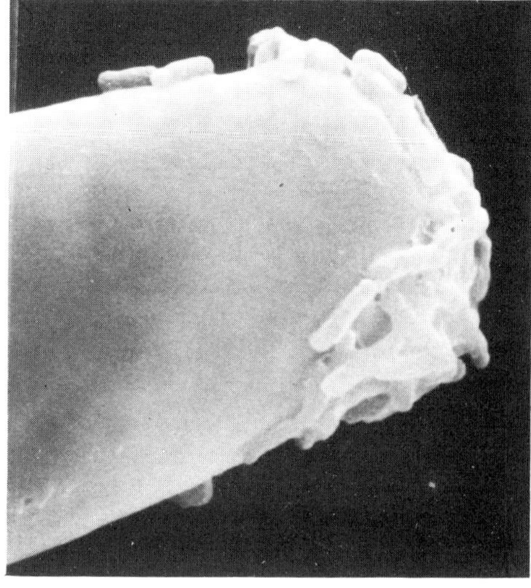

Figure 1.
Attachment of *Rhizobium trifolii* 0403 to a clover root-hair tip after 15 min. incubation, as examined by scanning electron microscopy (from F.B. Dazzo & W.J. Brill (1979) *J. Bacteriol.* 137, 1362, and courtesy of the American Society for Microbiology).

from *R. meliloti,* to block the binding of the labeled polysaccharide (Dazzo & Brill, 1977). This experiment has been reproduced with *R. meliloti*/alfalfa (Dazzo & Brill, 1977), *R. japonicum*/soybean (Hughes *et al.,* 1979; T. Hughes & G. H. Elkan, unpublished data), and *R. leguminosarum*/pea (Kato *et al.,* 1980). In each case, the specific binding of the rhizobial polysaccharides to the host occurred in the region of young root hairs. That the sugar haptens for the corresponding host lectin specifically inhibited the binding of the labeled rhizobial polysaccharide is evidence that the root lectins were involved in this recognition process.

Lectins may be situated on the root in a number of ways. Bowles *et al.* (1979) have proposed that some root lectins may become intercalated in membranes and require detergents for their solubilization. Other root lectins can be solubilized by buffers containing sugar haptens, suggesting that they are anchored to glycosylated receptors. The removal of trifoliin A from intact seedling roots with 2-deoxyglucose (Dazzo & Brill, 1977; Dazzo *et al.*, 1978) suggests that some of this lectin falls within the latter category. The hapten-eluted root lectin was antigenically cross-reactive with the seed lectin (Dazzo *et al.,* 1978). Similar hapten-facilitated elution of pea root lectin has been found (van der Schaal & Kijne, 1981; W. Kamberger, personal communication). Pea root lectins have the same sugar-binding specificity and are serologically very similar to seed lectins (Kamberger, 1979b; personal communication). Some of the pea lectin integrated seems to be through the plant cell wall, which clarifies the difficulties in isolating significant amounts of pea root lectins by the hapten elution method (van der Schaal & Kijne, 1981).

One of the possible consequences of lectin/polysaccharide interaction would be that the bacterial cell could attach and then firmly adhere to the target host cell. Our model for selective adhesion of *Rhizobium* to root hairs of its host involves a lectin-mediated cross-bridging of similar saccharide receptors on the bacterium and the root hair cell wall (Dazzo & Hubbell, 1975b; see Figure 2). By mediating the adhesion of specific cells, the lectin could also function as a "cell recognition molecule," influencing which cells associate in sufficient proximity to the root hairs that subsequent recognition steps can occur.

Light and electron microscope studies (Dazzo & Hubbell, 1975b; Chen & Phillips, 1976; Dazzo *et al.,* 1976; Dazzo & Brill, 1979; Dazzo 1980a; b; d), have revealed at least two stages in the process of microsymbiont attachment. During the initial attachment phase, docking of the bacteria is initiated by contact of the fibrillar capsule with electron-dense, globular aggregates lying on the outer periphery of the root hair wall (Dazzo & Hubbell, 1975b). Quantitative microscopic studies during this period have shown a correlation between the ability of rhizobial cells to attach in high numbers to the root hairs of the host and the ability of these bacteria to infect the host (Dazzo *et al.,* 1976; Dazzo, 1980a; Stacey *et al.,* 1980; Kato *et al.,* 1981). Such

Figure 2.
Model of cellular recognition during attachment of *Rhizobium trifolii* to clover root hairs (from F.B. Dazzo & D. Hubbell (1975) *Appl. Microbiol.* 30, 1017, and courtesy of the American Society for Microbiology).

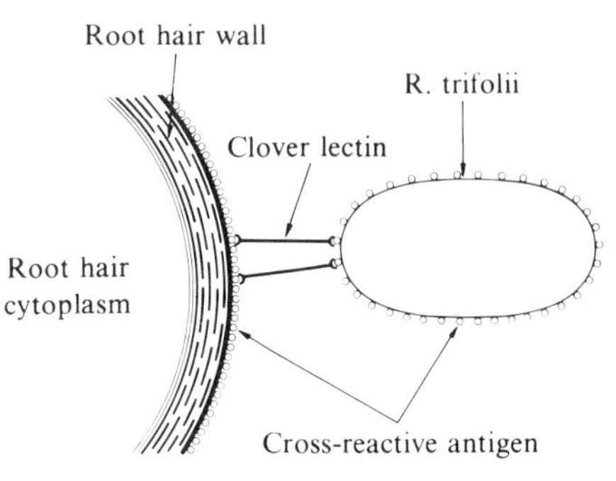

attachment is specifically inhibited by the sugar that is an effective hapten of the root lectin (Dazzo *et al.,* 1976; Kato *et al.,* 1980; Stacey *et al.,* 1980). After several hours of incubation, rhizobial adhesions are less localized on the root surface and fibrillar material associated with the bacteria adhering to root hairs is more easily resolved in scanning electon micrographs (Dart, 1971; Dazzo, 1980b; c; d).

According to the cross-bridging hypothesis, the ability of a *Rhizobium* strain to adhere to root hairs on the host should be influenced by conditions that effect the accumulation of lectins on the root surface or saccharide receptors on the bacterium. Evidence in support of this includes:

Antigenically altered mutant strains of *R. trifolii* (Dazzo & Hubbell, 1975a) have significantly fewer or nondetectable trifoliin A receptors (Dazzo & Hubbell, 1975b) and are attached to clover root hairs only at low background levels (Dazzo *et al.,* 1976);

Levels of trifoliin A and the attachment of *R. trifolii* to root hairs decline as the concentrations of either NO_3^- or NH_4^+ in the rooting medium increase (Dazzo & Brill, 1978);

Under certain growth conditions, the transient appearance of trifoliin A receptors on *R. trifolii* coincides with their ability to attach in greatest quantity to clover roots; and

Intergeneric hybrids of *Azobacter* that express *R. trifolii* genes for trifoliin A receptors (Bishop *et al.*, 1977) acquire specific binding to clover root hair tips (Dazzo & Brill, 1979).

It now also appears that more than one polysaccharide on the *Rhizobium* cell surface may act as lectin receptor. These include capsular polysaccharides; (Dazzo & Brill, 1979); lipopolysaccharide (Wolpert & Albersheim, 1976; Dazzo *et al.*, 1981); and a glycan (Planque & Kijne, 1977). Both host-specific lectin-LPS interactions (*R. meliloti*/alfalfa) and exopolysaccharide-lectin interactions (*R. japonicum*/soybean) have been found (Kamberger, 1979a). Pea and clover lectins will bind to both the LPS and capsular polysaccharides of their symbiont rhizobia only at certain culture ages (Kamberger, 1979a; Hrabak *et al.*, 1981). Kamberger (1979b) has proposed that root hair attachment is mediated by lectins cross-bridging the capsular polysaccharides as a preliminary recognition event, followed by a more critical recognition event involving the host-specific binding of the lectin to the underlying bacterial LPS which then triggers successful infection.

IMPLICATIONS OF THE LECTIN-RECOGNITION HYPOTHESIS IN BNF TECHNOLOGY DEVELOPMENT

A number of environmental and soil factors, many of which operate at least in part through effects on legume/*Rhizobium* recognition mechanisms, can affect nodule development and limit N_2 fixation.

A major cause for concern is that lectin binding sites on rhizobia are both strain dependent and transient in nature, with most lectin-binding cells and the greatest number of sites per cell in the early- and mid-log phases of growth (Bhuvaneswari *et al.*, 1977). Other strains react best at early stationary phase. Chemical and immunological changes in the surface polysaccharides and lipopolysaccharides have been reported as the cell ages (Dazzo *et al.*, 1979; Dazzo *et al.*, 1981; Hrabak *et al.*, 1981). The underlying mechanism that controls these chemical changes is not known, but a number of soil conditions including waterlogging, oxygen depletion, mineral imbalance and temperature could have implications for the expression of lectin receptor molecules. Other aspects of the legume/*Rhizobium* symbiosis in which host/strain recognition is important include combined N, soil acidity, soil temperature, and competition for nodulation sites.

Combined N

It has been known for many years that combined N can limit the development and the success of the *Rhizobium*/legume symbiosis (Fred *et al.*, 1932). While a number of possible mechanisms have been suggested, root hair infection is known to be inhibited by critical concentrations of NO_3^- or NH_4^+. We have demonstrated in white clover (Dazzo & Brill, 1978; see Figure 3) that the immunologically detectable levels of trifoliin A and the level of binding of *R. trifolii* to root hairs are both affected by increasing concentrations of NO_3^- in the culture medium. Interestingly, low levels of nitrate (1 mM NO_3^-) enhanced the levels of trifoliin A and rhizobial attachment, while higher levels of nitrate reduced them.

We have begun to search for an explanation of this effect of nitrate on recognition. Ligand-binding studies with radiolabeled $^{13}NO_3^-$ (generated in a cyclotron) have shown that NO_3^- effects on trifoliin A and rhizobial

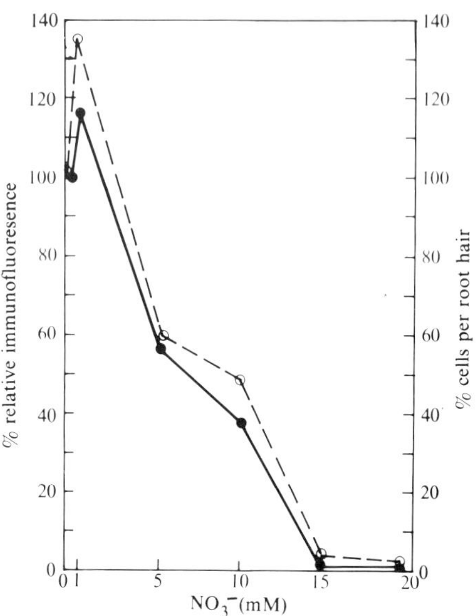

Figure 3.
Effect of N on adsorption of *Rhizobium trifolii* to root hairs (solid line) and immunologically detectable trifoliin A (dotted line) in the root hair region of clover seedlings. Bacterial adsorption was measured by direct microscopy and trifolin A by quantitative immunocytofluorimetry (from F.B. Dazzo, and W.J. Brill (1978) *Plant Physiol.* 62, 18, and courtesy of the American Society for Plant Physiology).

accumulation on clover roots are not due to the direct interaction of receptors with this anion (Dazzo *et al.,* 1981). Rather it seems that the availability of combined N will dictate how well the legume can recognize its symbiont *Rhizobium.* Recent studies with clover (Dazzo *et al.,* 1981) and peas (Diaz *et al.,* 1981) have shown that the supply of NO_3^- influences root cell wall composition, a finding consistent with the observation that accessability of trifoliin A receptors on purified root cell walls is reduced appreciably when clover seedlings are grown in 15 mM nitrate. Further experiments should be done to determine whether the *increased* accumulation of root lectin and concommitant rhizobial colonization of the root surface at a critical low level of NO_3^-(1 mM) account for the stimulation of root hair infection (Dart, 1977) and nodulation (Wilson & Wagner, 1935; Raggio & Raggio, 1962) commonly observed. Studies aimed at answering this question may lead to better control of nodulation under field conditions.

Soil acidity

The infection of legume root hairs by *Rhizobium* includes early acid-sensitive steps with infection significantly reduced below pH 5 (Munns, 1968), a level of H^+ that is common in acid soils of the tropics. This observation led us to examine the stability at low pH of the cross-reactive antigen on *R. trifolii* that binds trifoliin A. The acid instability of this antigen corresponded closely with observed effects on root hair infection (Dazzo & Hubbell, 1975b, see Figure 4). It is theoretically possible that genetic manipulations could result in modifications of acid-labile groups, giving them protection from soil acidity without modification of lectin binding properties.

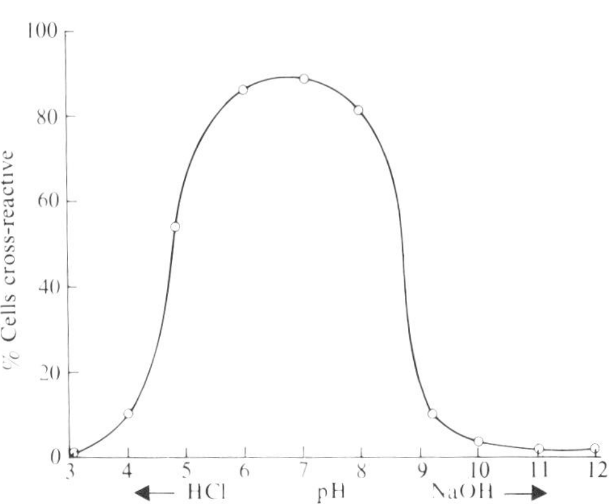

Figure 4.
The effect of pH on the cross-reactivity of encapsulated cells of *Rhizobium trifolii* 0403 with anti-clover root antiserum, as measured by indirect immunofluorescence (from F.B. Dazzo, and D. Hubbell (1975) *Appl. Microbiol.* 30, 1017 and courtesy of the American Society for Microbiology).

Soil temperature

Genes important to symbiotic specificity and nodulation, including the genes responsible for the 2-deoxyglucose inhibitable attachment of *R. trifolii* to clover root hairs, are encoded on large transmissable plasmids (Johnson *et al.,* 1978; Zurkowski & Lorkiewicz, 1978; van der Schaal & Kijne, 1979; Zurkowski, 1980). Growth of *Rhizobium* at high temperatures (35° C) either eliminates these important plasmids or induces large deletions in them and can result in modified nodulation performance (Zurkowski & Lorkiewicz, 1978). Thus, the high temperatures of tropical soils may exert serious constraints on the population of nodulation plasmids and, therefore, on the long-term persistence of effectiveness in *Rhizobium.* Perhaps genetic manipulation leading to increased temperature stability of the DNA polymerases responsible for plasmid replication may improve the performance of rhizobia in hot soils of the tropics.

Competition for nodulation sites

It is attractive to hypothesize that the ability of strains to outcompete others in a mixed population is related to their ability to interact efficiently with the lectin at the time they encounter the host root. Circumstantial evidence supporting the hypothesis has been found:

Inoculum prepared from *R. trifolii* or *R. japonicum* at a culture age when the majority of the cells bind the corresponding clover and soybean lectins will induce more root hair infections and nodules, respectively, than an equivalent inoculum dose from a culture age when few cells bind the lectin (Napoli, 1976; Hrabak *et al.,* 1981).

The one strain of *R. japonicum* (311b123) found to accumulate the lectin-binding capsule during the early stationary phase (Bhuvaneswari *et al.,* 1977) belongs to the serogroup found most frequently in nodules of soybeans from many soils of the central USA (Damirgi *et al.,* 1967; Ham *et al.,* 1971).

The delay in appearance of the capsule surrounding cells of *R. trifolii* TA1 (Dudman, 1968; Humphrey, & Vincent, 1969) may contribute to its competitiveness in soil (Dudman, 1968).

Rhizobia coated with appropriate host lectin, a substance the availability of which could limit the nodulation process, induced more root hair infections and nodulated earlier than equivalent, untreated rhizobia (B. Solheim, personal communication; F.B. Dazzo, unpublished data).

Under certain conditions, and using strains of *R. trifolii* that were only moderately competitive, we have shown that treatment of the rhizobia with lectin preparations can enhance their competitive ability. This raises the question of whether it is feasible to improve inoculant technology by providing a lectin-coated inoculant. Interestingly, this modification of the inoculant did not further improve the competitiveness of strains that were already highly competitive. Although the results were not uniformly reproducible (instability of the lectin in the inoculant?), they do suggest that an understanding of the cellular recognition process could have important implications for strain selection and post-inoculation competition between inoculant strains and native rhizobia in soil.

CONCLUSION

Despite the extensive support presented here in favor of the lectin-recognition hypothesis, the proof is not conclusive. We assume the attitude that adhesion of the infective rhizobia is only one in a sequence of steps leading to nodule initiation. Whatever the final details prove to be, it must be clear from the above presentation that the process of cellular recognition in the legume/*Rhizobium* symbiosis has major implications for BNF in the tropics.

REFERENCES

Bhuvaneswari, T.V., Pueppke S.G. & Bauer, W.D. (1977) *Plant Physiol.* 60, 486.

Bishop, P.E., Dazzo, F.B., Applebaum, E., Maier, R.J., & Brill, W.J. (1977) *Science* 198-938.

Bohlool, B.B. & Schmidt, E.L. (1974) *Science* 185, 260.

Bowles, G., Lis, H. & Sharon, N. (1979) *Planta* 145, 143.

Chen, A.J. & Phillips, D.A. (1976) *Physiol. Plant.* 38, 83.

Damirgi, D.M., Frederick, L.R. & Anderson, I.C. (1967) *Agron. J.* 59, 10.

Dart, P.J.. (1971) *J. Expl. Bot.* 22, 163.

Dart, P.J. (1977) Infection and development of leguminous nodules *In:* Treatise on dinitrogen fixation. Vol. III. R.W.F. Hardy & W. Silver (Eds). Wiley, New York, NY. USA. p. 367.

Dazzo, F.B. (1980b) Infection process in the legume-*Rhizobium* symbiosis *In*: *In:* Adsorption of microorganisms to surfaces, G. Britton & K. Marshall (Eds.). Wiley. New York, NY, USA. p.253.

Dazzo, F.B. (1980b) Infection process in the legume *Rhizobium* symbiosis *In;* Advances in legume science, R.J. Summerfield & A.H. Bunting (Eds.). Royal Botanic Gardens, Kew, England. p. 49.

Dazzo, F.B. (1980c) Lectins and their saccharide receptors as determinants of specificity in the *Rhizobium* legume symbiosis *In:* The cell surface: Mediator of development processes, S. Subtelny & N. Wessells (Eds.). Academic Press, New York. NY. USA. P.277.

Dazzo, F.B. (1980d) Determinants of host specificity in the *Rhizobium*-clover symbiosis *In:* Nitrogen fixation, W.E. Newton & W. Orme-Johnson (Eds.). University Park Press, Baltimore, MD, USA P.165.

Dazzo, F.B. & Brill, W.J. (1977) *Appl. Environ. Microbiol.* 33, 132.

Dazzo, F.B. & Brill, W.J. (1978) *Plant Physiol.* 62, 18.

Dazzo, F.B. & Brill, W.J. (1979) *J. Bacteriol.* 137, 1362.

Dazzo, F.B., Hrabak, E.M., Urbano, M.R., Sherwood, J.E., & Truchet, G. (1981) Regulation of recognition in the *Rhizobium*-clover symbiosis *In:* Current perspectives in nitrogen fixation, A.H. Gibson & W.E. Newton (Eds.). Aust. Acad. Sci., Canberra, Australia. Pp. 292-295.

Dazzo, F.B. & Hubbell, D.H. (1975a) *Appl. Microbiol.* 30, 172.

Dazzo, F.B. & Hubbell, D.H. (1975b) *Appl. Microbiol.* 30, 1017.

Dazzo, F.B.. Napoli, C.A. & Hubbell, D.H. (1976) *Appl. Environ. Microbiol.* 32, 168.

Dazzo, F.B.. Urbano, M.R. & Brill, W.J. (1979) *Curr. Microbiol.* 2, 15.

Dazzo, F.B., Yanke, W.E. & Brill, W.J. (1978) *Biochem. Biophys. Acta* 539, 276.

Diaz, C., Kijne. J.W. & Quispel, A. (1981) Influence of NO_3^- on pea root cell wall composition. *In*: Current perspectives in nitrogen fixation, A.H. Gibson & W.E. Newton (Eds.). Austr. Acad. Sci., Canberra, Australia. P 426.

Dudman. W.F. (1968) *J. Bacteriol.* 95, 1200.

Fred, E.B.. Baldwin, I.L. & McCoy, E. (1932) Root nodule bacteria and leguminous plants. University of Wisconsin Press, Madison, WI, USA.

Ham, G.E.. Frederick, L.R. & Anderson, I.C. (1971) *Agron. J.* 63, 69.

Hamblin. J. & Kent. S.P. (1973) *Nature* (Lond.) 245, 28.

Hrabak, E., Urbano, M. & Dazzo, F.B. (1981) *J. Bacteriol.* 148, 697.

Hughes. T.. Leece. J. & Elkan, G.H. (1979) *Appl. Environ. Microbiol.* 37, 1243.

Humphrey. B. & Vincent, J.M. (1969) *J. Gen. Microbiol.* 59, 441.

Johnston, A.W., Beynon, J.L., Buchanan-Woolaston. A.V., Setchell, S.M., Hirsch. F.R., & Beringer, J.E. (1978) *Nature* (Lond.) 276, 634.

Kamberger. W. (1979a) *Arch. Microbiol.* 121, 83.

Kamberger. W. (1979b) *FEMS Microbiol. Letters* 6, 361.

Kato, G., Maruyama, Y. & Nakamura, M. (1980) *Agric. Biol. Chem.* 44, 2843.

Munns. D.N. (1968) *Plant Soil* 28, 129.

Napoli. C.A. (1976) PhD. Thesis, Univ. of Florida, Gainesville, FL USA.

Planqué. N. & Kijne. J.W. (1977) *FEBS Letters* 73, 64.

Raggio. M. & Raggio. N. (1962) *Ann. Rev. Plant Physiol.* 13, 109.

Schaal. I. van der & Kijne, J.W. (1979) Surface polysaccharides of a *Rhizobium leguminosarum* inf$^-$ strain. *In*: North Amer. *Rhizobium* Conf., College Station, TX. USA. P. 17.

Schaal. I. van der & Kijne, J.W. (1981) Pea lectins and surface carbohydrates of *Rhizobium leguminosarum*. *In:* Current perspectives in nitrogen fixation, A.H. Gibson & W.E. Newton (Eds.). Austr. Acad. Sci. Canaberra, Australia. P. 425.

Stacey. G.. Paau. A. & Brill, W.J. (1980) *Plant Physiol.* 66, 609.

Vincent. J.M. & Humphrey, B. (1969) *J. Gen. Microbiol.* 59, 411.

Wilson. P. & Wagner. F.C. (1935) *Trans. Wisc. Acad. Sci. Arts Lett.* 30, 43.

Wolpert, J.S. & Albersheim, P. (1976) *Biochem. Biophys. Res. Commun.* 70, 729.

Zurkowski, W. (1980) *Microbios* 27, 27.

Zurkowski, W. & Lorkiewicz, Z. (1979) *Arch. Microbiol.* 123, 195.

TECHNOLOGY FOR INOCULANT PRODUCTION

MODERN CONCEPTS IN LEGUME INOCULATION

J.C. Burton[1]

Summary

Inoculant technology has advanced considerably over the last century. Problems in host-range specificity have been addressed, and save for a limited number of tropical legumes, largely resolved. Rhizobia can be cultured to populations guaranteeing adequate numbers even in unsterile peat. While peat continues to be the favored inoculant carrier, various coal and compost formulations show promise for regions where the peat supply is inadequate. Processing or sterilization of the carrier is also being increasingly adopted. Thus, provided quality control is adequate, there is every reason to expect success in the routine inoculation of new lands or crops.

A number of new problems are emerging and will require intensive investigation, especially in the tropics. These include the failure of inoculant rhizobia to compete with native soil rhizobia in traditional areas of production for crops such as soybeans and beans, the need for an inoculant technology suited to the needs of the small farmer, and problems experienced as population pressure forces agriculture development into previously underexploited regions.

INTRODUCTION

When compared to the thousands of years that leguminous crops have been valued and cultured for their nutritional and soil-building properties, our knowledge of the microsymbiont *Rhizobium* is recent.

Since it is reasonable to assume that prior to this century dissemination of the nodule bacteria was slow and often inadequate, it is reassuring to think that legumes achieved the niche they hold in agriculture without inoculation. Nonetheless, the challenge to successful legume agronomy today, with new crop species being emphasized and existing crops being expanded into new

[1] Nitragin Co., Milwaukee, WI 53209, USA.

countries or onto more marginal lands, is perhaps greater than at any time in history. Some of these challenges are already being met through advances in inoculation technology.

Development of the inoculant industry in the USA, as in other countries, was largely motivated by the desire to introduce leguminous species to new areas with immediate success. Early attempts to culture these legumes were often failures, since even the transfer of large volumes of soil to new fields did not provide the rhizobial numbers needed for adequate nodulation. An inoculant technology was necessary that recognized host-plant specificity and effectiveness groupings, introduced suitable carriers, solved distribution problems, established regulatory controls, etc. Technological development has also permitted 1000-fold increases in the expected quality of inoculants (Date & Roughley, 1977). Introduced legume species that have profited from the improvements in inoculant technology include soybean (*Glycine max* (L.) Merr.), introduced from China, and alfalfa (*Medicago sativa* L.), introduced from Persia. Currently almost 80% of US-produced inoculants are for these two species (see Table 1).

This review will look at modern strain selection and inoculant production technology and will try to identify those areas where additional research is needed to meet the challenges of tropical legume cropping systems.

HOST SPECIFICITY AND *RHIZOBIUM* STRAIN SELECTION

One of the first steps in legume inoculant manufacture is to obtain effective nitrogen (N_2) fixing strains of rhizobia for the legumes to be inoculated. In Australia, New Zealand, Brazil, and possibly other countries, the *Rhizobium* strains to be used are specified and provided by government or regulatory agencies. In the United States and Mexico individual manufacturers must screen their own strains or procure them from other sources.

The importance of matching host-genotypes and *Rhizobium* strains has long been recognized. Date (1976) summarized the attributes needed in an inoculant strain as:

- Ability to form N_2 -fixing nodules on the host for which it is recommended, under a range of field conditions;
- Competitiveness in nodule formation; and
- Survival and multiplication in soil.

Brockwell *et al.* (1968) proposed, as well:

- Prompt effective nodulation over a range of root temperatures;
- Good growth in culture;
- Good growth and survival in peat; and
- Survival on the seed.

Many of these traits are discussed in detail elsewhere in these proceedings.

Since it is not economically feasible nor desirable to provide a different inoculant strain for each of the numerous legumes grown in the USA, wide-

TABLE 1: Legume inoculant production for 1980.

Legume crop for which produced	Broth culture (x 10^3 l)	Peat inoculant (kg)	Area inoculated (x 10^3 ha)	Percent of total
Lathyrus, Pisum and *Vicia* spp.	67	201	466	5.0
Vicia faba	13	39	93	0.1
Glycine max	950	2,851	7,847	72.8
Powder for seed	(730)	(2,190)	(7,604)	(56.0)
Granular	(220)	(661)	(243)	(16.8)
Vigna and *Lespedeza*	7	22	91	0.5
Arachis hypogaea Granular	114	342	128	8.6
Medicago sativa	114	342	4,904	8.6
Trifolium spp.	47	131	2,040	3.6
Miscellaneous				0.8
Total		3,928	15,569	100.0

spectrum strains are preferred, and strain selection must balance effective response with the preferred host against strain response with other legumes it can nodulate. Thus, on the one hand such phylogenetically diverse genera as *Coronilla*, *Onobrychis*, *Leucaena* and *Petalostemum* can each symbiose effectively with the same strain of *Rhizobium*; on the other hand, *Trifolium* spp. show marked specificity in symbiosis with 13 different inoculants needed for this genus alone (Burton, 1967; 1979).

More examples of effectiveness groups are given on page 30. Many of the major tropical legumes show diversity in response to *Rhizobium* strains. These interactions have not yet been adequately studied but can be complex (Date & Norris, 1979).

CULTURING RHIZOBIA IN MASS

Media and methods for culturing rhizobia are detailed by Burton (1967; 1979), Roughley (1970) and Date & Roughley (1977). See also p. 127.

Rhizobia are not fastidious in their growth and nutrient requirements. They can be cultured in shake culture, glass bottles equipped for aeration with sterile air, or in fermentors of various designs. Carbon steel or stainless steel drums can be modified to serve as fermentors, providing they allow autoclaving and aeration with sterile air. Suitable openings must be provided for adding the inoculum and sampling at various times. Sucrose, mannitol, glycerol, and arabinose are the most common source of carbon, though slow-growing rhizobia do not metabolize sucrose. Yeast products are generally used to provide organic nitrogen and growth factors for those strains that need them. The rhizobia should reach a population of 10^9 in 48-71 hours and should be mixed with the carrier material while in the logarithmic growth phase to attain maximum growth.

It is argued that when multiple strain inocula are to be made, each strain should be grown separately to avoid one strain dominating others (Date & Roughley, 1977). When various strains are to be grown together it is certainly advisable to select compatible strains with similar growth rates, but whether separate fermentors are needed for each strain remains to be determined. Certainly, the use of separate fermentors could have economic implications as fermentor costs are disproportionate to fermentor capacity.

CARRIER MEDIA FOR RHIZOBIA

Peat

Peat has been the most commonly used base for commercial inoculants, and is generally considered the most dependable (Fred, Baldwin & McCoy, 1932; Burton, 1979). Many, but not all peats (Graham, Morales & Cavallo, 1974) satisfy the requirements for a good *Rhizobium* carrier. Carriers must be:

Highly absorptive and easy to process;
Nontoxic to rhizobia;
Easy to sterilize;
Available locally; and
Inexpensive.

Peats used in making legume inoculants are diverse in nature and may vary widely even in the same deposit (Date & Roughley, 1977). Composition of the peat used most extensively in the United States is given in Table 2. Fine peat, with 70-95% passing through a 200-mesh screen is considered most suitable for seed inoculants as fine particles tend to adhere to small seeds better than coarse ones. Fine particles are also essential when inoculants are to be applied in aqueous suspension directly to the soil (R.R. Gault & J. Brockwell, personal communication). Large particles settle out quickly from a suspension and can cause plugging of the spray nozzles.

TABLE 2: Analysis of Demilco Sedge Peat.[1]

	Sieve Analysis		Chemical Analysis		Ash Analysis	
Particle Size	Powder inoculant	Granular inoculant				
850-12,00 µm** (16-20 mesh)	0.0	0-10	Organic matter	86.60	Potassium	1.12
			Total nitrogen	1.62	Phosphorus	0.33
600-850 µm (20-30 mesh)	0.0	30-40	Crude ash	13.20	Calcium	5.21
300-600 µm (30-50 mesh)	1.0	50-60	Exchangeable K	62 ppm	Magnesium	1.14
150-300 µm (50-100 mesh)	5.10	4.0	Nitrogen as NH_4^+ and NO_3^-	94 ppm	Iron	2.10
			Available P	12 ppm	Silicon	28.00
60-150 µm (100-200 mesh)	5-10	Trace	pH	4.5-5.0	Aluminium	6.32
-60 µm (through 200 mesh)	80-90	Trace	Moisture	7.8	Sodium	0.52

[1]Demilco, a subsidiary of Nitragin Co., Inc., Milwaukee, WI, USA.
[2]Micrometers - Mesh - ASTM (Amer. Soc. Testing Methods).

With granular inoculants, coarse particles (16 to 40 mesh) are essential for flowability and uniform distribution with the mechanical applicators available for granular products (see Table 2). Care must be taken with strains used for granular preparations. Unpublished results from my laboratory have shown that peanut strains vary greatly in ability to grow in the granular inoculant carrier.

Sterilization of peat carriers

It is generally agreed that as an inoculant base, sterile peat is superior to nonsterile peat, and that heat-treated or autoclaved peat is better than air-dried peat. Systems of sterilizing peat have not been studied sufficiently to justify firm conclusions or generalizations. Further work in this area is indicated.

A common practice in preparation of inoculants with slow-growing rhizobia in Australia is to irradiate peat prepackaged in polyethylene bags with five megarads of gamma rays. The broth culture is then injected into the carrier using a sterile hypodermic syringe (Date & Roughley, 1977). Sterilization of the peat by gamma irradiation apparently makes the carrier more suitable for growth of the rhizobia than autoclaving at 121°C for four hours and shelf life of the inoculant is increased. However, this method of producing inoculants is very labor intensive and it is not readily adapted to large-scale production of inoculants. In many tropical countries access to a radioactive source may be limited, and the cost of packed and irradiated peat may be high. Whether the extended shelf life justifies the extra cost will have to be determined.

Other inoculant carriers

Many countries, particularly those in tropical regions, do not have a local supply of peat. The peat available in some countries can also be unsatisfactory (J. Halliday, personal communication). A number of alternate carriers have been proposed, and appear to show promise. Strijdom & Deschodt (1976) found a coal bentonite lucerne combination (CBL) almost as good as peat. However, they pointed out that *Rhizobium* strains differ in their ability to grow in different carriers and that two cowpea strains grew very poorly in the CBL base. It is, of course, essential to know characteristics of strains before attempting to make an inoculant with them.

A maize cob compost was prepared by mixing maize cobs with 2.5% ground limestone, 0.8% single superphosphate and 1.1% ammonium nitrate, adding moisture and allowing to ferment for 30 weeks (Corby, 1976). The mixture was kept under plastic, turned at various intervals, and remoistened. Following fermentation, the compost was air dried, hammer milled, sifted, placed in containers, and sterilized. Survival of the rhizobia was very good.

Coals and lignite have recently attracted interest as carriers for rhizobia. Only one of three coals used as an inoculant base by Halliday & Graham (1978) proved satisfactory, and it was not recommended for use in inoculants because the particles tended to aggregate into hard lumps during storage and were very difficult to wet at the time of seed inoculation. Paczkowski & Berryhill (1979) reported good results from six of eight coals tested with *Rhizobium phaseoli*. However, a bituminous coal from Illinois and a Texas lignite, with a pH of 5.0 and 4.7, respectively, were unsatisfactory.

Various other materials - bagasse, coconut coir dust, coconut shell flour, sugarcane filter mud, vermiculite, charcoal, silt and other substances - have been studied, with favorable results (Farag *et al.*, 1976; Philpotts, 1976; Dommergues, Diem & Divies, 1979). Thus, while lack of a suitable carrier medium is commonly cited as a constraint to inoculant production in tropical countries, it is problem which appears readily resolvable.

EMERGING PROBLEMS IN INOCULANT USE

From the preceding comments it should be clear that the technology already exists for the production of high-quality inoculants. Despite this, inoculant strains may produce only 2% of the nodules on soybeans in the USA (Ham, Lawn & Brun, 1976), while in Brazil less than 1% of farmers elect to inoculate plantings of *P. vulgaris* (Araujo, 1974). Clearly there are gaps in our knowledge, and we must consider what is wrong with our technology and how inoculants or inoculation methods might be improved.

Strain competition for nodule sites

After growing a legume, an ordinary soil may contain up to 10^{20} rhizobia/ha in the top 10 cm (Nutman, 1975). These rhizobia may persist for many years spanning varietal and inoculant strain changes. (Elkins *et al.*, 1976). They may subsequently compete with inoculant rhizobia for nodulation sites, and since seed inoculation at recommended rates supplies only 10^9 rhizobia/ha for inoculated white clover or 10^8 rhizobia/ha for soybean, they will often predominate in nodules (Ham *et al.*, 1976).

Solution of this problem will not be easy. Selection of more aggressive rhizobia that are better able to colonize the soils and rhizosphere, and of varieties that are selective for the inoculant strain, will undoubtedly prove important.

The importance of selecting competitive strains in the establishment of subclover (*Trifolium subterraneum*) on a California soil heavily infested with native, ineffective *R. trifolii* was shown by Jones, Burton, & Vaughn (1978). Strains of rhizobia were first screened and selected for competitiveness against native clover rhizobia before being used as inoculants for seed planting. This procedure made it possible to establish good stands of sub-clover in the California rangelands. Moreover, the effective rhizobia persisted in the soils laden with the ineffective rhizobia for several years.

Improved inoculant methodologies will also play a part in overcoming competition, since the number of inoculant cells added to the soil is obviously critical. On first glance it would appear to be difficult to raise the number of rhizobia/g already in peat. One should bear in mind however the 1000-fold range in number of viable rhizobia/g of peat among inoculants examined by Hiltbold, Thurlow & Skipper (1980) in the USA, and the often poor-quality inoculants available in the tropical countries. This is not a technology problem *per se*, but rather one of quality control. On the other hand, greater quantities of inoculant can be added to the soil as granular or liquid preparation and placed in the optimum position for rapid colonization of the developing rootlets. Much greater attention needs to be paid to inoculant form, especially in the tropics where higher soil temperature, low pH, and Mn or Al excess could affect the survival and competitiveness of inoculant strains.

Inoculant technology for small farm situations

In many countries in the tropics grain legume production is undertaken mainly by small farmers who use multiple cropping systems and minimal technical inputs. Planting is by hand and at low population densities. Current inoculation technologies are not appropriate. Pre-inoculated seeds obtained through extension or credit sources would be ideal, but have a poor reputation even in temperate climates (Brockwell & Roughley, 1967).

CONCLUSION

During the first two-thirds of this century, research on legume inoculants was primarily concerned with methods of culturing rhizobia, determining suitable carrier media, and the selection of strains for leguminous species being introduced into virgin soil under relatively favorable conditions. Production technology is now adequate for such conditions. The need in the area of production technology is to transfer present technology to workers in the tropics and to develop control systems that would ensure the quality of inoculants.

The resolution of other inoculation problems in the tropics will be more difficult. Tropical legumes are frequently promiscuous and commonly nodulated by rhizobia which do not enhance growth. Large numbers of highly infective strains, with excellent potential for N_2 fixation, will be needed to bring about effective nodulation. Furthermore, *Rhizobium* strains will need to be selected for their tolerance of high soil temperatures, and for their ability to multiply and persist in acid soils hostile to nodule bacteria. Systems for the distribution of inoculants to farmers in remote areas are also problematical. Nonetheless, these objectives are realistic and should be achieved

REFERENCES

Araujo, S.C. (1974) Producão de inoculantes para feijao. *In*: Primer reunião sobre nodulaçaõ e fixaçaõ de nitrogeno en *Phaseolus vulgaris* L. Vicosa, Brazil. Pp. 44-48.

Brockwell, J., Dudman, W.F., Gibson, A.H., Hely, F.W., & Robinson, A.C. (1968) *Trans. 9th Intern. Cong. Soil Sci.* Adelaide, Australia. Vol. 2, 103-114.

Brockwell, J. & Roughley, R.J. (1967) *J. Aust. Inst. Agric. Sci.* 33, 204-207.

Burton, J.C. (1967) *Rhizobium* culture and use. *In*: Microbial technology, H.J. Peppler (Ed.). Reinhold Publishing Co., New York, NY, USA. Pp. 1-33.

Burton, J.C. (1979) *Rhizobium* species. *In*: Microbial technology, 2nd Ed. H.J. Peppler and D. Perlman (Eds.). Academic Press, New York, NY, USA. Pp. 29-58.

Corby, H.D.L. (1976) A method of making pure-culture, peat type legume inoculant, using a substitute for peat. *In*: Symbiotic nitrogen fixation in plants, P.S. Nutman (Ed.). Cambridge Univ. Press, Cambridge, England. Pp. 169-173.

Date, R.A. (1976) Principals of *Rhizobium* strain selection. *In*: Symbiotic nitrogen fixation in plants, P.S. Nutman (Ed.). Cambridge Univ. Press, Cambridge, England. Pp. 137-150.

Date, R.A. & Norris, D.O. (1979) *Aust. J. Agric. Res.* 30, 85-104.

Date, R.A. & Roughley, R.J. (1977) Preparation of legume seed inoculants. *In*: A treatise on dinitrogen fixation, Sec. IV, Agronomy and ecology. R.W.F. Hardy & A.H. Gibson (Eds.). Wiley, New York, NY, USA. Pp. 243-276.

Dommergues, Y.R., Diem, H.G. & Divies, C. (1979) *Appl. Environ. Microbiol.* 37, 779-781.

Elkins, D.M., Hamilton, G., Chan, C.K.Y., Briskovich, M.A. & Vanderventer, J.W. (1976) *Agron. J.* 68, 513-517.

Farag, F.A., El-Nady, M.A., Haroun, A.F.T. & Lotfi, M. (1976) *Agric. Res. Rev. Egypt* 54. 221-226.

Fred, E.B., Baldwin, I.L. & McCoy, E. (1932) Root nodule bacteria and leguminous plants. *In*: Univ. of Wisconsin *Studies in Sci.* No. 5. Univ. of Wisc. Press, Madison, WI, USA.

Graham, P.H., Morales, V.M. & Cavallo, R. (1974) *Turrialba* 24, 47-50.

Halliday, J. & Graham, P.H. (1978). *Turrialba* 28. 348-349.

Ham, G.E., Lawn, R.J. & Brun, W.A. (1976) Influence of inoculation, nitrogen fertilizers and photosynthetic source-sink manipulations on field grown soybeans. *In*: Symbiotic nitrogen fixation in plants, P.S. Nutman (Ed.). Cambridge Univ. Press, Cambridge, England. Pp. 239-253.

Hiltbold, A.E., Thurlow, D.L. & Skipper, H.D. (1980) *Agron. J.* 72, 675-681.

Jones, M.B., Burton, J.C. & Vaughn, C.E. (1978). *Agron. J.* 70, 1081-1085.

Nutman, P.S. (1975) *Rhizobium* in the soil. *In*: Soil microbiology - A critical review, M. Walker (Ed.). Wiley, New York, NY, USA. Pp. 111-121.

Paczkowski, M.W. & Berryhill, D.L. (1979) *Appl. Environ. Microbiol.* 38, 612-615.

Roughley, R.J. (1970) *Plant Soil* 32, 675-701.

Strijdom, B.W. & Deschodt, C.C. (1975) Carriers of rhizobia and the effects of prior treatment on the survival of rhizobia. *In:* Symbiotic nitrogen fixation in plants, P.S. Nutman (Ed.). Cambridge Univ. Press, Cambridge, England. Pp. 151-168.

THE STORAGE, QUALITY CONTROL, AND USE OF LEGUME SEED INOCULANTS

R.J. Roughley[1]

Summary

The survival of rhizobia in peat-based inoculants during storage and distribution depends on both the strain used and its immediate environment. The type of carrier used and its freedom from toxic factors, the number of non-*Rhizobium* micro-organisms present when inoculated, the moisture potential of the inoculant, the regulation of the composition of its gas phase, and temperature of storage are all important factors of that environment.

The quality of inoculants depends both on the number of rhizobia they contain and the ability of such rhizobia to fix nitrogen with the intended host. Quality control, therefore, should not only monitor the number of viable cells in the inoculant but also control the strains used. The standard applied to inoculants in a particular country should be considered in the light of the agronomic demands made on the culture — the harsher the sowing conditions and the smaller the seed, the greater the number of rhizobia that will be required per unit of inoculum.

The method of introducing rhizobia into the soil is also important. For grain legumes, slurry inoculation with the inoculum stuck to the seed with dilute methyl cellulose or gum arabic is the most common method. However, if the seed is treated with agrochemicals either solid inocula or liquid injection should be used. The latter is more applicable to large sowings. Granular inoculum can be used for smaller holdings. Rhizobia on seed to be aerially sown are best protected by pelleting with either agricultural lime or rock phosphate.

INTRODUCTION

The initial number of rhizobia in an inoculant and how the rhizobia survive during storage and distribution is influenced both by the procedures used in

[1] Horticultural Research Station, Gosford, 2250, NSW, Australia.

inoculant preparation (see p. 127) and by the conditions that pertain after manufacture. The storage temperature of the inoculant, its relative humidity, and gas interchange capability are all critical to *Rhizobium* survival in the inoculant, but current recommendations have been based on only a few studies (Roughley & Vincent, 1967; Roughley, 1968), with differences in strain response now recognized. Given these problems and the natural variation to which strains of *Rhizobium* are prone (Herridge & Roughley, 1975), it is essential that the quality of inoculants be monitored; not only during the development phase of an inoculant industry, but continually thereafter. Roughley (1976) has documented some of the problems which can develop in an established industry.

This review considers factors affecting growth and survival of *Rhizobium* during the storage and distribution of inoculants and the control procedures guaranteeing high-quality products for the farmer. It briefly discusses common methods of inoculation and their relative advantages and disadvantages.

FACTORS AFFECTING GROWTH AND SURVIVAL OF RHIZOBIA DURING STORAGE AND DISTRIBUTION

Temperature of storage and sterility of the carrier

The effect of storage temperature on growth and survival of rhizobia is influenced by both the purity of the culture and the amount of moisture lost during storage. With cultures prepared in sterilized peat, incubation at 26° C immediately after inoculation promotes rapid growth of rhizobia and, if the moisture content is maintained, has little or no effect on survival up to six months. In experiments on long-term storage of unsterilized peat cultures, the weekly log death rate of clover rhizobia increased from 0.04 at 5° C to 0.094 at 25° C (Roughley, 1968; Date & Roughley, 1977). In contrast, preliminary results obtained by the Australian Inoculants Research and Control Service (AIRCS) suggest that strains such as CB 82 (for fine stem stylo), CB 627 (for *Desmodium*) and CB 1024 (for *Lablab purpureus*) survived better when stored at 26° C than at 4° C (see Table 1).

Survival of *Rhizobium* in soil is known to be adversely affected by high temperatures, particularly when the soil is moist (Bowen & Kennedy, 1959). Despite this the study of *Rhizobium* survival in moist peat cultures subject to high temperatures during storage and distribution had been neglected until Wilson & Trang (1980) compared the survival of unknown strains of the cowpea miscellany stored at temperatures between 25° C and 55° C and at 50% relative humidity (RH). Numbers were constant over a 21-week period at 25° C and 35° C but declined significantly at 45° C and 55° C. Also of concern was a suggested decline in infectivity of the survivors at 35° C and above. Although infectivity was regained following subculture, it may be that

TABLE 1: The effect of temperature of storage on survival of rhizobia in peat inoculants after 12 months.*

Strain	Host	Storage temperature			
		4°C		26°C	
		Inoculants tested	Mean log no. cells/g	Inoculants tested	Mean log no. cells/g
CB1809	*Glycine max*	27	9.56	27	9.22
CB1015	*Vigna mungo*	22	8.98	10	9.13
CB756	*Vigna unguiculata*	11	8.93	6	9.08
CB627	*Desmodium*	7	6.27	2	9.22
CB1923	*Centrosema*	5	6.91	2	8.92
CB1024	*Lablab purpureus*	10	7.32	4	9.35
CB82	*Stylosanthes* (fine stem stylo)	4	5.94	1	9.52

*Data kindly supplied by G. Bullard.

numbers of rhizobia surviving storage in the tropics are not always indicative of the usefulness of the inoculant. This aspect warrants further investigation.

Effects of aeration

Since an early report that rhizobia grew better on both solid and liquid media when provided free access to air, there have been conflicting reports on the gaseous exchange requirements of *Rhizobium* for growth and survival in peat culture. Canadian and European workers observed rapid death of rhizobia in sealed containers, but with access to air the numbers of cells remained high until the carrier became desiccated (Hedlin & Newton, 1948; van Schreven, Otsen & Lindenberg, 1954). In contrast, other workers found that rhizobia were able to multiply 10- to 100-fold and then survive satisfactorily in either screw-capped jars or sealed cans (Newbould, 1951; Spencer & Newton, 1953; Gunning & Jordan, 1954). Some of this confusion was possibly caused by the fact that the demand for gas exchange in peat cultures, though definite, is not high. Most reports compared only "unrestricted exchange" with sealed containers. Where the latter were not sealed under vacuum, the proportion of air trapped to carrier material could have affected survival of the rhizobia.

In a study of packaging materials, Roughley (1968) examined the growth and survival of clover, medic, and cowpea-type rhizobia in sterilized peat, in cotton wool-stoppered tubes, sealed cans, and plastic film packets with various gas-exchange properties. The survival of rhizobia in the sealed cans and a laminated mylar-polythene film of very low gas exchange was completely unsatisfactory. However, growth and survival in a low-density and a medium-density polythene film and in a polyamide film with only 6% of the gas exchange capability of the low-density polythene film was comparable to that in plugged tubes.

Effects of moisture content and sodium chloride

The moisture content of the inoculant has a marked effect on numbers of rhizobia: not only is the initial moisture level critical, but there is a marked relationship between the death rate of rhizobia and the rate of water loss during storage. Such loss can occur also from some containers when cultures are stored under refrigeration. Further, since the interaction of *Rhizobium* and contaminant micro-organisms varies with moisture content, the effect of moisture content on rhizobial survival in unsterile peat is often different from that obtained in sterile peat.

Because peats and peat/soil mixtures vary widely in their ability to absorb moisture, the expression of moisture as either a percentage of the wet or dry weight of carrier is misleading. This ability of different carriers to absorb different amounts of moisture may explain the different optima reported for growth and survival of *Rhizobium*. Future comparisons should be made on the basis of moisture potential. Using this method of expression, the moisture contents in Badenoch peat could be expressed as pF values of 4.88, 4.15, 3.42, and 2.69, equivalent to 30, 40, 50, and 60% moisture on a wet weight of peat, respectively.

In sterilized peat, strains tolerate higher levels of moisture, with growth and survival optimal in the pF range 3.42-2.69 (50-60% moisture).

In determining the effect of moisture content on the survival of rhizobia, it is important to separate the direct effect of moisture from indirect effects on the concentration of soluble salts (Steinborn & Roughley, 1974). Two inoculants with the same concentration of chloride (dry weight) but with moisture contents of 55% and 45% would, assuming all the chloride were dissolved, differ by a factor of 1.5 in the concentration of chloride in solution. This is not generally taken into consideration when determining optimum moisture contents or when comparing different carrier materials.

Sources of peat, otherwise suitable as carriers of rhizobia, may be contaminated with sodium chloride, either by the saltwater origins of the swamp, or through proximity to the sea and spray contamination. The level of sodium chloride in peat beds may fluctuate both between and within years, depending on the rainfall. Leaching with water of low salt content can reduce the sodium chloride level to satisfactory limits. The tolerance of strains of rhizobia to salt varies widely. Strains for lucerne (*R. meliloti*) survive well at levels up to 0.89% chloride (expressed on a dry weight of peat basis), whereas for clover (*R. trifolii*) the upper limit is 0.17% with cultures of 50% moisture on a dry weight basis (Steinborn & Roughley, 1974).

QUALITY CONTROL OF INOCULANTS

The aim of a quality control program should be to anticipate and, therefore, to avoid problems during production and storage and so to ensure the sale of high quality cultures. This requires an understanding of the many factors which affect quality of inoculants and of how and when they are likely to operate.

Experience in Australia suggests that production and quality control should be conducted by separate bodies and that, for greater consumer protection, quality control from strain selection through to preparation and distribution is preferable to a system that tests only the final product obtained from retail outlets. The quality control group should be an official body with powers sufficient to enforce its standards on all producers. In this way a uniform product, assessed by standard procedures by a central, or at least centrally directed, control group provides maximum consumer protection and more direct assistance to manufacturers by early detection of such problems as loss of effectiveness, poor survival in peat culture, or failure to grow in broth culture.

Standards for inoculants

The quality of legume inoculants depends on both the number of rhizobia they contain and the effectiveness of these rhizobia in fixing nitrogen with the intended host. Standards by which inoculants are judged are ultimately determined by field performance in different situations, and because these differ widely, it would be unrealistic to set a rigid standard to apply for a wide range of environments. Where legumes are to be established in *Rhizobium*-free soil with good conditions, 100 rhizobia per seed provides a satisfactory inoculum level. Where large numbers of ineffective rhizobia occur and/or conditions for *Rhizobium* survival are poor, numbers in excess of 10^6 per seed may be required. Ireland & Vincent (1968) showed that lime-pelleting clover seed improved the relative performance of inoculants for a given number of rhizobia per seed. This made it possible to establish rhizobia in soil that contained large numbers of rhizobia and that would otherwise have required extremely heavy inoculation. Within the bounds of inoculum technology, therefore, it is the agronomic demands made on cultures that determine the standards by which they need to be judged.

The minimum number of rhizobia in peat cultures required in Australia has increased 1000-fold since 1957; those now accepted by the AIRCS are 1000 x 10^6 rhizobia/g at manufacture and 100 x 10^6/g at expiry, with less than 0.1% contamination. These changes, which illustrate the dynamic nature of standards in practice, resulted largely from changes in technology that enabled manufacturers to consistently produce inoculants containing more rhizobia.

Standards should also take into consideration the legumes for which the inoculants are to be used. For example, used at the recommended rate, approved Australian inoculants would provide 33,000 rhizobia per seed of *Desmodium*, 16 x 10^5 for cowpea and 2 x 10^6 rhizobia for soybean. There is no agronomic basis for this difference, which is due solely to differences in seed size. Therefore, if soybeans can be consistently well-nodulated by an inoculant providing only 10^6 rhizobia/g of culture (2,000 rhizobia/seed) but produced locally with adapted strains, this could be considered a suitable inoculant. It would, of course, be inadequate for smaller-seeded legumes such as *Desmodium*.

Testing inoculants

The development of a routine system of quality control for Australian inoculants has been described many times (Date, 1969; 1970; Date & Roughley, 1977; Thompson, 1980). This system is based on testing representative samples from all batches of inoculant and must be concluded before such inoculants are released for sale. The tests vary in number and type according to whether sterile or nonsterile peat has been used and depending on the competence and experience of the manufacturers. Where sterilized carriers are the only form of culture prepared, detailed quantitative tests on the broth used to inoculate the carrier are not normally necessary, since the final number of rhizobia in the peat is independent of the number added in the broth (Roughley, 1968).

However, when manufacturers are inexperienced, or the carrier non sterile, it is essential that the broth cultures used to prepare each batch of inoculant are also tested. Testing at this stage reduced nodulation failures in the early days of commercial inoculant production in Australia.

Tests on broth cultures

Before mixing with the peat, the identity of the *Rhizobium* strain in the broth culture should be verified by agglutination against a specific antiserum. Freedom from contamination should also be demonstrated by the absence of growth on glucose-peptone agar streaked with inoculant culture, while gram-stain preparations should show no gram-positive cells. Results of these tests are available within 24 hours and are the basis on which the producer is permitted to impregnate the peat.

Broth cultures must also be evaluated for invasiveness and effectiveness by inoculating plants growing on N-free medium in tubes, and where nonsterile carriers are to be used, the number of viable rhizobia should be counted using the plate count method.

Tests on peat cultures

After maturation of the inoculant, and before distribution, plate counts on sterile peats should be made to determine the number of rhizobia present and to ensure that contamination is low. Where unsterile peats are used, plant-infection tests should also be done. Only after completion of these tests should the inoculant be released for use and an expiry date assigned. It is impossible to set general expiry dates since the useful life of the culture will depend on the packaging and carrier materials, storage conditions, and methods of distribution and sale. However, Australian experience has shown that inoculants for all temperate and most, but not all, tropical legumes, after storage for five months at 4°C followed by six months storage either under refrigeration or on open shelves, are still satisfactory as inoculants. Thus, manufacturers may store newly manufactured cultures under refrigerated conditions for up to six months before allocating the normal six-month expiry date. Cultures stored in this way, particularly those prepared in sterilized peat, may be resubmitted for testing within four weeks of expiry date, and if they meet the original standard and have adequate moisture (equivalent to pF 3.78) may be approved for a further six months.

An important part of the control scheme is the random testing of inoculants purchased from retail outlets. Such tests provide information on the effect of storage conditions, early information on variation in the performance of particular strains, and a check on the labeling of packets by manufacturers.

USE OF LEGUME INOCULANTS

Predicting the need to inoculate

Forecasting the need to introduce rhizobia into a soil is one of the most important practical considerations faced by the agricultural adviser. Some guidelines are available, but the exceptions are sufficiently common to lead to uncertainty.

Occurrence of naturally occurring rhizobia

Brockwell & Robinson (1970) and Roughley & Walker (1973) attempted to relate the occurrence of rhizobia in soil to climate, vegetation, topography, previous history (including cropping data), fertilizer applications, vegetation before sowing, soil type, and pH. None of these characteristics except vegetation had any consistent relationship, except as they affected the occurrence of leguminous plants. Consistent relationships did occur between the presence of a legume host and the number and type of rhizobia in soil, but even so, it was impossible to consistently predict the need to inoculate.

Host-plant requirements

Some knowledge of the origin of a legume, its growth requirements, its distribution, and its promiscuity in forming nodules with a range of rhizobia is also useful as a guide. Specificity between host and *Rhizobium* is well known, for example *Lotononis* sp., *Trifolium ambiguum,* and soybeans (*Glycine max)* require specific inoculants, whereas legumes such as siratro (*Macroptilium atropurpureum*) are promiscuous and nodulate with a wide range of rhizobia. There is, therefore, a greater likelihood that highly specific hosts will require inoculation, especially when grown in an area for the first time, than hosts that are compatible with a wider range of strains.

Effectiveness of native strains

Apart from predicting a need to inoculate based on the numbers of the indigenous soil rhizobia, there is the question of the effectiveness of naturalized strains. There have been few extensive surveys to assess the effectiveness of naturalized rhizobia, one in southeastern Australia indicated a general level of effectiveness of *R. trifolii* of approximately 50% that of the inoculum strain TA1 (Bergersen, 1970). Failure to establish a more effective strain in such situations would not necessarily lead to crop failure, but would result in reduced production.

Date (1976) recommended a simple, three-treatment experiment to assess the numbers and effectiveness of naturalized rhizobia in new situations. The three treatments were:

An uninoculated control to check for the presence or absence of naturalized rhizobia and their effectiveness;

An inoculated treatment using a strain of *Rhizobium* known or reported to be effective with the host; and

The same inoculated treatment plus nitrogen (N).

Results from such a trial allow assessment of the need to introduce rhizobia, determine the suitability of the applied strain, and show whether native, ineffective strains occur and if so, how well the introduced strain competes with them. Comparison of the growth of inoculated plants with those supplied combined N gives a measure of strain effectiveness and indicates whether factors other than N may be limiting growth.

Methods of inoculating legume seeds

Inoculants have generally been applied directly to the seed. However, the presence in some legumes of seed coat factors toxic to *Rhizobium* (Thompson, 1960; Bowen, 1961; Masterson, 1962) and the increasing use of toxic agrochemicals have heightened interest in indirect inoculation methods.

Direct application of peat cultures

Legume inoculants prepared in organic carriers promote better survival of rhizobia, both in storage and when inoculated onto seed, than do agar or broth cultures (Date, 1970). Further, the method used to inoculate seed also affects survival of the rhizobia, and adhesives and coating materials may also improve survival (Herridge & Roughley, 1974).

Dry inoculation: This method, involving only application of the powdered inoculum to the seed, is the simplest method of inoculation but is inefficient, as the powder adheres poorly and the survival of the rhizobia that do adhere is suboptimal. This method is still used for inoculating very large quantities of grain legumes in areas where high numbers of rhizobia/seed are not essential, but it cannot be recommended.

Slurry inoculation: The inoculant, prepared as a suspension in water, is applied to the seed, which must then be allowed to dry before sowing. Adhesion to the seed coat may be improved by suspending the inoculant in 10% sucrose, but this may encourage seed and seedling pathogens. Either gum arabic (10% solution) or methyl cellulose (1%) adhesives may be used to improve adhesion and survival of rhizobia on seed. It is essential to ensure that no preservatives have been added to the adhesive. This method is particularly suitable for inoculating grain legumes when sowing small areas.

Seed pelleting: This method improves the survival of some rhizobia on seed. It involves the use of gum arabic (40% w/v) or methyl cellulose (1.5% w/v of 4000 c.p.) as adhesives for the inoculum, with the inoculated seeds rolled in, and coated by, finely grown calcium carbonate or rock phosphate. There is some controversy as to whether tropical legumes should be pelleted with lime (Norris, 1967), and rock phosphate is more generally recommended for this group of legumes. Seed pelleting is particularly suitable for small-seeded legumes to be sown in soils of pH 5.5-6.0, or when seed is sown in contact with acid fertilizers. It has proved the most suitable method of inoculation for seed to be aerially sown.

Indirect inoculation

The introduction of rhizobia into soil separately from the seed is best when seed treated with pesticides harmful to rhizobia is to be used, when sowing seeds that have a very toxic seed coat, or when sowing large areas of grain legumes where, because of seed size, the large volume of seed makes other methods of inoculation impractical. Two general techniques have been investigated; one involves spraying liquid inocula directly into the soil, the second applies solid inocula in one of several forms.

Liquid inocula: These may be prepared by suspending peat cultures in water in a tank mounted on the seed drill. The liquid may then be sprayed either into the row or beneath the seed. This method was used successfully in Israel for inoculating groundnuts (Schiffman & Alper, 1968). A suitable spray system was described in detail by Brockwell *et al.* (1979). It comprises a tank of sufficient size to apply 112 liters/ha, a pump, and a pressure regulator by-pass set to approximately 140 kpa in order to deliver one-third of the total flow of liquid to the spray jets and return the rest to the tank for agitation. The manifold should be made of noncorrosive material and the spray jets of copper tubing of 1.5-2 mm internal diameter located behind the seed boot and 2.5-5 cm above the bottom of the furrow.

Solid inocula: These may consist of compressed peat impregnated with rhizobia, granules of calcium sulphate semihydrate and carboxymethyl-cellulose sprayed with a mixture of *Rhizobium* broth, skim milk powder and sucrose (Fraser, 1966), or a solid inert core such as sand or "Alkathene" beads inoculated and lime-coated as for seed (Corbin, Brockwell & Gault, 1977).

Solid inocula consisting of coarse particles of peat impregnated with rhizobia are available commercially in the USA (Burton, 1975). These granules are sown in the drill row at a rate to provide 10^7 rhizobia/2.25 cm. The rate can be increased where necessary and the granules sown deeper to avoid high soil temperatures.

CONCLUSIONS

It is likely that there will be an increased need to apply higher numbers of rhizobia to the seed or directly to the soil as less favorable sites are sown with legumes or established areas are to be resown using improved strains. Either the number of rhizobia in peat cultures must be increased or their survival following inoculation must be improved. General experience has shown that with the exception of a few strains that reach populations of 10^{10}/g in peat, most rarely exceed 5×10^9. It is, therefore, likely that the chances of increasing numbers lies in improved methods of using inoculants. Further work on agents to protect rhizobia during drying and to protect them from toxic factors in the seed coat, as well as work on improved adhesives, offers perhaps the best approach to meet the challenges of the future.

REFERENCES

Bergersen, F.J. (1970) *Plant Soil* 32, 727-736.

Bowen, G.D. (1961) *Plant Soil* 15, 155-165.

Bowen, G.D. & Kennedy, M. (1959) *Queensl. J. Agric. Sci.* 16, 177-179.

Brockwell, J. & Robinson, A.C. (1970) Proc. XI Intern. Grassl. Congr. Pp. 438-431.

Brockwell, J., Gault, R.R., Carlin, C. & Lund, R. (1979) Spray inoculation for lupins. *In*: Lupin production in 1979. NSW Department of Agriculture, Australia. Pp. 35-38.

Burton, J.C. (1975) Proc. Fifth Soybean Seed Res. Conf., Chicago, IL, USA. Pp. 41-52.

Corbin, E.J., Brockwell, J. & Gault, R.R. (1977) *Aust. J. Expl. Agric. Anim. Husb.* 17, 126-134.

Date, R.A. (1970) *Plant Soil,* 32, 703-725.

Date, R.A. (1969) *J. Aust. Inst. Agric. Sci.* 35, 27-37.

Date, R.A. (1976) Inoculation of tropical pasture legumes. *In*: Exploiting the legume-*Rhizobium* symbiosis in tropical agriculture. J.M. Vincent, A.S. Whitney & J. Bose (Eds.). Univ. Hawaii, Coll. Trop. Agric. *Misc. Pub.* No. 145. Pp. 293-311.

Date, R.A. & Roughley, R.J. (1977) Preparation of legume seed inoculants *In*: A treatise on dinitrogen fixation. R.W.F. Hardy & A.H. Gibson (Eds.). Wiley, New York, NY, USA. Pp. 243-275.

Fraser, M.E. (1966) *J. Appl. Bacteriol.* 29, 587-595.

Gunning, C. & Jordan, D.C. (1954) *Canad. J. Agric. Sci.* 34, 225-233.

Hedlin, R.A. & Newton, J.D. (1948) *Canad. J. Res.* 26, 174-187.

Herridge, D.F. & Roughley, R.J. (1974) *Plant Soil 40, 441-444.*

Herridge, D.F. & Roughley, R.J. (1975) *J. Appl. Bact.* 38, 19-27.

Ireland, J.A. & Vincent, J.M. (1968) IX Internat. Congr. Soil. Sci. Trans II, 85-93.

Masterson, C.L. (1962) *Irish J. Agric. Res.* 1, 343-344.

Norris, D.O. (1967) *Trop. Grassl.* 1, 107-121.

Newbould, F.H.S. (1951) *Sci. Agric.* 31, 463-469.

Roughley, R.J. (1968) *J. Appl. Bacteriol.* 31, 259-265.

Roughley, R.J. (1976) The production of high quality inoculants and their contribution to legume yield. *In*: Symbiotic nitrogen fixation in plants, P.S. Nutman (Ed.). Cambridge, Univ. Press, Cambridge England. Pp. 125-136.

Roughley, R.J. & Vincent, J.M. (1967) *J. Appl. Bacteriol.* 30, 362-376.

Roughley, R.J. & Walker, M.H. (1973) *Aust. J. Expl. Agric. Anim. Husb.* 13, 284-291.

Schreven, D.A. van, Oestn. D. & Lindenberg, D.J. (1954) *Antonie van Leeuwenhock, J. Microbiol. Serol.* 20, 33-37.

Schiffman, J. & Alper, Y. (1968) *Expl. Agric.* 4, 219-226.

Spencer, J.F.T. & Newton, J.D. (1953) *Canad. J. Bot.* 31, 253-264.

Steinborn, J. & Roughley, R.J. (1974) *J. Appl. Bacteriol.* 37, 93-99.

Thompson, J.A. (1960) *Nature* (Lond.) 187, 169.

Thompson, J.A. (1980) Production and quality control of legume inoculants *In*: Methods for evaluating biological nitrogen fixation, F.J. Bergensen, (Ed.). Wiley, New York, NY, USA. Pp. 489-534.

Wilson, D.O. & Trang, K.M. (1980) *Trop. Agric.* (Trinidad) 57, 233-238.

CULTURING *RHIZOBIUM* IN LARGE-SCALE FERMENTORS

A.P. Balatti[1]

Summary

This paper considers the different types of fermentors, with and without agitation, that can be used in laboratories, pilot plants, and in large-scale fermentations. Using a balanced medium and either a mechanically stirred or airlift type fermentor, it is possible to obtain cellular concentrations of about 1.5×10^{10} cells/ml of *R. japonicum* in 48 h.

INTRODUCTION

Although the legume inoculant industry started in the early 1900's, it is only relatively recently that attention has been given to the production of high-count broth cultures of *Rhizobium* with which to inoculate carriers or for direct field use. This paper considers some aspects of the technology by which *Rhizobium* are propagated.

LABORATORY SCALE FERMENTORS

To obtain a *Rhizobium* culture of a high concentration, the fermentation method in submerged process is used. It is convenient to start the first step in a rotary shaker. This operation is normally done in Erlenmeyer flasks using 1/5 part of the volume of the liquid medium in relation to the volume of the flask. It is common to transfer an agar slant culture from a tube to an Erlenmeyer flask of 500 ml with 100 ml of medium. The Erlenmeyer flasks are placed in a rotary shaker at a constant temperature (26-30° C).

Figure 1 shows two different types of fermentors, used in laboratories and in small-scale industrial production. Both of them are suitable for the development of *Rhizobium*. One works with mechanical agitation. It has an

---

[1] Centro de Investigación y Desarrollo de Fermentaciones Industriales, 47 y 115, La Plata, Argentina.

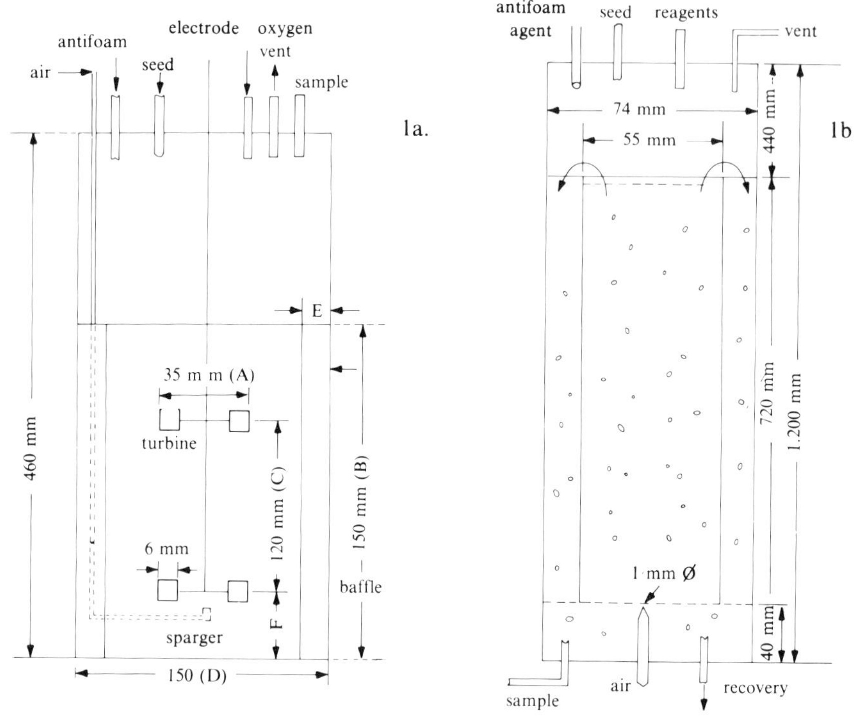

Figure 1a. Typical dimensions of mechanically stirred fermentor (A/D) 0.34 (F/A) 0.8 to 1; (B/D) 1.0; C/A 1.0 to 2.0; ED 0.08 to 0.10.
1b. Airlift - type fermentor.

air entry, baffles, and a turbine-type impeller. The principal objective of the baffle is to produce turbulence and so to increase the interfacial area of the bubbles in the liquid. This is important in meeting the oxygen requirements of the growing organism; it is also helpful in the heat transfer process. The other fermentor shown in Figure 1 is of the airlift type, without mechanical agitation. In this case agitation is achieved by circulation of the liquid medium following air injection. This type of fermentor is very easy to build (Mazza, Lopreto & Balatti, 1976), as it essentially consists of two concentric pyrex glass tubes stoppered at each end with synthetic rubber stoppers. The drawing shows air intake and sampling ports set into the base, and tubes in the top for adding medium, inoculum, and antifoam, as well as for air escape. Both fermentors can be sterilized empty, by passing through fluent steam for 60 min; alternatively they can be autoclaved with the medium at 121°C for 20 min. Counts of up to 1.5×10^{10} cells/ml can be obtained with this type of fermentor using a sucrose, yeast extract medium containing KNO_3. Figure 2 shows the growth curve for a strain of *R. meliloti* in a mechanically agitated

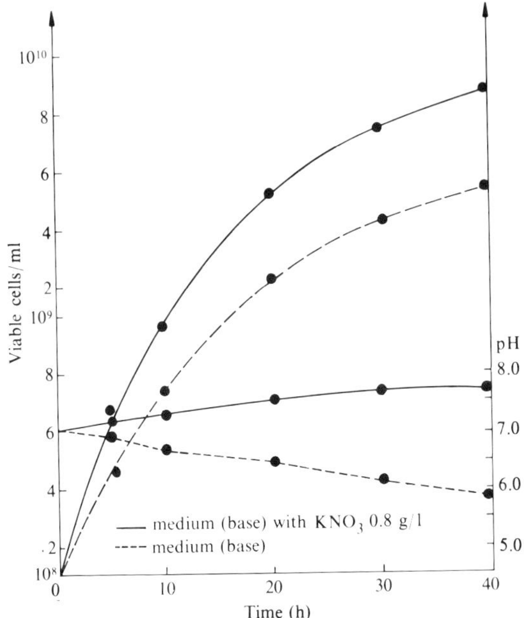

Figure 2. Growth curves of *Rhizobium meliloti* in a mechanically stirred fermentor. Operation condition: 250 rpm and 0.5 vol air/vol. medium per minute. Medium (base): sucrose, 10 g/l; $MgSO_4 .7\ H_2O$, 0.6 g/l; NaCl, 0.1 g/l; yeast extract, 3.0 g/l; $MnSO_4$, (10%) 0.1 ml; $FeCl_3$, (10%) 0.1 ml; pH=7.2.

fermentor when an agitation rate of 250 rpm, an air flow of 0.5 air volumes/ medium volume per minute, and 3 1 of medium in a 5 1 fermentor, were used. The figure shows clearly that addition of KNO_3 to the medium both favors high cell counts and controls pH.

Figure 3 shows the results of a similar fermentation using a strain of *R. japonicum*. Note that, in this case, glycerol has been used as the carbon source, because *R. japonicum* cannot metabolize sucrose.

INDUSTRIAL FERMENTATION

While many inoculant producers employ small fermentors of 10-20 1 capacity, industrial fermentors with capacities up to 30,000 1 can be used to grow *Rhizobium*. The sequence by which a stock culture is built up in volume until it can be used as inoculum for a production-stage fermentor is shown in Figure 4. At each stage the inoculum must comprise 5-6% of the volume to be inoculated; otherwise there will be a prolonged lag phase with greater opportunity for contamination.

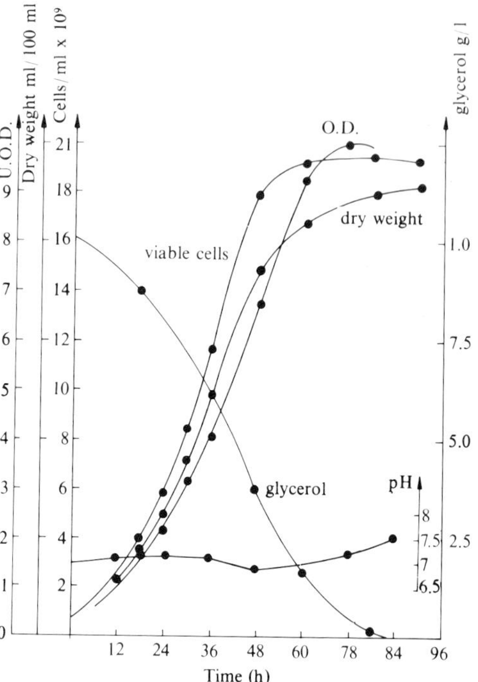

Figure 3.
Growth curves of *Rhizobium japonicum* in a mechanically stirred fermentor. Operation condition: 250 rpm and 0.5 vol. air/vol. medium per minute. Medium: glycerol 10 g/l; K_2HPO_4, 0.5 g/l; $(NH_4)_2HPO_4$, 0.3 g/l; NaCl, 0.1 g/l; KNO_3, 0.8 g/l; $MgSO_4.7H_2O$, 0.2 g/l; yeast extract, 4 g/l; $MnSO_4$, (10%) 0.1 ml/l; $FeCl_3$, (10%) 0.1 ml/l.

A typical production tank with its most important auxiliaries is shown in Figure 5.

Stainless steel is the usual material for fermentation vessels. The fermentation tanks are conventionally designed with a height:diameter ratio in the range of 2-3:1, and with an operating volume of about 75% of the total capacity to allow some room for foam to build up. Mechanically agitated tanks have four baffles; coil and jackets are used for heating and temperature controls. The up-to-date fermentors have an external coil around the tank wall. This sytem helps to achieve a better heat transfer. The agitation is provided by some type of turbine impeller mounted either singly or in multiples on a central shaft. The shaft enters the fermentor through a stuffing box or rotating seal. The air enters through a sterilized filter, air pipe, and sparger at a pressure of about 1.5 atm. The sparger most commonly used is the one that consists of a circular ring with holes drilled at intervals. A high velocity nozzle can also be used. The control devices most commonly used are: air pressure flow recorder controller, temperature recorder and antifoam addition-controller. Water is needed to cool the tank and a supply of sterile air to meet the organism's need for oxygen. Cellulose filters are usually used to provide sterile air.

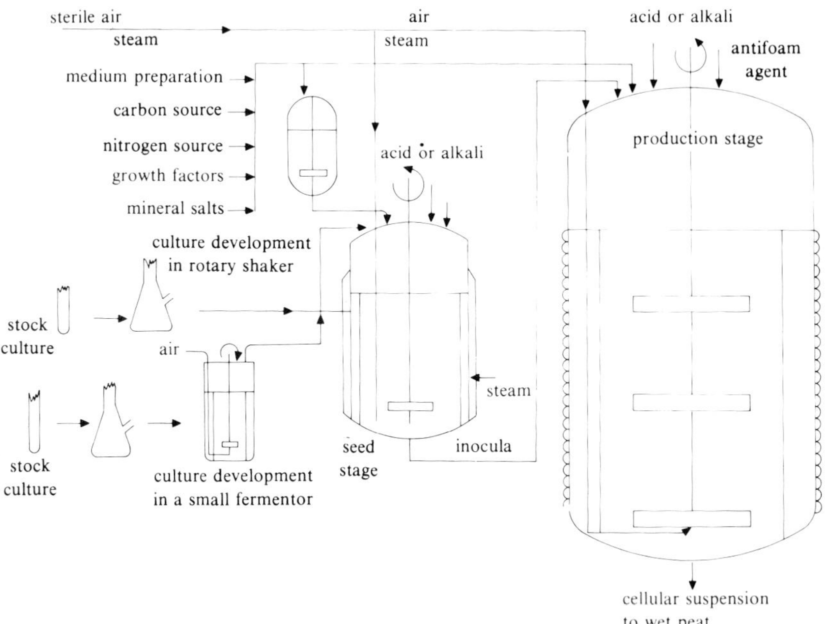

Figure 4. Culturing *Rhizobium* in a large fermentor. Flow diagram of fermentation process.

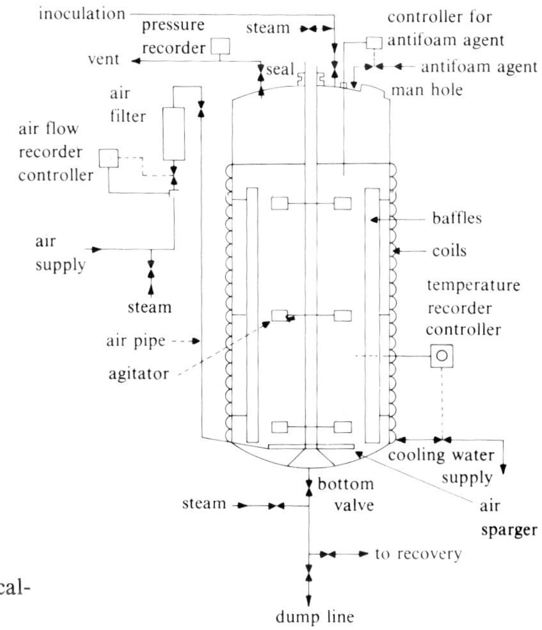

Figure 5.
Typical large-scale mechanically stirred fermentor.

In the scale up from pilot equipment to industrial production it is common to use similar rates of power consumption per unit volume of liauid. The power of agitation used in most fermentors is from 1-3 watt/liter (Balatti, Morisi & Gualandi, 1968). This guarantees a good mixing of the culture and adequate biomass production.

REFERENCE

Mazza, L.A., Lopreto, C.P.& Balatti, A.P. (1976) *Rev. Assoc. Argen. Microbiol.* 8, 99-103.

Balatti, A.P., Morisi, G. & Gualandi, G.G. (1968) Ann. I Super Sanita 4, 626-632.

ENVIRONMENTAL FACTORS AFFECTING SYMBIOTIC N_2 FIXATION

SOIL CONSTRAINTS TO LEGUME PRODUCTION

D.N. Munns[1] and A.A. Franco[2]

Summary

Lack of information and response criteria make it impossible for us to assess accurately the extent to which soil constraints might limit legume productivity. The following are estimates: **Erosion hazard** on 75% of tropical land; excepting only the deep, level cohesive alluvial and Oxisol soils. **Droughtiness** on 45%; especially shallow and sandy soils, Oxisols with few pores of intermediate size, Alfisols and Ultisols with impeding subsoil. **Excessive compactability or cohesiveness** on 25-30%; mainly Vertisols and weakly structured Alfisols. **Salinity and alkalinity** on 7%; mainly coastal and semiarid inland areas. **Acidity** and/or Mo deficiency on 35%; mainly humid Oxisols, Ultisols, some Alfisols; with high lime requirement on 10 of the 35%. **Phosphate deficiency** on 80%; exceptions mainly alluvial and basaltic. **Other deficiencies** on 5-10%; mainly S, K, Zn in high rainfall areas and Zn elsewhere; likely to increase with time.

Erodibility, droughtiness, compaction/cohesiveness and severe salt, being economically difficult conditions to alter, are usually "capability limiters" to which land use, crop type and management practices must be adjusted. By contrast, acidity and nutrient deficiencies can often be corrected economically. Costs for P and lime are greatest where the soil is high in reactive colloids (acid Andosols and clayey Oxisols, for example). Fertilizer costs also depend on transport availability and proximity. Inputs could be made more efficient by improving root growth and mycorrhizal development, by better soil management, and by selection of legume and *Rhizobium* for tolerance to low P, acidity, and salinity. It is especially desirable to raise the salt and acid tolerance and reduce the P and S requirement of the legume to levels comparable with other crops in the system.

---

[1] Dept. Land, Air and Water Resources (LAWR), University of California, Davis, CA 95616, USA.

[2] Empresa Brasileira de Pesquisa Agropecuaria - SNLCS - PFBN, 23460, Seropedica, Rio de Janeiro, Brazil.

INTRODUCTION

The following sets of soil properties are likely to constrain production of legumes:

- Droughtiness, due to shallowness, impedances, pore characteristics;
- Excessive strength, cohesiveness, and ease of compaction;
- Excessive erodibility;
- Salinity, alkalinity, sodicity;
- Acidity and related properties; and
- Nutrient deficiencies.

The constraints are not peculiar to legumes or to the tropics. They operate on crops worldwide and underlie most schemes for assessing or rating land capability or fertility (USDA, 1971; Sopher & McCracken, 1973; Buol *et al.*, 1975; Lal *et al.*, 1975).

In general, the physical properties and severe salinity are unlikely to be altered easily or economically. They appear, therefore, in capability classifications as "capability limiters." Their main influence is to restrict the options for land use and crop choice, and to limit the benefits derived from improvements in technology. By contrast, acidity and nutrient deficiencies can often be economically remedied. They define inputs that are a recognized part of biological nitrogen (N_2) fixation technology and, therefore, receive most emphasis in this paper.

The severity of a constraint depends on what one is trying to do and the resources available. For the purposes of this paper we propose two reasonable short-term goals in legume development:

- Moderate extension of grain and pasture legumes onto land with the least severe physical capability limitations (certainly excluding most of the 50% of tropical land that is above 3000 m, steeper than 10%, and/or drier than 250 mm annual rainfall); and
- Improvement of yield to levels that are now easily achieved on experimental fields. "Soil constraints" then, include all those properties that need to be modified in order for these goals to be achieved.

Assessing the extent and severity of soil constraints is difficult. What is needed are comprehensive field trials and supporting research at a large number of sites that accurately represent the diversity of tropical conditions. Without this information, we must resort to available response data and general knowledge about soils, and attempt to develop vaguely quantitative estimates, only some of which can be checked against soil surveys, local fertilizer recommendations, and published papers. (There is probably a wealth of unpublished information in files of experiment stations, extension offices and the like. Some priority could be given to a project intended to extract this information, assess it, compile it, and publish it.)

As our first approximation, Table 1 relates the likelihood of major problems to the soil orders of the USDA Soil Taxonomy. These orders can be translated into the categories used in other soil classifications (Sánchez, 1976; Isbell, 1978). Figure 1 suggests the distribution of the soil orders in the tropics.

TABLE 1: Limitations of tropical soils for agriculture.

Soil order	% total area	Problems and their likelihood of ocurrence[1]					
		Water	Strength	Erosion	Salt	Acid	Nutrient
Aridisols	18	***	*	***	***	0	* P,Zn
Vertisols	3	*	***	0	*	0	* P,Zn
Molli-, Enti- Inceptisols							
Fine	8	0	0	*	*	0	0
Sandy	8	***	0	**	0	*	* P,K,S,Zn
Ando (ash)	4	*	0	***	0	*	** P
Alfisols	18	**	**	***	0	**	** P,S,Zn,K
Ultisols	12	*	0	***	0	***	*** P,S,Mo,K,Zn
Oxisols	20	**	0	*	0	***	*** P,S,Mo,K,Zn

[1]From 0, little likelihood, to ***, very high likelihood.

PHYSICAL CONSTRAINTS

Shallowness, low water retention, impeding horizons

Growth reduction by drought is more likely and more severe if soil profile characteristics limit the storage of water accessible to the plant. These characteristics are particularly important where rainfall is low and unreliable.

Shallowness is undoubtedly important, though there are few good data (Lal, 1979). By itself it is likely to be a severe problem in soils less than 70 cm deep; or about 5% of the tropical lowlands and much more of the uplands.

Pore size distribution that is unfavorable to water retention at potentials in the available range can make even deep soils droughty. These soils include sandy and rocky Entisols that occupy some 10% of the tropical lowlands, mainly in West and Southwest Africa (Ahn, 1970; Moorman & Greenland, 1980), and some Oxisols (Sharma & Uehara, 1968). Sánchez & Cochrane (1980) rate nearly all Oxisols of tropical America in this category. Even halving their estimate would still leave 10% of the tropics occupied by droughty Oxisols.

Subsurface clay, hardpan, plinthite, and gravel impede root extension, water movement, and gas movement. They can aggravate temporary

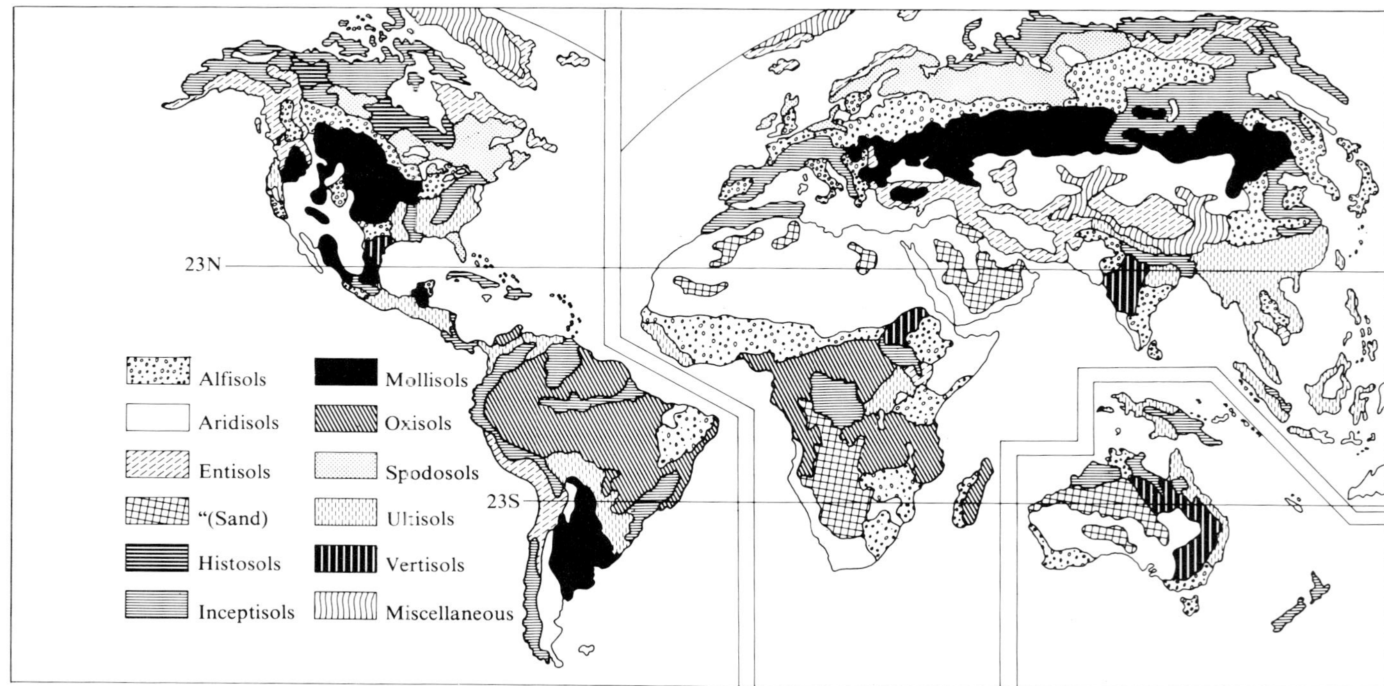

Figure 1. Probable distribution of soil orders. Adapted from US Department of Agriculture, Soil Survey Division, and P.A. Sánchez, 1976.

waterlogging and erosion due to runoff as well as aggravate the effects of drought. Improvement by deep plowing or ripping is possible but usually not economically feasible (Nicou & Charreau, 1980). Soils with serious subsurface impedances are mainly Alfisols and Ultisols on land surfaces of low or moderate relief. They probably amount to about 25% of the tropical land surface (Lal, 1979) and include few of the soils that are droughty for other reasons.

Excessive strength, cohesiveness, compaction

In the topsoil these properties can impair emergence and root development to the point of precluding production of root and tuber crops. They can make machine cultivation difficult and manual cultivation impracticable, and they can lead to increased runoff, erosion, and drought stress.

Vertisols in particular, though usually level, fertile, deep, water-retentive, and potentially highly productive, are difficult to till and irrigate. Broad-based furrows and other management practices for easier water management have been worked out (Kampen & Burford, 1980). Vertisols occupy about 4% of the tropical land area, mainly in Australia, East Africa, and India.

Surface crusting and compaction can be alleviated by minimizing traffic and tillage, and by mulching and residue incorporation (Lal, 1979; Nicou & Charreau, 1980). Nevertheless, or because of the need for these practices, crusting and compaction tendencies are significant constraints in most soils and serious constraints under mechanization and on the 20% or so of soils with particularly weak surface structure.

Erodibility

Erodibility depends on soil and site properties. It limits use and management options mainly by requiring that ground cover be maintained at critical times. Acceptable soil loss rates consistent with sustained productivity can be as high as 5 t/ha per year in deep soils with medium texture, high fertility, and subsoils favorable for growth; but almost no loss is acceptable in shallow soils with strong or gravelly subsoil (Wischmeier & Smith, 1978). Erosion due to wind is greatest in soils with silty or fine-sandy, weakly structured topsoil that is exposed during dry windy periods. Erosion by rain, which is, in general, greater than wind erosion, is predictable in principle from the equation:

$$\text{Annual soil loss} = R \cdot K \cdot S \cdot L \cdot C \cdot P \cdot$$

where the terms are scaled factors for erosiveness of the rainfall (R), erodibility of the soil (K), angle and length of slope (S and L), effectiveness of cover and management (C), and effectiveness of control practices (P). Tropical soils are not inherently more or less erodible than others: values of K for samplings of soils from both Hawaii and the temperate continental USA ranged between 0.1 and 0.5, and the Oxisols and Ultisols were within the normal range (Wischmeier & Smith, 1978).

Nevertheless, erosion and erodibility might be the single most extensive and serious soil constraint to crop production in the tropics. Highly erosive rainfall patterns are common, especially where long dry spells and intense storms alternate. Population pressure and poverty also combine to force cultivation of steep or semiarid land with inadequate protection from rain or wind. Severe erosion has already damaged much fertile land of the tropics (Ahn, 1970; Kampen & Burford, 1980; Moorman & Greenland, 1980; Sánchez & Cochrane, 1980).

Two groups of soils on which erosion hazard is minimal both occur on land surfaces of low to moderate relief. They are deep Oxisols with favorable subsoils, and Vertisols and Entisols of alluvial origin. These soils occupy, respectively, about 15% and 10% of the tropical land surface. On the remaining 75%, erodibility is a serious constraint.

Erodibility is more important for annual grain legumes than for perennials, cover crops, pasture, forage, and timber legumes. Indeed one of the best reasons for cultivating the latter groups is the need for erosion control. Among grain legumes, erosion might sometimes be a factor in favor of using sprawling types rather than inherently more productive, upright determinate types.

SALINITY AND ALKALINITY

Salinity is common in coastal, arid and irrigated soils. There are also some very alkaline soils of only moderate salinity. Alkalinity appears to be the more severe, though less frequent, stress for legumes (Munns, 1977). Salt effects on legumes have received little study; alkalinity effects even less.

Salt tolerance varies between legumes. *Pisum sativum*, *Phaseolus* spp., *Cicer arietinum*, and certain *Trifolium* spp. are highly sensitive. *Medicago sativa*, *Vigna unguiculata* and *Vicia faba* are moderately sensitive (like maize, wheat and rice) and *Melilotus* spp. are slightly sensitive (like barley and ryegrass) (Richards, 1954; D.J. Lauter, and V.A. Marcarian,unpublished data.). These sensitivity categories reflect 50% growth reduction at electrical conductivities of about 4, 8, and 12 mho/cm, respectively (25° C, saturated soil paste). If these data are typical, few legumes are as salt tolerant as the major crop species. There are, however, claims for tolerance among legume species that are at present little used for agriculture (National Academy of Sciences, 1979). Dependence on N_2 fixation seems to lower the salt tolerance of legumes for poorly understood reasons that involve more than just interference with N_2 fixation (Lauter *et al.*, 1981).

Because rhizobia tolerate much higher salt concentrations than do agricultural plants, selection for tolerance would be useful only to eliminate the odd sensitive strain (Graham & Parker, 1964; Lauter *et al.*, 1981) On the other hand, selection in the host to reduce salinity constraints appears promising, at least for some species (V.A. Marcarian, personal communication).

Coastal lands that are saline, but otherwise capable of agricultural development, occupy about 30 million ha in southern Asia (Ponnamperuma & Bandyopadhya, 1980), and there may be comparable areas in tropical Africa and America. The expense of reclaiming these soils might be justified for highly productive crops such as rice.

Estimates of the extent of inland saline areas vary. Thus, for India, estimates range between 7 million ha (Kampen & Burford, 1980) and 20 million ha (Ponnamperuma & Bandyopadhya, 1980). The difference may depend on what level of salinity is considered significant. If so, the larger estimate (equal to 7% of the land area) seems preferable for the more sensitive legumes. Similar areas might exist in tropical Africa. Again, intensification would depend on irrigation, and legumes would be minor members of a system with other crops. Improving their salt tolerance to match that of the main crops would have obvious advantages.

SOIL ACIDITY

Low soil pH is often associated with aluminum toxicity, manganese toxicity and calcium deficiency. All four disorders are corrected by liming. They interfere with legume growth and N_2 fixation in several ways: stopping growth of the rhizobia and nodule initiation, impairing nodule function, and slowing growth of the plant.

The presence of aluminum and low pH itself can inhibit growth of rhizobia. Most slow-growing strains are more tolerant than most fast growers, but not all slow growers are equally tolerant. A screening procedure, in which growth is evaluated in medium containing 50 µmolar Al at pH 4.5, has been used to identify strains of cowpea rhizobia tolerant of acid soil stresses (Keyser & Munns, 1979a), and has shown good agreement with glasshouse tests of strain performance in acid soils (Keyser *et al.*, 1979). Manganese toxicity and calcium deficiency seem unlikely to be important inhibitors of growth of rhizobia in soils (Keyser & Munns, 1979b).

Improvement of acid soil tolerance also requires attention to the plant. Even with adequate rhizobial numbers on the root, nodule initiation is inhibited by acid soil factors. This has been shown for low pH and Ca in temperate species (reviewed by Munns, 1977); for Al in *Stylosanthes* spp. (Carvalho *et al.*, 1981); and for Mn and low pH in *Phaseolus vulgaris* (see Figure 2; Döbereiner, 1966).

The plant's own sensitivity may cause symbiotic failure more often than older literature would suggest. Thus, in US soybean and Al-sensitive cowpea cultivars, Al toxicity has been found to stop legume growth in acid soil

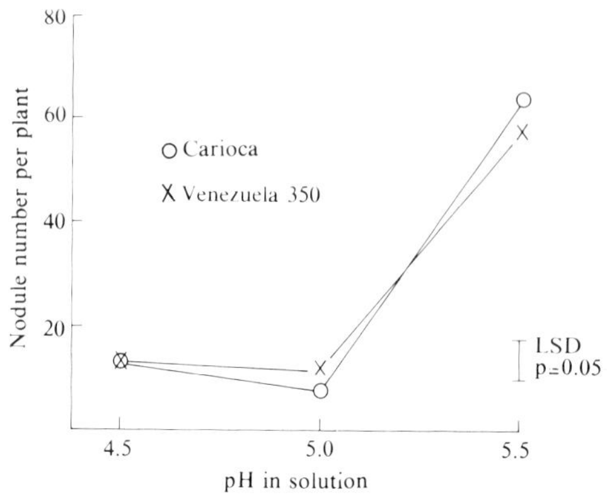

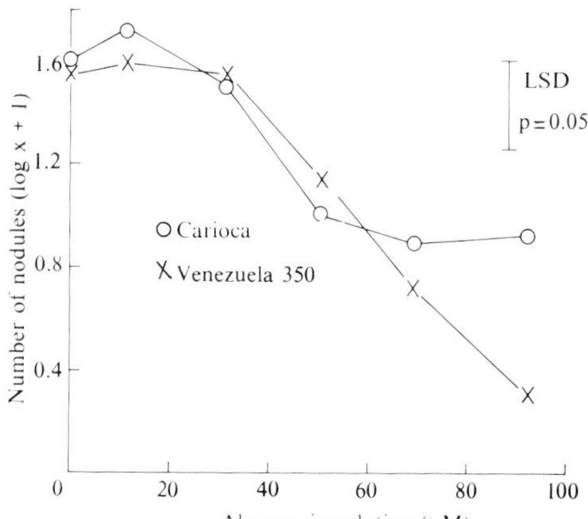

Figure 2.
Nodulation response of varieties of *Phaseolus vulgaris* to variation in pH and Al concentration in solution culture. Authors' unpublished data.

without inducing nodulation failure or N starvation (Munns, *et al.*, 1981; D.N. Munns, unpublished data). Variation in acid-soil tolerance has been shown in a few legume species (Foy *et al.*, 1967; Spain *et al.*, 1975; Munns, 1977). Plant selection would appear to be a useful way to lower the lime requirement for legumes.

Soil acidity results from prolonged leaching with input of biologically generated acids. The most acid soils coincide with high rainfall, low relief, old stable land surfaces, and free drainage (though hardpan development may have eliminated the latter). The acids responsible are mainly carbonic, sulfuric and nitric acids, the latter originating via oxidation from N_2 fixation. The acidification that results indirectly from N input depends little on whether the N was fixed biologically or industrially. It is maximal if N is put in as ammonium or N_2 rather than nitrate, if nitrate is leached, and if large amounts of plant nutrient cations are removed in the harvest (Nyatsanga & Pierre, 1973; Helyar, 1976).

The relative importance of H, Al, Ca, and Mn varies from soil to soil. Manganese toxicity is most common in acid soils, where temporary or local anoxia results from wetness, high organic matter, or impeding layers; but it can also occur in well-drained Oxisols (Vidor & Freire, 1972). Calcium deficiency seems to be most important as a factor aggravating acidity and Al or Mn toxicities. Occasionally it may be the dominant factor by itself, as in moderately acid Oxisols with low Al (pH above 5), and in acid Histosols where Al is immobilized in humic chelates (Evans & Kamprath, 1970; Pearson, 1975). In most acid soils, Al toxicity is dominant. Exchangeable and solution Al correlate closely with pH (Adams & Lund, 1966; Kamprath, 1970; 1978) so that Al toxicity can be expected in sensitive species as pH falls toward 5.0 (and solution Al approaches 20μM) and in tolerant species as pH falls toward 4.5 (60μM Al) (Adams, 1978; Helyar, 1978; Munns, 1978).

Soils acid enough to need lime include Ultisols, many Oxisols (especially the acric and ultic subgroups), many Alfisols, and some Entisols, Inceptisols, and Histosols. Appropriate recommendations for most tropical situations are to lime to pH 5.5 or 6.0, or to reduce exchangeable Al to below 10% of the exchange capacity (Adams, 1978; Kamprath, 1978). Few field trials show benefits from liming to higher pH, and adverse effects are common (Kamprath, 1971). This should not preclude testing a full range of rates in research (Munns & Fox, 1977)

Quantities of lime required range between 500 and 5000 kg/ha depending on the crop and on the soil's initial pH and buffering capacity. Buffering increases with the amount of exchangeable Al and the variable charge on humus, amorphous, and oxide colloids. The most expensive soils to lime are, therefore, very acid Andosols, clayey Oxisols, and soils high in humus. Cost of liming also depends heavily on transport costs. Some large acid-soil areas have well-distributed deposits of limestone, but other areas are less fortunate. Investment in lime can last several years, but sometimes (for unknown reasons) the residual effect dissipates in a year or two (Pearson, 1975).

Soils likely to need lime for crops of moderate sensitivity represent about 35% of the tropical land area. This estimate agrees with the reported frequency of lime responses in field trials with *Phaseolus* (Franco, 1977), and with the lower frequency reported in trials with more tolerant species, e.g., *Stylosanthes* and *Arachis* (Bruce & Bruce, 1972). Soils with high lime requirements, above 4 tons/ha, may account for 10% of the tropical land area. These figures may underestimate the importance of acidity: it is a major feature of the extensive, potentially productive Oxisols and Ultisols that remain to be developed.

In large areas of Oxisols and Ultisols, subsoils that are low in Ca and high in Al restrict root growth and aggravate drought stress. A cheap technology for modifying subsoil acidity is needed. Incorporating lime as deep as is

Measures to improve efficiency of P utilization are unlikely to eliminate the need to apply P. Phosphorus requirement is commonly 200 to 500 kg P/ha initially, followed by maintenance rates of 10 to 100 kg/ha per year. Residual effects in most soils are high, especially if crop offtake and erosion loss are properly accounted (Brams, 1973; Fox, 1978). Leaching is rarely significant.

From the above, it is clear that phosphate deficiency can be expected wherever N limitation is alleviated. Field and greenhouse trials indeed indicate P responses in 80-90% of such cases (Fassbender, 1967; Bruce & Bruce, 1972; Franco, 1977) even where the test plants are P efficient (*Stylosanthes, Centrosema*). Large initial requirements are mainly in soils with large contents of amorphous or poorly crystallized (large surface) oxides in their upper horizons (Fox & Kang, 1977; Moorman & Greenland, 1980). These soils include some, but certainly not all, Oxisols and Andosols; perhaps 10% of humid tropical soils.

Costs of P fertilizer are variable and uncertain. Without acid treatment, phosphate rock can be effective in acid soils, and cheaper than conventional fertilizers. Rock phosphates of inferior quality are being successfully utilized after silicate fusion in Brazil (W.A.G. Braun, personal communication). The larger question in most countries is the availability of commercial quality rock, whether for direct or indirect application. If the more generous estimates of the world's reserves are correct we have several centuries' supply (IFDC, 1978), but these reserves are concentrated in a few countries. Elsewhere, dependence on imports could make critical issues of P supply and P-use efficiency.

Micronutrients

Sánchez (1976) and Lopes (1980) have reviewed the general micronutrient status of tropical soils and Andrew (1976), Munns (1977) and Franco (1978) the specific situation of plants growing on N_2. In general, three main cases may be recognized:

Alkaline soils where Fe, Mn and B may be deficient;
Unlimed acid soils where Mo is most limiting; and
Limed soils where deficiencies of Zn, Mn, B, and Cu may appear.

Molybdenum is the most widely reported micronutrient deficiency in N_2-dependent legumes on acid soils. Lime can alleviate the deficiency. Large differences in plant response have been observed. In bean, lack of response to Mo application at low pH cannot be attributed to impairment of Mo uptake (Franco & Munns, 1981). Large differences in Mo accumulation in seed arise from varietal and soil differences and suggest the possibility of using high-Mo seed for deficient areas (see Table 2). For annual legumes applications of Mo with seed may also be successful.

Zinc deficiency is general in the Oxisols and Ultisols of the central plateau of Brazil and the Oxisols of Colombia and central Africa, especially when they

TABLE 2: Concentration of Mo in seeds of several field grown bean cultivars in Goiania, Go, Brazil and in Davis, CA, USA.

Cultivar	Grown in:	Mo concentration (µg)	
		Per g seed	Per seed
Venezuela 350	Goiania	0.091	0.024
	Davis	2.030	0.385
Rico 23	Goiania	0.177	0.040
	Davis	2.206	0.453
Carioca	Goiania	0.099	0.023
	Davis	1.864	0.402
Chief	Davis	6.568	1.064
Light R. Kidney	Davis	1.860	1.180
Sultan Pink	Davis	2.460	0.700
L.S.D. (P = 0.05)[1]			

[1]Valid only for the cultivars grown in both locations.

are limed and put under intense cultivation. Zinc deficiency has also been recognized as a major limiting factor in calcareous and saline alkaline soils of India, Pakistan and the Philippines.

Responses to B, Mn, and Cu are less frequent. However, soil analyses show a large numbers of cases where levels are below or near critical, and responses have been observed in greenhouse experiments (Franca & Carvalho, 1970; De-Polli *et al.*, 1975; Lopes, 1980).

The use of fritted trace elements (FTE) containing one or several nutrients seems to be promising for humid and hot conditions (Franco, 1978). The long-term effects of FTE containing all micronutrients are exemplified by a four-year field trial with pastures containing siratro, centrosema and stylo (De-Polli *et al.*, 1979). Siratro almost disappeared from the pasture without FTE, but after four years it still comprised 25% of the herbage when FTE were applied.

Sulfur

Sulfur deficiency in legumes reduces protein content and protein quality (Andrew, 1978; Robson, 1978). Reduction of yield and indirectly of N_2 fixation has been mostly attributed to inhibition of protein synthesis, effects on nodulation being mainly indirect (Robson, 1978). We know of no studies on S nutrition of *Rhizobium*.

Buol, S.W., Sánchez, P.A. & Granger, M.A. (1975) Soil fertility capability classification. *In*: Soil management in tropical America, E. Bornemisza and A. Alvarado (Eds.). N. Carolina State Univ., Raleigh, NC, USA. Pp. 126-144.

Carvalho, M.M. de, Edwards, D.G., Andrew, C.S., & Asher, C.J. (1981) Aluminum toxicity, nodulation and growth of *Stylosanthes* species. *Agron. J.* 73, 261-265.

Cassman, K.G., Munns, D.N. & Beck, D.P. (1981) Growth of *Rhizobium* strains at low concentrations of phosphate. *Soil Sci. Soc. Amer. J.* 45, 520-523.

Cassman, K.G., Whitney, A.S. & Fox, R.L. (1981) Phosphorus requirements of cowpea and soybean as affected by mode of N nutrition. *Agron. J.* 73, 17-22.

Crush, J.R. (1974) Plant growth response to vesicular arbuscular mycorrhizas. VII. Growth and nodulation of some herbage legumes. *New Phytol.* 73, 743-749.

De-Polli, H., Suhet, A.R. & Franco, A.A. (1975) Micronutrientes limitando a fixação de nitrogenio atmosférico e produção de *Centrosema* em solo Podzólico Vermelho Amarelo. *Anais XV Congr. Brasileiro de Cienc. Solo* Pp. 151-156.

De-Polli, H., Carvalho, S.R., Lemos, P.F., de & Franco, A.A. (1979) Efeito de micronutrientes no estabelecimento e persistencia de leguminosas em pastagens de marro em solo Podzólico Vermelho-Amarelo. *Rev. Bras. Ci. Solo* 3, 154-157.

Döbereiner, J. (1966) Manganese toxicity effects on nodulation and nitrogen fixation of beans in acid soils. *Plant Soil* 24, 153-166.

Evans, C.E. & Kamprath, E.J. (1970) Lime response as related to percent Al saturation, solution Al and organic matter content. *Soil Sci. Soc. Amer. Proc.* 34, 893-896.

Fassbender, H.W. (1967) La fertilización del frijol. *Turrialba* 17, 46-82.

Fox, R.L. (1978) Studies on phosphorus nutrition in the tropics *In*: Mineral nutrition of legumes in tropical and subtropical soils, C.S. Andrew & E.J. Kamprath (Eds.). CSIRO, Melbourne, Australia. Pp. 164-188.

Fox, R.L. & Kang, B.T. (1977) Some major fertility problems of tropical soils. *In*: Exploiting the legume-*Rhizobium* symbiosis in tropical agriculture, J.M. Vincent, A.S. Whitney & J. Bose (Eds.), Univ. Hawaii Coll. Trop. Agric. *Misc. Publ.* 145. Pp. 183-210.

Foy, C.D., Armiger, W.H., Fleming, A.L., & Zaumeyer, W.J. (1967) Differential tolerance of dry bean, snapbean, and lima bean varieties to an acid soil high in exchangeable aluminum. *Agron. J.* 59, 561-563.

Franca G. E., & Carvalho, M.M. de (1970) Ensaio exploratório de fertilização de cinco leguminosas tropicais em um solo de cerrado. *Pesq. Agropec. Bras.* 5, 147-153.

Franco, A.A. (1977) Nutritional restraints for tropical grain legume symbiosis. *In*: Exploiting the legume-*Rhizobium* symbiosis in tropical agriculture, J.M. Vincent, A.S. Whitney & J. Bose (Eds.). Univ. of Hawaii. Coll. Trop. Agric. *Misc. Publ.* 145. Pp. 237-252.

Franco, A.A. (1978) Micronutrient requirements of legume-*Rhizobium* symbiosis in the tropics. *In*: Limitations and potentials for biological nitrogen fixation in the tropics. J. Döbereiner, *et al.* (Eds.). Plenum Press, New York, NY, USA. Pp. 161-171.

Franco, A.A. & Munns, D.N. (1981) Response of *Phaseolus vulgaris* to Mo under acid conditions. *Soil Sci. Soc. Amer. J.* (In press.)

Graham, P.H. & Parker, C.A. (1964) Diagnostic features in the characterization of the root-nodule bacteria of legumes. *Plant Soil* 20, 383-396.

Helyar, K.R. (1976) Nitrogen cycling and soil acidification. *J. Aust. Inst. Agric. Sci.* 42, 217-221.

Helyar, K.R. (1978) Effects of Al and Mn toxicities on legume growth. *In*: Mineral nutrition of legumes in tropical and subtropical soils, C.S. Andrew & E.J. Kamprath (Eds.). CSIRO, Melbourne, Australia. Pp. 207-232.

International Fertilizer Development Center (IFDC) (1978) Fertilizer manual. IFDC, Muscle Shoals, AL, USA.

Isbell, R.F. (1978) Soils of the tropics and subtropics: Genesis and characteristics. *In*: Mineral nutrition of legumes in tropical and subtropical soils, C.S. Andrew & E.J. Kamprath (Eds.). CSIRO, Melbourne, Australia. Pp. 1-21.

Jones, R.K. (1974) Phosphorus response of a wide range of accessions from the genus *Stylosanthes*. *Aust. J. Agric. Res.* 25, 847-862.

Kampen, J. & Burford, J. (1980) Productions systems, soil-constraints and potentials in the semiarid tropics. *In*: Soil constraints to food production in the tropics, J.F. Metz & N.C. Brady (Eds.). IRRI, Los Baños, Philippines. Pp. 141-166.

Kamprath, E.J. (1970) Exchangeable aluminum as a criterion for liming leached mineral soils. *Soil Sci. Soc. Amer. Proc.* 34, 252-254.

Kamprath, E.J. (1971) Adverse effects of overliming. *Soil Crop Sci. Soc. Florida Proc.* 31, 200-203.

Kamprath, E.J. (1978) Lime in relation to Al toxicity in tropical soils. *In*: Mineral nutrition of legumes in tropical and subtropical soils, C.S. Andrew & E.J. Kamprath (Eds.). CSIRO, Melbourne, Australia. Pp. 233-246.

Kemmler, G. (1980) Potassium deficiency in soils of the tropics as a constraint to food production. *In*: Soil constraints to food production in the tropics, J.F. Metz & N. C. Brady (Eds.). IRRI, Los Baños, Philippines. Pp. 253-276.

Keyser, H.H. & Munns, D.N. (1979a) Tolerance of rhizobia to acidity, aluminum, and phosphate. *Soil Sci. Soc. Amer. J.* 43, 519-523.

Keyser, H.H. & Munns, D.N. (1979b) Effects of Ca, Mn, and Al on growth of rhizobia in acid media. *Soil Sci. Soc. Amer. J.* 43, 500-503.

Keyser, H.H., Munns, D.N. & Hohenberg, J.S. (1979) Acid tolerance of rhizobia in culture and in symbiosis with cowpea. *Soil Sci. Soc. Amer. J.* 43, 719-722.

Lal, R. (1979) Physical characteristics of soils of the tropics. *In*: Soil physical properties and crop production in the tropics, R. Lal & D.J. Greenland (Eds.). Wiley, New York, NY, USA. Pp. 7-44.

Lal, R., Kang, B.T., Moorman, F.R., Juo, A.S.R., & Moomaw, J.C. (1975) Soil management problems and solutions in western Nigeria. *In*: Soil management in tropical America, E. Bornemisza & A. Alvaredo (Eds.). N. Carolina State Univ., Raleigh NC, USA. Pp. 372-408.

Lauter, D.J., Munns, D.N. & Clarkin, K.L. (1981) Salt response of chickpea as influenced by nitrogen supply. *Agron. J.* (In press.)

Little, D.A. & Shaw, N.H. (1979) Superphosphate and stocking rate effects on a native pasture oversown with *Stylosanthes humilis* in Central Coastal Queensland: Bone phosphorus levels in grazing cattle. *Aust. J. Expl. Agric. Anim. Husb.* 19, 646-651.

Lopes, A.S. (1980) Micronutrients in soils of the tropics as constraints to food production. *In*: Soil constraints to food production in the tropics, J.F. Metz & N.C. Brady (Eds.). IRRI, Los Baños, Philippines. Pp. 277-298.

Meissner, A.P. & Clarke, A.A. (1977) Response of mown pasture to potassium fertilizer in south-eastern Australia. *Aust. J. Expl. Agric. Anim. Husb.* 17, 765-775.

Moorman, F.R. & Greenland, D.J. (1980) Major production systems related to soil properties in humid tropical Africa. *In*: Soil constraints to food production in the tropics, J.F. Metz & N.C. Brady (Eds.). IRRI, Los Baños, Philippines. Pp. 55-77.

Mosse, B. (1977) Role of mycorrhiza in legume nutrition. *In*: Exploiting the legume-*Rhizobium* symbiosis in tropical agriculture, J.M. Vincent, A.S. Whitney & J. Bose (Eds.). Univ. of Hawaii. Coll. Trop. Agric. *Misc. Publ.* 145. Pp. 275-292.

Munns, D.N. (1977) Mineral nutrition of legume symbioses. *In*: A treatise on dinitrogen fixation. IV. Agronomy, R.W.F. Hardy & A.H. Gibson (Eds.). Wiley, New York, NY, USA. Pp. 353-392.

Munns, D.N. (1978) Soil acidity and nodulation. *In*: Mineral nutrition of legumes in tropical and subtropical soils. C.S. Andrew & E.J. Kamprath (Eds.). CSIRO, Melbourne, Australia. Pp. 247-264.

Munns, D.N. & Fox, R.L. (1977) Comparative lime requirements of tropical and temperate legumes. *Plant Soil* 46, 533-548.

Munns, D.N., Righetti, T.L., Hohenberg, J.S., & Lauter, D.L. (1981) Soil acidity tolerance in symbiotic and nitrogen-fertilized soybeans. *Agron. J.* 73, 407-410.

National Academy of Sciences. (1979) Tropical legumes: Resource for the future. NAS, Washington, D.C., USA.

Nicou, R. & Charreau, C. (1980) Mechanical impedance related to land preparation as a constraint to food production. *In*: Soil constraints to food production in the tropics, J. F. Metz & N. C. Brady (Eds.). IRRI, Los Baños, Philippines. Pp. 371-422.

Nyatsanga, T. & Pierre, W.H. (1973) Effect of nitrogen fixation by legumes on soil acidity. *Agron. J.* 65, 936-940.

Nye, P.H. & Foster, W.N.M. (1958) A study of the mechanism of soil-phosphate uptake in relation to plant species. *Plant Soil* 9, 338-352.

Pearson, R.W. (1975) Soil acidity and liming in the humid tropics. *Cornell Intern. Agric. Bull.* No. 30, Cornell Univ., Ithaca, NY, USA.

Ponnamperuma, F.N. & Bandyopadhya, A.K. (1980) Soil salinity as a constraint on food production in the humid tropics. *In*: Soil constraints to food production in the tropics. J.F. Metz & N.C. Brady (Eds.). IRRI, Los Baños, Philippines. Pp. 203-216.

Richards, L.A. (Ed.). (1954) Saline and alkali soils. Agric. Handbook No. 60. US Dept. Agriculture, Washington, D.C., USA.

Ritchey, K.D., Souza, D.M.G., Lobato, E., & Correa, O. (1980) Calcium leaching to increase rooting depth in a Brazilian Savannah Oxisol. *Agron. J.* 72, 40-44.

Robson, A.D. (1978) Mineral nutrients limiting nitrogen fixation in legumes. *In*: Mineral nutrition of legumes in tropical and subtropical soils, C.S. Andrew & E.J. Kamprath (Eds.). CSIRO, Melbourne, Australia. Pp. 277-294.

Russell, J.S. (1978) Soil factors affecting growth of legumes on low fertility soils. *In*: Mineral nutrition of legumes in tropical and subtropical soils, C.S. Andrew & E.J. Kamprath (Eds.). CSIRO, Melbourne, Australia. Pp. 75-92.

Sánchez, P.A. (1976) Properties and management of soils in the tropics. Wiley, New York, NY. USA.

Sánchez, P.A. & Cochrane, T.T. (1980) Soil constraints in relation to farming systems in tropical America. *In*: Soil constraints to food production in the tropics, J.F. Metz & N.C. Brady (Eds.). IRRI, Los Baños, Philippines. Pp. 107-139.

Schenck, N.C. & Hinson, K. (1973) Response of nodulating and nonnodulating soybeans to species of endogone mycorrhiza. *Agron. J.* 65, 849-880.

Sharma, M.L. & Uehara, G. (1968) Influence of soil structure on water relations in Latosols. *Soil Sci. Soc. Amer. Proc.* 32, 765-774.

Shaw, N.H. & Andrew, C.S. (1979) Superphosphate and stocking rates on a native pasture oversown with *Stylosanthes humilis. Aust. J. Expl. Agric. Anim. Husb.* 19, 426-436.

Sopher, C.D. & McCracken, R.J. (1973) Relationships between soil properties, management and corn yields in S. Atlantic coastal plain soils. *Agron. J.* 65, 595-600.

Spain, J.M., Francis, C.A., Howeler, R.H., & Calvo, F. (1975) Differential species and varietal tolerance to soil acidity in tropical crops and pastures. *In*: Soil management in tropical America, E. Bornemisza & A. Alvarado (Eds.). N. Carolina State Univ., Raleigh, NC, USA. Pp. 308-329.

US Dept. of Agriculture. (1971) National inventory of soil and water conservation needs, 1967. Statistical Bulletin No. 461. Washington, D.C., USA.

Vidor, C. & Freire, J.R.J. (1972) Control of Al and Mn toxicity in *Glycine max* by lime and phosphate *Agron. Sulriogr.* 8, 73-87.

Wischmeier, W.H. & Smith, D.D. (1978) Predicting rainfall erosion losses. US Dept. of Agric., Agric. Handbook No. 537. Washington D.C., USA.

Yost, R.S., & Fox, R.L. (1979) Contribution of mycorrhizae to P nutrition of crops growing in an Oxisol. *Agron. J.* 71, 903-908.

EFFECTS OF INOCULATION, NITROGEN FERTILIZER, SALINITY, AND WATER STRESS ON SYMBIOTIC N_2 FIXATION BY *VICIA FABA* AND *PHASEOLUS VULGARIS*

A.S. Abdel-Ghaffar, H.A. El-Attar, M.H. El-Halfawi, and A.A. Abdel Salam[1]

Summary

This study reports the effects of inoculation, salinity, water stress and nitrogen (N) fertilization on N_2 fixation by faba beans and beans. Inoculation of faba beans increased nodulation and nitrogenase activity, while addition of N fertilizer (180 kg N/ha) suppressed nodulation and N_2 fixation but increased yields. Saline conditions also depressed nodulation and N_2 fixation and decreased crop yield in the absence of fertilizer N. Water stress inhibited nitrogenase activity in faba beans, but had no marked effect on nodulation.

Inoculation of *P. vulgaris* markedly enhanced nodulation and N_2 fixation, plant dry weight, N content and final yield. The granular inoculum had a better effect than either the powder form or liquid culture. Application of N fertilizer (100 kg N/ha) reduced nodulation and depressed nitrogenase activity but resulted in yields less than those obtained through inoculation. Salinity and water stress inhibited nodulation, depressed nitrogenase activity, and decreased the yield of bean plants. Maximum N_2 fixation and yield were obtained when plants were irrigated every 7-12 days.

INTRODUCTION

Environmental factors such as soil moisture stress (McKee, 1961; El Nadi, Brouwer & Locher, 1969; Hamdi, 1971; Sprent, 1971; 1976), salinity (Ibrahim, Kamel & Khader, 1970; Wilson, 1970), and availability of combined N (McEwen, 1970; Candlish & Clark, 1975; Gibson, 1976; Hamdi,

[1] Dept. of Soil and Water Science, Faculty of Agriculture, Univ. of Alexandria, Alexandria, Egypt.

1976; Dean & Clark, 1977; Richards & Soper, 1979) can affect the nodulation and nitrogen (N_2) fixation of grain legumes.

Nodulation of *Phaseolus vulgaris* under Egyptian field conditions is scarce (Hamdi, 1976), but faba beans (*Vicia faba*) are usually well nodulated even without inoculation. The yield of both crops can be affected by salinity and by infrequent irrigation that causes water stress. The experiments reported in this paper test the effects of inoculation, salinity, and water stress, in the presence and absence of added N fertilizer, on symbiotic N_2 fixation by *Vicia faba* and *Phaseolus vulgaris*.

MATERIALS AND METHODS

Field and pot experiments were conducted at the Farm of Alexandria University, Alexandria and Sakha Experimental Station, Kafr El-Sheikh, using *Vicia faba* 'Giza 3' and *Phaseolus vulgaris* 'Giza 3'. In pot experiments seeds were planted in earthenware pots containing 7 kg soil and were given water as needed. In field experiments, plot dimensions were 7 x 6 m; each plot contained 10 rows, 60 cm apart and only plants from the center rows were used for subsequent analyses. All plots received superphosphate applied at locally recommended rates, and were replicated at least five times.

In all experiments inoculants were added to the soil or seed at planting. Local and imported (Nitragin Co., Milwaukee, WI, USA) inoculants were used. Plants were sampled for nodulation and N_2 (C_2H_2) fixation at several stages in the growth cycle. C_2H_2 assays followed the method of Dart, Day & Harris (1972) and used a Varian model 1400 gas chromatograph with hydrogen flame ionization detector. Specific treatments evaluated three factors.

Salinity: Effect of salinity was studied only in pot experiments. In one experiment, the soil was salinized with NaCl and $CaCl_2$ (1:1 by wt) before potting. In a second experiment, the plants were irrigated with water salinized with the same salt mixture. The electrical conductivity (EC) of the salinity levels tested was 2, 5, 7.5, and 10 mmhos/cm.

Water stress: Effects of water stress on cultivated faba beans were evaluated by comparing plants irrigated when 25% or 75% of the available soil moisture had been depleted. In the experiment with beans, plants were irrigated every 7, 12, 17, or 22 days during the growing season.

N fertilization: Field as well as pot experiments were carried out with and without N fertilizer. In the pot experiments, N fertilizer was added before seeding, while in the field experiments, N was applied before the first irrigation after sowing. The form and dose used are indicated in the results.

RESULTS AND DISCUSSION

Vicia faba

Table 1 shows the response of faba beans to inoculation and N fertilization. As indicated earlier, nodulation was abundant, even in uninoculated plots. Even so, inoculation in the absence of combined N enhanced N_2 (C_2H_2) fixation and improved dry matter production and yield. As to be expected, N fertilization reduced nodule number per plant and N_2 (C_2H_2) fixation. Maximum dry matter production was achieved in N fertilized plots, but grain yields in inoculated and +N treatments were not significantly different.

TABLE 1: Effect of inoculation and N fertilizer[1] on nodulation, acetylene reduction and yield of a faba bean pot experiment (planted Nov. 6, 1979).

	Uninoculated		Inoculated	
	N_0	N_1	N_0	N_1
Nodules/plant[2]	126	70	382	132
umol C_2H_4/g dry nod. per h	19	82	113	97
umol C_2H_4/plant per h	0.81	7.14	12.79	4.61
Yield of dry matter (g/plant[3])	11.21	12.85	14.12	16.37
Seed yield (g/plant)	3.53	4.15	4.63	4.45

[1] N_1: 180 kg N/ha as ammonium nitrate.
[2] Age of plants: 70 days
[3] Age of plants: 120 days

The effect of soil salinity on nodulation and N_2 fixation in *Vicia faba* is shown in Table 2. In this experiment faba beans proved very susceptible to salinization with yields reduced almost 13% by the use of irrigation water with an EC of only 2 m mhos/cm. While the nodulation and N_2 (C_2H_2) fixation of inoculated, but not N fertilized, plants of *V. faba* were also highly sensitive to salt, plants that had also been N fertilized showed enhanced nodulation and total N_2 (C_2H_2) fixing activity at the 5 mmho/cm level of salinization.

Though reducing the frequency of irrigation reduced the N_2 (C_2H_2) fixation of faba bean from 19 to only 6 μmol C_2H_4 produced/plant per hour, this difference was not reflected in yields. Nodule number was also little affected by irrigation frequency.

TABLE 2: Effect of salinity and N fertilizer[1] on nodulation, acetylene reduction and yield and N content of a faba bean pot experiment (planted Nov. 6, 1979).

		EC of irrigation water, mmhos/cm				
		0	2	5	7.5	10
		EC of soil extract at harvest				
		1.5	8.8	15.5	21.0	26.0
Nodules/plant[2]	N_0	382	97	79	17	4
	N_1	132	274	321	102	51
µmol C_2H_4/g dry	N_0	113	171	120	6	3
nodules per h	N_1	97	184	193	96	37
µmol C_2H_4/	N_0	12.8	7.2	7.6	0.4	0.9
plant per h	N_1	4.6	21.3	28.5	17.6	2.6
Yield[3]: Dry matter	N_0	14.12	12.72	11.56	8.03	3.05
(g/plant)	N_1	16.37	14.18	11.14	7.77	3.99
Seeds	N_0	4.63	4.02	3.35	1.85	0.25
(g/plant)	N_1	4.45	4.21	3.62	1.67	0.33

[1]N_1: 180 kg N/ha as ammonium nitrate.

[2]Age: 70 days.

[3]Age: 120 days.

Phaseolus vulgaris

The response of *Phaseolus vulgaris* to inoculation is shown in Table 3). In this case uninoculated control plants bore no nodules and gave very low dry matter production. While the rates of N_2 (C_2H_2) fixation cited are low in comparison with nodule number and dry weight, there was a very clear dry matter increase with inoculation, granular inoculation being most effective.

Saline conditions depressed the nodulation, N_2 fixation, and yield of bean plants (see Table 4), with N yield reduced more than 50% when the soil salinity was increased from two to five mmhos/cm.

Effects of irrigation interval on parameters of nodulation, N_2 (C_2H_2) fixation and yield in *P. vulgaris* are shown in Table 5.

Generally, nodulation and nitrogenase activity, as well as seed yields of beans decreased as the time intervals between irrigations increased. Although N fertilizer increased seed yield in this experiment, it depressed nodulation

TABLE 3: Effect of type of inoculum on nodulation and acetylene reduction by beans *(P. vulgaris)* in a field experiment (planted April 18, 1980, sampled after 48 days).

	Inoculum type[1]			
	Liquid	Powder	Granular	Control
Nodules/plant	72	49	146	0
Nodule dry wt (mg/plant)	61	43	106	–
µmol C_2H_4/g dry nod per h	6.2	18.1	20.6	–
µmol C_2H_4/plant per h	0.37	0.61	1.94	–
Dry matter (g/plant)[2]	25.47	34.59	37.16	6.67

[1] The liquid culture was supplied by the Microbiology Research Dept., Agricultural Research Center, Cairo, Egypt; the powder and granular inoculants by the Nitragin Company, Milwaukee, WI, USA.

[2] Age of plants: 82 days.

TABLE 4. Effect of salinity and N fertilizer[1] on nodulation, acetylene reduction, yield and N content of beans *(P. vulgaris)* in a pot experiment (planted May 10, 1970).

		Soil salinity, m mhos/cm			
		2.0	5.0	7.5	10.0
Nodules/plant[2]	N_0	25	15	6	3
	N_1	21	15	3	3
µmol C_2H_4/g dry wt nod per h	N_0	16.9	–	14.9	7.7
	N_1	15.8	5.2	1.6	–
µmol C_2H_4/plant per h	N_0	350	350	63	40
	N_1	290	60	4	2
Yield: Dry matter (g/plant)[3]	N_0	3.02	1.26	0.74	0.48
	N_1	3.09	1.11	0.64	0.52
N (mg/plant)	N_0	57.70	24.70	13.80	6.50
	N_1	64.90	21.50	11.20	8.20

[1] N_1: 100 kg N/ha as ammonium sulphate.

[2] Using plants 30 days old.

[3] At 60 days.

INFLUENCE OF MOLYBDENUM ON NITROGEN FIXATION BY WHITE CLOVER IN THE BOGOTA SAVANNA

A. Lozano de Yunda and N. Mora de González[1]

Summary

In a glasshouse experiment with white clover, two soils from the Bogota savanna responded differently to the application of molybdenum (Mo). With soil from the Tibaitatá series, application of 250 g/ha of ammonium molybdate to the soil increased the yield and nitrogen content of white clover by 23%, and raised nitrogenase activity 32%, but the changes were not statistically significant. By contrast, soil from the Techo series responded strongly to Mo application with 750 g/ha ammonium molybdate applied giving the best results.

INTRODUCTION

Production of dairy cattle on the Bogota savanna (altitude 2600 m above sea level, average temperature 14° C, and average annual rainfall, 941 mm) has in recent years, moved toward legume-based pastures, with white clover (*Trifolium repens* L.) and *Pennisetum clandestinum* emphasized. (Carrera, Pichott & Alexander, 1968). Good responses to inoculation have been obtained, especially when basal applications of phosphorus (P), potassium (K), and boron (B) were applied (Gonzalez & De Rozo, 1979; Lozano de Yunda, 1981. The objectives of the present study were:

To determine the response to molybdenum (Mo) of white clover grown in these soils;
To compare methods of application of Mo; and
To determine the interaction of lime and Mo.

---

[1] Depto. de Química, Universidad Nacional de Colombia, Ciudad Universitaria, Bogotá, Colombia.

RESULTS AND DISCUSSION

Application of Mo to the Tibaitatá soil at the rate of 250 g ammonium molybdate/ha enhanced the yield and N content of tissues 23%, and increased N_2 (C_2H_2) fixation by 32%. However, neither of these increases proved statistically significant (see Table 2). Higher levels of application had negative effects on yield and N_2 fixation, and the other methods for the application of Mo were without effect. Lime, in the treatment without Mo, produced a nonsignificant yield increase of 30% and increased the N content of tissues 36%, but nitrogenase activity declined.

The application of Mo to Techo soil resulted in a significant increase in yield and in the N content of tissues (see Table 3). Highest yields were obtained with the addition of 750 g/ha of ammonium molybdate to the soil. Similar yields were obtained by applying 2.5 mg/1 of ammonium molybdate in the inoculant.

TABLE 3: Effect of molybdenum application on growth and N_2 fixation by white clover in Techo soil.

Molybdenum treatment	Yield (mg/pl)	N (mg/pl)	n mol C_2H_4/ plant · hr
Soil applied, 250 g/ha	202 b[1]	6.1 c	122 a
Soil applied, 500 g/ha	262 ab	9.6 b	120 a
Soil applied, 750 g/ha	341 a	13.8 a	211 a
Inoc. applied, 1.5 mg/1	307 a	9.2 ab	92 a
Inoc. applied, 2.5 mg/1	322 a	11.0 a	153 a
Inoc. applied, 3.5 mg/1	268 a	8.1 b	74 a

[1]The variance analyses for each method of application were made independently. For each method of application means followed by the same letter are not significantly different.

REFERENCES

Carrera, E., Pichiott, J. & Alexander, E. (1968) Instituto Geográfico Agustín Codazzi, Depto. Agrológico, Vol. IV. Pp 53-73.

González, E. & De Rozo, E. (1979) *Suelos Ecuatoriales* 10, 32-38.

Lozano de Yunda, A. (1981) Influencia del molibdeno en la fijación simbiótico de nitrógeno en suelos de la sabana de Bogotá. Tesis de Magister, Univ. Nacional de Colombia, Bogotá, Colombia.

NITROGEN AND PHOSPHORUS REQUIREMENTS FOR THE GROWTH AND NODULATION OF *CAJANUS CAJAN* IN PANAMANIAN SOILS

B.C. Hernández[1], J.M. Mendez-Lay[1] and D.D. Focht[2]

Summary

Chemical analysis and missing element trials with *Sorghum vulgare* L. showed that three Panamanian soils, representative of three great soil groups, were deficient in both nitrogen (N) and phosphorus (P). When a greenhouse trial was undertaken to test the response of *Cajanus cajan* to rhizobial inoculation, N and P fertilization in these soils, no response was obtained in either the Río Hato or Los Santos soils. There was a definite response to P and a slight response to inoculation in the Pacora soil, which had the poorest fertility level. N applications depressed nodulation. The lack of response of *Cajanus cajan* to P in the Río Hato soil was attributed to the high incidence (55%) of VA mycorrhizal infection. Inoculation of *Cajanus cajan* with both *Rhizobium* and *Glomus* may be important in low-fertility soils.

INTRODUCTION

Inoculation trials with tropical legumes can give extremely variable results, in part because many of the legumes used are symbiotically promiscuous and so will nodulate with native soil rhizobia (Norris, 1972a; 1972b), but also because elements other than nitrogen (N) can limit plant growth. Phosphorus (P) is frequently a problem in tropical soils, especially latosols, and has been reported to be more limiting than N for tropical legumes (Loneragan, 1972). Soluble P is highly variable in tropical soils; moreover, the soluble P concentration for maximum yield varies between crops (Fox, 1973). S deficiency is also recognized as a problem in some tropical soils (Bolle-Jones, 1964). No general rule can be made regarding micronutrient deficiencies.

---

[1] Escuela de Biología and Escuela de Agronomía, Universidad de Panamá, Republic of Panama, respectively.

[2] Dept. of Soil and Environmental Sciences, Univ. of California, Riverside, CA 92521, USA.

The present study was undertaken to establish the limiting nutrients in Panamanian soils that could affect the response of *Cajanus cajan* to *Rhizobium* inoculation.

MATERIALS AND METHODS

The three soils studied represent great soil groups important in Panama. Their physical and chemical properties are detailed in Table 1. All soils were initially screened for response to N, P, S, Ca, Mg, B, Zn, Fe, K, Cu, Mn, and Mo in replicated missing-element trials with *Sorghum vulgare* L. Control pots received no fertilization, while the complete plots received all 12 elements. After 30 days, plants were topped, dried and weighed. The same three soils were used to assess the effects of N and P addition on response to inoculation in pigeonpea (*Cajanus cajan*). In this study, elements other than N and P, shown to be deficient in the missing-element trial, were added at a single prescribed rate as appropriate to the different soils. Since the Río Hato soil responded only to N and P, it received no supplemental fertilizer. Given the differences in P fixation for the three soils, each received different levels of P:

Río Hato: 0, 50, 100 and 200 ppm P.
Los Santos: 0, 35, 70 and 140 ppm P.
Pacora: 0, 100, 200 and 300 ppm P.

Thirty ppm N was used in the +N treatments; the inoculant for *Cajanus cajan* was provided by J.C. Burton.

After 50 days plants were topped, the roots washed free of soil, the nodules excised; then plants and nodules were dried and weighed.

Mycorrhizal infection of pigeonpeas in the Río Hato soil was also determined. Fifty root sections/plant were stained with trypan blue and examined microscopically for infectivity as recommended by Daft & Nicholson (1969).

RESULTS AND DISCUSSION

Yield responses of *Sorghum vulgare* in the missing-element trial are shown in Table 2. All three soils responded strikingly to nutrient additions, with N and P responses found in all three soils. Even with complete fertilization, the Pacora soil gave only moderate yields. There was a direct correlation between organic matter content of the soils and their control ($y=0.49x - 0.64$, $r^2=0.99$) and complete ($y=1.14x+1.20$, $r^2=0.97$) yields.

Surprisingly there was no response to either inoculation or P in the Los Santos and Río Hato soils. This may have been due to the presence of both native rhizobia effective for *Cajanus* and endotrophic mycorrhiza. In the Río Hato soil the percent infection with endotrophic mycorrhiza ranged from 62% at 50 ppm P to 46% with 200 ppm P.

TABLE 1: Characteristics of soils. Pacora (Oxisol), Los Santos (Mollisol), Río Hato (Oxisol).

Soil	Depth	Texture S- Si- C (%)	pH	P	K	Ca	Mg	Al	O.M	Mn	Fe	Zn	Cu
				(ppm)		(meq/100 g)			(%)	(ppm)			
Pacora	6"	36-14-50	5.5	Tr	45	0.5	0.05	5.3	1.45	2.0	9.0	–	Tr
Los Santos	6"	32-16-52	7.15	13.6	1000	12.0	5.75	0.11	5.46	92.0	18.0	–	2.0
Río Hato	6"	62-16-22	6.5	12	85	35.0	0.74	0.2	2.46	41.0	29.0	–	Tr

TABLE 2: Yield response (mg dry weight/pot) of *Sorghum vulgare* L.

Soil	Complete	Control	Highest[2] response level	Missing-element response[3]
Los Santos	7.31 a[1]	2.40 c	5.75	Zn, B, Mo, Fe, N, Mn, Cu, S, P
Río Hato	4.54 b	0.72 d	1.83	N, P
Pacora	2.31 c	0.06 e	0.74	Ca, S, Mg, N, P

[1]Means sharing the same letter are not significantly different at $P < 0.05$.
[2]Highest yield that was significantly different ($P < 0.05$) than the complete treatment.
[3]Listed in respective order from left to right as yield response was greater.

On the Pacora soil there was a strong response in dry matter production and nodule dry weight to P application, a substantial response to applied N, but little response to inoculation (see Figures 1 and 2). We assume that native

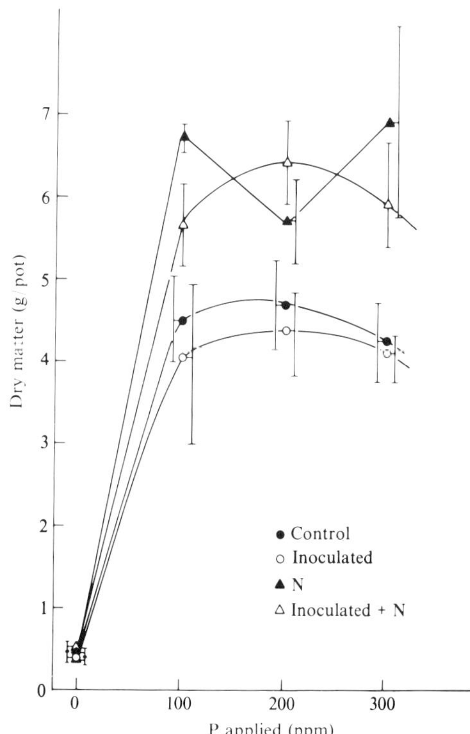

Figure 1.
Dry matter response of pigeonpea to P additions to the Pacora soil.

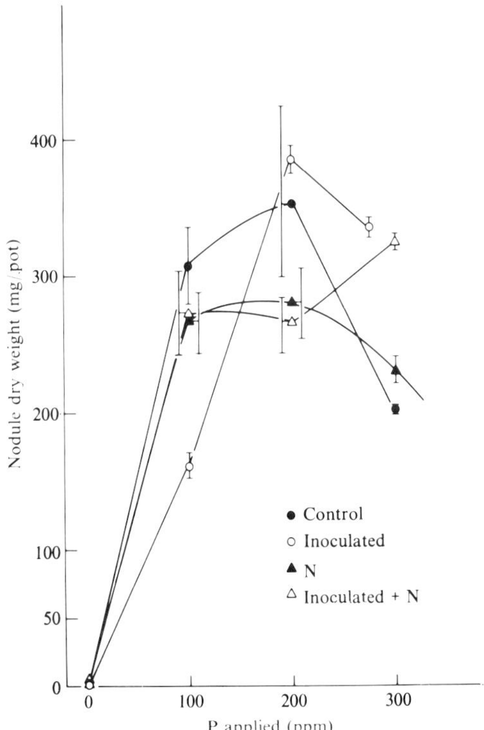

Figure 2.
Nodule mass of pigeonpea in response to P additions to the Pacora soil.

soil rhizobia were competing for nodule sites with the added rhizobia, and by this competition limiting the capacity for N_2 fixation of the host. Certainly, plants receiving N fertilizer performed better than those that were only inoculated.

REFERENCES

Bolle-Jones, E.W. (1964) *Emp. J. Expl. Agric.* 32, 241-248.

Daft, M.J. & Nicholson, T.H. (1969) *New Phytol.* 68, 945-952.

Fox, R.L. (1973) *Soil Crop Sci. Soc. Fla. Proc.* Vol. 33.

Loneragan, J.F. (1972) *IAEA Tech. Rept.* 149, 17-54.

Norris, D.O. (1972a) *Aust. J. Expl. Agric. Anim. Husb.* 12, 152-158.

Norris, D.O. (1972b) *Trop. Grassl.* 5, 159-170.

THE LEGUME/*RHIZOBIUM* ASSOCIATION AS AFFECTED BY HIGH ROOT TEMPERATURE

F. Munévar[1] and A.G. Wollum II[2]

Summary

Selection of *Rhizobium* strains and plant genotypes was studied as a means to alleviate the effects of high temperature stress on the *Rhizobium*/legume symbiosis. Pure culture studies, in which 42 strains of *Rhizobium japonicum* were grown in liquid medium at 19 different temperatures (27.4 to 54.1°C), indicated that strains of this species differ in their tolerance of increasing temperature. The effect of high root temperature on the nodulation, nitrogen (N_2) fixation and dry matter production of soybean plants inoculated with different strains from the pure culture study was examined in the greenhouse. Temperature effects on the symbiotic response were dependent on the rhizobial strain and were related to the response of the strains to temperature in pure culture. Screening of rhizobial strains could, therefore, help to identify strains that are tolerant of high temperature and, thus, better able to symbiose with legumes under tropical conditions. Differences in high temperature tolerance were also found among soybean cultivars and may be an alternative means to overcome high soil temperature stress.

INTRODUCTION

Temperature is one of the major environmental factors influencing the legume/*Rhizobium* association (Gibson, 1971). Both low and high temperatures are detrimental to the symbiotic system and to the symbionts grown independently (Gibson, 1977; Parker, Trinick & Chatel, 1977). In tropical areas, high temperatures will constitute a limitation under many circumstances, whereas low temperatures may be limiting only at very high elevations. Although high temperatures affect the response of both the roots

---

[1] Programa de Suelos, Instituto Colombiano Agropecuario (ICA) A.A. 151123, Bogotá, Colombia.

[2] Dept. of Soil Science, North Carolina State Univ., Raleigh, NC 27650, USA.

and the shoots, it has been suggested that root temperatures are more critical for the symbiosis than shoot temperatures (Gibson, 1976; Possingham, Moye & Anderson, 1964). For these reasons this paper emphasizes the effects of high root temperature.

Both tropical and temperate soils may reach temperatures detrimental to rhizobial survival (Bowen & Kennedy, 1959) and the legume/*Rhizobium* symbiosis (Gibson, 1977). Among the processes affected by high soil temperature are:

The survival in soil of essentially all the *Rhizobium* species (Marshall, 1964; Parker *et al.*, 1977; Vincent, 1977);

Root hair formation in *Pisum sativum* (Frings, 1976), *Phaseolus* spp. (Lie, 1974), and *Trifolium* spp. (Kumarasinghe & Nutman, 1979);

Binding of the *Rhizobium* to root cells of *Pisum sativum* (Frings, 1976);

The formation of infection threads in *Lotus corniculatus* (Rao, 1977a), *Trifolium subterraneum* (Pankhurst & Gibson, 1973) and *Pisum sativum* (Frings, 1976);

Nodule initiation and growth in *Glycine max* (Dart *et al.*, 1975; Munévar & Wollum, 1981), *Stylosanthes* and *Lotus* spp. (Rao, 1977a), *Pisum sativum* (Roponen, Valle & Ettala, 1970), *Phaseolus vulgaris* (Roponen *et al.*, 1970; Small *et al.*, 1968), and *Trifolium subterraneum* (Pankhurst & Gibson, 1973);

Leghemoglobin content in *Trifolium subterraneum* (Gibson, 1976), *Vigna sinensis* (Gibson, 1974) and *Pisum sativum* (Frings, 1976); and

Nitrogenase activity in *Glycine max* (Aprison, Magee & Burris, 1954; Dart *et al.*, 1976; Munévar & Wollum, 1981), *Cicer arietinum* (Dart *et al.*, 1976), *Pisum sativum* (Lie, *et al.*, 1976), *Phaseolus vulgaris* (Pankhurst & Sprent, 1976; Graham, 1979), *Lotus* spp. and *Stylosanthes* spp. (Rao, 1977b), and *Medicago sativa* (Barta, 1978).

As a consequence of the effects of high root temperature on one or more of the processes mentioned above, lower nitrogen (N) contents and biomass production of the host plant have been found for a number of species, including *Desmodium* spp., *Glycine wightii, Macroptilium atropurpureum,* and *Stylosanthes humilis* (Gibson, 1974), when grown at high root temperature.

While the processes mentioned have different critical temperatures (Gibson, 1977), the fact that all are affected by high root temperature suggests that the whole system is very susceptible and that ways must be found to alleviate the effects of high root temperature. Among promising alternatives are the identification of *Rhizobium* strains and legume genotypes tolerant to high soil temperature (Gibson, 1971).

This paper presents some studies conducted with the objective of selecting *Rhizobium japonicum* strains and *Glycine max* genotypes tolerant of high root temperature.

MATERIALS AND METHODS

Pure culture studies

The tolerance of 42 strains of *R. japonicum* to high temperature was evaluated in pure culture. The strains were isolated from nodules of soybean plants grown in different locations of the United States, Brazil, Malaysia, and Japan (Munévar, 1981). Liquid cultures of rhizobia grown on HEPES-MES-gluconate (HMG) broth (Upchurch & Elkan, 1977) were incubated for 96 hours at 19 different temperatures ranging from 27.4 to 54.1°C. The temperature treatments were imposed using a "Poly-Temp" apparatus, with bacterial growth monitored by measuring the optical density (OD) of the cultures at 600 nm. At the end of the incubation period cultures were transferred to an incubator maintained at 28°C, and their ability to grow after removal of the temperature treatments was determined. A bacterial culture was considered to have survived the temperature treatment when its OD increased at any time during a six-day period following the removal from the Poly-Temp apparatus. The maximum survival temperature (MST) of a strain was the highest temperature at which survival following heat treatment was recorded. A detailed description of these procedures is presented by Munévar (1981).

Strain evaluation based on the response of inoculated plants to high root temperature

To establish whether there was a relationship between the temperature response of strains in pure culture and their performance as symbionts, 13 strains from the pure culture study were inoculated onto six-day-old soybean plants (cv. Lee) grown in polyvinyl chloride pots containing vermiculite and supplied N-free nutrient solution (McClure & Israel, 1979). Root temperature treatments were imposed by submerging inoculated pots in thermostatically controlled water baths providing constant root temperature of 28°, 33°, and 38° $\pm$ 0.5%. Quantitive observations of nitrogenase activity (C_2H_2 reduction), nodulation, biomass and plant N content were made at harvest time (34 days). Four experiments were conducted, in which four strains were compared at a time. Procedures are detailed elsewhere (Munévar & Wollum, 1981).

Cultivar evaluation

Two experiments were conducted to study the influence of plant genotype on symbiotic response to high root temperature. The cultivars used (Gasoy-

17, Bragg, Hutton, and Ranson) were inoculated either with strain USDA 110 or 587. Plant culture conditions were as described in the previous section. Three root temperature treatments were factorially combined with the cultivar and strain treatments.

RESULTS AND DISCUSSION

Pure culture studies

Strains differed markedly in response to temperature in pure culture, with four general responses identified among the different strain/temperature combinations studied. For each strain there was a temperature range, within which OD increased continuously during the incubation period (Response A in Table 1). The upper limit of this temperature range for each strain was designated the maximum permissive temperature (MPT). Within the same range a specific temperature value gave the highest OD for each strain at the end of the incubation period. That value was considered as the optimum temperature (OT) for growth of the particular organism.

The other three growth responses shown in Table 1 are:

An initial increase in the OD of the cultures at certain temperatures followed by a decrease in OD with time;

A continuous decrease in the OD throughout the course of the incubation;

No noticeable change in culture OD at high temperature.

The results presented in Table 1 show a diversity in strain growth response to temperature. Thus, for the 42 strains tested, the OT ranged from 27.4 to 35.2° C, the MPT from 29.8 to 38.0° C, and MST from 33.7 to 48.7° C. Strains 587, TAL 102, NC 1005, TAL 184, and NC 1033 appeared to be most tolerant of high temperatures, while the more susceptible strains included NC 1016, USDA 123, and 572.

Relation between the response of strains to temperature in pure culture and as symbionts

The response of inoculated soybean plants to high root temperature varied with the *R. japonicum* strain used as inoculant as indicated by a significant temperature x strain interaction (probability <0.05) for fresh weight of nodules per plant, and the total N content of the plants (see Table 2). That interaction was also significant for the specific nitrogenase activity (C_2H_2 reduction) of attached nodules and the dry weight of the plants (data not included).

Strains 587 and TAL 184 had higher OT, MPT, and MST, as determined in the pure culture studies, than strains USDA 110 and USDA 122 (see Table 1). Concomitantly, plants inoculated with the former two strains had higher

TABLE 1: Response of *Rhizobium japonicum* strains to high temperatures.

Strain	Temperature (° C)													
	27.4 to 29.8	31.1	32.5	33.7	35.2	36.7	38.0	39.1	40.5	42.3	43.7	45.5	47.2	48.7	50.5 to 54.1
587	A[1]	A	A	A	A*	A	A	B/72	B/48	BΔ/48	B/48	B/48	B/48	B/48	B/48
TAL 102	A	A	A	A*	A	A	AΔ	B/48	B/24	B/24	B/24	B/24	B/24	B/24	C
NC 1033	A	A	A	A*	A	A	BΔ/96	B/48	B/48	B/24	B/24	B/24	C	C	C
NC 1005	A	A	A	A	A*	A	BΔ/96	B/48	B/48	C	C	C	C	C	C
NC 1029	A	A*	A	A	A	A	B/72	B/48	BΔ/48	B/24	B/24	B/24	B/24	C	C
USDA 110	A*	A	A	A	A	A	B/72	B/48	BΔ/24	B/24	B/24	C	C	C	C
TAL 184	A	A	A	A*	A	A	B/48	B/48	B/48	B/72	B/48	D	D	DΔ	D
TAL 183	A	A*	A	A	A	A	BΔ/24	B/24	B/48	B/24	B/24	C	C	C	C
USDA 122	A*	A	A	A	AΔ	B/48	B/48	B/48	B/24	B/24	B/24	B/24	C	C	C
NC 1016	A*	A	A	A	A	B/24	BΔ/24	B/24	B/24	C	C	C	C	C	C
572	A*	A	A	A	B/96	B/72	BΔ/24	B/24	C	C	C	C	C	C	C
527	A*	A	A	A	B/96	BΔ/48	B/48	C	C	C	C	C	C	C	C
USDA 123	A*	A	A	BΔ/48	B/24	B/24	B/24	B/24	C	C	C	C	C	C	C
NC 1031	A	B*/96	B/96	B/95	B/96	B/24	B/72	B/72	B/72	BΔ/24	B/48	B/48	B/48	D	D

[1]Letters indicate the responses as follows: A = Continuous increase in optical density during the 96 hours of incubation; B = Initial increase in optical density followed by a decrease (the number after the slash indicates the time in hours when the decrease in optical density was first observed); C = continuous decrease in optical density; D = no detectable change in optical density with time. * indicates the optimum temperature, and Δ indicates the maximum survival temperature. The highest temperature at which response A was observed for each strain, is the maximum permissive temperature.

TABLE 2: Effect of root temperature and *Rhizobium* strain on the fresh weight of nodules and the total N content of soybean plants (adapted from Munévar & Wollum, 1981).

Strain	Nodule weight (mg/plant)			N content (mg/plant)		
	Temperature (° C)			Temperature (° C)		
	28	33	38	28	33	38
587	456.0	550.2	32.8	41.4	32.7	6.1
USDA 110	392.1	384.0	0.9	39.2	19.3	5.4
USDA 122	440.6	327.5	0.0	40.6	12.4	5.2
TAL 184	394.4	728.8	39.8	37.6	49.4	5.1
LSD[1] .05:	T, 145.3; S, 88.2, T x S, 196.0			T. 9.3; S, ns; T x S, 17.9		

[1]Least significant difference at the 0.05 level of probability to compare temperature (T), strain (S), and any two (T x S) means, respectively; ns: nonsignificant at the 0.05 level.

nodule weights than plants inoculated with the latter two strains at a root temperature of 33° C, in spite of the similar nodule weights obtained at 28° C. Although the N content of plants did not differ with strains at the 28° C root temperature, higher N contents were found for the plants inoculated with 587 and TAL 184 at 33° C than for plants inoculated with USDA 110 and USDA 122. Plants inoculated with the temperature-tolerant strains formed nodules at a root temperature of 38° C, whereas nodulation at that temperature was almost nil when the plants were inoculated with heat-susceptible strains.

The results presented in Table 2 along with those of four additional experiments including a total of 13 strains (data not shown), suggest a close association between the tolerance of the strains to high temperature in pure culture and the response of inoculated plants to high root temperature. Correlation analyses were therefore used to quantitatively estimate the relationship between temperature profiles of the strains in pure culture and their symbiotic performance at different root temperatures. No statistically significant correlations were found between OT, MPT, and MST and any plant variable at 28° C; however, significant positive correlations were found at 33° C (see Table 3).

Results of the correlation analysis indicate that the ability of inoculated soybean plants to form and sustain nodule development, to fix and accumulate N, and to produce dry matter at high root temperature (33° C) is related to the ability of the *Rhizobium* strain applied to grow in pure culture at

TABLE 3. Correlation coefficients between variables measured in the pure culture studies (OT, MPT, and MST) of *Rhizobium japonicum* strains and variables measured for plants inoculated with the same strains and grown at a root temperature of 33° C. A total of 45 observations is included. (Adapted from Munévar & Wollum, 1981).

Variables from the inoculated plants	Variables from the pure culture studies		
	OT	MPT	MST
Nodule number/plant	0.333	0.436	ns[1]
Fresh wt of nodules/plant	0.554	0.568	0.678
Nitrogenase activity/plant	0.581	0.612	0.541
Nitrogenase activity/g of nodules	0.450	0.546	ns
N content of tops and roots	0.608	0.552	0.738
Dry wt of tops and roots	0.544	0.446	0.553

[1]ns: nonsignificant at the 5 % level. All other correlations were statistically significant ($P < 0.05$).

high temperatures. Therefore, pure culture evaluation can be used as a preliminary screening procedure to identify strains that are tolerant of high temperature as potential symbionts for soybean.

Cultivar differences

Cultivars Bragg and Gasoy-17 responded somewhat differently to the root temperature treatments (see Table 4). When strain USDA 110 was used as inoculant, the changes in nodule weight and plant N content were inversely proportional to root temperature for both cultivars. Nodule weight and plant N content also decreased with increasing temperature for cv. Bragg inoculated with strain 587. However higher nodule weights were obtained at 33°C than at 28°C for cv. Gasoy-17 in association with strain 587. For that association, no significant difference was observed in the N content of plants grown at a root temperature of 33°C compared to those grown at 28°C.

A significant temperature x cultivar interaction (probability<0.05) was found for the parameters included in Table 4 as well as for the number of nodules and the dry weight of the plants (data not shown). In the second experiment in which cvs. Hutton and Ransom were compared, the temperature x cultivar interaction was significant for the number and weight of nodules, but not for the N content or the dry weight of the plants (data not shown).

TABLE 4: Effect of root temperature on the fresh weight of nodules and the N content of 'Bragg' and 'Gasoy-17' soybean plants inoculated with the *R. japonicum* strains USDA 110 or 587.

Temperature	Strain USDA 110		Strain 587	
(°C)	'Bragg'	'Gasoy-17'	'Bragg'	'Gasoy-17'
	Nodule fresh weight (mg/plant)			
28	701.5	566.7	781.2	728.3
33	593.8	554.3	600.6	790.7
37	0.0	0.0	0.0	3.4
	N content (mg/plant)			
28	62.4	41.4	47.5	41.9
33	22.5	22.7	28.2	43.7
37	7.2	8.0	6.6	8.4

These results suggest that soybean genotypes could differ in their high root temperature tolerance and that selection of soybean cultivars with characteristics of tolerance to high root temperature in symbiotic association with *R. japonicum* could be a means to reduce high soil temperature stress.

REFERENCES

Aprison, M.H., Magee, W.E. & Burris, R.H. (1954) *J. Biol. Chem.* 208, 29-39.

Barta, A.L. (1978) *Crop. Sci.* 18, 637-640.

Bowen, G.D. & Kennedy, M.M. (1959) *Qld. J. Agric. Sci.* 16, 177-197.

Dart, P., Day, J., Islam, R., & Döbereiner, J. (1976) Symbiosis in tropical grain legumes: Some effects of temperature and the composition of the rooting medium. *In:* Symbiotic nitrogen fixation in plants, P.S. Nutman (Ed.). Cambridge Univ. Press, Cambridge, England. Pp. 361-384.

Frings, J.F.J. (1976) The *Rhizobium*-pea symbiosis as affected by high temperatures. Medelingen Landbouwhogeschool. 76-7. Wagenigen, The Netherlands. 76 p.

Gibson, A.H. (1971) *Plant Soil* Special Vol, 139-152.

Gibson, A.H. (1974) *Ind. Nat. Sci. Acad. Proc.* 40B, 741-767.

Gibson, A.H. (1976) Limitations to dinitrogen fixation by legumes. *In:* Proc. First Intern. Symp. Nitrogen Fixation. W.E. Newton & D.J. Nyman (Eds.). Washington State Univ. Press. Pullman, WA, USA. Vol. 2 Pp. 400-428.

Gibson, A.H. (1977) The influence of the environment and managerial practices on the legume-*Rhizobium* symbiosis. *In:* A treatise on dinitrogen fixation IV. Agronomy and ecology. R.W.F. Hardy & A.H. Gibson (Eds.). Wiley, New York, NY, USA. Pp. 393-450.

Graham, P.H. (1979) *J. Agric. Sci.* (Camb.) 93, 365-370.

Kumarasinghe, R.M.K. & Nutman, P.S. (1979) *J. Expl. Bot.* 30, 503-515.

Kuo, T. & Boersma, L. (1971) *Agron. J.* 63, 901-904.

Lie, T.A. (1974) Environmental effects on nodulation and symbiotic nitrogen fixation. *In:* The biology of nitrogen fixation. A. Quispel (Ed.). North - Holland Publ. Co. Amsterdam, The Netherlands. Pp. 555-582.

Lie, T.A., Hille, D., Lambers, R. & Houwers, A. (1976) Symbiotic specialisation in pea plants: Some environmental effects on nodulation and nitrogen fixation. *In:* Symbiotic nitrogen fixation in plants, P.S. Nutman (Ed.). Cambridge Univ. Press, Cambridge, England. Pp. 319-333.

Marshall, K.C. (1964) *Aust. J. Agric. Res.* 15, 273-281.

McClure, P.R. & Israel, D. W. (1979) *Plant Physiol.* 64, 411-416.

Munévar, F. (1981) Studies of the soybean-*Rhizobium* association as affected by high root temperature. PhD thesis. North Carolina State Univ., Raleigh, NC, USA.

Munévar, F. & Wollum II, A.G. (1981) *Soil Sci. Soc. Amer. J.* 45. 1113-1120.

Pankhurst, C.E. & Gibson, A.H. (1973) *J. Gen. Microbiol.* 74, 219-231.

Pankhurst, C.E. & Sprent, J.I. (1976) *J. Expl. Bot.* 27, 1-19.

Parker, C.A., Trinick, M.J. & Chatel, D.L. (1977) Rhizobia as soil and rhizosphere inhabitants. *In:* A treatise on dinitrogen fixation IV: Agronomy and ecology. R.W.F. Hardy & A.H. Gibson (Eds.). Wiley, New York, NY, USA. Pp. 311-352.

Possingham, J.V., Moye, D.V. & Anderson, A.J. (1964) *Plant Physiol.* 39, 561-563.

Rao, V., R. (1977a) *J. Expl. Bot.* 28, 241-259.

Rao V., R. (1977b) *J. Expl. Bot.* 28, 262-268.

Roponen, I., Valle, E. & Ettala, T. (1970) *Physiol. Plant.* 23, 1198-1205.

Small, J.G.C., Hough, M.C., Clarke, B., & Grobbelaar, N. (1968) *South Afr. J. Sci.* 64, 218-224.

Upchurch, R.G. & Elkan, G.H. (1977) *Can. J. Microbiol.* 23, 1118-1122.

Vincent, J.M. (1977) *Rhizobium:* general microbiology. *In:* a treatise of dinitrogen fixation. III. Biology. R.W.F. Hardy & W.S. Silver (Eds.). Wiley, New York, NY, USA. Pp. 277-366.

MICROBIAL CONSTRAINTS TO LEGUME SYMBIOSIS

C. Vidor[1]

Summary

Symbiotic nitrogen (N_2) fixation in the legume/*Rhizobium* association can be reduced markedly by antagonistic microbial interactions in the soil and rhizosphere. Besides their efficiency in N_2 fixation, *Rhizobium* strains used in inoculants must be able to compete actively with native *Rhizobium* strains for nodule sites. Microbial interactions that limit nodulation, N_2 fixation, and *Rhizobium* survival are discussed in this paper.

INTRODUCTION

The symbiotic association between *Rhizobium* and legume can provide most of the nitrogen (N) required for the growth and productivity of the host plant. However, for this to be true, the legume host must be efficiently nodulated by its homologous *Rhizobium.* In some soils large populations of rhizobia that are effective with the legume to be planted are already present, and no inoculation is needed. More commonly, however, the natural population of *Rhizobium* in the soil will be small or the strains that are present will be ineffective. Inoculation will then be necessary and must aim at the long-term establishment in the soil of an efficient strain of *Rhizobium* under conditions that permit it to form a high percentage of the nodules produced on the homologous host. Inoculant strains, therefore, must not only be of proven ability to fix N_2 with the appropriate host, but also must be capable of survival as saprophytes in soil and be able to compete with other rhizobia in the soil for nodulation sites. This paper examines some aspects of the survival and strain competition problems.

---

[1] Depto. de Solos, UFRGS and IPAGRO, Secretaría de Agricultura, Porto Alegre, Brazil. Bolsista do CNPq.

SURVIVAL OF RHIZOBIA IN SOIL

Survival and establishment of an inoculant strain in soil is influenced by host, strain and soil factors. Nonbiotic soil factors are considered separately (see p. 133). There are situations where introduced strains easily colonize the soil, and conversely, where they do not even establish in the rhizosphere of the host. While numerous examples can be given, the factors involved in strain survival in soil remain unclear.

The survival of strains of *R. phaseoli* in Brazilian soils of different pH is reported elsewhere in this volume (see Vidor, Lovato & Miller, p. 201). While the effect of pH was evident, especially in the Erechim soil, *Rhizobium* survival in all soils was excellent until 63 days after incubation.

Bohlool & Schmidt (1973) studied the persistence of the *R. japonicum* strain USDA 110 in clarion silt loam. At an initial population of 2.2. x 10^3 cells/g this organism produced 85% of the nodules. However, on incubation of the soil for 10 and 30 days the percentage of nodules due to strain 110 dropped to 55% and 45%, respectively. This decline was related to the inability of the strain to survive in soil.

ANTAGONISTIC INTERACTIONS

Antagonistic interactions exerted by the soil microbial population against *Rhizobium* have much to do with the degree of persistence achieved by different strains of *Rhizobium*. Figure 1 shows the population change over time of effective strains of *R. japonicum* introduced into a soil with an indigenous population of this *Rhizobium* species (Vidor & Miller, 1980). All strains multiplied and survived well in sterile soil. However, in nonsterile soil all strains decreased in number during the seven-week incubation period. The most rapid death rate was observed with strain USDA 123 which declined 1000-fold during the first five days. There was a direct relationship between the population decline of this strain and the simultaneous population increase of a lytic organism, probably a bacteriophage (see Figure 2). Numbers of the isolate 10/74 (serogroup 123), originally isolated from a Miamian soil, were unaffected by the presence of this organism, nor did the number of plaques increase significantly.

Serogroup 123 is the dominant serogroup in field plots of the Miamian soil, occurring in 50-70% of soybean nodules. Bacteriophage specific for this serogroup are, thus, more likely to be present in this soil because of previous contacts. Isolate 10/74 is likely to survive because of changes in cell surface configuration or lysogeny, changes that are of ecological significance for it.

Similarly Chatel & Parker (1973a) report that a number of the problems of pasture establishment in Australia can be explained by antagonistic interactions between *Rhizobium* and other soil micro-organisms. Specifically, they showed the second-year clover mortality problem in Western Australia to be due to such an interaction (Chatel & Parker, 1973b).

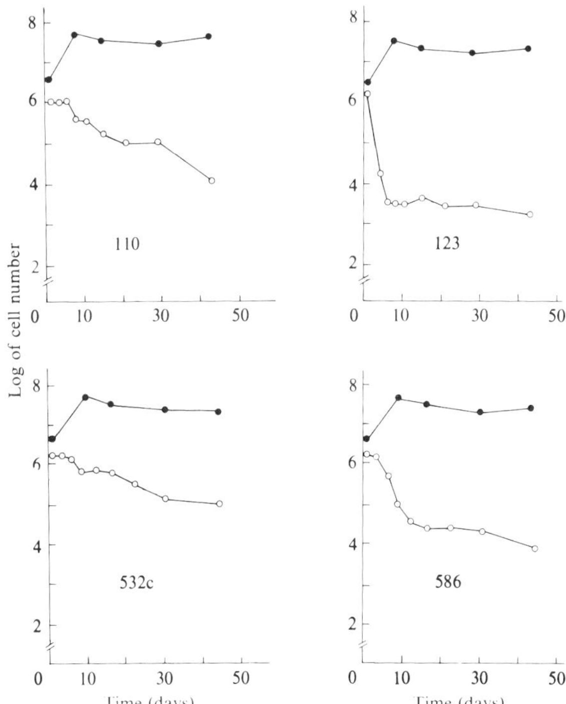

Figure 1. Survival of *R. japonicum* strains (110, 123, 532c, and 586) in sterilized (—•—) and nonsterilized (—○—) Miamian silt loam as determined by quantitative fluorescent antibody techniques (Vidor & Miller, 1980).

According to Chowdhury (1977) the antagonistic interactions exerted by the microbial population against rhizobia in soil include competition, amensalism, predation, parasitism, and lysis.

Competition for nutrients in the soil needs to be considered under two situations. The first is in the soil rhizosphere, where *Rhizobium* populations of 10^6 cells per g dry soil, or higher, are reached (Nutman, 1965), and the second is in the soil away from the root zone. In the first case, *Rhizobium* may have an advantage for nutrient uptake in comparison to specific groups of micro-organisms because of the stimulus exerted by root excretions and the attraction of the *Rhizobium* to the host legume root (Munns, 1968; Currier & Strobel, 1976; 1977). Conversely, in the soil away from the root influence, the competition for nutrients is directly related to the saprophytic competence exhibited by the *Rhizobium* population. Low *Rhizobium* cell densities, usually less than 10^3 cells/g dry soil, may be an indication of its disadvantage in competing for nutrients with the microbial population, which is frequently above 10^6 cells/g dry soil.

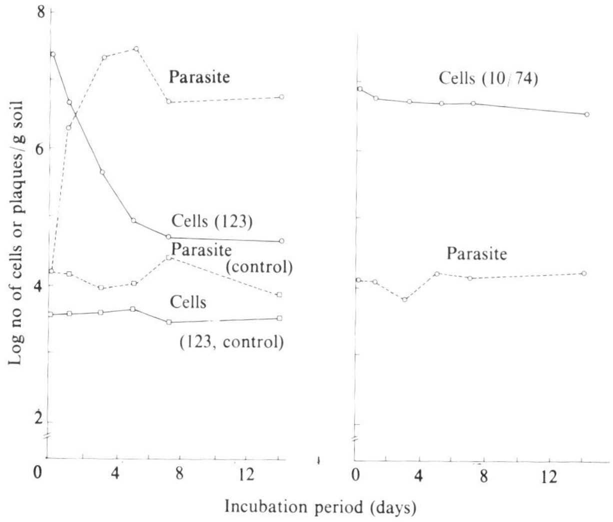

Figure 2. Survival of added cells of *R. japonicum* strain 123 and isolate 10/74 in Miamian silt loam compared to the number of plaques formed by an unknown parasite. Number of cells of serogroup 123 and parasite in an unamended control soil are included for comparative purpose (Vidor & Miller, 1980).

The ability to persist in the soil for extended periods under starving conditions would be a useful attribute for a *Rhizobium* strain. Survival under such conditions may be due to higher amounts of reserve polymers such as poly-β-hydroxybutyrate or production of extracellular polysaccharides (Wong & Evans, 1971; Chen & Alexander, 1972; Patel & Gerson, 1974; Vincent, 1974).

Bacteria, actinomycetes and fungi can all exercise amensalism with respect to *Rhizobium*. Among the bacteria *Pseudomonas* and *Bacillus* spp. have been reported as the principal antagonistic organisms against *Rhizobium* (van Schreven, 1964; Damirgi & Johnson, 1966; Patel, 1974). According to van Schreven (1964) antagonistic actinomycetes can reduce nodulation of the legume host. Members of *Aspergillus* and *Penicillium* have been demonstrated as the principal inhibitors among an appreciable number of harmful genera of fungi (Chowdhury, 1977).

The importance of streptomycin resistance to the establishment of rhizobia for soybean and *Stylosanthes* in "cerrado" soils in Brazil is detailed on page 195. Use of antibiotic-resistant rhizobia in inoculants, together with soil amendments that encourage the growth of *Streptomyces* in soil, might be one means to establish an inoculant strain in soils with high indigenous populations of *Rhizobium*. A similar approach with fungicide-resistant rhizobia applied to treated seeds has already been used experimentally.

Bacteriocinogeny is the ability of a bacterium to produce bacteriocins, proteinaceous compounds with antibacterial action (Schwinghamer, 1971). Schwinghamer (1975) also demonstrated that two different bacteriocins were produced by strains of *R. trifolii:* one of low molecular weight and the other a phage-like compound. Since bacteriocins exhibit strain specificity, bacteriocin-producing strains can limit the growth of other rhizobia in mixed culture or in multi-strain inoculants. According to Schwinghamer (1975), about 5% of the *R. trifolii* strains from the Canberra culture collection (Australia), or isolated from clover nodules, were bacteriocinogenic.

The holozoic group of protozoa feed directly on bacteria. Alexander (1961) reported that when pure cultures of bacteria and protozoa were inoculated into sterile soil, bacterial growth was initially rapid, but that the protozoa then began to multiply with a corresponding drastic decrease in the number of bacteria. He estimated that one species of *Sarcodina* required about 4 x 10^4 bacteria per cell division. Danso, Keya & Alexander (1975) stated that the *Rhizobium* population decline is a matter of energy relationships in which the equilibrium is reached when the energy required by the protozoa to find suitable prey equals or exceeds the energy obtained from the feeding process. Figure 3 shows the fluctuation in the population of *R. meliloti* when incubated during a period of 42 days in sterile and nonsterile Valois silt loam (Danso *et al.,* 1975). The authors demonstrated that predation by protozoa assumed an important role in the *Rhizobium* population decline (see Figure 4). They inoculated samples of nonsterile Lima silt loam with *Rhizobium* strain K04S (effective on cowpea and resistant to streptomycin) and estimated the protozoa and *Rhizobium* population using appropriate selective media.

Since the initial report on the occurrence of the bacterial predator *Bdellovibrio bacteriovorus* by Stolp & Starr (1963) a wide range of bacterial and *Bdellovibrio* interactions have been reported (Sullivan & Casida, 1968). Parker & Grove (1970) demonstrated the ability of *B. bacteriovorus* to parasitize *R. meliloti* and *R. trifolii* in soils of Western Australia. Keya &

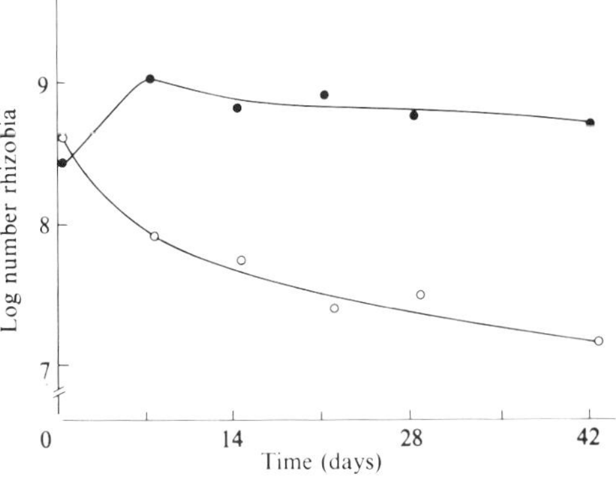

Figure 3.
Survival of *Rhizobium meliloti* in sterile (—•—) and non-sterile (—○—) Valois silt loam. Data expressed as log number of rhizobia/g dry soil (Danso *et al,* 1975).

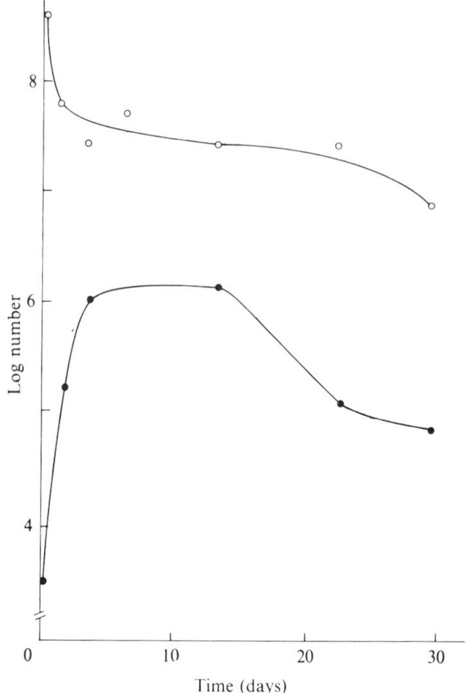

Figure 4.
Increase in number of protozoa (—●—) in Lima silt loam inoculated with streptomycin-resistant mutant *Rhizobium* K04S (—○—) effective on cowpea. Data expressed as log number/g dry soil (Danso *et al*, 1975).

Alexander (1975) studied the influence of different factors on the growth of *Bdellovibrio* and *Rhizobium*. They showed, for example, that *Bdellovibrio* is adsorbed more strongly to clay minerals than is *Rhizobium*, reducing the extent of parasitism in the presence of montmorillonite, kaolinite, and vermiculite.

Bacteriophage are a potentially important biotic factor affecting rhizobial multiplication in the rhizosphere. According to Bruch & Allen (1955), the occurrence of rhizobiophage was first demonstrated by Laird in 1932. Since then, several reports have shown that bacteriophage limit the *Rhizobium* population in soils. Further, strain specificity (Golebiowska, Sawicka & Sypnieska, 1971; Atkins & Hayes, 1972; Barnet, 1972; Kowalski *et al.*, 1974; Patel, 1975) could cause population shifts.

COMPETITION FOR NODULE SITES

Competition for nodule sites can be both host (see p. 27) and *Rhizobium* mediated. The mechanism that enables some strains to occur in nodules with greater frequency than they are found in the surrounding rhizosphere and soil, though extensively studied, is still not understood. Johnson and Means (1964) observed that only 13 of 299 *R. japonicum* strains were more competitive for nodule sites than the chlorosis-inducing strain 76. Table 1 shows remarkable differences in competitiveness for nodule sites among *R. japonicum* strains when used as a mixture on soybean cultivars. Strain 29 W was dominant, occurring in 86-100% of the nodules when strain 587 was not mixed in the inoculum (Vidor, Brose & Pereira, 1979). When strain 587, considered highly competitive for nodule sites, was mixed in the inoculant, the percentage of nodules due to 29 W fell. The other strains —even though highly efficient in N_2 fixation— were not able to compete actively for nodule sites (Peres & Vidor, 1980a). This is not to say that highly efficient strains tend to be noncompetitive. A study by Franco & Vincent (1976) showed clearly that the efficiency of strains was not correlated with ability to compete for nodule sites.

TABLE 1: Competitiveness for nodule sites among *R.: japonicum* on soybean cultivars grown on sand N-free nutrient solution (Vidor, Brose & Pereira, 1979; Peres & Vidor, 1980a).

Cultivars	Percentage of nodules due to:						
	513Re	527	532c	566	586	587	29 W
Pérola	0	0	2	0	0	NS	98
Missoes	0	0	5	0	2	NS	93
Bragg	0	2	4	0	2	NS	92
Paraná	0	3	11	0	0	NS	86
Hardee	0	0	0	0	0	NS	100
Planalto	0	0	0	0	0	NS	100
Santa Rosa	2	0	0	0	0	NS	98
Prata	0	0	0	0	0	NS	100
Pampeira	5	3	2	0	2	NS	88
Bragg	NS	12	7	NS	0	15	69
Santa Rosa	NS	16	8	NS	4	21	49
UFV-1	NS	18	3	NS	2	42	45
IAC-2	NS	0	0	NS	0	29	71

NS – not studied.

While studies on the competitive ability of inoculant strains are obviously important and must be considered an essential step in strain selection, we must also consider the effect of environmental factors on the survival and competitiveness of strains, as a function of time. Table 2 demonstrates the different abilities of *R. japonicum* strains to compete for nodule sites when

TABLE 2: Competition for nodule sites among *R. japonicum* strains used as a mixture on 12 soybean cultivars grown under field conditions (Freire *et al.*, 1976).

Cultivars	Percentage of nodules due to:							
	527		532c		566		587	
	1975	1976	1975	1976	1975	1976	1975	1976
Bragg	37	6	33	5	0	2	30	83
Bossier	15	17	12	5	0	3	73	62
Davis	55	11	10	6	0	1	35	76
Hardee	37	0	9	0	0	2	54	94
IAS-1	12	13	15	10	0	0	73	40
IAS-4	34	1	45	6	0	3	21	81
IAS-5	38	9	12	7	0	9	50	68
Pérola	39	5	26	3	3	3	66	88
Pampeira	29	15	5	2	0	0	66	83
Planalto	25	0	30	0	0	3	45	95
Prata	13	15	38	3	0	1	49	78
Santa Rosa	27	11	25	3	0	0	47	76

used as mixture on 12 soybean cultivars (Freire *et al.*, 1976). In the first year, all strains save strain 566 occurred with more or less similar frequency in nodules. Strain 587 was dominant in the second year, occurring in more than 70% of the nodules of most soybean cultivars. Since this strain is tolerant of high temperature (A.G. Wollum, personal communication) and high aluminum and manganese concentrations (R.H. Miller, personal communication), the better performance of strain 587 in the second year could well be due to its ability to survive adverse soil conditions.

Different concentration ratios of strains can effect their distribution in nodules of the legume host, especially when they are highly competitive and used as a mixture (Peres & Vidor, 1980b). However, when a highly competitive strain is mixed with a noncompetitive one, the former one can still dominate, even at very low ratios (Robinson, 1969; Skrdleta & Karimova, 1969). Table 3 shows the effect of concentration ratios between strains 587 and 29 W on the frequency of serogroup distribution in a soil with a low population of *R. japonicum* (Peres & Vidor, 1980b). There was no dominance for nodule sites when both strains were mixed at ratio 1:1. However, at ratio 10:1, the strain present in greater number occupied 80% of the nodules, while at ratios of 100:1 or higher, there was a complete dominance of the strain that was present in greater number.

TABLE 3: Occurrence of *R. japonicum* strains 587 and 29 W in nodules of soybeans grown in a *R. japonicum*-free soil inoculated with different concentration ratios (Peres & Vidor, 1980b).

Inoculum level	Number of crushed nodules	Strain		
		587 (%)	29 W (%)	No reaction (%)
Control	63	17	51	32
A_3B_3	123	45	52	3
A_3B_4	341	16	79	5
A_3B_5	389	2	98	0
A_3B_6	391	0	100	5
A_4B_3	201	78	17	5
A_5B_3	60	57	37	6
A_6B_3	321	93	6	1

Letters A and B represent, respectively, strains 587 and 29 W. Numbers 3 to 6 represent the log number of cells per gram of inoculum.

The need to increase inoculation rates to favor the introduced strains has been reported by many investigators (Johnson, Means & Weber, 1965; Holland, 1970; Kapusta & Rouwenhorst, 1973; Hamdi *et al.*, 1974). In soils containing an indigenous population of *R. japonicum* (above 10^3 cells/g dry soil) it is unlikely that inoculation at rates recommended by inoculant manufacturers (7.3×10^4 cells/seed for *R. japonicum*) can increase nodule formation (Weaver & Frederick, 1974a). In further research the same authors (1974b) observed that to obtain 50% of the nodules from the introduced strain, an inoculum rate at least 1000-fold greater than the soil population (per g dry soil) is needed. According to them, most manufacturers cannot supply an inoculant to meet this requirement.

The examples sited above emphasize *R. japonicum*. Similar work has also been done using *R. trifolii* in Australia, with essentially identical results (Ireland & Vincent, 1968; Marques Pinto, Yao & Vincent, 1974; Gibson *et al.*, 1976).

CONCLUDING REMARKS

Even though a great many papers deal with antagonistic interactions among the microbial population and rhizobia, it is not known what really happens in the natural and complex system that is the soil. One of the great limitations in most studies to date is that they were undertaken using culture media or sterile soils.

Since strains introduced by inoculation into soils with low natural rhizobial populations usually establish without problems, it must be assumed that antagonistic mechanisms do not often limit the survival or establishment of introduced strains. Predation by protozoa and parasitism by *Bdellovibrio* and bacteriophage are more likely to be constraints in soils cropped to the same legume for many years. Even in these soils it is likely that antagonistic factors will be of secondary importance behind interstrain competition for nodule sites.

Improved competitiveness by inoculant strains must be achieved. Research examining the use of higher inoculation rates, better inoculation methods, and the use of soil amendments that favor introduced competitive strains must be implemented.

REFERENCES

Alexander, M. (1961) Introduction to soil microbiology. (First edition.) Wiley, New York, NY, USA. 472 pp.

Atkins, G.J. & Hayes, A.H. (1972) *J. Gen. Microbiol.* 73, 273-278.

Barnet, Y.M. (1972) *J. Gen. Virol.* 15, 1-5.

Bohlool, B.B. & Schmidt, E.L. (1973) *Soil Sci. Soc. Amer. Proc.* 37, 561-564.

Bruch, C.W. & Allen, O.N. (1955) *Soil Sci. Soc. Amer. Proc.* 19, 175-179.

Chatel, D.L. & Parker, C.A. (1973a) *Soil Biol. Biochem.* 5, 415-423.

Chatel, D.L. & Parker, C.A. (1973b) *Soil Biol. Biochem.* 5, 425-432.

Chen, M. & Alexander, M. (1972) *Soil Biol. Biochem.* 4, 283-288.

Chowdhury, M.S. (1977) Effects of soil antagonists on symbiosis. *In:* Exploiting the legume-*Rhizobium* symbiosis in tropical agriculture, J.M. Vincent, A.S. Whitney & J. Bose (Eds.). Univ. Hawaii College Trop. Agric. *Misc. Publ.* 145. Pp. 385-411.

Currier, W.W. & Strobel, G.A. (1976) *Plant Physiol.* 57, 820-823.

Currier, W.W. & Strobel, G.A. (1977) *Science* 196, 434-436.

Damirgi, S.M. & Johnson, H.W. (1966) *Agron. J.* 58, 223-224.

Danso, S.K.A., Keya, S.O. & Alexander, M. (1975) *Can. J. Microbiol.* 21, 884-895.

Franco, A.A. & Vincent, J.M. (1976) *Plant Soil* 45, 27-42.

Freire, J.R.J., Kolling, J., Godinho, I.T., & Pereira, J.S. (1976) Competicão, sobrevivencia e especializacão simbiótica de estirpes de *Rhizobium japonicum* em variedades de soja. Ata da IV Reuniao Conjunta de Pesquisa da Soja - RS/SC. Santa Maria, RS, Brazil. Pp. 93-102.

Gibson, A.H., Date, R.A., Ireland, J.A., & Brockwell, J. (1976) *Soil Biol. Biochem.* 8, 395-401.

Golebiowska, J., Sawicka, A. & Sypnieska, U. (1971) *Soil Fert. Abst.* 36, 110. 1973.

Hamdi, Y.A., Abd-el-Samea, M.E. & Lofti, M. (1974) *Soil Fert. Abst.* 38, 509. 1975.

Holland, H.H. (1970) *Plant Soil* 32, 293-302.

Ireland, J.A. & Vincent, J.M. (1968) *Trans. 9th Intern. Cong. Soil Sci.* Adelaide, Australia. Vol. 2, pp. 85-93.

Johnson, H.W., & Means, U.M. (1964) *Agron. J.* 56, 60-62.

Johnson, H.W., Means, U.M. & Weber, C.R. (1965) *Agron. J.* 57, 179-185.

Kapusta, G. & Rouwenhorst, D.L. (1973) *Agron. J.* 65, 916-919.

Keya, S.O. & Alexander, M. (1975) *Arch. Microbiol.* 103, 37-43.

Kowalski, M., Ham, G.E., Frederick, L.R., & Anderson, I.C. (1974) *Soil Sci.* 118, 221-228.

Marques Pinto, C., Yao, P.Y. & Vincent, J.M. (1974) *Aust. J. Agric. Res.* 25, 317-329.

Munns, D.N. (1968) *Plant Soil* 28, 129-146.

Nutman, P.S. (1965) The relation between nodule bacteria and the legume host in the rhizosphere and in the process of infection. *In:* Ecology of soil-borne plant pathogens, K.F. Baker & W.C. Synder (Eds.). Univ. of California Press, Los Angeles, CA, USA. Pp. 231-247.

Parker, C.A. & Grove, P.L. (1970) *J. Appl. Bact.* 33, 253-255.

Patel, J.J. (1974) *Plant Soil* 41, 395-402.

Patel, J.J. (1975) Virulent phages of *Lotus* rhizobia, their ecology, morphology and host range. *Proc. 5th Aust. Legume Nodulation Conf.*, Brisbane, Australia. Pp. 11-13.

Patel, J.J. & Gerson, T. (1974) *Arch. Microbiol.* 101, 211-220.

Peres, J.R.R. & Vidor, C. (1980a) *Agron. Sulriogr.* 16. (In press.)

Peres, J.R.R. & Vidor, C. (1980b) *Rev. Soc. Bras. Ciencia do Solo* 4, 139-143.

Robinson, A.C. (1969) *Aust. J. Agric. Res.* 20, 827-841.

Schreven, D.A. van (1964) *Plant Soil* 21, 283-302.

Schwinghamer, E.A. (1971) *Soil Biol. Biochem.* 3, 355-363.

Schwinghamer, E.A. (1975) Types of bacteriocins produced by *Rhizobium trifolii*. *Proc. 5th Aust. Legume Nodulation Conf.*, Brisbane, Australia. Pp. 1-6.

Skrdleta, V. & Karimova, J. (1969) *Arch. Microbiol.* 66, 25-28.

Stolp, H. & Starr, M.P. (1963) *Antonie van Leeuwenhoek* 29, 217-248.

Sullivan, C.W. & Casida, L.E. (1968) *Antonie van Leeuwenhoek* 34, 188-196.

Vidor, C. (1977) Studies of saprophytic competence in strains of *Rhizobium japonicum* (Kirchner) Buchanan. PhD Dissertation. Ohio State Univ. Columbus, OH, USA. 189 pp.

Vidor, C. & Miller, R.H. (1980) *Soil Biol. Biochem.* 2, 483-487.

Vidor, C., Brose, E. & Pereira, J.S. (1979) *Agron. Sulriogr.* 15, 227-238.

Vincent, J.M. (1974) Root-nodule symbioses with *Rhizobium*. *In:* The biology of nitrogen fixation, A. Quispel (Ed.). North-Holland Research Monographs: Frontiers of Biology. 33, 265-341.

Weaver, R.W. & Frederick, L.R. (1974a) *Agron. J.* 66, 229-232.

Weaver, R.W. & Frederick, L.R. (1974b) *Agron. J.* 66, 233-236.

Wong, P.P. & Evans, H.J. (1971) *Plant Physiol.* 47, 750-755.

SUSCEPTIBILITY OF *RHIZOBIUM* STRAINS TO ANTIBIOTICS: A POSSIBLE REASON FOR LEGUME INOCULATION FAILURE IN CERRADO SOILS

M.R.M.M.L. Scotti,[1] N.M.H. Sa,[1] M.A.T. Vargas,[2] and J. Döbereiner[3]

Summary

Soybean nodulation problems in the Brazilian "cerrados" (a type of edaphic savanna) were solved by the introduction of strains, 29W and 587, each resistant to 80-160 μg/ml of streptomycin. A survey in representative areas of this region showed that 86% of 218 *R. japonicum* strains isolated were resistant to high levels of streptomycin (80 μg/ml or more). Among 149 strains of *Rhizobium* sp. isolated from *Stylosanthes* spp. collected in cultivated cerrado soils, 43% were resistant to 40 μg/ml of streptomycin, while only 16% of 68 *Stylosanthes* isolates from undisturbed cerrado savannas supported this level. It is suggested that the ecological changes caused by cultivation of the virgin savanna resulted in survival advantages for streptomycin-resistant *Rhizobium* strains.

INTRODUCTION

One hundred and eighty million ha of the Central Highland of Brazil are "cerrados," an edaphic type of savanna (Goodland, 1971). Now that economically viable fertilization practices have been developed, this area is being opened to intensive agriculture. Soybeans are among the legumes suited to the region, with some 1 million ha planted in 1980. Inoculation problems seemed initially to restrict this crop, but two new *Rhizobium* strains (29 W and 587) were found that nodulated soybeans effectively when applied at five times the rate commercially recommended (Vargas & Suhet, 1980a; 1980b; Peres, Vargas & Suhet, 1981).

---

[1] Dept. of Microbiology, Univ. Federal de Minas Gerais, 30.000, Belo Horizonte, M.G., Brazil.

[2] Centro de Pesquisa Agropecuaria dos Cerrados, EMBRAPA, CP 70/0023, 73.300, Brasilia, D.F., Brazil.

[3] Programa de Fixacao Biologica do Nitrogeno, Km 47, 23460 Seropedica, R.J., Brazil.

Since *Rhizobium* establishment problems in some virgin soils have been attributed to the predominance of antagonistic micro-organisms, especially actinomycetes (Damirgi & Johnson, 1966; Patel, 1974), with soybean nodulation in sterile soil inhibited by the inoculation of antagonistic actinomycetes (Damirgi & Johnson, 1966), and since in virgin cerrado soils 75-94% of the total microflora were found to be *Streptomyces* spp. (Coelho & Drozdowicz, 1979), it seemed possible that resistance to certain antibiotics could be needed for legume root infection and nodule formation in cerrado soils. The present paper demonstrates that spontaneous streptomycin-resistant *Rhizobium* strains dominate in newly cleared cerrado soils.

MATERIALS AND METHODS

Soybean nodules were collected at 11 sites in the vicinity of Brasilia, Ituiutaba, Araxá, Uberaba, and Uberlandia, representative areas of cerrado savanna. Soils were red yellow or dark red Oxisols with very low base exchange capacity, that had been cleared, limed and fertilized three to five years before and had been planted with soybeans for at least three years. Inoculants were used during the first years but not in the year of sampling (1979). The soybean cultivars sampled were Sta. Rosa, UFV-1, Paraná, IAC-2, IAC-5 and Bossier. At each site 20 plants were collected and two nodules per plant stored in vials with $CaCl_2$. *Rhizobium* were isolated from the dry nodules using the isolation procedure of Vincent (1970).

Stylosanthes nodules were sampled within two major areas: native cerrado near Brasilia, where many spontaneous *Stylosanthes* plants can be found, and near Sete Lagoas and Uberaba where *Stylosanthes* spp. are cultivated after cash crops that are limed and fertilized. In neither area had these forage legumes been inoculated. The isolation of *Rhizobium* strains from *Stylosanthes* was carried out from fresh nodules, within 2-24 after harvest.

Two hundred and eighteen *Rhizobium* strains were isolated from soybeans and 149 from three *Stylosanthes* spp. (*S. guianensis*, *S. grandifolia* and *S. bracteata*). All isolates were plant-tested in sterilized Leonard jar assemblies or sterile test tubes (Norris, 1964) using either the soybean cultivar IAC-2 or the *Stylosanthes* sp. from which the strains had been isolated. For comparison nine strains of *R. japonicum* and eight strains for *Stylosanthes* spp., each used in commercial inoculants, were included in the study.

Level of resistance to streptomycin was determined using agar pour plates of yeast mannitol medium (Eagle, Levy & Fleishman, 1952) with a pH of 6.8-6.9. Increasing concentrations of streptomycin sulphate were sterilized by filtration and added to the agar after cooling to 45° C. The inoculant was standardized to an optical density of 100-120 Klett units. Six strains were streaked in star-like design on each plate, using four replicate plates for each streptomycin level. Growth of *Rhizobium* was observed after three to four days at 29° C in both the control (streptomycin-free medium) and the test plates. Single colony growth after seven days was considered negative. The level of streptomycin-resistance achieved by a strain was considered to be the highest level of antibiotic at which growth comparable to that of the controls was achieved in at least three of the four replicate plates.

RESULTS

Eighty-six percent of the *R. japonicum* strains isolated from cerrado soils were resistant to more than 80µg/ml of streptomycin sulphate (see Table 1). This suggests that streptomycin resistance is needed for survival and legume nodulation in cerrado soils and explains why strains 29 W and 587, each naturally resistant to relatively high levels of streptomycin, have performed so well in the cerrados (Peres *et al.*, 1981).

In Table 2 the streptomycin resistance of other *Rhizobium* strains used in commercial inoculants can be compared with that of strain 29 W and 587. The commercial strains that failed to nodulate soybeans in the cerrado soils showed a streptomycin-resistance level of only 5-20µg/ml.

The data in Tables 1 and 2 also indicate that *Stylosanthes* isolates, in general, are more sensitive to streptomycin than are soybean strains, with most commercial strains tolerating only 2 to 5 µg/ml of streptomycin sulphate. The isolates from native cerrado showed a near normal distribution in resistance to streptomycin, in which the majority of strains were resistant to only 5-20µg/ml of streptomycin. The isolates from cultivated cerrado areas showed an extended peak for resistance with 34 of 81 strains resistant to at least 40 µg/ml streptomycin. Six very highly resistant strains occurred in native cerrado, and one occurred among the commercial strains, indicating the need for further study. Strain Brla, which was the only one among the commercial strains which tolerated 600µg/ml streptomycin, was isolated from a hydromorphic soil formerly planted to rice in Rio de Janeiro State. This strain was tested in a field inoculation experiment in cerrado soil (A.M.Q. Escuder, personal communication) and was found to cause profuse nodulation and to increase dry weight of *Stylosanthes guianensis* by a significant amount.

DISCUSSION

The great proportion of spontaneous high level (> 80µg/ml) streptomycin-resistant *Rhizobium* strains found in the nodules of soybeans grown on cerrado soils, and the competitive advantage these strains have against common inoculant strains, seems remarkable. Spontaneous streptomycin-resistant strains are usually few (Gareth-Jones & Hardarson, 1979) and resistance levels of 5-10µg/ml are considered normal (Schwinghamer, 1967). A group of *R. japonicum* isolates obtained in Iowa State (USA) contained

TABLE 1: Levels of resistance to streptomycin among isolates of *Rhizobium* from *Glycine max* and *Stylosanthes* spp. found in cerrado soil.

Origin of strain	Host species	No. of strains tested	Streptomycin levels (µg/ml)									
			1	2	5	10	20	40	80	150	300	600
			Number of tolerant strains[1]									
Brasilia	*Glycine max*	114	–	–	1	1	0	18	47	43	1	3
Ituiutaba		8	–	–	0	0	0	0	6	2	0	0
Araxá		32	–	–	1	0	2	4	11	13	0	1
Uberaba		17	–	–	0	1	0	0	6	8	0	2
Uberlandia		47	–	–	0	0	1	1	23	16	2	4
	% of total		–	–	1	1	1	11	43	38	1	5
Cultivated cerrado[2]	*Stylosanthes* spp.	81	2	7	17	11	10	15	7	7	1	4
Undisturbed cerrado		68	3	8	15	18	13	4	1	2	0	4

[1]Tolerant to indicated streptomycin level when grown on YMA plates.

[2]Strains isolated from cultivated regions that had received lime and fertilizers.

TABLE 2: Levels of resistance to streptomycin among strains of *Rhizobium* used in commercial inoculants for *Glycine max* and *Stylosanthes* spp.

Inoculant for:	Strains tested	Level of resistance (μg/ml)			
		< 20	40-80	150-300	600
Glycine max	9	7	1[1]	1[2]	–
Stylosanthes spp.[3]	8	6	1	–	1

[1]Strain 29W

[2]Strain 587

[3]Strains for *Stylosanthes* inoculants were kindly provided by P.H. Graham (CIAT, Colombia), J. Döbereiner (EMBRAPA, Brazil) and W.P.L. Sandmann (Ministry of Agriculture, Zimbabwe).

19% resistant strains (100μg/ml) while 44% tolerated only 10μg/ml (Cole & Elkan, 1979). Mutation to streptomycin resistance was not observed to interfere with symbiotic performance (Josey *et al.*, 1979; Franco & Vincent, 1976) but competitive ability against other strains was reduced (Gareth-Jones & Bromfield, 1978). These studies, however, were performed in sterile test-tube cultures and did not take in consideration interactions and competition with the soil microflora.

Changes in the microbial equilibrium caused by the drastic modification of the ecosystem, when virgin soils are taken into agriculture, should be expected. The very high proportion of actinomycetes in cerrado soils (Coelho & Drozdowicz, 1979) indicates changes in favor of this potentially antibiotic-producing group, and a build up in streptomycin concentration seems possible. While streptomycin is readily inactivated in soil (Pramer, 1958), it can remain active in plant tissue for several weeks (Schwinghamer, 1967). Selective and active assimilation of this antibiotic by plant roots and its translocation to stems and leaves has also been reported (Crowdy & Pramer, 1955; Pramer, 1956). The possibility that streptomycin is produced on the root surface and assimilated by the plant can also not be discounted.

The use of antibiotic-resistant *Rhizobium* strains in inoculants, in conjunction with agricultural practices that have enhanced antibiotic production in soil and/or on the root surface, opens a promising new field of research.

REFERENCES

Cole, M.A. & Elkan, G.H. (1979) *Appl. Environ. Microbiol.* 37, 867-879.

Coelho, R.R.R. & Drozdowicz, A. (1979) *Rev. Ecol. Biol. Sol.* 15, 459-473.

Crowdy, S.H. & Pramer, D. (1955) Movement of antibiotics in higher plants. *Chemistry and Industry* (London), 160-162.

Damirgi, S.M. & Johnson, H.W. (1966) *Agron. J.* 58, 223-224.

Eagle, H., Levy M. & Fleischman, R. (1952) *Antibiotics Chemotherapy* 11, 563-574.

Franco, A.A. & Vincent, J.M. (1976) *Plant Soil* 45, 27-48.

Gareth-Jones D. & Bromfield, E.S.P. (1978) *Ann. Appl. Biol.* 88, 448-450.

Gareth-Jones, D. & Hardarson, G. (1979) *Ann. Appl. Biol.* 92, 221-228.

Goodland, R. (1971) *J. Ecol.* 59, 411-419.

Josey, D.P., Beynon, J.L., Johnston, A.W.B., & Beringer, J.E. (1979) *J. Appl. Bacteriol.* 46, 343-350.

Norris, D.O. (1964) Techniques used in work with *Rhizobium*. *In*: Some concepts and methods in sub-tropical pasture research. Farnham Royal Bucks Com. Agric. Bur. (Bull. 47). Pp. 86-193.

Patel, J.J. (1974) *Plant Soil* 41, 395-402.

Peres, J.R.R., Vargas, M.A.T. & Suhet, A.R. (1981) *Rev. Bras. Ci. Solo.* (In press.)

Pramer, D. (1956) *Arch. Biochem. Biophys.* 62, 265-273.

Pramer, D. (1958) *Appl. Microbiol.* 6, 221-224.

Schwinghamer, E.A. (1967) *Ant. van Leeuwenhock. J. Microbiol. Serol.* 33, 131-136.

Vargas, M.A.T. & Suhet, A.R. (1980a) *Pesq. Agropec. Bras.* 15, 343-347.

Vargas, M.A.T. & Suhet, A.R. (1980b) *Rev. Bras. Ci. Solo.* 4, 17-21.

Vincent, J.M. (1970) A manual for the practical study of root-nodule bacteria. Blackwell Sci. Publ., Oxford, England. 164 pp.

SURVIVAL OF STREPTOMYCIN-RESISTANT MUTANTS OF *RHIZOBIUM PHASEOLI* IN NONSTERILE SOIL

C. Vidor,[1] P.E. Lovato[1] and R.H. Miller[2]

Summary

Antibiotic-resistant mutants of *Rhizobium phaseoli* were used to follow fluctuations in the population density of this organism in five different soils. There were remarkable differences in cell survival rates in the different soils. In some soils cell numbers declined from 10^8 cells/g at time 0 to about 10^4 cells/g after 63 days incubation, presumably because of low pH and related factors. In the Vila soil, with a natural pH higher than the others, cell numbers declined by less than two log units during the incubation period. The implications of these results for nodulation and N_2 fixation in acid soil are discussed.

INTRODUCTION

Mutants resistant to antibiotics and fungicides have emerged as a useful tool for ecological studies of *Rhizobium* in soil (Obaton, 1971, Schwinghamer & Dudman, 1973; Danso & Alexander, 1974; Odeyemi & Alexander, 1977), particularly when introduced rhizobia bear antigenic similarities to the indigenous population.

Resistance to streptomycin has been the most common marker used in genetic and ecological studies of *Rhizobium* species (Brockwell, Schwinghamer & Gault, 1977). In most cases, effectiveness was maintained by the streptomycin-resistant mutants (Schwinghamer & Dudman, 1973).

The failure of nodulation in *Phaseolus vulgaris* in southern Brazil has triggered research to identify the factors limiting the symbiosis between this leguminous plant and its homologous *Rhizobium*. As a part of this research population changes and possible differences in survival of two streptomycin-resistant mutants of *R. phaseoli* inoculated into soils with different physical and chemical properties were examined.

[1] Depto. de Solos, UFRGS and IPAGRO, Secretaria de Agricultura, Porto Alegre, Brazil.
[2] Agronomy Dept., Ohio State University, Columbus, OH 43210, USA.

MATERIALS AND METHODS

Bulk soil samples from the surface (0-20 cm) were taken from five different localities in Rio Grande do Sul, Brazil. The samples were kept at field moisture, sieved (2 mm), and stored at 4° C.

The soils were incubated for three weeks with two levels of lime: zero, and half the amount required to raise the soil pH to 6.0, according to the modified SMP method (Mielniczuk, Ludwick & Bohnen, 1969). Selected physical and chemical properties of these soils are given in Table 1.

Rhizobium phaseoli strains 484-6 and 487-1, resistant, respectively, to 5000 and 500 μg of streptomycin per ml of medium were grown on yeast mannitol extract-agar (YMA) slants for one week, washed off with saline solution, dispersed with a Vortex mixer, and the cell population adjusted to approximately 10^9 cells/ml.

Aliquots of one ml from each cell suspension were individually added to replicate test tubes containing 10 g of nonsterile soil. The moisture was adjusted with sterile distilled water to 60% of the field capacity for each soil and maintained during incubation by periodically weighing each test tube and adding sterile distilled water as needed. All tubes were stored in the laboratory at room temperature.

Survival of the mutant strains was estimated by plate count on the day of inoculation and at 3, 5, 7, 14, 21, 42, and 63 days after inoculation using a selective medium (YMA) containing 500 μg of streptomycin/ml.

TABLE 1: Selected physical and chemical properties of the experimental soils.

Soil	Order	Sand (%)	Silt (%)	Clay (%)	pH	C (%)	N (%)	CEC (meq/100g)	Al^{3+} (meq/100g)
Bom Jesus	Haplumbrept	14	30	56	4.4	2.79	0.24	20.0	5.2
Vacaria	Haplohumox	8	31	61	4.5	2.64	0.20	16.4	4.5
Erechim	Haplorthox	2	21	77	3.9	1.52	0.13	13.7	5.4
Vila	Argiudoll	4	60	36	5.6	1.32	0.19	23.0	0.2
Tupancireta	Paleudult	82	8	10	4.4	0.68	0.05	3.7	0.9

RESULTS AND DISCUSSION

Both mutant strains showed similar survival patterns in soil; bacterial populations in all soils declined from 10^8 cells/g at time zero to 10^3-10^6 cells/g by day 63. The rate of the decline varied, however, according to soil type and pH (see Table 2).

TABLE 2: Survival of *R. phaseoli* strains 484-6 and 487-1, natural streptomycin resistant mutants, in nonsterile soils. Data expressed as log number of cells per g dry soil.

Soil	pH	Incubation period (days)							
		0	3	5	7	14	21	42	63
					Strain 484-6				
Erechim	3.9	7.92	6.22	7.73	7.63	4.84	5.00	–	3.48
	5.4	8.01	8.45	8.00	7.96	7.64	7.01	5.01	5.83
Bom Jesus	4.4	8.06	7.94	7.44	6.80	6.41	6.03	4.67	4.12
	5.2	8.01	7.82	7.43	7.68	6.76	6.31	4.67	4.61
Vacaria	4.5	8.02	7.54	7.02	7.12	6.52	5.60	5.52	4.15
	5.3	7.96	7.96	7.34	8.03	6.72	6.00	5.70	5.86
Vila	5.6	7.96	8.45	8.57	8.48	8.33	7.25	6.10	6.24
	6.1	8.07	8.46	8.49	8.44	8.00	7.45	6.60	6.26
Tupancireta	4.4	8.00	7.66	6.94	7.75	5.67	5.70	5.48	4.84
	5.4	8.02	8.55	7.60	7.75	6.83	6.48	6.12	5.78
					Strain 487-1				
Erechim	3.9	7.63	6.80	7.14	6.20	4.94	–	3.48	3.60
	5.4	7.76	7.63	7.40	7.40	7.31	7.13	5.90	5.94
Bom Jesus	4.4	7.63	6.86	6.88	6.34	6.10	5.32	4.60	3.36
	5.2	7.70	6.99	6.89	7.43	6.41	6.05	5.20	4.45
Vacaria	4.5	7.70	6.78	6.41	6.36	5.90	5.33	4.45	3.76
	5.3	7.74	7.52	7.53	6.89	7.16	6.91	5.90	5.95
Vila	5.6	7.63	8.20	8.00	7.50	7.70	7.38	7.04	6.96
	6.1	7.23	8.20	8.08	7.61	7.63	7.51	6.95	6.97
Tupancireta	4.4	7.50	6.93	6.26	6.57	4.84	5.23	4.11	3.00
	5.4	7.54	8.34	7.88	7.65	7.57	7.33	5.89	5.89

In some unlimed soils (e.g., the Erechim soil) cell populations were reduced by more than four log units in the unlimed treatment, with liming definitely beneficial to *Rhizobium* survival. By contrast, *Rhizobium* survival in the Vila soil, where the natural pH was higher, was not affected significantly by liming.

The poor response to liming in the Bom Jesus soil could be due to the high organic matter content of this soil; liming may have stimulated the growth of antagonistic micro-organisms. Vincent (1974) reported that other soil micro-organisms could share the advantage of raised pH in nonsterile soils and hence depress *Rhizobium* multiplication.

The effect of low pH on different species of *Rhizobium* has been studied extensively (Vincent, 1974; Munns, 1977). Some species are highly sensitive to pH below 5.0, whereas others are tolerant even at pH around 4.0 (Graham & Parker, 1964). According to Nutman (1972), nodule formation is much more sensitive to low pH than the *Rhizobium* strain itself. While this in undoubtedly true, several recent reports have suggested a close correlation between ability to survive in acid medium and the strain's capacity to nodulate its host legume in acid soils (Munns *et al.*, 1979; P.H. Graham, personal communication). In this experiment inoculant levels were above those normally used. While survival levels undoubtedly reflected this, the rate of decline in soil *Rhizobium* levels was not great, and even at more conventional rates of inoculation, enough cells should have been available for the critical period of root hair infection and nodulation.

In soils, acidity cannot be viewed as the exclusive action of the hydrogen ion concentration, but rather as an "integrated soil acidity," involving acidity, calcium deficiency, aluminum toxicity, and manganese toxicity, as well as organic matter content (Munns, 1977). Soil properties, therefore, may play an important role in ameliorating or intensifying the action of low soil pH.

REFERENCES

Brockwell, J., Schwinghamer, E.A. & Gault, R.R. (1977) *Soil Biol. Biochem.* 9, 19-24.

Danso, S.K.A. & Alexander, M. (1974) *Soil Sci. Soc. Amer. Proc.* 38, 86-89.

Graham, P.H. & Parker, C.A. (1964) *Plant Soil* 20, 383-396.

Odeyemi, O. & Alexander, M. (1977) *Soil Biol. Biochem.* 9, 247-251.

Obaton, M. (1971) *C.R. Acad. Sci. Paris. Série D,* 272, 2630-2633.

Munns, D.N. (1977) Soil acidity and related factors. *In*: Exploiting the legume-*Rhizobium* symbiosis in tropical agriculture, J.M. Vincent, A.S. Whitney & J. Bose (Eds.). Univ. Hawaii Coll. Trop. Agric. *Misc. Publ.* 145. Honolulu, HI, USA. Pp. 211-236.

Munns, D.N., Keyser, H.H., Fogle, V.W., Hohenberg, J.S., Righetti, T.L., Lauter, D.L., Zaroug, M.G., Clarkin, K.L., & Whitacre, K.W. (1979) *Agron. J.* 71, 256-260.

Mielniczuk, J., Ludwick, A. & Bohnen, H. (1969) Recomendacão de adubo e calcário para os solos e culturas do Rio Grande do Sul. Univ. Fed. Rio Grande do Sul, Fac. Agron., Porto Alegre, Brazil. Boletin Técnico No. 2, 29p.

Nutman, P.S. (1972) *IAEA Rept.* 149, 55-84.

Schwinghamer, E.A. & Dudman, W.F. (1973) *J. Appl. Bact.* 36, 263-272.

Vincent, J.M. (1974) Root-nodule symbioses with *Rhizobium*. *In*: The biology of nitrogen fixation, A. Quispel (Ed.). North-Holland Research Monographs, Frontiers of Biology. Pp. 265-341.

SURVIVAL OF COWPEA RHIZOBIA AS AFFECTED BY SOIL TEMPERATURE AND MOISTURE

Nantakorn Boonkerd[1] and R.W. Weaver[2,3]

Summary

Successful inoculation of peanut and cowpea can depend on the survival of rhizobia in soils undergoing marked fluctuations in temperature and water content. To determine the survival of rhizobia in sterile and nonsterile soils under various environmental conditions, two cowpea and two peanut strains were studied. Each was incubated under three moisture conditions; air dry, moist (-.33 bar) and saturated. The temperatures used were 25 and 35°C for nonsterile soil and 40°C for sterile soil. Populations were measured periodically for 45 days. Strain 201 survived relatively well under all environmental conditions in nonsterile soil. The 35°C temperature in conjunction with the air dry or saturated soil was the most detrimental to survival. At this temperature, the populations of strains T-1, 309 and 3281 declined by as much as 99% during the 45 days of incubation. In moist sterilized soil, the populations of all strains except CB756 (replacing 3281 in this experiment) increased during the two-week incubation. All strains declined in number when incubated in sterile dry soil. However, in contrast to the nonsterile soil, the populations did not decline under saturated soil conditions.

INTRODUCTION

Some effects of environmental stress on *Rhizobium* survival have been reported. Day *et al.* (1978) reported that some cowpea rhizobia were able to survive on seed at 45°C for three days, whereas other strains survived poorly at 42°C and did not survive at 45°C. Wilkins (1967) found strains isolated from a dry area with high temperatures were better survivors at high

[1] Dept. Agriculture, Bangkhen, Bangkok - 9, Thailand.

[2] Dept. Soil & Crop Sciences, Texas A&M University, College Station, TX, USA.

[3] The financial support of USAID under project AG/TAB 610-9-76 is gratefully acknowledged.

temperatures than strains isolated from cooler areas. Survival of cowpea rhizobia on seed (Herridge & Roughley, 1974) and in inoculants (Wilson & Trang, 1980) was better at 25° C than at 35° C or above. Several investigators (Marshall, 1964; Chatel & Parker, 1972; Bushby & Marshall, 1976; Philpotts, 1977) have reported that slow-growing rhizobia are comparatively more resistant to high soil temperatures than *R. trifolii* and *R. meliloti.* Moisture level in soil is also important for survival of rhizobia. Pena-Cabriales & Alexander (1979) reported the decline of *R. japonicum* populations in soil to be biphasic with initial, rapid decline as the soil dried, and subsequent slow decline in viability when soil was relatively dry. Osa-Afiana & Alexander (1979) reported that *R. trifolii* and *R. japonicum* survived better at 10% soil moisture content than at 22%, 35% or 40%. Mahler & Wollum (1980) found the survival of *R. japonicum* to be from one to three orders of magnitude lower under water potentials of -15 bars than when soil was incubated near field capacity.

Survival of *R. japonicum* strains in sterile and nonsterile soils was compared by Vidor & Miller (1980) who found all strain numbers increased about 100-fold in sterile soil but decreased about 10-fold in nonsterile soil. Our objective was to determine changes in the population of cowpea rhizobia as a function of moisture and temperature conditions in both sterile and nonsterile soils.

MATERIALS AND METHODS

Survival of cowpea rhizobia under nonsterile conditions was studied in two soils, one from Thailand and one from Texas. The Thai soil used was a sandy loam with pH 5.7. The Texas soil was a sandy clay loam with pH 6.8. Four strains of cowpea rhizobia were selected: 3281 (n15), TAL 309, 201 (Thailand) and T-1 (Texas A&M). Three moisture regimes (dry, - 0.33 bar, and saturated) and two temperatures (25° C and 35° C) were used. All treatments were replicated twice.

Only the Thai soil was used for the sterile soil experiment. In this experiment strain 3281 (n15) was replaced by CB756. The moisture regimes were as before, but an incubation temperature of 40° C was used. All treatments were replicated twice.

Each strain of *Rhizobium* was inoculated into either 10 g samples of soil in small plastic bags (nonsterile soil) or small test tubes with plastic caps (sterile soil); then their moisture content adjusted to the desired level by the addition of sterile distilled water or by drying. The samples were incubated for periods of 0, 5, 15, and 45 days; then enumerated by either the MPN plant-infection technique with siratro (*Macroptilium atropurpureum* (D.C.) Urb) (Weaver & Frederick, 1972) or by plate count.

RESULTS AND DISCUSSION

Nonsterile soils

As no statistically significant differences (0.05 level) in the survival of rhizobia in the two soils were obtained, the results were averaged. The composite data for each treatment are provided in Table 1.

TABLE 1: Survival of cowpea rhizobia in nonsterile soil incubated at different temperatures and moistures.[1]

Strains	Moisture status	Temperature							
		25° C				35° C			
		Incubation time (days)				Incubation time (days)			
		0	5	15	45	0	5	15	45
		(log. no. per gram soil)							
201	Dry	4.37	4.11	3.92	3.80	4.37	3.24	3.63	3.53
	Moist	4.37	5.00	4.49	4.39	4.37	4.80	3.93	3.95
	Saturated	4.37	4.38	4.46	3.81	4.37	3.99	3.56	2.89
T-1	Dry	4.23	4.07	3.29	2.69	4.23	3.42	2.43	2.82
	Moist	4.23	4.63	4.49	4.72	4.23	4.54	3.96	3.92
	Saturated	4.23	4.39	3.61	4.06	4.23	3.66	2.46	2.30
309	Dry	4.17	3.75	3.43	3.93	4.17	3.24	3.11	2.57
	Moist	4.17	4.59	4.72	4.34	4.17	4.80	3.73	3.43
	Saturated	4.17	3.42	3.98	3.83	4.17	3.06	2.93	1.43
3281	Dry	4.35	3.71	3.23	3.08	4.35	3.80	2.90	2.64
	Moist	4.35	4.61	4.03	3.96	4.35	3.23	2.57	1.95
	Saturated	4.35	4.14	3.03	3.26	4.35	3.23	2.57	1.95

[1]Each number represents an average of four samples.
The C.V. is 16 % and the L.S.D. (.05) is 1.25.

In moist soil (– 0.33 bars) the numbers of strain 201 were increased after five days of incubation at both 25° C and 35° C. By 15 days of incubation at 35° C the population had declined to slightly below the initial numbers, and this level was maintained for the following 30 days. However, at 25°C the rhizobial numbers remained higher than the initial numbers for the entire experimental period. Strain 201 also survived well at 25° C when incubated in either dry or saturated soil but showed reduced survival at 35° C under both dry and saturated conditions. This notwithstanding, the population remained relatively large.

Survival of strain T-1 in moist soil at either temperature was similar to that of strain 201. The rhizobial numbers in dry soil at 25° C and in dry and saturated soil at 35° C decreased more rapidly for strain T-1 than for strain 201. The populations of strain TAL 309 at 25° C were similar to those of strain 201 for all moisture conditions, but at 35° C, the population changes were similar to those of strain T-1. Survival of strain 3281 in moist soil at 25° C was similar to that of the other strains but in dry or saturated soil the population declined somewhat more. At 35° C, the population decline was similar to that of the other strains.

The data show good survival of all strains tested in moist soil (—0.33 bar) at 25° C. At this temperature strains 201 and 309 also survived well in dry and saturated soil conditions but strains T-1 and 3281 were affected by the stress conditions.

At 35° C, survival of all strains at —0.33 bar was again satisfactory although numbers had declined slightly by day 45. Under moisture stress, the population of all strains except 201 was approximately an order of magnitude lower. Strain 201 was originally isolated from a relatively hot environment.

Sterile soil

Survival of cowpea strains in sterile soil is illustrated in Table 2. The population of strains 201 and T-1 in moist soil increased from 10^7 to 10^8 within five days and was maintained for 45 days, but for strain 309, the increase was less dramatic. In contrast to other strains, cell numbers of CB756 decreased approximately 1 log by 45 days.

All strains survived well in saturated sterilized soil at 40° C, but populations did not significantly increase. Under dry conditions the population of all strains decreased at least an order of magnitude within five days. Strain T-1 was most severely affected; its population decreased more than two orders of magnitude within five days and three orders of magnitude within 45 days.

The results of this investigation indicate that dry and hot soil conditions affect the survival of cowpea rhizobia. Under these conditions, the order of survival was: 201 > CB756 >309 > T-1. Day *et al.* (1978) observed that strain NGR9 could survive on seed for three days at 45° C, whereas other strains including CB756 failed to survive. The data on survival of cowpea rhizobia in this study support the results of Vidor & Miller (1980) and indicate that abiotic factors do not limit survival or rhizobia in moist soil exposed to moderate temperatures.

TABLE 2: Survival of cowpea rhizobia in sterile soil incubated under different moistures stresses at 40° C.[1]

Strain	Moisture status	Incubation time (days)			
		0	5	15	45
		(log. no. per gram soil)			
201	Dry	7.53	6.53	6.25	6.41
	Moist	7.53	8.15	8.20	8.17
	Saturated	7.53	7.32	7.28	7.92
T-1	Dry	7.53	4.99	5.00	4.30
	Moist	7.53	8.15	8.20	8.17
	Saturated	7.53	7.32	7.28	7.92
309	Dry	7.25	6.32	6.28	5.43
	Moist	7.25	7.30	7.66	7.36
	Saturated	7.25	6.80	6.84	6.84
CB756	Dry	7.61	6.40	5.97	5.93
	Moist	7.61	7.46	7.17	6.32
	Saturated	7.61	7.17	6.662	7.94

[1]Average standard deviation ± 0.32.

Survival of cowpea rhizobia was good in moist soil, whether or not it was sterilized before inoculation. Under saturated conditions the survival of all rhizobial strains in nonsterile soil at 35°C was poor but survival was good in sterile soil at 40°C. This suggests that the death of rhizobia in nonsterile, flooded soil may be due to biotic effects as suggested by Osa-Afiana & Alexander (1979) who indicated that populations of indigenous protozoa increase appreciably in saturated soil, and that the increase coincided with a rapid decline in numbers of rhizobia.

REFERENCES

Bushby, H.V.A. & Marshall, K.C. (1976) Some factors affecting the survival of root-nodule bacteria on desiccation. *Soil Biol. Biochem.* 9, 143-147.

Chatel, D.L. & Parker, C.A. (1972) Survival of field-grown rhizobia over the dry summer period in Western Australia. *Soil Biol. Biochem.* 5, 415-423.

Day, J.M., Roughley, R.J., Eaglesham, A.R.J., Dye, M., & White, S.P. (1978) Effect of high soil temperatures on nodulation of cowpea, *Vigna unguiculata*. *Ann. Appl. Biol.* 88, 476-481.

Herridge, D.F. & Roughley, R.J. (1974) Survival of some slow-growing *Rhizobium* on inoculated legume seed. *Plant Soil* 40, 441-444.

Mahler, R.L. & Wollum, A.G. (1980) Influence of water potential on the survival of rhizobia in a Goldsboro loamy sand. *Soil Sci. Soc. Amer. J.* 44, 988-992.

Marshall, K.C. (1964) Survival of root-nodule bacteria in dry soils exposed to high temperatures. *Aust. J. Agric. Res.* 15, 273-281.

Osa-Afiana, L.O. & Alexander, M. (1979) Effect of moisture on the survival of *Rhizobium* in soil. *Soil Sci. Soc. Amer. J.* 43, 925-930.

Pena-Cabriales, J.J. & Alexander, M. (1979) Survival of *Rhizobium* in soils undergoing drying. *Soil Sci. Soc. Amer. J.* 43, 962-966.

Philpotts, H. (1977) Effect of inoculation method on *Rhizobium* survival and plant nodulation under adverse conditions. *Aust. J. Expl. Agr. Anim. Husb.* 17, 308-315.

Vidor, C. & Miller, R.H. (1980) Relative saprophytic competence of *Rhizobium japonicum* strains in soils as determined by the quantitative fluorescent antibody technique (FA). *Soil Biol. Biochem.* 12, 483-487.

Weaver, R.W. & Frederick, L.R. (1972) A new technique for most-probable-number counts of rhizobia. *Plant Soil* 36, 219-222.

Wilkins, J. (1967) The effects of high temperatures on certain root-nodule bacteria. *Aust. J. Agric. Res.* 18, 299-304.

Wilson, D.O. & Trang, K.M. (1980) Effects of storage temperature and enumeration methods on *Rhizobium* spp. numbers in peat inoculants. *Trop. Agric.* 57, 233-238.

STUDY OF *RHIZOBIUM* IN THE LEGUME RHIZOSPHERE

M.P. Salema, C.A. Parker, D.K. Kidby,[1] and D.L. Chatel[2]

Summary

A selective method for the study of both fast- and slow-growing rhizobia, double-marked with resistance to streptomycin and chloramphenicol at relatively low levels, has been developed and tested.

Rhizosphere counts of marked *Rhizobium trifolii* WU 1 (= TA 1) on subterranean clover (*Trifolium subterraneum* (L.) cv. Dwalganup) and *R. japonicum* CB 1809 on soybean (*Glycine max* (L.) Merr.) were successfully made using this medium. In these studies, only 1% and 0.4%, respectively, of the marked WU 1 and CB 1809 cells applied to the seedling were present on the radicle of the host plant 24 h after radicle emergence. The cells that got into the rhizosphere multiplied faster than those on the seed, indicating a strong stimulation of inoculant rhizobia in the rhizosphere of its homologous host. It is suggested from these results that attention should not only be focused on applying large numbers of rhizobia to the seed, but also on those rhizobia that are capable of rapid colonization of the rhizosphere.

INTRODUCTION

Knowledge of numbers of rhizobia in the rhizosphere of the emerging root of a legume is important in understanding the potential of inoculant *Rhizobium* to initiate nodulation and nitrogen (N_2) fixation rapidly. Various methods available for the examination of soil and rhizosphere populations have been reviewed by Parker, Trinick & Chatel (1977). Direct agar plate count is the most convenient and accurate method of estimation of numbers providing that the growth of other micro-organisms can be suppressed. The aims of this study were to develop a selective medium for both fast- and slow-

---

[1] Dept. Soil Science & Plant Nutrition, University of Western Australia, Nedlands 6009, Australia.

[2] West Australian Dept. Agriculture, Jarrah Road, South Perth, Western Australia.

growing rhizobia, marked with resistance to relatively low levels of antibiotics, and to employ this medium in rhizosphere studies of rhizobia double marked with streptomycin and chloramphenicol (McKay, Salema & Kidby, 1979).

MATERIALS AND METHODS

Strains used

The parent strains were *R. trifolii* WU 1 (=TA 1), a commercial clover strain used in Australia, and *R. japonicum* CB 1809, a commercial soybean strain. Mutants of these strains were obtained as described by Schwinghamer & Dudman (1973). When mutants had acquired resistance to 200 µg/ml of streptomycin, they were exposed to chloramphenicol and isolates were selected that were tolerant of 50 µg/ml. The double-marked strains derived from WU 1 and CB 1809 are hereafter referred to as WU 1 str^r chl^r and CB 1809 str^r chl^r, respectively. Infectiveness and effectiveness tests on the mutants showed them to behave similarly to the parent cultures.

Selective medium

The medium used for the enumeration of the mutants consisted of (µg/ml) streptomycin sulphate, 200; chloramphenicol, 50; bacitracin, 50; actidione, 20; pimaricin, 10; and nystatin, 5 in Yeast Mannitol Agar (YMA) medium. The YMA was of the following composition: mannitol, 2.0 g; glucose, 3.0 g; sucrose, 5.0 g; K_2HPO_4, 0.5 g; NaCl, 0.1 g; $MgSO_4.7H_2O$, 0.2 g; $CaSO_4.2H_2O$, 0.05 g; NH Cl, 0.1 g; and Yeast Extract Powder (Difco), 1.0 g; agar (Difco certified), 20 g per 1000 ml of medium. The pH was adjusted to 6.8-7.0. Bacitracin was used in addition to streptomycin and chloramphenicol to suppress other soil bacteria, while actidione, pimaricin and nystatin were used to suppress fungal growth. The bacitracin and the fungicides did not suppress the growth of the marked strains when counted on this medium. The concentration of actidione could be increased to 100 µg/ml for WU 1 $str^r chl^r$ and 500 µg/ml for CB 1809 str^r chl^r without affecting numbers.

Rhizosphere counts

Subterranean clover (*Trifolium subterraneum* L. cv. Dwalganup) and soybean (*Glycine max* (L.) Merrill cv. Clark 63) were used as host legumes for WU 1 str^r chl^r and CB 1809 str^r chl^r, respectively. A 48-hour culture of WU 1 str^r chl^r and 72-hour culture of CB 1809 str^r chl^r were used to inoculate seeds. Cells were suspended in 2% methyl cellulose (Methocel) to adhere the rhizobia onto the seed (Salema *et al.*, 1981). Seeds were left to air dry for 1 hour before being planted in coffee cups with 300 g Carnamah gray sand moistened to 60% of its water-holding capacity (Piper, 1944). A control with uninoculated seeds was also included in the experiment. Cups with sub-clover were stored at 20°C, and those with soybean were stored at 28°C. Counts on the seed and emerging radicle were made using the Miles and Misra drop count technique (Vincent, 1970). Duplicate samples of 50 sub-clover seeds or seedlings and 10 soybean seeds or seedlings were vigorously shaken for 10 minutes in YM broth to wash off the rhizobia. Necessary serial dilutions were made in 9 ml deionized water. Seed counts for soybean after 48 hours could not be made because the germinating seeds had shed their seedcoat.

RESULTS

The uninoculated controls gave no growth of rhizobia on the selective medium, indicating that the medium used was successful in controlling resident unmarked rhizobia.

Changes in the numbers of WU 1 str^r chl^r on the seed and rhizosphere are shown in Figure 1a. There was overall decrease in numbers in the first 24h, followed by a relatively more rapid decrease in the ensuing 24. At 24h germination had just started. From 48h-72h numbers on the seed and radicle increased steadily. At 48h after sowing, only 1% of the total number of rhizobia on the seedling were actually in the rhizosphere; the rest were on the seed. The rhizobia on the radicle did, however, multiply more rapidly than those on the seed.

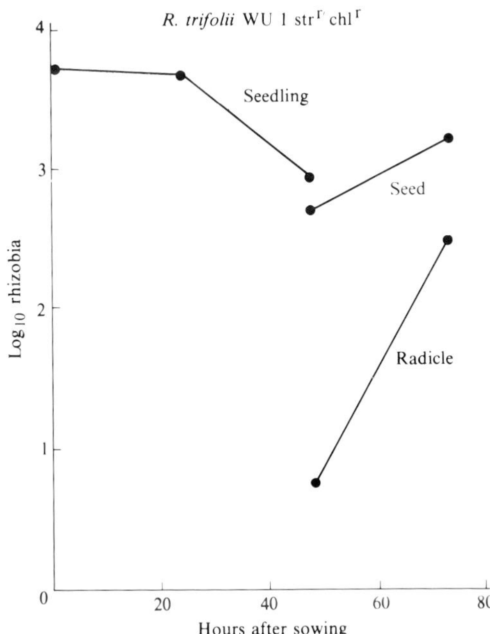

Figure 1a.
Changes of numbers of rhizobia on germinating seed. *R. trifolii* WU 1 str^r chl^r on subterranean clover seed.

Changes in the numbers of CB 1809 str^r chl^r (see Figure 1b) showed a similar trend, except that numbers started increasing on the seedling soon after germination. Only 0.04% of the rhizobia counted on the seedling after 48 were on the emerging soybean radicle.

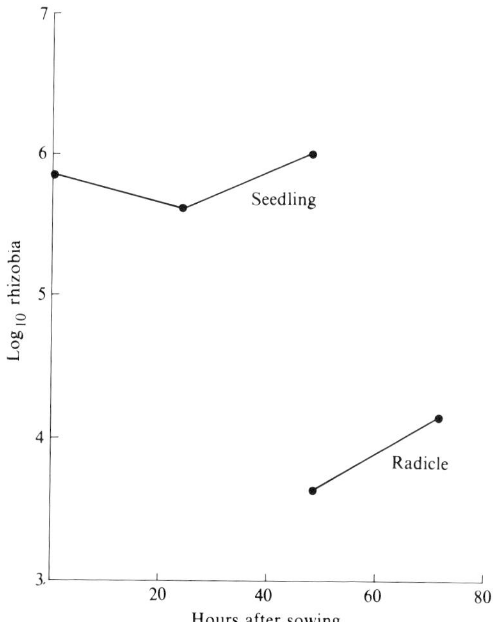

Figure 1b.
Changes in numbers of rhizobia on germinating seed. *R. japonicum* CB 1809 str^r chl^r on soybean.

DISCUSSION

The medium developed for this study required only that the rhizobia be marked at relatively low levels of antibiotic resistance. In this way, risks of altering infectiveness or effectiveness (Zelazna-Kowalska, 1971) were minimized. Apart from that, the medium has the other advantages of a selective medium—none of the ingredients or materials used in the experiment had to be sterilized, and the experiment was conducted in a nonsterile environment.

Radicle counts showed that only a small percentage of those rhizobia counted on the seedling were actually on the radicle, although they multiplied rapidly there. This is because the radicle contacts the inoculant rhizobia on the seed surface only at the point of emergence from the seed. This is a disadvantage of seed inoculation. Solid and liquid inoculants introduced directly into the seedbed (Brockwell, *et al.,* 1980) place the inoculum in a strategic position to contact the radicle as it grows through the soil containing the inoculum. The more rapid multiplication of rhizobia on the radicle than on the seed is another example of the so called "rhizosphere effect" (Bowen & Rovira, 1976); the small number of inoculant cells reaching the radicle emphasize the need to select inoculant strains capable of rapid multiplication in the rhizosphere.

The fall in numbers following germination of sub-clover seeds implies the liberation of seed-coat toxins (Hale & Mathers, 1977) when the radicle breaks the seed-coat. Soybean, the seed-coat of which is not known to harbor diffusable toxins for rhizobia, showed an increase in numbers, especially with the formation of the radicle which has a stimulatory effect on rhizobia.

REFERENCES

Bowen, G.D. & Rovira, A.D. (1976) *Ann. Rev. Phytopath.* 14, 121-144.

Brockwell, J., Gault, R.R., Chase, D.L., Hely, F.W., Zorin, M., & Corbin, E.J. (1980) *Aust. J. Agric. Res.* 31, 47-60.

Hale, C.N. & Mathers, D.J. (1977) *N.Z.J. Agric. Res.* 20, 69-73.

McKay, I.A., Salema, M.P. & Kidby, D.K. (1979) Genetic markers for the study of rhizobia in the field. *In:* Proceedings, Sixth Australian Legume Nodulation Conference. Perth, Western Australia. Pp. 37-41.

Parker, C.A., Trinick, M.J. & Chatel, D.L. (1977) Rhizobia as soil and rhizosphere inhabitants. *In:* A treatise on dinitrogen fixation. Section IV, Agronomy and ecology. R.W.F. Hardy & A.H. Gibson (Eds.). Wiley, New York, NY, USA. Pp. 311-352.

Piper, C.S. (1944) Soil and plant analysis. University of Adelaide, Adelaide, Australia.

Salema, M.P., Parker, C.A., Kidby, D.K., & Chatel, D.L. (1981) *In:* Proceedings, IV International Symposium on Nitrogen Fixation, Canberra, Australia.

Schwinghamer, E.A. & Dudman, W.F. (1973) *J. Appl. Bact.* 36, 263-272.

Vincent, J.M. (1970) A manual for the practical study of root-nodule bacteria. IBP Handbook No. 15. Blackwell Sci. Pubs., Oxford, England. 164 pp.

Zelazna-Kowalska, I. (1971) *Plant Soil* Special Volume, 67-71.

THE PHYSICAL EFFECT OF DRYING AND REHYDRATING *RHIZOBIUM* ON INOCULATED SEED

M.P. Salema, C.A. Parker, D.K. Kidby,[1] and D.L. Chatel[2]

Summary

Electron microscopy of *Rhizobium* on inoculated seed revealed that the drying process did not affect the morphology of cells of *R. trifolii* WU 1 (= TA 1). However, when dried cells were rehydrated, the cell envelope ruptured, resulting in distorted shapes and cellular materials oozing out from the cell.

The practical implications of these findings for the survival of *Rhizobium* on the seed and in soil are discussed.

INTRODUCTION

While it is well established that rhizobia die rapidly on the surface of seeds, little is known about the cause of such death. Since all methods for determining viability of dried cells involve rehydration it has proved difficult to demonstrate whether death occurs during drying, rehydration, or both. In this paper we report on the morphology of fresh, dried and rehydrated cells as observed by electron microscopy.

MATERIALS AND METHODS

Cells of *Rhizobium trifolii* WU 1 (= TA 1) were grown on yeast mannitol broth (YMB), pH 6.8-7.0, for 48 h. Fresh cells, cells dried on glass cover slips, and cells dried on seed and then rehydrated, were then examined under the electron microscope (Hitachi type HU-118) at 75 KV.

Preparation of cells was as follows:

Fresh cells: Cells were negatively stained on carbon coated grids with 0.4% uranyl acetate (Haschemeyer & Myer, 1972).

---

[1] Dept. of Soil Science and Plant Nutrition, Univ. of Western Australia, Nedlands, WA, Australia.

[2] Western Australian Dept. of Agriculture, Jarrah Road, South Perth, WA, Australia.

Dried cells: To avoid rehydrating the cells it was necessary to use shadowing. Cover slips were inoculated with broth cultures of *Rhizobium*, then air dried. They were then coated at 90°C with 100 A° of evaporated carbon and shadowed at 18°C with platinum in a Siemens vacuum evaporator. The carbon/platinum coat was floated off the glass in water, picked up on a carbon coated grid and observed under the E.M.

Dried and rehydrated cells: Seed of mung bean (*Vigna radiata* (L.) were inoculated with *Rhizobium*, air dried; then stored at 26°C for 24 h. The rhizobia were then rehydrated for 30 min by placing the seed in YMB, and the seed agitated gently to ensure resuspension. The rehydrated cells were negatively stained as already described. They were also shadowed to rule out possible effects of the stain on cell morphology.

RESULTS AND DISCUSSION

Fresh negatively stained and air-dried and stored cells were morphologically similar, and had the normal rod shape with three subpolar flagella visible.

Negative staining of rehydrated cells revealed, in addition to normal cells (see Figure 1a):

Collapsed cells with cytoplasmic membrane withdrawn from the cell wall (see Figure 1b),

Cells with distorted shapes (see Figure 1c), and

Cells with cellular materials oozing from the cell (see Figure 1d).

Shadowed rehydrated cells gave similar results, indicating that the observations with stained cells were not artifacts of staining. The shadowed pictures did not show withdrawn cytoplasm, as shadowing only provides cell outlines.

This study has shown that dried *Rhizobium* cells look morphologically similar to undried ones, but that on rehydration, major structural changes occur that must result in the death of many cells.

Chatel (1975) observed a fall in the population of *R. lupini* on sown, inoculated lupin seeds after successive wetting and drying of soil. Recently, Pena-Cabriales & Alexander (1979) reported reduction in population size of *R. japonicum* in a silt loam with each wetting and drying cycle. The results obtained in this study offer an explanation for the results of these workers and perhaps for other cases of death in bacteria associated with rehydration.

Can these effects be minimized? Clearly one should aim to reduce the number of cycles of wetting and drying, by planting when there has been sufficient rain to ensure seed germination, and not at the beginning of the rainy season when showers can be spasmodic.

Bad effects can also be avoided if freshly inoculated seeds are sown into moist soil while still wet, in order to avoid the initial drying and rehydration cycle. Although this is not feasible in mechanized, large-scale farming where operations like sowing take up to several days, it should be quite possible in

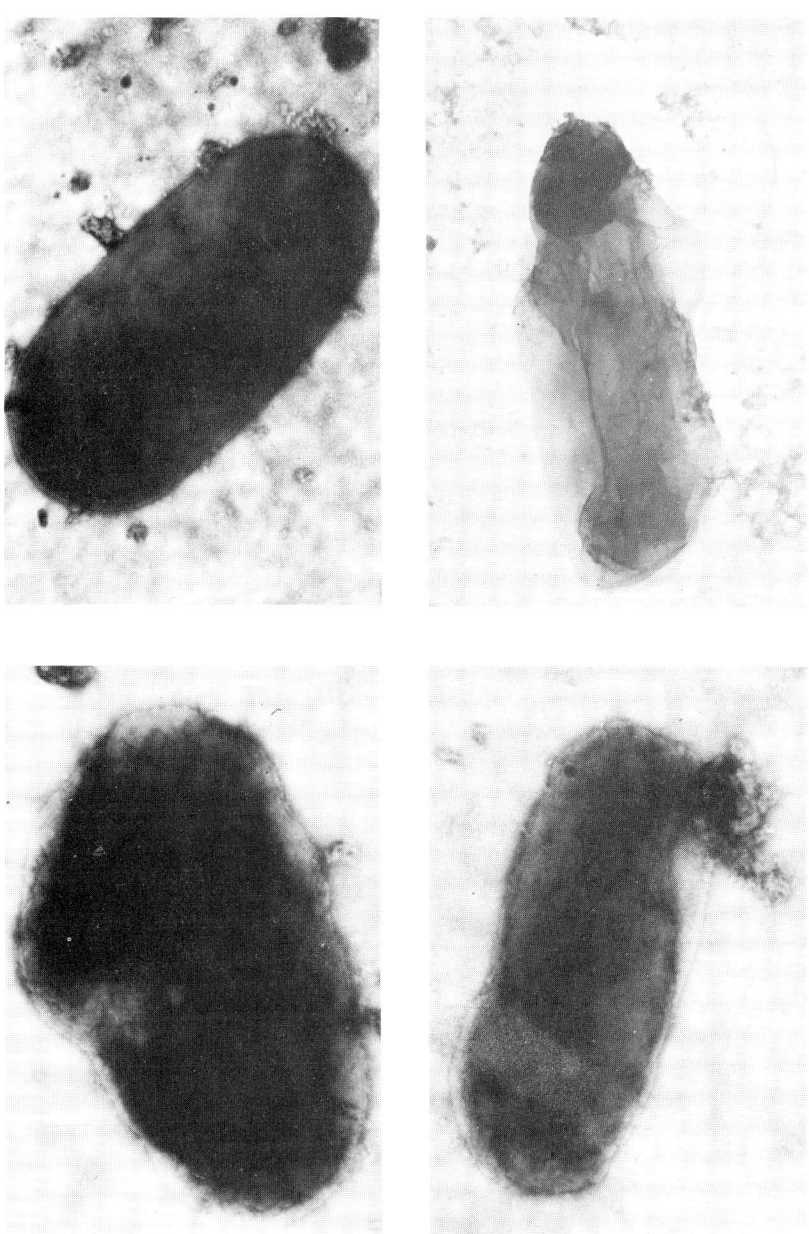

Figure 1. Rehydrated cells of *Rhizobium trifolii* WU 1 a) Normal looking; b) collapsed; c) distorted cellular materials x 45,000 (negatively stained); d) ruptured with oozing cellular materials x 45,000 (negatively stained).

small-scale peasant farming situations, where family labor is available and sowing can sometimes be done in one day.

The use of liquid inocula for direct application to the seedbed (Brockwell, Gault & Hely, 1979) is another alternative, which apart from minimizing the number of wetting and drying cycles, places the inoculum at a strategic position for the emerging radicle to be colonized by the inoculant rhizobia.

REFERENCES

Brockwell, J., Gault, R.R. & Hely, F.W. (1979) Field experiments with solid and liquid inoculants introduced directly into the seedbed. *In*: Proc. Sixth Australian Nodulation Conference, Perth, Western Australia, Australia. Pp. 54-60.

Chatel, D.L. (1975) The survival of *Rhizobium lupini* on lupin seed. *In*: Supplement to *Rhizobium Newsletter* 20, 62-64.

Haschemeyer, R.H. & Myers, R.J. (1972) Negative staining. *In*: Principles and techniques of electron microscopy. Biological applications, Vol. 2. M.A. Hayat (Ed.). Van Nostrand Reinhold Co., New York, NY, USA. Pp. 101-147.

Pena-Cabriales, J.J. & Alexander, M. (1979) *Soil Sci. Soc. Am. J.* 43, 962-966.

INOCULATION TRIALS

THE INTERNATIONAL BEAN INOCULATION TRIAL (IBIT): RESULTS FOR THE 1978-1979 TRIAL

P.H. Graham, C. Apolitano, R. Ferrera-Cerrato, J. Halliday, R. Lepiz, O. Menendez, R. Rios, S.M.T. Saito, and S. Viteri[1]

Summary

Response to the inoculation of dry beans (*Phaseolus vulgaris* L.) in Latin America has been extremely variable. Because of this a collaborative multi-location inoculation trial using ten highly efficient strains of *Rhizobium phaseoli* was initiated. This paper reports results obtained in 1978-1979.

Twelve IBIT trials were sown in seven countries. Significant yield responses (39-61% increase above control plants without nitrogen) were obtained at five sites, with the strains CIAT 632 and 640 generally among the most effective. CIAT 57 (syn. CC511) was disappointing. Extensive nodulation of uninoculated control plants occurred at several sites highlighting the problem likely to occur with native soil rhizobia in traditional bean-growing regions. At one site in Piracicaba, Brazil, one inoculant strain produced only 35% of nodules.

INTRODUCTION

Inoculation trials for dry beans (*Phaseolus vulgaris* L.) in Latin America have tended to use only a few strains of *Rhizobium phaseoli* and to include no strains of recognized efficiency. Inoculant quality has also been suspect at times. These and other factors have contributed to highly variable field inoculation results with this crop, a high proportion of investigators obtaining no response to inoculation (Pessanha *et al.,* 1970; Sistachs, 1970; Fontes, 1972; Nuñez & Valdes, 1976; Cuautle, 1979). To overcome these problems a collaborative multi-locational field trial was developed to evaluate the response of *P. vulgaris* to selected and highly efficient strains of *R. phaseoli.* This paper reports results from the first year of testing.

[1] c/o CIAT, AA 67-13, Cali, Colombia.

FORMAT OF THE 1978-1979 IBIT TRIAL

No attempt was made in this first trial to impose standard conditions. Guidelines were provided, but the scientist implementing the trial was free to select the site, determine the need for liming and/or fertilizer application and select the variety and the cultural system to be used. Plot size could also be modified according to labor availability and expertise.

For each location the experiment contrasted ten selected strains of *R. phaseoli* with -N and +N controls in a randomized block design having four replications. The inoculant strains were selected from among 60 isolates provided by collaborators, and all had been retested for nodulation and nitrogen(N_2)fixation at the Centro Internacional de Agricultura Tropical (CIAT). The strains used, and their histories, are detailed in Table 1. Inoculants were normally provided to collaborating scientists as high-quality peat cultures, air mailed or hand carried to their destination less than six weeks before the intended planting date.

Again because of labor availability and expertise the data taken at each site could be varied. Yield data was required, but most collaborators also gave details of nodulation and some $N_2(C_2H_2)$ fixation data.

TABLE 1: Strains of *Rhizobium phaseoli* used in the 1978-1979 IBIT trial.

CIAT No.	Original No.	Source
45	F310	IPEACS, km 47, Campo Grande, Brazil
57	CC511	CSIRO, Canberra, Australia
255	Z272	Isolated from the Danli region, Honduras
632	21	Isolated by R. Aguilera, ICTA, Guatemala
640	Z632	Isolated by P. Graham, La Buitrera, Colombia
676	3620	Rothamsted Exp. Station, England
893	M20	Isolated by G. Ocampo, Carmen de Viboral, Colombia
903	TAL182	NifTAL, Maui, Hawaii, USA
904	487	UFRGS, Porto Alegre, Brazil
905	127K17	Nitragin Co., USA, Courtesy of J.C. Burton

RESULTS FROM THE 1978-1979 IBIT TRIAL

Sites used in the 1978-1979 IBIT series are characterized in Table 2. As is obvious from this table, sites varied appreciably in pH, soil organic matter, and available P and in climate. The varieties used and the planting systems adopted were also highly variable. Thus, while bush bean cultivars were used in most trials, four trials were planted to climbing beans; in three of these beans were grown associated with maize.

TABLE 2: Sites used in the 1978-1979 IBIT trial.

Location of trial	Soil type	Soil pH	Organic matter (%)	P (ppm)	Rainfall (mm)	Mgst[2] (°C)
Chapingo, Mexico[1]	sand	6.6	1.11	27.0		
Chiclayo, Peru	clay loam	7.8	1.43	6.8	irrigated	22.6
Cochabamba, Bolivia	clay loam	5.7		4	176	18.5
Jalisco, Mexico	clay loam	6.0	2.0	2.9	473	
La Selva, Colombia	sandy loam	5.0	22.5	2.0		
Maui, Hawaii, USA	silty clay	5.7		1.0		
Piracicaba, Brazil-Site 1	clay loam	5.8	1.5	1.0	210	18.6
Piracicaba, Brazil-Site 2	clay loam	6.1	2.4	5.0	211	18.6
San Andres, El Salvador[1]	clay	6.3		76.0	260	24.5
Santander de Quilichao, Colombia	clay loam	4.9	7.1	1.8	irrigated	22.0

[1]Two experiments on same site.
[2]Mean growth season temperature (°C)

Yield data for the 12 experiments of the 1978-1979 series is included in Table 3. As might be expected from the diversity of soils and cropping systems, yields are extremely variable. This notwithstanding, a significant response to inoculation was obtained in five trials including two with relatively high soil *Rhizobium* populations. Yields of the best of the inoculated treatments at the five sites were 39.9-61.1% greater than those of -N control treatments. The yield response to inoculation with the strains CIAT 632 and CIAT 640 was consistently superior to that of the other strains. In contrast, CIAT 57 (syn. CC511) fared poorly. This strain has been widely used in inoculants and was considered a standard, but it gave very poor yields at the higher-temperature Santander location. In early trials of the 1979-1980 IBIT, this strain has again performed poorly, raising the possibility that it has undergone some modification of symbiotic properties.

The yield data is also of interest for the number of sites with low soil organic matter at which the -N controls yielded at least as well as those receiving N fertilizer. In our experience, this is sometimes due to a higher incidence of foliar pathogens on the more luxuriant +N plants. Disease-resistant cultivars or heavy pesticide applications are needed.

As might be expected from the long history of bean cultivation in Latin America, there were a number of locations at which competition for nodule sites limited the opportunity for response to inoculation. This is evident in the nodulation data provided in Tables 4 and 5. Thus, uninoculated plants in the first Chapingo trial averaged more than 100 nodules/plant. For this location R. Ferrera-Cerrato (personal communication) has concluded that less than 2% of nodules are likely to come from the inoculant strain. High nodule numbers/plant were also evident at the San Andres, Piracicaba 2, Jalisco, and Cochabamba sites. For the noncompetitive site at Piracicaba S.M.T. Saito (personal communication) has shown that the inoculant strains produced 50-100% of nodules. In the second trial on a bean soil having approximately 10^4 rhizobia/gram, the percentage of nodules derived from the inoculant varied from 35%-90%, with CIAT 904 the least competitive strain. This finding parallels other results at CIAT.

FUTURE OF THE IBIT SERIES

The 1979-1980 IBIT series with new strains of *R. phaseoli* included has already been distributed. For the 1981 trial we are proposing to use again the better strains from the previous two years of testing, but a number of them will be distributed as antibiotic-resistant mutants, the competitive abilities of which can be followed in soil. Simultaneously, we propose more intensive collection of additional isolates, with particular attention to those from acid soils or regions of high temperature. We do not propose to reissue already tested strains repeatedly, but will only continue the IBIT trials if additional select isolates can be identified.

TABLE 3: Yield (g/plant) by location for the 1978-1979 IBIT trial.

Location of trial	Yield -N	Yield +N	Yield range in inoculated treatments	Best strains	% yield increase with best strains
Chapingo, Mexico 1	11.0	9.5	7.7 - 11.1	640	0 n.s.
Chapingo, Mexico 2	6.7	5.4	5.0 - 7.2	632	7.4 n.s.
Chiclayo, Perú	48.5	38.8	30.1 - 51.6	255	6.3 n.s.
Cochabamba, Bolivia	8.6	7.6	6.8 - 9.1	893, 904	5.5 n.s.
Jalisco, Mexico	15.7	14.9	12.9 - 16.8	632, 640	7.3 n.s.
La Selva, Colombia	11.5	19.3	13.2 - 17.9	632, 640	56.3 *
Maui, Hawaii, USA	7.2	6.3	7.3 - 11.6	57, 893	61.1 *
Piracicaba, Brazil 1	30.2	37.4	27.2 - 44.8	632, 640, 903	48.3 *
Piracicaba, Brazil 2	1.3	3.6	1.0 - 1.9	903	46.1 *
San Andres, El Salvador	8.6	7.9	6.8 - 9.1	57	5.5 n.s.
San Andres, El Salvador	5.1	5.3	4.8 - 7.7	632, 640, 905	39.9 *
Santander, Colombia	5.3	5.5	4.8 - 6.1	632, 640	15.5 n.s.

TABLE 4: Nodule number per plant for locations in the 1978-1979 IBIT trial.

Location of trial	-N	+N	Range among inoculated treatments
Chapingo, Mexico 1	102.5	102.7	68.0 - 223.7
Chapingo, Mexico 2	147.2	154.7	64.5 - 173.7
Chiclayo, Peru	15.4	7.1	12.2 - 32.4
Cochabamba, Bolivia	26.7	26.2	31.0 - 205.2
Jalisco, Mexico	45.9	32.4	36.1 - 60.9
La Selva, Colombia		data not taken	
Maui, Hawaii, USA	0.1	0	0.1 - 26.2
Piracicaba, Brazil 1	13.9	3.6	24.6 - 50.7
Piracicaba, Brazil 2	50.2	42.2	50.5 - 88.1
San Andres, El Salvador 1	36.1	0.8	28.8 - 54.3
San Andres, El Salvador 2	22.8	0	33.3 - 40.3
Santander, Colombia		data not taken	

TABLE 5: Nodule fresh weight for locations in the 1978-1979 IBIT trial.

Location of trial	-N	+N	Range among inoculated treatments
Chapingo, Mexico 1	42.5	69.5	27.5 - 143.0
Chapingo, Mexico 2	131.0	95.5	57.0 - 176.5
Chiclayo, Peru	72.0	12.0	33.0 - 171.0
Cochabamba, Bolivia	7.5	11.0	15.4 - 79.5
Jalisco, Mexico	190.0	82.0	80.0 - 247.0
La Selva, Colombia		data not taken	
Maui, Hawaii, USA	0	0	0 - 18.6
Piracicaba, Brazil 1	11.8	2.4	20.6 - 73.4
Piracicaba, Brazil 2	104.8	10.6	93.4 - 183.8
San Andres, El Salvador	15.5	7.4	11.0 - 30.0
San Andres, El Salvador	15.0	0	14.0 - 26.0
Santander, Colombia	38.4	2.6	14.8 - 34.4

REFERENCES

Cuautle, M.E. (1979) Thesis, Colegio de Postgraduados, IEICA Chapingo, Mexico. 142 pp.

Fontes, L.A.N. (1972) *Revista Ceres* 19, 211-216.

Nuñez, R. & Valdes, M. (1976) Avances en la enseñanza y la investigación. Colegio de Postgraduados, IEICA, Chapingo, Mexico. Pp. 136-137.

Pessanha, G.G., Franco, A.A., Döberiener, J., Groszmann, A., & de Souza Britto, D.P.P. (1970) V Reunión Latinoamericana de *Rhizobium*. Rio de Janeiro. Pp. 36-45.

Sistachs, E. (1970) *Rev. Cubana Ci. Agric.* 4, 233-237.

MULTI-LOCATIONAL FIELD RESPONSES OF *PHASEOLUS VULGARIS* TO INOCULATION IN EASTERN AFRICA

S.O. Keya, V.R. Balasundaram, H. Ssali, and C. Mugane[1]

Summary

Field experiments undertaken in Kenya, Tanzania, and Uganda examined the response of *Phaseolus vulgaris* to inoculation. In Kenya a survey of 68 bean producing regions showed that most soils contained *Rhizobium phaseoli* and that bean plants could symbiose effectively with the native rhizobia. Despite this, yield responses to inoculation ranging from 7-47% were obtained in field trials. Among inoculation treatments best results were usually obtained using the commercial, imported inoculant culture.

INTRODUCTION

Phaseolus vulgaris L. is a major grain legume in Eastern Africa where production is mainly by small farmers. The yields of beans are relatively low with the national average in Kenya only 500 kg/ha. Beans are traditionally grown in rotations or mixtures with cereal crops, and little or no inoculation is practiced.

Efforts to increase yields through inoculation in East Africa have not been particularly successful (Macartney & Watson, 1966; Stephens, 1967; de Souza, 1969 Mughogho, 1979). Nevertheless, some responses to inoculation have been obtained in areas where beans have not been grown before (Macartney & Watson, 1966; de Souza, 1969). More recently Keya (1976) in Kenya and A. Hakizimana (personal communication) in Rwanda have shown that yield increases of up to 20% can be obtained through inoculation.

Beans, however, do respond to the application of nitrogen (N) fertilizers. In FAO-organized trials on farmers' fields in Kenya, responses to N fertilizer were recorded even for landrace cultivars. The current recommendation in Kenya is to apply 20 kg N/ha.

[1] University of Nairobi, Nairobi, Kenya.

TABLE 2: Effect of form of inoculant, cultivar and treatment on the yields of beans grown during the period September through December on a small farm near Turin.

Inoculant form	Cultivar	Treatment	Yield (kg/ha)
Granular	Rojo de Seda	CIAT inoculant	592 bc[1]
		Nitragin inoculant	697 ab
Pellet	Rojo de Seda	CIAT inoculant	563 c
		Nitragin inoculant	742 a
–	Rojo de Seda	Control	615 bc
		Fertilized	656 abc
Granular	Nahuizalco Rojo	CIAT inoculant	706 b
		Nitragin inoculant	1007 a
Pellet	Nahuizalco Rojo	CIAT inoculant	750 b
		Nitragin inoculant	1007 a
–	Nahuizalco Rojo	Control	981 a
		Fertilized	928 a
Granular	S-184N	CIAT inoculant	398 b
		Nitragin inoculant	487 b
Pellet	S-184N	CIAT inoculant	451 b
		Nitragin inoculant	504 b
–	S-184N	Control	481 b
		Fertilized	685 a
Granular	Porrillo 70	CIAT inoculant	908 b
		Nitragin inoculant	964 ab
Pellet	Porrillo 70	CIAT inoculant	909 b
		Nitragin inoculant	936 b
–	Porrillo 70	Control	873 b
		Fertilized	1066 a

[1]Any two means within a cultivar followed by the same letter do not differ at the 5 % level of probability as judged by DNMRT.

inoculation. The granular form of the Nitragin inoculant produced as high a yield as applied N on 'Porrillo 70', whereas the observed response to the pelleted form was not different from the control.

TABLE 3: Effect of cultivar treatment on the yield of beans grown during the period of September through December on a small farm near Quezaltepeque.

Cultivar	Yield (kg/ha)	Treatment	Yield (kg/ha)
Rojo de Seda	522 a[1]	CIAT	529 b[1]
S-184N	513 a	Nitragin	671 a
Nahuizalco Rojo	496 a	Control	366 c
		Fertilized	313 c

[1]Any two means within a cultivar or treatment followed by the same letter do not differ at the 5 % level of probability as judged by DNMRT.

TABLE 4: Effect of location and treatment on the nodule number and weight of five plants at 25 days after planting, for beans grown in the Ahuachapan, Quezaltepeque, and Turin trials.

Site	Treatment	Nodule number	Nodule weight (g)
Ahuachapan	CIAT strains	168	0.70
	Nitragin strains	166	0.51
	+N control	70	0.32
	-N control	67	0.32
Quezaltepeque	CIAT strains	161	0.68
	Nitragin strains	170	0.85
	+N control	115	0.35
	-N control	104	0.48
Turin	CIAT strains	132	0.65
	Nitragin strains	119	0.64
	+N control	84	0.38
	-N control	111	0.52

Bean yields were uniformly low, and unaffected by cultivar, at the Quezaltepeque site. Fertilization did not enhance yield though a significant response to inoculation was achieved with both the Nitragin and CIAT inoculants (see Table 3).

In these experiments fixation parameters varied markedly between sites, and in their relation to yield. Thus at Ahuachapan nodule weight was not affected by cultivar or treatment, while nodule number was negatively correlated with yield (r = -0.41); at Turin, nodule number was unaffected by treatment and nodule weight was negatively correlated with yield (r = -0.20); and at Quezaltepeque, positive correlations between nodule number (r=0.28) and nodule weight (r= 0.40) and yield were observed. This, together with the variable response to the two sources of inoculant used, and extensive nodulation of the uninoculated controls at each location (see Table 4) highlights the need for additional experimentation on the use of inoculant technologies under small-farmer production systems.

RESPONSE OF GROUNDNUT (*ARACHIS HYPOGAEA*) TO INOCULATION

P.T.C. Nambiar, P.J. Dart, B. Srinivasa Rao and H.N. Ravishankar[1]

Summary

Though groundnut is nodulated by a number of rhizobia belonging to the cowpea miscellany, the nodulation and nitrogen (N_2) fixation achieved under farmers' conditions is often inadequate. Studies at ICRISAT have attempted to overcome this by examining a large number of inoculant strains and various methods of inoculation.

Large variability between groundnut rhizobia in ability to fix N_2 exists, but poor correlations between nodule mass and plant dry weight gains can occur. Inoculum size is important with nodule number and distribution and N_2 fixation enhanced by heavier inoculation rates. Liquid inoculants have provided greater increases in yield than either granular or seed slurry inoculation, the latter method reducing germination and stand establishment. Several field trials at ICRISAT, both in the rainy and irrigated, post-rainy seasons, have given significant responses to inoculation, even though the soil already contains 10^4 rhizobia/g. The cultivar Robut 33-1 with strain NC 92 has given most consistent results.

INTRODUCTION

Though groundnut (*Arachis hypogaea* L.) is nodulated by rhizobia of the cowpea miscellany (Fred, Baldwin & McCoy, 1932), and can, under optimum conditions, fix most of the nitrogen (N_2) needed by the plant (Pettit *et al.*, 1975; Burton, 1976), nodulation in farmers' fields in southern India is generally poor. In one survey, 52 of 95 fields examined showed inadequate nodulation, with rates of N_2 (C_2H_2) fixation less than one-tenth that which can be obtained under reasonable field conditions. Poor nodulation and N_2

[1] ICRISAT, Patancheru P.O., Andra Pradesh 502 324, India.

fixation are undoubtedly one reason for low groundnut yields in India, currently averaging about 800 kg/ha.

ICRISAT maintains a collection of *Rhizobium* for groundnut and has experimented extensively with strain evaluation and inoculation method. This paper reports some of these studies.

MATERIALS AND METHODS

Pot trials using the methods detailed by Nambiar & Dart (1980) were undertaken to determine the nodulation and dry matter production achieved following inoculation with 14 selected strains for groundnut. N-free plants and plants supplied nitrate were used as controls in this study.

Similar methods were used to evaluate the number of rhizobia required to achieve profuse nodulation and active N_2 fixation in the groundnut cultivars TMV-2 (bunch), Kadiri 71-1 (runner) and Robut 33-1 (semispreading). Strain NC 92 was applied as a broth culture inoculant to the base of eight-day-old plants at inoculation rates ranging from 2.2 x 10^2 to 3.2 x 10^9 cells/seedling. Plants were supplied sterile, N-free nutrient medium during growth and were harvested 57 days after planting, when nodule number, total N/plant and shoot dry weight were determined. Plants supplied nitrate were again used as controls.

Inoculation trials with groundnut have been undertaken at ICRISAT since 1977. These have included a range of cultivars (TMV 2, Kadiri 71-1, Robut 33-1, Argentine, AH 8189, and MH2) and strains (5a/70, IC6006, ICG 60, NC 92, NC 43.3 and NC 7.2) and have used both granular and liquid inoculation. Fertilization in these trials has been at recommended local levels.

Finally, inoculation method has been studied using granular and liquid soil-applied inoculation in comparison with conventional slurry inoculation. All seeds in this trial were treated with thiram before planting.

RESULTS AND DISCUSSION

Response of groundnut to inoculation with selected strains of *Rhizobium* is shown in Figures 1a and 1b. Strains varied markedly in nodule development, and in ability to promote plant growth. While a good correlation between nodule development and plant growth was observed under the -N conditions of the experiment, the strains IC6083, IHP 100 and IHP 2 developed appreciable nodule mass without obvious benefit to the plant.

Tables 1 and 2 show the response of groundnut cultivars to inoculant level. From these results it is apparent that groundnut requires a heavy inoculation rate (10^7 rhizobia/seed) for adequate nodulation and N_2 fixation. Nodulation and fixation were reduced when only 10^4 rhizobia/seed were applied, while no primary root nodules and only a few secondary root nodules developed when only 10^2 rhizobia/plant were applied. The changing pattern of nodulation as

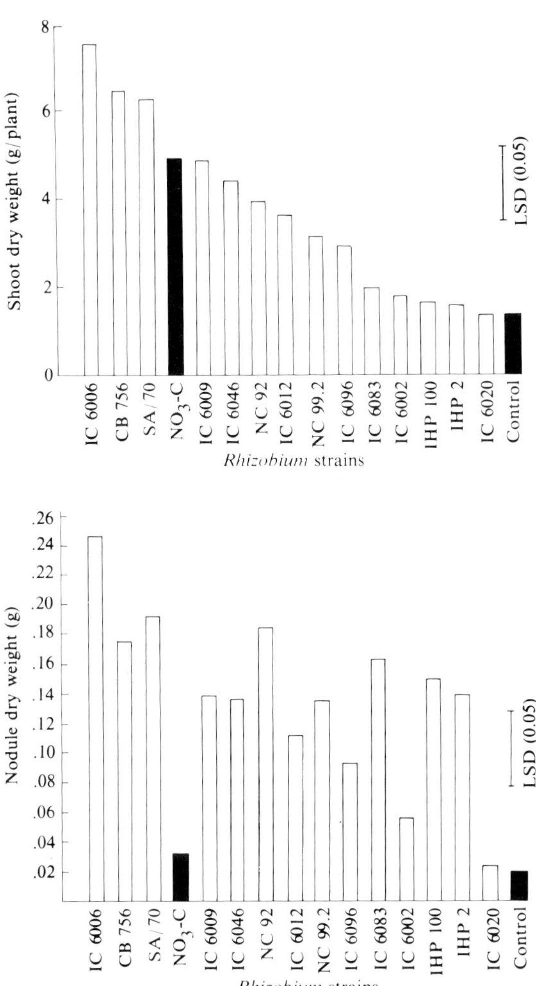

Figure 1: Shoot production and nodule formation by groundnut inoculated with different *Rhizobium* strains. Three plants per 20 cm x 20 cm pot.

the inoculation rate was reduced resembled the response to delayed inoculation reported by Dart & Pate (1959). Similar responses to inoculation rate are reported by Weaver & Frederick (1972) in soybean.

Table 3 summarizes the results of field inoculation trials conducted at ICRISAT from 1977-1980. Although response to inoculation was not always obtained, 'Robut 33-1', which is in the final stages of national release in India, gave substantial increase in pod yield in four of the eight experiments. Tables 4 and 5 show the excellent response of 'Robut 33-1' to inoculation with strain

TABLE 1: Influence of *Rhizobium* inoculum level on nodulation and N_2 fixation by groundnut cv. Kadiri 71-1.

Level of *Rhizobium* applied as broth (no./seed)	Shoot dry wt (g/plant)	Nodule dry wt (g/plant)	Total N (mg/plant)
3.2×10^9	3.38	0.13	73.2
5.5×10^7	2.38	0.12	50.3
4.8×10^4	1.08	0.03	18.6
6.1×10^2	0.97	0.02	14.3
Nitrate control	4.34	0	89.8
SEM ±	0.39	0.011	2.1
LSD (5 %)	1.13	0.031	21.7

TABLE 2: Effect of *Rhizobium* inoculum population on nodule dry weight production and N_2 fixation by groundnut.[1]

Rhizobium inoculum (cells/seed)	Nodule weight (mg/plant)		N_2 fixation (mg N/plant)	
	Robut 33-1	TMV-2	Robut 33-1	TMV-2
2.7×10^2	18	18	25	17
2.7×10^4	36	79	23	31
2.7×10^6	125	101	48	39
2.7×10^8	119	120	-	48
LSD[2] (5 %)	90		4.1	

[1]Harvested at 61 days after planting.
[2]For comparison within a particular cultivar.

NC92. One significant feature of those responses to inoculation is that they were obtained in fields containing more than 10^4 cowpea group rhizobia per gram of soil and uninoculated plants were well nodulated and yield levels were high.

Inoculation with a liquid culture applied to the soil below the seed proved superior to either granular or conventional slurry inoculation. Not only did the liquid inoculant cause fewer problems in the germination of seedlings (see Table 6), its use resulted in significantly enhanced grain yield (see Table 7).

TABLE 3: Summary of inoculation trials conducted at ICRISAT.

Year/season	Soil type	Cultivars	Strain	Pod yield response
Rainy season 1977	HF,[1] Alfisol	TMV-2 Kadiri 71-1	5a/70	Nil
Rainy season 1977	LF, Alfisol	Kadiri 71-1 Robut 33-1, TMV-2	5a/70	TMV-2, 25 %, Robut 33-1, 32 %
Rainy season 1977	HF, Vertisol	Kadiri 71-1 TMV-2	5a/70 IC 6006	Nil
Rainy season 1978	HF, Alfisol	Robut 33-1 Argentine AH-8189	5a/70 ICG-60 IC 6006 Mixture	Nil
Rainy season 1978	LF, Alfisol	MH-2 Argentine Robut 33-1	5a/70 ICG-60 6S Mixture	Robut 33-1, 26 % (NS)
Post-rainy season 1979	HF, Alfisol	MH-2 Robut 33-1 AH-8189	NC 92 IC 6009 Mixture	Robut 33-1, 28.5 %
Rainy season 1979	HF, Alfisol	Kadiri 71-1 Robut 33-1 AH-8189	5a/70 IC 6006 NC 43.3 NC 7.2 NC 92	Robut 33-1, 25.7 %
Post-rainy season 1980	HF, Alfisol	Robut 33-1	NC 92	Nil

[1]HF = High Fertility LF = Low Fertility.

TABLE 4: Response of groundnut yield (kg/ha) to *Rhizobium* inoculation in the 1978-79 post-rainy season, ICRISAT.

Cultivars	Inoculum strain			
	Uninoculated	IC-6009[1]	NC 92[2]	Mixture (IC 6009 + NC 92)[1]
MH-2	2220	1890	1940	2030
Robut 33-1	3510	3330	4520[3]	2810[4]
Ah-8189	2830	2860	2680	2810

[1]Inoculum applied as granule.
[2]Inoculum applied as liquid.
[3]Significant at the 1 % level.
[4]Significant at the 5 % level.

Coefficient of variation, 15 % ; LSD, 291 kg/ha.

TABLE 5: Effect of *Rhizobium* inoculation on groundnut yield (kg pods/ha) in the 1979 rainy season, ICRISAT.

Rhizobium strain	Cultivar		
	Kadiri 71-1	Robut 33-1	Ah 8189
5a/70	360	800	420
IC 6006	480	790	290
NC 43.3	460	960	480
NC 7.2	450	950	420
NC 92	570	1160[1]	480
Control	500	870	470

SEM ± 24 CV = 20%

[1]Significant at 5 % level.

TABLE 6: Effect of method of inoculation on percentage germination of groundnut.

Method of inoculation	Germination	
	ICRISAT Center	Solipur (outside ICRISAT station)
Control, uninoculated	83	77
Seed slurry inoculated	46	71
Liquid inoculant in furrow	98	79
Granular inoculant	73	57
L S D (5 %)	9.6	9.1
Coeficient of variation %	8	13

TABLE 7: Effect of different methods of inoculation on groundnut yield (kg/ha), 1980 rainy season, ICRISAT.

Rhizobium strain	Method of inoculation		
	Granular	Liquid	Seed
5a/70	1290	1770	240
NC 92	1020	1640	1020
6006	1000	1630	930
Mixture (5a/70 + NC 92 + 6006)	1050	1520	1000
SEM ±		134	
Uninoculated control		1345 ± 77.4	
Coefficient of variation		15 %	

CONCLUSION

The data presented above indicate that it is possible to obtain increase in pod yield of groundnut by inoculating with *Rhizobium* even in fields where a substantial native population already exists. It may be possible to achieve inoculation responses in many farmers' fields where nodulation is found to be poor, provided other major constraints which limit yields are overcome. Methods of applying inoculum in liquid or granular form below the seed need to be developed for the small farmer.

REFERENCES

Burton, J.C. (1976) Pragmatic aspects of the *Rhizobium*: leguminous plant association. *In*: Proc. First Internat. Symp. Nitrogen Fixation, Vol. 2. W.E. Newton & C.J. Nyman, (Eds.). Pullman, Washington State Univ. Press, Pullman, WA, USA. Pp. 429-446.

Dart, P.J. & Pate, J.S. (1959) *Aust. J. Biol. Sci.* 12, 427-444.

Fred, E.B., Baldwin, I.L. & McCoy, E. (1932) Root nodule bacteria and leguminous plants. Univ. of Wisconsin Studies, No. 52.

Nambiar, P.T.C. & Dart, P.J. (1980) Studies on nitrogen fixation by groundnut at ICRISAT. *In*: Proc. Internat. Symp. Groundnut, R.W. Gibbons (Ed.). ICRISAT, Patancheru, AP, India. Pp. 110-124.

Pettit, R.E., Weaver, R.W., Taber, R.A., & Stichler, C.R. (1975) Beneficial soil microorganisms. *In*: Peanut production in Texas, J.E. Miller, (Ed.). Texas Agricultural Experimental Station, Texas A&M Univ. College Stn., TX, USA. Pp. 26-33.

Weaver, R.W. & Frederick, L.R. (1972) *Agron. J.* 64, 597-599.

INOCULATION TRIALS ON GROUNDNUTS (*ARACHIS HYPOGAEA*) IN SUDAN

M.A. Hadad,[1] T.E. Loynachan [1] and M.M. Musa[2]

Summary

Field plots established on heavy cracking clays near Wad Medani, Sudan, examined the effect of inoculation method, rate, and depth of placement of inoculant on the nodulation and yield of two adapted groundnut cultivars, Ashford and Barberton.

Most probable number (MPN) counts with siratro as host indicated approximately 2 x 10^4 cowpea-group rhizobia/g of soil at Wad Medani. These were highly infective on groundnut, but did not supply the crop with all the nitrogen (N) it required. Thus, addition of 40 kg N/ha increased the yield of 'Barberton' by 38%, while 120 kg N/ha increased yields of 'Barberton' by 52% and of 'Ashford ' by 23%. The added inoculant had little effect on any trait associated with N_2 fixation. This might suggest the need for inoculant strains competitive with the naturally occurring rhizobia that are infective for groundnut.

A survey of 30 sites throughout Sudan indicated only one location — in the sandy soils of western Sudan — with less than 10^2 cowpea-type rhizobia/g of soil.

INTRODUCTION

Groundnuts (*Arachis hypogaea* L.) are both a source of protein for the local inhabitants and a major cash crop for the Sudan. Currently more than 385,000 ha are planted, but the area sown is increasing, and the crop could occupy several million ha in the near future if current rates of expansion are maintained.

Research in the Sudan on groundnut as a nitrogen (N_2) fixing legume has been limited (Musa, 1972; Muktar & Yonsif, 1979). Inoculation of groundnut with effective compatible rhizobia may result in yield increases, especially if

[1] Agronomy Dept., Iowa State University, Ames, Iowa, USA.

[2] Agricultural Research Corporation, Wad Medani, Sudan.

the indigenous strains are not effective (Ham, 1980). Deeper placement of the inoculant may be necessary to protect the rhizobia from surface temperatures as high as 60°C (Musa, 1972).

As Sudanese soils are known to be deficient in N (Said, 1973) a series of experiments was undertaken to test the response of groundnuts to inoculation and N fertilization at Wad Medani, and to survey outlying areas of Sudan to determine the incidence, and efficiency in symbiotic N_2 fixation, of native cowpea-type rhizobia in soil.

MATERIALS AND METHODS

Field study at Wad Medani

Initial experiments were undertaken at the Research Center, Agricultural Research Corporation, Wad Medani, Sudan. The soils were heavy cracking clays classified as Vertisols, containing free $CaCO_3$ and with a pH close to 8.5. The site was previously sown to cotton.

Two cultivars, Ashford, which is late maturing, semispreading, and alternately branched, and Barberton, an early maturing, sequentially branched cultivar, were used in a randomized complete block design having eight treatments (see Table 1). The inoculant used contained four groundnut *Rhizobium* strains (176A22 and 25B7 from the Nitragin Company, Milwaukee, WI; 3G4b4, from the USDA collection at Beltsville, MD; and TAL 309, obtained from North American Plant Breeders, Princeton, IL). The strains were selected on the basis of greenhouse results at Iowa State University (ISU) with the two Sudanese cultivars. Two rates of inoculum (10^4 and 10^8 rhizobia/two seeds) were applied to plots fertilized with P, K, S, and all the micronutrients except Mo, while the 10^8 treatment was applied both with the seed and 8 cm below the seed. The two rates of N (40 and 120 kg N/ha) were applied as ammonium sulfate.

Five plots each 3 x 9.6 m with five ridges 60 cm apart, were sown for each treatment, and irrigated within 24 h after application of the inoculant. Two samplings were made to monitor growth during the season; the first at the flowering stage (six weeks after sowing) and the second during pod filling (10 weeks after sowing). Both samples were taken from 50 cm of the outer two rows. Nodule number, nodule dry weight, shoot dry weight, and N content were determined. Harvest of the plots for yield was at 90 days after sowing of 'Barberton' and 120 days after sowing for 'Ashford'.

Most probable number (MPN) counts for the Wad Medani location used siratro (*Macroptilium atropurpureum*) as the test plant, and the method detailed by Vincent (1970).

TABLE 1: Summary of treatments imposed in the field study.

Treatment	*Rhizobium*	N P K	S and micronutrients[1]
1	–	–	–
2	–	1 – –	–
3	–	3 1 1	1
4	10^4/2 seeds	– 1 1	1
5	10^8/2 seeds	– 1 1	1
6	10^8/2 seeds	– – –	–
7	10^8/2 seeds	– 1 1	–
8[2]	10^8/2 seeds[2]	– – –	–

[1]Fertilizer rates are as follows:

N_1: 40 kg N per ha as $(NH_4)_2SO_4$; N_3 : 120 kg N per ha as $(NH_4)_2SO_4$
P_1: 40 kg P_2O_5 per ha as triple superphosphate
K_1: 40 kg K_2O per ha as mutriate of potash

S and micronutrients

S : 45 kg S per ha as elemental S
B : 0.5 kg B per ha as borax
Fe: 0.5 kg Fe per ha as chelate (6 % Fe)
Cu: 2 kg Cu per ha as $CuSO_4.5H_2O$
Mn: 15 kg Mn per ha as $MnSO_4.H_2O$
Zn: 0.6 kg Zn per ha as chelate

[2]Deep placement.

Survey of outlying regions

To gain a better understanding of groundnut rhizobia throughout Sudan, samples were collected from the surface 15 cm of soil from outlying regions of the Sudan and taken to Wad Medani for a MPN determination using siratro as the test plant. The history of the field at each site was obtained. Also at Wad Medani and at several of the outlying areas, quantities of the inoculum previously used in the Wad Medani study were supplied to cooperators who established observation trials with a varying number of cultivars with and without inoculation. The inoculated cultivars were grouped together to minimize contamination while the same cultivars, without inoculation, were grown in an adjacent area. Fifty cm of the planted rows were dug for evaluation of nodulation and to determine an average shoot dry weight of the inoculated and control plants. This study was designed mainly to gain survey information and the treatments were not replicated.

RESULTS AND DISCUSSION

Field study at Wad Medani

Native rhizobia and the need for inoculation

MPN counts with siratro showed that the Wad Medani site contained approximately 2 x 10^4 rhizobia/g in the top 15 cm at planting. Many of these rhizobia were apparently infective with both groundnut varieties tested, as there was heavy nodulation of all control plots (see Table 2). Despite this, plants in the control plots of both cultivars were decidedly chlorotic during the early flowering stage when compared with N-fertilized treatments. This indicated both the inefficiency of the native rhizobia in supplying the plants with sufficient N, and the need for N fertilization or inoculation with effective and competitive strains of *Rhizobium*. Pod yields at harvest were 4638, 5628, and 5725 kg/ha respectively for the control, 40, and 120 kg/ha treatments with 'Ashford'; and 2335, 3229, and 3559 kg/ha, respectively, for the same treatments with 'Barberton'. By evaluating orthogonal comparisons (treatment 1 vs. treatment 2, etc.), 40 kg N/ha with 'Barberton' produced greater yield than the control, and at 120 kg N/ha (treatment 3 vs. treatment 4), yields of both 'Ashford' and 'Barberton' were statistically increased over the control.

Response to inoculation

Little benefit from inoculation was observed in this study (see Table 2), and yields following inoculation were not significantly different from control plots. Since identification of nodule rhizobia was not attempted in this study, the ability of the introduced rhizobia to compete for nodule sites under the high-temperature conditions of this trial cannot be evaluated. Further studies with marked or identifiable strains are required.

Survey of outlying regions

MPN counts with siratro as host showed that cowpea-group rhizobia abounded in most of the soils tested, irrespective of the time since peanuts were last planted (see Table 3). The one exception was a sandy soil from El Obeid which contained only 3 x 10^2 rhizobia/g of soil. High numbers were even found in virgin soils not previously planted to groundnut. Apparently the native leguminous plants in the Sudan can serve as an inoculant source.

Trial plantings were made at Wad Medani, Abu Naama, Rahad, El Obeid, and Sennar. Fourteen experimental cultivars were included in the Medani study, and six at Rahad. Since the study was not replicated, only general observations can be made. All of the cultivars at the five locations were nodulated without the addition of an inoculant (see Table 4). It appears, however, that there was a slight advantage in overall nodule numbers to added inoculum. The variety MH383, at Wad Medani and Rahad, had considerably more nodules with inoculation. This is a variety that is being considered for replacement of 'Ashford' as an irrigated variety within the country. Overall growth of shoots at all sites appears to have benefited from inoculation.

TABLE 2: The effect of added inoculant on nitrogen-fixing traits.

Trait		6 weeks after sowing		10 weeks after sowing	
		'Ashford'	'Barberton'	'Ashford'	'Barberton'
Lateral-root nodules (no/plant)					
Control	(trt 1)	39.2 a[2]	20.4 abc	55.7 a	16.2 a
1N	(trt 2)	36.7 a	11.0 c	49.6 a	24.4 a
3N	(trt 3)	22.6 a	7.5 c	56.1 a	17.6 a
10^8	(trt 6)	41.9 a	16.6 abc	26.2 a	23.7 a
10^8	(trt 8)[1]	42.0 a	33.0 ab	53.5 a	24.1 a
Main-root nodules (no/plant)					
Control	(trt 1)	33.0 ab	24.1 a	45.4 a	17.0 a
1N	(trt 2)	30.8 ab	14.2 a	43.2 a	13.2 a
3N	(trt 3)	17.2 b	12.2 a	67.6 a	15.6 a
10^8	(trt 6)	25.4 ab	14.7 a	36.5 a	17.6 a
10^8	(trt 8)[1]	45.0 a	25.2 a	52.1 a	24.9 a
Total nodule dry wt (mg/plant)					
Control	(trt 1)	19 b	11 a	395 a	227 a
1N	(trt 2)	15 b	9 a	441 a	225 a
3N	(trt 3)	10 b	6 a	376 a	184 a
10^8	(trt 6)	17 b	10 a	264 a	320 a
10^8	(trt 8)[1]	117 a	10 a	471 a	323 a
Shoot dry wt (g/plant)					
Control	(trt 1)	3.6 a	5.3 a	15.1 b	15.1 a
1N	(trt 2)	4.9 ab	4.3 a	26.9 a	17.6 a
3 N	(trt 3)	6.9 a	7.2 a	23.8 ab	21.6 a
10^8	(trt 6)	4.4 b	3.6 a	16.0 ab	13.8 a
10^8	(trt 8)[1]	4.8 ab	4.6 a	23.5 ab	23.7 a

[1]Inoculant placed at 8 cm below the seed.

[2]Means, within the same column having common letters are not significantly diferent at the 0.05 level by DMRT.

TABLE 3: The number of viable cowpea-group rhizobia found in Sudanese soils.

Number of soils	Years since last planted to groundnut	Ave. MPN count with siratro (Viable cells/g soil)
11	1	2.3×10^5
6	2	3.6×10^4
4	3	2.9×10^4
3	4	3.7×10^4
6	–[2]	4.9×10^5

[1] One of the six samples had 2.4×10^6 rhizobia/g soil; one sandy sample from western Sudan had fewer than 3×10^2 rhizobia/g (lowest detection limit of the test), and was not included in the average.

[2] Never planted to groundnut.

FUTURE RESEARCH

Many areas for future research are evident from this initial study with some additional studies already underway at ISU. Thus:

Five isolates collected during the survey of outlying regions are being evaluated for efficiency in comparison with other known groundnut strains (25B7, 26Z6, 176A22, TAL309, 8A11, 3Gb10, 3Gb20). Tests of efficiency and infectivity with both 'Ashford' and 'Barberton' will be made;

Antibiotic-resistant markers are being developed in the above strains to determine their competitive ability in the field. Antiserum will also be developed for the best selected strains in order to evaluate their characteristics against those of the Sudanese strains;

The Sudanese and other strains are being evaluated for resistance to high temperatures and desiccation in a growth chamber study at ISU. Inoculant strains must be able to compete with the native strains in the hot, dry soils of Sudan in order to form nodules.

If facilities permit, the field work in Sudan will be extended to important production areas other than Wad Medani. With the low number of native rhizobia and the potential for groundnut expansion in the El Obeid region, this is a logical choice for future work.

TABLE 4: Summary of observation plots in groundnut-producing regions of Sudan.

Location	Cultivar	Nodules/plant[1]		Top dry wt[1]	
		Inoculated	Uninoculated	Inoculated	Uninoculated
Wad Medani:	Ashford	150	(missing)	70.0	13.3
	MH383	244	55	32.5	15.0
	Virginia	59	135	50.0	4.0
	C/5/B-2	30	32	30.0	6.8
	C/5/B-1	77	94	60.0	5.0
	MH372	76	125	53.3	11.7
	C/5-1	132	71	57.5	7.5
	Wadie No. 2	223	44	16.7	25.0
	NA/2/40	108	86	22.0	20.0
	AM-22	196	157	40.0	24.0
	Nigerian	141	176	23.3	33.0
	430AD9G	80	164	60.0	11.7
	NC-2	81	194	15.0	20.0
	C/5/6	98	99	38.0	14.3
	Average	121	110	40.6	15.1
Rahad:	Ashford	95	71	10.0	28.0
	MH383	136	78	21.3	16.7
	MH372	119	95	15.0	20.0
	Wadie No. 2	99	82	20.8	17.0
	Nigerian	111	83	16.0	28.0
	430AD9B	99	106	18.0	16.0
	Average	110	86	16.9	16.0
Abu Naama:	Ashford	85	93	10.3	7.6
	Barberton	75	75	6.2	7.6
	Average	80	84	8.3	7.6
El Obeid:	Barberton	75	71	5.0	4.4
Sennar:	Ashford	35	21	2.0	1.5
	Barberton	34	15	2.1	1.4
	Average	35	18	2.1	1.5

[1]Values are averages of 1/2 m of row, and depending upon plant density, ranged from four to eight plants.

REFERENCES

Ham, G.E. (1980) Inoculation of legumes with *Rhizobium* in competition with naturalized strains. *In:* Nitrogen fixation, W.E. Newton and W.H. Orme-Johnson (Eds.). Univ. Park Press, Baltimore, MD., USA. Vol. II. Pp. 131-138.

Mukhtar, N.O. & Yousif, Y.H. (1979) *Zbl. Bakt. II Abr.* 134, 25-33.

Musa, M.M. (1972) Annual Report, Gezira Res. Station, Wad Medani, Sudan.

Said, M.B. (1973) *Plant Soil* 38, 9-16.

Vincent, J.M. (1970) A manual for the practical study of root nodule bacteria. IBP Handbook No. 15. Blackwell Sci. Publ. Oxford, England. 164 pp.

FIELD RESPONSES TO *RHIZOBIUM* INOCULATION IN *ARACHIS HYPOGAEA, VIGNA* SPP. AND *DOLICHOS* SPP. IN INDIA

S.V. Hegde[1]

Summary

This paper reviews recent information on the response of some grain legumes to inoculation in India.

INTRODUCTION

Grain legumes (pulses) are important food crops in India where they are used extensively in the preparation of dhal, and are consumed in different forms with cereals in the daily diet. Pulses are the most economical source of protein in India, and consequently, the per capita daily consumption of these grains is high. While the production and yield of cereals in India and elsewhere has increased appreciably in recent years, pulse yields have changed little. Because of this, the Indian Council of Agricultural Research (ICAR) has given great emphasis to improving the quality and quantity of pulse production, and has set up a network of research centers to work, in coordination, on pulse crops.

Pulses and groundnut together occupy about 30 million ha annually in India. Groundnut (*Arachis hypogaea* L.) is one of the principal legume oilseed crops in the country. The crop is grown over an area of 7 million ha with an annual production of approximately 5 million tons. This represents about 46% of the total area under oilseeds and provides 60% of the edible oil produced in the country. Most of the area under groundnut is planted under rainfed conditions in the kharif (monsoon) season; only 8% of the acreage is grown under irrigation during the rabi (winter) season (George, Shrivastav & Desai, 1978). Groundnuts are grown both as a monoculture and mixed with

[1] Microbiology Dept., University of Agricultural Sciences, Bangalore, India.

cereals and other pulses. Compared with the maximum yields reported of 5000 kg/ha, and the Brazilian average of 1308 kg/ha, the Indian average from 1972-1975 was a low 709 kg/ha.

Pulse crops occupy about 23.5 million ha annually in India. Mungbean (*Vigna radiata* (L.) Wilczek), blackgram (*Vigna mungo* (L.) Hepper) and horsegram (*Macrotyloma uniflorum* (Lam.) Verdc. Syn. *Dolichos biflorus* L.) are grown on 2.8, 2.4, and 2.0 million ha, respectively. Cowpea (*Vigna unguiculata* (L.) Walp.) and lablab (*Lablab purpureus* (L.) Sweet) occupy a comparatively small area but have local importance in some states. In the State of Kerala more than 40% of the total area under pulses is occupied by cowpea.

Field-grown groundnut, mungbean, blackgram, pigeonpea, horsegram and cowpea are generally well nodulated by naturally occurring "cowpea-group" rhizobia in Indian soils (Dadarwal *et al.,* 1977). with the number of rhizobia nodulating groundnut in cultivated soils of India as determined by plant infection technique, ranging from 10^2 to 10^6/g of dry soil, (Sheth, 1979). However, reports of poor nodulation in the field are not uncommon (Nair, Ramaswamy & Porumal, 1971), especially in the close to 7 million ha of saline/alkali soil, where pulse crops do not nodulate, though native rhizobia are known to be present (Bhardwaj, 1974). Both fast-growing, acid-producing and slow-growing, alkali-producing rhizobia have been isolated from the root nodule of groundnut (Sheth, 1979) and horsegram (Siddaramaiah, 1977) and all the above isolates nodulated siratro (*Macroptilium atropurpureum* (DC) Urb.) Some *Rhizobium* isolates from the wild species of groundnut, *Arachis duranensis,* were also very effective on the cultivated species *A. hypogaea* (Dadarwal *et al.,* 1974). Thus, groundnut is a promiscuous legume host nodulating freely with a wide range of *Rhizobium* strains (Dart, 1974). Döbereiner & Campelo (1977) suggested that 30% of cowpea-group rhizobia nodulate groundnut effectively, and the remainder ineffectively.

The high yields reported in northern Nigeria suggest that groundnut nodules can fix appreciable amounts of nitrogen (N), and estimates of as much as 240 kg N/ha, or 80% of the plant's N uptake, have been reported (Dart & Krantz, 1977). In India the necessity to inoculate groundnut has neither been shown conclusively nor investigated thoroughly. The reports on the field performance of inoculant *Rhizobium* strains of groundnut vary widely, from no response (Gaur, Sen & Subba Rao, 1974) to a significant increase in yields (Sunder Rao, 1971; Bajpai, Lehri & Pathak, 1974; Iswaran & Sen, 1974; Nagaraja Rao, 1974).

Sheth (1979) studied the field performance of five selected *Rhizobium* isolates of groundnut at three different locations in Gujarat. A yield increase was obtained with one isolate at one location and was equivalent to the yield obtained with applications of 25 or 50 kg N/ha to uninoculated plots. In other studies application of phosphorus (P) alone or in combination with inoculation increased oil and protein contents of groundnut but reduced the total soluble carbohydrates. Free fatty acids and pod yields were unaffected (Arora, Saini & Gandhi, 1970). Lack of response to nodulation and low yield in groundnut are probably due to competition from strains in soil ineffective with this host, and require that inoculant strains be both effective and competitive (Guar *et al.*, 1974). Antagonism from other organisms in soil can also play a part (Jain & Rewari, 1974; Kumar Rao, Sen & Shende 1974). Using inoculation rates 3 x standard and the application in the inoculant of molybdenum and boron at 1.6 ppm and 4.0 ppm, respectively, was also helpful in overcoming nodulation by ineffective indigenous rhizobia (Iswaran & Sen, 1974). Sheth (1979) found inoculant strains for peanut to occupy 24-64% of nodules.

Field response of *Vigna* spp. to *Rhizobium* inoculation has been studied since 1975 in multi-locational trials under the auspices of the All India Coordinated Pulse Improvement Project. Significant seed yield increases following *Rhizobium* inoculation in mungbean, blackgram and cowpea have been spasmodic (see Tables 1 and 2), and unrelated to host variety, inoculant strain, year of trial, or locations tested. In other studies inoculation trials with *Vigna* spp. have resulted in varied responses ranging from no response (Sheriff *et al.*, 1970) to a significant seed yield increase in cowpea (Bajpai *et al.*, 1974; Pawar, Shirshat & Ghulgule, 1977; Bagyaraj & Hedge, 1978; Thimme Gowda, Hedge & Bagyaraj 1979), mungbean (Ramaswamy & Nar, 1965; Oblisami, Balaraman & Natarajan, 1976), and blackgram (Sahu, Behera, 1972; Lehri, Gangwar & Mehrotra, 1974). Inoculants prepared with more than one *Rhizobium* strain were found to be superior over single strain inoculants in some (Oblisami *et al.*, 1976), but not all studies (Bagyaraj & Hedge, 1978; Ramachandran, Menan & Alyer, 1980).

Damage of root nodules of pulse crops by soil insects is also a problem in many parts of India, with the maggots of *Rivellia* sp. and other soil insects causing widespread and heavy damage to the root nodules of cowpea, mungbean, blackgram, redgram, and groundnut. 10-98% of nodules may be affected, the damage being most severe in July and in late-sown crops. Side dressing of aldicarb or disulfotan or carbofuran applied at the rate of 1 kg active ingredient/ha gives complete protection from nodule damage by insects and resulted in significant yield increases in insect-infested soils (Iswaran, 1975; Rai *et al.*, 1976).

In India pulse crops are largely cultivated under rainfed situations in the monsoon season. Prolonged moisture stress can occur due to irregular distribution of rain. Nodule development and N_2 fixation were markedly reduced under soil moisture stress (Prabhashankar, 1979). Soil mulching with maize or ragi/straw at the rate of 3 ton/ha, three weeks prior to sowing, reduced moisture stress and markedly improved N_2 fixation in cowpea (S.V. Hegde, unpublished).

TABLE 1: Incidence of significant seed yield increases due to *Rhizobium* inoculation in mungbean and blackgram.

Location	Mungbean						Blackgram					
	1977		1978		1979		1977		1978		1979	
	V[1]	S[2]	V	S	V	S	V	S	V	S	V	S
Madurai	1/1	5/5	2/2	2/4	0/2	0/4	1/1	10/11	–[3]	–	2/2	2/4
				4/4								
Coimbatore	–	–	1/1	4/4	–	–	–	–	1/1	2/5	2/2	4/4
Kaveripatnam	–	–	1/1	2/4	–	–	–	–	1/1	2/5	–	–
Bangalore	0/2	0/3	0/2	0/4	0/2	0/4	1/2	3/3	0/2	0/4	0/2	0/4
								0/3				
Gulbarga	0/2	0/4	0/2	0/2	–	–	0/2	0/4	–	–	–	–
Hyderabad	–	–	1/2	4/5	–	–	0/2	0/16	–	–	–	–
Badnapur	0/4	0/5	2/2	3/4	0/2	0/4	–	–	1/2	1/4	0/2	0/4
Dholi	0/2	0/7	–	–	2/2	4/4	2/2	7/7	–	–	2/2	4/4
												2/4
Durgapura	1/1	5/8	–	–	–	–	–	–	–	–	0/2	0/4
Delhi	–	–	–	–	0/2	0/4	–	–	–	–	0/2	4/5
											1/2	0/4
Ludhiana	–	–	3/3	4/4	3/3	6/7	–	–	–	–	2/2	3/3
				2/4		5/7						
Kanpur	–	–	2/2	5/12	–	–	2/2	6/6	–	–	–	–
				4/4				5/6				
Hissar	0/1	0/9	0/2	0/4	0/2	0/6	0/1	0/8	0/2	0/5	0/1	0/5

[1] Varieties tested [2] *Rhizobium* strains tested [3] Trial not conducted

TABLE 2: Incidence of significant seed yield increase due to *Rhizobium* inoculation in cowpea.

Year	Trial number	Location			
		Bangalore		Durgapura	
		V[1]	S[2]	V	S
1975	1	0/1	0/6	–[3]	–
1976	1	1/1	1/11	–	–
	2	1/1	2/11	–	–
1977	1	1/1	2/2	1/1	5/9
	2	1/1	6/17	–	–
	3	1/3	1/3 0/3 0/3	–	–
1978	1	0/1	0/8	1/1	4/13
	2	0/1	0/8	1/2	3/4 0/4
	3	0/1	0/4	–	–
1979	1	2/3	4/4 2/4 0/4	0/1	0/9
	2	0/1	0/9	1/1	2/5 0/5

[1]Cowpea varieties tested,
[2]*Rhizobium* strains tested
[3]Trial not conducted

The transfer of fixed N from grain legumes to associated crops in mixed cropping systems, and to successive crops in relay, has been studied extensively in India. In legume/cereal mixed-cropping systems, inoculation of cowpea and lablab increased grain, straw, and N yields of associated finger millet. Yields of finger millet grown with inoculated lablab were on par with the yields of finger millet sole cropped and supplied with 50 kg N/ha. (Hegde & Bagyaraj, 1980). In a grass/legume mixture involving Dharwar Hybrid-2 grass and lablab, grass yields of 110.94, 91.15, and 76.5 ton fresh wt/ha per yr were produced in the inoculated, uninoculated and control treatments, respectively. On a fresh weight basis uninoculated and inoculated lablab transferred 18.75 and 40 kg N/ha per yr, respectively, to the associated grass. The contribution of inoculated and uninoculated lablab to the N economy of the soil were 68.6 and 33.6 kg N/ha per yr, respectively; thus inoculation contributed 35.0 kg N/ha per yr. Pure grass plots showed a deficit of 106 kg N/ha per yr (Venkataswamy, 1975).

Enrichment of soil N following the growth of inoculated legumes has been reported for cowpea (Sahu & Behera, 1972) and groundnut (Badami, 1930;

Mahta & Janoria, 1933). Mungbean grown in rotation with cereal crops also benefited the latter (Misra & Misra, 1975). The general consensus is that pulse crops are better suited as relay crops than as companion crops with cereals.

It is clear from these comments that much remains to be done if India is to maximize benefits from symbiotic N_2 fixation. Priority areas include strain evaluation, problems of competition, varietal development and the evaluation of legume and *Rhizobium* tolerance to alkaline soil conditions.

REFERENCES

Arora, S.M.K., Saini, T.S. & Gandhi, R.C. (1970) Study of chemical composition and yield of groundnut as affected by *Rhizobium* inoculation. *Oleagineaux* 25, 279-280.

Badami, V.K. (1930) Groundnut in Mysore. *J. Mysore Agric. Expt. Un. Stn.* 11, 113-119.

Bagyaraj, D.J. & Hegde, S.V. (1978) Response of cowpea (*Vigna unguiculata* (L.) Walp.) to *Rhizobium* seed inoculation. *Curr. Sci.* 47, 543-549.

Bajpai, P.D., Lehri, L.K. & Pathak, A.N. (1974) Effect of seed inoculation with *Rhizobium* strains on the yield of leguminous crops. *Proc. Indian Nat. Sci. Acad.* 40(B), 571-573.

Bhardwaj, K.K.R. (1974) Growth and symbiotic effectiveness of indigenous *Rhizobium* species in a saline-alkali soil. *Proc. Indian Acad. Sci.* 40(B), 540-543.

Dadarwal, K.R., Prabha, S., Tauro, P., & Subba Rao, N.S. (1977) Serology and host range infectivity of cowpea group rhizobia. *Indian J. Expl. Biol.* 15, 462-465.

Dadarwal, K.R., Singh, C.S., & Subba Rao, N.S. (1974) Nodulation and serological studies of rhizobia from six species of *Arachis*. *Plant Soil* 40, 535-544.

Dart, P.J. (1974) Development of root-nodule symbioses. *In*: The biology of nitrogen fixation. A. Quispel (Ed.). North-Holland Publ. Co., Amsterdam, The Netherlands. Pp. 381-429.

Dart, P.J. & Krantz, B.A. (1977) Legumes in the semi-arid tropics. *In:* Exploiting the legume-*Rhizobium* symbiosis in tropical agriculture, J.M. Vincent, A.S. Whitney & J. Bose (Eds.). Univ. Hawaii, Coll. Trop. Agric. *Misc. Publ.* 145. Pp. 119-154.

Döbereiner, J. & Campelo, A.B. (1977) Importance of legumes and their contribution to tropical agriculture. *In:* A treatise on dinitrogen fixation, Vol. 4. R.W.F. Hardy & A.H. Gibson (Eds.). Wiley, New York, NY, USA. Pp. 191-220.

Gaur, Y.D., Sen, A.N. & Subba Rao, N.S. (1974) Problem regarding groundnut inoculation in tropics with special reference to India. *Proc. Indian Nat. Sci. Acad.* B 40, 562-570.

George, P.S., Shrivastava, U.K. & Desai, E.M. (1978) Groundnut. *In*: The oilseeds economy of India. MacMillan (India) Ltd., Delhi, India. Pp. 44-71.

Hegde, S.V. & Bagyaraj, D.J. (1980) Benefits of *Rhizobium* inoculation of legumes to ragi (*Eleusine coracana*) in mixed cropping system. Proc. National Symp. Biological Nitrogen Fixation in Relation to Crop Production. Tamil Nadu Agricultural University, Coimbatore, India.

Iswaran, V. (1975) Seed pelleting with systemic insecticide (Aldicarb) for the control of pests of mungo (*Phaseolus aureus* L.) *Z. Bakt.* Abt. 11. 130, 365-366.

Iswaran, V. & Sen, A. (1974) Some studies on the groundnut *Rhizobium* symbiosis. *Z. Bakt.* Abt. II. 129, 477-480.

Jain, M.K. & Rewari, R.E. (1974) Isolation of seed-borne microflora from leguminous crops and their antagonistic effect on *Rhizobium. Curr. Sci.* 43, 151.

Kumar Rao, J.V.D.K., Sen, A. & Shende, S.T. (1974) Inhibition of groundnut *Rhizobium* in Indian soils. *Proc. Indian Nat. Sci. Acad.* 40B, 535-539.

Lehri, L.K., Gangwar, B.R. & Mehrotra, C.L. (1974) Bacterization experiments with *Rhizobium. J. Indian Soil Sci.* 22, 66-69.

Mahta, D.N. & Janoria, D.L. (1933) Groundnut as a rotation crop with cotton. *Indian J. Agric. Sci.* 3, 917-932.

Misra, A. & Misra, H.C. (1975) Effect of legumes on associated and subsequent crops. *Indian J. Genet. Plant Br.* 35, 329-341.

Nagaraja Rao, H.S. (1974) Response of groundnut variety TMV to rhizobial inoculation. *Proc. Indian Nat. Sci. Acad.* 40B, 650-651.

Nair, K.S., Ramaswamy, P.P. & Porumal, R. (1971) Studies on the causes of poor nodulation in groundnut in soils of Tamil Nadu. *Madras Agric. J.* 53, 5-8.

Oblisami, G., Balaraman, K. & Natarajan, T. (1976) Effect of composite cultures of *Rhizobium* on two pulse crops. *Madras Agric. J.* 63, 587-589.

Pawar, N.B., Shirsat, A.M. & Ghulgule, J.N. (1977) Effect of seed inoculation with *Rhizobium* on grain yield and other characters of cowpea (*Vigna unguiculata*). *Tropical Grain Legume Bull.* 7, 3-5.

Prabhashankar, M.R. (1979) Potential of rhizobial inoculation of fieldbean (*Lablab purpureus* (L.) Sweet) under rainfed farming in a mixed cropping system with ragi (*Eleusine coracana* (L.) Gaertn.) M.Sc. thesis submitted to Univ. of Agric. Sci., Bangalore, India.

Rai, P.V., Madhava Rao, A.R., Bopaiah, B.M., & Davaiah, M.A. (1976) Biochemical changes in the nodules of cowpea damaged by insects. *Curr. Res.* 3, 158-159.

Ramachandran, K., Menon, M.R. & Aiyer, R.S. (1980) Effect of composite rhizobial culture inoculation on cowpea (*Vigna unguiculata* (L.) Walp.). *Indian J. Microbiol.* 20, 220-224.

Ramaswamy, P.P. & Nair, K.S. (1965) A study on the response to greengram to bacterial seed inoculation. *Madras Agric. J.* 52, 241-242.

Sahu, S.K. (1973) Effect of *Rhizobium* inoculation and phosphate application on blackgram. *Madras Agric. J.* 60, 989-993.

Sahu, S. & Behera, B. (1972) Note on effect on *Rhizobium japonicum* inoculation on cowpea, groundnut and greengram, *Indian J. Agron.* 17, 359-360.

Sheriff, M.R., Ratnaswamy, R., Selvakumari, G., Ragupathy, A., & Krishnan, R.H. (1970) Effect of bacterial inoculation for pulses cultivated in Tamil Nadu. *Madras Agric. J.* 57, 181-185.

Sheth, R.D. (1979) Studies on the development of rhizobial inoculants for groundut (*Arachis hypogaea* L.). Ph.D. Thesis, Univ. of Agric. Sci., Bangalore, India.

Siddaramaiah, V.K. (1977) Isolation, testing and development of inoculant strain of *Rhizobium* for horsegram (*Macrotyloma uniflorum* (Lam.) Verdc.) M.Sc. Thesis Univ. Agric. Sci., Bangalore, India.

Sundera Rao, W.V.B. (1971) Field experiments on nitrogen fixation by nodulated legumes. *Plant Soil* (Special Volume), 237-291.

Thimme Gowda, S., Hedge, S.V. & Bagyaraj, D.J. (1979), *Rhizobium* inoculation and seed pelleting in relation to nodulation, growth and yield of cowpea (*Vigna unguiculata* (L.) Walp.) *Curr. Res.* 8, 42-43.

Venkataswamy, D.R. (1975) Studies on rhizobial inoculation of *Lablab purpureus* (L.) Sweet and its contribution to fodder yields in Dhaswes hyland - *L. purpureus* mixtures. M. Sc. Thesis, Univ. Agric. Sci., Bangalore, India.

RESPONSE OF PIGEONPEA TO *RHIZOBIUM* INOCULATION IN NORTHERN INDIA

R.P. Pareek[1]

Summary

Pigeonpea *(Cajanus cajan* (L.) Millsp.) occupies about 11.34% of the area devoted to grain legumes in India, comprising about 15.8% of the grain legume production. Nodulation surveys conducted through the All India Coordinated Pulse Improvement Project suggest that pigeonpea nodulation in northern India is commonly inadequate. In inoculation trials carried out at Ludhiana, Jabalpur, Sardar Krishinagar, Varanasi and Hissar during 1978-79, significant responses to inoculation were only obtained at the Ludhiana and Jabalpur locations, and for 18 of the 32 strain/cultivar combinations. Cultivar T21, in particular, responded well to inoculation. Trials in three locations showed a strong interaction between inoculation and P_2O_5 supply.

INTRODUCTION

Pigeonpea *(Cajanus cajan* (L.) Millsp.) is an important pulse legume of the tropics and subtropics, and is particularly important in India, where it occupies roughly 11.34% of the area sown to grain legumes and comprises about 15.8% of total grain legume production. The greatest production comes from the States of Uttar Pradesh, Madhya Pradesh, Andhra Pradesh, Bihar, and Karnataka. Successful cultivation of the crop depends, in part, on an effective symbiosis with *Rhizobium* (Dart, Isalam & Eaglesham, 1975). This presentation summarizes briefly the available information on the response of pigeonpea to inoculation and P fertilization in northern India.

NODULATION SURVEY

A small survey of the nodulation status of pigeonpea in northern India was carried out in 1978-79 through the All India Coordinated Pulse Improvement

[1] Dept. Soil Science, G.B. Pant University of Agriculture & Technology, Pantnagar, Nainital, UP, India.

Project (AICPIP) with more than 300 locations surveyed. In Haryana only 9 of the 233 sites evaluated over the two-year period showed reasonable nodulation (more than 10 nodules/plant). Similarly, in the Varanasi district of Uttar Pradesh, only 8 of 23 locations surveyed showed reasonable nodulation, while in Pantnagar plants at all 37 locations were poorly nodulated. The survey also showed poor nodulation in Dholi and Gujurat.

When soil samples from the Pantnagar region were potted and pigeonpeas raised in the glasshouse under more controlled conditions, plants contained only 1-10 nodules, while nodule dry weight varied from 14-78 mg/plant.

RESPONSE TO INOCULATION

Responses to inoculation in Uttar Pradesh have proved variable. Singh, Prasad & Choudhary (1976) obtained no response to inoculation on a Mollisol near Pantnagar, but inoculation gave favorable responses at Kanpur (Gupta & Prasad, 1979), Bulandshahar (Pareek, 1979) and Bijnor (R.P. Pareek, unpublished data).

Table 1 shows the inoculation responses obtained in AICPIP trials in northern India during 1978-79. Compounded over varieties and strains, the trials show an average yield increase in Ludhiana of only 12% in 1978, but a highly significant increase for all strain x variety combinations in 1979. In sum, 18 of the 32 strain/cultivar combinations tested in these and in other trials near Ludhiana and Jabalpur have shown a significant response to inoculation, with yields increased as much as 67%.

Of the strains and cultivars tested in these and other trials, strain F4 with cultivar T21 has given most promising results, with consistent and statistically significant yield increases following inoculation at both Ludhiana and Jabulpur.

RESPONSE TO PHOSPHORUS

Northern India is generally deficient in phosphorus (P) (Bains & Choudhary, 1971; Choudhary & Bhatia, 1971; Manghi, Choudhary & Karatkar, 1973; Rathi, Singh & Malik, 1974; Singh, Prasad & Choudhary, 1976). At Pantnagar Singh *et al.* (1979) observed a significant interaction between variety, strain and P uptake in a loamy soil high in organic matter. In Kanpur district, Gupta & Prasad (1979) observed an 11-13% increase in grain yield with 50 kg P_2O_5/ha applied (see Table 2). Yields were increased substantially, however, when both inoculation and P were supplied. The interaction of P and inoculation was not apparent in trials in Bulandshahah and Bijnor.

TABLE 1: Response of pigeonpea to inoculation at three sites in northern India in 1978/79.

Location	Variety	Strain used	1978 yield (q/ha)	1979 yield (q/ha)
Ludhiana	T21	Uninoculated	6.21	11.71
		F4	7.49	15.72*
		KA-1	6.49	14.06*
		IPH-195	6.29	17.10*
	P4-4	Uninoculated	6.44	9.60
		IPH-195	8.02	16.10*
Jabalpur	T21	Uninoculated	4.82	5.4
		F4	6.93*	7.80*
		KA-1	5.95	6.70*
		JN-2	6.27*	7.35*
	KH2	Uninoculated	4.85	6.12
		F4	5.83	7.33*
		JN-1	6.60*	7.12*
		CC-1	5.90	7.98*
Sardar Krishnagar	T21	Uninoculated	14.76	6.17
		F4	17.49	6.67
		KA-1	14.57	8.18
		CC-1	17.00	7.28
		BON-2	16.19	6.90
	T15-15	Uninoculated	14.61	9.25
		F4	15.24	16.56
		KA-1	16.26	11.01
		CC-1	14.51	15.67

*Significantly different from the uninoculated control at the P = 0.05 level.

TABLE 2: Yield response of pigeonpea (q/ha) to inoculation and P fertilization at four locations in Uttar Pradesh.[1]

Treatment	Kampur, 1979		Bulandshahar, 1979	Bijnor, 1979
	Site 1	Site 2		
Uninoculated	16.31	12.63	14.43	13.56
Inoculated	17.56	13.56	17.56	15.22
P applied	18.42	13.97	–	12.11
Inoculated + P	20.17	15.64	17.41	15.33

[1]The amount of P applied was: Kanpur, 50 kg P_2O_5 /ha; Bulandshahar, 100 kg P_2O_5 /ha; and Bijnor, 30 kg P_2O_5 /ha.

REFERENCES

Bains, S.S. & Choudhary, S.L. (1971) Agronomy of pulse crops. *In*: New vistas of pulse production. IARI, New Delhi, India. Pp. 24-26.

Choudhary, S.L. & Bhatia, P.C. (1971) *Ind. Farm.* 20, 27-31.

Dart, P.J., Isalam, R. & Eaglesham, A. (1975) Proc. Internat. Workshop on Grain Legumes. ICRISAT, Hyderabad, India. Pp. 63-83.

Gupta, B.R. & Prasad, S.N. (1979) AICPIP, Kharif pulse progress report. Pp. 39-46.

Manghi, S., Choudhary, S.L. & Karatkar, A.G. (1973) *Ind. J. Agric. Sci.* 43, 998-1001.

Pareek, R.P. (1979) Research on Kharif pulses at Pantnagar. Pp. 31-41.

Rathi, S.S., Singh, D. & Malik, R.S. (1974) *Fert. News* 19, 27-31.

Singh, K.S., Prasad, R. & Choudhary, S.L. (1976) *Ind. J. Agron.* 21, 49-53.

Singh, H.P., Baghel, R.A., Singhania, R.A., & Pareek, R.P. (1979) *Ind. J. Microbiol.* 19, 170-172.

RESPONSE OF GREEN GRAM (*VIGNA RADIATA*) AND COWPEA (*VIGNA UNGUICULATA*) TO INOCULATION WITH RHIZOBIA FROM WILD LEGUMES

J.S. Srivastava and V.P. Tewari[1]

Summary

Rhizobium cultures obtained from 14 legumes growing wild or cultivated in the Varanasi area of India were tested for efficiency in nitrogen (N_2) fixation with green gram (*Vigna radiata*) and cowpea (*Vigna unguiculata*) in sand and agar culture. Seven of the cultures were effective with cowpea and increased the total N of inoculated plants 12-48%. The most effective strains were from *Uraria picta* and *Zornia diphylla*. With green gram in sand culture, only the *Rhizobium* isolated from a plant classified locally as *Phaseolus psoraleoides* was effective in promoting plant development. In tube culture, however, isolates from *Cassia absus* and *Zornia diphylla* were also highly effective. Known strains of *Rhizobium* for *V. unguiculata* and *V. radiata*, included in this trial as controls, were generally poor in N_2 fixation with these hosts.

INTRODUCTION

The ability of rhizobia from wild legumes to symbiose with agriculturally important species can affect the need to inoculate and the ease of establishment of these species (Lange & Parker, 1961). In Varanasi there are many wild and cultivated species. This paper examines the symbiotic performance of rhizobia obtained from 14 of them with *Vigna radiata* (green gram) and *V. unguiculata* (cowpea).

MATERIALS AND METHODS

Rhizobia were isolated from the nodules of 14 legumes growing wild or cultivated in the Varanasi area of India, using the methods of Vincent (1970).

[1] Dept. of Mycology and Plant Pathology, Banaras Hindu University, Varanasi 221005, India.

The legumes from which isolates were made were: *Alysicarpus publeurifolius*, *A. monilifer*, *Aeschynomene americana*, *Cassia absus*, *Clitoria ternatea*, *Desmodium gangeticum*, *D. triflorum*, *D. triquetrum*, *Rhynchosia minima*, *Tephrosia purpurea*, *Uraria picta*, *V. triloba*, *Zornia diphylla*, and a legume classified locally as *Phaseolus psoraleoides*.

Ability of these isolates to symbiose effectively with *V. radiata* and *V. unguiculata* was tested in replicated trials in the glasshouse using sand culture and Thornton's nutrient medium without N. The host varieties used were cv. T44 for *V. radiata* and 'Pusa do Fasli' for *V. unguiculata*. Known strains for these host legumes were included in each trial.

TABLE 1: Effectiveness of *Rhizobium* strains isolated from wild legumes in sand culture with *Vigna radiata*.

Host from which isolated	Nodule number per plant	Size of nodules (mm)		Total dry weight plant (mg)	N content/ plant (mg)
		1-2.5	Above 2.5		
Control	–	–	–	237.6	4.90
Alysicarpus publeurifolius	14.0	12.6	1.4	257.8	5.48
A. monilifer	11.2	10.4	0.8	255.8	5.59
Aeschynomene americana	10.2	9.4	0.8	262.4	5.68
Clitoria ternatea	12.2	11.6	0.6	258.6	5.45
Desmodium gangeticum	7.4	7.4	–	236.4	5.32
D. triflorum	6.2	6.2	–	220.8	4.96
D. triquetrum	6.8	6.8	–	261.2	5.39
Phaseolus psoraleoides	15.6	12.4	3.2	347.6	7.06
Rhynchosia minima	8.6	8.6	–	255.6	5.71
Tephrosia purpurea	8.9	8.9	–	238.0	4.98
Usaria picta	9.2	9.2	–	248.2	5.28
Vigna radiata-I	12.4	12.4	–	277.8	5.68
V. radiata-II	11.8	11.8	–	242.0	4.94
V. radiata-III	6.3	6.3	–	237.4	5.35
V. triloba	11.4	10.0	1.4	257.4	5.11
Zornia diphylla	12.2	12.2	–	250.2	5.45
S.E.M. ±	–	–	–	12.75	0.31
C.D. at 5 %	–	–	–	24.99	0.60

The nodulation and N_2 fixation of *V. radiata* was also assayed in a light room using tube culture (Vincent, 1970). Tubes 200 x 38 mm were used, with the inoculated plants grown at 30°C at 3000 lux. Additional nutrient solution was provided to tubes as needed. Five replicates were used for each host/strain combination.

Both experiments were terminated six weeks after inoculation, and determinations were made on nodule number, nodule weight, plant dry weight, and plant N content.

RESULTS AND DISCUSSION

Results of the sand culture test with *V. radiata* are shown in Table 1. While only the *Rhizobium* from *P. psoraleoides* induced substantial increases in dry weight compared to the -N control, a number of the isolates did enhance the N content of plants. When this experiment was repeated using agar slants, the *P.*

TABLE 2: Effectiveness of *Rhizobium* strains isolated from wild legumes on *Vigna radiata* grown on agar slants.

Host from which isolated	Nodule number per plant	Nodule dry weight plant (mg)	Dry weight of plant (mg)
Control	–	–	104.6
Alysicarpus publeurifolius	15.3	6.3	245.0
A. monilifer	8.6	4.0	215.0
Aeschynomene americana	15.0	6.3	173.3
Cassia absus	19.0	8.3	301.3
C. ternatea	13.0	5.3	190.6
Desmodium gangeticum	12.9	9.0	224.0
D. triflorum	14.6	4.6	185.0
D. triquetrum	4.0	2.6	117.0
Phaseoloides psoraleoides	27.0	9.3	316.6
Rhynchosia minima	5.6	5.6	276.0
Tephrosia purpurea	6.6	6.3	167.0
Uraria picta	22.0	8.0	292.3
Vigna radiata-I	9.3	7.0	248.3
V. radiata-II	10.3	5.3	280.0
V. radiata-III	6.0	4.6	205.0
V. triloba	9.0	6.3	260.6
Zornia diphylla	18.6	9.0	304.6

psoraleoides isolate was again best, but several other isolates induced substantial increases in plant dry weight (see Table 2). However, at least five of the isolates were weak in N_2 fixation, and these could well cause less than adequate growth of the host if competing with inoculant rhizobia under field conditions.

When *V. unguiculata* was used as host, the isolates from *Uraria picta* and *Zornia diphylla* were most effective (see Table 3). Surprisingly, a number of the isolates, including all three inoculant strains for cowpea included in this trial, were weak in N_2 fixation with plant dry weight and N content only a little better than the -N control. Again, N_2 fixation in the field in the presence of these rhizobia could be less than adequate, and their presence could limit inoculation response.

TABLE 3: Effectiveness of *Rhizobium* strains isolated from wild legumes in sand culture tests with *Vigna unguiculata.*

Host from which isolated	Nodule number per plant	Size of nodules (mm)		Dry weight/ plant (mg)	N content/ plant (mg)
		1-2.5	Above 2.5		
Control	–	–	–	379.0	7.81
Alysicarpus publeurfifolius-II	11.4	1.0	10.4	439.0	8.76
A. monilifer	8.4	3.0	5.4	381.6	7.87
Clitoria ternatea	9.2	0.0	9.2	408.2	8.08
Desmodium gangeticum	12.4	3.2	9.2	408.0	8.14
D. triflorum	15.8	2.0	13.8	471.0	9.55
D. triquetrum	4.6	0.0	4.6	389.4	7.83
Phaseolus psoraleoides	14.6	2.8	11.8	449.0	9.13
Tephrosia purpurea	8.2	0.0	8.2	387.2	8.59
Uraria picta	23.6	3.4	20.2	539.4	11.60
Vigna triloba	18.0	6.2	11.8	447.2	8.95
V. unguiculata-I	17.6	2.8	14.8	399.8	8.01
V. unguiculata-II	10.4	7.2	5.2	383.1	7.87
V. unguiculata-III	15.0	3.2	11.8	398.8	8.61
Zornia diphylla	22.8	5.0	17.8	492.0	10.50
S.E.M. ±	–	–	–	15.36	0.41
C.D. at 5 %	–	–	–	30.10	0.80

REFERENCES

Lange, R.T. & Parker, C.A. (1961) *Plant Soil* 15, 193-198.

Vincent, J.M. (1970) A manual for the practical study of root nodule bacteria. Blackwell Scientific Publ. Oxford, England.

N_2 FIXATION IN GRAIN LEGUMES

THE CHARACTERIZATION OF NEW *RHIZOBIUM JAPONICUM* GERMPLASM

H.H. Keyser and D.F. Weber[1]

Summary

A collection of isolates of *R. japonicum* from the People's Republic of China is being evaluated for biochemical, serological and symbiotic characteristics. The vast majority of the isolates have properties typical of the soybean rhizobia already held in the USDA *Rhizobium* collection. The PRC isolates exhibit a range of effectiveness on 'Siratro' and on soybean. A large percentage of them do not react with common *R. japonicum* antisera, though representation is found within certain serogroups. Some of the isolates are non-infective on 'Lee' soybean.

INTRODUCTION

Soybean (*Glycine max* (L.) Merrill) is the most extensively planted grain legume in the world, since it is utilized in both tropical and temperate agriculture (FAO, 1979). Soybean has the potential to fix most or all of its required nitrogen (N) when in symbiosis with *Rhizobium japonicum*, but N_2 fixation under field conditions can be limited by host/ *Rhizobium* specificity and by competition from native soil rhizobia. New germplasm of this bacterium could prove useful in overcoming these and other constraints limiting BNF in this species.

The Organization for International Cooperation and Development, an agency of the US Department of Agriculture, sponsored a tour of the People's Republic of China (PRC) for American soybean germplasm workers during August and September of 1979. Two of these workers, Kuell Hinson and Walt Fehr, cooperated with microbiologists of the USDA Beltsville *Rhizobium*

---

[1] USDA/SEA/AR, Cell Culture and Nitrogen Fixation Laboratory, Beltsville, MD 20705, USA.

Culture Collection by collecting soybean root nodules from plants growing in agricultural institute farms, commune farms, and garden plots. Forty-one nodule samples from 12 locations between 35 and 45° N latitude were obtained (provinces of Heilongjiang, Liaoning, Shandong, Henan, and Shanxi), and from these 240 strains were isolated. This material comes from the center of origin of *G. max* and its putative wild ancestor (*G. soja* Sieb & Zucc. (ussuriensis Regel & Maack)) (Hadley & Hymowitz, 1973), and has probably evolved with the soybean over numerous centuries.

This paper examines some biochemical and serological properties of these strains, and their symbiotic response to some currently important US soybean cultivars.

CHARACTERIZATION OF THE ISOLATES

Characteristics of these new (hereafter referred to as PRC) soybean rhizobia that have been, or will be, evaluated include:

- Growth rate on yeast-extract mannitol agar (YMA) (Vincent, 1970);
- Biochemical tests, including pH reaction on YMA, reaction in litmus milk, growth on glucose peptone agar, and in some cases, growth with different carbon sources (Vincent, 1970);
- Symbiotic effectiveness on *G. max* and other hosts, including an evaluation of cultivar specificity;
- Competitiveness for nodule formation; and
- Identification of serological groupings among the isolates, and of affinities with *R. japonicum* serotypes in the Beltsville collection.

LABORATORY TESTS

With the exception of 28 isolates, the PRC isolates were typical of other *R. japonicum* in their slow growth rate, alkaline reaction on bromthymol blue YMA, and sparse early growth on glucose peptone agar. The exceptional isolates exhibited a faster growth rate on YMA and produced an acid reaction on bromthymol blue YMA.

Serological comparisons have been made on the first 100 PRC isolates with the 17 *R. japonicum* serogroups in the Beltsville collection. Only 52% of these isolates reacted with any serum in somatic antigen agglutination tests. In contrast 82% of 800 isolates from nodules in the major soybean producing areas of the USA reacted with these antisera. Serogroup 123 was found in the greatest relative abundance in both the PRC and USA survey collections. Serogroup 123 has been reported previously to be dominant in soils in the Midwest USA (Damirgi, Frederick & Anderson, 1967; Ham, Frederick & Anderson, 1971; Kapusta & Rouwenhorst, 1973). Serogroup cI-123 was also found fairly frequently in both collections.

Antisera are being prepared against representative strains from the PRC collection to determine their serological relatedness.

PLANT TESTS

Subsequent to laboratory tests, verification of the PRC isolates as *Rhizobium* was carried out in growth pouches (diSPo Seed-Pack, Scientific Products) with *Macroptilium atropurpureum* (DC) Urb. cv. Siratro as the host. This small seeded legume is convenient for this purpose, and with over 260 *R. japonicum* isolates tested we have yet to find one which will not nodulate 'Siratro.' The ability of soybean rhizobia to nodulate 'Siratro' has been noted previously (van Rensburg, Strijdom & Kriel, 1976; J.M. Vincent, personal communication). Of the 226 PRC isolates tested on 'Siratro' all were infective, with 40% rated fully effective (yield greater than 75% of the +N control), 24% partially effective (yield greater than 50% of the +N control), and 36% ineffective (yield less than 50% of the +N control).

Evaluation of the effectiveness of the isolates on the soybean cultivar Kent was carried out in sand jars in the greenhouse. Parameters measured were top dry weight of plants and nodulation abundance and pattern. With 191 PRC isolates tested, 39% were fully effective, 39% partially effective, and 22% ineffective. Further comparisons with a range of cultivars will be made in sand jars between the most effective PRC isolates and the recommended USDA *R. japonicum* strains.

A comparison of the effectiveness ratings of these 191 PRC isolates on 'Kent' soybean and 'Siratro' revealed that while effectiveness on soybean cannot be predicted by that on 'Siratro', a distinct trend was apparent. Of those isolates (56) rated ineffective on 'Siratro', 39% were ineffective and 20% fully effective on 'Kent'. Those isolates (88) rated fully effective on 'Siratro' gave 11% as ineffective and 55% as fully effective with 'Kent'. Other workers (Barua & Bhaduri, 1967; Doku, 1969) have shown the ability of *R. japonicum* to nodulate and fix N_2 with some legumes that normally symbiose with cowpea rhizobia.

HOST CULTIVAR SPECIFICITY

Further evaluation of some of the fast growing PRC isolates revealed a striking cultivar interaction. 'Peking' and 'Lee' cultivars of soybean were grown together in growth pouches and inoculated separately with 16 of the fast-growing isolates. Uninoculated and +N controls were included; also pouches in which USDA 110 was used as inoculant. All of the PRC isolates were infective and effective with 'Peking', and were non-infective with 'Lee'. 'Peking' is an "unimproved" line, whereas 'Lee' is a product of selective breeding. Further examination of nodulation by this group of isolates with "improved" lines of soybean is focusing on the possibility that their non-infectiveness is associated with cultivars that have a substantial pedigree.

REFERENCES

Barua, M. & Bhaduri, P.N. (1967) *Can. J. Microbiol.* 13, 910-913.

Damirgi, S.M., Frederick, L.R. & Anderson, I.C. (1967) *Agron. J.* 59, 10-12;

Doku, E.V. (1969) *Plant Soil* 30, 126-128.

Hadley, H.H. & Hymowitz, T. (1973) Speciation and cytogenetics. *In:* Soybeans: Improvement, production, and uses, B.E. Caldwell (Ed.). Amer. Soc. Agronomy, Monograph Series, No. 16. Pp. 97-116.

Ham, G.E., Frederick, L.R. & Anderson, I.C. (1971) *Agron. J.* 63, 69-72.

Food and Agriculture Organization (1979) 1978 Production yearbook. FAO, Rome, Italy.

Kapusta, G. & Rouwenhorst, D.W. (1973) *Agron. J.* 65, 916-919.

Rensburg, H.J. Van, Strijdom, B.W. & Kriel, M.M. (1976) *Phytophylactica* 8, 91-96.

Vincent, J.M. (1970) A manual for the practical study of root-nodule bacteria. IBP Handbook No. 15, Blackwell Sci. Pubs., Oxford, England.

MANAGEMENT OF THE COWPEA/ *RHIZOBIUM* SYMBIOSIS UNDER STRESS CONDITIONS

V. Marcarian[1,2]

Summary

High temperatures and saline/alkaline soils adversely affect the legume/ *Rhizobium* symbiosis. With cowpeas (*Vigna unguiculata* (L.) Walp.) grown in desert environments there is little natural nodulation, and even plants inoculated using peat inoculants fail to nodulate.

In experiments on a clay-loam soil of pH 7.65 to 8.40 near Safford, Arizona, the use of granular inoculants applied in the seed row or placed 10 to 15 cm below seed level, resulted in nodulation. The distribution of nodules along the root was correlated with inoculant placement. Despite the improved nodulation, inoculation did not significantly affect yield or other parameters of plant development.

INTRODUCTION

Cowpeas are grown extensively in the lowland tropics and are the most important grain legume for the dry, semi-arid regions of Africa and northeastern Brazil (Dart & Krantz, 1977). In some of these areas, cowpeas are affected by both high soil temperatures and saline/alkaline soils.

Negative effects of salinity on cowpea growth and development have been reported (Imbamba, 1973; Narain, Singh & Pal, 1977). Gill (1979) found soil alkalinity to affect the growth and yield of cowpeas with a reduction in their chlorophyll, protein, RNA and DNA content. Effects of salt on the cowpea/ *Rhizobium* symbiosis have also been reported (Totowat & Saxena, 1970; Chonkar, Iswaran & Jauhri, 1971; Balasubramanian & Sinha, 1976; Joe & Allen, 1980). Similarly, Minchin, Huxley, & Summerfield (1976) have

---

[1] University of Arizona, Tucson, AZ 85721 USA. Univ. of Arizona Agricultural Experiment Station, Journal Paper No. 396.

[2] The financial support of USAID under project AG/TAB610-9-76 is gratefully acknowledged.

shown that temperatures above 32° C affect the vegetative development of cowpeas appreciably, with nodule activity reduced at 35.4° C.

Genetic variability in tolerance to soil salinity has been identified in our field testing program, with over 15% of the lines screened lost through sodium toxicity. Paliwal & Maliwal (1973) have also reported variation among genotypes at both germination and seedling stages. The range in electrical conductivity at which germination occurred was from 3 to 12 mmhos/cm but salt tolerance at germination was not necessarily related to seedling performance. Variability in the tolerance of slow-growing rhizobia to salinity also exists (Graham & Parker, 1964; Steinborn & Roughley, 1975), though the commonly used cowpea strain, CB756, tolerated only 0.5% NaCl.

We feel it is important to use a bi-directional approach in our studies, the identification of superior adapted cowpea germplasm and rhizobial strains going hand in hand with the development of inoculant technologies for stress situations. The present study examines the response of selected cowpea lines to granular inoculation at different levels in the soil profile.

EXPERIMENTAL METHODS

Conventional inoculation methods using peat inocula applied to the seed are ineffective in the low desert areas of the southwest. Soil temperatures at planting in excess of 30° C (see Figure 1) and high sodium levels (see Table 1) are contributing factors. Nodulation with native soil rhizobia is also rare. When results of preliminary experiments proved encouraging, formal studies to evaluate the value of granular inoculants were initiated.

In this trial eight cowpea lines and cultivars were used: P.I. 293518 (Entry no. 1), P.I. 353332 (2), 'Speckled Purple Hull' (3), P.I. 211642 (4), 'California

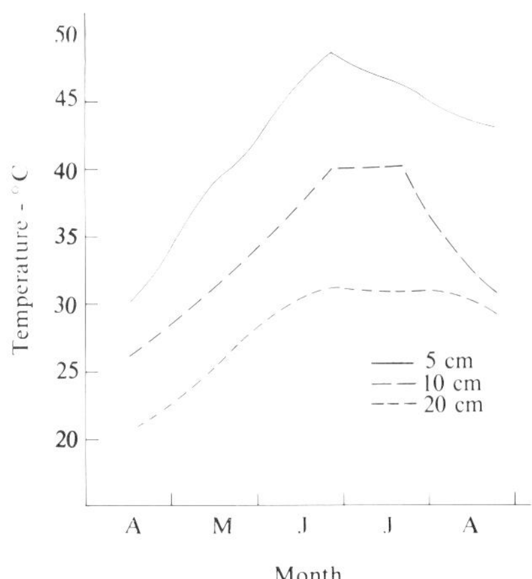

Figure 1.
Bi-weekly averages of daily soil temperatures at 5, 10 and 20 cm depth. Growing season, 1980.

TABLE 1: Soil data - 1980 salt tolerance screening trials.University of Arizona Experimental Farm, Safford, Arizona.

Plot no.	Soil depth (cm)	Soil type	pH	$Ece_3 x 10^3$	Soluble salts (ppm)	Na (meq/1)	ESP	N (ppm)
3	0-10	Clay loam	8.00	5.44	5,327	0.53	0.90	22.80
3	10-20	Clay loam	8.30	2.32	1,624	13.79	7.58	5.05
19	0-10	Clay loam	7.65	42.01	29,407	154.00	15.57	16.00
19	10-20	Clay loam	8.40	1.58	1,106	12.66	12.34	8.80

No. 5' (5), P.I. 353011 (11), P.I. 353380 (12), and P.I. 180494 (19). Each had performed consistently well over four seasons of field testing for salt tolerance. Inoculant was prepared with strain CB756. The Nitragin Company, Milwaukee, Wisconsin, USA, formulated and provided the granular peat inocula.

Since a moist seedbed appeared conducive to rhizobial survival, cowpeas were planted on pre-irrigated beds with 1.2 m centers. For the deep placement of inoculant, an Ortho fertilizer applicator was used that delivered 16 kg/ha of inocula 10 to 15 cm in the soil at planting. Uninoculated controls and cowpeas inoculated with 32 g of granular inoculant per 33 m of row at seed level were included in the trials. The experiment was planted in a randomized complete block with four replications. Seeds were placed approximately 7.5 cm deep and the plots "capped" prior to seedling emergence. Soil conditions at planting are shown in Table 1. Ten plants per plot were collected for evaluation of vegetative growth, nodulation, and acetylene reduction assay at 23, 39, 53, and 93 days, while final harvest occurred at 124 days.

RESULTS AND DISCUSSION

Both deep inoculation and the use of granular inoculants at seed level resulted in nodulation of cowpea plants. Uninoculated controls produced no nodules (see Table 2). In general the total dry weight of nodules/plant (see Figure 2) and nodule numbers (see Figure 3) were enhanced by deep placement of the inoculant. Deep placement of inoculant also affected nodule distribution as nodules occurred significantly lower in the soil profile with this treatment than when inoculant was placed at seed level (see Figure 4). No significant correlation was found between ethylene production (see Table 3), yield (see Figure 5), and total plant dry weights and leaf weights.

Interestingly, a band of granular inoculant was still evident in the soil 93 days after planting. The lower soil temperatures, reduced soil salt micro-

TABLE 2: Influence of inoculation placement and cultivar on percentage of plants nodulated over the growing season.

Cultivar	Days after planting											
	23			39			53			93		
	Uninoculated	Inocula depth		Uninoculated	Inocula depth		Uninoculated	Inocula depth		Uninoculated	Inocula depth	
		7.5cm	10-15cm		7.5cm	10-15cm		7.5cm	10-15cm		7.5cm	10-15cm
1	0	0	0	0	0	40	0	0	11	0	0	0
2	0	0	0	0	20	30	0	0	100	0	0	83
3	0	10	0	0	40	0	0	100	0	0	100	75
4	0	30	0	0	10	100	0	100	100	0	100	100
5	0	10	8	0	30	10	0	0	0	0	100	100
11	0	0	100	0	0	100	0	100	100	0	100	100
12	0	0	40	0	30	70	0	100	100	0	100	90
19	0	0	17	0	40	60	0	100	0	0	100	75

climate, and available moisture, in conjunction with the protection offered by granules at 10 to 15 cm depth, may account for enhanced nodulation.

While nodulation was influenced by inoculant method and host genotype, this was not reflected in final yields. There were, however, significant differences among cultivars in yield under these hot, saline soil conditions.

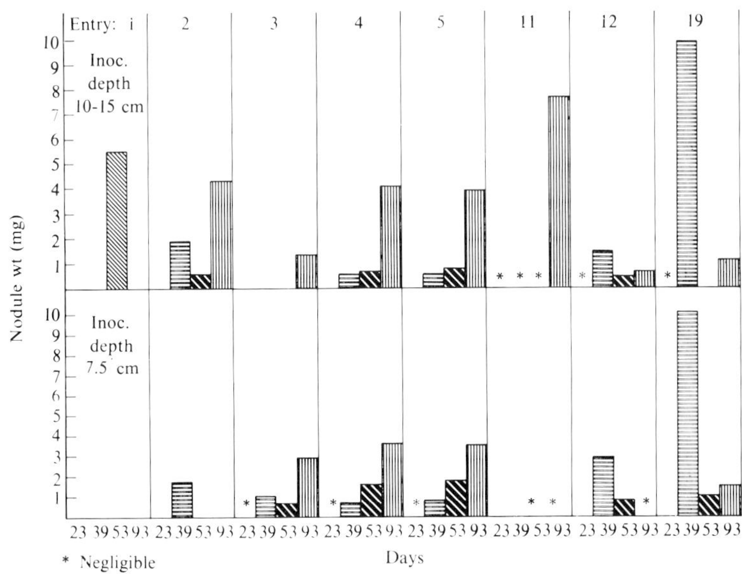

Figure 2. Average dry weight of nodules/plant at 23, 39, 53 and 93 days.

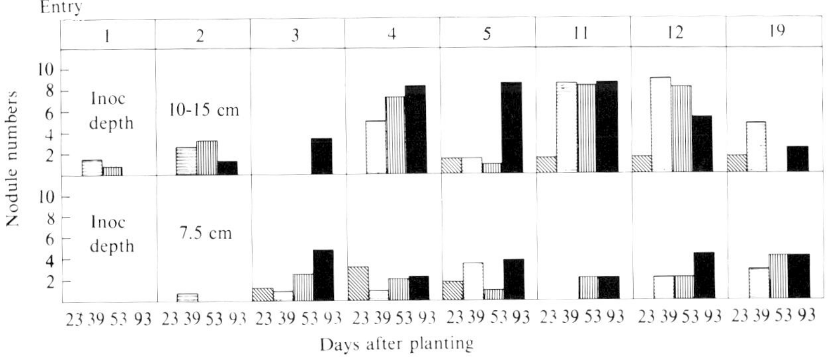

Figure 3. Average numbers of nodules/plant on cowpea roots inoculated at two depths with granular inoculant.

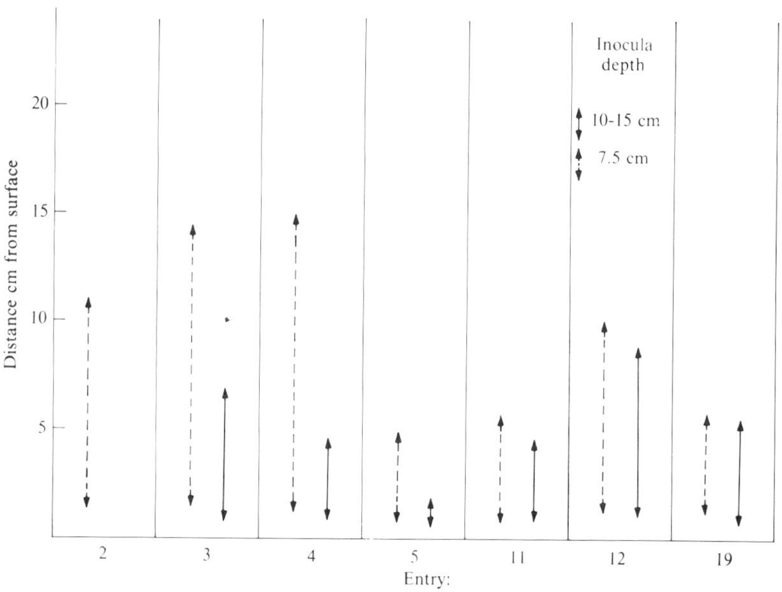

Figure 4. Effect of inoculant placement on distribution of nodules on cowpea roots after 93 days.

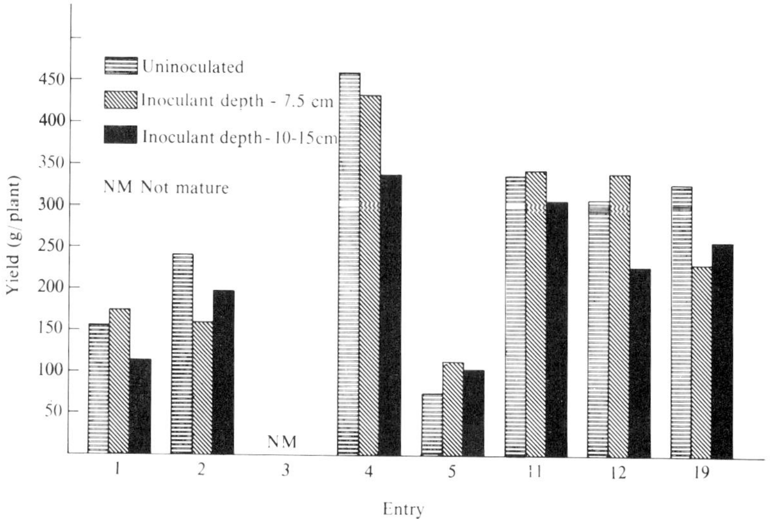

Figure 5. Average yields of cowpeas inoculated at two depths with granular inoculant.

TABLE 3: Ethylene production of cowpeas inoculated at two depths with granular inocula (µ moles/plant per h).

Entry	39 days			53 days			93 days		
	Uninoculated	Inocula depth		Uninoculated	Inocula depth		Uninoculated	Inocula depth	
		7.5cm	10-15cm		7.5cm	10-15cm		7.5cm	10-15cm
1	–	–	28.43	–	–	113.02	–	–	–
2	–	53.71	33.35	–	–	12.25	–	–	26.04
3	–	26.33	–	–	56.69	–	–	66.13	51.64
4	–	*	9.13	–	26.15	14.13	–	72.31	*
5	–	12.55	91.99	–	–	–	–	*	21.37
11	–	–	10.21	–	31.50	11.62	–	9.50	*
12	–	40.13	17.95	–	64.40	13.84	–	6.77	*
19	–	25.80	13.05	–	11.67	–	–	*	*

* Negligible.

REFERENCES

Balasubramanian, V. & Sinha, S.K. (1976) *Physiol. Plant.* 36, 197-206.

Chonkar, P.K., Iswaran, V. & Jauhri, K.S. (1971) *Plant Soil* 35, 449-452.

Dart, P.J. & Krantz, B.A. (1976) Legumes in the semi-arid tropics. *In*: Exploiting the legume-*Rhizobium* symbiosis in tropical agriculture, J.M. Vincent, A.S. Whitney & J. Bose (Eds.). Univ. Hawaii College Trop. Agric. *Misc. Publ.* 145, Pp. 119-154.

Gill, K.S. (1979) *Ind. J. Agric. Sci.* 49, 7-12.

Graham, P.H. & Parker, C.A. (1964) *Plant Soil* 20, 383-396.

Imbamba, S.K. (1973) *Physiol. Plant.* 28, 346-349.

Joe, W. Hwan-E. & Allen, J.R. (1980) *Comm. Soil Sci. Plant Anal.* 11, 1077-1085.

Minchin, F.R., Huxley, P. & Summerfield, R.J. (1976) *Expl. Agric.* 12, 279-288.

Narain, P., Singh, B. & Pal, B. (1977) *Indian Farm.* 27, 15-17.

Paliwal, K.V. & Maliwal, G.L. (1973) *Ann. Arid Zone* 12, 135-144.

Steinborn, J. & Roughley, R.J. (1975) *J. Appl. Bact.* 39, 133-138.

Totowat, K.L. & Saxena, S.W. (1970) *Plant Soil* 33, 43-47.

RESEARCH ON THE INOCULATION OF *GLYCINE MAX* AND *VICIA FABA* IN EGYPT

Y.A. Hamdi and M.N. Alaa El-Din[1]

Summary

Though soybeans (*Glycine max*) are a relatively new crop for Egypt, their response to inoculation has been variable. Failure to inoculate has been attributed to insufficient rhizobia applied/seed, death of the rhizobia applied, poor inoculant methodologies, seed treatment with toxic fungicides, and management problems, especially irrigation.

Vicia faba, by contrast, has been grown in Egypt for more than 2000 years, and its rhizobia occur in most soils there. Even so, significant increases in plant weight, nodule number and nodule weight at flowering have been common in inoculation trials undertaken in Egypt. Significant yield increases were obtained in five of fourteen inoculation experiments

INTRODUCTION

Soybeans (*Glycine max* (L.) Merr.) were introduced into Egyptian agriculture in the 1960's and now occupy about 40,000 ha. By contrast field beans (*Vicia faba* L.) were known to the pharaohs, and have been grown in Egypt since at least 2100 BC (Abdalla, 1979). This paper considers some aspects of the symbioses between these two legumes and their respective rhizobia under Egyptian conditions.

SOYBEANS

Response to inoculation

Most Egyptian soils do not contain *Rhizobium japonicum* (Abd El-Ghaffar, 1976; Sayed, 1980). Marked differences in response to inoculation

[1] Dept. of Microbiology, Institute of Soil and Water Research, Giza, Egypt.

have been obtained. While nodule number and weight and plant weight are usually enhanced by inoculation (Hamdi, Abd El Samea & Loufti, 1974; Abd El-Ghaffar, 1976; Sayed, 1980) soybean growth and development is often inadequate due to factors such as strain inefficiency (Abd El-Ghaffar, 1976) and soil type (Abd El-Ghaffar, 1976; Sayed, 1980). Above-normal rates of inoculation can be necessary. Hamdi *et al.* (1974) reported that yield when 28 x 10^4 rhizobia/seed had been applied was less than half that achieved with inoculation at 28 x 10^6 *R. japonicum* cells/seed (see Table 1).

Field experiments in the Beni-Suef and Manufiya Governorates suggest that the variable inoculation response may be due to poor *Rhizobium* survival in the Okadin inoculant, which is prepared from Nile silt. Thus, M.E. Abd El Samea (personal communication) found soybean yield in the Beni-Suef Governorate increased from 14 g/plant in the uninoculated control to 20.3 g/plant when the Okadin inoculant was used. However, when the same strains were used in a liquid culture, or in sterile peat, yields were in excess of 32 g/plant. Similar results were obtained in the Manufiya experiment. Because of these results, and the unavailability of peat, experiments are being undertaken to identify alternate carriers.

TABLE 1: Response of soybean var. Clark to the number of *R. japonicum* cells/seed used as inoculum (Hamdi *et al.*, 1974a).

Inoculation rate (cells/seed)	Plant dry wt (g)	Nodule fresh wt (g/plant)	No pods	Pod dry wt (g/plant)
Uninoculated control	9.8 ±1.0	0	33.0 ±2.63	8.7 ±1.8
28 x 10^6	12.1 ±1.2	1.30	46.5 ±6.41	17.7 ±3.0
28 x 10^5	10.5 ±1.9	0.70	28.0 ±5.9	14.7 ±3.7
28 x 10^4	9.7 ±1.4	0.30	31.1 ±9.1	8.5 ±2.2

Agronomic factors affecting symbiotic response in soybean

Attempts have been made to use nitrogen (N) fertilization in association with legume inoculation. Soybeans responded to N application at both the Beni-Suef and Menufiya sites, but even with 45 kg N applied/acre, yields were substantially less than in inoculated treatments receiving no N. At both sites yield with inoculation plus 15 kg/acre N was slightly better than in the inoculated-only plots (M.E. Abd El Samea, unpublished data), but higher rates of N fertilization generally depressed both nodulation and N_2 fixation.

Salt stress is of major significance in Egyptian agriculture. Strains N2 and E 45 of *R. japonicum*, selected, respectively, for tolerance and susceptibility to salt in culture medium, were used as inoculants in pot experiments with soils having different salt concentrations (Alaa El-Din, 1976). Nodule fresh weight, N_2 (C_2H_2) reduction, N content, and yield of all salt treatments was less than that of the corresponding controls, but in general strain N2 was less affected by salt than was E 45. In a similar experiment with soils having electrical conductivities between 3.36 and 10.00 m mho/cm, nodulation and yield were markedly reduced at all levels of electrical conductivity from 4.00-10.00, though the effect was most severe in a calcareous soil (Sayed, 1980).

Seed treatment with fungicides such as spergon, phygon and captan (Hamdi, Moharram & Loutfi, 1974) and benlate or vitavax/captan (Loutfi *et al.*, 1980) also depressed nodulation and N_2 fixation in soybean. Similar results were obtained in a pot experiment using the herbicides aretit, phanaum, cobex, linaron and treflan at rates of 0.75 to 10 kg or 1 to 7.5 litres/acre. (Alaa El-Din *et al.*, 1980).

FIELD BEANS *(VICIA FABA)*

Response to inoculation

As field beans have been grown in Egypt for many centuries most soils contain populations of *R. leguminosarum*. Uninoculated plants will bear an average of 79-94 nodules/plant depending on the location, rotation and water status of the crop (Loutfi *et al.*, 1980). Loutfi *et al.* (1980) also showed major population fluctuations over time at each of six sites tested, with *R. leguminosarum* numbers ranging from less than 10^2 to more than 10^6 rhizobia/g soil.

Despite the high background populations significant yield responses to inoculation were obtained in two of four trials undertaken by M. Loutfi and co-workers and in three of the ten trials undertaken by Hamdi & co-workers (Y.A. Hamdi, unpublished data). In the latter case, nodule number and weight/plant were enhanced by inoculation at all sites. Little is known of the ability of *R. leguminosarum* strains to compete with naturalized soil rhizobia under field conditions in Egypt. In one study, Hamdi and co-workers (Y.A. Hamdi, unpublished data) found that the percentage of nodules due to the inoculant strain varied from 60-100%. Of the strains commonly used at present Leg 1 appears the most highly competitive.

REFERENCES

Abd El-Ghaffar, S.A.M. (1976) MS thesis, Faculty of Agriculture, Univ. of Alexandria, Egypt.

Alaa El-Din, M.N. (1976) First Conf. Microbiol. Soc. Iraq, Baghdad.

Alaa El-Din, M.N., Mahmoud, S.A.E., El-Bassid, A.A., Abd El-Nasser, M., & Herzallah, N.A. (1980) *J. Res. Agric. Dev. Minia Univ.* (In press.)

Hamdi, Y.A., Abd El Samea, M.E. & Loutfi, M. (1974a) *Zent. fur Bakt.* (Abt. 2) 120, 574-578.

Hamdi, Y.A., Moharram, A.M. & Loutfi, M. (1974b) *Zent. fur Bakt.* (Abt. 2) 120, 129-135.

Loutfi, M., Risk, S.G. & Hamdi, Y.A. (1980) Final report to PL 480 Project No. 127. Presented to US Agency for International Development, Washington, DC, USA.

Sayed, K.M. (1980) MS thesis, Univ. of Tanta, Kafr El Sheikh, Egypt.

COWPEA-GROUP *RHIZOBIUM* IN SOILS OF THE SEMIARID TROPICS

J.V.D.K. Kumar Rao, P.J. Dart and M. Usha Khan[1]

Summary

Population of "cowpea-group" *Rhizobium* in fields at ICRISAT were estimated by the most probable number (MPN) method using siratro (*Macroptilium atropurpureum*) as host. There was usually a large variability in *Rhizobium* numbers between sampling sites in the same field. The populations were more consistent in Alfisols (range from 10^4 to 3 x 10^5/g soil) than in Vertisols (0 to 10^6/g soil) and decreased with depth. In paddy fields, the numbers were very low. Pigeonpea cultivars ICP-7332 (small seeded) and ICP-1 (medium sized), grown in test tubes, could also be used for the MPN method. In four of five soils tested, counts with pigeonpea as host were less than when siratro was used.

INTRODUCTION

Grain legumes such as groundnut, pigeonpea, and green gram are important agricultural crops in the semiarid tropics. Though nodulated by "cowpea-group" rhizobia, they have sometimes been shown to be poorly nodulated in farmers' fields (Nair, Ramaswamy & Porumal, 1971; Rewari, Kumar & Subba Rao, 1980; J.V.D.K. Kumar Rao & P.J. Dart, unpublished data), perhaps due to low numbers of the appropriate *Rhizobium* in soil. Because there is little data available on number of *Rhizobium* in arable soils of the semiarid tropics, we have examined the number and distribution of cowpea-group rhizobia in some soils typical of the region, using siratro (*Macroptilium atropurpureum*) and pigeonpea (*Cajanus cajan*) as trap hosts in most probable number (MPN) counts.

---

1 CP No. 62, ICRISAT, Patancheru P.O, Andra Pradesh 502324, India.

MATERIALS AND METHODS

The sampling unit for 0-30 cm depth samples was generally an area of approximately 0.1 ha, from which a number of random samples, each nearly 100 g, was collected, bulked, and subsampled to provide a final sample of 100 g. Of this amount, about 10 g was suspended in water and the remainder used for moisture determination. When soils were relatively loose, a split soil sampling tube or 4 cm mechanical corer were used. When soil was hard, pits were dug.

Rhizobium populations in soil samples were estimated by a serial dilution, plant infection method using siratro and/or pigeonpea as the test plant. Siratro seedlings were grown aseptically from sterilized seed sown directly into 18 mm x 150 mm test tubes containing Jensen's nitrogen (N) free agar medium (Vincent, 1970). Pigeonpea seeds were pre-germinated in plates before transfer to 25 mm x 200 mm tubes with the same medium. When the plants were about one week old, each tube was inoculated with a 1 ml aliquot of a 10-fold serial dilution of soil and incubated in a light chamber with a 16 h light and 8 h dark period at a temperature of 28 ± 2°C for 30 days. The MPN counts of rhizobia present in samples were calculated from the proportion of plants that nodulated, using MPN tables (Fisher & Yates, 1963; Brockwell *et al.*, 1975).

Siratro is normally used as a trap host for cowpea rhizobia. Initial tests of pigeonpea as a trap host favored the use of a small-seeded cultivar ICP-7332 (100 seed weight, 5.3 g), but subsequently cv. ICP-1, a commonly grown cultivar (100 seed weight, 10 g), was also found to grow and nodulate satisfactorily in 25 x 200 mm tubes. When siratro and pigeonpea were used to count the rhizobia in artificial soil/*Rhizobium* mixtures, MPN counts correlated well with plate counts (see Table 1). It is evident from Table 1 that nodules form when only a few rhizobia are present in the aliquot. This method

TABLE 1: Counts of *Rhizobium* added as pure cultures to ICRISAT soil using the plate count and MPN count methods.

Method of counting	Strain used		
	IHP-147	IHP-195	IHP-224
Plate count	5.0×10^8	1.0×10^7	5.0×10^6
MPN using pigeonpea	1.0×10^9	4.0×10^6	1.0×10^7
MPN using siratro	1.7×10^9	2.0×10^6	4.2×10^6

was then used to count the number of *Rhizobium* in fields at ICRISAT, to determine how distribution varied with depth, and to evaluate the cowpea-group and pigeonpea *Rhizobium* in a number of soils in India.

RESULTS AND DISCUSSION

Rhizobium populations in the fields at ICRISAT

Samples from 15 Vertisols and 8 Alfisols were collected, and MPN values were calculated using siratro as host. MPN counts for these 23 non-paddy soils are shown in Table 2. The MPN counts in Alfisols proved fairly uniform, but in the Vertisols, counts ranged from 0 to more than 10^6 rhizobia/g soil. There was no obvious relationship between population and present crop, nor any apparent reason why some fields should have such low numbers. The exception was field BA-10, where salinity was a problem. Samples were also taken from paddy soils at ICRISAT. *Rhizobium* populations in paddy soils

TABLE 2: Populations of cowpea group rhizobia ($\log_{10}$ MPN/g dry soil) in some Vertisols and Alfisols of ICRISAT, Hyderabad.

Vertisols				Alfisols			
Sample No.	Field	$\log_{10}$ MPN		Sample No.	Field	$\log_{10}$ MPN	
1	BW-2	6.1	(25)[1]	1	RW-2D	5.4	(3)[1]
2	BA-25	5.1	(34)	2	RA-17	5	(11)
3	ST-1	5.1	(32)	3	RA-25	5	(16)
4	BW-4	4.3	(25)	4	RW-2	5.0	(5)
5	BW-7	4.3	(23)	5	R-10	5.0	(3)
6	B-5	4.3	(22)	6	RA-26	4.7	(8)
7	M-14	4.2	(5)		(Healthy		
8	BW-6	3.7	(21)		Pigeonpea)		
9	BW-3	3.3	(25)	7	RA-26	4.2	(10)
10	B-2	3.1	(29)		(Sterility		
11	B-4	2.3	(29)		mosaic)		
12	BW-5	2.3	(26)				
13	BW-8	2.0	(15)	8	R-1	4.2	(11)
14	BA-10	1.7	(18)				
15	BW-1	0	(21)				
Mean over all Vertisols		3.4		Mean over all Alfisols		4.8	

[1]Moisture percentage of soil sample.

were low; generally less than 100/g of soil. In many rice growing areas of India it is common practice to grow a legume after the main crop of paddy, if water is limiting. If pigeonpea or other members of the cowpea inoculation group of legumes are planted after a paddy crop, it may be necessary to re-inoculate in order to ensure adequate nodulation.

Variation in *Rhizobium* population with depth

Pigeonpea is a deep-rooted crop, and roots grow to a depth of 200 cm. We examined the distribution of cowpea-group *Rhizobium* at soil depths ranging from 0-160 cm in small areas of different fields (see Table 3). In one Alfisol field (A), the *Rhizobium* population remained high (10^4/g dry soil) throughout most of the profile, whereas in field B, the population declined rapidly with depth, especially below 100 cm. Similar differences were observed in Vertisol fields. It is not known whether pigeonpea rhizobia travel along with the root system in the rhizosphere as the root grows through the soil. Further studies on the relationship of soil populations to nodulation and the response to inoculation are being initiated.

TABLE 3: Population of cowpea group rhizobia (log_{10} MPN/g dry soil) at different depths of two Alfisol and two Vertisol fields.

Soil depth (cm)	Alfisol		Vertisol	
	Field A[1]	Field B[2]	Field C[3]	Field[4]
0-5	3.2 (10)[5]		3.2 (2)	
		4.5[6] (9)		5.4[6] (21)
5-10	4.3 (10)		3.2 (25)	
20-30	5.0 (7)	4.0 (9)	3.8 (24)	4.9 (21)
50-60	4.7 (11)	2.5 (12)	2.8 (28)	4.6 (14)
100-110	4.2 (13)	1.7 (12)	1.6 (34)	3.0[7] (13)
150-160	3.3 (13)	0 (17)	1.6 (30)	2.8 (19)

[1] Average of 2 replications on a 4 x 16 m grid covering 0.1 ha in RW2B field, ICRISAT site, Patancheru.
[2] Average of 10 replications in Nursery field, ICRISAT, Patancheru.
[3] Average of 4 replications on a 4 x 16 m grid covering 0.1 ha in BW 4 field, ICRISAT site, Patancheru.
[4] Average of 3 replications in M-11 field, ICRISAT site, Patancheru.
[5] Value in brackets is moisture percent of sample on dry wt basis.
[6] Sample collected from 0-10 cm soil depth.
[7] Sample collected from 90-100 cm soil depth.

Specificity of pigeonpea

In the above studies, siratro was used as the trap legume for cowpea-type rhizobia. Subsequently both siratro and pigeonpea were used in MPN counts of cowpea-group rhizobia in different soils. With the marked exception of the soil from ICRISAT, where MPN estimates with the two legumes were similar, the estimates obtained using siratro as host were always higher than when pigeonpea was used (see Table 4). This suggests some degree of specificity between pigeonpea and cowpea-group rhizobia.

In the present study, rhizobial numbers varied within the same field, with soil type and depth: there was little relationship between present crop and *Rhizobium* population. Given this variation, seed inoculation could be worthwhile insurance, even in fields where the population of *Rhizobium* appears to be relatively high.

TABLE 4: Soil populations of cowpea *Rhizobium* when tested on siratro and pigeonpea.

Source of soil (India)	Numbers of rhizobia/g soil nodulating	
	Siratro	Pigeonpea
Kashmir	190,000	3270
Hissar (1)	3440	64
Hissar (2)	4300	0
Maharashtra	43000	92
ICRISAT	19300	19300

REFERENCES

Brockwell, J., Diatloff, A., Grassia, A., & Robinson, A.C. (1975) *Soil Biol. Biochem.* 7, 305-311.

Fisher, R.A. & Yates, F. (1963) Statistical tables (6th Ed.). Oliver & Boyd, London, England.

Nair, K.S., Ramaswamy, P.P. & Porumal, R. (1971) *Madras Agric. J.* 58, 5-8.

Rewari, R.B., Kumar, V. & Subba Rao, N.S. (1980) Pigeonpea response to inoculation in India. *In:* Proc. Internat. Workshop on Pigeonpeas, ICRISAT, Patancheru, Andhra Pradesh, India. (In press.)

Vincent, J.M. (1970) A manual for the practical study of root-nodule bacteria. IBP Handbook No. 15, Blackwell Scientific Publ. Oxford, England.

THE EFFECTS OF FERTILIZER NITROGEN AND *RHIZOBIUM* INOCULATION ON THE YIELD OF COWPEAS AND SUBSEQUENT CROPS OF MAIZE

S.K. Mughogho,[1] J. Awai,[1] H.S. Lowendorf,[2] and D.J. Lathwell[2]

Summary

Field experiments carried out on a Piarco fine sand and River Estate loam in Trinidad measured the response of cowpeas to fertilizer nitrogen (N) and to inoculation. On Piarco fine sand (a highly acid, poorly drained Tropudult) grain yields were initially low but improved in subsequent plantings. Yield responses to both fertilizer N and *Rhizobium* inoculation were small, indicating that factors other than N supply were limiting yield. On the Inceptisol, River Estate loam, yields were higher, but again there was little response to fertilizer N or *Rhizobium*. The yield of subsequent maize crops was increased by the incorporation of cowpea residues that made available to the maize crop the equivalent of 40-80 kg fertilizer N/ha. Much room for improvement in the yield of cowpeas remains, and only when the yield potential in the field is realized, can full advantage be taken of the legume/*Rhizobium* symbiosis.

INTRODUCTION

Grain legumes such as cowpeas (*Vigna unguiculata*) are important components of many cropping systems. When *Rhizobium* strain and host plant are compatible, and edaphic and climatic conditions favorable, the legume requires little or no additional nitrogen (N).

Currently, though grain legumes continue to be an important source of dietary protein, yields are low. While many soils in tropical regions are deficient in N (Diaz-Romeu, Balerdi & Fassbender, 1970; Bazan, 1975) the response to both *Rhizobium* inoculation and N fertilization has often proved

[1] Dept. of Soil Science, Univ, of the West Indies, St. Augustine, Trinidad.

[2] Agronomy Dept., Cornell University, Ithaca, NY, 14853 USA.

disappointing. As little data on this topic was available for Trinidad, we examined the effect of fertilizer N and/or *Rhizobium* inoculation on the symbiotic N_2 fixation and grain yields of cowpeas and on the yield of subsequently planted maize (*Zea mays*).

MATERIALS AND METHODS

The effect of fertilizer N and/or *Rhizobium* inoculation on N_2 fixation in cowpea was studied in two experiments on Piarco fine sands and one on River Estate loam. The first-named soil is highly acid and has a high degree of aluminum (Al) saturation (see Table 1). It has very restricted drainage in the subsoil. In contrast, the River Estate loam is an Inceptisol in which the upper portion of the profile is high in bases (see Table 1). It is a well-drained soil, derived from micaceous phyllite alluvium.

TABLE 1: Some chemical properties of the Piarco fine sand and River Estate loam soils.

Sample depth (cm)	pH	Ca	Mg	Al	Organic matter (%)	Total N (%)
			(meq/100g)			
Piarco fine sand						
0-15	4.6	0.40	0.19	2.37	2.2	0.14
15-20	4.7	0.35	0.17	2.69	1.6	0.08
River Estate loam						
0- 8	6.6	10.3	1.1	-	2.0	0.26
8-24	6.6	3.4	0.4	-	0.7	0.08
24-56	6.6	1.8	0.3	-	0.7	0.07

On the Piarco fine sand, all plots received a basic dressing of superphosphate, muriate of potash, and limestone, rotovated into the soil before each experiment was established. In addition, the site was camber bedded to improve surface drainage. Treatments included three levels of applied N (0, 60, 120 kg N/ha) with or without *Rhizobium* inoculation. Fertilizer N was applied as urea and banded beside the seed at planting. Where 120 kg N/ha was applied, half was applied at planting, the remainder four weeks after emergence. Inoculated seed was prepared by wetting the seed with inoculant the night before planting. Cowpea seed in all experiments was planted in rows spaced 50 cm apart with 15 cm between seeds. Grain was harvested and yields calculated. On the River Estate loam the same procedure was followed, except that no lime was applied.

Two experiments to investigate the effects of cropping system, N fertilization and inoculation on subsequent maize crops were undertaken — one at each site. The Piarco experiment compared maize productivity in soil previously cropped to maize or cowpea with that of land previously in fallow. For each cropping treatment four N fertilization rates were used (0, 30, 60, 120 kg N/ha). All residues from the previous crop plus additional P and K were rotovated or spaded into the plots prior to planting the maize in rows 90 cm apart with 30 cm between plants. N fertilizer was applied as in the previous experiment.

On the River Estate loam no N fertilizer was applied, so that any differences were due to previous cropping history, N fertilization, or inoculation.

RESULTS AND DISCUSSION

Cowpea yields in the first trial on the Piarco fine sands were very low — control plots yielded only 190 kg/ha. Yield was increased significantly by the application of 60 kg fertilizer N/ha, but application of further N or *Rhizobium* inoculation failed to enhance yield levels. As the maximum yield obtained in this trial was only 540 kg/ha, factors other than those under investigation were obviously limiting yield. In another fertilization and inoculation trial at this location, yields were appreciably higher (average 1075 kg/ha) but there was no response to either fertilizer N or *Rhizobium* inoculation. Despite the poor response to applied N and to *Rhizobium* inoculation some advantage did accrue to maize following cowpea (see Table 2). When the responses of maize to fertilizer N are compared, the advantage of comparing cowpeas-maize to maize-maize was equivalent to the addition of about 80 kg N/ha, and for the cowpea-maize to fallow-maize, the advantage was equivalent to about 45 kg N/ha. Thus, the cowpea residues were quite effective in supplying N to the following maize crop compared to fertilizer N.

Grain yields of cowpeas grown on River Estate loam were higher than those on Piarco fine sands (see Table 3). Total grain yield was not affected by fertilizer N application, at this site, but *Rhizobium* inoculation resulted in a small but significant yield increase. There was a trend for increased yield of marketable peas with additions of fertilizer N. Maturity was delayed in the uninoculated and zero N plots, with increased disease incidence resulting in fewer marketable peas. This is interesting, as fertilizer N is often considered to delay maturity in crop plants.

When maize followed cowpea on the River Estate loam, yields were definitely enhanced (see Table 4). Mughogho *et al.* (1981) estimated that an average of 45 kg N/ha remained after cowpea grain had been harvested. In this experiment differences in N uptake between maize after fallow and maize

TABLE 2: The effect of fertilizer N application on maize yield following fallow, maize or cowpea grown on Piarco fine sand. October, 1977-March 1978.

Fertilizer N rate (kg/ha)	Maize yield (kg/ha)			
	After fallow	After maize	After cowpea	Mean
0	2505	2065	2705	2425
30	2610	2450	2845	2635
60	2800	2655	3035	2830
120	3325	2985	3345	3220
Mean	2810	2540	2985	

Differences among fertilizer N treatments were significant (P = 0.01).
Differences among cropping treatments were significant (P = 0.06).

TABLE 3: The effect of *Rhizobium* inoculation and fertilizer N application on grain yield of cowpeas grown on River Estate loam, March-May, 1980.

Fertilizer N rate (kg/ha)	Cowpea grain yield (kg/ha)					
	Uninoculated		Rhizobium 13B		Mean	
	Total	Marketable	Total	Marketable	Total	Marketable
0	1725	1270	1770	1485	1750	1380
30	1685	1340	1950	1690	1820	1515
60	1795	1470	1895	1575	1845	1525
Mean	1735	1360	1870	1585		

Differences between *Rhizobium* treatments were significant (P = 0.05).
No significant differences among fertilizer N treatments were found.

after cowpea suggest that the maize recovered about 12 kg N/ha of this. Inoculation of the preceding cowpea crop had little effect on maize yields or N content. Both cowpea treatments were well nodulated, whether inoculum had been added or not. Apparently, little residual fertilizer N remained in the soil, as evidenced by the yields obtained following the fallow or the cowpea plots.

TABLE 4: The effect of fertilizer N application on maize yield following fallow, uninoculated cowpeas, and inoculated cowpeas on River Estate loam.

Fertilizer N rate (kg/ha)	Maize yield (kg/ha)			
	After fallow	After cowpeas (uninoculated)	After cowpeas (inoculated)	Mean
0	1885	3070	3225	2720
30	2070	2895	3030	2665
60	2115	2940	3270	2775
Mean	2025	2970	3175	

No significant difference due to fertilizer N was found.
Differences among cropping treatments were significant ($P = 0.05$).

The contribution of residues of cowpeas to the N economy of the subsequent crop, at least in these experiments, was relatively small. Shrader, Fuller & Cady (1966) in Iowa found a good legume crop contributed about 110 kg/ha of N to a subsequent crop. Bartholemew (1972) argued that legumes may not be able to supply enough N to meet the needs of high yielding crops. The only way increased N supply from residues can be achieved is to increase significantly the N_2 fixation of the legume crop. These results indicate we have a long way to go to achieve this objective.

REFERENCES

Bartholomew, W.V. (1972) Soil nitrogen and organic matter. *In:* Soils of the humid tropics. National Academy of Sciences, Washington D.C., USA. Pp. 63-81.

Bazan, R. (1975) Nitrogen fertilization and management of grain legumes in Central America. *In:* Soil management in tropical America, E. Bornemisza & A. Alvarado (Eds.). North Carolina State Univ. Raleigh, N.C., USA. Pp. 228-245.

Diaz-Romeu, R., Balerdi, F. & Fassbender, H.W. (1970) *Turrialba* 20, 185-192.

Mughogho, S.K., Awai, S.K., Lowendorf, H.S., & Scott, T.W. (1981) Biological nitrogen fixation in cropping systems. (In press.)

Shrader, W.D., Fuller, W.A. & Cady, F.B. (1966) *Agron. J.* 58, 397-401.

EFFECT OF NITROGEN FERTILIZATION ON LEAF NITRATE REDUCTASE AND NODULE NITROGENASE ACTIVITY IN SOYBEANS

T.C. Juang,[1] C.C. Tann[1] and S.C.S. Tsou[2]

Summary

The nitrate reductase activity of pot-grown soybean leaves showed a Michaelis-Menten relationship with soil nitrate nitrogen (N) content at all growth stages, but maximum inducible nitrate reductase activity decreased as the plant aged. A certain level of nitrate-N in soil was needed for optimum nitrogenase activity in the later growth stages.

Nitrate reductase and nitrogenase activities were negatively correlated in four-week-old seedlings, but showed a parabolic relationship six and ten weeks after germination.

INTRODUCTION

In a period of rapidly increasing fertilizer prices it is important that fertilizer nitrogen (N) be used effectively and, where it is applied to legumes, that it be compatible with symbiotic N_2 fixation. In soybean, the activity of leaf nitrate reductase (the primary enzyme in nitrate metabolism) is high during early growth but declines rapidly after flowering (Harper & Hageman, 1972; Thibodeau & Jaworski, 1975; Hatam & Hume, 1976). N_2 fixation by the root nodules gives a peak during flowering and pod-fill; then declines (Hardy *et al.*, 1968; AVRDC, 1976).

The Asian Vegetable Research and Development Center (AVRDC) (1976) has reported that leaf nitrate reductase activity before flowering was significantly correlated with yield. We hypothesize that both nitrate reductase and nitrogenase activity are important to soybean seed production, the former during the early growth stage, the latter at a subsequent stage in the

[1] Research Institute of Soil Science, National Chung Hsing University, Taiwan, Republic of China.

[2] Asian Vegetable Research Development Center (AVRDC) Taiwan, Republic of China.

growth cycle. In this paper we look at the effect of fertilizer N on soil N status and on the activities of nitrate reductase and nitrogenase.

MATERIALS AND METHODS

Plant and soil materials

Soybean seeds (AVRDC breeding line 30182-2-6) were inoculated with a commercial inoculant (Nitragin Co., Milwaukee, WI, USA); then planted into pots containing 6 kg of loamy soil with an organic matter content of 1.50%, a total N content of 0.072% and a pH of 7.4. All pots received a basal dressing of Ca $(H_2PO_4)_2$ and KCl before planting. Three forms of N fertilizer $(NH_4)_2SO_4$, urea, and sulfur-coated urea (SCU, 24% N) were used, and applied at rates of 300 or 600 mg/pot. The $(NH_4)_2SO_4$ and urea were applied in split dressings at planting and 35 and 60 days after germination; the SCU was applied as a single dosage at planting. All treatments were replicated three times.

Nitrate reductase and nitrogenase assay

Leaf nitrate reductase activity was assayed using the method of Streeter & Bosler (1972). N_2 (C_2H_2) activity was measured using two washed root systems per inoculation vessel, with ethylene production measured on a Shimadzu model CC 5A gas chromatograph using a flame ionization detector and a 2 m stainless steel column packed with Poropak N.

Plant and soil analysis

Plant tissue samples were oven dried at 70° C, ground, and then stored in a desiccator. Total N was determined by the Kjeldahl method. Available NO_2^-, NO_3^- and NH_4^+ in soil samples were determined by Kjeldahl distillation and back titration with diluted H_2SO_4 .

RESULTS AND DISCUSSION

Effect of N fertilization on leaf nitrate reductase activity

Time course studies on leaf nitrate reductase activity showed that N fertilization increased nitrate reductase activity (see Figure 1). Leaf nitrate reductase showed a Michaelis-Menten relationship with soil NO_3^- (see Table 1) at all stages of plant growth. Soil NH_4^+ effects on leaf nitrate reductase activity could not be detected. This finding is contrary to that reported by Orebamjo & Stewart (1975) who noted nitrate reductase formation and activity in *Lemna minor* inhibited by NH_4^+.

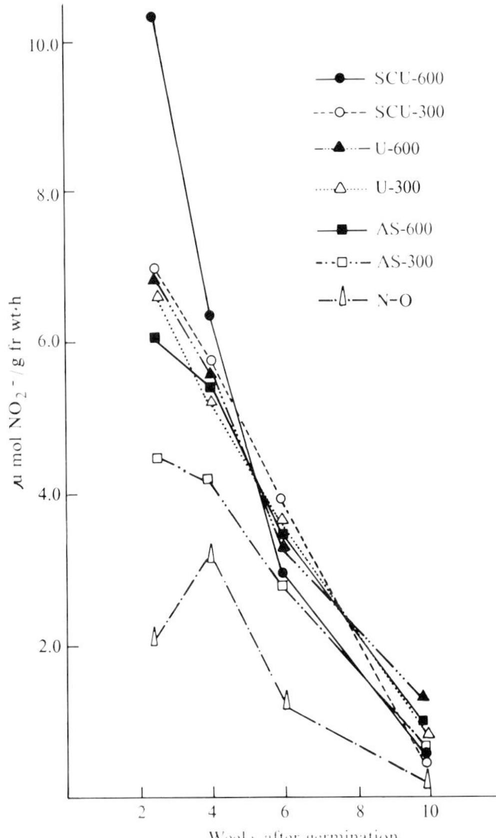

Figure 1.
Time course of soybean leaf nitrate reductase (NR) activity as affected by ammonium sulfate (AS), urea (U) and sulfur-coated urea (SCU) application at rates of 300 mg and 600 mg N per pot.

By using double reciprocal plots, the maximum inducible nitrate reductase activity and Km values could be calculated (see Table 1). The maximum inducible activity of nitrate reductase was 8.7 μmoles NO_2^-/g fresh weight per hour at four weeks after germination, but it decreased as the plant aged. By contrast Km values increased from 7.3 to 12.3 ppm of nitrate N as the plants aged.

Effect of N fertilizer on nodule nitrogenase activity

Total N and nitrate N in the soil at no stage exceeded 40 and 30 ppm, respectively. Effects of N fertilization on N_2 (C_2H_2) fixation are shown in Figure 2. While the levels of activity given are generally low, there is evidence of early inhibition of N_2 (C_2H_2) fixation following N fertilization. However,

TABLE 1: Correlation of leaf NR activity and nodule N_2-ase activity to soil mineral nitrogen content.

	Soil N (X)	
	Nitrate-N	Ammonium-N
NR activity (Y)		
4 wk	$1/Y = 0.114 + 0.831/X$ ($r = 0.73^*$) Vmax[1] = 8.7 Km = 7.3	NS
6 wk	$1/Y = 0.152 + 2.144/X$ ($r = 0.95^{**}$) Vmax = 6.6 Km = 14.1	NS
10 wk	$1/Y = 0.539 + 6.574/X$ ($r = 0.74^*$) Vmax = 1.9 Km = 12.3	NS
N_2-ase activity (Y)		
4 wk	$Y = 0.048 + 4.200/X$ ($r = 0.86^{**}$)	NS
6 wk	NS	NS
8 wk	NS	NS
10 wk	NS	NS

[1]Vmax: μmol NO_2^-/g fresh wt per h. Km: ppm nitrate-N. NS: nonsignificant.

by eight weeks after germination most N-fertilized pots showed fixation rates greater than that of the unfertilized control.

Relationship between leaf nitrate reductase and nitrogenase activity

At the four-week harvest there was a negative linear correlation between leaf nitrate reductase and N_2 (C_2H_2) fixation. However at the six-week and ten-week harvests, leaf nitrate reductase activity showed a parabolic relationship with N_2 (C_2H_2) fixation (see Figure 3). This suggests that a certain level of nitrate N may be beneficial to symbiotic N_2 fixation promoting early plant development and, thus, providing greater pools of photosynthate for nodules. Similar results have been obtained by Hashimoto (1976).

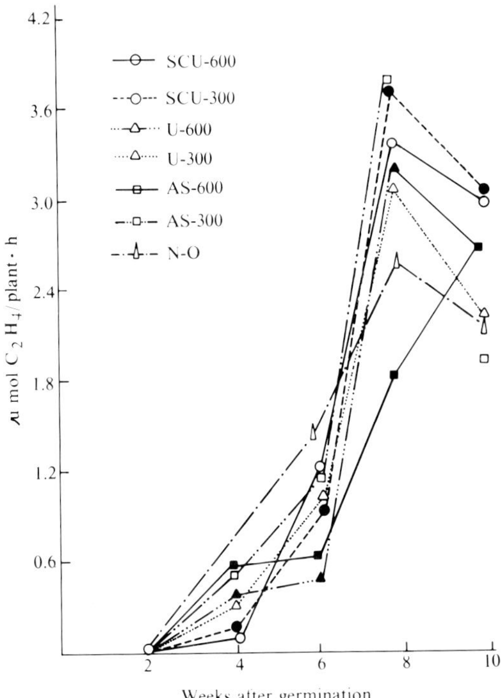

Figure 2.
Soybean nodule nitrogenase (N_2-ase) activity as affected by ammonium sulfate (AS), urea (U) and sulfur-coated urea (SCU) application at rates of 300 mg and 600 mg per pot.

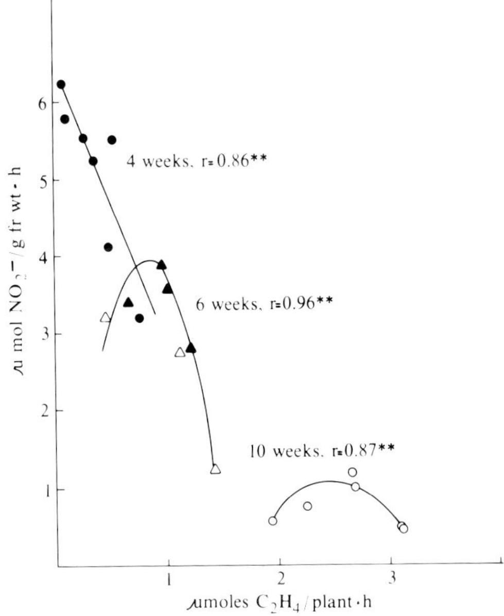

Figure 3.
Regression analysis of leaf nitrate reductase (NR) activity in relation to nodule nitrogenase activity.

REFERENCES

Asian Vegetable Research and Development Center (AVRDC) (1976) Soybean report for 1975. AVRDC, Shanhua, Taiwan, Republic of China.

Hardy, R.W.F., Holsten, R.D., Jackson, Z.K., & Burns, R.C. (1968) The acetylene reduction assay for N_2 fixation: Laboratory and field evaluation. *Plant Physiol.* 43, 1185-1207.

Harper, J.F. & Hageman, R.H. (1972) Canopy and seasonal profiles of nitrate reductase in soybeans (*Glycine max* (L.) Merr.). Plant Physiol. 49, 146-154.

Hashimoto, K. (1976) The significance of nitrogen nutrition to the seed yield and its relating characters of soybeans. *Res. Bull. Hokkaido Natl. Agric. Exp. Stn.* 114, 1.

Hatam, M. & Hume, D.J. (1976) Relations between nitrate reductase activity and nitrogen accumulation in soybeans. *Can. J. Plant Sci.* 56, 337-384.

Orebamjo, T.O. & Stewart, G.R. (1975) Ammonium repression of nitrate reductase formation in *Lemna minor* L. *Planta* (Berl.) 122, 27-36.

Streeter, J.G. & Bosler, M.E. (1972) Comparison of *in vitro* and *in vivo* assays for nitrate reductase on soybean leaves. *Plant Physiol.* 49, 448-450.

Thibodeau, P.S. & Jaworski, E.G. (1975) Patterns of nitrogen utilization in the soybean. *Planta* (Berl.) 127, 133-147.

STUDIES ON THE PERSISTENCE OF INTRODUCED STRAINS OF *RHIZOBIUM JAPONICUM* IN SOIL DURING FALLOW, AND THE EFFECTS ON SOYBEAN GROWTH AND YIELD

V. Ranga Rao, G. Thottapilly and A. Ayanaba[1]

Summary

Inoculation experiments with the American soybean cultivars TGm 80 ('Bossier') and TGm 294-4 in Nigeria in 1978 showed striking responses to inoculation. Because African farmers practice shifting cultivation, we examined the persistence of the inoculant strains in soil, and their ability to sustain soybean yields after a two-year fallow period.

After the fallow period, significant increases in nodule mass, shoot weight, and grain yield were again observed in the inoculated plots, where TGm 80 and TGm 294-4 were grown, in comparison to the uninoculated treatments. With 'Orba' the differences were not significant. Serological typing of the nodules using the Enzyme Linked Immunosorbent Assay (ELISA) revealed that most of the nodules formed on the three soybean cultivars were from the strains introduced in 1978. We conclude that the nitrogen fixed by these nodules could sustain the growth and yield of soybean cultivars after a two-year fallow period, thus encouraging a possible low-input soybean cultivation by subsistence farmers in Africa.

INTRODUCTION

Tropical soils not previously used for the cultivation of soybean contain few rhizobia capable of effectively nodulating this species. There is, therefore, great potential for achieving high soybean yields with no fertilizer nitrogen (N) input, by introducing known effective strains of *Rhizobium japonicum*. In 1978, a series of field experiments were undertaken throughout Nigeria to screen strains of *R. japonicum* and select those that proved most efficient. In

[1] International Institute of Tropical Agriculture (IITA), PMB 5320, Ibadan, Nigeria.

this study, seed yield of American soybean cultivars was increased as much as 100% by inoculation, but cultivars having Asiatic origins did not respond significantly (Kang, 1975; Pulver *et al.*, 1978; Nangju, 1980; Rao *et al.*, 1980).

In the shifting cultivation pattern practiced in Africa, it is common to leave the field in fallow after cropping. The present study was designed to evaluate the persistence of *R. japonicum* strains introduced in 1978 as seed inoculants, after a two-year fallow period, and to assess the ability of surviving rhizobia to sustain soybean growth and yield.

MATERIALS AND METHODS

The experiment was conducted in predominantly clayey upland soils (Egbeda series) low in N (0.12% total N) at the International Institute of Tropical Agriculture (IITA), Ibadan, Nigeria.

Twelve single-strain inoculants and one multi-strain commercial inoculant (Nitragin Co. Milwaukee, WI, USA) had been used in the 1978 study. The single strains used were *R. japonicum* 46 (Zambia); G3 ENSA (Ivory Coast); 67 (Zambia); 18 (IITA); SM 35 and SM 31 (mutants of 61A76, USA); 110, 110 mutant (USA); 142, 143, 138, 122 (USA). These had been applied to the seed as peat based inoculants using a Nitracoat adhesive (Nitragin Co.), and inoculated seed was planted in a moist soil.

Uninoculated and fertilizer N treatments had also been used in this trial, urea (150 kg/ha) being applied as a split dressing at sowing, flowering, and early pod-fill.

After a two-year fallow, the plots were cleared and uninoculated seed of the cultivars TGm 80 ('Bossier'), and TGm 294-4 (both of American origin) and the Indonesian cultivar Orba were replanted into the plots they had occupied in 1978. An additional treatment, that of freshly inoculated seed was added as a control, while plots under N in the 1978 trial received a further 150 kg/ha as urea.

The ELISA serological technique (Enzyme Linked Immunosorbent Assay) was used to determine what percentage of the nodules formed were due to the previously applied inoculant. For preparing antisera, *Rhizobium* strains were grown on the liquid medium for 3 days at 27 $\pm$ 1°C. Bacterial cells were harvested by centrifugation at 12,000 g for 10 minutes and resuspended in 0.85% NaCl solution. The cells were thoroughly washed in saline and centrifuged again. The antisera were prepared by intramuscular injection of rabbits using 1 ml of bacterial suspension (containing approximately 2×10^{12} cells/ml) and an equal volume of Freund's incomplete adjuvant. Three such injections were given at weekly intervals. The rabbits were bled 2 weeks after the last injection and weekly thereafter. For the preparation of antigens, single nodules were crushed in a solution of phosphate-buffered saline (pH 7.4) containing 0.05% Tween-20 and 2% polyvinylpyrrolidone. The "double antibody sandwich" form of the ELISA assay (Voller *et al.*, 1976; Clark &

Adams, 1977) was used. The reactions were carried out in polystyrene microtitre plates (Cooke M 129 A; Dynatech Laboratories, Alexandria, VA, USA). The coating of the plates with γ-globulin was done after dilution in 0.05 M carbonate buffer (pH 9.6) with the plates then incubated overnight at 4-6° C (Thottapilly & Rossel, 1980). After washing the plates, 0.02 ml of the test samples was added to each well with further overnight incubation. After washing, 0.2 ml of γ-globulin-alkaline phosphatase conjugate was added to each well and incubated at 4-6°C for 10-12 hours. The plates were again washed and 0.2 ml of enzyme substrate solution (0.5 mg/ml of p-nitrophenyl phosphate in 10% diethanolamine, pH 9.8) was added to each well. Positive reactions produced a yellow coloration due to the action of antibody-linked alkaline phosphate on the enzyme substrate; negative reactions remained colorless.

RESULTS AND DISCUSSION

Significant increase in nodule mass was noticed in all three cultivars following inoculation in the 1978 planting, though uninoculated plants of cv. Orba, had 6-20 times more nodule mass than those of cv. Bossier and cv. TGm 294-4, indicating the wider compatibility of indigenous rhizobia with 'Orba'. Earlier studies had shown that 'Orba' is nodulated by cowpea-group rhizobia, while the occasional nodules seen on 'Bossier' and TGm 294-4 were due to *R. japonicum* strains that have found their way into African soils. Also, many strains of rhizobia isolated from 'Orba' were not compatible with 'Bossier' and TGm 294-4, showing a clear host/strain specificity pattern between the Asian and American soybean cultivars (IITA, 1978; 1979). Significant increases in shoot weight and grain yield were obtained with all inoculant treatments in TGm 80 and TGm 294-4, but in 'Orba' such a response was visible with only a few inoculants (Ranga Rao *et al.*, 1980).

Significant differences in the nodule mass between inoculated and uninoculated treatments were again observed in 1980 for the varieties TGm 80 and TGm 294-4, but not for 'Orba'. For most of the inoculation treatments nodule mass in the 1980 planting was considerably below that of the 1980 inoculated check, and less than had been reported in 1978 (see Table 1). This is indicative of a possible drop in *Rhizobium* numbers during the fallow period.

Similarly, grain yields in the 1980 planting tended to be less than those achieved by the 1980 inoculated check, and below those that had been achieved in 1978. However the inoculation response in 'Bossier' and TGm 294-4 was still clear with most of the 1978 inoculation treatments yielding as much as the plots receiving 150 kg N/ha. No such response was evident with the 'Orba' variety (see Table 2). The yield responses with the 'Bossier' and TGm 294-4 varieties clearly reflect the persistence and effectiveness of at least some of the introduced rhizobia over the two-year fallow period.

TABLE 1: Nodule dry weight (mg/plant, 6 weeks after planting) in three cultivars of soybean after inoculation in 1978, and following a two-year fallow period.

Treatments		Cultivars					
		Bossier		TGm 294		Orba	
		1978	1980	1978	1980	1978	1980
Uninoculated	-N	14	14	46	68	287	208
	+100N	46	68	30	72	275	135
R. japonicum:							
	46	251	190	186	125	351	236
	G3 ENSA	386	129	472	215	569	161
	67	349	181	317	102	505	193
	18	362	206	300	199	473	175
	SM 35	609	140	552	249	679	225
	SM 31	650	93	509	216	695	156
	110	431	120	306	126	443	178
	110 Mut.	479	148	388	115	538	175
	142	458	121	303	100	488	225
	143	765	168	410	213	495	244
	138	532	160	344	225	452	213
	122	391	122	406	133	348	175
	Nitragin	645	107	424	96	648	152
SM 35 inoculated in 1980			367		392		584

L S D (0.05) for comparison of means of different treatments:

1978 = 185; 1980 = 77

Using the ELISA technique for four strains of rhizobia, we found that nearly all nodules formed in 1980 by 'Bossier' and TGm 294-4 were from the strains introduced in 1978. In 'Orba', the nodulation was not entirely due to introduced rhizobia. Because 'Orba' is compatible with indigenous, cowpea-type rhizobia, the performance of *R. japonicum* 110 and 138 in 1980 is suggestive of the poor competitiveness of these strains with indigenous rhizobia. When heavy doses of inoculum were used, as in the case of *R. japonicum* SM 35 introduced in 1980, all the nodules formed on the three cultivars were of this strain (see Table 3). There was a small increase in the nodule mass of TGm 80 and TGm 294-4 in the uninoculated plots. ELISA

TABLE 2: Grain yield (kg/ha) of three cultivars of soybean after inoculation in 1978 and following a two year fallow period.

Treatments		Cultivars					
		Bossier		TGm 294		Orba	
		1978	1980	1978	1980	1978	1980
Uninoculated	-N	1643	1526	1079	1655	2124	1924
	+150N	2726	2314	2682	2151	2671	1848
R. japonicum:							
	46	2781	2429	2947	2279	2251	1915
	G3 ENSA	3180	2331	2872	2540	2559	1670
	67	2978	2422	2848	2309	1857	1772
	18	3125	2690	2843	2503	2622	1657
	SM 35	3034	2387	2525	2576	2368	1978
	SM 31	2816	2451	2943	2120	1734	2046
	110	3170	2736	2872	2834	2660	1789
	110 Mut.	2792	2934	3069	2598	2748	1950
	142	3173	2271	2590	1936	2353	2044
	143	2533	1847	2318	1807	2090	1758
	138	2871	2433	3152	1997	2523	1471
	122	3126	2362	2860	2188	2426	1857
	Nitragin	3032	2616	2878	2335	2620	2067
SM 35 inoculated in 1980			3031		2935		2205

L S D (0.05) for comparison of means of different treatments:

1978 = 309; 1980 = 508

results showed also that nodules formed in the uninoculated plots on TGm 80 and TGm 294-4 were almost entirely due to contamination originating from the introduced strains while in **'Orba' they were largely due to native rhizobia** (see Table 4). From our study with *R. japonicum* cultures and with soybean nodules, and from earlier work on groundnut (Kishnevsky & Bar-Joseph, 1978) and lentil nodules (Berger *et al.*, 1979), the ELISA technique appears to be a promising serological tool for rapid detection of rhizobia in nodules and in culture, facilitating analysis of large numbers of samples with very little antiserum.

TABLE 3: Percent of nodules formed by inoculant strain after a two-year fallow period.[1]

Rhizobium japonicum strains	Cultivars		
	Bossier	TGm 294	Orba
SM 35	81	98	72
SM 31	93	100	78
110	98	88	16
138	90	94	45
SM 35 (1980)	100	100	100

[1]Based on 192 nodules/treatment.

TABLE 4: Percent of nodules formed in the uninoculated plants due to contamination by *R. japonicum* strains.[1]

Contaminating strain	Cultivars		
	Bossier	TGm 294	Orba
SM 35	25	19	17
SM 31	27	20	26
110	6	6	0
138	47	41	0

[1]Based on 192 nodules/cultivar.

CONCLUSION

The following conclusions can be drawn from the above studies:

Rhizobium inoculants offer a great hope for increasing the yields of high-yielding US soybean cultivars in Africa;

Effective strains of rhizobia introduced as inoculants survive short fallow periods and can sustain soybean yields after fallow without further inoculant or fertilizer N input; and

Cultivars of Asian origin do not respond to inoculants significantly because of their ability to nodulate with the indigenous rhizobia.

The soybean breeding program at IITA is aiming to transfer the nodulating characteristics of Asian cultivars to agronomically superior, American-bred cultivars.

REFERENCES

Berger, J.A., May, S.N., Berger, L.R., & Bohlool, B.B. (1979) *Appl. Environ. Microbiol.* 27, 642-646.

Clark, M.F. & Adams, A.N. (1977) *J. Gen. Virol.* 34, 475-483.

International Institute of Tropical Agriculture (1978) Ann. Rept. IITA, Ibadan, Nigeria.

International Institute of Tropical Agriculture (1979) Ann. Rept. IITA, Ibadan, Nigeria.

Kang, B.T. (1975) *Expl. Agric.* 11, 23-31.

Kishinevsky, B. & Bar-Joseph, M. (1978) *Can. J. Microbiol.* 24, 1537-1543.

Nangju, D. (1980) *Agron. J.* 72, 403-406.

Pulver, E.L., Brockman, F., Nangju, D., & Wien, H. (1978) IITA's programme on N_2 fixation. *In*: Isotopes in biological dinitrogen fixation. Internat. Atomic Energy Agy., Vienna, Austria. Pp. 269-283.

Ranga Rao, V., Ayanaba, A., Eaglesham, A.R.J., & Kueneman, E.A. (1980) Exploiting symbiotic nitrogen fixation for increasing soybean yields in Africa. *In*: Proceedings GIAM VI Conference. (In press.)

Thottapilly, G. & Rossel, H.W. (1980) ELISA technique for the detection of viruses of economically important food crops in humid tropics of West Africa. *IITA Research Brief* 1, 1-2.

Voller, A., Barlett, A., Bidwell, D.E., Clark, M.F., & Adams, A.N. (1976) *J. Gen. Virol.* 33, 165-167.

EFFECTS OF SUPPLEMENTAL NITROGEN ON NODULATION, ASSIMILATION OF NITROGEN, GROWTH AND SEED YIELD OF *PHASEOLUS VULGARIS* AND *VIGNA UNGUICULATA*

M.S. Fernándes, M.C.P. Neves and M.F.M. Sá[1]

Summary

Supplemental nitrogen (N) equivalent to 60 kg N/ha was applied to inoculated plants of *Phaseolus vulgaris* and *Vigna unguiculata* at flowering, either as nitrate N or ammonium N + Nitrapyrin to soil, or as urea applied foliarly in repeated dressings. Plants harvested at weekly intervals thereafter were assayed for nitrogenase and nitrate reductase activity, nodule development, and the ureide content of the xylem exudate.

Bean plants had lower nodule dry weight and were weaker in N_2 (C_2H_2) fixation than cowpea, but profiles of activity were similar for both species. The nitrate reductase activity of bean plants was about three times greater than that of cowpea. Applied N affected nitrate reductase activity in cowpea, but in beans the sharp increase in nitrate reductase activity soon after flowering occurred with or without supplental N.

For cowpea the ureide content of xylem sap was greatest during early vegetative growth, while in beans maximum ureide content was found during flowering and decreased just after application of supplemental N.

Yield of green bean pods was enhanced considerably with applied nitrate-N, whereas for cowpeas maximum yield was obtained using urea in foliar applications. Cowpeas outyielded beans in all treatments, but were less efficient in utilization of nitrate-N.

INTRODUCTION

The availability of nitrogen (N) to plants at critical stages of growth is essential for high yield. Legumes are fortunate in that they not only have the

[1] Dept. of Soil Science, UFRRJ, Itaguai, 23460, Rio de Janeiro, Brazil.

ability to utilize soil and fertilizer N, but they can also fix N_2 from the atmosphere. Thus, under most field conditions both nitrate reductase and nitrogenase enzymes will be operating, though at different levels of activity. For nitrogenase (N_2-ase), maximum activity has been reported during vegetative and early reproductive growth, whereas peaks in nitrate reductase activity (NRA) can occur both in the early-vegetative (Streeter, 1972; Franco, Pereira & Neyra, 1979) and post-flowering periods (Franco *et al.,* 1979).

Given the increasing cost of N fertilizer, it is essential that methods of fertilization are developed that are compatible with, and complementary to, N_2 fixation. In this paper we report the effects of post-flowering N fertilization on the N uptake, metabolism and yield of nodulated beans (*Phaseolus vulgaris*) and cowpea (*Vigna unguiculata*) plants.

MATERIALS AND METHODS

The experiment was undertaken on a red yellow podzolic soil having 51.8 ppm K, 3.2 ppm P, 0.05 meq/100 g Al, 5.2 meq/100 g Ca + Mg, 0.13% N, and a pH of 5.9

Prior to planting, the experimental area was fertilized with 80 kg/ha P_2O_5 as triple superphosphate, 30 kg/ha K_2O as KCl, and 20 kg/ha N as $(NH_4)_2SO_4$. Test plants were *Phaseolus vulgaris* cv. Rio Tibagi and *Vigna unguiculata* cv. Vita 34. For each cultivar three replicate blocks were sown using 60 cm between rows and 5 cm between seeds. Seeds were inoculated with *Rhizobium* (C-05 and F413 mixed for *P. vulgaris,* I_{1a} for *V. unguiculata*) just before planting.

Supplemental N was applied at the onset of flowering. Nitrogen (60 kg N/ha) was applied to the soil either as $NaNO_3$ or as $(NH_4)_2SO_4$ plus 20 ppm Nitrapyrin. Urea was applied as a foliar spray in four applications (12 kg/ha each) at weekly intervals.

Assays for nitrogenase and nitrate reductase activity were initiated seven days after emergence, and continued at weekly intervals thereafter. For nitrogenase two plants were analyzed per treatment using the method of Franco *et al.* (1979).

Nitrate reductase activity was measured in the leaflets of mid-stem internodes of five plants using the method of Jaworski (1971). Plant N was determined by a Kjeldahl procedure. To follow patterns of ureide movement over time four plants/treatment were used each week in the collection of xylem exudates. Stems were cut 3 cm from soil surface and exudates collected for 1 hour. Samples were kept at -20°C until analyses were performed. Ureides in the exudates were determined colorimetrically by the method of Young and Conway (1942).

RESULTS

In cowpeas without N supplementation the differences in NRA during the life cycle were not significant. Following N supplementation at flowering, NRA increased, reached its maximal level two to three weeks after flowering; then declined to the same level as unfertilized controls (see Figure 1). NRA in bean plants began to decline soon after germination and reached its minimum in the week after flowering (days 35 to 42). NRA then began to increase, even in control plants (see Figure 2). The NRA level of bean plants was, on average, four times higher than that found in cowpea.

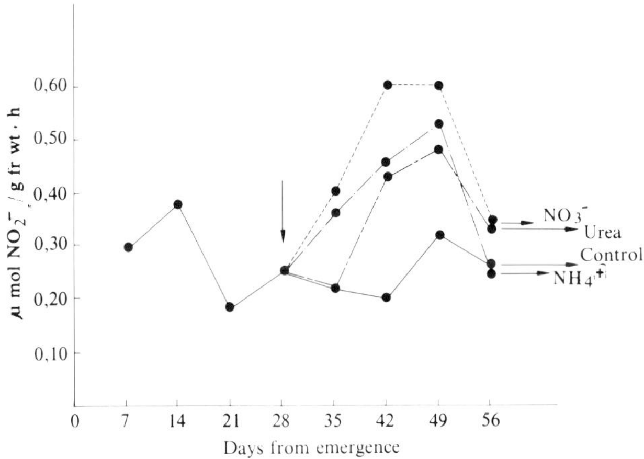

Figure 1. Effects of supplemental N on the NRA of cowpea. The arrow indicates when treatments were initiated.

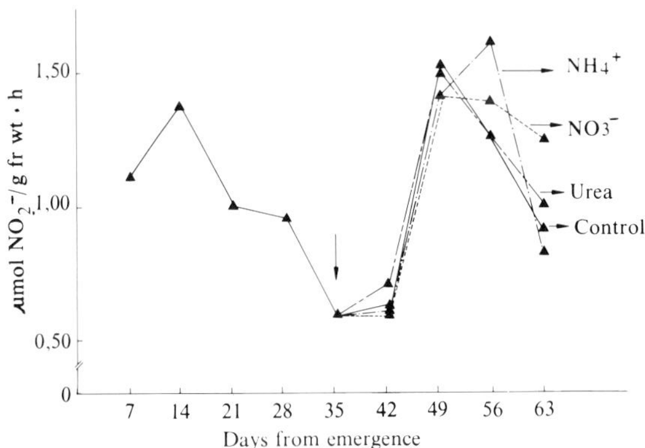

Figure 2. Effect of supplemental N on the NRA of beans.

The seasonal patterns of NRA in this experiment were similar to those observed for beans by Franco *et al.* (1979), but for cowpea, seasonal NRA patterns showed much less variation than observed by Minchin *et al.* (1980) using phytotron-grown plants and 200 ppm nitrate-N.

Nodule development in cowpeas was markedly superior to that of beans, especially from the first to the third week after germination when nodule dry weight in cowpeas increased exponentially, but changes in beans were small (see Figure 3). N fertilization at flowering had little effect on nodule development in either species, since by the time fertilizer treatments were imposed nodule dry weight was already on the decline. The nodule weights observed in this experiment fall within the range reported for these species by other workers (Graham & Rosas, 1977; F.F. Duque, personal communication).

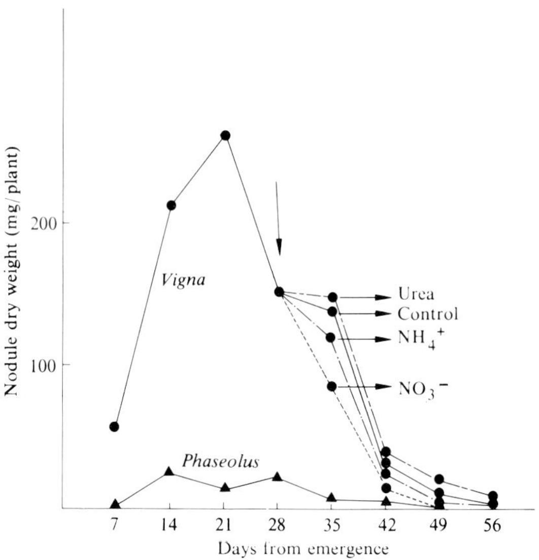

Figure 3. Effects of supplemental N on nodule dry weight of cowpea and beans. The arrow indicates when treatments were initiated.

Seasonal variation in N_2-ase activity for the two species (see Figure 4) followed a pattern similar to that observed with nodule dry weight. Nitrogenase activity in cowpea declined sharply at flowering, and 42 days after emergence could no longer be detected. As for nodule dry weight, the effect of N supplementation on N_2 fixation was very small.

The pattern of ureide accumulation in the xylem sap of beans and cowpeas did not coincide with the patterns observed for nodule dry weight and N_2-ase activity (see Figures 5, 6). In beans, there was also a negative correlation

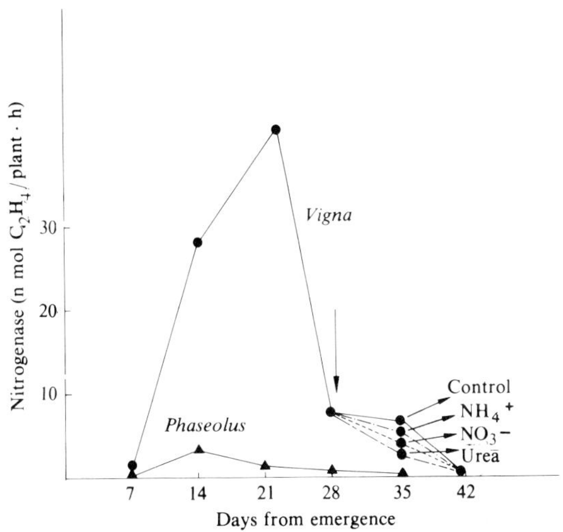

Figure 4. Effects of supplemental N on N_2 fixation activity of cowpea and beans. The arrow indicates when treatments were initiated.

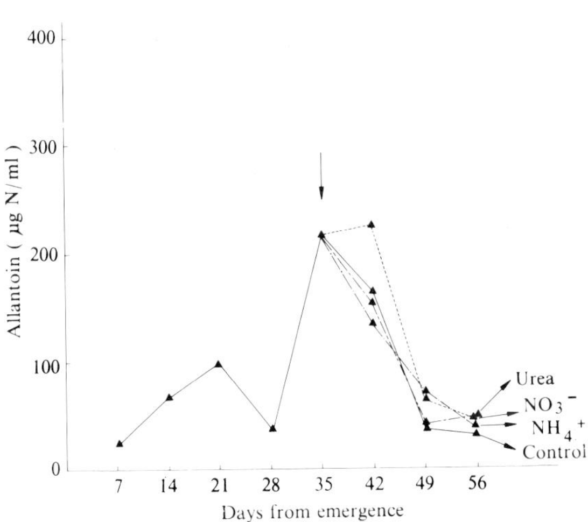

Figure 5. Effects of supplemental N on ureide content of the xylem sap of beans.

(r = - 0.79**) between xylary ureide content and leaf NRA. There was no such correlation found for cowpea. Ureide accumulation in the xylem sap of cowpea showed a tendency to decline from the first to seventh week after germination. Application of fertilizer N to the soil or as a spray resulted in only smaller modifications of this trend (Figure 6).

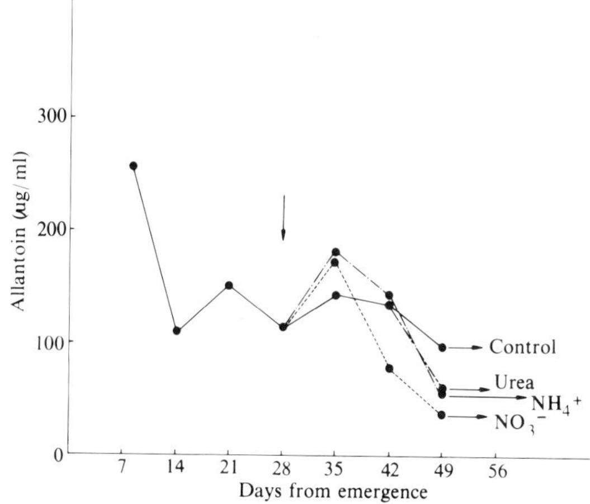

Figure 6. Effects of supplemental N on ureide content of the xylem sap of cowpea. The arrow indicates when treatments were initiated.

Figure 7 shows the pattern of nitrate accumulation in bean plants and Figure 8 the amino acid accumulation in the leaves of beans. Accumulation of amino N in bean leaves parallels the decline in nitrogenase activity in these plants, and is coincident with the beginning of nitrate-N accumulation. Nitrate accumulation in bean tissues reached a maximum of 49 to 56 days after emergence, by which time the amino-N content of leaves had begun to drop sharply. This indicates that nitrate accumulation for seed development continues even while the leaves are beginning to mobilize N to the pods. Uptake of nitrate-N in cowpea (see Figure 9) was not as marked as with beans, though cowpeas also showed extensive amino acid accumulation in leaves (see Figure 8). N fertilization again did not markedly affect these traits.

Seed production (kg/ha) and N accumulation in seeds (kg N/ha) of beans and cowpea are shown in Table 1. Seed production was significantly higher (statistical data not shown) over all the treatments for cowpea than for bean plants. Bean plants seemed to use nitrate more efficiently than cowpea. Foliar sprayed urea resulted in an increase in seed production by cowpea. Accumulation of N by plants (kg N/ha) is also shown in Table 1. Beans with supplemental nitrate had the highest N accumulation level of all treatments, whereas urea-supplemented cowpea showed the second highest N accumulation level.

DISCUSSION

Cowpea showed better nodulation than beans and also greater nitrogenase activity. The poor nodulation in beans may have led to its greater use of soil N.

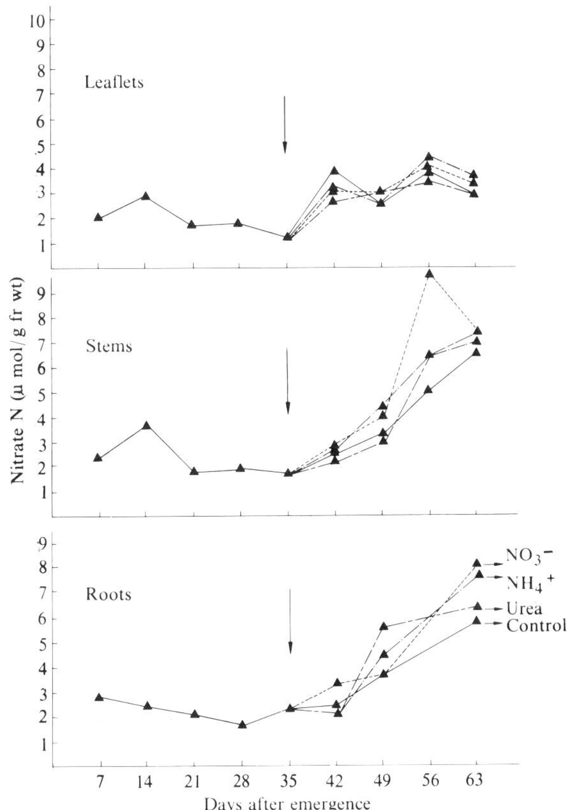

Figure 7. Effects of supplemental N of the NO_3^--N distribution in beans. The arrows show when treatments were initiated.

This is indicated not only the higher NRA level of beans compared to cowpea, but also by the sharp increase of NRA in beans at the onset of reproductive activity. Supplementation of plants with mineral N, either applied to soil or sprayed onto leaves, at the beginning of flowering had little effect on nodulation and N_2-ase activity of beans and cowpea. However, supplemental N affected NRA, nitrate accumulation in roots and stems, and amino-N accumulation patterns of leaves.

No direct relationship was shown between ureide accumulation in the xylem sap of beans and cowpea, and the seasonal patterns of N_2-ase activity. However, a negative relationship between NRA in leaves and ureide in the xylem sap of beans was found. Although the NRA of roots and the ureide content of leaves were not measured, the patterns of N accumulation in roots and stems, together with NRA changes in leaves, leads us to speculate that at

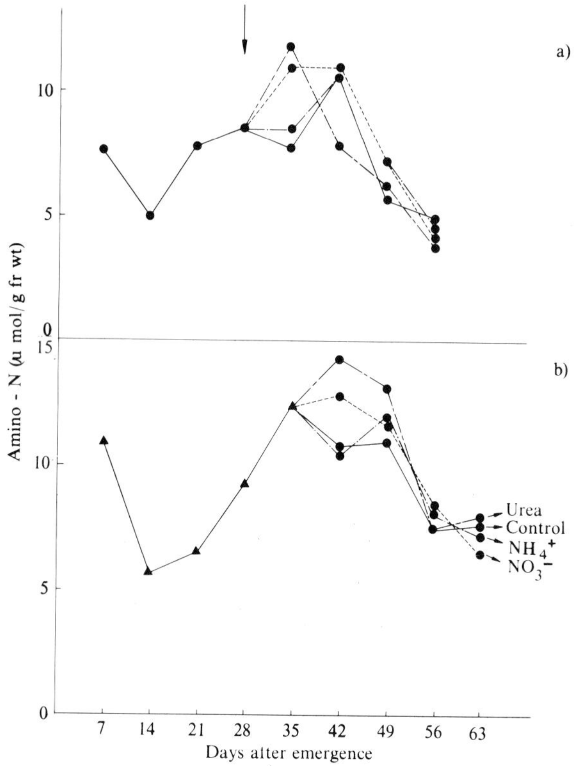

Figure 8. Effects of supplemental N on amino-N accumulation in leaves of cowpea (a) and beans (b). The arrow indicates when treatments were initiated.

TABLE 1: Seed production (kg/ha) and N accumulation (kg N/ha) in seeds of beans and cowpea with and without supplemental N.

Legume	Treatment			
	0	NO_3^-	NH_4^+	Urea
	Seed production (kg/ha)			
P. vulgaris	813	1274	968	966
V. unguiculata	1041	1121	1027	1389
	N accumulation (kg/ha)			
P. vulgaris	26.8	47.2	34.8	36.7
V. unguiculata	31.2	39.2	32.9	45.8

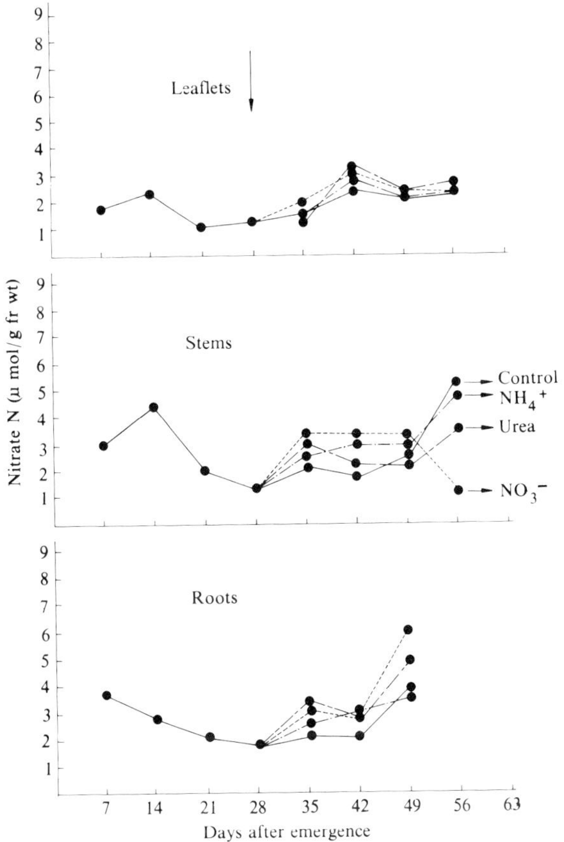

Figure 9. Effects of supplemental N on the NO_3^- - N distribution in cowpea.

least some of the ureides in bean plants may come from nitrate reduction in the roots.

Applications of fertilizer N at the onset of the reproductive stage resulted in higher yields for beans when nitrate was used, while cowpea had an increase in seed production when urea was applied.

Our data show that, although cowpea and beans produce seed having similar characteristics, their N uptake and metabolism is different and they may require different management techniques.

REFERENCES

Franco, A.A., Pereira, J.C. & Neyra, C.A. (1979) *Plant Physiol.* 63, 421-424.

Graham, P.H. & Rosas, J.C. (1977) *J. Agric. Sci.* (Camb.) 88, 503-508.

Jaworski, E.G. (1971) *Biochem. Biophys. Res. Comm.* 43, 1274-1279.

Minchin, F.R., Summerfield, R. & Neves, M.C.P. (1980) *J. Expl. Bot.* 31, 1327-1345.

Streeter, J.G. (1972) *Agron. J.* 64, 315-319.

Young, E.G. & Conway, C.F. (1942) *J. Biol. Chem.* 142, 839-853.

PROFILES OF UREIDES AND AMINO ACIDS IN EXUDATES FROM SENESCING SOYBEAN NODULES

L.L. Shearman and R.V. Klucas[1,2]

Summary

The concentration of ureides (allantoin, allantoic acid, and urea), amino acids, and total nitrogen (N) in nodule exudates were monitored over the production cycle of field- and glasshouse-grown soybeans, and related to levels of N_2 (C_2H_2) fixation in these plants.

In both glasshouse and field studies, specific N_2-fixing activity peaked at mid-flowering and initiation of pod fill, with a slight secondary peak at the full seed stage. As N_2 fixation per nodule correlated with nodule fresh and dry weight ($r = 0.70$), two populations of nodules are suggested.

Nodule exudates from greenhouse-grown plants had higher amino acid concentrations than field-grown plants. Asparagine was the major amino acid and reached a concentration of 1.6 mM during reproductive development. Asparagine, glutamine, serine, alanine and aspartate were found in all samples; glycine, isoleucine, threonine, valine, and proline appeared in only some samples. Ureides accounted for most of the N exported from nodules, but the ureide:amino acid ratio declined during peak fixation.

Nodule exudates from field-grown plants contained a high proportion of ureides — mostly as urea, but again the proportion of amino acid N tended to increase during peak fixation.

Although changes were observed in the various N fractions during the study, they were not consistent for both greenhouse and field-grown plants and could not be related to nodule senescence.

---

1 Dept. of Agricultural Biochemistry, Univ. of Nebraska, Lincoln, NE, 68583, USA.

2 Research Support from the USDA/SEA-CRGO (Grant No. 7800083) and the Nebraska Soybean Development, Utilization and Marketing Board is gratefully acknowledged.

INTRODUCTION

Although the gross morphological consequences of nodule senescence are easy to observe and describe, the physiological and biochemical events contributing to senescence are unknown. The loss of nitrogen (N_2) fixation is a useful and convenient indicator of nodule senescence (Klucas, 1974). Though profiles of N_2 fixation versus plant age are quite variable and depend on the types of legumes, rhizobia, and growth conditions, the use of tap root nodules that are approximately the same age (Bergersen, 1958), or the use of conditions that restrict secondary infections (Stipf & Werner, 1978), yield reproducible profiles in which the N_2 fixation peak is followed by a moderate or sharp decline in activity.

During the active life of a nodule, ammonia formed by N_2 fixation is assimilated into nitrogenous compounds before translocation from the nodules. In soybean nodules (Matsumoto, Yatazawa & Yamamoto, 1977; McClure & Israel, 1979; Streeter, 1979), as well as in the nodules of certain tropical legumes (Herridge & Pate, 1977; Herridge *et al.*, 1978), ureides are the primary and amino acids are the secondary nitrogenous products that are translocated. The distribution of N between ureides and amino acids is dependent on the plant type (Pate, 1980), availability of inorganic N (Tajima, Yatazawa & Yamamoto, 1977; McClure, Israel & Volk, 1980) and possibly plant development. Nodule senescence may also change the distribution, not only by altering pathways involved in assimilation of N, but also by increasing catabolism of proteins and nucleic acids. Catabolism of proteins could yield differences in the amount and distribution of N among amino acids, whereas breakdown of nucleic acids could yield increases in ureides.

The primary objective of the present study was to determine whether changes in metabolism that accompany nodule senescence were reflected in the N-containing exudates from legume nodules.

MATERIALS AND METHODS

Both a field and a glasshouse study were undertaken. For the field study seeds of soybean (*Glycine max* (L.) Merr. cv. Woodworth), inoculated with a commercial inoculant (Nitragin Co., Milwaukee, WI, USA) were grown without fertilization, but were irrigated as needed. Greenhouse-grown plants of the same cultivar, inoculated with strain 110 of *R. japonicum* were sown into Turface (Wyandotte Chemicals of Canada Ltd., Scarborough, Ontario, Canada) and irrigated with N-free mineral medium (Evans, Koch & Klucas, 1972). At each sampling date, randomly selected plants were harvested approximately five hours after sunrise and characterized according to stage of development (Fehr & Caviness, 1977), after which the root systems were used either to measure $N_2(C_2H_2)$ fixation or for the collection of nodule exudates.

To obtain exudate samples, nodules were removed from roots, washed with distilled water and placed on moist filter paper (Pate, Gunning, & Briarty, 1969). Xylem tubes from the nodule that were exposed during excision from the root were enclosed by a 5 μl glass capillary tube and approximately 5 μl of exudate were collected from each of 20 nodules. The pooled exudates were quickly frozen and stored at -80°C until used for analysis.

N_2 (C_2H_2) fixation was estimated by a method similar to that of Pedersen *et al.* (1978), using methane (42 μmol) as an internal standard.

Nodule exudates were analyzed for amino acids, ureides, and total N. Amino acid analyses were done on an amino acid analyzer (Hitachi-Perkin-Elmer KLA-3B Norwalk, MA, USA) using a procedure for physiological fluids (Benson, 1972). The lower limit of detection for these amino acids, except proline, was approximately 1 nmole. Because of limited amounts of sample, basic amino acids were not measured in this study.

Allantoic acid, allantoin and urea in nodule exudates were separated by thin layer chromatography on silica gel plates of 250 μm thickness (EM Reagents, Darmstadt, Germany). Plates were developed twice in a solvent system containing methyl ethyl ketone:chloroform:glacial acetic acid:water (14:2:3:3). Urea, allantoin, allantoic acid and ammonia had R_f values of 0.86, 0.71, 0.49, and 0.1, respectively, in this system. Areas of the gel pertaining to allantoic acid and allantoin were scraped from the plate and scrapings were eluted two times with 1.50 ml hot 0.1 N NaOH. A 2 ml aliquot of the eluate was assayed using the procedure described by Young and Conway (1942). Urea was quantitated by eluting from the silica gel with water, incubating with urease at pH 7, and assaying for ammonia by a microdiffusion procedure using Nessler's reagent as described by Burris (1972). To measure total N, exudates were subjected to microdigestion (Ballentine, 1957) to form ammonia and the ammonia was quantitated by Nessler's reagent.

RESULTS AND DISCUSSION

Two, possibly three, peaks in specific nodule activity (SNA) were observed in each study (Figures 1 and 2), and corresponded to the periods between onset of flowering and full bloom and initiation of pod development and full pod development. SNA was highly correlated with fresh weight of nodules (r = 0.83 and 0.70, fresh weight basis for the field and glasshouse studies, respectively). From this data it appears that two cycles of nodule formation might have occurred.

Concentrations of total acidic and neutral amino acids in nodule exudates varied from 0.33 mM to 2.20 mM in the greenhouse study (see Table 1) and from 0.002 mM to 0.48 mM in the field study (see Table 2). Asparagine was the amino acid present in the greatest concentration in nodule exudates throughout the reproductive stages of soybean development. Concentrations ranged from 0.28 to 1.78 mM and accounted for 20% to 80% of the amino

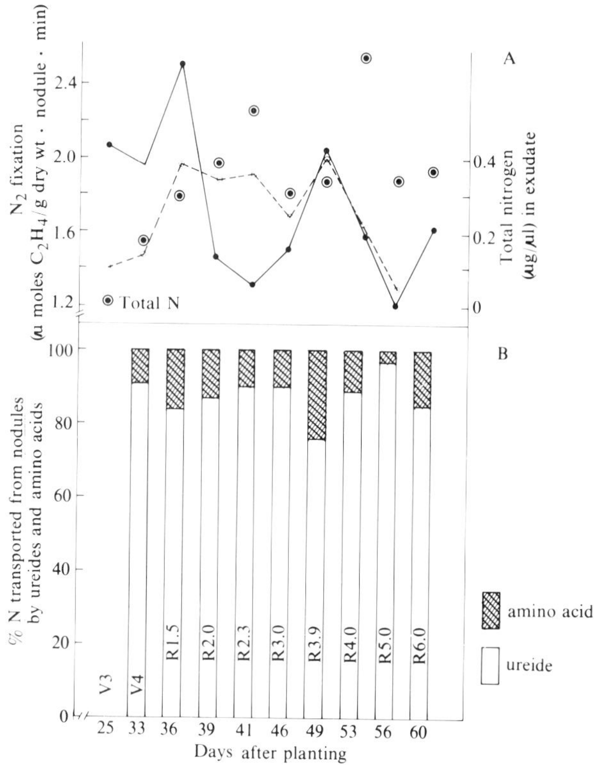

Figure 1. Total N in nodule exudates, distribution of N between ureides and amino acids in nodule exudates and N_2 fixation by attached nodules from greenhouse-grown plants of various ages. a. Acetylene reduction was used to measure N_2 fixation (——). Total nitrogen (- - -) was measured after digestion of nodule exudates or calculated (⊙) from amino acid and ureide values. b. Neutral and acidic amino acids (hatched) and ureides (unhatched) were measured as described in "Materials and Methods." Plant stage of development depicted for each sample.

acids in the greenhouse study (see Figure 3) and from 0.06 to 0.33 mM, accounting for 40% to 85% of the amino acids, in the field study (see Figure 4). However, the composition of amino acids in nodule exudates varied substantially with plant development and growth conditions. In the greenhouse study, glutamine was the second most abundant amino acid, and its levels in nodule exudates correlated very well with rates of N_2 fixation. Serine, aspartate, and alanine were also detected in exudates. In nodule exudates from field-grown plants, the concentrations of amino acids were lower, and fewer of them were detected. Serine, with lesser amounts of alanine

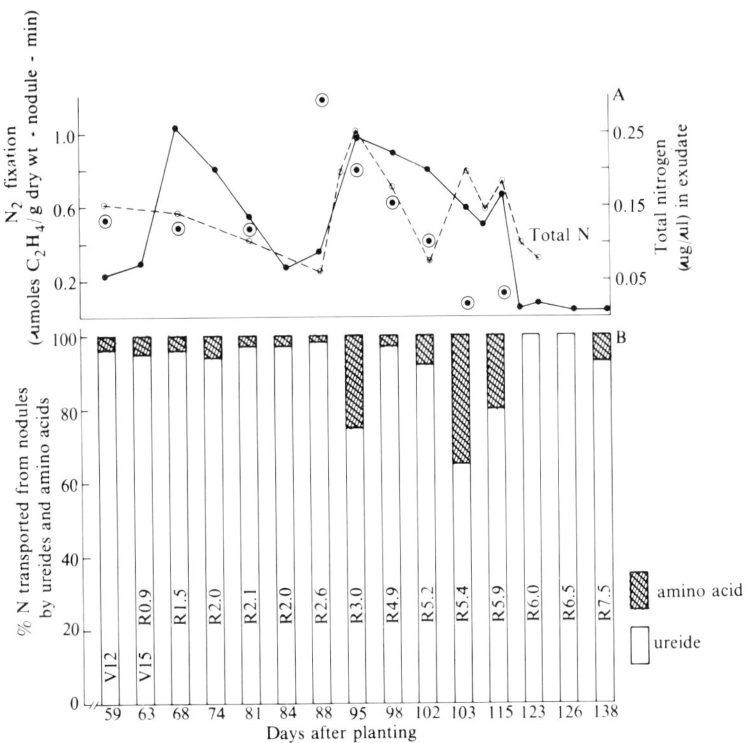

Figure 2. Total N in nodule exudates, distribution of N between ureides and amino acids in nodule exudates and N_2 fixation by attached nodules from field-grown plants of various ages. Legend as Fig. 1a and 1b.

and aspartate were the secondary amino acids in most samples, and little glutamine was detected. However, the presence of glutamine in nodule exudates from field-grown plants did coincide with peaks of nitrogenase activity. From the amino composition of nodule exudates, it was apparent that asparagine concentration was lowest, and consequently the percentage of other amino acids was highest, when nitrogenase activity was relatively low. However, none of the exudates, including those collected during the later stages of plant development, possessed a large complement of amino acids, suggesting nodular destruction.

Levels of ureides in nodule exudates at each sampling time are shown in Tables 1 and 2. Exudates of nodules from greenhouse-grown plants had high ureide concentrations (10 mM - 46 mM as N) including allantoin, allantoic acid, and urea in all but the late vegetative stages of plant development.

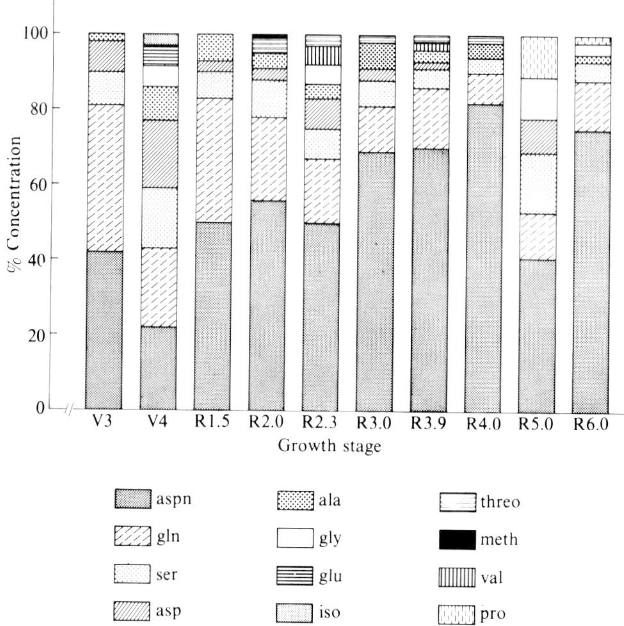

Figure 3. Distribution of acidic and neutral amino acids in nodule exudates as a function of stage of development for greenhouse-grown soybeans.

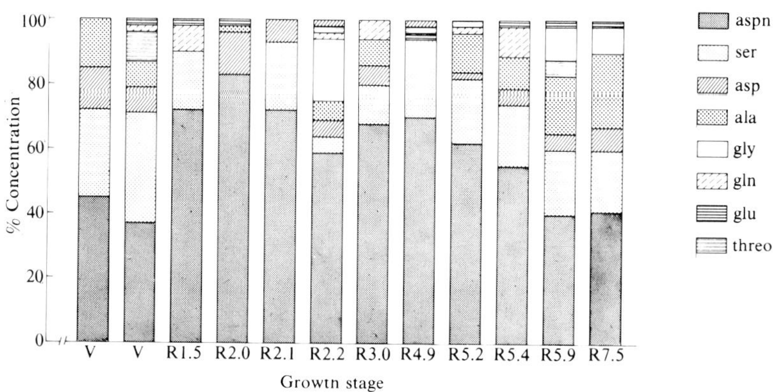

Figure 4. Distribution of acidic and neutral amino acids in nodule exudates as a function of stage of development for field-grown soybeans.

TABLE 1: Ureide and amino acid concentrations in nodule exudates from soybeans grown under greenhouse conditions.

Age	Stage	Allantoin	Allantoate	Urea	Ureide N[1]	Total Amino acids[2]
Days				mM		
25	V3	0	0	–	–	0.65
33	V4	0.6	0.7	2.5	10.3	0.49
36	R1.5	2.3	1.4	2.0	18.7	1.02
39	R2.0	2.9	2.3	2.1	25.0	1.36
41	R2.3	5.4	2.6	1.7	35.6	1.41
46	R3.0	2.1	1.9	2.2	20.6	0.91
49	R3.9	2.3	0.7	3.6	19.1	2.20
53	R4.0	5.3	4.9	2.5	45.7	2.07
56	R5.0	1.2	2.7	4.3	24.4	0.33
60	R6.0	2.5	1.6	3.0	22.5	1.54

[1]Ureide N was obtained by summation of N in allantoin, allantoate and urea.
[2]Total amino acid values are obtained by summation of individual acidic and neutral amino acids in nodule exudates.

During the reproductive stages of plant development, allantoin concentrations ranged from 1.2 mM to 5.4 mM and accounted for 20-60% of the total N recovered in ureides. Allantoic acid concentrations were somewhat lower ranging from 0.68 mM to 4.88 mM and accounting for 14-45% of the ureide N. Urea was also detected at levels between 1.72 mM and 4.33 mM, which was 10-37% of the ureide N. The level of ureides (1.8 mM - 20 mM as N) in nodule exudates from field-grown plants was consistently lower (see Table 2). In many samples, urea was the predominant or only ureide detected with concentrations ranging from 0.3 mM to 9.3 mM. High urea levels could be artifacts resulting from the breakdown of allantoin and allantoic acid (Trijbels & Vogels, 1966; Tajima & Yamamoto, 1975; Tajima *et al.*, 1977; McClure & Israel, 1979).

Total N levels in nodule exudates as determined directly after digestion, and as calculated by summation of amino acid and ureides, are shown in Figures 1a and 2a. Values for total N from direct analysis varied between 3.6 mM and 28.9 mM in the greenhouse study and between 4.3 mM and 17.9 mM in the field study. The correlation between the two methods of estimating total N was generally good; thus, most of the N in the nodule exudates must have been in the neutral and acidic amino acid fractions and in ureides. The divergence

TABLE 2: Ureide and amino acid concentrations in nodule exudates from soybeans grown under field conditions.

Age	Stage	Allantoin	Allantoate	Urea	Ureide N[1]	Total Amino acids[2]
Days		mM				
59	V	0	0	4.3	8.6	0.13
63	V	0	0	4.1	8.2	0.25
68	R1.5	0.9	0.6	1.0	8.0	0.19
73	R2.0	0	0	2.9	5.8	0.19
76	R1.9	0.5	0.7	–	–	0.32
81	R2.1	0	0	7.0	14.0	0.20
84	R2.0	0	0	5.4	10.8	0.12
88	R2.6	0	0.4	9.3	20.2	0.06
90	R2.6	0.3	0	0	. 1.2	0.17
95	R3.0	0.1	0.3	0.5	2.6	0.48
98	R4.9	0	0.2	5.1	11.0	0.12
102	R5.2	0.1	0	2.8	6.0	0.32
105	R5.4	0.2	0	0.3	1.4	0.36
109	R5.9	0.2	0.1	0.6	2.4	–
115	R5.9	0	–	0.5	–	0.27
118	R5.8	0	0	0.9	1.8	–
123	R6.0	0	0	3.3	6.6	$<$0.01
126	R6.5	0.1	0.1	1.4	3.6	$<$0.01
138	R7.5	1.0	0	1.7	7.4	0.32

[1]Ureide N was obtained by summation of N in allantoin, allantoate and urea.
[2]Total amino acid values were obtained by summation of individual acidic and neutral amino acids.

between measured and calculated N was greatest in samples collected late in the growth cycle and varied with growing conditions.

The percentage of N translocated as acidic and neutral amino acids appeared to parallel nitrogenase activity in both studies. By contrast, the percentage of ureides in nodule exudates was lowest during periods of peak nitrogenase activity.

Changes were observed in various nitrogenous compounds of nodule exudates as a function of stage of plant development or N_2 fixation in both studies. However, changes in metabolism that accompany nodule senescense were not reflected in the N containing compounds found in nodule exudates.

REFERENCES

Ballentine, R. (1957) Determination of total nitrogen and ammonia. *In*: Methods in enzymology, S.P. Colowick & N.O. Kaplan (Eds.). Academic Press, New York, NY, USA. Pp. 993-994.

Benson, J.V. (1972) Multipurpose resins for analysis of amino acids and ninhydrin positive compounds in hydrolysates and physiological fluids. *Annal. Biochem.* 50, 477-493.

Bergersen, F.J. (1958) The bacterial component of soybean root nodules; changes in respiratory activity, cell dry weight, and nucleic acid content with increasing nodule age. *J. Gen. Microbiol.* 19, 812-828.

Burris, R.A. (1972) Nitrogen fixation-assay methods and techniques. *Methods Enzymol.* 24, 421-422.

Evans, H.J., Koch, B. & Klucas, R.V. (1972) Preparation of nitrogenase from nodules and separation into components. *Methods Enzymol.* 24, 470-476.

Fehr, W.R. & Caviness, C.E. (1977) Stages of soybean development. Iowa State Univ. Ames, IO, USA *Spec. Report* No. 80.

Herridge, D.F., Atkins, C.A., Pate, J.S., & Rainbird, R.M. (1978) Allantoin and allantoic acid in the nitrogen economy of the cowpea (*Vigna unguiculata* (L.) Walp). *Plant Physiol.* 62, 495-498.

Herridge, D.F. & Pate, J.S. (1977) Utilization of net photosynthate for nitrogen fixation and protein production in an annual legume. *Plant Physiol.* 60, 759-764.

Klucas, R.V. (1974) Studies on soybean nodule senescence. *Plant Physiol.* 54, 612-616.

Matsumoto, T., Yamamoto, Y. & Yatazawa, M. (1976) Role of root nodule in the nitrogen nutrition of soybeans. (II). Fluctuations of allantoin concentration in the bleeding sap. *J. Sci. Soil Manure* (Japan) 47, 463-469.

Matsumoto, T., Yatazawa, M. & Yamamoto, Y. (1977) Distribution and change in the contents of allantoin and allantoic acid in developing nodulating and non-nodulating soybean plants. *Plant Cell Physiol.* 18, 353-359.

McClure, P.R. & Israel, D.W. (1979) Transport of nitrogen in the xylem of soybean plants. *Plant Physiol.* 64, 411-416.

McClure, P.R., Israel, D.W. & Volk, R.J. (1980) Evaluation of the relative ureide content of xylem sap as an indicator of N_2 fixation in soybeans. *Plant Physiol.* 66, 720-725.

Pate, J.S. (1980) Transport of partitioning of nitrogenous solutes. *Ann. Rev. Plant Physiol.* 31, 313-340.

Pate, J.S., Gunning, B.E.S. & Briarty, L.G. (1969) Ultrastructure and functioning of the transport system of the leguminous root nodule. *Planta* (Berlin) 85, 11-34.

Pedersen, W.L., Chakrabarty, K., Klucas, R.V., & Vidaver, A.K. (1978) Nitrogen fixation (acetylene reduction) associated with roots of winter wheat and sorghum in Nebraska. *Appl. Environ. Microbiol.* 35 (1), 129-135.

Streeter, J.G. (1979) Allantoin and allantoic acid in tissues and stem exudate from field-grown soybean plants. *Plant Physiol.* 63, 478-480.

Stripf, R. & Werner, D. (1978) Differentiation of *Rhizobium japonicum*, II. Enzymatic activities in bacteroids and plant cytoplasm during the development of nodules of *Glycine max*. *Z. Naturforsch.* 33c, 373-381.

Tajima, S. & Yamamoto, Y. (1975) Enzymes of purine catabolism in soybean plants. *Plant Cell Physiol.* 16, 271-282.

Tajima, S., Yatazawa, M. & Yamamoto, Y. (1977) Allantoin production and its utilization in relation to nodule formation in soybeans. *Soil Sci. Plant Nutr.* 23(2), 225-235.

Trijbels, F. & Vogels, G.D. (1966) Degradation of allantoin by *Pseudomonas acidovorans*. *Biochim. Biophys. Acta.* 113, 292-301.

Young, E.C. & Conway, C.F. (1942) On the estimation of allantoin by the Rimini-Schryver reaction. *J. Biol. Chem.* 142, 839-853.

N_2 FIXATION IN PASTURE LEGUMES

NATIVE LEGUMES IN MINAS GERAIS STATE, BRAZIL

N.M.S. Costa[1]

Summary

The multiplicity of soils, climates and vegetation types in Minas Gerais State has resulted in a large variation in the genera and species of legumes that occur naturally there. A number of these appear to have forage potential.

This paper reports on the occurrence, nodulation and resistance to stress conditions of some naturally occurring species, but emphasizes *Stylosanthes* spp. In observations of natural settings and field nurseries, six different rooting patterns were found in species of *Stylosanthes*. Three *Stylosanthes* species had unusually large nodules, while in *S. capitata* and *S. macrocephala* few or no nodules were found under natural field conditions. By contrast *S. guianensis* var. *vulgaris*, the new species *S. debilis*, and *S. grandifolia* showed good nodulation, even on poor soils. Anthracnose, caused by *Colletotrichum gloesporioides* was the most serious disease of *Stylosanthes* species in Minas Gerais, though *S. macrocephala* and *S. capitata* appeared less susceptible than other species. Root nematodes and stem borers were not a major problem in Minas Gerais.

INTRODUCTION

Ferreira & Antunes (1980) divided the State of Minas Gerais (MG), Brazil, into five homogenous soil, climatic, and vegetation regions, as summarized in Figure 1 and Table 1. The variation in soils and climate in these areas results in large variation between these ecosystems in the legumes found, and their relative importance. In those environments characterized by low soil fertility associated with other adverse conditions, the prevailing species have mechanisms of adaptation such as:

[1] Empresa de Pesquisa Agropecuaria de Minas Gerais, CP 295, Sete Lagoas 35700, MG, Brazil.

"Special" root systems;
Crowns located below the soil surface, protecting the plant against fire;
Efficiency of uptake and utilization of nutrients and/or tolerance to nutrient excesses (toxic elements); and
Resistance to some pests and diseases.

Abundant seed production, effectiveness of mycorrhiza, and nodulation are also important factors. On the other hand, in the regions with high fertility soils, adequate rainfall and favorable temperature, competition for light seems to be the main factor determining plant survival. Seedling vigor, initial growth rate, and plant habit determine the species that will remain in these ecosystems.

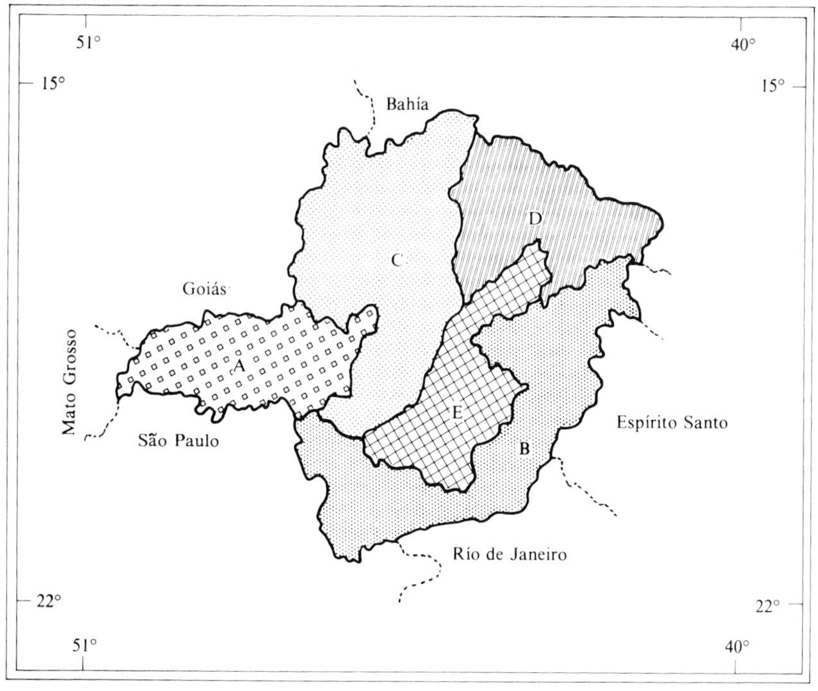

Figure 1. The five natural regions of Minas Gerais State.

GENERA WITH FORAGE POTENTIAL

After five years of observation in both natural settings and field nurseries, the following are considered the genera/species with greatest forage potential:

Aeschynomene - Ten species have already been described in MG. In general, they are found in the lowlands, and the plants show nodulation.

TABLE 1: Soil, climate and vegetation characteristics of the five natural regions in Minas Gerais State (from Ferreira & Antunes, 1980).

Regions	Climate		Soil	Vegetation
	Thermic Regime	Hydric Regime		
A	Ta-21-24° C Tf (July) 16-24° C	Pa-1300-1700 mm Da 100-200 mm June September Rainy season Oct-April	Oxisols Relief plane to gently undulated Vertisols	"Cerrado" (savanna) and "Cerradão"
B	ALTITUDE $<$ 600 m Ta-21-24° C Tf (July) 19° C ALTITUDE $<$ 600 m Ta-18-21° C Tf (June) 15° C	Pa-700-1200 mm Da 150 - 300 mm May-October Rainy season Oct-April Pa-1100-2000 mm Da $<$ 100 mm Rainy season Oct-April	Ultisols and Inceptisols High to medium fertility Relief rough	Rainy forest Some "Campo Limpo" and "Cerrado" (savanna)
C	Ta-21-24° C Tf (June) 19-22° C	Pa-900-150 mm Da-200-500 mm Rainy season Oct-March	50 % of area with Inceptisols and Oxisols Relief rough 50 % Oxisols Relief plane	Different types "Cerrado" (savanna)
D	Ta-21-24° C Tf (June) 18-23° C	Pa-600-1200 mm Da-600-1100 mm Da-200-600 mm highlands Rainy season Oct-March	Alfisols and Ultisols Relief plane and gently undulated Some fertile soils	"Cerrado" (deciduous forest)
E	Ta-19-22° C Tf (July) 13-18° C	Pa-1200-2000 mm Da-20-15 mm May-September Rainy season Oct-April	Ultisols Fertile soils on rough relief Oxisols, gently undulated Poor soils on plane relief	"Cerrado" (savanna)

Ta- Annual medium temperature; Tf- Medium temperature of the coldest mouth; Pa- annual rainfall; Da- Hydric deficiency.

Calopogonium - Few species occur in MG, the most promising being *C. mucunoides,* which is found in the south, east, and west. It presents good forage potential, good nodulation, and sometimes black nodules. The leaves are frequently attacked by fungi.

Canavalia - The most frequent species is *Canavalia gladiata,* which possesses high dry matter yield potential and good nodulation, but low palatability. It is very susceptible to nematode root damage.

Centrosema - It occurs frequently in MG and has high forage potential but sometimes is only poorly nodulated. Some species are susceptible to pests and diseases.

Cratylia - The few species occurring in MG are susceptible to pests and diseases. They present high forage potential, good nodulation, and good stem rooting capacity.

Desmanthus - There are only two species but both are drought resistant and have good dry matter yields. The leaves are sometimes attacked by viral and other diseases. They show deficient nodulation.

Desmodium - This genus is widespread in MG and many species occur. It presents medium forage yield, and its nodulation is plentiful.

Galactia - There are a few species in MG, and some have forage potential, but they do not show ample nodulation. It is attacked by pests and diseases.

Macroptilium - They are very frequent in MG, with some species having high forage potential. They are very susceptible to pests and diseases but usually have good nodulation.

Mimosa - While a large number of *Mimosa* spp. occur in MG, they usually show only low forage potential. They are susceptible to pests and diseases but generally are well nodulated.

Teramnus and *Rhynchosia* - Few species occur. Their cultivation is limited by their susceptibility to nematodes. Reasonable dry matter yield can be achieved together with good nodulation.

Zornia - Some ecotypes present a good forage potential and nodulation. Sometimes their leaves and stems are attacked by pests and diseases.

THE GENUS *STYLOSANTHES*

Among the many forage legumes found in Minas Gerais, the genus *Stylosanthes* has been considered the most promising because it has a large number of species and ecotypes with forage potential. It has been found in many different ecosystems throughout the state and adapts well to a range of soil and climatic conditions. *Stylosanthes* species are the most common legumes in soils with low nutrient availability and/or Al toxicity.

While the majority of *Stylosanthes* species have a normal root system with a well-developed tap root and thin, branched secondary roots (see Figure 2a) a number possess special root features that help their survival after annual burning. In *S. bracteata* and *S. linearifolia,* this takes the form of enlarged roots, 2-3 cm in diameter and 10-20 cm long; the root enlargements being visible from early vegetative development (see Figure 2c). Nodules appear on both normal and enlarged roots. Some root storage tissue is also found in the more finely rooted species *S. acuminata, S. gracilis* and *S. montevidensis* (see Figure 2b).

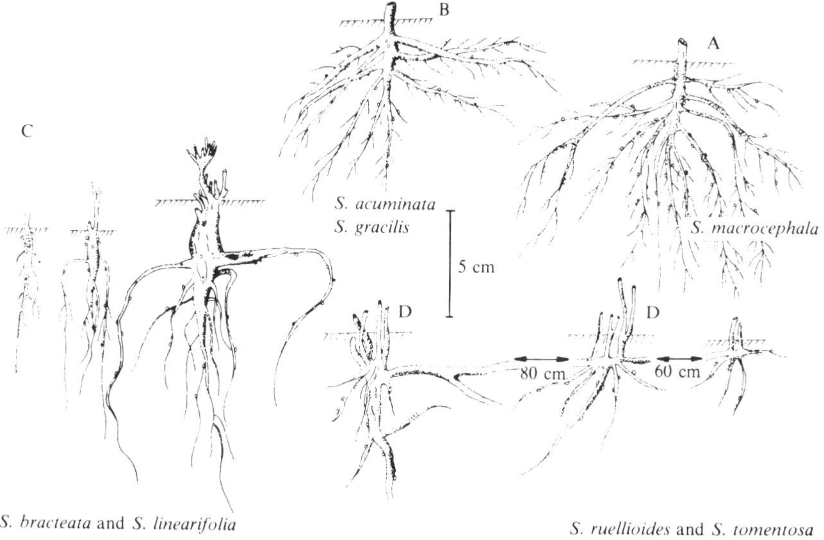

Figure 2. Some root types among *Stylosanthes* species found in Minas Gerais State.

Stylosanthes ruelliodes, S. tomentosa and some ecotypes of *S. guianensis* (see Figure 2d) present budding roots that develop at 2-4 cm depth and may reach up to 1 m from the mother plant. From these budding roots, new shoots may be formed if burning occurs. These species were found in sandy soils at Serra do Cipó, near Diamantina. Variation in stem-rooting capacity occurs both between species, and even within ecotypes of the same variety. In the species *S. guianensis,* the var. *microcephala* is usually believed to have the highest stem-rooting capacity. However, at Triángulo Mineiro and Serra do Cipó, some ecotypes of *S. guianensis*, var. *vulgaris* were found with thin, long stems, reaching up to 3 m in lenght and with rooting capacity. Possibly because of its semi-erect growth habit, *S. guianensis* var. *canescens* has less stem-rooting capacity than the two other varieties. In some ecotypes of *S. viscosa, S. macrocephala, S. capitata,* and *S. leiocarpa* some rooting may occur if the plant population is dense.

The position of the crown below the soil surface can also protect the basal buds against burning and trampling. Among *Stylosanthes* species the deepest basal crowns were noted for *S. bracteata* and *S. linearifolia* (2-3 cm depth). Some ecotypes of *S. guianensis* var. *vulgaris*, and the commercial Oxley "fine stem stylo" show buried crowns, but not to the same degree as found in *S. bracteata.*

Nodulation in *Stylosanthes* species

Stylosanthes guianensis belongs to the "cowpea nodulation group" (Norris, 1965), and it nodulates easily with native strains. However, the author has observed some ecotypes without nodulation or with few nodules even at the place of origin.

Costa & Ferreira (1977) classified *S. guianensis* into three varieties:

- *S. guianensis,* var. *vulgaris* possessing hairy and viscid stem and leaves;
- *S. guianensis,* var. *canescens* without hair, showing no viscidity of the stems or leaves, and with white pubescence on the spike; and
- *S. guianensis* var. *microcephala* with thin stems and small leaflets, both without hair, small pubescent spikes and few seeds per head.

The pattern of nodulation is different for the three varieties. *S. guianensis* var. *microcephala,* in general, shows abundant red nodules, spread throughout the root system. The *vulgaris* variety, found as diverse ecotypes, shows good nodulation even in poor soils. Compared to the two other varieties, var. *canescens* forms few or no nodules. The nodulation difficulties in this variety were stüdied by Souto, Cóser & Döbereiner (1978) using the cultivar IRI-1022, a cultivar that did not nodulate with some strains of cowpea-group rhizobia.

Australian commercial cultivars of *S. guianensis* belong to the *vulgaris* variety. They respond well to inoculation with CB756 under controlled conditions, but in tests in Angola rarely responded to inoculation in the field (Costa, 1970). From yield observation there appears to be little need for inoculation of the *vulgaris* variety under Brazilian soil conditions.

Nodulation data for 14 species of *Stylosanthes* is given in Table 2 with *S. debilis* and *S. grandifolia* outstanding in their nodulation under field conditions.

S. capitata, S. macrocephala, S. bracteata, S. linearifolia, S. acuminata, S. gracilis, and *S. aurea* present problems in nodulation. Sometimes they nodulate, but frequently they do not. In spite of the nodulation problem *S. capitata* and *S. macrocephala* have been recognized as having good forage

TABLE 2. Nodulation of some *Stylosanthes* species under natural conditions.

Species	Size			Quantity		
	Large 3 mm	Medium 1.5 mm	Small 1.5 mm	Many	Few	None
S. acuminata		+	+		+	
S. aurea			+		+	
S. campestris	+	+		+		
S. capitata		+	+		+	+
S. debilis		+		+		
S. gracilis		+	+		+	+
S. grandifolia		+		+		
S. guianensis var. *canescens*		+	+		+	+
S. guianensis var. *microcephala*		+	+	+		
S. guianensis var. *vulgaris*		+		+		
S. leiocarpa		+	+	+		
S. macrocephala		+	+		+	+
S. pilosa			+		+	
S. ruellioides	+	+		+		
S. scabra		+	+	+	+	
S. tomentosa	+	+		+		

potential. Effective strains for *S. capitata* have been isolated in acid soils at CIAT, Colombia. Collaborative work has been done with J. Döbereiner and her group at EMBRAPA in an attempt to isolate effective strains for *S. macrocephala*. Although *S. ruelliodes, S. tomentosa,* and *S. campestris* are morphologically different, the number, size, shape, and internal color of the nodules are similar. The nodules are located close to the crown and on the secondary roots. They are large compared with other *Stylosanthes* species reaching 2-4 mm in diameter (see Figure 3). It is not known yet if the size of nodules is related to the plant and/or to the *Rhizobium*.

PESTS AND DISEASES OF *STYLOSANTHES* IN MINAS GERAIS

Undoubtedly, anthracnose (*Colletotrichum gloesporioides*) is the factor most limiting the performance of *Stylosanthes* species as forage legumes. The disease is found in all countries where the genus occurs. Resistance or susceptibility to anthracnose depends not only on genetic characteristics of

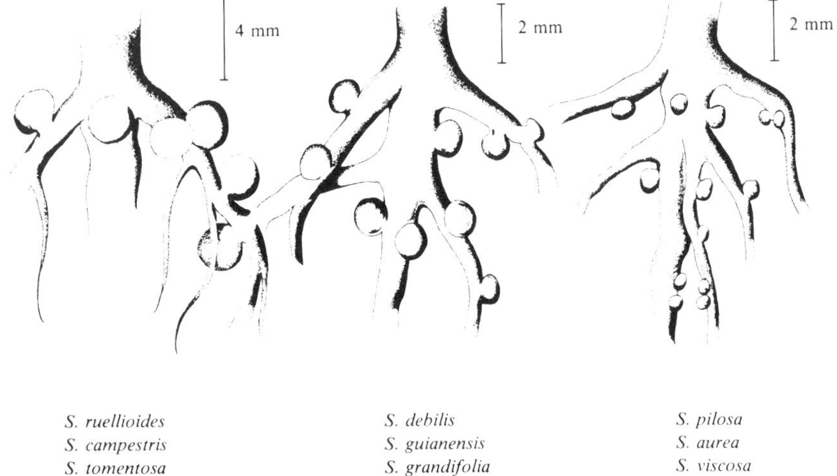

Figure 3. Some patterns of nodulation in *Stylosanthes* species.

the plant, but also on the races of fungus present and on environmental conditions. Some species seem to present a greater percentage of resistant ecotypes than others. Some ecotypes of *S. capitata* and *S. macrocephala* are good examples of the differences in adaptation to environmental conditions. *S. guianensis* var. *canescens* and var. *microcephala* show narrow genetic variability and are susceptible to anthracnose. On the other hand, *S. guianensis* var. *vulgaris* presents broader genetic variability and shows some ecotypes resistant to anthracnose.

Nematodes of the genus *Meloidogyne* limit the performance of a number of legumes in Minas Gerais and are particularly damaging to *Rhynchosia* and *Teramnus* species. The author has only rarely observed nematode damage on the majority of *Stylosanthes* spp. but has found *S. guianensis* var. *microcephala, S. pilosa,* and *S. ruellioides* to be heavily infected under field conditions (see Table 3).

A large number of *Stylosanthes* species are attacked by insect pests, which destroy the base of flowering buds and also the developing seeds. The main insect attacking the species is *Stagasta* sp. Some species or ecotypes are more susceptible than others. In Sete Lagoas, *S. acuminata, S. grandifolia, S. gracilis,* and *S. campestris* are frequently attacked. *S. guianensis* var. *microcephala, S. capitata* and *S. macrocephala* are hardly ever attacked by insects.

While *S. guianensis* and *S. scabra* have been reported as susceptible to attack by stem borers of the genus *Caloptilia,* certain resistance has been identified in *S. capitata* (CIAT, 1978). *Stylosanthes* species in Serra do Cipó,

TABLE 3. Diseases and pests of *Stylosanthes* species.

Species	Anthracnosis		Pests		
	Stems	Leaves	Stems	Spikes	Roots
S. acuminata	+++	++	o	+++	o
S. aurea	+++	+++	o	+++	o
S. campestris	o	+++	+++	++	+
S. capitata	+	+	+	+	o
S. debilis	+++	+++	o	o	o
S. gracilis	+++	+++	o	+++	o
S. grandifolia	++	+++	o	+++	o
S. guianensis var. *canescens*	+++	++	o	+	o
S. guianensis var. *microcephala*	+++	+++	o	o	+++
S. guianensis var. *vulgaris*	++	++	+	+	o
S. leiocarpa	+++	+++	o	+	o
S. macrocephala	+	+	o	+	o
S. pilosa	+++	+++	o	+	++
S. ruellioides	+	+++	++	+	++
S. scabra	++	++	+	o	o
S. tomentosa	++	+++	+	o	+
S. viscosa	++	++			

+ : Lightly attacked, ++ : Moderately attacked, +++ : Heavily attacked, o: Not attacked

[1]Empresa de Pesquisa Agropecuaria de Minas Gerais, CP 295, Sete Lagoas 35700, MG Brazil.

Minas Gerais, have also shown variation in susceptibility to this pest. Thus, *S. campestris, S. ruelliodes* and *S. tomentosa* were highly susceptible but *S. capitata* and *S. macrocephala* were not affected.

Minas Gerais State is considered one of the centers of diffusion of the genus *Stylosanthes*. The diversity in nodulation and pest or disease resistance cited here emphasizes the wide variation found in this genus and demands that extensive collection and evaluation of this genus be undertaken in Minas Gerais.

REFERENCES

Centro Internacional de Agricultura Tropical (CIAT) (1978) Annual report of the beef production program. 186 pp.

Costa, N.M.S. (1970) *Stylosanthes gracilis,* Contribuição para o estudo da sua introdução nas pastagenus naturais des regioes planálticas de Angola, Universidade Técnica de Lisboa, Instituto Superior de Agronomia, Lisboa, Portugal.

Costa, N.M.S. & Ferreira, M.B. (1977) O genero *Stylosanthes* no Estado de Minas Gerais. Empresa de Pesquisa Agropecuaria de Minas Gerais, Belo Horizonte, Brazil. 38 p.

Ferreira, M.B. & Antunes, F.Z. (1980) Fatores ecológicos de importancia para as pastagens de Minas Gerais: Solo, clima e vegetacao. *Informe Agropec.* (Belo Horizonte) 6(70).

Norris, D.O. (1965) *Rhizobium* relationships in legumes. *Anais IX Congr. Int. Pastagens,* Sao Paulo, Brazil Vol. 2, pp. 1087-1092.

Souto, S.M., Coser, A.C. & Döbereiner, J. (1972) Host plant specificity of a native variety of *Stylosanthes gracilis. Pesq. Agropec. Bras. Ser. Zootec.* 7, 1-5.

NITROGEN FIXATION AND FORAGE CHARACTERIZATION OF *AESCHYNOMENE* SPP. IN A SUBTROPICAL CLIMATE.

K.H. Quesenberry, S.L. Albrecht and J.M. Bennett[1]

Summary

Since some species of the genus *Aeschynomene* have been suggested for use as forages, we assembled a large collection of *Aeschynomene* accessions and undertook a series of greenhouse and field experiments to characterize the N_2 fixation and water-stress responses of *Aeschynomene* species.

The nitrogenase activity of greenhouse-grown *Aeschynomene* plants was saturated at 10% C_2H_2 and showed maximum activity at 34°C. Specific rates were highest in four-week-old plants and declined in older plants. Three accessions of *A. americana* L. and one of *A. villosa* Poir. had normal rates of $N_2(C_2H_2)$ fixation and leaf water and turgor potential after three days of flooding, while in *Desmodium heterocarpon* DC., nitrogenase activity was only 3% of the well-watered control and leaf turgor potential was reduced to near zero. Drought stress decreased nitrogenase activity in all accessions to less than 40% that of the controls.

Nitrogenase activity and nodule number of field-grown *A. americana* were not significantly affected by increased P and K fertilizer, application of 100 kg/ha N at planting, or application of *Rhizobium* spp. inoculum to seeds at planting. Dry matter and total N were significantly increased by the addition of higher levels of P and K fertilizer. The addition of 100 kg/ha N at the higher level of P and K produced significantly higher dry matter and total N yields than the inoculated treatment, but there were no differences between inoculated and uninoculated plots at either fertility level.

INTRODUCTION

Aeschynomene is primarily a genus of tropical origin with major collections reported from both Africa and the Americas. The taxonomy of American

[1] Dept. of Agronomy, USDA/SEA-AR, and Dept. of Agronomy, respectively, Univ. of Florida, Gainesville, FL 32611 USA.

species was reviewed by Rudd (1955), while Kretschmer & Bullock (1980) suggested that some species could have agronomic potential as pasture legumes. They stated that the genus comprises approximately 160 species, of which roughly one half are xeric and the remainder hydrophytic. Plant types range from low-growing herbs to tree-like shrubs 8 m tall.

The species *A. falcata* (Poir.) DC. and *A. americana* L. have been evaluated for agronomic use. Joint vetch (*A. falcata* cv. Bargoo) was released in Australia in 1973 (Hennessy & Wilson, 1974). American joint vetch (*A. americana*) has been used widely as a pasture legume in Florida, but no named cultivars have been released. Grazing results with mixtures of Bahia grass (*Paspalum notatum* Flugge) and *Aeschynomene* spp. have been promising (Hodges *et al.*, 1976; Ocumpaugh, 1979).

The results in grazing trials led to the collection and evaluation of additional accessions of *A. americana* and other species. Kretschmer & Bullock (1980) found broad genetic diversity among 98 accessions of *A. americana* for flowering date, plant height, adventitious rooting, insect feeding, and perennial habit. Quesenberry & Ocumpaugh (1981) reported percentage nitrogen (N) to range from 2.52 to 4.38%, while the N yield of spaced plants at one harvest varied from 10-113 kg/ha. Total seasonal yields in excess of 150 kg N/ha have been obtained. Another advantage for *Aeschynomene* spp., revealed in preliminary studies under glasshouse conditions, is that most accessions show no significant reduction in nitrogenase activity under flooded conditions (Albrecht, Bennett & Quesenberry, 1981).

The experiments reported here fall into three groups. The first experiments examine the effect of assay time, C_2H_2 concentration and temperature on the nitrogenase activity of four to eight-week-old plants; look at seasonal variation in N_2 (C_2H_2) reduction by *Aeschynomene* cultivars; and examine the effects of defoliation. A further glasshouse trial then details the response of *Aeschynomene* species to water stress, while the final experiment provides some information on N_2 fixation by *A. americana* under field conditions.

MATERIALS AND METHODS

To determine the appropriate conditions for N_2 (C_2H_2) assay of *Aeschynomene* spp., several accessions were grown on washed quartz sand and watered twice weekly with full strength Hoagland solution minus N. The effects of assay duration, C_2H_2 concentration and temperature were then examined using four to eight-week-old plants.

Another series of plants from accessions number 55, 57, and 64 of *A. americana* were grown as above, but assayed weekly from 4-15 weeks after germination. In this study an additional treatment was included in which plants received Hoagland solution plus 15 mM nitrate twice weekly.

The effects of defoliation on N_2 (C_2H_2) fixation were also studied, a group of eight-week-old plants being clipped to a height of 15 cm (about 6 nodes above the soil), after which their foliar regrowth and N_2 (C_2H_2) fixation were examined for 3-50 days more.

Except in the studies on assay time, C_2H_2 concentration, and incubation temperature, assay conditions for N_2 (C_2H_2) reduction were similar to those adopted by other authors, but we employed 75 ml serum vials with 10% by volume C_2H_2 injected, and assay periods of 30 and 60 minutes. In the aforementioned studies, the procedure was varied to permit sampling from 15 - 420 minutes, C_2H_2 concentrations from 0-25% and incubation temperatures from 5-50° C. In the latter case samples were equilibrated in incubators for 60 minutes; then the assay was run for 60 minutes.

In a second study, accessions of *Aeschynomene* species and *D. heterocarpon* were grown in sand:peat:perlite mixtures in 15 cm pots. Ten weeks after germination, pots were either flooded with water to surface level or were denied water. Nitrogenase activity and components of leaf water potential were then measured after three days. Leaf water potentials were measured with thermocouple psychrometers, and osmotic potentials were determined on the same samples after freezing and thawing of the tissue. Leaf turgor potentials were calculated as the difference between leaf water and osmotic potentials.

The final experiment was a field inoculation trial carried out on a Pomona sand known to contain a low population of indigenous rhizobia. Two levels of fertilization (12 kg P + 46 kg K/ha or 28 kg P + 105 K/ha, each with 16 g/kg of FTE 503 containing 3% B, 3% Cu, 18% Fe, 7.5% Mn, 2% Mo, and 7% Zn) and three inoculation treatments (uninoculated; uninoculated but with 100 kg/ha N as NH_4NO_3 applied at planting; and inoculated with a mixture containing strains TAL 309, CIAT 465 and CIAT 753) were used. Seeds of *A. americana* were planted at a depth of 1-2 cm in plots 2 x 7 m. After 13 weeks, 5 plants/plot were harvested and nodules counted. Six days later 2 plants/plot were harvested and assayed for nitrogenase activity using the acetylene reduction assay. Plots were harvested for dry matter after five months, and N content was determined by the micro-Kjeldahl technique of Gallagher *et al.* (1976).

RESULTS AND DISCUSSION

In the experiment on C_2H_2 concentration effects on C_2H_4 formation by *A. americana,* saturation occurred at 0.10 atm C_2H_2 with a maximum rate of greater than 70 μmoles C_2H_4 produced/gram of dry nodules per h. The apparent K_m for C_2H_2 determined from a Lineweaver-Burk plot was 0.0107 atm, similar to the range of values (0.004-0.010 atm) normally reported for this substrate.

Under standard conditions the rate of C_2H_4 formation was linear for at least 165 minutes; then decreased to a lower linear rate for up to seven hours after injection of the C_2H_2, a finding similar to that of Sprent (1969).

Accessions number 64 and 57 showed similar responses to incubation temperature with peak activity at 34°C and a plateau of optimal activity between 20° and 37°C (see Figure 1). Accession 55 had a significantly lower nitrogenase activity than the other accessions and maintained maximum values from 26° to 34°C. Cralle & Heichel (1980) found that short-term rates of nitrogenase activity in alfalfa (*Medicago sativa* L.) were optimum between 25° and 35°C.

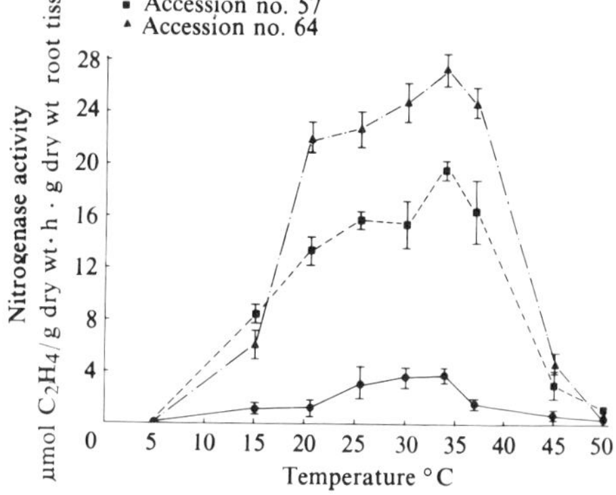

Figure 1.
Effect of incubation temperature on nitrogenase activity of nodulated *A. americana*. Bars show the standard error of the mean.

Weekly assays of nodule and nitrogenase development in *A. americana* showed greatest specific nodule activity (SNA) in four-week-old plants, irrespective of N treatment (see Figure 2). Activity decreased more rapidly with age in the +N treatment, but moderate rates of nitrogenase activity were measured at 10 weeks after germination with SNA still relatively high (45 µmoles/g of dry nodule per h) even after 13 weeks in the -N treatment. Nodule weight was significantly higher in the treatment without N for most of the experiment, but nodule biomass in the +N treament continually increased through the period of the experiment. This suggests that *A. americana* will nodulate and retain relatively high nitrogenase activity in the presence of fixed N.

Figure 3 shows the relationship of foliar regrowth and nitrogenase activity. Nitrogenase activity of defoliated Florida common *Aeschynomene* decreased to less than 10% of the activity of the nondefoliated control three days after defoliation, and even 50 days thereafter was only 60% that of nondefoliated control plants. Regression of nitrogenase activity on leaf biomass showed a tight linear relationship ($r^2 = 0.93$). Similar results have been reported by Fishbeck & Phillips (1980).

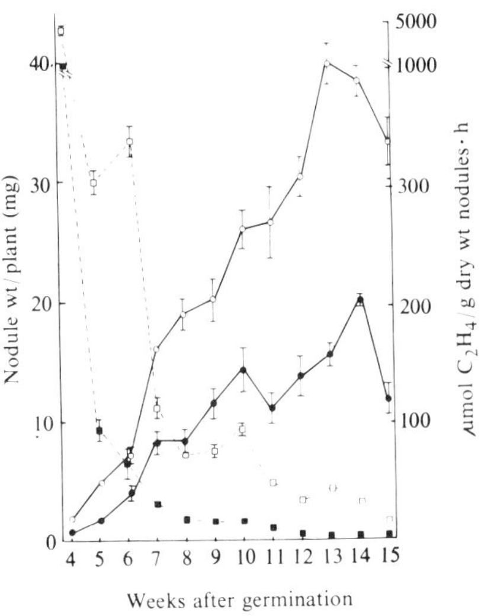

Figure 2.
Effect of plant age on nodule weight and C_2H_4 evolution of *A. americana*. Open symbols are -N treatment and closed symbols are +N treatment. Hatched lines show SNA and solid lines nodule weight. Bars show the standard error of mean.

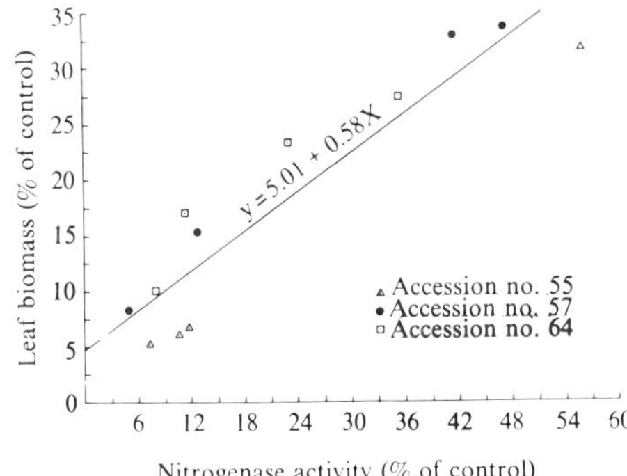

Figure 3.
Relationship of leaf biomass regrowth to nitrogenase activity of three accessions of *A. americana*.

The effects of water stress on nitrogenase activity in *Aeschynomene* spp. and *D. heterocarpon* are shown in Table 1. While all *Aeschynomene* accessions appeared normal, with nitrogenase activity similar to those of control plants, flooding for three days reduced the SNA of *D. heterocarpon* nodules to only 3% that of well-watered control plants. Leaf water, osmotic, and turgor potentials of *Aeschynomene* plants were also little affected by flooding (see Table 2), suggesting that *Aeschynomene* spp. are much more tolerant of flooding than is *Desmodium heterocarpon*. By contrast most of the *Aeschynomene* accessions were markedly affected in the dry treatment, though *A. americana* (UF186) and the *D. heterocarpon* accession showed greater nitrogenase activity and leaf water or turgor potential than the other accessions.

TABLE 1: Comparison of water stress effects on nitrogenase (C_2H_2) activity in *Aeschynomene* and *Desmodium* accessions.

Legume identification	Control	Flooded	Dry
	µmol C_2H_4/g nodule dry wt·h		
A. villosa UR 369	2.58 ± 0.67 (100)	2.43 ± 0.47 (95)	0.20 ± 0.06 (8)
A. americana UF 57	5.13 ± 0.27 (100)	5.65 ± 0.64 (110)	0.11 ± 0.03 (2)
A. americana UF 186	1.88 ± 0.63 (100)	1.94 ± 0.24 (103)	0.75 ± 0.12 (40)
A. americana UF 255	3.45 ± 0.81 (100)	3.97 ± 0.66 (114)	0.09 ± 0.03 (3)
D. heterocarpon UF 20	6.49 ± 0.89 (100)	0.18 ± 0.05 (3)	2.40 ± 0.55 (37)

[1] Indicates standard error of mean.

TABLE 2: Water stress effects on leaf water (ψ_l), osmotic (ψ_s), and turgor (ψ_p) potentials of *Aeschynomene* and *Desmodium* accessions.

Legume identification	Control			Flooded			Dry		
	ψl	ψs	ψp	ψl	ψs	ψp	ψl	ψs	ψp
	Bars								
A. viscosa UF 369	-3.1	- 5.6	2.5	-1.7	-4.8	3.1	- 7.0	- 5.8	-1.2
A. americana UF 57	-2.7	- 6.1	3.4	-3.7	-7.0	3.3	-16.0	-14.0	-2.0
A. americana UF 186	-4.4	- 7.4	3.0	-2.9	-7.4	4.5	-13.5	-16.4	2.9
A. americana UF 255	-7.2	-10.9	3.7	-3.0	-8.1	5.1	-12.0	-12.1	-0.1
D. heterocarpon	-3.4	- 5.8	2.4	-3.2	-3.1	-0.1	- 9.5	- 7.4	-2.1

[1]Calculation of ψ p yields some negative values as apoplastic dilution of cell sap after freezing causes slight underestimation of ψ p.

The results of the field inoculation trial are presented in Table 3, with no significant differences evident among the treatments for nitrogenase activity or nodule number. High SNA and nodule number were even obtained in the +N treatment, confirming the tolerance of the *Aeschynomene* symbiosis to soil N. Clearly, sufficient effective native rhizobia were present to limit the response to inoculation. At the same time, the increased dry matter production and N yield of the +N treatment implies that neither native rhizobia nor inoculant strains could satisfy the N requirements of the plant. Increased P and K fertilization did, however, enhance dry matter and N yield.

TABLE 3: Nitrogenase activity, nodule number and dry matter, and N yield of *A. americana.*[1]

Treatments		Nitrogenase activity (μmoles C_2H_4/ g root · h)	Nodule number	Yield (kg/ha)	
Fertility level[2]	Inoculation[3]			Dry matter	Nitrogen
1	1	9.46 a[1]	1620 a	5310 bc	96 bc
1	2	8.05 a	1341 a	4213 c	76 c
1	3	8.15 a	1421 a	3755 c	66 c
2	1	11.46 a	1573 a	6503 ab	118 ab
2	2	9.28 a	1545 a	8016 a	135 a
2	3	8.56 a	1715 a	5080 bc	95 bc

[1]Means followed by the same letter are not significantly different (P = 0.05).
[2]Fertility level 1 = 275 kg/ha 0-10-20 with 16 g/kg FTE 503. Fertility level 2 = 600 kg/ha 0-10-20 with 16 g/kg FTE 503.
[3]Inoculum treatments were: 1, un inoculated; 2, 100 kg/ha N from NH_4NO_3 applied at planting; 3, inoculated with NifTAL-prepared inoculum.

REFERENCES

Albrecht, S.L., Bennett, J.M. & Quesenberry, K.H. (1981) Growth and nitrogen fixation of *Aeschynomene* under water stressed conditions. *Plant Soil.* 60, 309-315.

Cralle, H.T. & Heichel, G.H. (1980) Temperature and chilling sensivity of alfalfa nodule nitrogenase activity. *Plant Physiol.* (Suppl.) 65, 108.

Fishbeck, K.A. & Phillips, D.A. (1980) Apparent photosynthesis, root carbohydrates, and nitrogen fixation in alfalfa following harvest. *Plant Physiol.* (Suppl.) 65, 109.

Gallaher, R.H., Weldan, C.O. & Boswell, F.C. (1976) A semi-automated procedure for total nitrogen in plant and soil samples. *Soil Sci. Soc. Amer. Proc.* 40, 887-889.

Hennessy, D.W. & Wilson, G.P.M. (1974) Nutritive value of 'Bargoo' joint vetch (*Aeschynomene falcata*) and companion grasses when fed to sheep. *J. Aust. Inst. Agric. Sci.* 40, 82-83.

Hodges, E.M., Peacock, F.M., Chapman H.L. Jr., & Martin, F.G. (1976) Grazing trials with tropical grasses and legumes in peninsular Florida. *Soil Crop Sci. Soc. Fla. Proc.* 35, 84-86.

Kretschmer, A.E. Jr. & Bullock, R.C. (1980) *Aeschynomene* spp.: Distribution and use. *Soil Crop Sci. Soc. Fla. Proc.* 39, 145-152.

Ocumpaugh, W.R. (1979) Creep grazing for calves. Beef Cattle Short Course, IFAS, Univ. of Florida, Gainesville, FL, USA. Pp. 159-165.

Quesenberry, K.H. & Ocumpaugh, W.E. (1981) Forage evaluation of *Aeschynomene* species in north central Florida. *Soil Crop Sci. Soc. Fla. Proc.* 40. (Submitted for publication.)

Rudd, V.E. (1955) American species of *Aeschynomene. US National Herbarium* 32:1-172. (US National Museum, Smithsonian Institution, Washington D.C., USA.)

Sprent, J.I. (1969) Prolonged reduction of acetylene by detached soybean nodules. *Planta* 88, 372-375.

LEGUME ESTABLISHMENT IN PANGOLAGRASS PASTURES IN THE HUMID TROPICS

W.B. Bryan[1] and E.R. Velásquez[2]

Summary

An experiment to compare two methods for establishing different forage legumes in a pangolagrass (*Digitaria decumbens*) pasture, was carried out on a loamy clay soil in the Orinoco Delta, Venezuela. Fourteen legumes, including *Centrosema plumieri* and three cultivars of *Stylosanthes guianensis*, were hand seeded into clipped pasture that had been either disk harrowed or rotovated twice and disk harrowed. Establishment of the legumes and recovery of the grass were observed over a 4½-month period. Six harvests were then made at six-week intervals, and the dry matter (DM) yield and the percentage crude protein (CP) of the pastures were determined.

Legumes with a climbing growth habit established more quickly where only the disk was used. All legume/pangolagrass associations yielded more DM and CP than grass only. Plots with *C. plumieri* or *S. guianensis* gave double the DM yield and triple the CP yield of grass only. The maximum DM yield of 1.8 metric tons/ha per 6 wks was produced by an *S. guianensis*/pangolagrass association which produced 0.33 metric tons of CP/ha per 6 wks. The majority of the plots had 30-50% legume. All legumes increased the CP content of the associated pangolagrass. Pangolagrass growing with *C. plumieri* contained 14.7% CP compared to 10.7% when grown alone.

INTRODUCTION

Pangolagrass (*Digitaria decumbens*) is grown widely in the humid tropics and supplies feed for the grazing animal. High production demands inputs of nitrogen (N) fertilizer even on fertile soils, and up to 800 kg N/ha per yr have

[1] Division of Plant and Soil Sciences, West Virginia University, Morgantown, W.VA., USA.
[2] Estación Experimental de Guara, Tucupita, Venezuela.

been recommended for pangolagrass pastures in the Orinoco Delta (Velásquez, Larez & Bryan, 1975). In a small plot trial 17.5 metric tons of dry matter (DM) per ha were produced annually over a four-year period from pangolagrass receiving 200 kg/ha per yr of phosphorus (P) and 800 kg/ha per yr N (Velásquez *et al.*, 1975).

The possibility of introducing legumes into pangolagrass pastures has aroused considerable interest, since feasibility analyses indicate that grass/legume associations may be more profitable for beef production than pastures based on grass alone (Burton & Bryan, 1981). In this study we compare two methods for the establishment of legumes in pangolagrass pastures.

EXPERIMENTAL METHODS

The experiment was carried out on the Estación Experimental de Guara, in the Orinoco Delta, Venezuela, using a pangolagrass pasture established more than eight years previously. The pasture was located on the Manamo soil series (dyke soils that vary from sandy to loamy clays with little organic matter content, low permeability, and irregular topography).

The pasture was rotary mowed and the clippings were removed. Plots 6x4 m were used. Half of each plot was cultivated twice with a rotovator, and then a disk harrow, set so that it made small slits in the ground, was passed once over the plots. Fourteen different legumes were evaluated (see Table 1). Each was hand planted into the narrow slits. Plots were hand weeded before cultivation and before each harvest (except the plot with pega-pega, a *Desmodium* species that volunteers in pastures in the region).

Establishment was observed over a 4½-month period. Plots were then cut (establishment cut), each plot divided into three, and the following fertilizer treatments applied to each division: control; 200 kg/ha of P as triple superphosphate; and 200 kg P as triple superphosphate with 100 kg K as KCl and 3000 kg lime/ha.

Six harvests were then made at approximately six-week intervals, using the cutting heights shown in Table 1. Two samples were cut from each plot using a 0.25 m^2 quadrat, and these were used to determine percentage of grass and legume. Cut herbage was hand separated into grass and legume and dried for 48 hours at 105° C. After sampling, the entire plot was cut with a rotary mower at the appropriate height (see Table 1) and clippings were removed. Crude protein (CP) was determined on the dried samples by the micro-Kjeldahl technique.

RESULTS AND DISCUSSION

Establishment

Rainfall was well distributed during the experiment with 21, 461 and 1058 mm precipitation during the pre-seeding, establishment, and cutting phases, respectively.

One week after seeding, all legumes save *Lablab purpureus* showed more seedlings in the disked-only subplot. One month after seeding, differences in seedling emergence were no longer evident, but the *Calopogonium mucunoides, Teramnus uncinatus, Pueraria javanica, P. phaseoloides*, and *Centrosema pubescens* plots all showed better growth where the rotovator had been used. Use of the rotovator checked regrowth of the grass and permitted deeper placement of the legume seeds. Monzote & Hernández (1977) recommended using a disk harrow and broadcasting the seed to establish *Glycine wightii* in pangolagrass pastures. Our results also suggest that legumes can be established successfully in pangolagrass pastures with minimum tillage.

Growth

Only two or three plants of *Desmodium* germinated; thus, the plot was used as a check at 10 cm cutting height. Following the establishment cut, *L. purpureus* also died out, and that plot was designated a check at 20 cm. Pega-pega was present in all plots and was removed by hand prior to the experiment, except in the plot designated to it.

Pangolagrass associated with legumes was a deeper green color and grew better than grass alone. Both grass and legumes also appeared to suffer less insect and fungal attack in association than in pure stand (legumes were compared with pure stands in plots in the introduction garden).

Dry matter yield

All legume/pangolagrass plots gave DM yields greater than the corresponding checks; in particular, plots with *C. plumieri* or *S. guianensis* yielded double the check (20 cm). The maximum DM yield (1.8 tons/ha per 6 wks) was derived from the *S. guianensis* IRI 2870/pangolagrass association (see Table 1).

Dry matter production was greater in the plots where the rotovator was used (see Table 2). Only plots with *Desmodium* sp. (pega-pega), *T. uncinatus* and *S. guianensis* yielded more where only the disk was used. Only in the case of *Clitoria ternatea* was the difference between establishment methods considered significant. In this case most of the seedlings did not survive after two months where only the disk was used.

TABLE 1: Average dry matter (DM) and crude protein (CP) yields, crude protein percentage of legume and pangolagrass, and the percentage of legume obtained in pangolagrass/legume associations.

Associated legume	Height of cut (cm)	DM yield (t/ha)	CP (t/ha)	% legume in pasture		% CP	
				First harvest	Last harvest	Legume	Grass
Stylosanthes guianensis IR 2870	15	1.8	0.33	62	90	21.0	12.4
Stylosanthes guianensis IRI 1022	20	1.6	0.26	55	78	19.6	11.9
Centrosema plumieri	15	1.6	0.33	78	37	25.8	14.3
Stylosanthes guianensis Q 8558	20	1.5	0.25	51	46	20.0	12.1
Teramnus uncinatus IRI 1286	20	1.3	0.22	64	44	20.5	13.3
Pueraria javanica IRI 1298	20	1.3	0.22	49	67	20.6	13.1
Pueraria phaseoloides	20	1.3	0.24	56	87	20.7	13.4
Clitoria ternatea	20	1.2	0.18	45	45	19.5	12.6
Centrosema pubescens IRI 1282	15	1.2	0.23	40	47	27.9	13.1
Calopogonium mucunoides IRI 1281	20	1.1	0.17	61	0	20.7	12.7
Glycine wightii IRI 1284	15	1.0	0.14	47	30	21.3	11.4
Macroptilium atropurpureum	20	1.0	0.14	50	18	20.2	11.4
Pega pega (*Desmodium* sp.)	10	0.6	0.07	38	35	17.4	10.9
Digitaria decumbens alone	20	0.8	0.08	–	–	–	10.7
Digitaria decumbens alone	10	0.3	0.03	–	–	–	10.6

TABLE 2: Average yield of dry matter (DM) for pangolagrass and legume associations as influenced by methods of legume seeding (average of six harvests).

Associated legume	Method of establishment	
	Disk only	Rotovator and disk
	(tons/ha)	
S. guianensis IRI 2870	1.5	2.1
S. guianensis IRI 1022	1.5	1.6
C. plumieri	1.5	1.7
S. guianensis Q 8558	1.6	1.3
T. uncinatus IRI 1286	1.4	1.3
P. javanica IRI 1298	1.3	1.4
P. phaseoloides	1.2	1.4
C. ternatea	0.8	1.4
C. pubescens IRI 1282	1.1	1.3
C. mucunoides IRI 1281	1.1	1.1
G. wightii IRI 1284	0.9	1.2
M. atropurpureum	0.9	1.0
Desmodium sp.	0.7	0.4
Check 20	0.8	0.8
Check 10	0.4	0.3
$\overline{x}$	1.1	1.2

There appeared to be no differences in DM yield due to fertilizer application. This is in agreement with data from limiting nutrient trials on the same soil series (Velásquez *et al.*, 1975). However, longer term trials are needed to examine fertilizer requirements.

Percentage of legume in the pasture

As the experiment progressed the percentage of *S. guianensis* 1022 and 2870, *P. phaseolides* and *P. javanica* in the pasture tended to increase while that of *Macroptilium atropurpureum*, *C. plumieri*, *S. guianensis* 8558 and *C. mucunoides* decreased. The percentage of the other legumes in their respective associations remained more or less constant (see Table 1) and in most cases contributed 30-50% of the dry matter yield. More frequent cutting, or cutting at a lower height could be used for those species that tended to dominate the pangolagrass; less frequent or higher cuts for those species that tended to disappear.

Dry matter percentage

The legumes with the lowest average DM percentages were *C. plumieri* (15%), *S. guianensis* 2870 (17%), and *P. phaseoloides* (17%). Pega-pega (*Desmodium* sp.) had the highest percentage of dry matter (26%). Pangolagrass associated with a legume had lower average DM percentage than when grown alone. Thus, pangolagrass with *C. plumieri* had 17% DM, while in the 10-cm and 20-cm check plots the DM percentages were 21% and 25%, respectively.

Crude protein

The crude protein concentration of pangolagrass associated with a legume was higher in all cases than when growing alone (see Table 1). The average CP content of pangolagrass associated with *C. plumieri* was 14.3%, representing a 33% increase in CP compared to the grass alone (10.7%). This is evidently the result of the use by the grass of N_2 fixed by the associated legume.

The legumes with the highest average CP content were *C. plumieri* (25.8%) and *C. pubescens* (27.9%). Thus, the associated legumes not only increased CP in the pangolagrass, but total CP in the sward grass was greatly increased by the direct contribution of the legumes. Yields of CP for *C. plumieri* and *S. guianensis* associations were over four times greater than for the pangolagrass alone (see Table 1).

REFERENCES

Burton, R.O. & Bryan, W.B. (1981) Proc. XIV Intern. Grassl. Cong. Lexington, KY, USA. (In press.)

Monzote, M. & Hernández, T. (1977) *Cuban J. Agric. Sci.* 11, 323-329.

Velásquez, E.R., Larez, O. & Bryan, W.B. (1975) IRI Research Institute, Bull. 43.

THE ROLE OF LEGUMES IN MIXED PASTURES

A.S. Whitney[1]

Summary

Legumes can contribute greatly to pasture production by providing high protein forage, especially during the dry season when grass quality is poor. Little nitrogen (N) is transferred underground by actively growing legumes, but aboveground transfer of N, principally in legume leaf litter, green leaf which is trampled into the soil by grazing animals, urine from animals grazing legumes, and feces, is significant. Management alternatives to maximize the legume N contribution are discussed.

INTRODUCTION

The potential for the improvement of tropical pastures by planting improved grasses and legumes can be impressive. In experiments conducted on the Colombian savannas by scientists from the Centro Internacional de Agricultura Tropical (CIAT), animals grazing *Andropogon gayanus* in combination with different legumes gained twice as much per animal and ten times as much per ha as animals grazing native savanna (CIAT, 1980b).

Species vary greatly in their ability to fix nitrogen (N_2) and to transfer some of the fixed N_2 to the grass. Thus, Whitney & Green (1969) found that *Desmodium canum* (kaimi clover) had a modest potential to fix N (about 100 kg/ha per yr) but transferred about 30% of the fixed N to the grass while *Desmodium intortum* had a far greater N_2 fixation potential (over 260 kg/ha per year), but provided only slightly more N to the grass fraction. Johansen & Kerridge (1979) sampled three pastures and found fixation in all but *Lotonanis bainesii* to be substantial (100-140 kg N/ha per year). *Lotononis* fixed only 51-74 kg N/ha per year but even so transferred 12-15% of this to the associated grass. In these two experiments clippings were removed from the plots; under grazed conditions N transfer would probably be much greater.

---

[1] University of Hawaii, Dept. of Agronomy and Soil Sci., Maui Agricultural Research Center, Kula, Hawaii.

Most ranches in the tropics could benefit substantially from grass/legume pastures. However the contribution of the legume must be reliable, and the establishment and management practices economically viable, while still assuring a good balance between grasses and legumes.

Obviously, a great many factors influence the legume contribution: disease and insect attack, nutrition of the legume plant (including competition by the associated grass), competence of the microsymbiont, and adaptation to the soil and climatic stresses present in the environment. This paper considers three aspects of post-establishment management of grass-legume pastures; maximizing N_2 fixation, transfer of N from grass to legume, and mineralization of N; all with the viewpoint of enhancing the contribution of the legume.

MAXIMIZING N_2 FIXATION

Defoliation regime

Defoliation regime is an important consideration in legume performance (Whitney, 1970). *Desmodium intortum* with both kikuyugrass (*Pennisetum clandestinum*) and pangolagrass (*Digitaria decumbens*) responded to lenient cutting with increased yield and N_2 fixation per unit of time (from 74 to 316 kg N fixed/ha per year depending on cutting height and interval). Only under lenient cutting was significant N transferred to the grass fraction (up to 56 kg ha per year). Jones (1967) also found that *Macroptilium atropurpureum* cv. Siratro yields of N and dry matter (DM) were reduced by both low height of clipping and short intervals between clippings.

Shade

Shading of low-growing legumes due to infrequent grazing, growth under plantation crops, or low light intensity during the rainy season can similarly result in reduced N_2 fixation due to a reduction in carbohydrate supply to the roots and nodules (Eriksen & Whitney, 1977). Legumes vary greatly in their tolerance to shade, with the less productive legumes generally more shade tolerant. Defoliation regime is, thus, especially important if the legumes are shaded, since the carbohydrate for regrowth and N_2 fixation would be even more limiting than under full sunlight. A legume can only be expected to fix appreciable N_2 when it has ample reserves to sustain regrowth after defoliation, and/or when defoliation is relatively lenient. The ideal situation therefore would be where the legume can make vigorous vegetative growth before being grazed. Fortunately, most tropical legumes are less palatable than the associated grass during the rainy season. There was a definite grazing pattern at CIAT-Quilichao for a mixture of grasses associated with *Desmodium ovalifolium* (CIAT, 1980a). Cattle grazed the legume only after the quality of the grass was reduced to a very low level. As expected this was accentuated in the high-grazing-pressure treatment. The legume was subsequently utilized to advantage by the animals to maintain the level of protein in the diet. Australian workers have also documented a preference for grasses in the rainy season; then, as grass quality declines, increased consumption of the legume (Stobbs, 1977; Gardener, 1980). This allows the legume to accumulate reserve carbohydrates to support regrowth.

N fertilization

Fertilization of a mixed sward almost always favors the grass, making it more competitive for light and/or nutrients relative to the legume (Jones, 1967; Whitney, 1970; Kitamura, *et al.*, 1981). Also N_2 fixation is depressed if the legume takes up soil N from fertilizer or urine patches. Soil N accumulation in the pasture can also reduce N_2 fixation by the legume (Hoglund & Brock, 1978). Vallis *et al.*, (1977) have shown that legumes vary greatly in their ability to compete with the grass for soil N. *Lotononis* was a good competitor compared to *Macroptilium atropurpureum*; however in no case was proportional uptake by the legume more than 25% over the growing season.

N TRANSFER FROM LEGUME TO GRASS

Underground transfer

Whitney & Kanehiro (1967) estimated N transfer from *Centrosema pubescens, D. intortum* and *D. canum* to companion pangolagrass using N-free nutrient solutions. Only when the legumes were cut was a significant quantity of N released to the grass, amounting to 1-9% of the total N mobilized from the roots to support regrowth.

Butler *et al.* (1959), among other reseachers, state that nodule shedding is important for N transfer to associated grasses in temperate pastures. Both defoliation and shading led to reduction in nodule number and weight. N from lost nodule tissue is rapidly mineralized by the rhizosphere bacteria (Haystead & Marriott, 1979). The importance of nodule shedding in tropical pastures is unknown.

Leaching of N from leaves

Less than 1% of their N can be leached from intact legume leaves (Whitney & Kanehiro, 1967). That which is leachable is mainly in the form of amino acids and is most leachable during the time that total N in the leaf is declining.

Leaf fall

Leaf fall from mature plants is another pathway of N transfer. From 1.6 to 3.5% of the N contained in the plant can be lost weekly through this means (Whitney & Kanehiro, 1967). Henzell *et al* (1966), found a layer of organic matter (mostly decomposing legume leaves and stolons) 2-3 cm thick in *Desmodium uncinatum* pastures fertilized for six years with superphosphate but no organic layer in unfertilized pasture. Soil in the fertilized pastures increased from 360 to 480 kg N/ha during the experiment, depending on the amount of superphosphate applied. Vallis (1972) also reported a significant increase in soil N at three sites; at Samford in S.E. Queensland, soil N increased on the average by 44 kg/ha per yr. Jones *et al.* (1967) reported a similar increase in soil N in a trial that was sampled and then grazed over a period of three years. Both legumes and N fertilizer increased soil N percentage, and this led to higher yields of a subsequent sorghum crop.

Animal excreta

A discussion of the N contribution of legumes to pasture must also take into account the transfer that takes place via animal excreta (Barrow, 1967; Mott, 1974; Wilkinson & Lowrey, 1973; Watkin & Clements, 1977). This is especially true of urine, since the N in excess of 8 g/kg of DM intake is excreted in the urine. Thus, animals grazing legume pastures would excrete significant quantities of N in the urine. However, losses of urine can be high due to high concentration (equivalent to up to 500 kg/ha in the patch), which can result in both volatization and leaching losses. Also some pasture is burned while N_2 fixation by legumes is inhibited in the patch. If dense vegetation occurs in the vicinity of urine patches, Denmeade *et al.* (1976) have shown that a closed ammonia cycle is operative in the vicinity of the horizon occupied by clover. However, this may be of limited importance to most tropical pastures.

Dung is also important in the N economy of pastures, but this N is in an organic form (microbial tissue) and in a rather low concentration. It is, therefore, subject to lower losses than in N from urine, but there is relatively little mineralization of N from dung in the short term. The distribution of excreta is also usually poor but is enhanced at high stocking rates (Rouguette, *et al.,* 1973).

MINERALIZATION OF LEGUME TISSUE IN SOIL

From data obtained by Henzell & Vallis (1977) it is probable that legume tissue must have at least 1.5% N for mineralization to show a net gain. Above that level, rates of N mineralization increased dramatically. In their study, 24% of the N from *Desmodium tortuosum* leaf mixed with the soil was recovered in only six weeks of inoculation by Rhodes grass (*Chloris guyana*), and 20% from siratro leaf. By contrast, *D. intortum* with a high concentration of tannin-bound protein in the green leaf, was slow to mineralize. With *D. intortum* excluded from the equation, N concentration explained 90% of the variation in recovery of N from legume tissue. Vallis & Jones (1973) reported similar data for 'Siratro' and 'Greenleaf desmodium'. There was no net mineralization of the desmodium leaf for four weeks, but after that the slope was the same as siratro leaf. They also sampled pastures of both 'Siratro' and 'Greenleaf desmodium'. Although siratro leaf decomposed more rapidly in pasture soils, there was no difference in mineralization rates between the two pastures after the initial flush, indicating that the N from desmodium leaf is probably equally available over time. In fact, the slow-release aspect might be beneficial where N losses by leaching or volatilization might occur.

Henzell & Ross (1973) estimate that the N remaining in the legume leaves is probably mineralized at a rate of only 1-2% per year, because the microbial N becomes rapidly stabilized against further degradation.

Trampling of green leaf by grazing animals is, thus, important because the green leaf is high in N and mineralizes rapidly. When trampling was allowed in a *Pennisetum clandestinum*/*D. intortum* pasture, the legume leaf material was 6-27% higher in N than where there was grazing only. Total N from leaf fall was doubled by trampling (A.B. Lwoga & A.S. Whitney, unpublished data).

CONCLUSIONS

To maximize the contribution of the legume, a good grass/legume balance is required, the grass will utilize the N_2 fixed to provide high quality feed during the rainy season when the legumes are unpalatable, at the same time protecting the legumes until they have made vigorous vegetative growth. It would seem, therefore, that where land is not limiting, "protein banks" should include a grass, with the legume planted in strips, the width of which would be determined by the spreading ability of the legume.

The potential for improving pastures through the use of legumes is contingent upon vigorous vegetative growth by the legume component. In addition, there may be scope for utilizing management practices designed to enhance the transfer of N to the associated grass.

REFERENCES

Barrow, N.J. (1967) Some aspects of the effects of grazing on the nutrition of pastures. *J. Aust. Inst. Agr. Sci.* 33, 254-262.

Butler, G.W., Greenwood, R. M. & Soper, K. (1959) Effect of shading and defoliation on the turnover of root and nodule tissue of plants of *Trifolium repens, Trifolium pratense* and *Lotus uliginosus*. *N.Z.J. Agric. Res.* 2, 415-426.

Centro Internacional de Agricultura Tropical (1980a) Annual report, Tropical Pastures 1979. CIAT, Cali, Colombia. P. 78.

Centro Internacional de Agricultura Tropical (1980b) CIAT Report, 1980. CIAT, Cali, Colombia. P. 82.

Denmeade, O.T., Freney, J.R. & Simpson, J.R. (1976) A closed ammonia cycle within a plant canopy. *Soil Biol. Biochem.* 8,161-164.

Eriksen, F. & Whitney, A.S. (1977) Performance of tropical forage grasses and legumes under different light intensities. Proc. Regional Seminar Pasture Res. & Develop. Hondura, Solomon Is. Pp. 180-190.

Gardener, C.J. (1980) Diet selection and liveweight performance of steers on *Stylosanthes hamata*-native grass pastures. *Aust. J. Agric.* Res. 31, 379-392.

Haystead, A. & Marriott, C. (1979) Transfer of legume nitrogen to associated grass. *Soil Biol. Biochem.* 11, 99-104.

Henzell, E.F., Fergus, I.F. & Martin, A.E. (1966) Accumulation of soil nitrogen and carbon under a *Desmodium uncinatum* pasture. *Aust. J. Exptl. Agr. Anim. Husb.* 6, 157-160.

Henzell, E.F. & Ross, P.J. (1973) The nitrogen cycle of pasture ecosystems. *In:* Chemistry and biochemistry of herbage, G.W. Butler & R.W. Bailey (Eds.). Academic Press, London, England. Pp 227-246.

Henzell, E.F. & Vallis I. (1977) Transfer of nitrogen between legumes and other crops. *In:* Biological nitrogen fixation in farming systems of the tropics, A. Ayanaba, & P.J. Dart (Eds.) Wiley, New York, NY, USA. Pp 73-88.

Hoglund, J.H. & Brock, J.L. (1978) Regulation of nitrogen fixation in a grazed pasture. *N.Z. J. Agric. Res.* 21, 73-82.

Johansen, C., & Kerridge, P.C. (1979) Nitrogen fixation and transfer in tropical legume-grass swards in south-eastern Queensland. *Trop. Grassl.* 13, 165-170.

Jones, R.J. (1967) Effects of close cutting and nitrogen fertilizer on growth of siratro (*Phaseolus atropurpureus*) pasture at Samford, south-eastern Queensland. *Aust. J. Exptl. Agric. Anim. Husb.* 7:157-161.

Jones, R.J., Griffiths Davies, J. & White, R.B. (1967) The contribution of some tropical legumes to pasture yields of dry matter and nitrogen at Samford, south-eastern Queensland. *Aust. J. Exptl. Agric. Anim. Husb.* 7, 57- 65.

Kitamura, Y., Guevara, A.B. & Whitney, A.S. (1981) Legume growth and nitrogen fixation as affected by plant competition for light and soil nitrogen. *Agron. J.* 73, 395-398.

Mott, G.G. (1974) Nutrient recyling in pastures. *In:* Forage fertilization, D. Mays (Ed.). Amer. Soc. Agron., Crop. Sci. Soc., and Soil Science Soc. Amer. Madison, WI, USA. Pp 323-339.

Rouquette, F.M. Jr., Matocha, J.E. & Duble, R.L. (1973) Recycling and recovery of nitrogen, phosphorus, and potassium by coastal bermudagrass: 11. Under grazing conditions with two stocking rates. *J. Environ. Qual.* 2, 129-132.

Stobbs, T.H. (1977) Seasonal changes in the preference by cattle for *Macroptilium atropurpureum* cv. Siratro. *Trop. Grassl.* 11, 87-91.

Vallis, I. (1972) Soil nitrogen changes under continuously grazed legume-grass pastures in subtropical coastal Queensland. *Aust. J. Exptl. Agric. Anim. Husb.* 12, 495-501.

Vallis, I., Henzell, E.F. & Evans, T.R. (1977) Uptake of soil nitrogen by legumes in mixed swards. *Aust. J. Agric. Res.* 28, 413-425.

Vallis, I. & Jones, R.J. (1973) Net mineralization of nitrogen in leaves and leaf litter of *Desmodium intortum* and *Phaseolus atropurpureus* mixed with soil. *Soil Biol. Biochem.* 5, 391-398.

Watkin, B.R. & Clements, R.J. (1977) The effects of grazing animals on pastures. *In:* Plant relations in pastures. J.R. Wilson (Ed.). CSIRO, Melbourne, Australia. Pp 273-287.

Wilkinson, S.R. and Lowrey, R.W. (1973) Cyling of mineral nutrients in pasture ecosystems. *In:* Chemistry and biochemistry of herbage, G.W. Butler & R.W. Bailey (Eds.). Academic Press, London, England. Pp. 247-315.

Whitney A.S. (1970) Effects of harvesting interval, height of cut and nitrogen fertilizer on the performance of *Desmodium intortum* mixtures in Hawaii. *Proc. XI Int. Grassland. Cong.,* 632-636.

Whitney, A.S. & Green, R.E. (1969) Legume contributions to yields and compositions of *Desmodium* spp.-pangolagrass mixtures. *Agron. J.* 61,741-746.

Whitney, A.S. & Kanehiro, Y. (1967) Pathways of nitrogen transfer in some tropical legume-grass associations. *Agron. J.* 59,585-588.

THE IMPORTANCE OF LEGUME COVER CROP ESTABLISHMENT FOR CULTIVATION OF RUBBER (*HEVEA BRASILIENSIS*) IN MALAYSIA

Chee Yan Kuan[1]

Summary

The most important legume cover crops for rubber production in Malaysia are *Calopogonium caeruleum*, *C. mucunoides*, *Centrosema pubescens*, *Mucuna cochinchinensis* and *Pueraria phaseoloides*. The plant characteristics of each species are described and their nutritive values, in terms of dry matter, crude protein, crude fiber, ether extract, ash, nitrogen-free extract, and gross energy, are presented. The beneficial effects of legume covers, in terms of nitrogen fixation and nutrient return, improvement of soil physical structure, growth of rubber, and soil erosion control, are given.

INTRODUCTION

Rubber (*Hevea brasiliensis*) occupies about two million ha and 55% of the cultivated area in Malaysia. It has an economic life span of about 30 years. Legume cover crop establishment is an important factor in the early years of rubber cultivation. The most important legume covers planted are *Calopogonium caeruleum*, *C. mucunoides*, *Centrosema pubescens*, *Mucuna cochinchinensis* and *Pueraria phaseoloides*. These legume covers are planted in the interrow of rubber, a space 7-10 meters wide.

The economic benefits of legume cover crops in rubber cultivation are enormous. Mainstone (1961; 1963) established that rubber trees grown in association with leguminous covers became tappable 12 months earlier and yielded 20% more than those in natural cover over a ten-year period of tapping. Ti *et al.* (1971) and Lim & Chai (1977) have shown that it is economically worthwhile to establish legume cover crops and maintain them

[1] Rubber Research Institute of Malaysia, Sugei Buloh, Selangor, Malaysia.

in pure stands between rubber plants. This paper discusses the types and characteristics of legume species, the beneficial effects of legume cover, soil and environmental barriers, agronomic gaps, and problems associated with legume use.

LEGUME SPECIES

Characteristics of the legume species commonly recommended as cover crops are:

Calopogonium caeruleum:	Shade and drought tolerant; not susceptible to pests and diseases. Persists under the shade of rubber trees for more than ten years. Animals do not feed on it.
Calopogonium mucunoides:	Rapid initial growth. Not persistent, and lasts for about a year under the canopy of rubber trees. Susceptible to pests such as *Pagnia signata*, *Chauliops bisonata*, and *Lamprosema diemenalis*. Can be grazed.
Centrosema pubescens:	Excellent cover. Drought tolerant; more shade tolerant than *Pueraria phaseoloides* and *Calopogonium mucunoides*. Persists for about five years under the canopy of rubber trees. Can be grazed.
Desmodium ovalifolium:	Slow to establish, but drought resistant. Will persist under rubber trees for more than ten years. Can be grazed.
Pueraria phaseoloides:	Vigorous grower and provides a thick cover. Can be grazed.
Mucuna cochinchinensis:	100% ground cover after four months growth in a pure stand. Can be grazed.

Because planting one species alone will entail risks from pests and diseases, mixed legume plantings are recommended, both for pest limitation and to permit an ecological succession of the legume covers. Thus, *C. mucunoides*, with initial rapid growth, dominates during the first months after sowing but does not persist; *P. phaseoloides* provides the bulk of the cover during the second and third year after planting, while *C. caeruleum*, *Centrosema pubescens* and *Desmodium ovalifolium* are more shade tolerant and will persist for longer than the other covers under the developing rubber trees. The following ratios for different legume mixtures were recommended by the Rubber Research Institute of Malaysia in 1972.

5:4:1 *C. mucunoides:C. pubescens:P. phaseoloides*
4:1 *C. pubescens:P. phaseoloides*
1:1 *C. pubescens:C. mucunoides*

The rate used was 2.2 to 5.7 kg/ha of scarified seeds. *C. caeruleum* and *D. ovalifolium*, which are shade tolerant, are added to the mixture at the rate of 0.21 kg/ha. The seeds are mixed with an equal weight of Christmas Island phosphate rock and inoculated with *Rhizobium* Compost RRIM strain 968. *M. cochinchinensis* is a vigorous legume cover for eight to ten months and it is effective against soil erosion on steep terrain. When grown too close to other legume creeping covers, it will suppress their growth. Teoh *et al.* (1979) showed that, in order to minimize competition, sowing of this cover should be delayed until about one and one-half to two months after planting of other legume species.

NITROGEN FIXATION BY LEGUMINOUS COVER CROPS

Nitrogen (N_2) fixation is of extreme importance for reducing the N fertilizer requirement of rubber. Many estimates of the total amount of N_2 fixed by nodulated legumes have been reported. Results vary with the host legume, the efficiency of the strains involved, and the environmental conditions governing the fixation process. Broughton & Parker (1976) found that the fixation rates varied from 200 - 650 kg N/ha per year for tropical legumes. In the *Hevea* cover crop system, a legume mixture of *P. phaseoloides*, *C. pubescens* and *C. mucunoides* gave an average of 150 kg/ha per year over a five-year period (Broughton, 1977).

Haines (1931) showed that, unlike grasses and lalang *(Imperata cylindrica)*, the growth of rubber trees is best when legumes are planted in the interrow. This is due to their high fixation of N_2 and to litter returns (see Table 1).

Watson, Wong & Naryanan (1964a, b) demonstrated the enormous advantage of growing leguminous cover crops compared with that of natural covers. The results in Table 1 and Table 2 show that leguminous cover crops returned large amounts of N to the soil, presumably as the result of N_2 fixation. In the sixth year after establishment the leaf litter from rubber trees in the legume cover crop areas contained twice as much N as did that from nonlegume areas. Loss of applied N in rubber plantations can be severe; Watson *et al.* (1962) found up to 24% of the applied N lost through volatilization. Against this background, the N_2 fixed and the form in which it is slowly released in the soil is of great importance.

TABLE 1: Amount of nutrients (kg/ha) in litter of different cover plants at 24 months after planting.

Cover plants	Dry weight of litter	N	P	K	Mg
Leguminous creepers	6038	140	11	31	19
Grasses	6140	63	9	31	16
Mikania	4096	68	7	23	16
Natural cover	5383	64	6	42	17

Leguminous creepers: mixed *P. phaseoloides, C. pubescens* and *C. mucunoides.*
Grasses: mixed *Axonopus compressus* and *Paspalum conjugatum*
Mikania: Mikania cordata
Natural cover: mixed indigenous bushes

TABLE 2: Total amounts of various elements (kg/ha) returned to the soil over a five-year period under different cover crops.

Cover plants	N	P	K	Mg
Leguminous creepers	226-353	18-27	85-131	15-27
Grasses	24-65	8-16	31-86	9-15
Mikania	74-119	9-14	63-99	9-24
Natural Cover	13-117	3-10	46-140	3-18

EFFECTS OF LEGUME COVER CROPS ON SOIL EROSION

Most of the rubber is grown on undulating to steep land, which is prone to soil erosion. Peninsular Malaysia has an annual rainfall between 1800 and 3000 mm (Ooi & Chia, 1979). Erosion is a serious problem during the time of replanting of rubber trees, after old trees are felled and when the land is cleared. The soil surface remains bare for up to six months before the legume covers form a protective layer over the soil.

The creeping legume plants maintained in the interrow of rubber protect soil from erosion and reduce the effect of extreme climatic conditions. The legume cover crops protect the topsoil in several ways:

Protection of the soil surface against falling rain;

Reduced rate of run-off;

Improved physical characteristics (Soong & Yap, 1971); and
Enhanced feeder root development of the rubber in the presence of legume covers.

NUTRITIVE VALUE OF LEGUME COVERS

Devendra (1979) reported the nutritive values of these cover legumes (see Table 3) and found them to have much higher nutritive values than cultivated grasses such as *Panicum maximum*, *Pennisetum purpureum* and *Brachiaria mutica*. These data are typical for similar legumes grown elsewhere in the tropics.

Chee & Devendra (1979) showed that the herbage under rubber, which consisted of natural cover and legumes, can support sheep rearing. A carrying capacity of 6 sheep/ha was possible.

SOIL AND ENVIRONMENTAL CONSTRAINTS TO HIGHER LEGUME YIELDS

In the tropics, the greatest limitation to increased yield of legume cover crops is poor mineral nutrition. The principal nutrient deficiencies are N, phosphorus (P), molybdenum (Mo) and calcium (Ca). P supply is intimately associated with N_2 fixation. The low P availability poses a major problem in successful legume cover establishment in Malaysia. Inoculation with selected strains of mycorrhiza may enable legume species to grow on soil low in available P, but little is known of the effectiveness of host/mycorrhiza associations and the ways in which such association may be encouraged for the benefit of legumes. Most soils in Malaysia have a pH of 4.0 - 4.5. The main effects of soil acidity are low pH, excessive levels of aluminum and manganese, and deficiency of Ca and Mo.

AGRONOMIC PROBLEMS ASSOCIATED WITH THE USE OF LEGUME COVER CROPS

The main disadvantage in using legume cover crops is the cost of establishment and maintenance. Teoh *et al.* (1979) found that the total cost of the first year of establishment in peninsular Malaysia was $410 to $470/ha, depending on soil type, terrain, and location. This poses no financial problem to the big plantation companies, but small farmers find it a burden to plant legume covers. For this reason the Rubber Smallholders Industry Development Authority is intensifying its campaign to plant legume covers by giving credits for the purchase of seeds, herbicides and fertilizer for legume establishment.

Poor legume seed quality is another important agronomic factor limiting successful legume planting. Most legume seeds are imported from Indonesia,

TABLE 3: Nutritive value of the leaves and stems of legume cover crops grown with rubber in Malaysia (Devendra, 1979).

Legume species	Dry matter (%) in fresh plant	% of dry matter					
		Crude protein	Crude fiber	Ether extract	Ash	N-free extract	Gross energy (M cal/kg)
Calopogonium mucunoides	25.6	15.6	31.5	2.3	6.2	44.4	2.60
Centrosema pubescens	24.3	22.2	30.9	2.5	9.5	34.9	3.62
Desmodium ovalifolium	24.0	9.2	40.0	2.1	9.2	39.5	3.10
Mucuna utilis	16.6	35.0	14.5	3.0	9.0	38.6	–
Pueraria phaseoloides	19.1	19.9	28.8	2.1	7.9	48.8	3.71
Mean	21.9	20.4	29.1	2.4	8.4	41.2	3.26

Sri Lanka, India and the Philippines. From 1972-1976, the average yearly cost of imported seeds was valued at 15 million Malaysian ringgit. Chee, Chin & Rashid (1979) found that most of the legume cover crop seeds had a germination percentage below 25%. This poor germination in legume cover crop seeds was also reported by Chin (1966), Hor (1973), and Yeoh (1578).

Weeds pose another big problem in rubber plantations, especially where poor germination results in uneven cover crop stands. Until recently weeds were removed manually, but the great increase in labor costs over the last ten years had made this impractical (Teoh & Chong, 1977). Because of this the Rubber Research Institute is giving priority to the search for better pre- and post-emergence herbicides.

CONCLUSION

Pure legume covers are very important in the N cycle in rubber cultivation. They benefit the growth and yield of rubber trees in terms of nutrient return and also reduce the cost of N fertilization of the rubber and of weed control. Using the evidence currently available on residual effects and extra fertilizer needed for nonlegume areas, Pushparajah & Tan (1977) calculated that the total N fertilizer saved per year by implementing a legume policy was about 64,665 t of N for the 56,330 ha replanted annually. This would represent a saving of over 80 million ringgit (Malyasian) at the current price. With improvement and refinement of biological N_2 fixation technology, improved management and cultural practices, and the use of better quality legume seeds, the saving of N fertilizer on rubber could be even greater. Also the high nutritive values of legumes grown in rubber are comparable to those of cultivated grasses (*Panicum maximum*, *Brachiaria mutica*, and *Pennisetum pureum*), and permit sheep to be reared, an extra source of income for the farmers.

REFERENCES

Broughton, W.J. (1977) *Agro-Ecosystems* 3, 147-170.

Broughton, W.J. & Parker, C.A. (1976) Microbial contributions to world nitrogen economy. *In*: Global impacts of applied microbiology: State of the art, W.R. Stanton & E. Da Silva (Eds.). McMillan Publ. Co., London, England.

Chee, Y.K., Chin, T.V. & Rashid, K.S. (1979) Proc. Rubber Research Institute of Malaysia Planters' Conference, Kuala Lumpur, Malaysia. Pp. 241-251.

Chee, Y.K. & Devenra, C. (1979) The nitrogen cycle: Role of legume and animals in rubber cultivation. Proc. Symp. Nitrogen Cycling in South East Asian Wet Monsoonal Ecosystems Workshop, Univ. of Chiang Mai, Thailand. (In press.)

Chin, N.F. (1966) *Serdang Sun*, 14, 45.

Devendra, C. (1979) Malayan feeding stuffs. Malysian Agricultural Research and Development Institute, Serdang, Selangor, Malaysia. 145 pp.

Haines, W.B. (1931) *J. Rubb. Res. Inst. Malaya*, 3, 110-113.

Hor, Y.L. (1973) *Malaysian Agric. Res.*, 2, 23.

Lim, K.P. & Chai, W. (1977) Leguminous covers versus natural covers — an economic exercise. *In*: Proc. Symp. Soil Microbiology and Plant Nutrition, W.J. Broughton, C.K. Ohn, J.C. Rajarao, & Beda Lim (Eds.). Univ. of Malaya Press, Kuala Lumpur, Malaysia.

Mainstone, B.J. (1961) Effect of ground cover type and continuity of nitrogenous fertiliser treatment upon the growth to tappable maturity of *Hevea brasiliensis*. Proc. Nat. Rubb. Conf., Rubb. Res. Inst. Malaya, Kuala Lumpur, Malaysia. Pp. 362-375.

Mainstone, B.J. (1963) *Rubber Research Inst. Malaysia Planters' Bulletin* 68, 130 pp.

Ooi, J.B. & Chia, L.S. (1974) The climate of West Malaysia and Singapore. Oxford Univ. Press, Singapore. 226 pp.

Pushparajah, E. & Tan, K.H. (1977) Legumes in the nitrogen economy of rubber cultivation. *In*: Proc. Symp. Soil Microbiology and Plant Nutrition. W.J. Broughton, C.K. Ohn, J.C. Rajarao, & Beda Lim (Eds.). Univ. of Malaya Press, Kuala Lumpur, Malaya. Pp. 513-534.

Rubber Research Institute of Malaya (1972) *Planters' Bulletin* 122, 170-180.

Soong, H.K. & Yap, W.C. (1975) *J. Rubber Res. Inst. Malaysia* 24, 145-159.

Teoh, C.H. & Chong, C.F. (1977) Use of pre-emergence herbicides during establishment of leguminous cover crop. Proc. Malaysian Inst. Agric., Oil Palm Conf., Kuala Lumpur, Malaysia. 485 pp.

Teoh, C.H., Adham, A. & Reid, W.M. (1979) Critical aspects of legume establishment and maintenance. Proc. Rubb. Res. Inst. Malaysia, Planters' Conf., Kuala Lumpur, Malaysia. Pp. 252-271.

Ti, T.C., Pee, T.Y. & Pushparajah, E. (1971) Economic analysis of cover policies and fertiliser used in rubber cultivation. Proc., Rubb. Res. Inst. Malaya, Planters' Conf. Kuala Lumpur, Malaysia. Pp. 214-233.

Watson, G.A., Chia, T.S. & Wong, P.W. (1962) *J. Rubber Res. Inst. Malaya* 17, 77-90.

Watson, G.A., Wong, P.W. & Naryanan, R. (1964a) *J. Rubber Res. Inst. Malaya* 18, 80-95.

Watson, G.A., Wong, P.W. & Naryanan, R. (1964b) *J. Rubber Res. Inst. Malaya* 18, 123-145.

Yeoh, C.H. (1978) *Rubber Res. Inst. Malaysia Planters' Bull.* 159, 54.

IMPROVING THE GROWTH AND NODULATION OF ALFALFA IN SOUTHERN CHILE WITH SELECTED *RHIZOBIUM* STRAINS, INOCULATION METHODS, CULTIVARS, AND NUTRIENT APPLICATIONS

W.M. Murphy,[1] L.E. Barber,[2] O. Romero Y.,[3] and M. Fernández del Pozo[4]

Summary

Soil problems affecting alfalfa nodulation and establishment limit its use for forage production to only 2500 of the 2.7 million ha of arable land in the six provinces of southern Chile. Pasture and forage production is below potential levels, especially on upland soils that become too dry to support shallow-rooted plants during midsummer.

Initially, strains of rhizobia and inoculation methods were tested to improve alfalfa growth. It soon became clear, however, that poorly adapted cultivars and soil nutrient deficiencies were also limiting seedling growth and development, and that all four constraints would need to be addressed simultaneously if pasture production was to be significantly enhanced. The combination of a Waterman-Loomis cultivar (WL512), inoculation with the "Balsac" strain of *Rhizobium meliloti*, Pelgel adhesive, and 50 kg sulfur/ha (as $CaSO_4$) significantly increased alfalfa seedling nodulation and forage yield. The enhanced seedling vigor should enable alfalfa to be established and to persist in areas where previously it could not be used.

INTRODUCTION

Soil problems limit the use of alfalfa *(Medicago sativa* L.) for forage production to only 2500 of the 2.7 million ha of arable land in the six provinces of southern Chile (Correa, 1972; Peralta, 1977). Most pastures are

[1] Dept. of Plant & Soil Science, Univ. of Vermont, Burlington, VT 05405 USA.

[2] N. Carolina State Univ., Raleigh, NC 27650, USA.

[3] Estación Experimental, Carillanca, Temuco, Chile.

[4] Estación Experimental La Platina, Santiago, Chile.

of red or white clover mixed with grasses. Pasture and forage production is less than it should be, especially in the upland regions, which are too dry for shallow-rooted plants during midsummer.

Red clays and Trumaos are the major soil groups in southern Chile. Red clays are generally adequate nutritionally, but are mainly composed of dense clays with extreme expansion-contraction characteristics, high water retention with a low percentage of available water, poor aeration, inhibited root penetration, and poor permeability. They are difficult to cultivate and are easily eroded. In contrast, Trumaos are composed mainly of allophanes that have very good physical properties. They are loose and deep, have excellent permeability and aeration, with high water retention and a high percentage of available water, but are acid (pH 5.5-6.0), contain large amounts of aluminum (Al), and have only limited decomposition of organic matter. Because of these factors, production levels of sensitive crops, especially legumes, are low (Binsack, 1964; Jara de la Maza, 1964; Urbina, 1964).

Resolving the problems of alfalfa nodulation and establishment would enable pasture and forage production levels to be increased. The objective of this research was to study the effects of selected *Rhizobium* strains, improved inoculation methods, and nutrient application on nodulation and yield of alfalfa seedlings grown on problem soils in southern Chile.

MATERIALS AND METHODS

The soil core method described by Vincent (1970) was used throughout with four replicate cores, each containing 10 seeds of alfalfa per treatment, randomized throughout the glasshouse. In all experiments plants were maintained for six weeks; then evaluated for effective nodulation and plant dry weight.

The soils used were from the Maipo, Arrayan, Candelaria, Santa Barbera, Vilcun, and Metrenco series. Chemical analysis of the soils is given in Table 1, together with a most probable number (MPN) count of *R. meliloti*, as determined by the plant dilution method (Vincent, 1970).

A number of different inoculant preparations and strains were used in this study, and were applied to seeds either as a slurry in a 25% sucrose solution or with Pelgel adhesive (Nitragin Co., Milwaukee, WI, USA). Inoculant preparations used included a Chilean peat inoculant, Nitrofix; the standard "A" Nitragin Co. inoculant for alfalfa; and special inoculants prepared by the Nitragin Co. and containing the acid-tolerant strains of *R. meliloti* C14, CE5, 102F51-56, R38 (selected in Oregon) and "Balsac" (selected by L.M. Bordeleau in Quebec). Seed pre-inoculated with strains 114, 118 and 120 of *R. meliloti* (Celpril Ind., Manteca, CA, USA) was also used in some trials. With the exception of the peats prepared with the Oregon strains, peat inoculants contained more than 10^7, and usually more than 10^8 cells/g and pre-inoculated seed 10^5-10^6 rhizobia/seed. Four experiments were conducted during this study.

Experiment 1

Treatments were uninoculated seed; uninoculated seed plus 100 kg nitrogen (N)/per ha; inoculated with the strain A or Balsac strains and Pelgel adhesive; inoculated with the Nitrofix preparation, slurry applied; and pre-inoculated seed using strains 114, 118 and 120. The variety Rayen was used throughout.

Experiment 2

All soils save Maipo received 200 g Mo/ha as sodium molybdate and 2 kg Co/ha as cobalt sulphate, applied as solutions. The Balsac strain was used as inoculant and applied with the Pelgel treatment. The Rayen variety was again used.

Experiment 3

The experiment compared inoculation treatments (uninoculated, inoculated with Nitrofix and slurry applied, inoculated with the Balsac, C14, Ce5, 102F51-5.6 or R38 strains of *R. meliloti* applied with the Pelgel treatment) and cultivar (B13-A14, an Al tolerant selection from 'Arc' selected by J.H. Elgin, Beltsville, MD; AT6, an Al-tolerant selection from L. Dessureaux, Ontario, Canada; WL 318 and WL 512 from the Waterman Loomis Co.; and Alta Francona, a cultivar used in Southern Chile) responses. Only the Candelaria and Vilcun soils were used.

Experiment 4

Treatments were uninoculated; inoculated with the Balsac or Nitrofix preparations; inoculated with the Balsac preparation plus 50 kg/ha S as $CaSO_4$; inoculated with the Balsac preparation plus MolyCoThi (a seed treatment preparation from the Rudy Patrick Co. (Princeton, IL, USA) containing Mo, Co, and the fungicide Thiram). The cultivars used were WL 318 and WL512. The soils studied were Candelaria, Metrenco, and Vilcun.

RESULTS AND DISCUSSION

From Table 1 it is evident that the Maipo soil collected near Santiago is well suited for alfalfa production, except for low phosphorus and potassium levels that could be corrected by fertilization. The Maipo soil developed under low rainfall (500 mm) from alluvial sediment and, as expected, was clearly

TABLE 1. Analyses of soils used in alfalfa nodulation studies in the greenhouse at the Carillanca Experiment Station, Temuco, Chile. November 1977-January 1978.

Sample location	Soil series	Soil group	Analysis						MPN per g
			N	P	K	Al	pH	OM	
			ppm					%	
Santiago	Maipo	Alluvial	19	8	93	0	7.7	2	$>10^5$
Chillan	Arrayan	Trumao	134	27	267	250	6.0	12	$<10^2$
Los Angeles	Candelaria	Trumao	55	13	237	371	6.0	13	<10
Cajon	Metrenco	Red clay	8	14	113	332	5.2	7	<10
Vilcun	Santa Barbera	Trumao	28	30+	50	665	5.4	21	<10
Vilcun	Vilcun	Trumao	12	14	37	612	5.9	16	<10

Soil analyses courtesy of the Soil Testing Laboratory, Carillanca Experiment Station, Temuco, Chile.

different from southern red clay and Trumao soils, which developed under high rainfall (1200-2400 mm) from volcanic ash, basalt, andesite, or alluvial sand and silt. The most striking aspects of the southern soils were their high Al content (250-655 ppm sodium acetate-extractable) and their low pH level (5.2-6.0). The Maipo soil was the only soil to have a significant population of native rhizobia able to nodulate alfalfa.

Experiment 1

The effect of inoculation treatment on the percentage of plants bearing effective nodules is shown in Table 2. As to be expected from the MPN data, only the Maipo soil showed significant nodulation in the uninoculated controls. Although selected strains of rhizobia and inoculation methods showed some improvement over Nitrofix peat inoculant in terms of percentage of plants nodulated, none of the treatments used gave good, effective nodulation.

Dry forage yields of plants did not differ significantly in any of the soils, suggesting that factors other than inoculant strain were limiting production.

Experiment 2

While Mo and Co applications increased the percentage of plants with effective nodules on the Arrayan soil, these treatments had no significant

TABLE 2: Inoculant treatment effects on the percentage of plants bearing effective nodules. Rayen alfalfa grown in the greenhouse at the Carillanca Experiment Station, Temuco, Chile. November 1977 - January 1978.

Soil	Treatment							
	Uninoculated control	100 kg N/ha	Pelinoc Nit A	Pelinoc "Balsac"	CP 114	CP 118	CP 120	Nitro-fix
	%							
Maipo	62 a[1]	0 b	64 a	58 a	40 a	38 a	65 a	57 a
Arrayan	0 a	0 a	25 a	13 a	25 a	37 a	4 a	0 a
Candelaria	0 b	0 b	29 ab	53 a	54 a	65 a	29 a	14 b
Metrenco	0 c	0 c	25 abc	32 abc	26 abc	45 ab	63 a	7 bc
Santa Barbera	0 a	0 a	0 a	20 a	15 a	0 a	16 a	0 a
Vincun	0 b	0 b	20 ab	19 ab	7 b	47 a	3 b	0 b
Avg	10 c	0 c	27 ab	32 a	28 ab	39 a	30 a	13 bc
Avg less Maipo	0 c	0 c	20 b	27 ab	25 ab	39 a	23 ab	4 c

[1]Means within a row followed by the same letter are not significantly different at the 0.05 probability level.

TABLE 3: Effects of cobalt (Co) and molybdenum (Mo) application on the percentage of plants bearing effective nodules.

Soil	Treatment					
	Uninoculated control	100 kg N/ha	Pelinoc "Balsac"	2 kg Co/ha	200 g Mo/ha	2 kg Co/ha + 200 g Mo/ha
	%					
Arrayan	0 bc[1]	0 c	13 bc	70 a	79 a	57 ab
Candelaria	0 b	0 b	53 a	54 a	84 a	75 a
Metrenco	0 bc	0 c	32 ab	37 a	24 abc	50 a
Santa Barbera	0 a	0 a	20 a	14 a	4 a	14 a
Vilcun	0 b	0 b	19 ab	27 a	43 a	15 ab
Avg	0	0	27	40	47	42

[1] Means within a row followed by the same letter are not significantly different at the 0.05 probatility level.

effects in the other soils (see Table 3). Once again changes in nodulation did not bring about enhanced dry matter production.

Experiment 3

None of the strains selected in Oregon nodulated plants. This may have been due to low numbers of rhizobia in the peat inoculants (1×10^3 to 2×10^6 rhizobia/g) resulting from problems with the peat, which were discovered after this experiment was completed.

Results with the Balsac and Nitrofix inoculants were similar to those reported in Table 2. The cultivar Alta Francona produced significantly fewer plants with effective nodules than did the other cultivars. Again this was not translated into yield differences though the cultivar WL 512 did produce more than the other cultivars in both inoculated and uninoculated treatments.

Experiment 4

Sulfur application markedly increased the percentage of nodulation (see Table 4). Nodules were larger and roots were better developed with many fine root hairs, compared to other treatments. In addition, average forage yields increased because of S application. These results indicated that S needs of alfalfa on the southern soils should be examined in depth. MolyCoThi applied to seeds did not improve nodulation or seedling growth. Amounts of Co and

TABLE 4: Inoculant and nutrient application effects on percentage nodulation (%) and dry forage (DF) yield of alfalfa seedlings grown in the greenhouse at the Carillanca Experiment Station, Temuco, Chile. November 1979 - January 1980.

Soil and cultivar	Treatment				
	Uninoculated control	Nitrofix	Nitragin "Balsac"	"Balsac" MolyCoThi	"Balsac" 50 kg S/ha
	%				
Candelaria					
WL 318	8	65	22	50	79
WL 512	0	26	42	2	85
Metrenco					
WL 318	0	8	8	10	60
WL 512	2	12	15	2	51
Vilcun					
WL 318	0	10	15	5	92
WL 512	0	3	10	19	60
Avg	2 c[1]	21 b	19 b	15 b	71 a
	DF, mg/plant				
Candelaria					
WL 318	40	30	28	36	32
WL 512	29	36	39	19	38
Metrenco					
WL 318	42	22	30	28	46
WL 512	36	36	60	37	62
Vilcun					
WL 318	34	36	46	40	63
WL 512	40	42	45	38	45
Avg	37 b	34 bc	41 b	33 bc	48 a

[1] Means within a row followed by the same letter are not significantly different at the 0.05 probability level.

Mo applied to seeds may have been insufficient to make a difference, but further research is needed on this aspect.

REFERENCES

Binsack S., R. (1964) Problemas de la fertilidad de suelos en el sur de Chile. *In*: Mesa redonda de suelos volcánicos. Soc. Agronómica de Chile, Santiago, Chile. Spec. Pub. No. 1.

Correa B., C. (1972) La alfalfa. *In*: El campesino. Soc. Nacional de Agricultura, Santiago, Chile.

Jara de la Maza, F. (1964) La fijación de fósforo en los suelos Trumaos de Chile y la respuesta a la fertilización fosfatada, en remolacha azucarera *(Beta vulgaris)*. *In*: Mesa redonda de suelos volcánicos. Soc. Agronómica de Chile, Santiago, Chile. Spec. Pub. No. 1.

Peralta P., M. (1977) Antecedentes sobre el potencial agrícola de Chile. *El Diario Austral*, (Temuco, Chile), December 12, p. 2.

Urbina, A. (1964) Interacción calcio-fósforo en suelos de cenizas volcánicas. *In*: Mesa redonda de suelos volcánicos. Soc. Agronómica de Chile, Santiago, Chile. Spec. Pub. No. 1.

Vincent, J.M. (1970) A manual for the practical study of root-nodule bacteria. IBP Handbook. No. 15. Blackwell Scientific Pub., Oxford, England.

NITROGEN AVAILABILITY IN A *BRACHIARIA DECUMBENS* PASTURE UNDER CONTINUOUS GRAZING

N.F. Seiffert[1]

Summary

A *Brachiaria decumbens* Stapf. pasture established in late 1976 under good growing conditions, but continuously grazed, maintained a nitrogen (N) content of about 1% until the end of the 1979 dry season. This represented the production of about 158 kg N/ha per year, corresponding to 1015 kg/ha of available crude protein. Growing Nelore cattle under these conditions gained 241 kg liveweight/ha per year.

During 1980 production declined 16.6% in dry matter and 50% in the available N in the pasture. Animal production, represented by average daily gains, dropped 42.6%.

INTRODUCTION

Pure grass pastures rapidly become nitrogen (N) deficient unless N is supplied by N_2 fixation or by fertilization (Henzell, 1970).

Vallis (1972) in Australia observed a decrease of 70 kg N/ha in pastures under continous grazing in a period of 29 months, involving three growing seasons and one severe dry period. The decrease was credited to the low level of N_2 fixation and to ammonia volatilization from excreta, enhanced by dry climatic conditions and reduced plant cover. On the other hand, the same author reported a linear increase in total N in the soil during a four-year period in mixed pastures, resulting in an addition of 40 kg N/ha per year.

Bruce (1965) measured the changes in total N and organic carbon in pastures of *Panicum maximum* and *P. maximum* plus *Centrosema pubescens* established without fertilization after clearing of tropical rain forest. The pasture with legume practically maintained the original N level in the soil. In the pure grass pasture, total N declined 35% in the first eight years, but then

[1] Centro Nacional de Pesquisa de Gado de Corte, EMBRAPA, C.P. 154, 79.100 Campo Grande Brazil.

TABLE 2: Grov
pastı
AU/

Period
Oct. 17 to Nov. 1
Nov. 16 to Dec.
Dec. 28 to Jan. 2
Jan. 26 to Feb. 2
Feb. 28 to Mar.
Mar. 23 to May
May 3 to May 3
May 31 to Jun.
Jun. 28 to Jul. 3
Jul. 30 to Aug.
Aug. 30 to Sep.
Sep. 27 to Oct.
Total

[1]Average of 10 sa
[2]Negative growth

A quite hig
aboveground
obtained from
the soil N mi

Forage N
season, appr
mance. In fa
obtained dur
season are v
kg/head per

DM and N

Dry matte
those obtair

N_2 FIXATION IN TREES

ENSURING EFFECTIVE SYMBIOSIS IN NITROGEN-FIXING TREES

Y. Dommergues[1]

Summary

The evaluation of the nitrogen (N_2) fixing potential of a given tree raises problems that are specific to perennial plants. Besides the establishment of an N balance, the acetylene reduction method can be helpful in identifying perennial species worthy of introduction and multiplication. Even trees that exhibit the highest N_2-fixing potential may fix little N_2 if limited by physical, chemical, or biological factors affecting nodulation and N_2 fixation. Examples illustrate the different approaches that can be used for increasing the N_2 fixation of tree species. As well as inoculation with *Rhizobium* or *Frankia*, ecto- and endomycorrhiza inoculants should be considered. These fungi have an important role in P-limited soils. Soil fertilization may also be required. Finally, one should not overlook the approach of plant breeding, which is still in a preliminary stage as far as N_2-fixing trees are concerned.

INTRODUCTION

People are becoming increasingly aware that nitrogen (N_2) fixing trees can contribute to the welfare of populations in the tropics both directly, by providing products as diverse as firewood, pulp, timber, forage for cattle, fruit, and gum, and indirectly by improving soil fertility and protecting the soil from erosion. The objective of this paper is to review our knowledge of the N_2-fixing potential of trees, to discuss the factors limiting this potential, and finally, to present the approaches (mostly of microbiological nature) that can be used to ensure effective symbiosis, both in perennial N_2-fixing legumes and N_2-fixing nonlegumes.

---

[1] ORSTOM/CNRS BP 1386, Dakar, Senegal.

ASSESSMENT OF N_2 FIXATION IN TREE SPECIES

The potential of leguminous tree species to fix N_2 varies a great deal. Thus, within the genus *Acacia*, *Acacia mearnsii* is active in N_2 fixation, whereas *A. albida* is not. Obviously one should recommend the use of trees exhibiting the highest N_2-fixing potential, and this necessitates an assessment of that potential. Since trees are perennials, this assessment should be made not only when they are at the seedling stage, which may extend from one to four years in nurseries, but also when they are planted or transplanted in the field.

Assessment of the potential for N_2 fixation in seedlings

The usual methods (Vincent, 1970) for the study of annual legumes can be adapted to tree seedlings. These methods are based on the measurement of the N accumulated by plants grown in tubes or larger assemblies (e.g., Leonard jars) containing N-free nutrient medium. These methods have been used successfully for tree seedlings of up to six months in age, but older plants can only be studied at the nursery or field level, where investigations of fertilization, fumigation, and other managerial practices can be carried out.

Assessment of the potential for N_2 fixation in the field

The simplest method of assessment is to evaluate the increment of soil N under the trees and the increment of N immobilized in the plant biomass that occurred during a given period of time. Caution is recommended for the interpretation of results, since observed increments cannot be attributed solely to N_2 fixation. Other processes may contribute to the accumulation of N in the soil under the canopy areas (see Figure 1), namely:

Concentration of soil nutrients, especially N extracted from the deeper soil horizons and eventually from the water table and returned to the soil surface with the leaf litter; and

Accumulation of wind-blown organic residue near the tree trunk.

Moreover, one should be aware that the N_2 fixation rate of trees will tend to decrease as the stand ages, since the N content of the soil progressively increases, impeding nodulation and N_2 fixation.

Table 1 gives a rough estimate of the potential for N_2 fixation of four tree species grown throughout the humid or arid tropics for their active N_2 fixation. *Leucaena leucocephala*, a plant that can be used for reforestation, animal feed, firewood, and soil mulches (National Academy of Sciences (NAS), 1977) appears to have a high potential for N_2 fixation when grown in favorable situations. *Acacia mearnsii* has been introduced in many parts of the world (e.g., southern and eastern Africa and Madagascar) as a source of tanbark, timber, and firewood, is also active in N_2 fixation, and is well adapted to a wide range of environmental conditions. When nodulated by

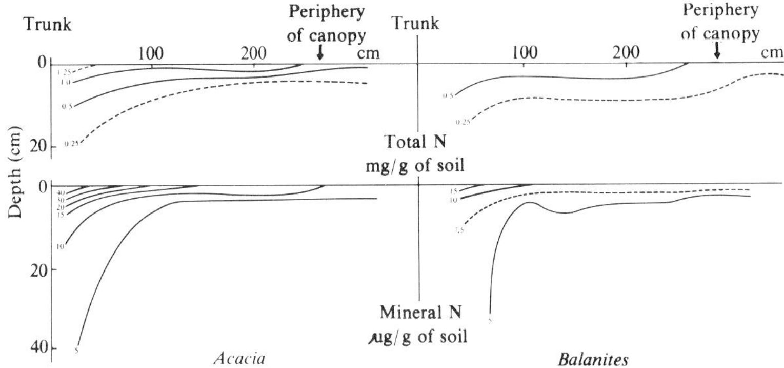

Figure 1: Distribution of total and mineral N in the soil beneath canopies of *Acacia senegal* and *Balanites aegyptiaca* (F. Bernhard-Reversat, unpublished data).

their specific endophyte (*Frankia* sp.), *Casuarina* sp. growing in favorable situations can fix 58-218 kg N_2/ha per year. According to Trinick (1980), *Parasponia andersonii*, a nonlegume fixing N_2 in association with a slow-growing *Rhizobium* can fix huge quantities of N_2 (850 kg N_2/ha per year). This explains its great potential as a source of fuel and as a colonizer and pioneer of disturbed land, low in fertility.

TABLE 1: Field estimates of N_2 fixed by trees in the tropics.

Species	Location	N_2 fixed (kg/ha·yr)	Reference
Leucaena leucocephala	Humid tropics	500[1]	NAS, 1977
Acacia mearnsii	Tropical highlands	200	Orchard & Darby, 1956
Casuarina equisetifolia	Arid zone	58	Dommergues, 1963
Casuarina littoralis	Humid tropics.	218	Silvester, 1977

[1]Estimates from studies undertaken at the University of Hawaii and at the Commonwealth Scientific and Industrial Research Organization (CSIRO), Queensland, Australia.

Another way to evaluate the N_2-fixing potential of tree species is to simultaneously estimate the total weight of the nodules of a tree and the specific acetylene reduction of the nodules (μmol acetylene reduced/g nodule tissue, designated here as SARA). One must be aware of three major difficulties in handling this data. The first problem is that the SARA of nodules decreases with age. This time course, which is well established for annual legumes (Hashimoto, 1976), was also observed in the case of perennial nodules of *Casuarina equisetifolia*. The SARA of four-month-old nodules of that plant was 55 to 93 μmol C_2H_4 produced/g dry wt per hour, whereas that of 13-month-old nodules was only 10 μmol C_2H_4 produced/g dry wt per hour (see Table 2). The second difficulty is that the theoretical 3:1 ratio for C_2H_2 reduced to fixed N_2 varies widely with the N_2-fixing systems under consideration and the environmental conditions prevailing at sampling time.

Finally, as evident in the paper by Roskoski *et al.* (p. 447), to harvest a significant percentage of the nodules of a tree species can be a difficult and demanding task. Despite these problems the measurement of SARA is usually worthwhile since it indicates quite rapidly whether the symbiosis is effective or

TABLE 2: Specific acetylene reduction activity (SARA) of tree nodules expressed as μmol C_2H_2 reduced per g fresh or dry weight per h.

Plant	SARA expressed on		Reference
	Fresh wt basis	Dry wt basis	
Legumes			
Acacia cyanophylla	12		Nakos, 1977
Sesbania rostrata			
root nodules	17		Dreyfus & Dommergues, 1981b
stem nodules	23-53		
Nonlegumes			
Casuarina rumphiana	12-15		Becking, 1976
Casuarina equisetifolia			
4-month-old nodules		55-93	D. Gauthier (unpublished data)
13-month-old nodules		10	
Myrica javanica	2	9	Becking, 1977
Parasponia parviflora		3-4	Becking, 1976
Parasponia parviflora	2-15		Akkermans *et al.*, 1978

not, whereas the classical method based on the comparison of the N content of non-nodulated and nodulated plants is more time-consuming and may be difficult to carry out in the field. $^{15}N_2$ dilution methods have, to the author's knowledge, not been applied to tree species.

Only a few estimates of SARA have been published to date (see Table 2). From our own experiments it appears that the maximum SARA of *Casuarina* nodules is probably similar to that of tree legumes, or of plants such as soybeans. Of course, more estimates of SARA are needed, and studies on the nodulation of trees growing in optimum conditions should be developed to determine the potential of the different systems. Trees may produce fresh nodules seasonally or bear perennial nodules that are adapted to persist for several years. Typical perennial nodules have been described for legumes such as *Lupinus arboreus* (Pate, 1977) or nonlegumes such as *Casuarina* sp. (Dommergues & Mangenot, 1970), but information concerning perennial tree nodules in general is still of fragmentary nature.

FACTORS LIMITING THE NODULATION AND N_2 FIXATION OF TREE SPECIES

As with annual legumes, a number of factors can limit the ability of tree legumes to fix N_2.

Physical factors

In arid and semi-arid areas, water stress is not only a major limiting factor for the plant itself, but also for the establishment and function of symbiosis. Water stress was reported to impede or reduce nodulation of *Acacia* sp. (Beadle, 1964; Habish, 1970) and *Casuarina equisetifolia* (Kant & Narayana, 1978) and waterlogging, as well as drought, was shown to drastically reduce the N_2 (C_2H_2) fixation of *Acacia cyanophylla* (Nakos, 1977).

Root temperatures higher than 30° C are known to affect nodulation in most tropical legumes. However, some species appear to be adapted to higher temperatures. Thus, *Acacia mellifera* still produces effective nodules at 30-35° C, which might be attributed to the resistance of rhizobia exposed to high temperatures (Habish, 1970). On the other hand, we observed that temperatures above 30° C severely retarded the nodulation of *Casuarina equisetifolia*. How temperature affects the nodule distribution in the deeper rooted tree species is not known.

Chemical factors

pH

The pH at which nodulation is affected varies with the legume species and the strain of *Rhizobium* (Munns, 1977). Thus, nodulation of *Acacia mellifera*, but not plant growth, is affected by pH values of 5.0-5.5, whereas in alkaline soils (pH 8.5-9.0) growth and nodulation of *A. mellifera* are reduced (Habish, 1970). Nodulation and growth of *Leucaena leucocephala* is markedly affected by soil acidity (Date, 1977), with strains of *Rhizobium* for this legume varying in pH tolerance (Norris, 1973). In the field it is difficult to determine the effect of soil pH by itself, because this factor cannot be isolated from other factors — calcium deficiency, manganese and aluminium toxicity. Field observations and laboratory experiments suggest that pH is not limiting for the nodulation of nonleguminous plants (Becking, 1976). Thus, *Casuarina cunninghamiana* nodulates well in perlite watered with half-strength Crone solution, pH 5.4 (Torrey, 1976). In the field, we observed satisfactory nodulation of *Casuarina equisetifolia* in the alkaline (pH 8.0) dune soils of the Senegalese coast.

Phosphorus

In many tropical soils, particularly those of acid pH, available phosphorus (P) is an important limiting factor for plant growth, nodulation, and N_2 fixation. In some forest soils, where N has accumulated with time, P may be the major limiting factor. The effects of mycorrhizal fungi on the phosphate supply of trees are discussed subsequently.

Combined N

The effect of combined N on nodulation and N_2 fixation is well documented (Houwaard, 1980). The effect of N accumulation in older stands of legumes on nodulation and N_2 fixation has already been mentioned. In Senegal the absence of nodules on *Acacia senegal* may be due to active nitrification of organic N (Bernard-Reversat & Poupon, 1979).

Biological factors

A number of factors that can be termed biological in nature may affect the nodulation and N_2 fixation of tree species. The most harmful biological agents are pathogens, especially nematodes and insects. Nematodes have been reported by G. Germani (personal communication) to attack tree species such as *Acacia pyrifolia* (*Meloidogyne* sp.), *A. holocericea* (*Meloidogyne* sp.), *A. cyanophylla* (*Meloidogyne* sp.), and *A. tumida* (*Rotylenchulus* sp. and *Meloidogyne* sp.) There is little doubt that nematode attacks reduce nodulation, with consequent harmful effects on N_2 fixation, in the same way as reported for annual legumes such as soybeans or peanuts (Baldwin *et al.*, 1979; Germani, 1979). Roskoski *et al.*, in this volume (p. 447), report the effects of defoliation by insects on SARA in *Inga jinicuil.*

INCREASING SYMBIOTIC N_2 FIXATION IN TREE SPECIES

The different approaches for increasing symbiotic N_2 fixation have been described recently in excellent reviews (Hardy & Gibson, 1977; Vincent *et al.*, 1977). However, the examples given were mainly related to annual crops. Here we shall concentrate on perennial trees.

Inoculation with the proper endophyte

Rhizobium

Responses to inoculation depend on the presence of suitable strains of *Rhizobium* in the soil and on the specificity of the legume, that is, on its ability to nodulate with a limited or a wide range of strains of *Rhizobium*.

Except in the case of very poor soils, inoculation is rarely necessary for those tree legumes such as *Acacia mearnsii* that are nodulated by cowpea-type *Rhizobium*, widespread in tropical soils. With a specific legume to be introduced in an area where it has never been grown before, an understanding of the likely nodulation response is required. Preliminary trials either in hydroponic or sand cultures are most useful. However, one should be aware of the fact that the results of these trials may not be reflected in the nursery or field because limiting factors, such as acidity, may alter the behavior of the legume/*Rhizobium* system. Thus, strain NGR 8, which was most effective in sand culture, was recommended for *Leucaena latisiliqua* (*ieucocephala*), but its performance in the field was so poor that strain CB81, formerly used, was "reinstated as the preferred strain for general use" (Jones, 1977). Beside *Leucaena leucocephala*, other specific tree legumes have been reported to benefit from the inoculation of seed beds, especially *Acacia* and other Mimosoideae in South America (Döbereiner, 1967).

Preliminary investigations indicate that the *Rhizobium* requirements of tree legumes are as complex as those of annual legumes. Thus, investigations on 13 species of *Acacia* (see Table 3) showed that these species fell into three inoculation groups according to the type of *Rhizobium* that nodulated them. The first group, including species such as *A. albida*, nodulated only with slow-growing strains; the second group, including species such as *A. senegal*, nodulated only with fast-growing strains; while the remainder, including promiscuous species such as *A. seyal*, nodulated with both fast- and slow-growing strains. Table 4 summarizes the results of inoculation trials with *Acacia senegal* in nursery conditions, using plastic pouches filled with unsterile soil.

Frankia

To date, inoculation of *Casuarina equisetifolia* has been achieved through the application of suspensions of crushed nodules to the seedlings. This simple

TABLE 3: Nodulation[1] of 13 *Acacia* species and *Leucaena leucocephala* by fast- and slow-growing strains of *Rhizobium* (Dreyfus & Dommergues, 1981 a).

Plant species	Fast-growing strains					Slow-growing strains				
	ORS 901	ORS 902	ORS 908	ORS 911	NGR 8	ORS 801	ORS 802	ORS 803	ORS 806	CB 756
Native African species										
A. albida	O	O	O	O	O	E	E	E	E	E
A. nilotica (var. neb-neb)	E	E	E	E	E	O	O	O	O	O
A. nilotica (var. tomentosa)	E	E	E	E	E	O	O	O	O	O
A. raddiana	E	E	E	E	e	O	O	O	O	O
A. senegal	E	E	E	E	E	O	O	O	O	O
A. seyal	E	e	E	E	I	E	e	e	E	I
A. sieberiana	e	I	e	O	O	E	e	E	e	O
Introduced species										
A. bivenosa	I	I	E	I	I	E	e	E	I	e
A. farnesiana	E	E	E	E	E	O	I	O	O	I
A. holosericea	O	O	O	O	O	E	e	e	e	E
A. linaroides	O	O	O	O	O	E	e	e	I	I
A. mearnsii	O	O	O	O	O	E	E	e	E	e
A. tumida	O	O	I	I	O	e	e	I	O	I
Leucaena leucocephala	E	e	E	e	E	O	O	O	e	O

[1]E = Effective nodulation.
e = Partially effective nodulation.
I = Completely ineffective nodulation.
O = No nodules produced.

TABLE 4: Effect of inoculation of *Acacia senegal* with fast- and slow-growing strains of *Rhizobium*[1] (I. Gueye & B. Dreyfus, unpublished data).

Rhizobium strain	Host plant	Height (cm)	Shoots (g dry wt/plant)	Nodule number	Nodules (g fresh wt/plant)
Fast-growing					
ORS 901	*Acacia senegal*	31	1.0	20	0.3
ORS 902	*Acacia senegal*	32	0.9	17	0.2
ORS 903	*Acacia senegal*	28	0.7	15	0.2
ORS 906	*Acacia senegal*	31	0.9	13	0.2
ORS 507	*Sesbania pachycarpa*	22	0.4	3	0.1
Slow-growing					
CB 756	*Vigna unguiculata*	20	0.4	3	0.1
ORS 801	*Acacia holosericea*	19	0.3	2	0.05
Uninoculated control		18	0.2	2	0.02

[1]Plants were harvested when 3 months old; plants grown in nursery conditions (unsterile Hann soil in plastic pouches).

method has been used successfully for the three last years in the nurseries of *Casuarina* in Senegal. Plants inoculated in this manner thrive after they have been transplanted from the nursery to the field. Such results, however favorable, should not divert soil biologists from attempting to prepare inoculants with pure cultures of *Frankia*. The isolation of this endophyte, reported recently by Gauthier *et al.* (1981), will probably permit this technology to be adopted in nurseries. Unfortunately, up to now, nodulation tests with the isolated strains have been unsuccessful.

Vesicular-arbuscular endomycorrhiza (VAM)

It is now well established that, by favorably affecting P uptake, VAM can contribute to the N_2 fixation of legumes (Mosse, 1977). In some soils, mycotrophic plants might even be unable to grow when not infected by VAM (Janos, 1980). A recent experiment in our laboratory indicates that VAM can also improve the uptake of N from soil by the host plant (see Table 5). *Acacia raddiana* was grown in a sterile, *Rhizobium*-free, P-deficient, N-containing soil. Seedlings that were inoculated with *Glomus mosseae* absorbed P and N much more actively than the control. VAM inoculation was even more effective than phosphate application. The conclusion of such an experiment is that VAM inoculation should always be recommended, together with *Rhizobium* inoculation, when the nursery soil has been sterilized, or in any soil type characterized both by P deficiency and low populations of VAM.

A similar recommendation is probably required in the case of *Casuarina*, a tree that has been recently shown to be infected by endomycorrhiza (Wlliams, 1979; Diem *et al.*, 1981). The indifference of *Parasponia* to soil fertility is probably due to the fact that, like those of *Casuarina*, the roots of this tree are heavily infected with VAM and exhibit proteoid-like roots (Trinick, 1980).

Representatives of the family *Podocarpaceae* of the *Gymnospermae* exhibit nodular structures that have sometimes been assumed to be the site of N_2 fixation. Actually, these nodules, which are induced by VAM fungi, do not seem to show any significant N_2-fixing activity (Becking, 1974). This symbiosis allows *Podocarpus* to colonize eroding and skeletal soils where soil P is more likely to be the major limiting factor (Silvester, 1977).

Ectomycorrhiza

The only report of ectomycorrhizal infection of a tropical N_2-fixing tree, is that of *Casuarina* sp. by *Hymenogaster cerebellum* (Trappe, 1962), but the effect of ectomycorrhizal infection upon the plant growth has not yet been investigated.

TABLE 5: Effect of inoculation with *Glomus mosseae* of *Acacia raddiana* grown in a P-deficient, but N-containing, sterile Dek soil[1,2] (F. Cornet & H.G. Diem, unpublished data).

Treatment	Infection		Shoots and root weight (g dry wt/plant)	Total N (mg/plant)	Total P (mg/plant)
	Frequency	Intensity			
Control	0	0	0.36 a[3]	4.1 a	0.18 a
Glomus mosseae	75	44	1.33 b	19.7 b	2.06 b
Phosphate	0	0	0.94 c	14.3 c	1.24 c

[1]Plants grown in pouches (1.2 kg soil) were inoculated with *Glomus mosseae* when 2 weeks old and harvested when 10 weeks old.
[2]Phosphate (KH_2PO_4) addition: 0.20 g/kg of soil.
[3]Numbers not followed by the same letter are significantly different at the $P = 0.05$ (shoot and root weight) and $P = 0.01$ (Total N and total P) levels.

Soil fertilization

Inoculation even with specific endophytes, namely *Rhizobium*, *Frankia* or VAM, is unsuccessful if chemical factors in the soil impede plant growth or the functioning of the symbiosis. Such limiting factors are often encountered, since areas to be forested are often leftover soils, abandoned by farmers because of their poor physical and chemical properties. Such soils are often deficient, not only in N, but also in P. If the P deficiency results from a very low soil content in total P, the addition of phosphate fertilizers is required. Due to high costs, soluble phosphate is not often used. An interesting possibility is the application of rock phosphate together with elemental sulfur (S) inoculated with thiobacilli (as suggested by Swaby, 1975) to nursery soils. Table 6 shows that such treatment applied to an annual legume, *Vigna unguiculata*, significantly increased the growth, total P and total N content of the plant. If the P deficiency is moderate, inoculation with mycorrhiza can definitely help the trees. If the P deficiency is attributable to the insolubility of soil total phosphorus, inoculation of the soil with thiobacilli on a carrier containing elemental S should be beneficial to the trees, provided the original soil pH is not too low.

Soil amendment

In acid soils, liming may dramatically improve the yield. Thus, liming increased six-fold the yield of *Leucaena leucocephala* grown in an N-deficient Hawaii Oxisol of pH 4.7 (Munns & Fox, 1977).

Plant breeding

One promising approach for increasing symbiotic N_2 fixation is to select the most active "host genotype x strain of *Rhizobium*" combinations. Such an approach has already been advocated for annual legumes such as *Phaseolus vulgaris* and *Vigna unguiculata*. A major aim of the breeding work with *Leucaena leucocephala* is to increase both dry matter and protein yield (Hutton & Bonner, 1960). New advances could be expected if plant breeders took the microbial situation more seriously into account.

Recently Dreyfus & Dommergues (1981b) reported that *Sesbania rostrata*, a stem-nodulated legume, not only exhibited a high N_2-fixing potential, but was also able to actively fix N_2, even in the presence of high levels of inorganic N in the soil. The authors speculated on the possibility of transferring these unique properties to other *Sesbania* species, especially *S. grandiflora*.

CONCLUSION

To date the use of N_2-fixing trees (legumes or nonlegumes) in forestry and agroforestry has been largely neglected. However, the success of the

TABLE 6: Effect of soil inoculation with thiobacilli upon the growth and P uptake of *Vigna unguiculata,* grown in a soil amended with rock phosphate[1] (B. Ollivier & H.G. Diem, unpublished).

Treatment	Shoots and roots (g dry wt/plant)	Nodules (mg dry wt/plant)	Total N (mg/plant)	Total P (mg/plant)
Control	2.19 a	25 a	25 a	1.5 a
Rock phosphate + S[2]	3.72 b	46 b	39 b	2.2 b
Rock phosphate[3] + thiobacilli + S	5.00 c	64 c	55 c	3.1 c

[1]Plants grown in pots (1.5 kg sterile Dek soil/pot) were inoculated with the strain of *Rhizobium* CB 756. They were harvested when 60 days old. Numbers not followed by the same letter differ at the P = 0.05. level.
[2]Addition of rock phosphate (Taïba) was 40 ppm P; addition of S (elemental) was 200 ppm.
[3]Same treatment as (2) plus thiobacilli that had been obtained by enrichment of a soil from Guadeloupe.

introduction of species with a high N_2-fixing potential, for example, *Leucaena leucocephala* (NAS, 1977) *Casuarina equisetifolia* (Dommergues, 1963) and *Lupinus arboreus* (Caradus & Silvester, 1979) is such that interest in N_2-fixing trees is increasing. Further use of N_2-fixing trees requires, as a first step, screening of species to determine which exhibit the highest N_2-fixing potential. Surveys of legumes such as that published by Hecht (1978) may help in the search for such trees. As a second step, it appears necessary to improve our knowledge of the requirements of the selected trees with regard to their effective endophyte *Rhizobium* or *Frankia*, in order to prepare appropriate inocula.

Even if the N_2-fixing endophytes are properly harnessed, the success of their inoculation may often be impeded by the interaction of limiting factors, especially P-deficiency. Since VAM markedly improve the growth of plants in such a situation, VAM inoculation should be performed simultaneously with *Rhizobium* inoculation. Fortunately, perennial plants are more easily handled than annual crops, since they can be inoculated in the nursery itself before they are transplanted (Hayman, 1980). Synthetic inoculum carriers that were proposed a few years ago for *Rhizobium japonicum* (Dommergues *et al.*, 1979) could probably prove useful for tree inoculation with their N_2-fixing endophytes and with ecto- or endomycorrhiza.

Whereas inoculation can be carried out at the nursery level without raising insuperable difficulties, the success of such inoculation in the field may be unpredictable, since our knowledge of the maintenance of symbiosis in aging trees is still limited to some tree species. More investigations in the field are obviously needed.

REFERENCES

Akkermans, A.D.L., Abdulkadir, S. & Trinick, M.J. (1978) *Plant Soil* 49, 711-716.

Baldwin, J.G., Barker, K.R. & Nelson, L.A. (1979) *J. Nematology* 11, 156-160.

Beadle, N.C.W. (1964) *Proc. Linn. Soc. New South Wales* 89, 273-286.

Becking, J.H. (1974) Putative nitrogen fixation in other symbioses. *In*: The biology of nitrogen fixation. A. Quispel (Ed.). North-Holland, Amsterdam, The Netherlands. Pp. 583-613.

Becking, J.H. (1976) Root nodules in non-legumes. *In*: The development and function of roots. J.H. Torrey & D.T. Clarkson (Eds.). Academic Press, London, England. Pp. 507-566.

Becking, J.H. (1979) *Plant Soil* 51, 289-296.

Bernhard-Reversat, F. (1981) Biochemical cycle of soil nitrogen in a semi-arid savanna. (In preparation.)

Bernhard-Reversat, F. & Poupon, H. (1979) Nitrogen cycling in a soil tree system in a Sahelian savanna: Example of *Acacia senegal*. *In:* Nitrogen cycling in West African ecosystems, T. Rosswall. (Ed.) Royal Swedish Academy of Sciences, Stockholm, Sweden. Pp. 363-369.

Brenan, J.P.M. & Melville, R. (1960) *Kew Bull.* 14, 37-39.

Caradus, J.R. & Silvester, W.B. (1979) *N.Z.J. Agric. Res.* 22, 329-334.

Date, R.A. (1977) Inoculation of tropical pasture legumes. *In*: Exploiting the legume-*Rhizobium* symbiosis in tropical agriculture, J.M. Vincent, A.S. Whitney and J. Bose (Eds.). Univ. Hawaii Coll. Trop. Agric. *Misc. Publ.* 145. Pp. 293-312.

Diem, H.G., Gueye, I., Gianinazzi-Pearson, V., Fortin, J.A., & Dommergues, Y.R. (1981) *Acta Oecologica* 2, 53-62.

Döbereiner, J. (1967) *Pesq. Agropec. Brasil.* 2, 301-305.

Dommergues, Y.R. (1963) *Agrochimica* 105, 179-187.

Dommergues, Y.R. & Mangenot, F. (1970) Ecologie microbienne du sol. Masson, Paris, France. 795 pp.

Dommergues, Y.R., Diem, H.G. & Divies, C. (1979) *Appl. Environ. Microbiol.* 37, 779-781.

Dreyfus, B.C. & Dommergues, Y.R. (1981a) *Appl. Environ. Microbiol.* 41, 97-99.

Dreyfus, B.C. & Dommergues, Y.R. (1981b) *FEMS Letters* 313-317.

Gauthier, D., Diem, H.G. & Dommergues, Y.R. (1981) *Appl. Environ. Microbiol.* 41, 306-308.

Germani, G. (1979) Nematicide application as a tool to study the impact of nematodes on plant productivity. *In*: Soils research in agroforestry, H.O. Mongi & P.A. Huxley (Eds.). International Council for Research in Agroforestry (ICRAF), Nairobi, Kenya. Pp. 297-313.

Habish, H.A. (1970) *Plant Soil* 33, 1-6.

Hardy, R.W.F. & Gibson, A.H. (Eds.) (1977) A treatise on dinitrogen fixation, Section IV: Agronomy and ecology. Wiley, New York, NY, USA. 527 pp.

Hashimoto, K. (1976) *Res. Bull. Hokkaido Nat. Agric. Expt. Sta.* 114, 1-87.

Hayman, D.S. (1980) *Nature* 287, 487-488.

Hecht, S. (1979) Spontaneous legumes of developed pastures of the Amazon and their forage potential. *In*: Pasture production in acid soils of the tropics, P.A. Sánchez & L.E. Tergas (Eds.). CIAT, Cali, Colombia. Pp. 65-78.

Houwaard, F. (1980) *Plant Soil* 54, 271-282.

Hutton, E.M. & Bonner, I.A. (1960) *J. Aust. Inst. Agric. Sci.* 26, 276-277.

Janos, D.P. (1980) *Ecology* 61, 151-162.

Jones, R.J. (1977) Yield potential for tropical pasture legumes. *In*: Exploiting the legume-*Rhizobium* symbiosis in tropical agriculture, J.M. Vincent, A.S. Whitney & J. Bose (Eds.). Univ. Hawaii Coll. Trop. Agric. *Misc. Publ.* 145. Pp. 39-65.

Kant, S. & Narayana, H.S. (1978) *Annals of Arid Zone* 17 (2), 216-221.

Mosse, B. (1977) The role of mycorrhiza in legume nutrition on marginal soils. *In*: Exploiting the legume-*Rhizobium* symbiosis in tropical agriculture, J.M. Vincent. A.S. Whitney & J. Bose (Eds.). Univ. Hawaii Coll. Trop. Agric. *Misc. Publ.* 145. Pp. 275-292.

Munns, D.N. (1977) Mineral nutrition and the legume symbiosis. *In*: A treatise on dinitrogen fixation. Section IV: Agronomy and ecology. R.W.F. Hardy & A.H. Gibson (Eds.). Wiley. New York, NY, USA. Pp. 353-391.

Munns, D.N. & Fox, R.L. (1977) *Plant Soil* 46, 533-548.

Nakos, G. (1977) *Soil Biol. Biochem.* 9, 131-133.

National Academy of Sciences (US) (1977) *Leucaena*: Promising forage and tree crop for the tropics. NAS. Washington, D.C., USA. 115 pp.

National Academy of Sciences (US) (1979) Tropical legumes: Resources for the future. NAS, Washington, D.C., USA. 331 pp.

Norris, D.O. (1973) *Aust. J. Expl. Agric. Anim. Husb.* 13, 98-101.

Orchard, E.R. & Darby, G.D. (1956) Fertility changes under continued wattle culture with special references to nitrogen fixation and base status of the soil. C.R. 6éme Congrés International Science Sol, Paris, France. Section D. Pp. 305-310.

Pate, J.S. (1977) Functional biology of dinitrogen fixation by legumes: *In*: A treatise of dinitrogen fixation. Section III. Biology. R.W.F. Hardy & W.S. Silver (Eds.). Wiley, New York, NY, USA. Pp. 473-517.

Silvester, W.B. (1977) Dinitrogen fixation by plant associations excluding legumes. *In*: A treatise on dinitrogen fixation, IV: Agronomy and ecology. R.W.F. Hardy & A.H. Gibson (Eds.). Wiley, New York, NY, USA. Pp. 141-190.

Swaby, R.J. (1975) Biosuper - biological superphosphate. *In*: Sulphur in Australian agriculture. K.D. MacLachlan (Ed.). CSIRO, Glen Osmond, Australia. Pp. 213-222.

Torrey, J.G. (1976) *Amer. Botany* 63, 335-344.

Trappe, J.M. (1962) *Botanical Rev.* October-December, 538-606.

Trinick, M.J. (1976) *Rhizobium* symbiosis with a non-legume. *In*: Proc. First Internat. Symp. Nitrogen Fixation, W.E. Newton & C.J. Nyman (Eds.). Washington State Univ. Press. Pullman, WA, USA. Vol 2, pp. 507-517.

Trinick, M.J. (1980) The effective *Rhizobium* symbiosis with the non-legume *Parasponia andersonii*. *In*: Proc. IV Internat. Symp. N_2 Fixation. Canberra, Australia. (In press.)

Vincent, J.M. (1970) A manual for the practical study of root-nodule bacteria. IBP Handbook No. 15. Blackwell Sci. Pubs., Oxford, England 164 pp.

Vincent, J.M., Whitney A.S. & Bose, J. (Eds.). (1977) Exploiting the legume-*Rhizobium* symbiosis in tropical agriculture. Univ. Hawaii Coll. Trop. Agric. *Misc. Publ.* 145. 469 pp.

Williams, S.E., (1979) *Bot. Gaz.* (Suppl.) S115-S119.

NITROGEN-FIXING TREE RESOURCES: POTENTIALS AND LIMITATIONS

J.L. Brewbaker, R. Van Den Beldt and K. MacDicken[1]

Summary

Nitrogen (N_2) fixing trees are discussed with special attention to their use as fuelwood. forage or green manure in the tropics. Severe deforestation is viewed as leading to a "balding of the tropics" that could jeopardize the genetic resources of many legume trees. Increasing fuel and fertilizer costs mandate the planting and husbandry of tropical fuelwood and green manure tree crops. High population densities giving maximal annual biomass yields, and the use of trees with little concern about conformity or beauty, will provide attractive targets for breeder and/or agronomist/silviculturist.

N_2-fixing genera with special value as fuelwoods, forages, green manures or nurse trees. ornamentals, and as timber are listed. Characteristics are given for 18 fast-growing N_2-fixing trees in current University of Hawaii network trials.

THE BALDING OF THE TROPICS

It is traditional for man to plant and grow his food, but not to grow the wood with which to cook it. In the world of 1900 AD, the hunting and collection of fuelwood from native forests presented little challenge. There were only 1.6 billion people in the world, and approximately seven billion ha of forests. In the world of 2000 AD, however, the challenge of finding fuelwood will be awesome (Food and Agriculture Organization (FAO), 1980). A world population of 6.4 billion is predicted for 2000 AD, with only 3.0 billion ha of remnant forests (down from 4.8 billion in 1950).

The "people vs. trees" problem is greatly exacerbated in the tropics, where most countries have doubled their human populations in only the past three decades, while cutting their forest lands by half. Forest depletion figures for developing countries are startling (see Table 1). Forest areas with closed

[1] Dept. of Horticulture. University of Hawaii, Honolulu, Hawaii, 96822 USA.

TABLE 1: World forest resources as totals of closed forest area and stock growing (adapted from Barney, 1978).

Region	Total closed forest area (10^6 ha) 1978	2000[1]
Tropics		
Latin America	640	380
Africa	230	180
Asia/Pacific	400	200
Total	1270	760
Temperate[2]	1620	1610

[1]By comparison, total world forests in 1950 exceeded 5000 million ha.
[2]North America, Europe, USSR, Japan, Australia, New Zealand.

canopy (including growing stock) that totaled 1,270 million ha in 1978 are predicted to drop to 760 million ha by the end of this century (Barney, 1978). The ramifications of this loss are staggering, but include possible effects on atmospheric carbon dioxide and world climate (Woodwell, 1978). In contrast, only a slight loss is anticipated from the 1,620 million ha of closed forests in developed countries. This may be recalled as the century when Planet Earth grew a giant bald ring around its equator. The planting and husbandry of fuelwood in the tropics is clearly mandated for the future.

It has also been traditional for man in the tropics either to allow nature to repair the soil losses to agriculture by the fallowing of land for 15-20 years, or to use inorganic fertilizer. The slash and burn tradition can no longer continue into the 21st century, as the forest depletion and man's population pressure simply obviate it. Neither can inorganic fertilizers be an economic option except for the limited, wealthy fraction of farmers. Thus, the planting and husbandry of green manure crops also becomes a mandate for the future.

The majority of tropical legumes are woody perennials, many of which are both energy producing and nitrogen (N_2) fixing. It may be asserted that the health of many tropical forests relies initially on leguminous trees for N_2 fixation. Wild populations of native or aggressive introduced leguminous trees are increasingly valued as fuelwoods (National Academy of Science (NAS), 1980) and to a lesser extent as green manure trees (NAS, 1979). Notable among these are the mimosoids, a subfamily of legumes that includes about 2800 species, predominantly tropical trees and shrubs.

Maximization of biomass/ha per year must be the immediate target for both fuelwood and fertilizer production by trees. Reduced to essentials, the number of carbon and N atoms fixed annually per unit area becomes the goal, with little consideration of tree form or appearance. It is a target more familiar to agronomists than to foresters, and one that gives the plant breeder free rein.

It is safe to predict that fuelwood and fertilizer tree production will be dominated within a few decades by trees that are agriculturally versatile and easily bred and managed. The future improvement of these legumes could, however, be limited by the availability of appropriate germplasm. With the accelerating loss of virgin tropical forests, these native resources are dwindling and are often endangered.

GENETIC RESOURCES FOR N_2-FIXING TREES

The Nitrogen-Fixing Tree Association (NFTA), a new international organization that aims to encourage research and communication on leguminous trees, was incorporated in Hawaii in 1981. A primary thrust of the NFTA is to help identify genetic resources and stimulate their careful preservation and expansion. Our present impression is that the genetic resources of N_2-fixing trees are in a tragic state. There are no major international repositories of legume tree germplasm, whether as seed, or in arboreta, and very few tree species have been the subject of botanical expeditions for germplasm collection. Additionally many of the genera of N_2-fixing trees are taxonomically confused, from unknown centers of origin, or from areas that are rapidly becoming treeless. Seeds available for distribution are often of unknown origin. Genetically distinct varieties are available for only a few species, and these are predominantly ornamentals.

The opportunities for exploitation of the genetic diversity in legume trees can be illustrated from studies with *Leucaena leucocephala* (known also as ipil-ipil, huaxin, guaje, leadtree, lamtoro, koa haole, or kubabul). These have been reviewed by Brewbaker & Hutton (1979) and other authors (NAS, 1977; Brewbaker, 1980). The arboreal leucaenas did not become naturally dispersed through the tropics, but only a shrub known as the "common-type" or "Hawaiian-type" *Leucaena*. Though our collection of this heavily flowering shrub includes more than 500 accessions from numerous countries in the tropics, there is little genetic variability. We surmise that all originated from a narrow gene base. The species was dispersed from its native Mexico mainly through Spanish galleons departing from Acapulco and Mazatlan. In this region a highly flowering shrub is the only representative of the species, and it is clearly this one self-pollinated variety that circled the world.

The tree form and other genetic variants of *Leucaena* occur in southern Mexico and in Central America, a center of diversity for this tetraploid species (which is an evident hybrid of two other species). The arboreal types were first considered a distinct species by botanists; then came to be known as the

"Salvador type." This type first came to Hawaii from Central American seed collectors in the 1930's, and was then widely dispersed in the 1960's as a result of research in Hawaii and in Australia (Brewbaker, 1975). As a source of fuelwood, the Salvador type exceeds the common type by over 100% in wood yield; yet differs by very few genes.

It is virtually certain that genetic gains similar to those in *Leucaena* await the first plant explorers for species grown solely as C or N_2 fixers. Since many of these species are outcrossing, unlike *Leucaena,* the identification of genetic superiority will require more care in seed production. However, such species may well afford greater genetic gains —as occurred in poplar and pine— through exploitation of hybrid vigor in controlled crosses or from seed orchard synthetics.

The hazards of endangerment of species are evident in *Leucaena.* The center of origin of the Salvador type appears to be in the Morazan province of southern Salvador, a region now virtually treeless. Salvador-type leucaenas are now to be found only in the city squares and in backyards, a poor genetic sample of what existed as little as 50 years ago. Leguminous trees are often selectively browsed by feral animals and are, thus, more apt to extinction than many others. Following fire, however, they often regrow with ferocity from the fire-scarified seeds that have long lain dormant in the soil.

IMPORTANT GENERA OF N_2-FIXING TREES

The 18,000 species of legumes (Family: Leguminosae) include the vast majority of important N_2-fixing trees and shrubs, many of which are in the predominantly woody subfamilies Mimosoideae (2800 spp.) and Caesalpinioideae (2800 spp.). Relatively few of the 12,000 species of Papilionoideae are arboreal, but some of these are of great economic importance. A high proportion of the tested mimosoids (92%) are able to fix N_2, contrasted with the papilionoids (94%) and the caesalpinioids (34%). A few nonleguminous tree genera also fix N_2, notably the temperate genus *Alnus* and the tropical *Casuarina* (Stewart, 1967; see p. 427).

Leguminous trees produce some of the outstanding luxury timber of the tropics (NAS, 1979). Notable among these are the papilionaceous genera *Dalbergia* (rosewood), *Perocopsis* (African teak), *Pterocarpus* (narra), and the caesalpinioid genus *Intsia* (ipil, Moluccan ironwood). Other important timbers include the mimosoids *Acacia, Lysiloma, Parkia,* and *Samanea.* Preferred timber species often exceed 30 m in height and are of slow-to-intermediate growth rates. With their high intrinsic value, such trees might wisely be interplanted at wide spacing (e.g., 100/ha) in plantations of fast-growing legumes, as a long-term investment.

The legume trees best known as ornamentals, offering striking displays of color when in flower, are predominantly in the Caesalpinioideae, many of which do not fix N_2. The ornamental legumes include:

Caesalpinioideae: *Amherstia, Barklya, Bauhinia, Brownea, Caesalpinia, Cassia, Colvillea, Delonix, Peltophorum, Saraca,* and *Schotia.*
Mimosoideae: *Calliandra, Samanea.*
Papilionoideae: *Butea, Erythrina, Sabinea, Sophora.*

Several tree legumes provide valuable gums (*Acacia* spp.) and the pods of several species are excellent human foods, including:
Caesalpinioideae: *Ceratonia* (carob), *Tamarindus* (tamarind).
Mimosoideae: *Inga, Parkia.*

The following discussions will focus on legume trees with special significance as sources of energy or green manure. As a generalization, most fast-growing legume trees are mimosoids. Genera to be considered in the discussions of energy and green manure are listed below, together with their approximate number of species:
Caesalpinioideae: *Acrocarpus* (3), *Cassia* (600), *Schizolobium* (5).
Mimosoideae: *Acacia* (600), *Albizia* (100), *Calliandra* (100), *Desmanthus* (40), *Enterolobium* (8), *Inga* (200), *Leucaena* (10), *Lysiloma* (35), *Mimosa* (450), *Parkia* (40), *Pithecellobium* (200), *Prosopis* (44), *Samanea* (1).
Papilionoideae: *Dalbergia* (250), *Erythrina* (100), *Flemingia* (35), *Gliricidia* (10).

WOOD AND FUELWOOD

World production of wood in 1975 exceeded 2.5 billion m^3 (World Bank, 1978). Less than a century ago, wood was the major energy source for all countries in the world. Today, only 45% of the wood harvested is for fuel, and this is almost entirely in the tropics. Industrial uses of wood (60% in construction, 25% for pulp, 15% for other uses) have increased far more rapidly than total world commodity trade. These uses govern the base price of wood and directly influence both the availability and cost of fuelwood in the tropics. Demand for industrial wood has been increasing at about a doubling rate every 25 years. Demands for fuelwood are also increasing and will soon exceed capacity in regions such as Asia, which has less than 0.18 ha of forest per person at present (Revelle, 1980).

Tree legume species considered of special significance for fuelwood are summarized in Table 2. Species with unusual adaptability to the arid tropics are distinguished. Although many of these species appear to be slow in growth in their native habitats, they are often fast growing under experimental conditions, notably with adequate water. Species of *Acacia* and *Inga* provide fuelwoods for tropical highlands, while temperate fuelwoods would also include species of *Gleditschia* and *Robinia.*

TABLE 2: Tropical tree legumes of special significance as fuelwood (adapted from NAS, 1980).

Genus	Species adapted to:	
	Humid tropics	Arid tropics
Acacia	*auriculiformis, mearnsii*[1]	*brachystigia, cambagei, cyclops, nilotica, saligna, senegal, seyal, tortilis*
Albizia		*lebbek*
Calliandra	*calothyrsus*	
Cassia		*siamea*
Derris	*indica*	
Gliricidia	*sepium*	
Inga	*vera*[1]	
Leucaena	*leucocephala*	
Mimosa	*scabrella*	
Pithecellobium		*dulce*
Prosopis		*alba, chilensis, cineraria, juliflora*[2]*, pallida, tamarugo*
Sesbania	*grandiflora*	

[1]Highland-adapted species.
[2]Widely considered an undesirable, thorny pest.

Dendrothermal power plants can be designed to use chips (conventionally) or roundwood. Choice of fuelwood stock is influenced primarily by heat production (combustion value), and by ease of sawing, chipping, and transportation. Combustion values and wood densities are summarized in Table 3 for the species included in the University of Hawaii studies. Combustion values (given for bone-dry wood) reflect wood chemistry; not density, and vary little for the species listed. These values decrease linearly as wood moisture increases (most fuelwoods contain about 50% moisture at harvest). Specific gravity of species like the fast-growing *Albizia falcataria* are too low to make commercial fuelwood, due to bulk density problems of transportation and handling for the boiler. On the other hand, some species are so dense (e.g., arid-zone *Acacia and Prosopis* spp.) that they present problems in sawing and chipping. An economic feasibility analysis in Hawaii (Brewbaker, 1980) concluded that giant leucaenas could be grown and

TABLE 3: Characteristics of N_2-fixing trees in University of Hawaii international network trials (Scale: 1, Good – 3, Poor).

Characteristics	*Acacia auriculiformis*	*Acacia mangium*	*Acacia mearnsii*	*Acrocarpus fraxinifolius*	*Albizia falcataria*	*Albizia lebbek*	*Calliandra callothyrsus*	*Casuarina equisetifolia*	*Dalbergia sissoo*	*Enterolobium cyclocarpum*	*Gliricidia sepium*	*Leucaena diversifolia*	*Leucaena leucocephala*	*Mimosa scabrella*	*Prosopis pallida*	*Samanea saman*	*Schizolobium parahyba*	*Sesbania grandiflora*
	Genus and species																	
Utility for:																		
Forage	3	3	2	3	2	1	2	3	2	2	1	1	1	3	1	2	3	1
Fuelwood	1	2	1		3	1	1	1	1	2	1	1	1	1	1	3	3	1
Roundwood	3	2	1		3	1	3	1	2	3	1	1	1		3	3		1
Lumber	3	1		1	2	2	3	3	1	1	3	3	3	2	2	1	3	3
Pulpwood	1	1	1		1		3	2	2	1	3		1	1	3	2	2	2
Green manure	3	3	2	3	2	1	1	3	2	3	1	1	1	1	2	3	3	1
Craftwood	3	2		2	3	1	3	3	1	1	2		2		1	1	3	3
Food	3	3	3	3	3	3	3	3	3	2	2	3	1	3	2	2	3	1
Tolerance of:																		
Acid soils	1	1			2?		2?	1				3	3					3
Cold soil	2	2	1	3	2	1	2	2	1	3	3	2	3	1	3	3	2	3
Drought	3	3	2	3	3	2	2	1	1	1	2	1	1		1	1	2	2
Min. rain (mm)	120	150	100	100	150	60	100	30	50	75	150	60	60		25	60	75	100
Coppicing ability	2	1	1		1	1	1	2	1		1	1	1		2			1

harvested profitably as boiler fuel, even with Hawaii's high costs of labor, land, and water. Energy returns from a 1000 ha tree farm, harvested incrementally on a four-year cycle, were calculated to be 28.6 million kwh annually. Wood drying and use of high efficiency boilers could increase this value by 20%.

Choice of fuelwood for home use involves many considerations. Local preferences dictate a wide array of species in the arsenal of the agroforester. Most simple stoves are designed to accomodate long pieces of wood that are fed into the stove as they burn. Most labor- and energy-efficient stoves are closed in order to minimize air intake, and so require specific, cut lengths. Split wood dries rapidly and is often favored over round wood, although marketing is conventionally by volume; not by weight. Irregular, heavily knotted woods (e.g., many acacias, prosopis) are difficult to prepare or split as fuelwood, but may be preferred for charcoal. Smokiness, ash content, explosive inclusions, thorniness, odor, and uniformity of burn can influence home fuelwood value. Many of these traits could be addressed profitably by the plant breeder and silviculturist. As an example, thornless mutants are found in several of the thorny mimosoids (Felker, 1979).

GREEN MANURE AND NURSE TREES

Leguminous shrubs and trees are of increasing interest as sources of "green gold" (Curran, 1976) for the fertilization or nursing of both herbaceous and tree crops in the tropics. Green manuring of herbaceous crops is a sadly neglected area of tropical research. Legume trees like *Leucaena* and *Sesbania* can be continously coppiced for harvest of leaf meal. The clippings, which are high in N, can be placed directly around an interplanted crop, or "cut and carried" for incorporation prior to planting. Guevara, Whitney & Thompson (1978) showed that annual N yields of 0.5 t/ha can be obtained from *Leucaena* harvested every three months. Similar estimates may be inferred from earlier studies in the authors' laboratory. The availability of inorganic fertilizers has discouraged research on green manures in the tropics until recently. Definitive, quantitative data on N recovery and utilization from leguminous forage remains a serious need. Initial studies of R.A. Bradfield (personal communication) on leucaena green manuring of maize at IRRI were very promising. Guevara (1976) later quantified this relationship in Hawaii, recording excellent maize yields and effective recovery of about 46% of the N applied as leaf meal. An extensive demonstration of these methods is underway by the Philippine National Food and Agriculture Council. Legume trees of special merit for green manure research include the widely used *Sesbania* spp., *Leucaena leucocephala* and *Gliricidia sepium* (annually deciduous); also *Acacia mearnsii, Albizia* spp., *Calliandra calothyrsus,* and *Mimosa scabrella.*

TABLE 4: Properties of N_2-fixing trees in University of Hawaii international network trials.

Property	*Acacia auriculiformis*	*Acacia mangium*	*Acacia mearnsii*	*Acrocarpus fraxinifolius*	*Albizia falcataria*	*Albizia lebbek*	*Calliandra callothyrsus*	*Casuarina equisetifolia*	*Dalbergia sissoo*	*Enterolobium cyclocarpum*	*Gliricidia sepium*	*Leucaena diversifolia*	*Leucaena leucocephala*	*Mimosa scabrella*	*Prosopis pallida*	*Samanea saman*	*Schizolobium parahyba*	*Sesbania grandiflora*
	Genus and Species																	
Specific gravity	.68	.65e[1]	.65	.63	.33	.58	.65	1.00	.68	.50	.75e	.55e	.54		.80	.52	.32	.42
Wood yield m^3/ha.yr.	15	30	20e		40	5	50	15		8e	8e	25e	45		8e	15e	20	22
Average caloric value (Kcal/g)	4.8					5.2	4.6	5.0	5.0		4.9		4.6					
Average annual height growth (m)	2.6	2.5	4e	2.0	5.0	1.4	6.0	2.1	2e	2e	25e	4.0e	4.5	4.5	2.5e	2.5e	1.9	3.3
Height at maturity (m)	30	30	25	60	45	30	10	30	30	30	10	20	20	15	20	45	30	10
DBH at maturity (cm)	60	25	50e	300	200	200	20	30	200	200	20e	20e	35	30	60	180	70	30

[1]e = estimated values..

The interplanting of leguminous trees as nurse crop to other trees evolved out of the tradition of shading crops like coffee and cacao. Shade may in fact be a disadvantage offset by the N-rich leaf drop in many plantations. Among the major nurse legumes for plantation crops are *Albizia carbonaria, Erythrina* spp., *Flemingia congesta, Inga* spp. and *Leucaena* spp. (*diversifolia, leucocephala* and *pulverulenta*). *Flemingia* is notable for its tolerance of acid rubber plantation soils, as is *Acacia auriculiformis.*

Tree legumes can also be used as living fences or support systems for other crops. Studies at the International Institute of Tropical Agriculture (IITA) (1979) have demonstrated the practicality of using *Leucaena* as living support for yams, winged beans and other crops (e.g., pepper, betel, vanilla, and passion fruit).

FORAGE

The leguminous trees commonly used for forage, following continuous clipping, include *Cassia sturtii, Desmanthus virgatus, Leucaena leucocephala,* and *Sesbania grandiflora.* Foliage of other species is palatable to animals and could be recovered during wood harvest, e.g., *Acacia mearnsii, Albizia lebbek, Gliricidia sepium* and *Mimosa scabrella* (see Table 4). *Leucaena,* the most intensively studied of the species listed above, can produce 10-15 tons (dry matter) of forage per hectare annually (Brewbaker *et al.,* 1972) when harvested regularly. The value of the foliage as co-product in fuelwood or pulpwood harvest may be great enough in the case of *Leucaena* to encourage use of chip-vacuum, leaf-meal recovery machines.

Many of the 600 *Acacia* spp. bear phyllodes (expanded petioles) as mature leaves that are generally fibrous and unpalatable. Mimosine (in all *Leucaena* spp.) and other alkaloids occur in some tree legumes and require caution in their use as forage. Breeding and management of the forage (e.g., silage preparation) may offer solutions to these problems (González, Brewbaker & Hamill, 1968; Rosas; Quintero & Gómez, 1980).

UNIVERSITY OF HAWAII TRIAL NETWORK FOR N_2-FIXING TREES

The US National Academy of Science reports on *Leucaena* and on tropical legumes prompted an expansion of genetic research in Hawaii on N_2-fixing trees, previously confined to *Leucaena* and *Acacia koa.* A major thrust of the expanded studies is to determine relative biomass yields of different species and varieties of leguminous trees. A trial network for *Leucaena* was initiated in 1978, and expanded with USDA support in 1980 to include other species.

The major species chosen for our studies are summarized in Tables 3 and 4. All are considered relatively fast growing, with most species exceeding 15 m^3/ha per yr of wood. Most are hardwoods with high intrinsic value as fuel or pulpwood, and several are valued for forage or lumber and craftwood. Acid and unusually arid soils, along with waterlogged and saline soils, present primary challenges to the forester. In this study *Acacia auriculiformis* was chosen for relative tolerance to acidity and *Prosopis pallida* for relative tolerance to aridity.

Yield trials are planted with dense spacing (5000 or 10,000/ha) using 3- to 4-month-old seedlings transplanted into small plots (minimally 28 m^2). Trials use the augmented block design (Federer & Raghavarao, 1975), and include several replications of 10-15 species, but can include additional unreplicated plots of other species or treatments. This is a flexible design that accommodates diverse entries and treatments at different locations, yet permits the pooling of replicated data for calculations of variety x location and error terms.

Initial results of such international trials with *Leucacena* have been gratifying. Giant varieties of *Leucaena* provide some of the fastest growth and greatest versatility of the tree legumes, probably equal to any nonlegume.

RESEARCH IMPERATIVES

With perhaps a thousand potentially significant N_2-fixing trees to study in the tropics, where should research emphasis be placed? It seems wise to focus on species providing both forage and fuelwood to the small farmer. Few nonlegumes bear consideration, and species achieving less than 2 m annual growth should be excluded. Thorniness must be considered undesirable, despite the protection it gives against animal depradation. The following dual-purpose species appear to deserve extensive collection, genetic evaluation, and site adaptability studies:

Acacia spp. (see Table 2)
Calliandra calothyrsus
Gliricidia sepium
Leucaena leucocephala
Prosopis spp. (Table 2)
Sesbania grandiflora

REFERENCES

Barney, G. (1978) The nature of the deforestation problem: trends and policy implications. *In:* Proceedings, US strategy conference on deforestation. US State Dept. Washington, D.C., USA.

Brewbaker, J.L.,Plucknett, D.L. & Gonzalez, V. (1972) *Hawaii Agric. Exp. Sta. Bull.* 166, 29 pp.

Brewbaker, J.L. (Ed.) (1980) Giant *Leucaena* (koa haole) energy tree farms: An economic feasibility analysis for the Island of Molokai. Hawaii Natural Energy Institute. Publ. No. 80-160. 90 pp.

Brewbaker, J.L. & Hutton, E.M. (1979) *Leucaena,* versatile tropical tree legume. *In:* New agricultural crops, G.A. Ritchie (Ed.). Amer. Assn. Adv. Sci., Westview Press. Boulder. CO. USA. Pp. 207-257.

Curran, H. (1976) Giant ipil-ipil: Green gold for the tropics. US Peace Corps, mimeographed.

Federer, W.T. & Raghavarao, D. (1975) *Biometrics* 31, 29-35.

Felker, P. (1979) Mesquite, an all-purpose leguminous arid land tree. *In:* New agricultural crops, G.S. Ritchie (Ed.). Amer. Assoc. Adv. Sci., Westview Press, Boulder. CO. USA. Pp. 207-257.

Food and Agriculture Organization (FAO) (1980) Forestry for rural communities. Forest Dept. Publ.. FAO, Rome, Italy. 52 pp.

González, V., Brewbaker. J.L. & Hamill, D.E. (1967) *Crop Sci.* 7, 140-143.

Guevara, A.B. (1976) Management of *Leucaena leucocephala* (Lam.) de Wit for maximum yield and nitrogen contribution to intercropped corn. PhD thesis, Univ. of Hawaii. Honolulu, Hawaii, USA.

Guevara, A.B., Whitney. A.S. & Thompson, J.R. (1978) *Agron. J.* 70, 1033-1037.

International Institute for Tropical Agriculture (IITA) (1979) Annual report. IITA, Ibadan, Nigeria.

National Academy of Science (NAS) (1977) *Leucaena:* promising forage and tree crop for the tropics. NAS. Washington, D.C., USA. 115 pp.

National Academy of Science (NAS) (1979) Tropical legumes: Resources for the future. NAS. Washington, D.C., USA 331 pp.

National Academy of Science (NAS) (1980) Firewood crops: Shrub and tree species for energy production. NAS, Washington, D.C., USA 237 pp.

Revelle, R. (1980) *Science* 209, 164-174.

Rosas, H., Quintero. S.O. & Gómez, J. (1980) *Leucaena Research Reports* 1, 17 pp.

Stewart, W.D.P. (1967) *Science* 158, 1426-1432.

Woodwell, G. (1978) Carbon dioxide-deforestation relationships. *In:* Proceedings, US Strategy Conference on Tropical Deforestation. US State Dept., Washington, D.C., USA.

World Bank (1978) Forestry sector policy paper. World Bank, Washington, D.C., USA. 65 pp.

CASUARINA: ACTINORHIZAL NITROGEN-FIXING TREE OF THE TROPICS

J.G. Torrey[1]

Summary

Casuarina is the most important actinorhizal plant of the tropics. The genus comprises well over sixty species of woody, dicotyledonous plants, most of which appear capable of symbiotic association with the filamentous bacterium *Frankia* of the Actinomycetales. The root nodules formed fix nitrogen (N_2), and so bring about an accretion of N in the soil environment at rates equivalent to those achieved by herbaceous legumes. This paper reviews the published literature on nodulation and N_2 fixation in *Casuarina* and assesses the experimental and practical measures which should be taken to improve the contributions made by *Casuarina* to agriculture and forestry in tropical and subtropical countries where this genus can be grown. The following topics are discussed: early studies on symbiotic N_2 fixation, the ecological role in the N economy, laboratory studies of N_2 fixation, nodule initiation and development, the ultrastructure of nodules, handling the micro-organism in culture and in nodule suspensions, inoculation of nursery seedling stock and the distribution of *Casuarina* and its actinomycetous endophyte.

INTRODUCTION

Casuarina is a woody dicotyledonous plant native to Australia but widespread in tropical and subtropical countries, where it has been disseminated by man. Its roots are nodulated following invasion of the filamentous soil bacterium, *Frankia* of the Actinomycetales and this symbiosis results in nitrogen (N_2) fixation at rates comparable to nodulated legumes (Torrey, 1978). These trees occupy a diversity of sites ranging from tropical rain forests to arid deserts and sandy coastal dunes. The genus

[1] Cabot Foundation, Harvard University, Petersham, MA, 01366 USA.
Research support from the Maria Moors Cabot Foundation and the National Science Foundation (Grant DEB 77-02249) is gratefully acknowledged.

encompasses more than sixty species, only a few of them presently of economic significance. In Australia, *Casuarina cunninghamiana,* the river sheoak, grows along fresh water river banks, reaches a height of up to 36 meters and produces a straight, hardwood trunk useful as timber. *Casuarina equisetifolia* is in common use in the tropics for shelter belts, for erosion control, land reclamation, and as a forage and fuel tree. By virtue of their symbiotic capacity, many *Casuarina* species serve as pioneers, preceding and making possible the establishment of forested stands. Despite such evidence of hardiness, the species diversity and adaptability to climatic variation and harshness of habitat within the genus have hardly been explored.

This paper brings together much of the available information on nodulation and N_2 fixation in *Casuarina* and aims thereby to encourage better understanding of the significance of the genus in its present habitats and of the possibilities for better utilization of these plants in worldwide tropical agriculture and forestry.

EARLY STUDIES ON N_2 FIXATION IN *CASUARINA*

Although Janse (1897) reported the presence of nodules on roots of *Casuarina* and later Miehe (1918) and McLuckie (1923) inferred that these nodules were implicated in N_2 fixation, the first direct studies of symbiotic N_2 fixation in *Casuarina* were made by Aldrich-Blake (1932) and Mowry (1933).

Aldrich-Blake (1932) planted surface-sterilized seeds of *C. equisetifolia* in sand watered with nutrient solution lacking N and inoculated them with ground nodule suspensions from mature plants collected in the field. Uninoculated plants lacking N or supplemented with NH_4NO_3 served as controls.

Uninoculated plants showed no root nodules. Inoculated roots showed numerous root nodules ranging in diameter up to 3.8 cm and representing 11.7% of the dry weight of the whole root system. Nodulated plants were more than three times taller than uninoculated ones, were more than 50 times heavier than control plants on a dry weight basis, and their average N content per plant was more than 100 times that of the uninfected control plants not provided fertilizer N.

Mowry (1933) reported the nodulation of nine different species of *Casuarina* seedlings grown in sterile soil following their inoculation with small pieces of fresh nodules from plants growing in the field. He concluded that a single strain of the infective organism nodulated all nine species, and that this organism, a bacterium, entered into a symbiotic relationship with the host resulting in N_2 fixation. In 20 different locations in Florida, on sand dunes and other sites of low fertility, he found no trees of any size which did not have nodules.

Other early workers reported the occurrence of root nodules on *Casuarina* (Kamerling, 1915; Narashimhan, 1918; Rao, 1923; Parker, 1932) and most of these observers made the connection between the presence of root nodules and satisfactory plant growth, probably related to N_2 fixation. These nodules were presumed to be produced by a soil micro-organism (Chaudhuri, 1931) and early efforts were made to isolate and culture it (Shibata & Tahara, 1917; Narashimhan, 1918).

Becking (1977) listed the earliest account in the literature of nodulation in each of the *Casuarina* species reported. He noted that 18 species of a total of 45 (as then interpreted) had been reported nodulated. The list could doubtless be extended, but this effort becomes fruitless in the face of changing views on the taxonomy of the group. In field collections of *Casuarina* nodules in Florida, Hawaii, and Australia, including 10-15 species (J.G. Torrey, unpublished), only one situation was found in which the plants were not nodulated. It is to be presumed that all of the species of the genus are capable of root infection and nodulation by the appropriate *Frankia*. Whether one or more strains of *Frankia* are involved remains to be demonstrated.

THE ECOLOGICAL ROLE OF *CASUARINA* SPP.

Evidence for a significant ecological role of *Casuarina* in the N economy of a given environment can be traced back to reports of agricultural practices involving *Casuarina* plantations. Silvester (1976) cited the role of *Casuarina* in traditional rotational agricultural practice in highland New Guinea, in which *Casuarina* is planted in cleared areas, grown for 5-10 years, then cleared for firewood or timber, after which the land is planted to yams or other crops that profit from the N accretion attributable to N_2 fixation and litter fall from *Casuarina*.

Estimates of the contribution to the N status of sandstone soils near Sydney, Australia, made by *Casuarina littoralis* were reported by Hannon (1956). Analyses of the plants of the low scrub forest showed 10,000-12,900 ppm N on a dry weight basis. Litter fall and dry matter increment represented 29.0 tons/ha per yr, which at 1% N represented an accretion of 290 kg N/ha per yr, largely attributable to symbiotic N_2 fixation.

Dommergues (1963; 1966) reported the N_2 fixation by *Casuarina equisetifolia* in sandy soils of the Cape Verde Islands off Portugal. By measuring soil and plant N, he was able to estimate a yearly increment of about 58 kg N/ha, mostly derived from N_2 fixation by nodulated plants. Beadle (1964) considered the role of *Casuarina* spp. in the N economy of arid areas in Australia.

Silvester (1977) reviewed the descriptive evidence for the importance of *Casuarina equisetifolia* in the revegetation of Krakatau Island, Indonesia, following volcanic destruction of the vegetation. On a small scale, a similar sequence of revegetation involving *Casuarina equisetifolia* can be observed on the Island of Hawaii. Opportunities for quantitative studies of establishment and succession of *Casuarina equisetifolia* exist in the Puna district near Hilo, where volcanic ash wiped out a stretch of vegetation from the volcano to the sea in 1960. New seedlings and young trees of *Casuarina* that invaded the site were well nodulated and flourished together with small sedges in a location otherwise devoid of vegetation (J.G. Torrey, unpublished data).

LABORATORY STUDIES ON N_2 FIXATION

Careful laboratory and greenhouse studies of symbiotic N_2 fixation by *Casuarina* are relatively sparse, though Bond and his associates have contributed significantly to our understanding of the symbiosis over a period of about twenty years.

Bond (1957a) determined shoot height, dry weight, and total N values for nodulated and non-nodulated plants and showed that a mean fixation of 50 mg N/plant occurred in seedlings of *C. cunninghamiana* over a six-month period in water culture. In similar studies Rodríguez-Barrueco (1973/74) reported that plants of *C. torulosa* showed accumulation of 430 mg N/plant in 12 months. Bond (1957b; 1964) demonstrated that detached nodules of *Casuarina* incorporated the N_2 from the atmosphere into fixed N. Nodules showed an N content of 3.0% on a dry weight basis and an increase in ^{15}N content of up to 0.368 atom percent of total N over the normal value during a 19-hour period. Bond (1961) also demonstrated the inhibition of N_2 fixation in detached nodules by molecular oxygen at concentrations above 20% and by gaseous hydrogen at 20% (>50% inhibition) and higher (Bond, 1960). This sensitivity was comparable to that found in N_2 fixation in nodules of legumes.

Bond and Hewitt also demonstrated the essentiality for N_2 fixation by *Casuarina* of molybdenum (Hewitt & Bond, 1961), cobalt (Bond & Hewitt, 1962; Hewitt & Bond, 1966), and copper (Bond & Hewitt, 1967).

Studies on the effects of combined N on nodulation and N_2 fixation have been made by Stewart (1963) and Rodríguez-Barrueco, Mackintosh & Bond (1970). Stewart showed that ammonium-N provided as $(NH_4)_2SO_4$ at 10 ppm N facilitated the nodulation and development of young seedlings inoculated with a nodule suspension and that NH_4^+-N up to 100 ppm did not significantly reduce the number of nodules formed. He concluded that under most field conditions *Casuarina* nodulation would not be affected by normal levels of soil N. Rodríguez-Barrueco (1972) also reported that low levels of N provided as NH_4^+ did not interfere with nodule development in seedlings of *C. cunninghamiana* although the ammonium ion became inhibitory at high levels. Fixation of N_2 was less efficient in the presence of the ammonium ion.

Rodríguez-Barrueco *et al.* (1970) grew nodulated *Casuarina* plants for 14 weeks in nutrient solutions containing different levels of $(NH_4)_2SO_4$ and provided $^{15}N_2$ in the atmosphere. Plants provided N as NH_4^+ grew well, more or less in proportion to the ammonium supplied, but the presence of fixed N reduced the N_2 fixation of all plants even at 10 ppm N. Nodule growth was likewise reduced. Plants not provided combined N, although well nodulated, did not grow as well as those provided NH_4^+-N, suggesting that N_2 fixation itself utilizes photosynthate that might otherwise go to growth. Coyne (1973) reported that 56 ppm N as $Ca(NO_3)_2$ inhibited nodule formation by as much as 75% under optimum pH conditions in water culture. According to Coyne, N_2 fixation was negligible in nodulated plants provided nitrate N.

Bond & Mackintosh (1975) using detached nodules incubated in $^{15}N_2$ found that fixation varied diurnally, being low in the early morning, relatively high for several hours in mid to late afternoon, and then decreasing. Light intensity and temperature together influenced fixation rates. According to these authors, the rate of N_2 fixation increased steadily from 10° to 36°C, with the maximum rate of fixation in *Casuarina cunninghamiana* nodules at 36°C. Waughman (1977) also observed a simple exponential response in nitrogenase activity in *C. equisetifolia* to increasing temperature. Rodríguez-Barrueco (1973/74) found that detached nodules of *C. torulosa* showed the highest fixation rates in the late afternoon and early evening rather than in mid morning.

NODULE INITIATION AND DEVELOPMENT

Structural studies of *Casuarina* root nodules attempted first to localize and identify the endophyte. Thereafter, attention was paid to the modification of root structure and the anomalous form and development of root nodules. More recently, ultrastructural studies have demonstrated root hair infection, root cortex invasion, and the proliferation of multilobed, modified, lateral root branches to form the typical nodules with nodule roots. Early anatomical studies of young nodules (Miehe, 1918; McLuckie, 1923; Aldrich-Blake, 1932) were reviewed by Torrey (1976).

Bond (1956; 1957a) first called attention to the presence of nodule roots growing vertically upward on *Casuarina* nodules. These nodule roots can be quite striking in young plants grown in water culture but may have dried up and shrivelled in field-collected nodules and so be totally missed or ignored.

Evidence to the present supports the view that the organism nodulating *C. cunnighamiana* gains entry by root hair penetration (Callaham *et al.*, 1979), as has been shown as well in *Alnus, Myrica,* and *Comptonia.* The endophyte within the root hair shows multiple filaments surrounded or encapsulated by a polysaccharide capsule formed by the host cytoplasm and characteristic nucleoid regions along the filament (Newcomb, Pankhurst & Torrey, 1981).

The filaments invade the cortical cells of the root, dissolving the cell walls and middle lamella and often forming wide strands of invading filaments (Torrey, 1976; Tyson & Silver, 1979). Filaments are septate and branched, approximately 1 μ in diameter, ramifying through the cells of the root cortex and causing cortical cell proliferation followed by cell hypertrophy (Torrey, 1976). The structure of the micro-organism is that of a filamentous bacterium of the group Actinomycetales.

Coincident with the first invasion by the actinomycete, the root at the site of invasion is stimulated to form multiple lateral root primordia that are in turn invaded in the newly formed cortex tissues, forming swollen lobes where N_2 fixation is presumed to occur (Torrey, 1976; Kant & Narayana, 1977). Only after the hypertrophy stage, when the endophyte has filled the cortical tissues, does the nodule root elongate from the pointed tip lobe of each successively formed nodule root. The result is the formation of a cluster of swollen nodule lobes at each infection site with upward-elongating nodule roots. The nodule roots remain uninfected by the bacterium. Silver *et al.* (1966) attempted to interpret the peculiar negative geotropism of nodule roots in terms of abnormal metabolism of the plant growth hormone, indole-3-acetic acid, within the developing nodules.

In nodules of actinorhizal plants, vesicles are the demonstrated site of the nitrogenase (see Tjepkema *et al.*, 1980; 1981) and have been reported to occur in mature nodule cortical cells in almost all actinorhizal plants studied structurally. By contrast, *Casuarina* nodules do not normally show the typical, terminal, swollen, filamentous structures termed vesicles (Torrey, 1976; Tyson & Silver, 1979; Newcomb *et al.*, 1981; P.J. Dart, personal communication) though one report claiming to illustrate nodule vesicles in *Casuarina* has been made (Gardner, 1976).

The lack of convincing evidence for the presence of vesicles in the endophyte in root nodules of *Casuarina* raises the question as to the site of nitrogenase activity in the nodules of this genus. More comprehensive and careful ultrastructural study of nodules fixed for microscopy at a time when nitrogenase activity is demonstrable are needed to resolve this question.

The evidence is good that the normal vesicle structure of cultured *Frankia* provides protection for the oxygen-labile nitrogenase against inactivation by ambient O_2 concentration (Tjepkema *et al.*, 1980). In the absence of a typical vesicular structure in *Casuarina*, how would nitrogenase be protected? Special modifications may have evolved in this case. Davenport (1960) reported the occurrence of hemoglobin in root nodules of *C. cunninghamiana*. Efforts of others to confirm this observation have not been successful. Here is another area needing further study.

HANDLING THE MICRO-ORGANISM

The ideal situation for the study of a host/micro-organism symbiosis is to be able to cultivate each of the components separately and to understand the behavior of each, independent of the other. While one can grow seeds of *Casuarina* independent of *Frankia*, it is not yet possible to grow in pure culture the *Frankia* that causes nodulation of *Casuarina* roots. Uemura (1961; 1964) attempted isolation of the micro-organism from nodules of *C. equisetifolia* and was able to grow a *Streptomyces*-like organism in nutrient medium. However, he failed to achieve reinfection of axenically grown seedlings inoculated with this isolate. I have used methods developed and applied successfully to the isolation of *Frankia* sp. from *Alnus, Comptonia, Elaeagnus* and other genera, but thus far have been unable to isolate the endophyte from nodules of *Casuarina* spp. collected in Florida, Hawaii, and Australia.

Gauthier *et al.* (1981) used microdissection methods and serial dilution to isolate an organism from *Casuarina* nodules, which when grown in culture, showed *Frankia*-like characteristics. The organism cultured by Gauthier *et al.* (1981) produced terminal vesicles *in vitro* and reduced acetylene, presumably due to nitrogenase activity. Unfortunately, attempts to demonstrate infection of *Casuarina* seedlings with this organism have so far failed. The reasons for this failure are not clear and further attempts at isolation and culture must be made.

In lieu of inocula prepared from the cultured organism, methods have been devised to inoculate seedlings with nodules collected in the field or from plants propagated in the greenhouse (Bond, 1957a; Torrey, 1976).

Coyne (1973) studied the importance of pH and nitrate-N for successful inoculation of plants grown in water culture. Initial pH was critical; almost no nodulation occurred in plants growing in solutions of pH 4.0 or pH 9.0. Optimum pH for nodule formation in two species (*C. glauca* and *C. cunninghamiana*) was pH 6.0 with good nodulation, still, at pH 7.0 and 8.0 but poor nodulation at pH 5.0. Bond (1957a) also reported good nodulation in *C. cunninghamiana* at pH 6 and 7. According to Coyne, the presence of nitrate-N reduced the number of nodules initiated but did not influence the optimum pH for nodulation.

Alternative methods for preparing inoculants have been described or discussed but not systematically studied. I have found that excellent nodulation can be obtained using dried nodule preparations. Small field samples of nodules of *C. equisetifolia* placed in a vial containing silica gel induced nodulation of the same species even after three months' storage. How long nodules can be safely stored in this way remains to be determined.

When ground in distilled water, fresh nodules rapidly turn brown and then grey, presumably because of the release of polyphenols and/or tannins. To limit the damage from such potentially toxic substances, nodules can be ground in the presence of polyvinylpyrrolidone (PVP). We have used 1% PVP-40 and found that its presence retards the blackening reaction. Activated charcoal (10% wt/volume) also can be used as adsorbent. Lalonde (1979) used 0.6-1% sodium chloride to grind *Alnus* nodules and found that this suspension also resulted in a clear light yellow fluid after filtration. No systematic study of the relative effectiveness of these methods has been made. All the methods suffer from the common difficulty that we do not know the chemical and physical requirements of the organism that must be present in the inoculum, the activity of which we are attempting to preserve.

There seems to be no published account of procedures for inoculating seedlings of *Casuarina* in the nursery. Observation of operations in government forestry nurseries in Hawaii, Australia, and New Zealand suggests that little attention has been paid by growers to ensuring the presence of the appropriate organism. Since most nursery operations routinely use sterilized soil mixes for seedling plantations, one cannot expect the infective actinomycete to be present in the root environment. Some arrangement must be made to introduce the organism into the rooting medium. Foresters have become most familiar with this problem in working with mycorrhizal fungus introductions.

Soil or leaf litter from around nodulated plants may serve as an adequate inoculum for seedlings planted in soil mixes in the nursery. Ground up nodules from field collections or nodulated plants in the plantation area are more likely to be effective.

Unfortunately, we still do not know whether a single *Frankia* strain from *Casuarina* will infect all species or whether there may be more than one strain (Allen & Allen, 1965). Coyne (1973) has suggested that there may be more than one type of *Frankia,* specific to different *Casuarina* host species. This question can only be resolved when an infective *Frankia* isolate is available in pure culture.

In nursery practice, as in the laboratory, successful inoculation of seedlings and nodulation in container-grown plants depends upon sustaining the seedlings in a healthy condition by providing combined N to the seedling until the nodules are actively fixing and can satisfy the N requirements of the plant. One must provide fixed N at low levels for plant maintenance, but not at levels or in forms inhibitory to nodulation. From the earlier discussions one can conclude that a container mix supplemented with ammonium N at rates not in excess of 100 ppm N should meet these needs. Nitrate N should be avoided in the soil mix. It might be possible to provide seedlings with a foliar spray of urea to sustain seedling growth while nodulation proceeds in inoculated soil mix.

Once seedlings are planted out, they depend upon adequate water supply. Plant height, weight of shoots and roots, and number, size, weight and N content of nodules are all affected by water shortage (Kant & Narayana, 1978).

DISTRIBUTION OF *CASUARINA* AND ITS ENDOPHYTE

Casuarina species are widespread throughout the tropics and subtropics, wherever they have been taken by man beyond their origins in Australia. They have adapted to many ecological sites in many countries. Most evidence from laboratory research indicates that the actinomycete is not transmitted with the seed —either within the seed or on its surface. Rather, *Frankia* is transported in nodule material or in the soil in a form that we do not yet certainly know.

The presumption, based on structural evidence, is that spores are the most resistant form and presumably can survive in a desiccated state for long periods and/or distances. The interesting question is how the micro-organism reached the many distant lands where nodulated *Casuarina* now occurs. One can find no reports in the older accounts suggesting that soil samples or nodules should accompany seeds for successful establishment. It is possible that *Frankia* spores can be circulated by the winds. This explanation seems a reasonable one for situations such as the Puna volcanic site in Hawaii, where existing stands of nodulated *Casuarina* plants are only a relatively short distance away. Greater distances are the source of great difficulties and puzzles.

In recent travels in New Zealand it was interesting to study the occurrence of *Casuarina* in planted sites or in forestry nurseries on the North and South Islands, where mild winter minimum temperatures allow *Casuarina* to survive as far south as Dunedin (at least in protected sites). Samples of *Casuarina* roots were made at various locations, and in some cases, excavations of whole root systems (in nursery plantations) were made. Several different species of *Casuarina* were examined including *C. cunninghamiana* and *C. stricta,* but root nodules were never observed! Plants were surviving on combined N available in the nurseries or field soils. Some plants were not very healthy.

Accounts were given of fairly extensive efforts in the North Island of New Zealand to develop *Casuarina* stands as a windbreak or fence rows but experimentation was abandonded as the plants failed to establish successfully. One would assume this failure occurred because the plants did not form nodules and, therefore, could not perform as they do in countries where the endophyte occurs. New Zealand has very strict laws concerning soil and plant material importation and it may be that *Frankia* that would be effective on an imported genus such as *Casuarina* has never reached that country. Examination of root systems of *Elaeagnus* and *Alnus* species at the nursery at Rotorua showed abundant nodulation by those *Frankia* species; so it seems unlikely that soils in New Zealand are deleterious to *Frankia.* New Zealand offers an interesting experimental situation for the careful and systematic introduction of the appropriate *Frankia* strains for use with *Casuarina* plantations. Other reports are scattered through the literature of areas where *Casuarina* occurs but where nodules have not been found or have occurred only sporadically. Bond (1976) quoted reports of studies made in Indonesia showing that of 83 trees of *C. equisetifolia* growing in a latosol soil only three plants were nodulated. Of 72 trees of *C. sumatrana* examined in another location, all were nodulated. Bond (1957a) also noted that specimens of *Casuarina* in botanical gardens in the British Isles seemed to lack nodules, a fact noted by Miehe (1918) in botanic gardens in Germany and also in Italy. These exotic plants were presumably sustained by regular N fertilization. The failure of nodulation suggests the difficulty of transport of *Frankia* by seed and the lack of distribution in soils in the temperate climatic areas.

Casuarina may also show mycorrhizal infection in addition to nodulation by *Frankia* (Dommergues, 1976), but the interaction of *Frankia* and fungus has been little studied. Recently, studies have been initiated by Bamber *et al.* (1980) in Australia. Effective mycorrhizal association may offer another mechanism to assure survival and adequate mineral nutrition.

REFERENCES

Aldrich-Blake, R.N. (1932) On the fixation of atmospheric nitrogen by bacteria living symbiotically in root nodules of *Casuarina equisetifolia. Oxford For. Mem.* 14.

Allen, E.K. & Allen, O.N. (1965) Nonleguminous plant symbiosis. *In:* Microbiology and soil fertility, G.M. Gilmour & O.N. Allen (Eds.). 25th Annual Biological Colloquium, Corvallis, OR, USA. Pp. 77-106.

Bamber, R.K., Mullette, K. & Mackowski, C. (1980) Mycorrhizal studies. *In:* Research report, 1977-1978. Forestry Comm. New South Wales, Sydney, Australia. Pp. 70-72.

Beadle, N.C.W. (1964) Nitrogen economy in arid and semi-arid plant communities. III. The symbiotic nitrogen-fixing organisms. *Proc. Linn. Soc. N.S.W.* 89, 273-286.

Becking, J.H. (1977) Endophyte and association establishment in non-leguminous nitrogen-fixing plants. *In:* Recent developments in nitrogen fixation, W. Newton, J.R. Postgate & C. Rodríguez-Barrueco (Eds.). Academic Press, London, England. Pp. 551-567.

Bond, G. (1956) A feature of the root nodules of *Casuarina. Nature* (Lond.) 177, 191-192.

Bond, G. (1957a) The development and significance of the root nodules of *Casuarina. Ann. Bot.* (Lond.) N.S. 21, 373-380.

Bond, G. (1957b) Isotopic studies of nitrogen fixation in nonlegume root nodules. *Ann. Bot.* (Lond.) N.S. 21, 513-521.

Bond, G. (1960) Inhibition of nitrogen fixation in non-legume root nodules by hydrogen and carbon monoxide. *J. Expl. Bot.* 11, 91-97.

Bond, G. (1961) The oxygen relation of nitrogen fixation in root nodules. *Zeitschr. Allg. Mikrobiologie* 1, 93-99.

Bond, G. (1976) The results of the IBP survey of root-nodule formation in non-leguminous angiosperms. *In:* Symbiotic nitrogen fixation in plants, P.S. Nutman (Ed.). Cambridge Univ. Press, Cambridge, England. Pp. 443-474.

Bond, G. & Hewitt. E.J. (1962) Cobalt and the fixation of nitrogen by root nodules of *Alnus* and *Casuarina*. *Nature* (Lond.) 195, 94-95.

Bond, G. & Hewitt. E.J. (1967) The significance of copper for nitrogen fixation in nodulated *Alnus* and *Casuarina* plants. *Plant Soil.* 27, 447-449.

Bond, G. & Mackintosh. A.H. (1975) Diurnal changes in nitrogen fixation in the root nodules of *Casuarina*. *Proc. Roy. Soc. Lond.* (Ser. B) 192, 1-12.

Callaham, D., Newcomb, W., Torrey, J.G., & Peterson, R.L. (1979) Root hair infection in actinomycete-induced root nodule initiation in *Casuarina, Myrica,* and *Comptonia*. *Bot. Gaz.* 140 (Suppl.), S1-S9.

Chaudhuri, H. (1931) Recherches sur la bactérie des nodosités radicularies du *Casuarina equisetifolia* (Fort.). *Bull. Soc. Bot. France* 79, 447-452.

Coyne, P.D. (1973) Some aspects of the autecology of *Casuarina,* with particular reference to nitrogen fixation. PhD thesis, Dept. of Forestry, Australian National Univ., Canberra, Australia.

Davenport, H.E. (1960) Haemoglobin in the root nodules of *Casuarina cunninghamiana*. *Nature* (Lond.) 186, 653-654.

Dommergues, Y. (1963) Evaluation du taux de fixation de l'azote dans un sol dunaire reboise en filao (*Casuarina equisetifolia*). *Agrochimica* 7, 335-340.

Dommergues, Y. (1966) La fixation symbiotique de l'azote chez les *Casuarina*. *Ann. Inst. Pasteur,* Paris. 111, 247-258.

Dommergues, Y. (1976) Mycorrhizes et fixation l'azote. *Ann. Edafol. Agrobiologia.* 35, 1039-1056.

Gardner, I.C. (1976) Ultrastructural studies of non-leguminous root nodules. *In:* Symbiotic nitrogen fixation in plants, P.S. Nutman (Ed.). Cambridge Univ. Press, Cambridge, England. Pp. 485-496.

Gauthier, D., Diem. H.G. & Dommergues, Y. (1981) *In vitro* nitrogen fixation by two actinomycete strains isolated from *Casuarina* nodules. *Appl. Environ. Microbiol.* 41, 306-308.

Hannon, N.J. (1956) The status of nitrogen in the Hawkesbury Sandstone soils and their plant communities in the Sydney district. I. The significance and level of nitrogen. *Proc. Linn. Soc. N.S.W.* 81, 119-143.

Hewitt, E.J. & Bond. G. (1961) Molybdenum and the fixation of nitrogen in *Casuarina* and *Alnus* root nodules. *Plant Soil* 14, 159-175.

Hewitt, E.J. & Bond. G. (1966) The cobalt requirement of non-legume root nodule plants. *J. Expl. Bot.* 17, 480-491.

Janse, J.M. (1897) Les endophytes radicaux de quelques plantes Javanaises. *Ann. Jard. Bot. Buitenzorg* 14, 53-201.

Kamerling, Z. (1915) Overhet voorkomen van Wortelknolletjes bij *Casuarina equisetifolia. Naturk. Tijdschr. Nederl. Indië.* 71, 73-75.

Kant, S. & Narayana, H.S. (1977) Preliminary studies on the development and structure of root nodules in *Casuarina equisetifolia* L. *Proc. Indian. Acad. Sci.* 85, 34-41.

Kant, S. & Narayana, H.S. (1978) Effect of water stress on growth, nodulation and nitrogen fixation in *Casuarina equisetifolia. Ann. Arid Zone.* 17, 216-221.

Lalonde, M. (1979) Techniques and observations of the nitrogen-fixing *Alnus* root nodule symbiosis. *In:* Recent advances in biological fixation, N.S. Subba Rao (Ed.). Oxford and IBH Publ. Co., New Delhi, India. Pp. 421-434.

McLuckie, J. (1923) Studies in symbiosis. IV. The root-nodules of *Casuarina cunninghamiana* and their physiological significance. *Proc. Linn. Soc. N.S.W.* xlviii, 194-205.

Miehe, H. (1918) Anatomische Untersuchung der Pilz-symbiose bei *Casuarina equisetifolia. Flora* 111/112, 431-449.

Mowry, H. (1933) Symbiotic nitrogen fixation in the genus *Casuarina. Soil Sci.* 36, 409-426.

Narashimhan, M J. (1918) A preliminary study of root nodules of *Casuarina. Ind. Forest.* 44, 265-268.

Newcomb, W., Pankhurst, C.E. & Torrey. J.G. (1981) *Casuarina montana, Coriaria arborea, Discaria toumaton* and *Dryas drummondii.* Abstract, IV Internat. Symp. N_2 Fixation, Canberra, Australia.

Parker, R.N. (1932) *Casuarina* root-nodules. *Ind. Forest.* 58, 362-364.

Rao, K.A. (1923) *Casuarina* root nodules and nitrogen fixation. (Preliminary contribution). *Yearbook Madras Agric. Dept.* 1923, 60-67.

Rodríguez-Barrueco, C. (1972) Effect of ammonium nitrogen on the fixation of atmospheric nitrogen by *Casuarina* nodules. *An. Edafol. Agrbiol.* 31, 905-916.

Rodríguez-Barrueco, C. (1973/74) Nitrogen-fixing ability of nodules of *Casuarina torulosa* L. *Agrochimica* 18, 119-27.

Rodriguez-Barrueco, C., Mackintosh, A.H. & Bond, G. (1970) Some effects of combined nitrogen on the nodule symbioses of *Casuarina* and *Ceanothus. Plant Soil* 33, 129-139.

Shibata, K. & Tahara, M. (1917) Studien über die Wurzelknollchen. *Bot. Mag.* (Tokyo) 31, 157-182.

Silver, W.S., Bendana, F.E. & Powell, R.D. (1966) Root nodule symbiosis. II. The relation of auxin to root geotropism in root and root nodules of non-legumes. *Physiol. Plant.* 19, 207-218.

Silvester, W.B. (1976) Ecological and economic significance of the non-legume symbioses. *In:* Proc. lst Internat. Symp. Nitrogen Fixation, W.E. Newton & C.J. Nyman (Eds.). Wash. State Univ. Press, Pullman, WA, USA. Pp. 489-506.

Silvester, W.B. (1977) Dinitrogen fixation by plant associations excluding legumes. *In:* A treatise on dinitrogen fixation, IV. Agronomy and ecology. R.W.F. Hardy & A.H. Gibson (Eds.). Wiley, New York, NY, USA. Pp. 141-190.

Stewart, W.D.P. (1963) The effect of combined nitrogen on growth and nodule development of *Myrica* and *Casuarina. Zeitschr. Allg. Microbiol.* 3, 152-156.

Tjepkema, J.D., Ormerod, W. & Torrey, J.G. (1980) On vesicle formation and *in vitro* acetylene-reduction by *Frankia. Nature* (Lond.). 287, 633-635.

Tjepkema, J.D., Ormerod, W. & Torrey, J.G. (1981) Factors affecting vesicle formation and acetylene reduction (nitrogenase activity) in *Frankia* sp. *Can. J. Microbiol.* 27, 815-823.

Torrey, J.G. (1976) Initiation and development of root nodules of *Casuarina* (Casuarinaceae). *Amer. J. Bot.* 63, 335-344.

Torrey, J.G. (1978) Nitrogen fixation by actinomycete-nodulated angiosperms. *Bio Science* 28, 586-592.

Tyson, J.H. & Silver, W.S. (1979) Relationship of ultrastructure to acetylene reduction (N_2 fixation) in root nodules of *Casuarina. Bot. Gaz.* 140 (Suppl.), S44-S48.

Uemura, S. (1961) Studies on the *Streptomyces* isolated from alder root nodules (*Alnus* spp.): Studies on the root nodules of Alder (*Alnus* spp.). VI. About the morphological and physiological properties of *Streptomyces* usually isolated from alder and some other non-leguminous root nodules (*Myrica rubra, Elaeagnus umbellata* and *Casuarina equisetifolia*). *Sci. Rep. Agr.* (Japan, For. and Fish Res. Counc). Vol. 7. 90 pp.

Uemura, S. (1964) Isolation and properties of micro-organisms from root nodules of non-leguminous plants. (A review with extensive bibliography.) Govt. For. Exp. Sta., Tokyo, Japan, *Bulletin* 167, 59-91.

Waughman, G.J. (1977) The effect of temperature on nitrogenase activity. *J. Expl. Bot.* 28, 949-960.

SESBANIA ROSTRATA AS A GREEN MANURE FOR RICE IN WEST AFRICA

G. Rinaudo, B. Dreyfus and Y. Dommergues[1]

Summary

We compared the effect of four treatments upon the yield and nitrogen (N) content of rice grown in 1 m^2 irrigated microplots: PK fertilization + inoculated *Sesbania rostrata* plowed in as green manure; PK fertilization + uninoculated *Sesbania rostrata* plowed in as green manure; PK fertilization + ammonium sulphate (60 kg N/ha); and PK fertilization alone (control). The effects of the first two treatments were not significantly different from each other. Both treatments dramatically increased grain and straw yield compared to the control and significantly increased the N content of both grain and straw.

INTRODUCTION

Nitrogen (N) inputs into rice fields can be increased by the cultivation of a green manure crop in rotation with, or intercropped with, the rice. This has already been done with winter vetch in California, and with *Astragalus sinicus* and the N_2-fixing nonlegume *Coriaria sinica* in Japan, Korea, and China (Watanabe & App, 1979; I. Watanabe, personal communication), as well as with *Sesbania cannabina* and *S. paludosa* in Vietnam and other Asian countries (D.T. Tuan, personal communication).

Recently Dreyfus & Dommergues (1981a) reported that *Sesbania rostrata,* a tropical legume colonizing waterlogged soils in the Senegal Valley, forms N_2-fixing nodules with *Rhizobium* on both the roots and the stem. Due to its profuse stem nodulation, this plant has five to ten times more nodules than most nodulated crop plants. Moreover, and because of its stem nodulation, *S. rostrata* could fix N_2 even when the N content of the nutrient medium was high (Dreyfus & Dommergues, 1980).

---

[1] ORSTOM/CNRS BP 1386 Dakar, Senegal.

This paper reports an experiment to determine the effect of *S. rostrata* as a green manure on yield and N uptake of rice.

MATERIALS AND METHODS

The experiments were carried out on microplots, each 1 m^2 (see Figure 1), during the rainy season at the ORSTOM Bel-Air Station in Dakar, Senegal. Soil characteristics are shown in Table 1. Twelve microplots were sown with *Sesbania rostrata* (seeds had been pre-treated in H_2SO_4 for 30 min.) on June 19, 1980; then later thinned to only 40 seedlings per microplot. All seedlings were treated with an insecticide, Curacron (Ciba-Geigy S.A.), to avoid insect attacks.

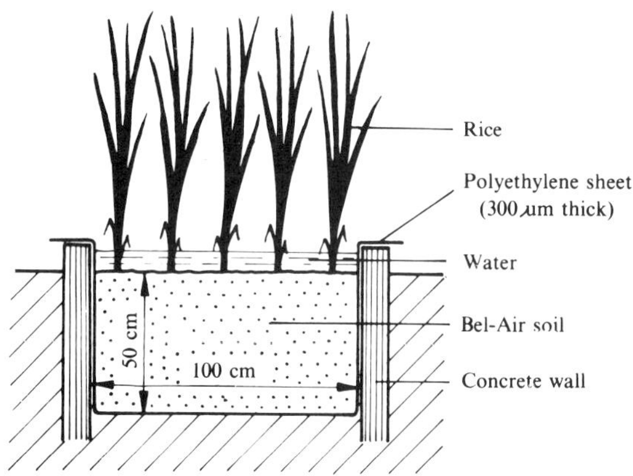

Figure 1: Section of a microplot. Each plot contained 560 kg homogenized Bel-Air soil.

Plants in 6 of the 12 microplots were inoculated by spraying the stems with a 2-day-old culture of the ORS 551 strain (Dreyfus & Dommergues, 1981b) on July 10 and 19. The remaining plots were not inoculated, but progressively developed stem nodules, indicating either native soil rhizobia or cross-contamination. A further 12 microplots were kept in bare fallow. All microplots were kept waterlogged until August 4.

On August 11, when the *Sesbania rostrata* plants were about 1.5 m tall, their stems were cut just above the soil; then chopped in 10 cm pieces and incorporated in the 0-30 cm horizon. All the plots were unirrigated until August 30, when 2-week-old rice (*Oryza sativa*) seedlings cv. Moroberekan were planted, with 25 hills per microplot. All microplots were then broadcast fertilized with K_2HPO_4, 17.44 g/m^2 and six plots received $(NH_4)_2SO_4$, 28.32 g/m^2. At this stage all the plots were waterlogged again. The rice was

TABLE 1: Characteristics of Bel-Air soil.[1]

pH (KCl, N)	7.0
Total C	0.4
Total N	0.025
Total P	0.037
Clay (0-2 µm)	3.8
Loam (2-50 µm)	2.1
Fine sand (50-200 µm)	48.4
Coarse sand (200-2000 µm)	44.5

[1]Ustropept.

harvested on December 29-30, when it was 120 days old (excluding the seedling stage in the nursery). The straw and grains were weighed, and the water content determined after drying at 65°C until a constant weight was obtained. N content was estimated using the Kjeldahl method.

RESULTS AND DISCUSSION

Microplots that had received *Sesbania rostrata* green manure yielded more than double the control plots and significantly more than microplots receiving the equivalent of 60 kg N/ha (see Table 2). The effect of stem inoculation was not significant, presumably because of the natural nodulation of uninoculated plants. The N content of the grain and straw of rice plants green manured with *S. rostrata* was significantly higher than that of control or +N plots. Thus, green manured rice contained four times the total N of control plots supplied only K_2HPO_4, and twice that of plots receiving 60 kg N/ha equivalent.

If we assume that an extrapolation to the field of the data reported here is valid, we can conclude that the use of *Sesbania rostrata* as green manure would allow us to obtain yields of rice grain as high as 6.0 t/ha in a soil with a lower-than-average fertility. However, more investigations are needed, especially in the field, to determine the best management practices, especially the timing for seeding and for plowing in *Sesbania rostrata* stems; the delay between plowing in *Sesbania rostrata* stems and rice planting; and the economic feasibility at the farmer's level.

Soil analyses are underway. These should allow us to establish a precise nitrogen balance, which will probably generate other useful information on the effect of *Sesbania rostrata* green manure on the soil nitrogen status in rice fields.

TABLE 2: Influence of *Sesbania rostrata* green manure on the yield and total N content of rice.[1]

Plot numbers	Treatments	Average dry yield (g/m^2)		N content (%)		Average N yield ($g N/m^2$)		
		Grain	Straw	Grain	Straw	Grain	Straw	Total
1 to 6	PK + green manure, inoculated	596 a	772 a	1.80 a	0.94 a	10.73 a	7.44 a	18.17
7 to 12	PK + green manure, uninoculated	571 a	762 a	1.73 a	0.98 a	9.90 a	6.92 a	16.82
13 to 18	PK + $(NH_4)_2SO_4$ (60 kg N/ha)	381 b	484 b	1.27 b	0.49 b	4.83 b	2.38 b	7.21
18 to 24	PK (control)	212 c	276 c	1.14 b	0.58 b	2.42 c	1.60 c	4.02

[1]Figures followed by the same letter do not significantly differ, P = 0.01.

REFERENCES

Dreyfus, B.L. & Dommergues, Y.R. (1980) C.R. Acad. Sci. Paris, D. 291, 767-770.

Dreyfus, B.L. & Dommergues, Y.R. (1981a) Stem nodules on the tropical legume, *Sesbania rostrata*. *In:* Current perspectives in nitrogen fixation, A.H. Gibson & W.E. Newton (Eds.). Australian Academy of Science, Canberra, Australia. P. 471.

Dreyfus, B.L. & Dommergues, Y.R. (1981b) *FEMS Letters* 10, 313-317.

Watanabe, I. & App, A. (1979) Research needs for management of nitrogen fixation in flooded rice crop systems. *In:* Nitrogen and rice. IRRI, Los Baños, Philippines. Pp. 485-490.

NITROGEN FIXATION BY TROPICAL WOODY LEGUMES: POTENTIAL SOURCE OF SOIL ENRICHMENT

J.P. Roskoski, J. Montano, C. van Kessel and G. Castilleja[1]

Summary

The urgent need for low-technology solutions to the problems of forage, firewood, and fertilizer scarcity in the tropics prompted a study to determine the multi-use potential of woody legumes in the State of Veracruz, Mexico. As part of this study, the nitrogen-fixing (C_2H_2-reducing) capacity of nine legume species was assessed: *Acacia pennatula, Albizia lebbek, Inga jinicuil, Pithecellobium lanceolatum, Caesalpinia cacalaco, Cassia fistula, Parkinsonia aculeata, Erythrina americana*, and *Gliricidia sepium*. All species save *C. cacalaco, C. fistula*, and *P. aculeata* fixed nitrogen (N_2) with rates from 2 to 18 μ moles N_2 fixed/g nodules per hour.

Nodule biomass and *in situ* N_2-fixing activity were then measured in stands of *I. jinicuil, A. pennatula*, and *G. sepium*, and approximate annual N_2 (C_2H_2) fixation by these species calculated. *I. jinicuil* is a common shade tree for coffee in Veracruz. In one coffee plantation, N_2 fixation by this species, about 35 kg N_2/ha per yr, approximated annual N inputs from fertilizers. Calculated fixation in 20-year-old stands of *A. pennatula* and *G. sepium* was estimated to be 34 and 13 kg N_2/ha per yr, respectively. These results suggest that N_2 fixation by tree legumes could make a significant N input to tropical agro-ecosystems.

INTRODUCTION

Insufficient forage for livestock (Quintero & Powers, 1976), lack of firewood for man (Villa-Sales, 1978), and diminishing soil fertility for agricultural production are problems common to Mexico and to most developing tropical nations (Myers, 1980). Technological solutions to these problems exist but are beyond the economic means of those most severely affected. Low-cost, low-energy-intensive alternatives are urgently needed.

[1] Instituto Nacional de Investigaciones sobre Recursos Bioticos, Apartado Postal 63, Xalapa, Veracruz, Mexico.

Woody legumes abound in Mexico and are utilized by rural populations as "living fences" (Sauer, 1979), shade for crops, and food for man and/or animals (Roskoski *et al.*, 1980). These facts suggested that some species could be used more widely and so help in resolving the forage, firewood, and fertilizer problems referred to above.

In 1979, studies were initiated to determine the multi-use potential of nine of the more than 250 species of woody legumes found in the State of Veracruz, Mexico. The species selected were: *Acacia pennatula* Schl. & Cham., *Albizia lebbek* L., *Inga jinicuil* Schl., *Pithecellobium lanceolatum* Humb. & Bonpl., *Caesalpinia cacalaco* Humb. & Bonpl., *Cassia fistula* L., *Parkinsonia aculeata* L., *Erythrina americana* Miller, and *Gliricidia sepium* Jacq. The species were chosen because they had at least one known use in Veracruz or other tropical areas (see Table 1).

While nitrogen (N_2) fixation by tree legumes could be an important factor in the N economy of tropical agro-ecosystems, most studies involving tree species have dealt with cross-inoculation reactions (Allen & Allen, 1936; Trinick, 1968; Habish & Khairi, 1970; Basak & Goyal, 1975) or reports of nodulation and N_2 fixation by previously untested species (McNeil & Carpenter, 1974; Bailey, 1976; Nakos, 1977; Tanwar, 1980). Ecological studies are exceedingly rare (Habish, 1970; Sheikh, 1978), and in general, have not sought to quantify fixation or assess the importance of this N input to the ecosystem.

This study, undertaken as part of the woody legume project, was to determine the potential for N_2 fixation of the nine test legumes under the soil

TABLE 1: Uses of nine species of tree legumes.[1]

Species	Food[2]	Forage	Firewood	Living fence	Green manure	Shade trees
Acacia pennatula		A	AB	A		A
Albizia lebbek		B	B		B	
Caesalpinia cacalaco	2 A			A		
Cassia fistula		B				
Erythrina americana	1 AB			A	B	AB
Gliricidia sepium	1 A	B		AB		
Inga jinicuil	3 A		A			A
Parkinsonia aculeata		B	AB	A		
Pithecellobium lanceolatum		A	A	A		

[1]A, in the State of Veracruz; B, in other tropical areas.
[2]Part consumed by man: 1 = flowers, 2 = green pods, 3 = succulent aril.

and climatic conditions existent in Veracruz, and to quantify annual fixation by these species.

CAPACITY FOR N_2 FIXATION

Given the difficulty of finding nodules on adult trees *in situ*, pot experiment were used to establish the levels of N_2 fixation for the nine species. Individual, uninoculated seeds of each species were planted in separate plastic bags containing either a coastal sandy loam or a volcanic ash-derived, clay soil from 1400 meters elevation. Half the bags were placed at sea level in the Institute field station, the remainder at 1400 meters in the Institute botanical garden. After seven months, the seedling in each bag was harvested and examined for the presence of nodules. When found, nodules from each plant were removed and assayed for N_2 fixation using the acetylene reduction technique.

The six species that fixed N_2 were: *A. pennatula*, *A. lebbek*, *G. sepium*, *I. jinicuil*, and *P. lanceolatum* (see Table 2). The three species from the sub-family Caesalpinioideae: *C. cacalaco*, *C. fistula*, and *P. aculeata* did not form nodules in any experimental treatment.

TABLE 2: Presence of N_2 fixation in nine species of tree legume.[1]

Species	Experimental Treatment[2]			F-test[3]
	Sandy soil Sea level	Clay soil Sea level	Clay soil 1400 m.	
G. sepium	<u>2.33</u>	18.40	8.57	.01
A. pennatula	4.79	6.55	<u>9.40</u>	.05
E. americana	5.58	6.41	<u>2.81</u>	NS
A. lebbek	not tested	4.25	2.91	NS
P. lanceolatum	<u>6.21</u>	not tested	not tested	
I. jinicuil	not tested	died	<u>7.04</u>	
C. fistula	not tested	no nodules	no nodules	
C. cacalaco	not tested	no nodules	no nodules	
P. aculeata	not tested	no nodules	no nodules	

[1] μ mol C_2H_4 produced/g nodules per h, underlined value indicates native soil and climate.
[2] Sea level, mean annual temperature 24°C, annual rainfall 1350mm.
1400 m, mean annual temperature 19°C, annual rainfall 1957mm.
Sandy soil, pH = 8.1, total N = .14 % , ppm P = 9.2.
Clay soil, pH = 5.5, total N = .33 % , ppm P = 29.0.
[3] F-test, values indicate significance level. NS, not significant.

No treatment differences in rates of N_2 fixation were found with either *E. americana* or *A. lebbek* (see Table 2). However, rates for *A. pennatula* and *G. sepium* did differ between treatments. *G. sepium* exhibited the highest level of activity when grown at sea level, where it normally occurs, but in bags containing the clay soil from 1400 meters elevation, and the lowest level of activity when grown both in its native soil and climate. *A. pennatula*, on the other hand, exhibited greatest N_2 (C_2H_2) fixation under its native soil and climate conditions, even though overall plant growth for this species was considerably greater in both sea level treatments.

RATES OF N_2 FIXATION

Although the seedling experiment established that six of the nine test species could fix N_2, the amount of N_2 fixed under field conditions remained to be determined. In a subsequent study, nodule biomass and *in situ* N_2-fixing activity were measured in stands of *A. pennatula*, *G. sepium*, and *I. jinicuil*. These data were used to estimate aerial fixation on an annual basis.

Acacia pennatula most commonly occurs as isolated individuals and *G. sepium* is usually found in living fences. Attempting to quantify nodule biomass in either system presents serious sampling problems. Fortunately, pure stands of these species are occasionally found in abandoned pastures or agricultural fields. Two such stands, one for each species, were located and sampled for nodule biomass. Soil cores, 25x25x15 cm, were randomly collected in each area. Nodules were separated from the soil, subsamples chosen for N_2 (C_2H_2) fixation assay, and the remaining nodules weighed fresh and after drying at 80° C for 48 hours. Nodule biomass for *I. jinicuil* was obtained in a commercial coffee plantation, which employs this species as a shade tree.

TABLE 3: N_2 fixation by three species of tree legumes.

Species	Trees/ha	Nodule weight (kg/ha)	SNA[1]	N_2 fixed[2] (kg/ha·yr)
A. pennatula	7200	6.8	20.54	34.26
G. sepium	2700	4.5	11.72	12.94
I. jinicuil	2.5	70.6	2.03	35.18

[1] SNA = μ mol C_2H_4 produced/g nodule weight per h.
[2] Assumes a 3:1 C_2H_2: N_2 ratio as suggested by Hardy *et al.* (1968).

Estimates of N_2 fixation, based on nodule mass and rates of N_2 (C_2H_2) fixation obtained from the preceeding study, or in the case of *I. jinicuil* from an experiment on yearly pattern of N_2 (C_2H_2) fixation, were calculated for the three species. While these estimates should be regarded as approximations, both *A. pennatula* and *I. jinicuil* fixed about 35 kg N/ha per yr, while *G. sepium* fixed 13 kg N/ha per yr (see Table 3). While the sites used in the studies on *A. pennatula* and *G. sepium* were not typical of the agricultural systems in which these species occur normally, the data for *I. jinicuil* is relevant to the N economy of coffee plantations in this region.

From 1976 through 1980, the site of the I. *jinicuil* study received between 45 and 157 kg N fertilizer/ha per yr. N_2 fixation could, therefore, be an important source of N to this system.

Although the bulk of the N_2 fixed by *I. jinicuil* is initially incorporated in its own biomass, much of the N_2 fixed undoubtedly becomes available to coffee trees and herbs following litter fall and decomposition. Interestingly, the area of the plantation with *I. jinicuil* also had higher coffee yields than adjacent areas with other shade trees (Jimenez & Martinez, 1979). However, whether the higher coffee production in the *I. jinicuil* site is wholly or even partly due to added fixed N_2 has yet to be determined.

DISTRIBUTION AND SEASONAL ACTIVITY OF *I. JINICUIL* NODULES

The magnitude of N_2 fixation by *I. jinicuil* and its potential importance to the coffee ecosystem justified further studies with this species.

Thus, it was found that *I. jinicuil* nodules were not randomly distributed throughout the soil but were concentrated around the trunks of coffee trees and within or just below the litter layer (Roskoski, 1981). This unusual distribution pattern could reflect fertilization practices employed in the plantation.

Prior to the rainy season in June, the leaf litter around coffee plants is scraped aside and N-P-K fertilizer applied at the base of the plants. Results show that as the distance from the coffee trunk increases, nodule biomass (Roskoski, 1981) and the P and N content of the soil decrease (van Kessel & Roskoski, 1981; see Table 4). Apparently, the stimulatory effect of P on nodule development and function overrides possible inhibitory effects from the combined N. Additional sampling in six other coffee plantations with *I. jinicuil* shade trees gave similar results (van Kessel & Roskoski, 1981).

To determine the yearly pattern of N_2 (C_2H_2) fixation by *I. jinicuil*, monthly nodule assays were made from March 1979 until October 1980, with nodule samples randomly collected every three hours up to 33 hours and

TABLE 4: Nodule biomass, distribution and soil chemistry.

Distance from coffee trunk (cm.)	Nodules (g/m^2)	Total N (%)	P (ppm)	pH
0-30	86.50	.32	64	4.1
30-60	15.74	.30	54	5.2
60-90	6.77	.24	44	5.8

assayed for N_2-fixing activity. Daily activity patterns from month to month were highly variable, but highest rates of activity were generally found at dawn and dusk, and lowest rates at 10:00 AM and 11:00 PM.

Flowering and leaf fall in *I. jinicuil* occur during the spring dry season from March through May (Jiménez & Martinez, 1979). After flowering in May 1979 and April 1980, N_2-fixing activity declined, perhaps as a result of the decrease in photosynthetic area (see Figure 1). As pods developed, during June and July, N_2-fixing activity increased, reaching a yearly maximum in July. Pods dropped in August with a subsequent decrease in activity. During the fall dry season (September-December) soil moisture levels dropped (E. Jiménez, personal communication), *I. jinicuil* again shed its leaves, and N_2 fixation declined. By January the *I. jinicuil* canopy was again fully occupied and nodular activity increased. This increase continued until the onset of the next dry season in March.

Since *I. jinicuil* is not a truly deciduous species, leaf fall and replacement are gradual processes occurring over several months. The continual presence of some photosynthetic area on the trees may explain why nodule activity persisted throughout the year. However, the largest number of young, white

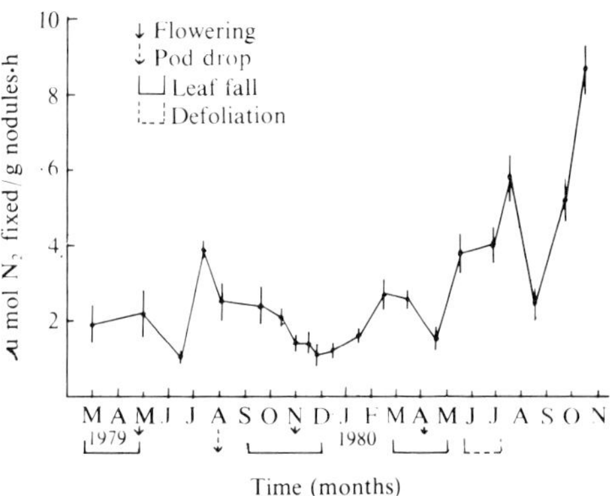

Figure 1.
Variation in specific nodule activity over time of *I. jinicuil* nodules taken from shade plants in a commercial coffee plantation.

nodules with pink centers was observed during the months of June and July. It was also during these months that white tips were seen on large, branched nodules, the size of which suggested that they were perennial structures.

Until September, the pattern for 1980 was similar to that for 1979. However, no pods were formed in 1980; insects defoliated the trees in June and July, and this apparently caused the abscission of immature fruits.

Following the defoliation, new leaf production began in September, at a time when *I. jinicuil* leaves are normally beginning to fall. Rates of N_2 fixation, rather than decreasing during this period, as occurred in 1979, dramatically increased, achieving the highest monthly values observed to date. It seems logical to assume that the severe physiological stress of defoliation not only caused the atypical production of leaves in the fall, but also indirectly led to the marked increase in N_2-fixing activity.

CONCLUSIONS

N_2 fixation was established for six species of tree legumes, most of which are presently used by farmers in Veracruz, Mexico, as integral parts of cropping systems. Rates of N_2 (C_2H_2) fixation for seedlings of these species differed depending on the soil type, and to a lesser extent, on the climate in which they were grown. Estimates of annual fixation for three of the species suggest that N inputs from fixation by tree legumes in tropical agro-ecosystems can be significant. Furthermore, the amount of N_2 fixed in these systems is apparently influenced by, and possibly amenable to, manipulation through simple management techniques; for example, phosphorus additions.

Leguminous trees, being long-lived organisms, undoubtedly exhibit changes in their capacity to fix N_2 as a function of age. In addition, there are daily and yearly changes as discussed here for one species. Therefore, obtaining realistic estimates for fixation by tree legumes will require studies of longer duration than are generally needed for their herbaceous relatives.

Once established, a tree legume should require minimal maintenance, and provide benefits aside from N_2 fixation. These include forage for cattle, firewood, erosion control, aesthetic benefits, and improvement of the enviroment. However, more field tests, physiological studies, and genetic improvements will be required before the full potential of tree legumes can be appreciated or realized.

REFERENCES

Allen, O.N. & Allen. E.K. (1936) *Soil Sci.* 42, 61-73.

Bailey, A.W. (1976) *J. Range Mgt.* 29, 479-481.

Basak, M.K. & Goyal. S.K. (1975) *Ann. Arid Zone* 14, 367-370.

H_2SO_4-scarified seeds of *Leucaena leucocephala* were planted. The *Rhizobium* strains used were SMS-436 (syn NGR 8), SMS-448, SMS-459 (syn CIAT 1923) and SMS-461 (syn CIAT 1967), applied after germination. Five replicates of each treatment were used with the pots randomized in the glasshouse.

Plants were harvested after 104 days, and the shoots separated, dried, weighed, and analyzed for N, as recommended by Bataglia *et al.* (1978). Nodules were also separated, dried and weighed.

RESULTS AND DISCUSSION

Soils limed with 1.0 or 1.8 g of dolomitic limestone/kg of soil were of similar pH and supported similar nodulation and growth of *Leucaena leucocephala.*

Three of the four strains tested induced a significant increase in plant dry weight; only SMS-459 failed to promote plant development (see Table 1). Nodule dry weight and shoot N were also enhanced by inoculation, but shoot N levels were not significantly different from those of uninoculated control plants.

The absence of nodules on uninoculated plants suggests again that *Leucaena* has specific *Rhizobium* requirements, and will benefit from inoculation under appropriate conditions.

TABLE 1: Dry matter, shoot N, and dry weight of nodules on *Leucaena* not inoculated, or inoculated separately with four rhizobia strains.[1]

Rhizobium strain	Shoot dry weight (g)	Nodule dry weight (mg)	Shoot N (mg)
SMS – 461	11.67 a	497.1 a	300.6 a
SMS – 436	10.72 a	729.8 a	289.5 a
SMS – 448	9.61 a	607.6 a	228.9 a
SMS – 459	6.60 b	337.8 a	146.2 a
Without inoculation	5.95 b	–	102.6 a

[1]Averages of five replications for the two liming rates per inoculation treatment.

REFERENCES

Bataglia, O.C., Teixera J.P.F., Furlani, J.P.F., & Furlani, A.M.C. (1978) Inst. Agronomico (Campinas) *Bulletin* No. 87, 31 pp.

National Academy of Science (US) (1977) *Leucaena*, promising forage and tree crop for the tropics. NAS. Washington, D.C., USA. 115p.

Norris, D.O. (1973) *Aust. J. Expl. Agric. Anim. Husb.* 13, 98-101.

ASSOCIATIVE N_2 FIXATION

FIELD INOCULATION OF GRASSES WITH *AZOSPIRILLUM*

Y. Okon[1]

Summary

Inoculation with *Azospirillum* clearly benefited the growth and commercial yield of *Zea mays, Sorghum bicolor, Setaria italica, Panicum miliaceum* and *Triticum* spp., grown under different environmental and soil conditions, at different levels of combined nitrogen (N), and in irrigated and unirrigated plots of commercial size. In one trial maize plants grown on inoculated plots contained up to 77.1 kg/ha more N than plants that were not inoculated.

INTRODUCTION

The isolation of *Azospirillum* sp. from the root system of the grass *Digitaria* (Döbereiner & Day, 1976) stirred wide interest in grass/bacteria associations and their potential to fix atmospheric nitrogen (N_2). Initial studies of the association used detached, pre-incubated roots (von Bülow & Döbereiner, 1975; Döbereiner & Day, 1976), and probably overestimated the rates of N_2 fixation obtainable *in situ* (van Berkum & Bohlool, 1980). Much lower activities have generally been reported in intact systems or in soil cores containing roots (van Berkum & Bohlool, 1980). Inoculation experiments carried out subsequently have given variable results with increases in plant dry weight, high acetylene reduction values, or ^{15}N uptake reported by some (De-Polli *et al.,* 1977; Neyra & Döbereiner, 1977; Bouton *et al.,* 1979; Rennie, 1980; Albrecht *et al.,* 1981) but not all (Barber *et al.,* 1976) workers. At the field level, early studies (Smith *et al.,* 1976; Taylor, 1979) showed that *Azospirillum* inoculation enhanced plant dry weight in *Panicum* and *Pennisetum* in soils fertilized with intermediate levels of N, but no increases in total N yield were demonstrated.

In Israel, increases in plant dry weight and total N have been obtained following the inoculation, in the greenhouse, of *Setaria*, maize, and other

[1] Dept. Plant Pathology and Microbiology, Faculty of Agriculture, Hebrew University of Jerusalem, Rehovot, Israel.

grasses (Cohen *et al.*, 1980; Nur, Okon & Henis, 1980a; 1980b; Kapulnik *et al.*, 1981a; 1981b; 1981c). The present paper extends these experiments to the field situation. It covers work undertaken in commercial fields in Israel from 1978-1980, under diverse soil and environmental conditions.

MATERIALS AND METHODS

Inoculant production

Azospirillum brasilense strain cd (Tarrand *et al.*, 1978) and a local strain, cd-1 (Nur *et al.*, 1980b), were used in the inoculation experiments. The bacteria were grown in a synthetic liquid medium, containing malate and supplemented with 0.05% NH_4Cl (Okon *et al.*, 1977) in a shaking bath at 33° C. The cell suspension was mixed with finely sieved sterile peat, which had been adjusted to pH 6.8 with $CaCO_3$, to give a final concentration of 10^8-10^9 cells/g, after which inoculant was stored in sealed polyethylene bags at room temperature. *Azospirillum* survived well in peat, giving counts of 10^7-10^8 viable cells/g after six months' storage.

Plant species tested

The cultivars tested in these experiments included four cultivars of *Zea mays* (cv. Jubilee, sweet corn from the Rogers Co., USA; cv. Rinat, sweet corn; cv. Hazera-nanasi, forage corn; and cv. Hazera 851, for corn meal), *Sorghum bicolor* (cvs. Hazera 226, and 6078), *Setaria italica, Panicum miliaceum, Triticum aestivum* (cvs. Miriam and Barkai) and *T. turgidum* var. durum cv. Inbar.

Experimental procedures

The 12 experiments reported in this paper were carried out near the Kibbutz Sede Yoav and Kibbutz Beth Kama (Northern Negev, Lachish area) on loess soils of pH 7.8, and near the Kibbutz Sede Eliahu (Jordan Valley, near Bet Shean) on Rendzina soils of pH 7.6-7.9.

The first experiment, carried out near Kibbutz Sede Yoav, followed an irrigated cotton crop. The soil was fertilized with 90 kg/ha P_2O_5, and four levels of N (0, 60, 120 and 240 kg/ha) applied, using liquid ammonia injected to a depth of 15 cm. The field was sown with sweet corn cv. Jubilee, leaving 1 meter between rows, and a final stand of 70,000 plant/ha. Total rainfall before sowing was 370 mm and total irrigation 360 mm water. The experiment was carried out in split plots in randomized blocks, with five replicates. Each N-treatment plot was 180 m² and each subplot 60 m², with 60 m² as guard area. Inoculation was carried out two weeks after emergence by applying a 1:1 mixture of *A. brasilense* strains cd and cd-1 near the plant row at the rate of

100 g inoculant/100m^2. The harvest area was 6 m^2/plot. The experiment was repeated the following year using only the 120 kg N/ha fertilizer level and the cultivars Jubilee and Rinat. A fourth maize experiment on this site used the cultivar Hazera-nanasi for forage following winter wheat. NO_3^- concentration in the soil (0-40 cm) was 68 ppm, and the plants were spaced 1 m between rows to a final density of 10,000 plants/ha. Total sprinkle irrigation was 220 mm water. The experiment was carried out as a randomized block in five replicates with 20 m^2 per treatment. Inoculation, with a peat inoculant mixture of cd and cd-1, was as described previously.

Two experiments with *Sorghum bicolor* were carried out on the Sede Yoav site, following unirrigated wheat. In the first, using cv. Hazera 226 on a soil with 130 ppm NO_3^-, a randomized block design with seven replicates was used. Plots were of 60 m^2 each with a final stand density of 60,000 plants/ha. Three inoculation treatments were used: inoculation with *A. brasilense* strain cd; inoculation with *Azospirillum* spp. strain cd-1; and inoculation with sterile peat. In each case 25 g of peat, moistened with 10% sucrose was applied/kg of seed. The experiment was not irrigated; total rainfall before sowing was 320 mm. A similar experiment was carried out in the summer of 1980 using *S. bicolor* cv. 6078.

The three other experiments carried out on the Sede Yoav site, with *Setaria italica* and *Triticum aestivum* cvs. Miriam and Barkai, used the format already described for sweet corn.

The corn experiment on the Sede Eliahu site (with cv. Hazera 851) used a randomized block design with five replicates of 60 m^2 each. The experiment was carried out on an "organic field" without chemical fertilization or pesticide treatment. It followed a clover crop for green manure and was fertilized with organic manure. NO_3^- concentration at 0-40 cm depth before sowing was 372 ppm. Afterwards, NO_3^- in soil decreased rapidly and, two months after sowing, only 50 ppm NO_3^- could be measured. Total sprinkle irrigation was 440 mm water. Samples for yield measurements were taken randomly from 6 m^2 of each plot.

The response of *Panicum miliaceum* to a mixed strain (cd, cd-1) inoculant was also tested at the Sede Eliahu site. Planting followed a carrot crop, and used a randomized block design with six replicates of 70 m^2. Soil NO_3^- concentration before sowing was 40 ppm. In this trial top weight was calculated from a 2 m^2 plant sample harvested at random and seed yield by harvesting each plot separately with a combine harvester.

Finally, at the Sede Eliahu site, effects of inoculation on *T. turgidum* var. durum cv. Inbar were evaluated using methods similar to the *Zea mays* cv. Jubilee experiment already described.

For all these experiments parameters appropriate to the crop in question were taken, and grain or leaf N determined by the Kjeldahl method of Hiller *et al.* (1948) after drying samples at 80°C for 96 h. Soil NO_3^- determinations followed the method of Bremner (1965).

RESULTS

Results for the different inoculation experiments with *Zea mays* are summarized in Table 1. In each of these trails inoculation with *Azospirillum* increased significantly the yield of maize. In the first trial with 'Jubilee' near Kibbutz Sede Yoav, inoculation enhanced maize yield at all levels of N fertilization tested. This was achieved mainly through greater ear number/plant, with average ear weight little affected. In the experiment with 'H-nanasi' at Sede Yoav, the N yield of inoculated plants exceeded that of uninoculated controls by 77.1 kg N/ha.

Results from the inoculation experiments with *Sorghum bicolor* are shown in Table 2. Again in these experiments there was a significant yield response to inoculation in both grain and forage cultivars, with the apparent N gain following inoculation of the forage sorghum more than 81 kg N/ha.

Positive responses to inoculation were also obtained with *Setaria italica* and *Panicum miliaceum* (see Tables 3 & 4). With *Setaria italica,* however, the apparent N gain following inoculation, while significantly better than that achieved in control plots, was of only 14.72 kg N/ha.

Results from the experiment with *Triticum turgidum* and *T. aestivum* are shown in Table 5. With cv. Miriam, inoculation with *Azospirillum* increased grain yield significantly at 0 and 40 kg N/ha (6.96%, 5.5%, respectively). Inoculation also significantly increased total plant dry weight (14.4%, 13.3%); percent N in leaves (17.7%, 11.2%), and the number of fertile tillers/m^2 (10.7%, 12.4%) (see Table 5). Nonsignificant differences in yield were obtained in inoculated plots fertilized with 80 and 120 kg N/ha. It is interesting to note that yields obtained in inoculated plots fertilized with 40 kg N/ha were not significantly different from those obtained in fully fertilized, uninoculated plots.

DISCUSSION

Inoculation with *Azospirillum* clearly benefited growth and increased the commercial yield of both grain and forage grass crops, grown under different environmental and soil conditions, at different levels of combined N, and in irrigated and unirrigated fields. Both vegetative and reproductive parameters were enhanced by inoculation. Thus, in sorghum there was an increase in fresh and dry weight of tops; in maize, sorghum and *Setaria* grown as forage crops as well as in wheat, there was an increase in the total weight of plants, while in *Setaria* plant height was significantly enhanced in inoculated plots. In maize the number of ears reaching market size, and in sorghum, the number of panicles per plant, the 1000 seed weight, and panicle weight were greater in inoculated than in control treatments.

TABLE 1: Response of cultivars of *Zea mays* to inoculation with *Azospirillum*.

Cultivar	Applied N (kg/ha)	Inoculation	Wt. fresh ears (t/ha)	Ears/ plant	Average ear wt (g)	Plant dry weight (t/ha)	Total N yield (kg/ha)	Average plant wt (g)
Jubilee	0	–	18.6	0.86	309	–	–	–
		+	20.2	0.95	304	–	–	–
	60	–	21.5	1.02	297	–	–	–
		+	23.3	1.05	322	–	–	–
	120	–	24.6	0.96	364	–	–	–
		+	28.0	1.14	353	–	–	–
	240	–	22.9	0.95	337	–	–	–
		+	25.7	1.09	344	–	–	–
Jubilee	120	–	21.4	1.01	402	–	–	–
		+	27.7	1.21	424	–	–	–
Rinat	120	–	13.3	1.00	227	–	–	–
		+	16.6	1.26	221	–	–	–
H-nanasi	0	–	–	–	–	11.93	103.8	–
		+	–	–	–	14.83	180.9	–
H-851	0	–	7.42	–	–	–	–	1.22
		+	8.20	–	–	–	–	1.48

TABLE 2: Response of cultivars of *Sorghum bicolor* to inoculation with *Azospirillum*.

Plant trait	Cultivar			
	H-226 (grain)		6078 (forage)	
	Inoculated	Uninoculated	Inoculated	Uninoculated
Panicle weight (t/ha)	3.89 b[1]	2.88 a	–	–
100 seed weight (g)	31 b	25 a	–	–
% N in seeds	1.67 b	1.52 a	–	–
No. panicles/plant	0.97 b	0.81 a	–	–
Weight/panicle (g)	67.8 b	59.2 a	–	–
Yield of forage (t/ha)	–	–	11.28 b	9.48 a
% N in forage	–	–	1.52 b	0.95 a
N yield (kg/ha)	–	–	171.4 b	90.06 a

[1]Numbers on the same line not followed by the same letter are significantly different at the P = 0.05 level.

TABLE 3: Response of *Setaria italica* (foxtail millet) to inoculation with *Azospirillum*.

Plant trait	Inoculation treatment	
	Control	Inoculated
Plant dry weight	1.4[1]	2.1
Total N yield (kg/ha)	11.48	26.20
Average plant height (cm)	73.5	90.8
Panicle dry weight (g)	248	366
Panicle lenght (cm)	9.9	10.7

[1]For each plant trait the difference between inoculated and uninoculated treatments is significant at the P = 0.05 level.

TABLE 4: Response of *Panicum miliaceum* to inoculation with *Azospirillum*.

Plant trait	Inoculation treatment	
	Control	Inoculated
Plant fresh weight (tons/ha)	10.31[1]	11.68
Seed yield (ton/ha)	2.80	3.17

[1]For each plant trait the difference between inoculated and uninoculated treatments is significantly different at the P = 0.05 level.

TABLE 5: Response of cultivars of *Triticum aestivum* and *T. turgidum* to inoculation with *Azospirillum*.

Cultivar	Applied N (kg/ha)	Inoculation	Grain yield (ton/ha)	% N in grain	Total plant dry weight (ton/ha)	% N in leaf	Fertile tillers/ m^2
Miriam	0	–	3.59	1.35	13.1	0.31	520
		+	3.84	1.41	18.9	0.55	560
	40	–	3.80	1.41	13.6	0.63	530
		+	4.01	1.45	18.1	0.73	655
	80	–	3.92	1.31	16.7	1.38	535
		+	3.99	1.35	17.4	1.75	555
	120	–	4.10	–	–	–	620
		+	3.90	–	–	–	550
Inbar		–	4.22				
		+	4.68				
Barkai		–	4.26				
		+	4.99				

Several interesting points emerge from this series of experiments:

While previous field studies with *Azospirillum* used small plots (Smith *et al.*, 1976; Taylor, 1979) the experiments reported here were carried out on a commercial scale. The increases in yield obtained could be translated into actual profit by farmers.

Unirrigated sorghum is known in Israel as a crop that does not respond to N fertilization. The upper layer of soil is dry after the winter rains, and sorghum roots reach a depth of 1.5 m to find moisture. The benefit of inoculation to this crop was highly significant.

The yields obtained in medium-level, N-fertilized, sweet corn and wheat were comparable to, or higher than, those achieved in fully fertilized, but uninoculated plots. Together with previous results (Smith *et al.,* 1976; Taylor, 1979), this suggests that *Azospirillum* inoculation could be used to save valuable N fertilizer.

Results in Israel suggest that plants can benefit more from inoculation with *Azospirillum* than hitherto believed possible (van Berkum & Bohlool, 1980). The high $CaCO_3$ content and pH (7.5 - 7.9) of Israel soils, together with prevailing high soil temperatures and light intensities, may favor the *Azospirillum* activities in association with grass roots in the field.

We plan to do further work on $^{15}N_2$ fixation and incorporation in plants in the field, and to search for better bacterial strains to be used with responsive grass cultivars, under optimal environmental conditions.

REFERENCES

Albrecht, S.L., Okon, Y., Lonnquist, J., & Burris R.H. (1981) *Crop Sci.* 21, 301-306.

Baldani, V.L.D. & Döbereiner, J. (1980) *Soil Biol. Biochem.* 12, 433-439.

Barber, L.E., Tjepkema, J.D., Russell, S.A., & Evans, H.J. (1976) *Appl. Environ. Microbiol.* 32, 108-113.

Berkum, P. van & Bohlool, B.B. (1980) *Microbiol. Rev.* 44, 491-517.

Bouton, J.H., Smith, R.L., Schank, S.C., Burton, G.W., Tyler, M.E., Little, R.C., Goller, R.N., & Quesenberry, K.H. (1979) *Crop Sci.* 19, 12-16.

Bremner, J.M. (1965) Nitrate by colorimetric methods. *In*: Methods of soil analysis, American Soc. Agron., Madison, WI, USA. Pp. 1212-1219.

Bülow, J.W.F. von & Döbereiner, J. (1975) *Proc. Natl. Acad. Sci.* (USA) 72, 2389-2393.

Cohen, E., Okon, Y., Kigel, J., Nur, I., & Henis, Y. (1980) *Plant Physiol.* 66, 746-749.

De-Polli, H., Matsui, E., Döbereiner, J. & Salati, E., (1977) *Soil Biol. Biochem.* 9, 119-123.

Döbereiner, J. & Day, J.M. (1976) Associative symbiosis in tropical grasses: characterization of micro-organisms and dinitrogen fixing sites. *In:* First Internat. Symp. on Nitrogen Fixation, W.E. Newton & C.J. Nyman (Eds.). Washington State Univ. Press, Pullman, WA, USA. Pp. 518-538.

Hiller, A., Plazin, J. & Slyke, D.D. von (1948) *J. Biol. Chem.* 176, 1409-1420.

Kapulnik, Y., Sarig, S., Nur, I., Okon, Y., Kigel, J., & Henis, Y. (1981a) *Expl. Agri.* 17, 171-178.

Kapulnik, Y., Okon, Y., Kigel, J., Nur, I., & Henis, Y. (1981b) *Plant Physiol.* 68, 340-343.

Kapulnik, Y., Kigel, J., Okon, Y., Nur, I., & Henis, Y. (1981c) *Plant Soil.* 61, 65-70.

Neyra, C.A. & Döbereiner, J. (1977) *Adv. Agron.* 29, 1-38.

Nur, I., Okon, Y. & Henis, Y. (1980a) *Can. J. Microbiol.* 26, 482-485.

Nur, I., Okon, Y. & Henis, Y. (1980b) *Can. J. Microbiol.* 26, 714-718.

Okon, Y., Albrecht, S.L. & Burris, R.H. (1977) *Appl. Environ. Microbiol.* 33, 85-88.

Rennie, R.J. (1980) *Can. J. Bot.* 58, 21-24.

Smith, R.L., Bouton, J.H., Schank, S.C., Quesenberry, K.H., Tyler, M.E., Milam, J.R., Gaskins, M.H., & Littell, R.C. (1976) *Science* 193, 1003-1005.

Tarrand, J.J., Krieg, N.R. & Döbereiner, J. (1978) *Can. J. Microbiol.* 24, 967-980.

Taylor, R.W. (1979) *Trop. Agric.* (Trin.) 56, 361-366.

EMERGING TECHNOLOGY BASED ON BIOLOGICAL NITROGEN FIXATION BY ASSOCIATIVE N_2-FIXING ORGANISMS

J. Döbereiner[1]

Summary

A large number of grasses and cereals have now been shown to support in their roots nitrogen (N_2) fixation measurable by acetylene (C_2H_2) reduction, N balance studies, or $^{15}N_2$ incorporation. Plant genotype and plant/bacteria interactions have been demonstrated. In addition to the high specificity of *Azotobacter paspali* for *Paspalum notatum* and *Bacillus* spp. for certain wheat lines, host-plant affinities for *Azopirillum* infection have also been shown. Maize, sorghum, and several C_4 forage grasses are infected by *A. lipoferum* while C_3 plants (rice, wheat, oat, rye, and barley) select for *A. brasilense*. The relationship between plant and bacteria is frequently very close. Attachment to, and penetration of, root hairs of *Pennisetum* was observed in N-deficient plants, while *Azozpirillum* infection of maize and sorghum roots extends into the root stele and stem tissues. Stem infections have also been found in rice, wheat, and *Brachiaria*.

Ecological and physiological data are available for *Azospirillum* spp. only. These organisms are found predominantly in soils under cultivation or pastures, but are scarce in equilibrium forests or savannas. So far only Gramineae and tuber plants have been found to associate with *Azospirillum* spp. Numbers in the range of 10^6 to 10^7/g soil or roots are frequently found in the tropics. Numbers within roots are generally lower, but peak during the reproduction growth stage of maize, rice, and wheat, when nitrogenase activity is highest. Root infection by *Azospirillum* spp. seems to be predominantly by strains that lack a dissimilatory nitrite reductase (nir^-).

These findings give a better basis for strain selection for inoculants. Inoculation of wheat with a *A. brasilense* nir^- strain

[1] Programa Fixacao Biologica de Nitrogenio, EMBRAPA/SNLCS - CNPq, Km 47, 23460 Seropedica, Rio de Janeiro, Brasil.

isolated from surface-sterilized wheat roots, and of maize with an equivalent maize strain (*A. lipoferum* nir$^-$) proportioned significant increases of plant N in the field (27 kg N/ha in wheat and 40 kg N/ha in maize). In the same experiment, application of 60 kg fertilizer N proportioned a plant N increase of 53 kg N/ha. Statistically significant grain yield increases due to *Azospirillum* inoculation have also been reported from India and Israel.

INTRODUCTION

A large number of plants, most of them Gramineae, have now been shown to support, in their roots, nitrogen (N_2) fixation which can be measured by C_2H_2 reduction (Balandreu *et al.*, 1977; Döbereiner, 1978; Purchase, 1978; Vlassak & Reynders, 1978a), $^{15}N_2$ incorporation (De-Polli, 1975; Ruschel, 1975; De-Polli *et al.*, 1977), ^{15}N dilution (Rennie, 1980), or by N balance studies (Döbereiner & De-Polli, 1980a). The amounts of N_2 fixed are variable and usually small, but economically significant rates of N_2 fixation have been reported, especially in the tropics (Jaiyebo & Moore, 1963; von Bülow & Döbereiner, 1975; Döbereiner, 1978). The major restriction seems to be the absence of a specific nodule-replacing structure that can protect the N_2-fixing bacteria against oxygen and other environmental effects. This review characterizes some rhizocoenoses, paying particular attention to *Azospirillum* associations; considers recent evidence for host-plant specificity in associative N_2 fixation, and evaluates the competitive advantages of streptomycin-resistant strains in the rhizosphere. It assesses recent evidence for yield increases following inoculation with *Azospirillum, Bacillus,* and other diazotrophic bacteria and suggests some areas where further research must be undertaken.

CHARACTERIZATION OF SOME RHIZOCOENOSES

Although many reports of rhizocoenoses are now available, most lack definition. In most cases information on the responsible bacteria is not provided (Jaiyebo & Moore, 1963; Giddens, 1977), or the isolation and enumeration of certain groups of bacteria from the rhizosphere is detailed without reference to specific plant/bacteria interactions (Barber *et al.*, 1976; Nelson *et al.*, 1976; Watanabe *et al.*, 1979). So far, the only reasonably defined diazotrophic associations seem to be:

Sugarcane/*Beijerinckia* (Döbereiner, 1961; Döbereiner, Day & Dart, 1972; Ruschel, 1981);

Paspalum notatum/*Azotobacter paspali* (Döbereiner, 1966; 1970);

The association of certain wheat lines with *Bacillus* sp. (Neal & Larson, 1976; Rennie & Larson, 1979);

The association of rice with *Pseudomonas*-like organisms (Watanabe & Barraquio, 1979); and

The various *Azospirillum* associations (von Bülow & Döbereiner, 1975; Döbereiner & Day, 1976; Vlassak & Reynders, 1978a; Baldani & Döbereiner, 1979; 1980).

No new results are available on the nature of the *Paspalum*/*Azotobacter* and sugarcane/*Beijerinckia* associations. The micro-organisms that multiply selectively in the rhizosphere of those root-rot resistant wheat lines that have limited exudation of organic matter into the rhizosphere have been identified as *Bacillus* spp. (Rennie & Larson, 1979). Inoculation of these organisms onto N-deficient wheat plants in Leonard jar assemblies enhanced total plant N. Recently Watanabe & Barraquio (1975) reported the occurrence of glucose-utilizing diazotrophic bacteria tentativcly identified as *Psuedomonas* sp. within the root of rice seedlings. These organisms comprised 81% of the total bacterial flora and were present in much greater numbers in stem and rhizosphere than in surrounding soil.

Diazotrophic, *Spirillum*-like organisms isolated from roots of *Potamogeton filiformis* (Sylvester-Bradley, 1976) and *Spartina alterniflora,* a C_4 marsh grass, were later identified as a *Campylobacter* sp. (McClung & Patriquin, 1980). In this plant, nitrogenase activity occurred in the endorhizosphere (Boyle & Patriquin, 1980), was correlated with the concentration of sugar in roots, and was CO_2 dependent (Patriquin & McClung, 1978). Additions of sugar or malate did not substantially increase the nitrogenase activity, indicating a large carbon pool (Boyle, 1978; Boyle & Patriquin, 1980). Diazotrophic *Enterobacteriaceae* and *Bacillus* sp. have also been found in high numbers in several other plants, but plant/bacteria interactions have yet to be shown.

Azospirillum associations

Since 1974, when the *Spirillum lipoferum* rhizocoenosis was first reported (Döbereiner & Day, 1976), a considerable volume of information has accumulated, and much of it has been reviewed (Balandreau *et al.,* 1977; Neyra & Döbereiner, 1977; Döbereiner, 1978; Döbereiner & De-Polli, 1980a).

The bacteria has been reclassified on the basis of DNA homology studies with 61 strains, and a new genus with two species (*Azospirillum lipoferum* and *A. brasilense*) has been described (Tarrand, Krieg & Döbereiner, 1978). Within each species two subgroups were distinguished according to their ability (nir^+) or inability (nir^-) to denitrify. These two subgroups could not be identified by DNA homology but gave distinct immunofluorescent reactions (De-Polli, Bohlool & Döbereiner, 1980). There are also differences among species in cell form, especially in older, alkaline cultures (Tarrand *et al.,* 1978). *A. lipoferum* is a very polymorphic organism while *A. brasilense* was only found to produce giant cells under extreme stress under wash-out conditions in chemostat cultures (M. P. Stephan, personal communication).

Azospirillum spp. are widely distributed (Döbereiner & De-Polli, 1980a) and can occur in high numbers in soil and grass roots (up to 10^6 or 10^7/g dry roots) (Pedersen *et al.,* 1978; Magalhães, Patriquin & Döbereiner, 1979; Freitas, Pereira & Döbereiner, 1981). *Azospirillum* can attach to grass roots within 24 h (Umali-Garcia, 1978) and growth substances emitted by the bacteria (IAA, giberellin, and cytokinin-like substances) (Tien, Gaskin & Hubbell, 1979) cause root hair multiplication and the shortening and thickening of the roots in monoxenic cultures (Umali-Garcia, 1978). Mucigel production is enhanced, and large numbers of *Azospirillum* are found embedded in it.

Azospirillum invades the root through the middle lamella of older root tissues and transparent areas around the invading cells suggest active hydrolysis of plant cell walls by pectolytic enzymes, such as have been found in culture media (Umali-Garcia, 1978). Vlassak & Reynders (1978b) suggested a role of growth substances produced from tryptophan by *Azospirillum* sp. All the studies mentioned above were performed with monoxenic test tube seedlings and with the type strain of *A. brasilense* nir^+, strain Sp 7 (ATCC 29145).

In maize grown in the field, the infection of healthy inner root tissues with bacteria that reduce tetrazolium (TTC) has been observed (Patriquin & Döbereiner, 1978; Magalhães *et al.,* 1979a; 1979b) but only in plants during the reproductive stage of the growth cycle (see Figure 1). The increase in the number of *Azospirillum* in surface-sterilized roots (one hour in Chloramine-T) at this time (10^4 increasing to 10^7), and the increase in infection in the stele around flowering (10% of examined root pieces infected increasing to 80%) indicates that deep root infection is a prerequisite for nitrogenase activity in maize roots (Magalhães *et al.,* 1979a; 1979b). It is now well documented that the maximum nitrogenase activity in many cereals occurs during flowering and grain fill (von Bülow & Döbereiner, 1975; Nery *et al.,* 1977; Watanabe, Lee & Guzman, 1978). During this period the spread of *Azospirillum* into the stem of plants such as maize (Magalhães *et al.,* 1979a; 1979b), rice (Watanabe & Barraquio, 1979), wheat (Kavimandan, Subba Rao & Mohrir, 1978) and *Brachiaria* (P.A.A. Pereira, personal communication) has been documented, but nitrogenase activity in stems has only been demonstrated for rice (Watanabe & Barraquio, 1979) and germinating sugarcane stem cuttings (Patriquin, Gracioli & Ruschel, 1980; Ruschel, 1981). The preference of *A. lipoferum* for glucose might be connected with the availability of sugars at the site where the bacteria occurs. *A. lipoferum* was shown to occur within the inner cortex and stele tissues of C_4 plants (Patriquin & Döbereiner, 1978) and, therefore, could have developed a pathway for the use of glucose. No data are available on the localization of *Azospirillum* in C_3 plant roots and infection of other root tissues might be the principal site.

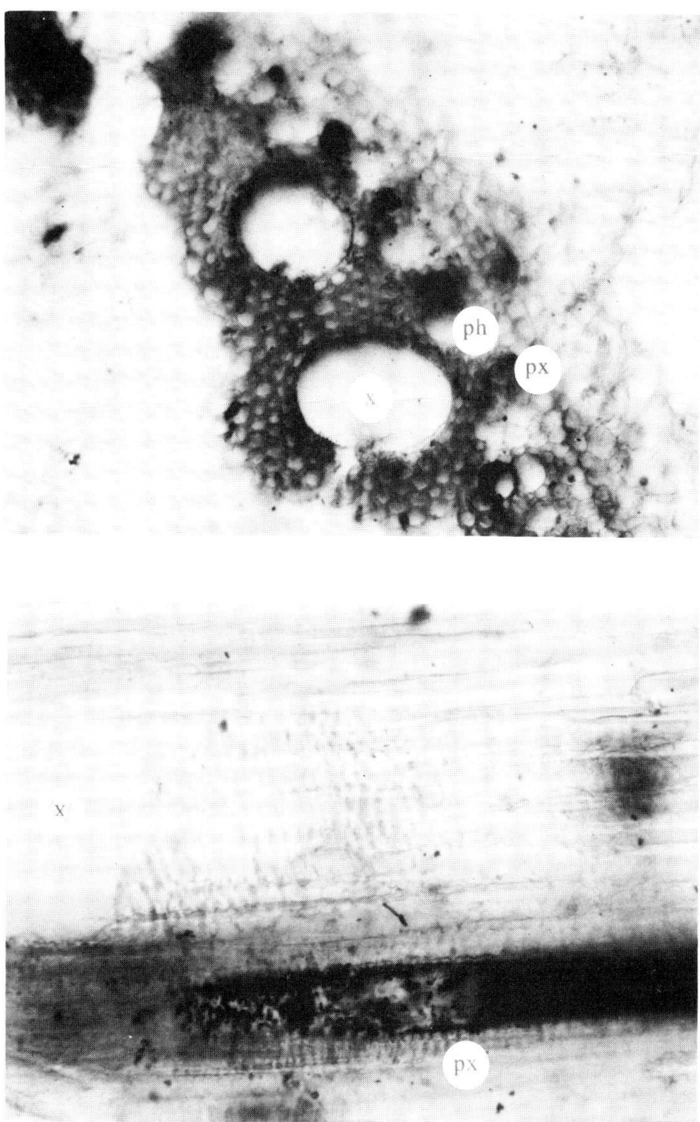

Figure 1. Infection of the central stele of field-grown maize roots by terazolium-reducing bacteria. Plants were harvested at grain filling stage and 2 cm segments of roots were incubated overnight at 35°C in a 0.15% solution of 2.3.5 Triphenyl tetrazolium chloride in 0.05 M phosphate buffer. The roots were cut on a cryostat and mounted in glycerol. The bar is 50 µm. Note the consistent infection of protoxylem vessels, which extends longitudinally x - xylem; px - protoxylem; ph - phloem.

HOST PLANT SPECIFICITY IN *AZOSPIRILLUM* ASSOCIATIONS

Once the infection of grass roots had been demonstrated, host-plant affinity or specificity groups were to be expected. *Azospirillum* isolates obtained from surface sterilized roots of plants grown in pots with soil containing nir⁻and nir+ forms of *A. lipoferum* and *A. brasilense* varied according to plant species. Fifty-eight percent of the maize isolates were *A. lipoferum* and 100% of the wheat isolates and 96% of the isolates from rice were *A. brasilense* (Baldani & Döbereiner, 1979; 1980). Very similar results were obtained in a field experiment (see Table 1). Also, most strains obtained from surface-sterilized roots do not denitrify (nir⁻) even when denitrifying strains are common in the soil (see Tables 1 and 2).

The strains obtained from maize roots in Belgium (Vlassak & Reynders, 1978a), also seem to be *A. lipoferum.* These authors and one Indian group (Lakshmi *et al.,* 1977) observed significant strain x plant interactions when plants grown in soil were inoculated with *Azospirillum.* Besides maize, sorghum, several C_4 forage grasses, and one Cyperaceae were infected predominantly by *A. lipoferum* and the major small grains (wheat, oat,

TABLE 1: Distribution of *Azospirillum* spp. groups among isolates from uninoculated maize or wheat grown in the field (Baldini & Döbereiner, 1979b).

Treatment	Sterilization[1]	No. of isolates[2]	% of isolates identified as		
			A. lipoferum	*A. brasilense*	
				nir⁺	nir⁻
Maize					
Soil	0	32	84	12	3
Roots	0	32	59	9	31
Roots	0.5	30	78	19	3
Roots	60	29	96	0	4
Wheat					
Soil	0	32	57	0	43
Roots	0	31	21	19	60
Roots	0.25	32	37	6	57
Roots	15	31	0	12	88

[1]Number of minutes exposed to Chloramine - T.
[2]Approximately 32 strains, 2 each of 4 replicate plots and four harvests (45, 60, 75, 95 days after planting).

TABLE 2: Selection for nir⁻ strains of *Azospirillum lipoferum* (during infection of maize roots (Baldini, 1980).

Growth stage of maize	Washed roots	Surface-sterilized roots	
		30 sec[1]	60 min[1]
	% nir⁻ strains		
Greenhouse			
Flowering	33	3	50
Grain filling	0	50	50
Maturation	0	33	3
Field			
Flowering	0	10	63
Grain filling	10	3	50
Maturation	3	3	10

[1]In 1 % Chloramine-T.

barley, rye and rice) by *A. brasilense* (Döbereiner & De-Polli, 1980a; da Rocha, Baldani & Döbereiner, 1981). It seems, therefore, that the infection of plants with the C_4 photosynthetic pathway is preferentially by *Azospirillum lipoferum* while C_3 plants are infected by *Azospirillum brasilense.* Whether there are further specificity groups within C_4 or C_3 plants is not yet known. The selection for nir⁻strains during infection, by both species in a variety of plants, suggests evolution pressure for a characteristic that seems rather of advantage to the plant than to the bacteria and indicates a certain dependence of the bacteria on actively growing plants. In contrast to attempts of other laboratories (Ruschel, 1981) that were unable to isolate *Azospirillum* from sugarcane, our observations (da Rocha *et al.*, 1981) and those of Hegazi & Vlassak (1977) indicate a role for this organism. The latter authors found *Azospirillum* predominant in nitrogenase active cane root pieces. It is not clear, however, whether these organisms, the ones isolated by Ruschel (1979), or *Beijerinckia* spp. are the most important bacteria. So far the only bacteria for which plant/bacteria interactions in sugarcane have been shown is *Beijerinckia* (Döbereiner, 1961). The sugarcane system certainly seems to be quite different from other Gramineae, a not-unexpected finding in view of the high sucrose content of this plant. Unlike the other grass biocoenoses, N_2 fixation in sugarcane was reported to occur mainly in the rhizosphere soil (Döberiner *et al.*, 1972; Ruschel *et al.*, 1978). Although activities per g soil were only one quarter of those of roots, the contribution in soils was calculated to be 30 times greater (67 kg/ha per yr). Also, in wheat and rice, more than one N_2-fixing bacteria seems to be of importance.

STREPTOMYCIN RESISTANCE AND STRAIN ESTABLISHMENT

When *Azospirillum* strains isolated from surface-sterilized roots were selected for low-level streptomycin resistance (20 µg/ml) and then inoculated into field-grown maize and wheat, more than 80% of the soil and rhizosphere isolates were identified as the inoculated strains, independently of strain or host (Baldani & Döbereiner, 1979; Döbereiner & Baldani, 1979b). Establishment of the inoculated strain within roots (1 h surface sterilized) was dependent, however, on the host plant. Only homologous strains (*A. lipoferum* from maize and *A. brasilense* from wheat) were recovered within roots, even if the heterologous streptomycin-resistant strain had been established in the rhizosphere by massive inoculation. These results show clearly the important role of plant specificity in *Azospirillum* rhizocoenoses.

Despite these results, the infection of cereals by N_2-fixing bacteria might, in some circumstances, be dependent on resistance to low levels of streptomycin. Higher proportions of low-level streptomycin- and/or penicillin-resistant bacteria than in soil were observed in the rhizosphere of legumes and vegetables (Brown, 1961), wheat (Brown, 1961; Döbereiner & Baldani, 1979a; 1979b), maize and sorghum. *Azospirillum* spp. are remarkably tolerant to several other antibiotics, especially penicillin (Döbereiner & Baldani, 1979a, 1979b; Reynders & Vlassak, 1978; Sampaio, Vasconcellos & Döbereiner, 1978). Increases in the number of actinomycetes in the rhizosphere (Rovira, 1965; Döbereiner & Boddey, 1980) and of the percentage of low-level, streptomycin-resistant bacteria in macerated maize roots have been reported. *Rhizobium* strains isolated from soybeans and cowpeas in newly claimed "cerrado" and Amazon soils showed resistance to even much higher antibiotic concentrations (Döbereiner *et al.*, 1980).

INOCULATION WITH N_2-FIXING BACTERIA

The need, especially in developing countries, to obtain cereals and grasses that satisfy at least part of their N requirement through biological N_2 fixation led to various studies in which immediately available strains of *Azotobacter* (Rubenchik, 1963) or *Azospirillum* (Smith *et al.*, 1977; Bouton *et al.*, 1979) were used as inoculants, irrespective of origin or adaptation to the test host. It is evident from the advances reviewed here that matching of microsymbiont and host is as important to the various biocoenoses as it is in the legume/*Rhizobium* symbiosis. Thus, for example, the role of dissimilatory nitrite reductase in *Azospirillum* remains to be determined.

Plant roots seem to select for nir$^-$ (not denitrifying) strains (Döbereiner & Baldani, 1981; Döbereiner & De-Polli, 1980b) but is not yet known whether the nitrite reductase is of advantage to the bacteria, to the plant, or to both. *Azospirillum* strains seem to interact with nitrate assimilation by the plant (Freitas *et al.*, 1981; Villas Boas & Döbereiner, 1981). Active dentrification occurs in nir+ *Azospirillum* cultures, but no information is as yet available on the role of such strains in soil, or in the rhizosphere. As much as 7% of the applied NO_3^- fertilizer was lost as N_2O or N_2 in *Brachiaria* swards in three days (Pereira & Döbereiner, 1981). Inoculation of maize with a nir+ *Azospirillum* strain caused plant N increases as well as decreases depending on the soil N status (Döbereiner, 1978).

In spite of many negative results (Barber *et al.*, 1976; Burris *et al.*, 1977) there is increasing evidence that inoculation with *Azospirillum* spp. can proportion significant increases in plant growth, plant N and even grain yields under field conditions (Kapulnik *et al.*, 1981; Subba Rao, 1981; Smith *et al.*, 1977). Recent data from Israel, presented in this symposium (p. 459), are particularly promising. Progress in strain selection and in the understanding of host-plant specificities have also permitted encouraging responses to

TABLE 3: Host-plant specificity in the inoculation of field-grown cereals with *Azospirillum* spp. (Döbereiner & De-Polli, 1980a; J.L.M. Freitas, R.E.M. da Rocha, P.A.A. Pereira & J. Döbereiner, unpublished data).

Plant	Inoculant[1]	Dry wt (g/plant)[2]	Total N (g/plant)[2]	Δ Total N due to inoculation (kg N/ha)	Grain yield (t/ha)[3]
Wheat	None[1]	2.73	0.045		0.87
	A. lipoferum[4]	2.67	0.048	4.1	1.17
	A. brasilense	3.17	0.059	26.9	1.19
d.m.s. (P = 0.01)		0.12	0.003		n.s.
Maize	None	151	2.19		2.59
	A. lipoferum	205	3.00	40.2	2.94
	A. brasilense	180	2.63	21.7	2.66
d.m.s. (P = 0.01)		43	0.62		n.s.

[1]The N added with the inoculant was less than 3 mg/plant and, therefore, was neglected in the controls.

[2]Means of 8 plants each from 4 field plots for wheat and 4 plants each from 16 field plots for maize.

[3]Based on 2 x 10^6 plants of wheat and 5 x 10^4 plants of maize per ha.

[4]*Azospirillum* strains isolated from surface-sterilized maize and wheat roots, respectively (Sp 107st and 242st), and low-level streptomycin resistant. Inoculation was made at planting by applying 10 ml of liquid culture grown with NH_4Cl containing 10^8 cells.

inoculation in Brazil (see Table 3). The maize experiment included additional treatments that permitted comparisons of the inoculation effects with those of N fertilizer. Organic matter (city dust compost) and fertilizer N did not seem to complement each other, inoculation with the maize strain of *Azospirillum* increased plant N by 36-44 kg N/ha above these two treatments, close to the increase obtained with 60 kg fertilizer N/ha. (See Table 4).

TABLE 4: Effect of organic matter, N fertilizer, and inoculation with *Azospirillum* spp. on N incorporation of maize in the field (flowering stage) (J.L.M. Freitas, R.E.M. da Rocha, P.A.A. Pereira & J. Döbereiner, unpublished data).

Treatment	Inoculant[2]	Total N incorporated (kgN/ha)			
		In plant tops[3]	Due to inoculation	Due to fertilization	Due to org. mat.
Organic matter + N fertilizer[1]	*A. lipoferum*	152	37	-26	-1
	A. brasilense	164	48	18	38
	None	115		-26	6
Organic matter	*A. lipoferum*	178	36		63
	A. brasilense	146	5		57
	None	141			70
N fertilization	*A. lipoferum*	153	44	38	
	A. brasilense	126	17	37	
	None	109		53	
Control	*A. lipoferum*	115	44		
	A. brasilense	89	17		
	None	71			

[1]40 t/ha of city dust compost (N % = 0.8) at planting and 60 kg N/ha applied 10 days before flowering as NH_4NO_3.

[2]Inoculation and all other experimental conditions as in Table 3.

[3]Effects or organic matter and inoculation, and interaction of organic matter x fertilizer N were significant at P = 0.01).

CONCLUSIONS

Technologies emerging from the last decade of research on N_2 fixation in grasses and cereals indicate the following possibilities:

Maximization of spontaneous N_2 fixation by the proper use of fertilizer (e.g., low N, high P levels, complemented with Mo.)

Plant breeding for increased N_2 fixation.

Inoculation with appropriately selected *Azospirillum* or other N_2-fixing bacteria. For this, strains must be selected in the field and tested in soils where few or no *Azospirillum* occur. In addition, competition experiments are necessary in soils where such bacteria do exist.

Interactions of plant genotype, bacteria, and low-level NO_3^- applications must be better explored since they are the key to complementing biological N_2 fixation with N fertilizer use in cereals and grasses.

REFERENCES

Balandreau, J., Ducerf, P., Hamad-Fares, I., Weinhard, P., Rinaudo, G., Millier, C., & Dommergues, Y. (1977) Limiting factors in grass nitrogen fixation. *In:* Limitations and potentials for biological nitrogen fixation in the tropics, J. Döbereiner, R.H. Burris & A. Hollander (Eds.). Basic Life Sciences Vol. 10, Plenum Press, New York, NY, USA. Pp. 275-302.

Baldani, V.L.D. (1980) Especificidade na infecção de raízes de milho, trigo e arroz para *Azospirillum* spp. MS thesis. UFRRJ, Rio de Janeiro, Brazil.

Baldani, V.L.D. & Döbereiner, J. (1979) *An. Acad. Brasil. Cien.* 51, 358-359.

Baldini, V.L.D. & Döbereiner, J. (1980) *Soil Biol. Biochem.* 12, 433-440.

Barber, L.E., Tjepkema, J.P., Russell, S.A., & Evans, H.J. (1976) *Appl. Environ. Microbiol.* 32, 108-113.

Boyle, C.D. (1978) Some characteristics of nitrogenase activity associated with diazotrophs in and around *Spartina alterniflora* roots. MS thesis, Dalhousie University, Halifax, Canada. 102 pp.

Boyle, C.D. & Patriquin, D.G. (1980) *Plant Physiol.* 66, 267-280.

Bouton, J.H., Smith, R.L., Schank, S.C., Burton, G.W., Tyler, M.E., Littell, R.C., Gallaher, R.H., & Quesenberry, K.H. (1979) *Crop Sci.* 19, 12-16.

Brown, M.E. (1961) *J. Gen. Microbiol.* 24, 369-377.

Bülow, J.F.W. von & Döbereiner, J. (1975) *Proc. Nat. Acad. Sci.* 72, 2389-2393.

Burris, R.H., Albrecht, S.L. & Okon, Y. (1977) Physiology and biochemistry of *Spirillum lipoferum*. *In:* Limitations and potentials for biological nitrogen fixation in the tropics, J. Döbereiner, R.H. Burris & A. Hollaender (Eds.). Basic Life Sciences Vol. 10, Plenum Press, New York, NY, USA. Pp. 303-315.

De-Polli, H. (1975) Ocorrencia de fixação de $^{15}N_2$ nas gramíneas tropicais *Digitaria decumbens* e *Paspalum notatum*. MS thesis, Univ. de São Paulo, Piracicaba, Brazil.

De-Polli, H., Bohlool, B.B. & Döbereiner, J. (1980) *Arch. Microbiol.* 126, 217-222.

De-Polli, H., Matsui, E., Döbereiner, J., & Salati, E. (1977) *Soil Biol. Biochem.* 9, 119-123.

Döbereiner, J. (1961) *Plant Soil* 15, 211-217.

Döbereiner, J. (1966) *Pesq. Agropec. Bras.* 1, 357-365.

Döbereiner, J. (1970) *Zentralbl. Bakt. Parasintek.* II, 124, 224-230.

Döbereiner, J. (1978) Nitrogen fixation in grass-bacteria associations in the tropics. *In:* Isotopes in biological dinitrogen fixation. IAEA, Vienna, Pp. 51-69.

Döbereiner, J. & Baldani, V.L.D. (1979a) *An. Acad. Brasil. Cienc.* 51, 359-360.

Döbereiner, J. & Baldani, V.L.D. (1979b) *Can. J. Microbiol.* 25, 1264-1269.

Döbereiner, J. & Baldani, V.L.D. (1981) Prospects of inoculation of grasses with *Azospirillum* spp. *In:* Associative N_2 fixation, P.B. Vose & A.P. Ruschel (Eds.) CRC Press, Palm Beach, FL, USA.

Döbereiner, J. & Boddey, R.M. (1981) Nitrogen fixation in association with gramineae. IV Internat. Symp. N_2 Fixation, Canberra, Australia.

Döbereiner, J. & Day, J.M. (1976) Associative symbioses in tropical grasses: Characterization of micro-organisms and dinitrogen- fixing sites. Proc. First Internat. Symp. Nitrogen fixation, W.E. Newton & C.J. Nyman (Eds.). Washington State Univ. Press, Pullman WA, USA. Pp. 518-538.

Döbereiner, J., Day, J.M. & Dart, P.J. (1972) *Plant Soil* 36, 191-196.

Döbereiner, J. & De-Polli, H. (1980a) Diazotrophic rhizocoenoses. *In:* Nitrogen fixation, D.P. Stewart & J.R. Gallon (Eds.). Pp. 301-334.

Döbereiner, J. & De-Polli, H. (1980b) Nitrogen fixing rhizocoenoses. Int. Symp. Root/Soil System, Londrina, Brazil.

Döbereiner, J., Scotti, M.R.M.M.L., Sá, N.M.H. & Vargas, M.A.T. (1980) Resistance to streptomycin of *Rhizobium* isolates from cerrado and Amazon soils. IV Internat. Symp. N_2 fixation, Canberra, Australia. (In press).

Freitas, J.L.M. de, Pereira, P.A.A. & Döbereiner, J. (1981) Effects of organic matter and inoculation with *Azospirillum* spp. on nitrogen metabolism of *Sorghum vulgaris*. *In:* Associative N_2 fixation, P.B. Vose & A.P. Ruschel (Eds.). CRC Press, Palm Beach, FL, USA.

Giddens, J. (1977) *Ga. Agric. Res.* 19, 12-13.

Hegazi, N. & Vlassak, K. (1977) Microscopic observations on the nitrogen-fixing *Spirillum* occurring in the rhizosphere of maize and sugar-cane. European Seminar on Biological Solar Energy Conversion Systems, Grenoble-Autrans, France.

Jaiyebo, E.O. & Moore, A.W. (1963) *Nature* 197, 317-318.

Kapulnik, Y., Sarig., Nur, I., Okon, Y., Kigel, J., & Henis, Y. (1981) *Expl. Agric.* 17, 179-187.

Kavimandan, S.K., Subba Rao, N.S. & Mohrir, A.V. (1978) *Curr. Sci.* 47, 96-98.

Lakshmi, V., Satyanarayana Rao, A., Vijayalaksmi, K., Lakshmi-Kumari, M., Tilak, K.V.B.R., & Subba Rao, N.S. (1977) *Proc. Indian Acad. Sci.* 86B, 397-404.

Magalhães, F.M.M., Patriquin, D. & Döbereiner, J. (1979a) *An. Acad. Brasil Cien.* 51, 358.

Magalhães, F.M.M. Patriquin, D. & Döbereiner, J. (1979b) *Rev. Brasil Biol.* 39, 587-596.

McClung, C.R. & Patriquin, D. (1980) *Can. J. Microbiol.* 26, 881-886.

Neal, J.L. & Larson, R.I. (1976) *Soil Biol. Biochem.* 8, 151-155.

Nelson, A.D., Barber, L.E., Tjepkema, J., Russel, S.A., Powelson, R., Evans, H.J., & Seidler, R.J. (1976) *Can J. Microbiol.* 22, 523-530.

Nery, M., Abrantes, G.T.V., Santos, O., & Döbereiner, J. (1977) *Rev. Bras. Ci. Solo* 1, 15-20.

Neyra, C.A. & Döbereiner, J. (1977) *Adv. Agron.* 29, 1-38.

Patriquin, D.G. & Döbereiner, J. (1978) *Can. J. Microbiol.* 24, 734-742.

Patriquin, D.G., Gracioli, L.A. & Ruschel, A.P. (1980) *Soil Biol. Biochem.* 12, 413-417.

Patriquin, D.G. & McClung, C.R. (1978) *Mar. Biol.* 47, 227-242.

Pedersen, W.L., Chakrabarty, K., Klucas, R.V., & Vidaver, A.K. (1978) *Appl. Environ. Microbiol.* 35, 129-135.

Pereira, P.A.A. & Döbereiner, J. (1981) Nitrogenase and nitrate reductase activities and denitrification in five genotypes of *Brachiaria* spp. *In:* Associative N_2 fixation, P.B. Vose & A.P. Ruschel (Eds.). CRC Press, Palm Beach, FL, USA.

Purchase, B.S. (1978) *Rhodesia Agric. J.* 75, 99-104.

Rennie, R.J. (1980) *Can. J. Microbiol.* 58, 21-24.

Rennie, R.J. & Larson, R.I. (1979) *Can. J. Microbiol.* 24, 2771-2775.

Rinaudo, G., Hamad-Fares, I. & Dommergues, Y.R. (1978) Nitrogen fixation in the rice rhizosphere: Methods of measurement and practices suggested to enhance the process. *In:* Biological nitrogen fixation in farming systems of the tropics, A. Ayanaba & P.J. Dart (Eds.). Wiley, New York, NY, USA. Pp. 313-322.

Rocha, R.E.M. da, Baldani, J.I. & Döbereiner, J. (1981) Host plant specificity in the infection of C_4 plants with *Azospirillum* spp. *In:* Associative N_2 fixation, P.B. Vose & A.P. Ruschel (Eds.). CRC Press, Palm Beach, FL, USA.

Rovira, A.D. (1965) *Ann. Rev. Microbiol.* 19, 241-266.

Rubenchik, L.I. (1963) *Azotobacter* and its use in Agriculture, A. Artman (Translator). Acad. Sci. Ulkrainian S.S.R./Nat. Sci. Foundation, Washington, 278 pp.

Ruschel, A.P. (1975) Fixação biológica de nitrogênio em cana-de-açucar. PhD thesis, Univ. de Sao Paulo, Piracicaca, Brazil. 73 pp.

Ruschel, A.P., Victoria, R.L., Salati, E., & Henis, Y. (1978) *Ecol. Bull.* (Stockholm) 26, 297-303.

Ruschel, A.P. (1981) Associative N_2 fixation by sugar-cane. *In:* Associative N_2 fixation, P.B. Võse & A.P. Ruschel (Eds.). CRC Press, Palm Beach, FL, USA.

Sampaio, M.J.A.M., Vasconcellos, L. & Döbereiner, J. (1978) *Ecol. Bull.* (Stockholm) 26, 364-365.

Smith, R.L., Schank, S.C., Quesenberry, K.H., Milam, J.M., & Hubbell, D.H. (1977) Univ. Florida, Dept. Agron., Soil Microbiol. Annual Report.

Subba Rao, N.S. (1981) Response of crops to *Azospirillum* inoculation in India. *In:* Associative N_2 fixation, P.B. Vose & A.P. Ruschel (Eds.). CRC Press, Palm Beach, FL., USA.

Sylvester-Bradley, R. (1976) *J. Gen. Microbiol.* 97, 129-132.

Tarrand, J.J., Krieg, N.R. & Döbereiner, J. (1978) *Can. J. Microbiol. 24, 967-980.*

Tien, T.M., Gaskin, M.H. & Hubbell, D.H. (1979) *Appl. Environ. Microbiol.* 37, 1016-1024.

Umali-Gracia, M. (1978) Early events in the establishment of an associative symbiosis of *Azospirillum brasilense* Sp7 with grass roots. PhD thesis, Univ. of Florida, Gainesville, FL, USA. 104 pp.

Villas Boas, F.C.S. & Dőbereiner, J. (1981) Efeito de diferentes níveis de N mineral na atividade de nitrato redutase e nitrogenase em arroz (*Oriza sativa*) inoculado com duas estirpes de *Azospirillum* spp. *In:* Associative N_2 fixation, P.B. Vose & AP. Ruschel (Eds.). CRC Press, Palm Beach, FL, USA.

Vlassak, K. & Reynders, L. (1978a) Associative dinitrogen fixation in temperate regions. *In:* Isotopes in biological dinitrogen fixation. IAEA, Vienna, Austria. Pp. 71-78.

Vlassak, K. & Reynders, L. (1978b) Conversion of tryptophan to auxins by *Azospirillum* spp. Proc. Steenbock Kettering Internat. Symp. N_2 Fixation, Madison, WI, USA. Abstr. 44.

Watanabe, I. (1981) Biological nitrogen fixation in rice. IV Internat. Symp. N Fixation. Canberra, Australia.

Watanabe, I., Lee, K.K. & Guzman, M.R. (1978) *Soil Sci. Plant Nutr.* 24, 465-471.

Watanabe, I. & Barraquio, W.L. (1979) *Nature* 277, 565-566.

Watanabe, I., Barraquio, W.L., Guzman, M.R. & Cabrera, D.A. (1979) *Appl. Environ. Microbiol.* 37, 813-819.

Each was then further subdivided, with half of the pots receiving, 52.5 g (equivalent to 25 m^3/ha) of farmyard manure (FYM).

To simulate natural conditions, waterlogging treatments were imposed two weeks before planting; then five seedlings/pot were transplanted. All pots received two applications of 0.7 g/pot of ammonium sulfate (52.5 kg N/ha), one four weeks after planting; the second eight weeks after planting.

Bacteriological determinations

Counts of N_2-fixing micro-organisms in rhizosphere and nonrhizosphere soil were made at planting and at 4, 6, 8, and 10 weeks thereafter. The method of Timonin (1940) was used to count rhizosphere micro-organisms. Most probable number (MPN) counts for *Azotobacter* were made on Ashby's medium (Abd El Malek & Ishac, 1968), for *Clostridium* on Winogradsky's medium incubated under anaerobic conditions (Allen, 1961), and for *Azospirillum* on lactate medium (Döbereiner *et al.*, 1976). Cochran's tables (Cochran, 1950) were used in calculating MPN values.

Assay of nitrogenase activity using N_2 (C_2H_2) reduction

N_2 (C_2H_2) reduction assays were carried out on the 10^{-2} dilution of the MPN counts for *Azospirillum* using the technique of Day & Döbereiner (1976). Determinations of N_2 (C_2H_2) reduction were also carried out on whole rice plants, using the technique of Balandreau & Dommergues (1973); on nonrhizosphere soil from planted pots; and on normally irrigated and inundated soils that had not been planted to rice.

RESULTS AND DISCUSSION

Azotobacter

MPN counts for *Azotobacter* in the different treatments are shown in Figure 1. The number of *Azotobacter* cells in the rhizosphere of plants without FYM rose gradually during the study period and achieved levels of 1.32 x 10^8 by week ten. The rhizosphere: soil ratio for *Azotobacter* was very high. After ten weeks it had reached 16.7 in the unmanured pots and 24.8 in pots with FYM. Root exudates are clearly important to the multiplication of this organism.

Application of FYM enhanced *Azotobacter* numbers in normally irrigated soil, but decreased the population of these organisms in unplanted waterlogged soil. The negative effect of FYM could have been due either to increasingly anaerobic conditions as oxygen was consumed by organisms decomposing the FYM, or to the production of a gas such as methane, which can be toxic to *Azotobacter* (Harrison & Aiyer, 1915-1916).

TABLE 1: Counts of *Azospirillum* in soil and rhizosphere and estimates of their ability to fix N_2.

Time and treatment	Nos. of *Azospirillum* (x 10^6/g dry soil)		$N_2(C_2H_2)$ fixation (n moles ml culture/h)[1]	
	-FYM	+FYM	-FYM	+FYM
Time, 0				
Rhizosphere soil	11.1	5.20	ND[2]	ND
Soil from planted pots	11.1	5.20		
Inundated, not planted	11.1	5.20		
Normally irrigated	11.1	5.20		
Time, 4 weeks				
Rhizosphere soil	ND	ND	67.8	23.3
Soil from planted pots			10.5	9.5
Inundated, not planted			13.3	12.0
Normally irrigated			52.9	9.7
Time, 6 weeks				
Rhizosphere soil	ND	ND	87.9	62.6
Soil from planted pots			22.9	20.3
Inundated, not planted			20.5	25.9
Normally irrigated			52.9	35.7
Time, 10 weeks				
Rhizosphere soil	44.9	12.50	94.5	56.3
Soil from planted pots	1.2	6.80	7.7	7.6
Inundated, not planted	6.6	1.10	10.4	7.7
Normally irrigated	7.3	0.97	31.2	6.4
R:S ratio	37.4	1.80		

[1]Determined on 10^{-2} dilutions in lactate medium.
[2]Not determined.

Burris, R.H., Okon, Y. & Albrecht, S.L. (1978) *Ecol. Bull.* (Stockholm) 26, 353-363.

Cochran, W.G. (1950) *Diometrios* 6, 105-115.

Day, J.M. & Döbereiner, J. (1976) *Soil Biol. Biochem.* 8, 45-50.

Döbereiner, J. (1974) Nitrogen fixation in the rhizosphere. *In*: The biology of nitrogen fixation, A. Quispel (Ed.). North-Holland Publ., Amsterdam, The Netherlands. Pp. 86-120.

Döbereiner, J., Marriel, I.E. & Nery, M. (1976) *Can J. Microbiol.* 22, 1464-1475.

Dommergues, Y.R. & Rinaudo, D. (1979) Factors affecting N_2 fixation in the rice rhizosphere. *In*: Nitrogen and rice. IRRI, Los Baños, Philippines. Pp. 241-260.

Grist, D.H. (1965) Rice (4th Ed.). Longmans, London, England. 221 pp.

Harrison, W.H. & Aiyer, P.A.S. (1915-1916) Mem. Dept. Agric. India (Pusa) Chem. Ser. 4, 1-14; 133-148.

Okon, Y., Albrecht, S.L. & Burris, R.H. (1976) *J. Bacteriol.* 127, 1219-1224.

Timonin, M.I. (1940) *Can. J. Res.* B 18, 444-456.

NITROGEN FIXATION IN ARTIFICIAL ASSOCIATIONS OF NONLEGUMES AND *RHIZOBIUM*

D. Hess[1]

Summary

This paper reviews recent work on the induction of nitrogenase activity in *Rhizobium* by agar grown plants of *Petunia*, *Triticum*, and *Sorghum*. On sterile vermiculite and soil, plants of *T. aestivum* showed both nitrogenase activity and enhanced plant dry weight. The possibility of practical wheat/*Rhizobium* associations is discussed.

INTRODUCTION

These proceedings have emphasized the importance of natural symbioses and associations between higher plants and nitrogen (N_2) fixing bacteria to improving world food production and nutrition. Recently there has also been much speculation as to whether the nif operon could be transferred from bacteria into higher plants. With the finding of a symbiotic N_2-fixing association between the nonlegume *Parasponia* and *Rhizobium*, a third possibility emerges: that of developing artificial associations of nonlegumes and bacteria, especially *Rhizobium*.

INDUCTION OF NITROGENASE ACTIVITY IN *RHIZOBIUM* BY NONLEGUMES

It has been demonstrated repeatedly in recent years that nonleguminous tissue cultures can induce nitrogenase activity in *Rhizobium* (Gibson *et al.*, 1976; Ranga Rao, 1976; Schetter & Hess, 1977). More recently it has been demonstrated that *Portulaca* cells can induce nitrogenase in *Rhizobium* sp. strain 32H1 through a membrane that is impermeable to bacteria, and that

[1] Lehrstuhl für Botanische Entwicklungsphysiologie, Univ. of Hohenheim, P.O. Box 70-05-62, D 7000, Stuttgart-70, FRG.

fixed N_2 could be incorporated into the normal pathway of ammonia utilization by the tissue culture (Lustig, Plischke & Hess, 1980a; 1980b; Hess & Lüstig, 1981).

Using plants of petunia *(Petunia hybrida)* grown with *Rhizobium* in agar, Hess & Götz (1977) and Götz (1980) demonstrated the ability of *Petunia* to induce N_2-ase activity in *Rhizobium*. The inducing capability increased with age and was enchanced more than 10-fold by the inclusion of plant growth regulators such as 6 benzyl-adenine in the medium (Hess & Feuereiszen, 1980).

Commercially important species such as tomato (*Lycopersicum esculentum*) and wheat (*Triticum aestivum*) also induced N_2-ase activity in *Rhizobium*. In tomatoes the inducing capability increased with plant age, as well, N_2 fixation being six-fold greater in plants inoculated at 22 days than in tomatoes inoculated nine days after germination (Hess, Schätzle & Dressler, 1981).

With wheat, nitrogenase activity could be induced in both *Rhizobium* sp. strain 32H 1 and in *R. japonicum* (Hess & Scholl, 1981), but when plants were removed the activity declined (Götz & Hess, 1980). N_2-ase activity could be enhanced by modification of the agar medium – especially the inclusion of mannitol (Hess & Kiefer, 1981) and of plant growth substances (Mertens & Hess, 1981).

When *Triticum aestivum* and *Sorghum nigricans* were inoculated under our artificial system with *Azospirillum lipoferum* strain 108 or *Rhizobium* sp. strain 32H1, both plant species induced nitrogenase activity in each bacteria. Ethylene accumulation was usually higher in *Sorghum* than in *Triticum,* but the maximum rates of N_2 (C_2H_2) fixation in sorghum were usually reached later, with no statistically significant difference between plant species and bacterial isolates (see Figure 1; Hess & Kiefer, 1981).

ATTACHMENT OF *RHIZOBIA* TO PLANT ROOT SURFACES AND UPTAKE INTO ROOT CELLS

With all the species used, rhizobia concentrated glove-like around the roots. Under the light microscope, a polar attachment of the bacteria to plant root surfaces; especially to root hairs, was shown (Gotz, 1980), and electron microscope studies showed that rhizobia had been taken into the roots of petunia and wheat. Rhizobia were detected in the intercellular spaces and, more interestingly, within parenchyma cells of wheat. Most of the rhizobia in wheat root cells showed a bacteroid-like structure. Furthermore, just as bacteroids they contained large granules of polyhydroxy-butyric acid. The question will be, whether bacteroids in wheat roots cells are able to fix nitrogen.

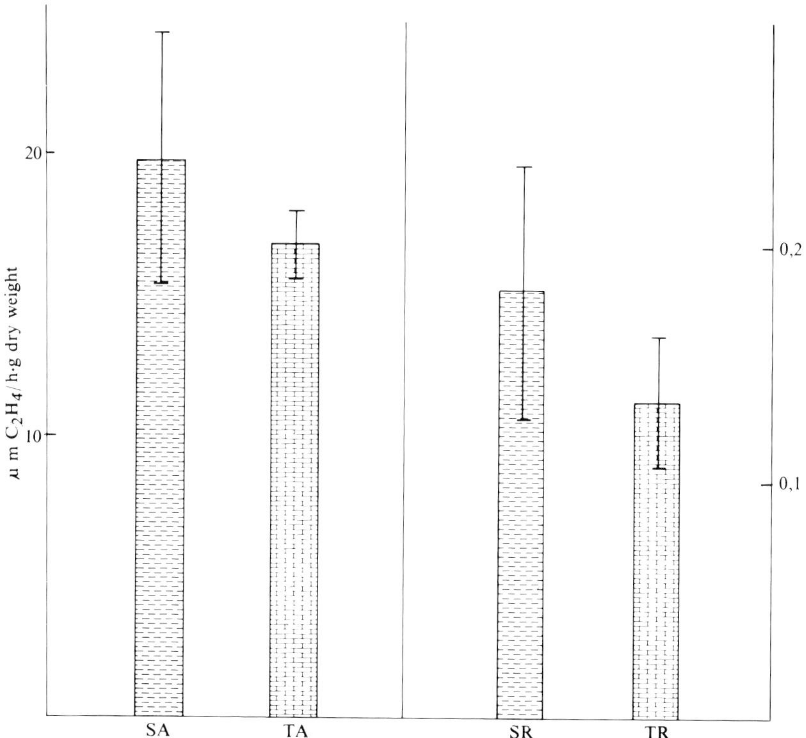

Figure 1. Nitrogenase activity in associations of *Triticum aestivum* and *Azospirillum* and *Rhizobium* strain 32H1 (TR), *Sorghum nigricans* and *A. lipoferum* (SA), *S. nigricans*, and *Rhizobium* strain 32H1 (SR), per plant dry weight and time (h = days from inoculation to evaluation). Evaluation was performed just before or after the final level of ethylene accumulation was reached. Bacteria alone showed no or a very low nitrogenase activity (from Hess & Kiefer, 1981).

REPLACEMENT OF AGAR

We are trying to replace the agar media by more natural media, and finally by soil under nonsterile conditions. The first steps are done: in associations of wheat and *Rhizobium* we replaced agar, under sterile conditions, with vermiculite and soil, and added liquid culture medium. On both substrates rhizobia concentrated around the roots as in agar media, and nitrogenase activity developed. Growth of the wheat plants on sterile vermiculite and soil was much better than on agar, and wheat plants associated with rhizobia showed enhanced dry weight on both substrates (Hess, 1981; see Figure 2).

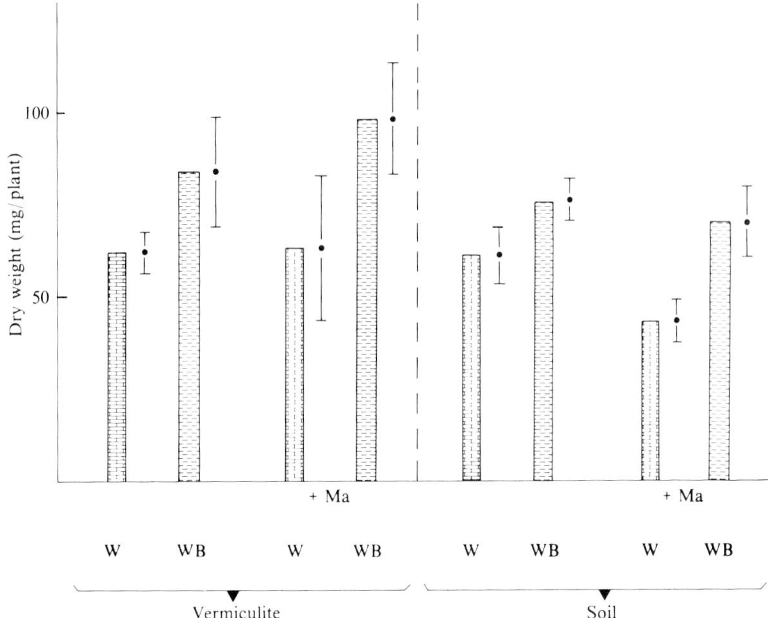

Figure 2. Increase of plant dry weight in associations of wheat and *Rhizobium* strain 32H1. Wheat was grown aseptically on vermiculite and soil, with the addition, of liquid culture medium, and with or without the addition of mannitol (Ma). The wheat plants were inoculated with rhizobia at an age of 18 days; 16 days later the plant dry weight was determined. W: wheat, WB: association wheat/rhizobia. (From Hess, 1981).

CONCLUDING REMARKS

What we have developed in the laboratory could have practical implications in the field. In fact Larson & Neal (1978) have already reported on natural associations between wheat and unknown N_2-fixing bacteria. Experiments on the *Triticum*/*Rhizobium* system in the field are justified. While it seems difficult to transfer all the gene material needed by a wheat plant for N_2 fixation, an association of *Rhizobium* and wheat would require much less manipulation.

REFERENCES

Gibson, A.H., Child, J.J., Pagan, J.D., & Scowcroft, W.R. (1976) *Planta* 128, 233-239.

Götz, E.M. (1980) *Z. Pflanzenphysiol.* 98, 465-470.

Götz, E.M. & Hess, D. (1980) *Z. Pflanzenphysiol.* 98, 453-458.

Hess, D. & Feureiszen, S. (1980) *Biochem. Physiol. Pflanzen* 175, 689-698.

Hess, D. & Götz, E.M. (1977) *Z. Pflanzenphysiol.* 85, 185-188.

Hess, D. & Kiefer, S. (1980). *Z. Pflanzenphysiol.* 101, 15-24.

Hess, D. & Lüstig, B. (1981) *Experientia.* (In press.)

Hess, D., Schätzle, H. & Dressler, K. (1981) (In preparation.)

Hess, D. & Scholl, M. (1981) (In preparation.)

Larson, R.I. & Neal, J.L. (1978) *Ecol. Bull.* (Stockholm) 26, 331-342.

Lüstig, B., Plischke, W. & Hess, D. (1980a) *Z. Pflazenphysiol.* 98, 277-281.

Lüstig, B., Plischke, W. & Hess, D. (1980b) *Experientia* 36, 1386-1387.

Mertens, T. & Hess, D. (1981) (In preparation.)

Ranga Rao, V. (1976) *Plant Sci.* Letters 6, 77-83.

Schetter, C. & Hess, D. (1977) *Plant Sci.* Letters 9, 1-5.

PERSPECTIVES ON BIOLOGICAL NITROGEN FIXATION IN SUGARCANE

A.P. Ruschel[1]

Summary

Micro-organisms capable of nitrogen (N_2) fixation were isolated from rhizosphere soil and from sugarcane roots, germinated stalks, and dry and green leaves. *Enterobacter cloacae*, *Klebsiella pneumoniae*, *Erwinia herbicola*, and *Bacillus polymyxa* were isolated from germinated stalks of sugarcane. Methods of evaluation of N_2 fixation in sugarcane are discussed. Future use for N_2 fixation in sugarcane will lie probably in the propagation of known varieties with high potential for N_2 fixation; however, studies must be done on the effect of climate, fertilizer and other agronomic practices, as well as the physiology and biochemistry of the N_2-fixing system.

INTRODUCTION

At one time there was a clear distinction between Leguminosae that fixed atmospheric nitrogen (N_2) and did not necessarily require N fertilizer, and Gramineae, which were not believed to support any N_2 fixation. The discovery of associative N_2-fixing systems in wheat, sorghum, tropical grasses, sugarcane, etc., has changed this simple picture. In Brazil, sugarcane does not respond in terms of yield to applications of N fertilizer in the first cropping year, but appears to require addition of N fertilizer to ratoon crops (Alvares, Segalla & Catani, 1958). This is probably because planting sets (sugarcane is propagated vegetatively) provide extra energy for N_2-fixing micro-organisms in the rhizosphere (Ruschel, Henis & Salati, 1975; Ruschel *et al.*, 1978), which, in turn, provide added N for sugarcane development.

In the last decade it has been possible to picture more clearly the micro-organisms and the nature of their association with sugarcane, as well as some

[1] Centro de Energía Nuclear na Agricultura (CENA), 13400 Piracicaba, São Paulo, Brazil.

quantitative aspects of the biological N_2 fixation system involved. A complete review of associative N_2 fixation in sugarcane has been presented recently (Ruschel, 1981); thus, this paper looks at a few major features of the association, examines some problem areas, and provides new information on the bacterial system.

THE NATURE OF THE ASSOCIATION

The finding that N_2-fixing micro-organisms were more abundant in the sugarcane rhizosphere than in surrounding soil (Döbereiner & Alvahydo, 1959; Anderson, 1962) suggested that this plant could be obtaining N via N_2 fixation. Nitrogenase activity was observed in roots (Döbereiner, Day & Dart, 1972; Ruschel & Ruschel, 1978; Purchase, 1980) and in the inner and outer parts of germinated cuttings (Ruschel & Ruschel, 1978), while N_2-fixing micro-organisms were obtained from enrichment cultures of roots (Ruschel *et al.*, 1978), germinated cuttings (Patriquin, Graciolli & Ruschel, 1980), node and internode (Graciolli & Ruschel, 1981; Costa & Ruschel, 1981) and phyllosphere (Graciolli & Ruschel, 1981).

Patriquin *et al.* (1980) observed that when surface-sterilized cuttings were germinated in sterile vermiculite, the vermiculite subsequently showed nitrogenase activity. Anatomical examination of the cuttings showed elongated ruptures or "holes" at the base of the roots around which the bacteria were clustered. Such holes could provide a means by which bacteria, carried initially in the stalks (planting sets), obtain ready access to the rhizosphere.

EFFECT OF PLANT CULTIVAR

Ruschel & Ruschel (1978) observed varietal differences in nitrogenase activity under both low and normal pO_2 conditions. Later they demonstrated that progeny resulting from crosses between cultivars differing in nitrogenase activity were intermediate between the parents (Ruschel & Ruschel, 1981) (see Table 1). When Ruschel (1979) exposed different varieties to $^{15}N_2$, not only were different rates of fixation observed, but evidence was obtained that fixation occurred in roots as well as in the seed piece (see Table 2). N in the shoots was due to translocation from roots, as demonstrated by Ruschel *et al.* (1979), who incubated shoots without roots under $^{15}N_2$ and observed no enrichment.

N_2-FIXING BACTERIA IN SUGARCANE

In some of the first work on N_2 fixation in sugarcane Döbereiner (1959) identified *Beijerinckia* as the principal N_2-fixing bacteria in this association. Ruschel *et al.* (1979) incubated segments of roots in different N-free glucose

TABLE 1: Nitrogenase activity (n mol C_2H_4 produced/plant per h) of parents and progenies from two different sugarcane crosses.[1,2]

Identification	Relation	Level of N_2 fixation
CP 36-105	P_1	108.2
CP 38-34	P_2	875.7
CP 48-124	F_1-A	260.9
CP 52-48	F_1-B	189.3
CO 301	P_1	166.1
CO 290	P_2	188.1
CB 45-3	F_1	335.6

[1]Data from ten vegetatively propagated plants per material, two months after planting.
[2]From Ruschel & Ruschel (1979).

TABLE 2: N enrichment (ug ^{15}N fixed/24 h) in roots, aerial parts, and "seed pieces" of three sugarcane varieties. Mean of three replications.

Varieties	Root	Aerial parts	Seed piece	Total[1]
CB 46-47	0.161	0.085	5.142	5.388 a
CB 41-76	0.126	0.358	4.788	5.272 b
CB 47-355	0.208	0.488	4.367	5.063 b
Mean	0.165 b	0.310 b	4.765 a	

[1]Tukey test.

and malate semisolid media, isolating in this way a range of organisms including *Azotobacter*, *Beijerinckia*, *Derxia*, *Caulobacter*, *Clostridium*, *Vibrio*, and *Bacillus polymyxa*. Following the demostration of N_2-fixing bacteria inside sugarcane stalks (Ruschel & Ruschel, 1978; Patriquin, *et al.*, 1980), *Enterobacter cloacae*, *Klebsiella pneumoniae*, *Erwinia herbicola* and *Bacillus polymyxa* were isolated and identified by the API[1] method (Rennie, 1980). Enterobacteriaceae that could not be classified into species by the API method were recovered from surface-sterilized cuttings of the variety CB41-76 (R.J. Rennie & A.P. Ruschel, unpublished data)(see Table 3).

[1] Analybad Products/Division of Ayerst Labs. Plainview, NY 11803, USA.

TABLE 3: Percent of bacteria isolated from plants obtained from unsterilized and surface-sterilized cuttings planted in sterilized vermiculite (R.J. Rennie and A.P. Ruschel, unpublished data).

Bacteria	Non sterilized		Sterilized	
	Root	Cutting	Root	Cutting
Klebsiella pneumoniae	17	17	0	0
Erwinia herbicola	67	50	0	0
Bacillus polymyxa	17	13	0	0
Unknown[1]	0	0	100	70

[1]Enterobacteriaceae

EVALUATION OF BIOLOGICAL N_2 FIXATION IN SUGARCANE

The use of $^{15}N_2$ is the most effective method of proving N_2 fixation in sugarcane (Ruschel *et al.*, 1975). However, due to the size of fully developed plants (2.0-2.5 m high) and the distribution of roots in the soil, it is difficult to find a good chamber in which to enclose a mature plant system for quantitative studies. In a previous attempt, when only the roots of the plant were enclosed (Matsui *et al.*, 1981), it was possible to demonstrate enrichment of $^{15}N_2$ in the soil around the roots, but the plant showed no enrichment. This was probably due not only to the high dilution of ^{15}N by N already present in the plant, but also to dilution of the ^{15}N-enriched gas by atmospheric N. E. Ralund (unpublished data), using a mixture of acetylene and propane, has demonstrated that atmospheric gas passes from leaves to the roots in only 30 minutes.

The isotope dilution method of estimating N_2 fixation requires the comparison of a N_2-fixing plant against one that doesn't fix N_2. It is difficult to find a proper control for sugarcane since it is a plant with a long growth cycle (14 months for plant cane under Brazilian conditions), and so far we have not tried this approach. The identification of a sugarcane variety which appears to support very little N_2 (C_2H_2) fixation may, however, now make it possible.

OTHER AREAS REQUIRING INVESTIGATION

There are sufficient differences between genotypes in nitrogenase activity to indicate that breeding for enhanced N_2-fixing capability is possible. At the same time loss in potential ability to fix N_2, brought about by varietal selection under conditions of high N fertilization, needs to be evaluated.

Preliminary results with Hawaiian varieties (sugarcane receives very high levels of applied N in Hawaii) suggested that selection under high N does not necessarily affect capacity to support an N_2-fixing system. Moreover, as the N_2-fixing micro-organisms are dependent on an energy supply for N_2 fixation, and since this energy must be consumed at the expense of sugar in the harvestable stalks, further studies on the physiological factors affecting fixation are needed.

The response of sugarcane to inoculation is not known, since most of the results obtained thus far have been obtained under nutrient solution conditions, or in soil and field using modified cultures. However, as we now have better knowledge of the micro-organisms isolated from stalks, we should be able to investigate the question of inoculation more scientifically. At the same time we also need better information on the effect of agronomic practices such as cultivation, irrigation, and supply of potassium and minor elements on N_2 fixation in sugarcane. Information on the pathway of newly fixed N in the plant is a priority as well.

REFERENCES

Alvares, R., Segalla, A.L. & Catani, R.A. (1958) Adubação de cana-de-açúcar. III. Fertilizantes nitrogenados. *Bragantia* 17, 141-146.

Anderson, J.R. (1962) Free-living nitrogen-fixing bacteria in Natal sugarcane soils. Proc. South African Sugar Technologists Assn. 36, 112-118.

Costa, J.M.F. & Ruschel, A.P. (1981) Seasonal variation in the microbial population of sugarcane stalks. *In*: Associative N_2 Fixation, P.B. Vose & A.P. Ruschel (Eds.). CRC Press, Boca Raton, FL, USA. Vol. 2, Ch. 15.

Döbereiner, J. (1959) Sobre a ocorrência de *Beijerinckia* em alguns estados do Brasil. *Rev. Bras. Biol.* 19(2), 151-160.

Döbereiner, J. & Alvahydo, R. (1959) Sobre a influência da cana-de-açúcar na ocorrência de *Beijerinckia* no solo. II. Influência das diversas partes do vegetal. *Rev. Bras. Biol.* 19(4), 401-412.

Döbereiner, J., Day, J.M. & Dart, P.J. (1972) Nitrogen activity in the rhizosphere of sugarcane and some other tropical grasses. *Plant Soil* 37, 191-196.

Graciolli, L.A. & Ruschel, A.P. (1981) Micro-organisms in the phyllosphere and rhizosphere of sugarcane. *In*: Associative N_2 Fixation, P.B. Vose & A.P. Ruschel (Eds.). CRC Press. Boca Raton, FL, USA. Vol. 2, Ch. 13.

Matsui, E., Vose, P.B., Rodriguez, N.S., & Ruschel, A.P. (1981) Use of ^{15}N enriched gas to determine N_2 fixation by undisturbed sugarcane plants in the field. *In*: Associative N_2 Fixation, P.B. Vose & A.P. Ruschel (Eds.). CRC Press, Boca Raton, FL, USA. Vol. 2, Ch. 21.

Patriquin, D.G., Graciolli, L.A. & Ruschel, A.P. (1980) Nitrogenase activity of sugarcane propagated from stem cuttings in sterile vermiculite. *Soil Biol. Biochem.* 12, 413-417.

Purchase, B.S. (1980) Nitrogen fixation associated with sugarcane. Proc. South African Sugar Technologists Assn. Pp. 173-176.

Rennie, R.J. (1980) Dinitrogen-fixing bacteria. Computer-assisted identification of soil isolates. *Can. J. Microbiol.* 26, 1275-1283.

Ruschel, A.P. (1979) Fixação biológica do nitrogênio. *In*: Fisiologia vegetal, M.G. Ferri (Ed.). EDUSP. Cap. 4: 167-178.

Ruschel, A.P. (1981) Associative N_2 fixation by sugarcane. *In*: Associative N_2 fixation, P.B. Vose & A.P. Ruschel (Eds.). CRC Press, Boca Raton, FL, USA. Vol. 2, Ch. 12.

Ruschel, A.P., Henis, Y. & Salati, E. (1975) Nitrogen-15 tracing of N-fixation with soil grown sugarcane seedlings. *Soil Biol. Biochem.* 7, 181-182.

Ruschel, A.P. & Ruschel, R. (1978) Varietal differences affecting nitrogenase activity in the rhizosphere of sugarcane. Proc. XVI Congress Internat. Soc. Sugarcane Technologists. Vol. 2, Pp. 1941-1948.

Ruschel, A.P., Victória, R.L., Salati, E., & Henis, Y. (1978) Environmental role of nitrogen-fixing blue-green algae and asymbiotic bacteria. *Ecol. Bull.* (Stockholm) 26, 297-303.

Ruschel, R. & Ruschel, A.P. (1981) Inheritance of N_2-fixing ability in sugarcane. *In*: Associative N_2 Fixation, P.B. Vose & A.P. Ruschel (Eds.). CRC Press, Boca Raton, FL, USA. Vol. 2, Ch. 18.

ASSOCIATIVE DINITROGEN FIXATION IN *DIPLACHNE FUSCA* (KALLAR GRASS)

K.A. Malik, Y. Zafar and A. Hussain[1]

Summary

Presence of nitrogen-fixing ability in the rhizosphere of kallar grass (*Diplachne fusca*), a salt-tolerant species, was demonstrated by the acetylene reduction method. High nitrogenase activity was observed in both washed and unwashed roots, indicating an active rhizocoenosis. Enrichment cultures from the roots were also able to reduce acetylene. N_2-fixing bacteria from the root samples were isolated on N-free medium, and characterized.

INTRODUCTION

Many tropical grasses establish diazotrophic rhizocoenoses with bacteria (Döbereiner & Day, 1975; Döbereiner, Marriel & Nery, 1976; Knowles, 1977; Neyra & Döbereiner, 1977; Nur *et al.*, 1980; Weier, 1980). During recent years such nitrogen (N_2) fixing associations have been recognized as important components of a range of ecosystems, including several extreme environments (Capone & Taylor, 1980; McClung & Patriquin, 1980).

Diplachne fusca (Linn.) Beauv. (locally known as kallar grass) is a highly salt-tolerant grass used as the primary colonizer of salt-affected soils in Pakistan (Sandhu & Malik, 1975). This grass, which grows luxuriantly in salt-affected and low-fertility soils, is a good animal fodder, providing three to four cuttings during the monsoon months even without N fertilization. Because of this we initiated studies to establish if biological N_2 fixation occurred in the rhizosphere of this species (Malik *et al.*, 1980). In this paper we report N_2 (C_2H_2) fixation by *D. fusca* from various salt-affected soils.

MATERIALS AND METHODS

Whole-plant samples, including roots to a depth of 20 cm, were collected

[1] Soil Biology Division, Nuclear Institute for Agriculture and Biology, Faisalabad, Pakistan.

from five salt-affected areas at different times during the year and transported to the laboratory.

Three root sample preparations were prepared from the plants taken at each site:

Unwashed sample;

Sample with the soil gently removed after which the roots were washed with tap water and distilled water; and

Clean samples as above but with the roots washed with 0.1% $HgCl_2$ for 30 sec and then rewashed several times with sterile distilled water.

Root samples were placed in McCartney vials, incubated overnight in 90% N_2:10% air; then N_2 (C_2H_2) fixation was measured using the technique of Hardy *et al.* (1968) and an incubation period of 3 h at 32° C.

Enrichment culture assays and isolation of the presumptive N_2-fixing bacteria were then carried out as described by von Bülow & Döbereiner (1975).

RESULTS AND DISCUSSION

Characteristics of the soils from which *D. fusca* plants were taken are summarized in Table 1. Four of the five soils were of high pH, electrical conductivity, and sodium adsorption ratio.

TABLE 1: Physico-chemical characteristics of the soils from which samples of *Diplachne fusca* were obtained.

Characteristic	Jhang area	NIAB field	Shahkot area	Shahkot area	Lahore (RDC)
pH (saturation paste)	8.7	7.75	9.8	9.6	8.8
Electrical conductivity (mmhos/cm)	43	1.60	11.5	11.5	11.2
Sodium adsorption ratio, (SAR)	28	11	342	340	50

Table 2 shows N_2 (C_2H_2) fixation for the variously treated roots of *D. fusca*. Fairly high N_2 (C_2H_2) fixation is evident in roots from four of the five sites. Samples obtained from fields at the Institute did not fix N_2 (C_2H_2).

For the locations where N_2 (C_2H_2) fixation was observed, greatest activity was found during the summer monsoon months. Nitrogenase activity declined toward the end of the growing season. N_2 (C_2H_2) fixation was also detected in $HgCl_2$-treated, and presumably surface-sterile root systems, suggesting the possibility of rhizoplane activity. Such associations have been reviewed recently by van Berkum & Bohlool (1980).

TABLE 2: Rates of C_2H_2-reduction (n moles C_2H_4 produced/g fresh weight/3 hours) of roots of kallar grass (*Diplachne fusca*) from different areas.

Areas	No of samples	Unwashed roots	Washed (H_2O) roots	Washed (0.1 % $HgCl_2$) roots
Jhang area 11.11.1979	10	210-420	30-1120	ND[1]
NIAB field 10-5-1980	35	0	0	0
Shahkot area 15.7.1980	15	30-1140	180-3000 (8070)[2]	30-390
Shahkot area 7.9.1980	28	15-450	60-330	30-300
Lahore (RDC) 6-12-1980	10	30-270 (1120)[2]	90-240	15-30

[1]ND = Not determined.
[2]Number in brackets corresponds to exceptional activity in only one sample.

For enrichment culture studies, selected pieces of surface-sterilized roots that showed N_2 (C_2H_2) fixation were transferred to N-free, semi-solid, sodium malate medium (von Bülow & Döbereiner, 1975). Acetylene reduction assays performed on the enrichment cultures revealed relatively high nitrogenase activity (see Table 3), with different areas sampled similar in activity.

The micro-organisms responsible for the N_2 (C_2H_2) fixation of root samples were isolated from enrichment culture and again checked for nitrogenase activity. They were gram negative, VP, MR and indole negative, highly motile, curved rods. They showed maximum activity with sodium malate and sodium succinate.

TABLE 3: Nitrogenase activity of enrichment culture after two days incubation on semisolid N-free mineral medium at 30°C.

No.	Samples (inoculum)	n moles C_2H_4/ml medium·h (ranges)
1.	Jhang area	30-1020
2.	NIAB field	Nil
3.	Shahkot area	210-630
4.	Shahkot area	150-600
5.	Lahore (RDC)	390-1500

REFERENCES

Berkum, P. van & Bohlool, B.B. (1980) Evaluation of nitrogen-fixation by bacteria in association with roots of tropical grasses. *Microbiol. Reviews* 44, 491-517.

Bülow, J.W.F. von & Dőbereiner, J. (1975) Potential for nitrogen fixation in maize genotypes in Brazil. *Proc. Nat. Acad. Sci. USA*. 72, 2389-2393.

Capone. D.G. & Taylor, B.F. (1980) N_2-fixation in the rhizosphere of *Thalassia testudinum*. *Can. J. Microbiol.* 26, 998-1005.

Döbereiner, J. & Day. J.M. (1975) Nitrogen fixation in the rhizosphere of tropical grasses. *In*: Nitrogen fixation by free living micro-organisms, W.D.P. Stewart (Ed.). Cambridge Univ. Press. Cambridge, England, Pp. 39-56.

Dőbereiner, J., Marriel, I.E. & Nery, M. (1976) Ecological distribution of *Spirillum lipoferum* Beijerinck. *Can. J. Microbiol.* 22, 1464-1473.

Hardy, R.W.F., Holsten, R.D., Jackson, E.K., & Burns, R.C. (1968) The acetylene-ethylene assay for N_2 fixation: Laboratory and field evaluation. *Plant Physiol.* 43, 1185-1207.

Knowles, R. (1977) The significance of asymbiotic dinitrogen fixation by bacteria. *In*: A treatise on dinitrogen fixation. Section IV: Agronomy and ecology. R.W.F. Hardy and A.H. Gibson (Eds.). Wiley, New York, NY, USA. Pp. 33-38.

Malik, K.A., Zafar, Y. & Hussain, A. (1980) Nitrogenase activity in the rhizosphere of kallar grass (*Diplachne fusca* (Linn.) Beauv.). *Biologia* 26, 114-118.

McClung, C.R. & Patriquin, D.G. (1980) Isolation of a nitrogen-fixing *Campylobacter* species from the roots of *Spartina alterniflora* Loisel. *Can. J. Microbiol.* 26, 881-886.

Neyra, C.A. & Döbereiner, J. (1977) Nitrogen fixation in grasses. *Advances in Agronomy.* 29, 1-38.

Nur, I., Okon, Y. & Henis, Y. (1980) Comparative studies of nitrogen-fixing bacteria associated with grasses in Israel with *Azospirillum brasilense. Can. J. Microbiol.* 26, 714-718.

Sandhu, G.R. & Malik, K.A. (1975) Plant succession-A key to the utilization of saline soils. *Nucleus* 12, 35-38.

Weier, K.L. (1980) Nitrogenase activity associated with three tropical grasses growing in undisturbed soil cores. *Soil Biol. Biochem.* 12, 131-136.

NONSYMBIOTIC NITROGEN-FIXING BACTERIA IN SOILS FROM PATAGONIA

M.G. Pozzo Ardizzi de Fidel[1]

Summary

Azospirillum was found in 67 of 86 soils examined in the Rio Negro, Neuquén and Chubut provinces of Argentina. Among spontaneous grasses found to associate with *Azospirillum* were *Piptochaetium*, *Stipa*, *Poa*, *Vulpia*, *Bromus*, *Festuca*, *Hordeum* and *Distichlis* species. Rates of N_2 (C_2H_2) fixation varied from 60.53-76.58 nmol/g roots per h.

INTRODUCTION

The Rio Negro, Neuquén and Chubut provinces in the Patagonia region of Argentina, at 40° to 42° south latitude, are characterized by a cool (average temperature 12° C), dry (annual rainfall less than 200 mm) climate. The area is devoted mainly to sheep raising, and spontaneous grass pastures provide the only animal feed. As nitrogen (N) in these soils is low, we have carried out examinations on various of the grass species present in the region to determine whether they associate with N_2-fixing bacteria.

MATERIALS AND METHODS

Soil and root samples

Samples were collected during August to November in the gramineous steppe and during April in the shrub steppe (see Figure 1). All samples were taken with care to avoid contamination. Soil and root samples were collected at each site, but soil samples were taken from areas without roots.

[1] Centro Univ. Reg. Viedma, Univ. Nacional del Comahue, C.C. 149-8500, Viedma, Rio Negro, Argentina.

Figure 1. Appearence of natural pastures in (a) the grass steppe and (b) the shrub steppe of Patagonia.

Culture methods

N-free semisolid malate medium was used to investigate the presence of N_2-fixing bacteria in soil and root samples, following the techniques described by Döbereiner, Marriel & Nery (1976). Peptone broth was also used to culture bacteria and observe their morphology. For the isolation and identification of an *Azospirillum*-like organism, N-free solid medium with 50 mg/l yeast extract was used.

Agar tetrazolium preparations were made with root pieces for the identification of N_2-fixing sites (Döbereiner & Day, 1976).

Acetylene reduction assays with washed roots, pre-incubated for 18 h, were carried out at 30% using 10% C_2H_2 and a 3 h incubation period.

RESULTS AND DISCUSSION

Of the 86 soil samples examined, 67 produced cultures with the typical *Azospirillum* pellicle in semisolid malate medium, and contained spiral cells with extensive lipid bodies. *Azotobacter* was identified in 51 soils and *Beijerinckia* in 17 (see Table 1).

TABLE 1: Occurrence of nonsymbiotic N_2-fixing bacteria in soils collected in Patagonia, Argentina.

Origin of samples	pH	No. of samples	No. of positive samples		
			Azospirillum	*Azotobacter*	*Beijerinckia*
Rio Negro	6.5 - 7.8	50	40	29	10
Chubut	6.8 - 7.2	15	15	7	3
Neuquén	7.2 - 7.5	21	12	15	4

N_2-fixing micro-organisms were found associated with many of the grasses that are important in this region (see Table 2). Only one plant species, *Stipa speciosa,* did not appear to associate with *Azospirillum* organisms. *Beijerinckia, Clostridium,* and other, filamentous bacteria were also found associated with roots.

Acetylene reduction assays carried out with roots of *Stipa neali*, *Distichlis scoparia*, and *Hordeum jubatum* gave rates of N_2 (C_2H_2) fixation of 76.58, 60.53 and 65.58 nmoles/g fresh wt of roots per h.

It is obvious from these results that nonsymbiotic, N_2-fixing bacteria occur widely in the soils, and are associated with the roots of grasses in this region.

TABLE 2: Occurrence of plant/root association in spontaneous grasses collected in soils from Patagonia, Argentina.

Subfamily	Tribe	Genus	Occurrence of	
			Azospirillum	*Azotobacter*
Festucoideas	Estipea	*Piptochaetium*	+	+
		Stipa humilis	x	+
		S. tenuis	+	+
		S. ambigua	x	+
		S. dusenii	+	+
		S. paposa	+	+
		S. speciosa	–	+
		S. neali	x	–
		S. fuliculmins	+	+
		Stipa sp.	+	+
	Festuceas	*Poa*	+	+
		Vulpia	x	–
		Bromus	+	–
		Festuca purpurascens	+	–
	Hordeas	*Hordeum jubatum*	x	–
		Hordeum murinum	x	+
Eragrostoideas	Eragrosteas	*Distichlis scoparia*	o	+
		D. spicata	x	+

+: S-shaped, short, and very motile.
x : S-shaped and helical long, and very motile.
o : Helical and comma-shaped, not very motile.

Further studies are needed to quantify their contribution to the N economy of the pastures.

REFERENCES

Döbereiner, J. & Day, J.M. (1976) Proc. First. Intern. Symp. Nitrogen Fixation. W.E. Newton & C.J. Nyman (Eds.). Washington State Univ., Pullman, WA, USA. Vol II, pp. 518-538.

Döbereiner, J., Marriel, J.E. & Nery, M. (1976) *Can. J. Microbiol.* 22, 1464-1472.

SOME PERTINENT REMARKS ON N_2 FIXATION ASSOCIATED WITH THE ROOTS OF GRASSES

P. van Berkum, C.R. McClung and C. Sloger[1]

Summary

The indirect measurement of nitrogenase (N_2-ase) activity using C_2H_2 is popular, but evidence that N_2 fixation is associated with grasses should be based on short-term assays immediately after sampling. Delaying the measurement of C_2H_2 reduction overestimates rates of N_2-ase activity and may erroneously identify N_2 fixation *in situ*. If N_2 fixation is occurring in grasses *in situ*, C_2H_2 reduction with excised roots should be detectable without delay and with immediately linear rates of C_2H_4 accumulation under the appropriate assay conditions. Root-associated N_2-ase activity in aquatic grasses is sensitive to O_2, but inactivation is temporary, causing nonlinear rates of immediate C_2H_2 reduction. N_2-ase activity associated with roots of *Oryza sativa* appears to be dependent upon a supply of O_2 from the leaves of the plants to the roots. Applications of KNO_3 to *O. sativa* and field plots of *Paspalum notatum* reduced the rate of N_2-ase activity, increased leaf NRA, and improved plant growth. At the present time associative N_2 fixation does not seem to be applicable to agriculture but may be of significance in maintaining soil fertility. It would seem desirable to re-examine the evidence that *Azospirillum* spp. are located inside grass roots and that rudimentary host plant/*Azospirillum* symbioses exist.

INTRODUCTION

Biological nitrogen (N_2) fixation is generally regarded as a mechanism by which applications of fertilizer N to crops could be supplemented or reduced and economic returns enhanced. The hypothesis that non-nodulated plants could derive significant benefit from nonsymbiotic N_2 fixation originates

[1] USDA/SEA/AR, BARC-West, Beltsville, MD 20705, USA.

from reports of N accumulation in N balance studies (Dart & Day, 1975; Greenland, 1977). Later it was suggested that *Azospirillum* and other bacteria could form N_2-fixing associations with the roots of grasses. The prospect that such associations offer a means of implementing biological N_2 fixation for the production of forage and cereal crops (Neyra & Döbereiner, 1977) stimulated intense research activity and has produced some anomalous results. This brief review examines three research areas in which this has occurred and attempts to provide needed perspective.

METHODS FOR THE MEASUREMENT OF N_2 FIXATION IN GRASSES

Nonsymbiotic and associative N_2 fixation are preferably measured using undisturbed, intact or *in situ* methods. The advantages and disadvantages of Kjeldahl analysis and measurements with isotopic $^{15}N_2$ are discussed elsewhere in these proceedings. However, the usefulness of these conventional methods to determine N_2 fixation in grasses may be limited because of delayed or slow transfer of fixed N from the bacteria to grasses (van Berkum, in press). Furthermore, we suggest that only unequivocal demonstration of N_2-ase activity *in situ* with C_2H_2 reduction justifies the subsequent use of $^{15}N_2$ to measure N_2 fixation in grass/soil systems.

MEASUREMENT OF C_2H_2 REDUCTION WITH SOIL CORES OF GRASSES

Day *et al.* (1975) developed a small soil core device with which to measure C_2H_2 reduction and so determine whether nonsymbiotic N_2 fixation was responsible for observed accumulations of N on the Broadbalk site, Rothamsted, England. Measurement of C_2H_2 reduction with soil cores of plants from the stubbed wilderness coincided with the N accumulation data, but samples from the wooded wilderness and the arable plots did not. The rates of N_2 fixation reported by Day *et al.* (1975) may be criticized because their estimates are based on arbitrary incubation times coupled with nonlinear rates of C_2H_2 reduction. Nonlinear rates of C_2H_2 reduction may have been caused by poor penetration of C_2H_2 into the soil (Day *et al.*, 1975) or the slow diffusion of C_2H_4 from microsites of N_2 fixation to the sampling ports (van Berkum & Day, 1980; van Berkum & Sloger, 1981a). Measurement of the diffusion rates of C_2H_2 and C_2H_4 through metal cylinders containing various soil types has indicated that long incubation times were required to saturate the samples with C_2H_2 (van Berkum & Day, 1980). On the other hand, C_2H_2 inhibits synthesis of NH_4^+ from N_2 and may induce N_2-ase activity, causing rates of N_2 fixation to be overestimated (van Berkum & Bohlool, 1980).

The soil core method developed by Day *et al.* (1975) has also been used to measure C_2H_2 reduction with tropical grasses in Brazil (Abrantes *et al.*, 1975; van Berkum & Day, 1980). Abrantes *et al.* (1975) were not able to detect C_2H_2 reduction in soil cores of grasses removed from the field and immediately assayed. They suggested that samples should be watered and incubated in the greenhouse for one to three days before measuring N_2-ase activity. Recently, van Berkum & Day (1980) reported that measurement of C_2H_2 reduction on soil cores of grasses kept and watered for several days before assay may seriously overestimate *in situ* N_2 fixation.

The measurement of C_2H_2 reduction in soil cores of grasses using short-term incubation times (up to 6 h) is possible when C_2H_2 diffuses rapidly throughout the samples (Tjepkema & van Berkum, 1977; van Berkum & Day, 1980). Immediately linear rates of C_2H_2 reduction have been reported with soil cores of *Paspalum notatum* and *Brachiaria mutica* (van Berkum, 1978; van Berkum & Day, 1980). However, C_2H_2 inhibits C_2H_4 oxidation by soil microflora and endogenously produced C_2H_4 may accumulate and contribute to the observed rate of C_2H_2 reduction (Witty, 1979). Another problem with soil cores is that it is not possible to distinguish microsites of N_2 fixation that may be associated with decaying organic matter as well as with the living roots of grasses. The evidence that N_2-ase activity is associated with living plant tissue has been based on measurements of C_2H_2 reduction with excised roots washed with distilled water.

MEASUREMENT OF C_2H_2 REDUCTION BY EXCISED ROOTS OF GRASSES

The foremost enigma of the excised root assay has been the initial 8 to 18-hour delay reported before C_2H_2 reduction begins. The delay before N_2-ase activity with excised roots is detectable is inconsistent with the kinetics of C_2H_2 reduction by all other N_2-fixing systems (van Berkum & Bohlool, 1980). Because it is difficult to interpret measurements of C_2H_2 reduction after this long delay, the excised root assay was modified to include an overnight pre-incubation period at reduced pO_2 (Döbereiner *et al.*, 1972a). The pre-incubation period was subsequently adopted as a routine method to prepare excised roots for the measurement of N_2 fixation in grasses (Abrantes *et al.*, 1975). It has also been suggested that the overnight pre-incubation period enables the potential rate of N_2 fixation in grasses to be measured (Day *et al.*, 1975; von Bülow & Döbereiner, 1975), but no evidence for this was provided (van Berkum, 1980). In contrast, it was shown that N_2-fixing bacteria proliferated and induced N_2-ase activity during the period before the onset of C_2H_2 reduction by excised washed roots (van Berkum, 1980). Recently, van Berkum & Bohlool (1980) concluded that the pre-incubated excised root assay not only overestimates rates of N_2-ase activity but also may erroneously extrapolate tissue to be fixing N_2 *in situ*.

The excised root assay has been shown to be useful in identifying N_2 fixation associated with grasses when C_2H_2 reduction is detected immediately and no pre-incubation period is used (van Berkum & Sloger, 1979; 1981), although C_2H_4 does not accumulate with linear rates (see Figure 1a).

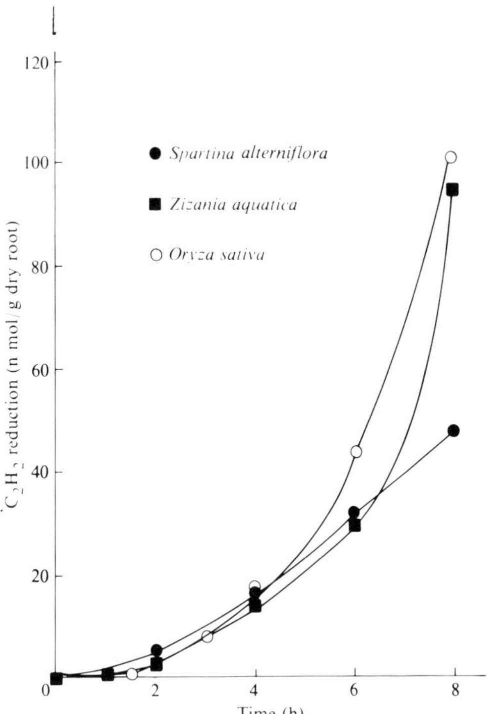

Figura 1a.
Reduction of C_2H_2 by roots of aquatic grasses in air immediately after excision from the plants (from van Berkum & Sloger, 1981).

MEASUREMENT OF C_2H_2 REDUCTION WITH INTACT AQUATIC GRASSES

The measurement of N_2-ase activity in aquatic grasses by exposing the plant tops to C_2H_2 (Patriquin & Denike, 1978; van Berkum & Sloger, 1979; 1981) exploits the ability of these plants to transport gases to the roots via the lacunae. Initial studies with this technique obtained rates of N_2(C H_2) fixation that were not immediately linear (van Berkum & Sloger, 1981a). However, immediately linear rates of C_2H_2 reduction were detected when the roots were protected from air during their removal from soil and measurement for N_2-ase activity (Figure 1b). This suggests that *in situ* plant-associated N_2-ase activity should result in inmmediate reduction of C_2H_2 and linear rates of C_2H_4 accumulation when the proper conditions are used.

N_2-ase activity is known to be sensitive to O_2 (Burns & Hardy, 1975), and N_2 fixation under fully aerobic conditions is not possible unless the enzyme is

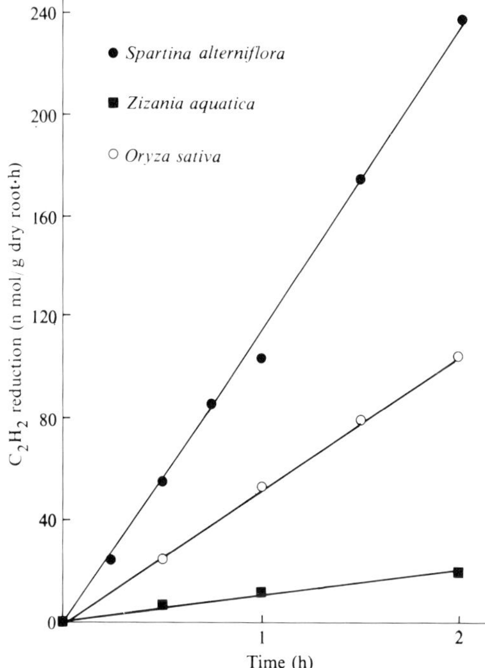

Figure 1b.
Immediately linear rates of C_2H_2 reduction by roots of intact aquatic grasses protected from air during preparation of plants for assay (from van Berkum & Sloger, 1981a).

protected. The pO_2 surrounding the roots of aquatic grasses *in situ* is extremely low, and the exposure of roots to O_2 during their preparation could cause an initial, but temporary, inactivation leading to the nonlinear profiles of C_2H_2 reduction. Similar initial nonlinear rates of C_2H_2 reduction have been reported with pre-incubated, excised sorghum roots (van Berkum, 1980), the roots of intact plants of *Scirpus olneyi* (van Berkum & Sloger, 1981), and nodulated soybean roots (van Berkum & Sloger, 1981), which had been exposed to air or O_2. The sensitivity of N_2-ase activity to O_2 could be due to poor O_2 protection mechanisms under *in situ* conditions. The initial accelerating rates of C_2H_2 reduction by roots treated with air may be caused by the recovery of N_2-ase activity as the pO_2 decreases in the film of water surrounding the respiring tissue. Alternatively, the recovery of N_2-ase activity may be mediated by the development of an O_2 protection mechanism for N_2-ase activity in the root-associated bacteria.

Van Berkum & Sloger (1981, in press) used *Oryza sativa* with the roots protected from exposure to air during sampling, to investigate the effect of O_2 on the initial rates of C_2H_2 reduction. As the concentration of O_2 in the assay chambers was increased, the linear rate of N_2-ase activity decreased (see Figure 2). This observation differs with reports of optimum O_2 concentrations for N_2 fixation by *Azotobacter* (Drozd & Postgate, 1970),

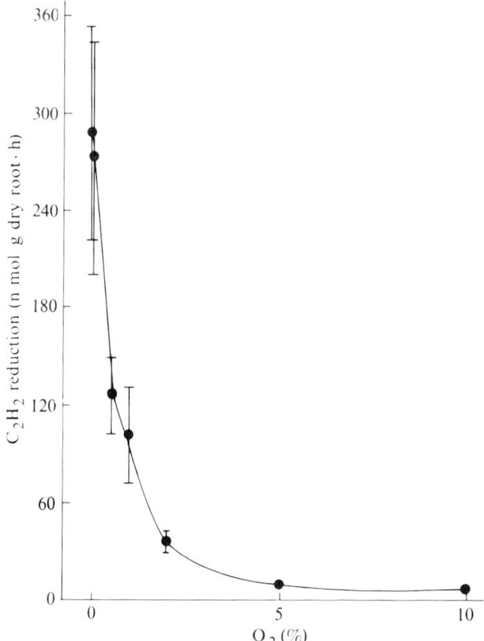

Figure 2.
The rate of C_2H_2 reduction by roots of *Oryza sativa* exposed to increasing concentrations of O in the assay chambers (from van Berkum & Sloger, 1981c).

Azospirillum (Day & Döbereiner, 1976), and pre-incubated, excised roots (Döbereiner *et al.,* 1972b). If the plant tops were removed and O_2 allowed to deplete in the remaining tissue for 4 h before assay, *O. sativa* was shown to have an optimal pO_2 for N_2-ase activity at 0.25% atm (see Figure 3). These observations suggest that N_2-ase activity associated with the roots of aquatic plants is dependent upon a supply of O_2 from the atmosphere (van Berkum & Sloger, 1981c), and that the intact assay method measures the rate of C_2H_2 reduction at pO_2's occurring in the roots of undisturbed grasses (van Berkum & Sloger, 1981a).

INFLUENCE OF COMBINED N ON ROOT-ASSOCIATED N_2-ASE ACTIVITY IN GRASSES

Grasses depend mainly on inorganic combined N for growth, but may stimulate N_2 fixation by bacteria associated with their roots. Combined N is known to inhibit N_2 fixation in legumes (Gibson, 1974; 1976) and has been suggested to inhibit or reduce the rate of root-associated N_2-ase activity in grasses.

Van Berkum (1978) used the soil core method developed by Day *et al.* (1975) in Brazil to follow the interaction of applied N with N_2-ase activity in field plots of *P. notatum.* Applications of KNO_3 (40 kg N/ha) reduced the rate of N_2-ase activity in *P. notatum* (see Figure 4), though the inhibition was temporary. Leaf nitrate reductase activity (NRA) in *P. notatum* was not detected in control plots, but was induced in plants receiving KNO_3. The percent N content of plants and the growth of *P. notatum* were also improved on plots receiving KNO_3 (van Berkum, 1978). This suggests that N_2 fixation is not able to provide all of the N needed for the growth of *P. notatum* and that fertilizer N could be incompatible with N_2 fixation.

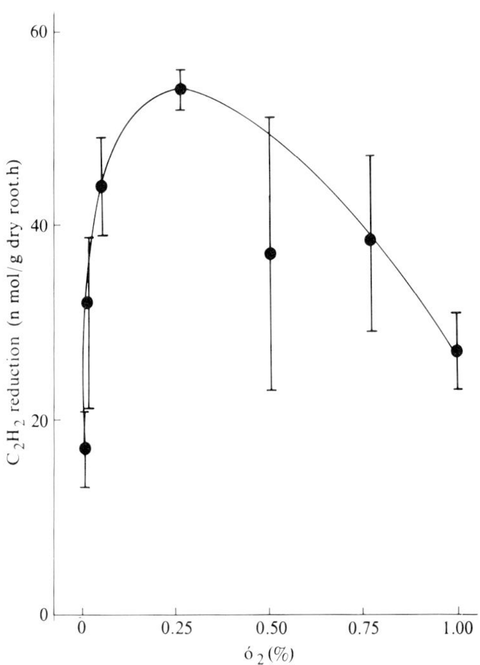

Figure 3.
The rate of C_2H_2 reduction by roots of *Oryza sativa* exposed to increasing concentrations of O_2 after they had been depleted of O_2 for 4 h before assay (from van Berkum & Sloger, 1981c).

Similar results have been obtained with *O. sativa,* with application of KNO_3 causing a delay in the development of, and reducing the rate of, root-associated N_2-ase activity during the growth cycle (see Figure 5). The rate of root-associated N_2-ase activity and the percent N of the roots of *O. sativa* in both treatments were negatively correlated, and again, the NO_3^- supplement resulted in the improvement of plant growth (van Berkum & Sloger, 1981b).

Meeker *et al.* (1974) suggested that changes in the observed rate of leaf NRA reflect changes in uptake, transport, and assimilation of NO_3^-, which in turn affect the rate of supply of reduced N to the plant. Therefore, low rates of leaf NRA and the observed inverse correlation of percent N of the roots of *O. sativa* with the rate of N_2-ase activity suggest that the development of N_2 fixation in grasses is the result of N deficiency. Because plant performance is improved by applying combined N, the farmer may sacrifice high yields with cereal grasses if he withholds fertilizer N to induce associative N_2 fixation. Therefore, at the present time, associative N_2 fixation does not seem to be applicable to agriculture, but in ecological terms it may be of significance for the maintenance of soil fertility.

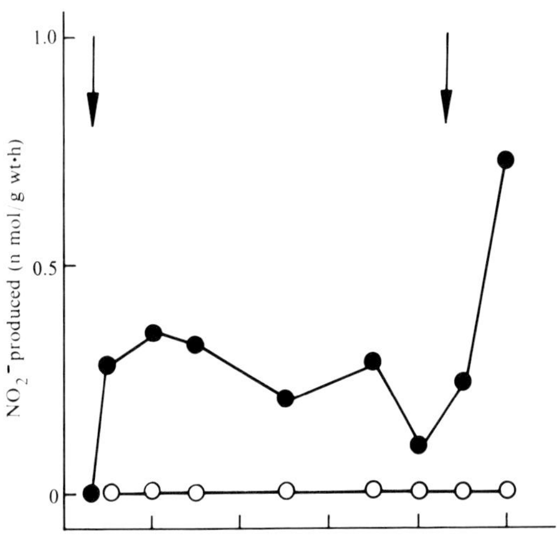

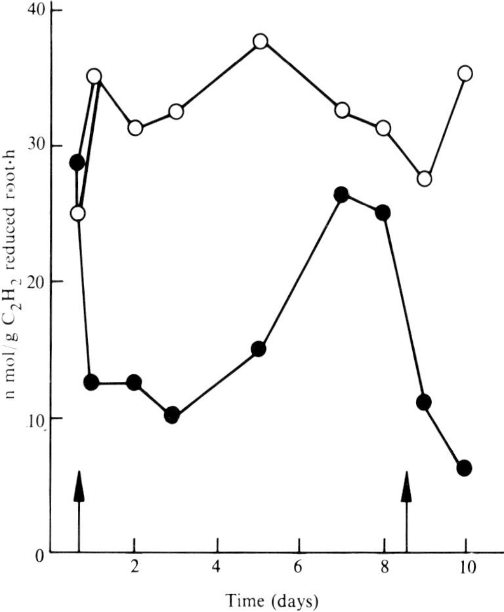

Figure 4.
The rate of N_2-ase activity associated with field plots of *Paspalum notatum* in Brazil measured with short-term assays of C_2H_2 reduction (6 h) immediately after sampling. Plots receiving 40 kg N/ha as KNO_3 (•) at times indicated by the arrows; control plots (○) (from van Berkum, PhD thesis, University of London, 1978).

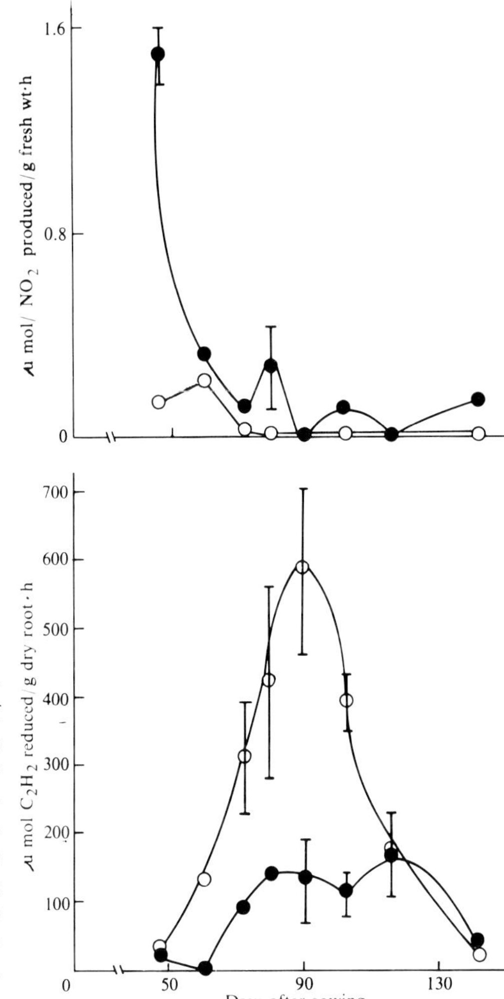

Figure 5.
The rate of N_2-ase activity associated with the roots of *Oryza sativa* during the life cycle of the plants. The linear rates of immediate C_2H_2 reduction were determined with short-term time-course assays (3 h). Plants receiving 10 kg N/ha as KNO_3 once every two weeks (•); control plants (○) from van Berkum & Sloger, 1981b).

MICROBIOLOGICAL ASPECTS OF ROOT-ASSOCIATED N_2 FIXATION IN GRASSES

The rhizosphere of the roots of grasses has been suggested as an ideal habitat for heterotrophic N_2-fixing bacteria (van Berkum & Bohlool, 1980). Certainly, N_2-fixing bacteria of many genera occur in high number in the rhizosphere of roots of a wide variety of grasses. *Azospirillum* is suggested to be of special significance when associated with the roots of tropical grasses, but has also been isolated from a diverse range of habitats.

An intimate internal association of N_2-fixing bacteria with the roots of grasses would be of great competitive advantage to the partners and be most useful, if associative N_2 fixation is to be implemented for the production of forage and cereal grasses. Evidence for the internal location of nonsymbiotic N_2-fixing bacteria in roots of grasses has been indirect. *Azospirillum* and *Campylobacter* have been isolated from roots "surface sterilized" with aqueous solutions of Chloramine-T (Döbereiner & Baldani, 1979; Baldani & Döbereiner, 1980; McClung & Patriquin, 1980). However, the procedures used were not demonstrated unequivocally to surface sterilize roots of grasses. McClung *et al.* (in preparation) have investigated the recovery of N_2-fixing bacteria from the surface of roots of *Spartina alterniflora, Zea mays,* and *Sorghum vulgare* after treatment with Chloramine-T and NaOCl solutions. Although these agents significantly reduced the recovery of bacteria from root surfaces, they did not result in surface sterility of the roots (see Table 1). The treatment of roots for 1 h with 5% NaOCl was more effective than 1% Chloramine-T for reducing the number of N_2-fixing bacteria on the root surfaces.

TABLE 1: Chloramine-T and NaOCl as chemical agents to surface sterilize roots of *Spartina alterniflora, Zea mays,* and *Sorghum vulgare* (from C.R. McClung, P. van Berkum, E.Davis, & C. Sloger, in preparation).

Treatment	*S. alterniflora*	*Z. mays*	*S. vulgare*
	(No. $\log_{10}$ /g fresh wt)[1]		
Water control			
root macerates	6.041	8.204	8.204
beads[2]	6.204	8.380	8.380
Chloramine-T (1 % , 60 min.)			
root macerates	4.591	6.380	5.732
beads	4.230	5.964	6.380
NaOCl (5 % , 60 min.)			
root macerates	3.415	4.833	3.914
beads	0.653	3.964	3.732

LSD - 0.603 (P = 0.05)

[1] Most probable number of malate-utilizing N_2-fixing bacteria.

[2] Most probable number of malate-utilizing N_2-fixing bacteria released into saline-phosphate buffer when roots were shaken with glass beads for 15 min at 400 rpm.

Two groups of N_2-fixing bacteria forming nonpigmented and pink colonies were isolated from serial dilutions of macerates of NaOCl-treated roots of *Spartina alterniflora* (see Table 2). The isolation of N_2-fixing bacteria from 10^{-3} to 10^{-5} serial dilutions of macerates of these roots coupled with the low number of N_2-fixing bacteria recoverable from their surfaces suggest that these isolates originated from internal sites. *Azospirillum*-like N_2-fixing bacteria were also observed to be associated with the roots of *S. alterniflora,* but were isolated only from controls or roots treated with Chloramine-T before they were macerated.

Based on these results it would seem desirable to re-examine the evidence that *Azospirillum* spp. are located inside grass roots and that rudimentary host plant/*Azospirillum* symbioses exist.

TABLE 2: N_2-fixing bacteria isolated from roots of *Spartina alterniflora* growing in a salt marsh of Chesapeake Bay (From McClung, van Berkum, Davis, & Sloger, in preparation).

Isolate	Source	NaCl tolerance
Pink-chromagens	10^3 to 10^5 dilutions of root macerates from 5 % NaOCl-treated samples	up to 7 %
Nonpigmented mucoid		up to 7 %
Azospirillum-like	Water and Chloramine-T-treated roots macerated or from the bead treatment	up to 3 %

No. *Campylobacter* have been isolated.

CONCLUSION

Grasses may indeed derive N from the atmosphere through the participation of nonsymbiotic or associative N_2-fixing bacteria. Whether or not this natural phenomenon can be put to use in agriculture for the production of forage and cereal grasses remains an open question. The *Azospirillum* grass associations have been suggested to offer the greatest prospect of fulfilling this role, but N_2 fixation by this combination, and significant fixed N transfer to crops under field conditions, remain to be demonstrated.

REFERENCES

Abrantes, G.T.V., Day, J.M. & Döbereiner, J. (1975) *Bull. Int. Inf. Biol. Sol Lyon* 21, 1-7.

Baldani, V.L.D. & Döbereiner, J. (1980) *Soil Biol. Biochem.* 12, 433-439.

Berkum, P. van (1978) PhD Thesis, University of London, London, England.

Berkum, P. van (1980) *Soil Biol. Biochem.* 12, 141-145.

Berkum, P. van & Bohlool, B.B. (1980) *Microbiol. Rev.* 44, 491-517.

Berkum, P. van & Day, J.M. (1980) *Soil Biol. Biochem.* 12, 137-140.

Berkum, P. van & Sloger. C. (1979) *Plant Physiol.* 64, 739-745.

Berkum, P. van & Sloger, C. (1981a) *Appl. Environ. Microbiol.* 41, 184-189.

Berkum, P. van & Sloger, C. (1981b) *Plant Physiol.* 68, 722-726.

Berkum, P. van & Sloger, C. (1981c) IV Internat. Symp. N_2 Fixation, Canberra, Australia. Abst. No. 165.

Bülow, J.W.F. von & Döbereiner, J. (1975) *Proc. Natl. Acad. Sic. (USA).* 72, 2389-2393.

Burns, R.C. & Hardy, R.W.F. (1975) Nitrogen fixation in bacteria and higher plants. Molecular biology, biochemistry and biophysics, Vol 21. Springer Verlag, Berlin, Germany. P. 189.

Dart, P.J. & Day, J.M. (1975) Non-symbiotic nitrogen fixation in soils. *In;* Soil microbiology - A critical review, N. Walker (Ed.). Butterworths, London, England. Pp. 225-252.

Day, J.M. & Döbereiner, J. (1976) *Soil Biol. Biochem.* 8, 45-50.

Day, J.M., Harris, D., Dart. P.J., & Berkum, P. van (1975) The Broadbalk experiment: An investigation of nitrogen gains from nonsymbiotic fixation. *In:* Nitrogen fixation by free-living micro-organisms, W.D.P. Stewart (Ed.). International Biological Programme Series, Vol 6. Cambridge University Press, Cambridge, England. Pp. 71-84.

Döbereiner, J. & Baldani, V.L.D. (1979) *Can. J. Microbiol.* 25, 1264-1269.

Döbereiner, J., Day, J.M. & Dart, P.J. (1972a) *J. Gen. Microbiol.* 71, 103-116.

Döbereiner, J., Day, J.M. & Dart, P.J. (1972b) *Soil Biol. Biochem.* 5, 157-159.

Drozd, J. & Postgate, J.R. (1970) *J. Gen. Microbiol.* 60, 427-430.

Gibson, A.H. (1974) The control of dinitrogen assimilation by nodulated legumes. *In:* Mechanisms of regulation of plant growth, R.L. Bieleski, A.R. Ferguson, & M.M. Cresswell (Eds.). Royal Soc. New Zealand, Wellington, NZ. Bulletin 12. Pp. 13-22.

Gibson, A.H. (1976) Limitation to dinitrogen fixation by legumes. *In*: Proceedings First. Inter. Symp. Nitrogen Fixation, W.E. Newton & C.J. Nyman (Eds.). Washington State Univ. Press, Pullman, WA, USA. Pp. 400-428.

Greenland, D.J. (1977) Contribution of micro-organisms to the nitrogen status of tropical soils. *In:* Biological nitrogen fixation in farming systems of the tropics, A. Ayanaba & P.J. Dart (Eds.). Wiley, New York, NY, USA. Pp. 13-26.

McClung, C.R. & Patriquin, D.G. (1980) *Can. J. Microbiol.* 26, 881-886.

Meeker, G.B., Purvis, A.C., Neyra, C.A., & Hageman, R.H. (1974) Uptake and accumulation of nitrate as a major factor in the regulation of nitrate reductase activity in corn (*Zea mays* L.) leaves: Effect of high ambient CO_2 and malate. *In*: Mechanisms of regulation of plant growth, R.L. Bieleski, A.R. Ferguson & M.M. Cresswell (Eds.). Royal Soc. New Zealand, Wellington, NZ. Bulletin 12. Pp. 49-58.

Neyra, C.A. & Döbereiner, J. (1977) *Adv. Agron.* 29, 1-38.

Patriquin, D.G. & Denike, D. (1978) *Aquat. Bot.* 4, 211-226.

Tjepkema, J.D. & Berkum, P. van (1977) *Appl. Environ. Microbiol.* 33, 626-629.

Witty, J.F. (1979) *Soil Biol. Biochem.* 11, 209-210.

STUDIES ON *AZOSPIRILLUM/AMARANTHUS* INTERRELATIONSHIPS

G. Oblisami & V. Udhayasurian[1]

Summary

Azospirillum populations in the phyllosphere, stem, and rhizosphere of *Amaranthus dubius*, *A. gangeticus*, *A. leucocarpus* and *A. edulis* were 1.06-1.68 x 10^2/cm^2, 3.34-4.14 x 10^3/g and 21.05-26.31 x 10^5/g dry soil, respectively. The rhizosphere-to-soil ratio for these four species was from 11.87 to 15.00. Grain type amaranths showed a better response to inoculation than did leafy types, with seed germination, root length, shoot length, and vigor all enhanced by inoculation. In a field trial with *Azospirillum* inoculation of *Amaranthus* sp., yield increases of 34.04 to 48.38% were obtained.

INTRODUCTION

Amaranths, widely consumed for their protein-rich leaves and high protein grains, have high photosynthetic activity and net assimilation rates. The incidence and importance of *Azospirillum* in the soil and rhizosphere of other C_4 grasses, including *Amaranthus spinosa* has been well documented (Döbereiner & Day 1975; Lakshmikumari, Kavimandan & Subba Rao, 1976; Hegazi, Amer & Monib, 1979). In this paper we examine the numbers of *Azospirillum* in the phyllosphere, stem, and rhizosphere of four different species of *Amaranthus* and demonstrate a field response to inoculation with *Azospirillum* in all four species.

MATERIALS AND METHODS

The prevalence of *Azospirillum* in the phyllosphere, stem, and rhizosphere of *Amaranthus dubius*, *A. gangeticus*, *A. leucocarpus*, and *A. edulis* at different stages of growth was assayed by the most probable number (MPN)

[1] Dept. of Agricultural Botany, Tamil Nadu Agricultural University, Coimbatore 641-003, India.

technique as well as other standard methods (Hegazi *et al.*, 1979; Watanabe *et al.*, 1979). *Azospirillum* cultures were isolated from amaranthus roots using the enrichment method of Day & Döbereiner (1976) and Neyra & Döbereiner (1977). Nitrogenase activity of *Azospirillum* cultures was then determined by acetylene reduction using the method of Day & Döbereiner (1976).

Response of *Amaranthus* to inoculation with *Azospirillum* was determined both in pot trials and in the field. In the pot trial the four species of *Amaranthus* mentioned above were again used, with measurements taken of green matter yield at the "tender green" (S_1), "Thandukeerai" (S_2), and harvesting (S_3) stages. Final grain yield (S_4) was also measured. In the field trial, four species of *Amaranthus* were again used, and the effect of *Azospirillum* inoculation on grain yield without N fertilization, or with 25, 50, or 75 kg N/ha added, was determined. A factorial randomized block design with two replications was adopted.

RESULTS AND DISCUSSION

Table 1 shows the number of *Azospirillum* found in the phyllosphere, stem, and rhizosphere of four *Amaranthus* species, and the rhizosphere effect at four different stages in plant development. The difference between species was not marked, although the leafy species (CO 1 and CO 2) did appear to have higher numbers of *Azospirillum* in the phyllosphere than the grain types (A. 62 and A. 90). In all species and tissues the numbers of *Azospirillum* found was greatest at the S_2 (Thandukeerai) stage, and declined as the plant matured. Greatest numbers of *Azospirillum* were found in the rhizosphere and there was a strong rhizosphere effect.

The *Azospirillum* isolates obtained from amaranth roots fixed varying amounts of nitrogen (N_2). An isolate from *A. dubius* fixed (21.36 mg N/g malic acid) and recorded the maximum nitrogenase activity (207.69 nmoles of C_2H_4/flask per hour), a value similar to those reported by Okon *et al.* (1976). This isolate showed greater ability to fix N_2 (C_2H_2) than that obtained from *A. spinosa* by Lakshmikumari *et al*; (1976).

The effect of seed inoculation with *Azospirillum* on green matter and grain yield under pot culture conditions is reported in Tables 2 and 3. Green matter yield was significantly increased at all stages of crop production, and in all species tested, with yields enhanced as much as 82% in the S_1 growth stage. Grain yields of the four amaranths increased 34.04-48.38% following inoculation, and tended to be higher with the grain than with the leafy cultivars.

Grain yield was again improved by inoculation with *Azospirillum* in the field trial, with the grain species again outyielding the leafy types (see Table 4). There was a strong response to N fertilization in this trial, but at 25 and 50 kg

TABLE 1: The prevalence of *Azospirillum* in the phyllosphere, stem, and rhizosphere of *Amaranthus* species, and the rhizosphere effect at four stages of plant development.[1]

Amaranth	Variety	Phyllosphere ($10^2/cm^2$)				Stem ($\times 10^3$/g dry sample)				Rhizosphere ($\times 10^5$/g dry soil)				R:S ratio			
		S_1	S_2	S_3	S_4	S_1	S_2	S_3	S_4	S_1	S_2	S_3	S_4	S_1	S_2	S_3	S_4
A. dubius	CO 1	1.59	2.22	1.78	1.14	4.00	5.10	4.33	3.14	15.20	20.20	42.10	21.40	8.53	13.28	20.43	10.33
A. gangeticus	CO 2	1.08	2.73	1.59	1.14	4.40	4.96	3.80	3.00	19.70	30.10	20.20	14.20	11.06	19.80	9.80	6.85
A. leucocarpus	A. 62	0.76	1.78	1.44	0.70	3.80	4.63	2.73	2.20	21.40	32.90	21.60	13.20	12.02	21.64	10.48	6.37
A. edulis	A. 90	0.82	1.59	1.08	0.76	4.70	5.83	3.12	2.50	24.70	41.10	21.40	18.07	13.87	27.03	10.38	8.72
	Mean	1.06	2.08	1.47	0.94	4.23	5.13	3.50	2.71	20.25	31.07	26.33	16.70	11.37	20.44	12.78	8.06
										Non-rhizosphere (control)							
										1.78	1.52	2.06	2.07				

[1] S_1, S_2, S_3, and S_4 are the four stages of growth at which samples were taken and are detailed in the text.

TABLE 2: Effect of *Azospirillum* inoculation on the green matter yield (g/plant) of *Amaranthus* species.

Amaranth species and variety	Tender green stage (S_1)		Thandukeerai stage (S_2)		Harvesting stage (S_3)	
	Control	Inoculated	Control	Inoculated	Control	Inoculated
A. dubius - CO 1	9.25	16.87	52.27	66.07	113.10	157.00
A. gangeticus - CO 2	13.97	22.85	56.33	75.33	90.26	119.53
A. leucocarpus - A.62	11.45	19.21	35.47	49.53	55.10	70.17
A. edulis - A.90	13.67	22.93	50.40	74.53	85.20	112.80
Mean	12.09	20.41	48.62	66.37	85.92	114.88
	P	SE_D	P	SE_D	P	SE_D
Variety	0.01	0.7152	0.01	2.1029	0.01	4.0191
Treatment	0.01	0.5057	0.01	1.4869	0.01	2.8419
Variety x treatment	NS	–	NS	–	0.05	5.6838

NS = not significant.

N applied/ha, inoculation with *Azospirillum* further enhanced yield. Yields with 50 kg N applied/ha and inoculation were similar to those with 75 kg N/ha applied, an appreciable saving.

TABLE 3: Effect of *Azospirillum* inoculation on the seed yield (g/plant) of *Amaranthus* species.

Amaranth species and variety	Control	Inoculated	% increase over control
A. dubius - CO 1	4.20	5.63	34.04
A. gangeticus - CO 2	5.40	7.30	35.18
A. leucocarpus - A.62	6.20	9.20	48.38
A. edulis - A.90	5.80	8.00	37.93
Mean	5.40	7.53	39.44[1]

[1]Differences due to variety and inoculation were each significant at the P = 0.01 level.

TABLE 4: Effect of *Azospirillum* inoculation on the seed yield (g/m^2) of *Amaranthus* species under graded levels of fertilizer nitrogen.

Treatment	Variety				
	CO 1	CO 2	A 62	A 90	Mean
$N_0 I_0$	18.2	104.0	180.0	130.0	108.05
$N_0 I_1$	23.2	122.0	204.0	144.0	123.30
$N_{25} I_0$	30.4	144.0	218.0	180.0	143.10
$N_{25} I_1$	51.8	176.0	260.0	196.0	170.95
$N_{50} I_0$	44.6	208.0	264.0	236.0	188.15
$N_{50} I_1$	57.2	252.0	340.0	296.0	236.30
$N_{75} I_0$	55.0	256.0	334.0	288.0	237.25
$N_{75} I_1$	56.8	264.0	322.0	300.0	235.25
Mean	42.15	190.75	265.25	221.26[1]	

[1]Differences due to variety, inoculation treatment and N level, and variety x treatment interactions were each significant at the P = 0.01 level.

REFERENCES

Day, J.M. & Döbereiner, J. (1976) Physiological aspects of N_2 fixation by a *Spirillum* from Digitaria roots. *Soil Biol. Biochem.* 8, 45-50.

Döbereiner, J. & Day, J.M. (1975) Nitrogen fixation in the rhizosphere of tropical grasses. *In*: Nitrogen fixation by free-living micro-organisms, W.D.P. Stewart (Ed.). Cambridge Univ. Press, Cambridge, England. Pp. 39-56.

Hegazi, N.A., Amer, H.A. & Monib, M. (1979) Enumeration of nitrogen fixing spirilla. *Soil Biol. Biochem.* 11, 437-438.

Lakshmikumari, M., Kavimandan, S.K. & Subba Rao, N.S. (1976) Occurrence of N_2 fixing *Spirillum* in roots of rice, sorghum, maize and other plants. *Indian J. Expl. Biol.* 14, 638.

Neyra, C.A. & Döbereiner, J. (1977) Nitrogen fixation in grasses. *Adv. Agron.* 29, 1-38.

Okon, Y., Albrecht, S.L. & Burris, R.H. (1976) Factors affecting the growth and nitrogen fixation of *Spirillum lipoferum*. *J. Bacteriol.* 127, 1249-1254.

Watanabe, I., Baraquio, W.L., De Guzman, M.R., & Cabreva, D.A. (1979) Nitrogen fixing (acetylene reduction) activity and population of aerobic heterotrophic nitrogen fixing bacteria associated with wetland rice. *Appl. Environ. Microbiol.* 27, 813-819.

EFFECT OF *AZOTOBACTER* INOCULATION AND NITROGEN FERTILIZATION ON THE YIELD OF SEED POTATOES IN THE COASTAL AREA OF PERU

J.M. Zapater R.[1]

Summary

Inoculation of seed potatoes (*Solanum tuberosum* cv. Mariva) with *Azotobacter* increased initial plant vigor and yield, but the differences were not significant. In the presence of 80 kg N/ha and high application rates of chicken manure, inoculation with *Azotobacter* resulted in a major yield loss.

INTRODUCTION

Inoculation of plants with *Azotobacter chroococcum* can affect their growth and sometimes increase crop yields (Brown, Burlingham & Jackson, 1964; Patel, 1969). *Azotobacter* can affect plant growth directly, either by the nitrogen (N_2) it fixes, or through growth-promoting substances (Rovira, 1963), or indirectly by changes in the microflora of the rhizosphere (Patel, 1969).

This study reports the effects of *Azotobacter* inoculation and N fertilization on seed potatoes (*Solanum tuberosum* cv. Mariva) in the coastal area of Peru.

METHODS

The site was an Entisol near La Molina, Peru, the description of which is given in Table 1. All plots received dressings of 10 tons/ha of chicken manure, 80 kg P_2O_5/ha as Fosfobayovar, and 50 kg K_2O/ha as K_2SO_4. A randomized complete block design with four replications was used: the treatments were 0, 80 or 160 kg N/ha, with or without *Azotobacter* inoculation.

[1] Universidad Nacional Agraria, La Molina, Peru.

TABLE 1: Surface soil analysis of Carapongo field (coast region).

Constituent	Amount		Units	Method used
	Sample 1	Sample 2		
Mechanical analysis:				
Sand	30	50	%	Hydrometer
Silt	54	40	%	Hydrometer
Clay	16	10	%	Hydrometer
Textural class	Silt loam	Loam		Textural triangle
pH	7.5	7.1		Potentiometric, soil-water 1:1
Free $CaCO_3$	0.57	0.95	%	Volumetric
Organic matter	2.34	1.58	%	Walkley and Black
Total nitrogen	0.110	0.075	%	Micro-Kjeldahl
Available elements:				
Phosphorus	14.4	18.7	p.p.m. P	Olsen. $NaHCO_3$ 0.5M, pH 8.5
Potassium	370	370	kg/ha K_2O	Peech
Cation exchange capacity	7.28	6.72	m.e./100g	Amonium acetate 1N, pH 7. 0
Exchangable cations:				Amonium extract
Ca^{++}	6.65	6.11	m.e./100g	E.D.T.A.
Mg^{++}	0.33	0.33	m.e./100g	Titan yellow
K^{+}	0.22	0.20	m.e./100g	Flame photometer
Na^{+}	0.08	0.08	m.e./100g	Flame photometer
Electric conductivity	1.80	2.50	mmhos/cm/25° C	Conductivity bridge (Saturation extract)

Plots were of 6 m x 3.25 m and contained 3 rows of 15 plants each. Seed potatoes were inoculated directly before planting and at 20 and 45 days thereafter and received broth cultures of *A. chroococcum* or sterile nutrient medium without carbohydrate.

Yield was determined 135 days after planting.

RESULTS AND DISCUSSION

Inoculated seed sprouted first and initially gave better growth than uninoculated seed. This initial benefit soon disappeared, and at harvest there was no significant effect of inoculation on potato seed yield in the 0-N treatment (see Table 2). Inoculation in the presence of fertilizer N had a strong negative effect on potato seed yield. This was presumably due to the effect of added nutrients on pathogens in the soil, rather than to the presence of *Azotobacter*. The results highlight the need for more compatible N-fertilization-inoculation practices.

TABLE 2: Yields (kg/ha) of potato, according to levels of N fertilizers and inoculation with *Azotobacter*.

	N fertilization (kg N/ha)			
	0	80	160	x N
Uninoculated	21,756	26,064	18,564	22,128
Inoculated with *Azotobacter*	24,987	19,692	18,448	21,042

$LSD_{0.05}$ = 5,471 kg

REFERENCES

Brown, M.E., Burlingram, S.K. & Jackson, R.M. (1964) *Plant Soil* 20, 194-214.

Patel, J.J. (1969) *Plant Soil* 31, 209-223.

Rovira, A.D. (1963) *Plant Soil* 19, 304-314.

THE *AZOLLA/ANABAENA* ASSOCIATION

CHINESE TECHNOLOGY FOR THE CULTIVATION OF *AZOLLA*

T.A. Lumpkin [1]

Summary

The People's Republic of China is the country most advanced in the practical application of *Azolla* for agricultural production systems. Methods for the cultivation and management of azolla in China vary with season and location. This paper reviews some of the methods used in the overwintering of azolla, spring nursery propagation, large-scale field cultivation, oversummering and autumn nursery propagation.

INTRODUCTION

Hundreds of years ago Chinese peasants discovered that *Azolla,* a genus of nitrogen (N_2) fixing aquatic ferns, was an effective green manure with which to increase rice yields. Azolla is now one of the most important green manures for rice in the southeastern provinces of China, where over 1.4 million ha are cultivated annually for the spring rice crop. Azolla is also used as a green manure for water bamboo (*Zizania aquatica*), arrowhead (*Sagittaria sagittfolia*) and taro (*Colocasia esculenta*); as a fodder for pigs, fish, and ducks; and is occasionally applied to upland crops, as well (Lumpkin & Plucknett, 1980). Geographically, azolla is cultivated from southern China to just north of the Yangtze River, in the Yellow River Basin and as far west as Sichuan and Shanxi provinces (see Figure 1).

Healthy azolla plants have a low carbon to N ratio (about 10:1) favoring rapid decomposition and release of N within a few weeks of soil incorporation. According to the results of over 1500 experiments by Chinese

[1] Dept. Agronomy & Soil Science, University of Hawaii, Honolulu, HI, 96822 USA.
[2] Research support from the USAID grant 58-9AH2-412 and the collaboration of scientists in the Zhejiang Academy of Agricultural Sciences, is gratefully acknowledged.

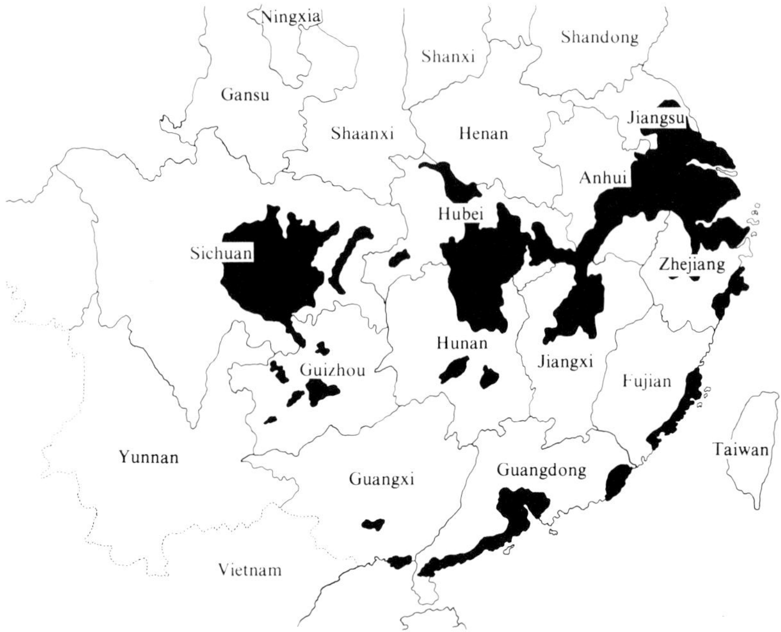

Figure 1. Most *Azolla* is cultivated within the intensively cropped rice regions of Vietnam and southeastern China, along the coast of Guangdong, Fujian, and Zhejiang provinces, north and south of the Changjiang River (Yangtze), and in the Sichuan basin. Black regions on the map indicate both intense cultivation of azolla and areas where extensive experimentation with this fern has been undertaken.

researchers in the paddy fields of Zhejiang, Guangdong, Fujian, Jiangsu, Hunan, Hubei and Yunnan provinces, cultivation of *Azolla pinnata* increased the yield of rice by 600-750 kg/ha above the yield of control plots (Zhejiang Academy of Agricultural Sciences, 1975). In experiments conducted in China by the author, rice manured preplanting, or pre- and post-planting, with *Azolla* yielded an average of over 1000 kg/ha more than the control (Lumpkin *et al.*, 1981). These increases are comparable with results obtained in California (Talley & Rains, 1980).

Since the use of spores is not yet possible, only vegetative material can be used for propagation. This means not only that cultivation of *Azolla* is a continual process requiring attention throughout the year, but also that methods of cultivation and management will vary according to the season and location. The methods discussed in this paper include: the overwintering of azolla, spring nursery propagation, large-scale field cultivation, over-summering, and autumn nursery propagation. This information was obtained both through personal observation and a review of Chinese fertilizer handbooks (Anon., 1976; Anwei Academy of Agricultural and Forestry Sciences, 1977; Beijing Agriculture University, 1979; Compiling Committee, 1975; Guangdong Department of Agriculture, 1979; Guangdong Academy of Agricultural Sciences, 1980; Hunan Agricultural College, 1979).

OVERWINTERING *AZOLLA*

Azolla can be killed by exposure to temperatures below -5° C for more than a few hours. Because of this covered nurseries are necessary for the safe overwintering of *Azolla* in the northern provinces of China's rice growing region (27-33° N). In the southern-most provinces, and along coastal areas further north, special covered nurseries are not necessary because the winter weather is mild.

The quantity of azolla maintained during the winter varies with the area to be inoculated in the spring, the cropping system, and the particular method of overwintering. While one ha of spring-transplanted rice requires the overwintering of 450-600 kg of azolla, a similar area of summer-transplanted rice requires only 7.5 to 15 kg. The quantity of azolla required for the summer rice crop is small since there is sufficient time to multiply overwintered azolla in spring nurseries before it is inoculated into the paddy fields.

Flooded nursery methods

The overwintering of azolla in cold areas usually requires the construction of plastic-covered or mud-roofed beds, as shown in Figure 2. These are usually 10 m long by 1.0-1.5 m wide and 13-20 cm deep and are oriented either to take advantage of afternoon sunlight or to give protection against cold Siberian winds. In extremely cold weather and at night, straw mats may be placed over the frames to retain the heat of water and soil; on days with mild weather the plastic sheeting can be rolled back for direct exposure to sunlight. In areas with mild winters, open nursery beds covered during cold weather with rollaway mats can be used. These usually measure 7 m long, 60 cm wide and 20 cm deep.

The structures pictured cover flooded nursery beds in which *Azolla* spp. are maintained. Generally, the azolla inoculum is checked carefully to ensure freedom from insects; then moved into the nursery beds in November. Azolla plants are maintained at a density of 0.75-1.0 kg/m^2 and are fertilized with 1-2 kg/m^2 of farmyard manure and 4-5 kg/m^2 of river mud. Superphosphate, ammonium sulphate and straw ash are applied in the early spring to accelerate the growth rate.

Figure 2. Structures used in the overwintering of azolla:

a) Arch-shaped overwintering nurseries are constructed of bamboo strips and plastic sheets in areas where occasional freezing occurs. The plastic sheets are pulled back during mild winter weather.

b) Mud wall overwintering nurseries with plastic sheet or glass panel roofs are the most effective protection against freezing weather. This type of nursery is commonly used for vegetable and rice seedlings as well.

Out-of-water winter storage

For this type of overwintering 50-75 kg of azolla is placed in a loosely piled stack, covered with 5-10 cm of straw ash and sprinkled routinely with water to prevent desiccation. A removable cone-shaped A-frame structure covering a circle of ground 1.5 m in diameter is placed over the stack and covered with straw mats. During the initial period of storage the stacks are monitored to ensure that they do not compost : temperatures should stay around 5-8° C, but should not be less than 0° C. Azolla is usually stored in these stacks during the coldest days of winter. In late winter or early spring, and before warm weather can cause the stored plants to rot, the stacks are opened up and allowed to reach ambient temperature; then placed in nursery beds; 50-80% of azolla is usually still alive.

Overwintering in warm water

Hot spring water has traditionally been used for overwintering azolla. With industrialization, warm uncontaminated waste water from factories, especially steam plants, has come into use. Usually, a field near the source of warm water is divided into small nursery beds. The irrigation system is arranged so that the warm water enters each bed directly without traveling through other beds. The movement of water is closely watched so that stagnation and then freezing does not occur.

Overwintering in subtropical areas

Many areas in southern China have a comparatively mild winter with air and water temperatures warm enough for survival of azolla. In these areas well-drained fields are raked and levelled, after which farmyard manure and superphosphate are applied. The fields are divided into long beds running east-west to prevent the north winds from blowing the azolla to one end. Screens prevent the loss of azolla during irrigation and windbreaks limit cold damage to the bed. Water level in the beds is manipulated to minimize cooling. With this type of overwintering 450 kg of azolla can be multiplied to provide the 5000 kg/ha needed to inoculated 1 ha of paddy field in the spring.

SPRING NURSERY PROPAGATION

The goal of spring nursery propagation is to multiply azolla as early and as rapidly as possible so that the largest possible area of paddy field can be inoculated. To meet this goal, intensive management is essential.

Spring nursery propagation takes place from mid-March to mid-April along the Yangtze River. At this time of year, azolla can double in mass every three to five days because of the mild air and water temperature. The azolla is continually subdivided by expanding the nursery areas. This is done to prevent crowding which could slow the growth rate. Every available paddy is used for the extension of the nursery. Once a nursery field is covered with an azolla mat two to three layers thick, it is subdivided to inoculate adjoining fields. Any extra azolla is used as fodder or is composted for upland crops.

LARGE-SCALE FIELD CULTIVATION OF *AZOLLA*

In China, three different cropping systems are used for the cultivation of azolla as a green manure for rice.

- Azolla is grown as a monocrop and incorporated into the paddy mud as a basal green manure before the rice is transplanted (see Figure 3).
- Azolla is grown after the rice is transplanted as an intercrop and incorporated as a topdressing manure.
- Azolla is grown as both a monocrop and intercrop.

Figure 3. Azolla is sometimes grown as a monocropped basal green manure. Cultivation begins in south China during mid-winter and later, in regions farther north, as the temperature rises above 15° C.

The cropping system used in any particular location varies each year depending upon the weather, tradition, and other factors in the cropping system. When azolla is monocropped, it is usually grown for 20-30 days and incorporated into the paddy mud once or twice during that period by plowing or harrowing. As an intercrop, it is grown until shaded out by the developing rice canopy, usually 20-40 days, and is partially incorporated once or twice during that period, by hand during weeding or, in a few locations, with a modified rotary rice weeder (see Figure 4). The final mat which develops before the rice canopy has completely developed either dies naturally after canopy closure, due to fungal rot, or is incorporated by hand before the maximum tillering stage of the rice.

Scientists in Fujian province promote the planting of rice in alternating wide and narrow row spacing (66 cm and 13 cm). They claim that this method does not reduce the rice yield, but allows the azolla to accumulate more N, since the ferns can grow for a longer period in the wide rows than in evenly spaced rows of rice. This method has not been adopted elsewhere.

In China there are three main rice crops: early rice (spring-summer), summer rice, and late rice (summer-autumn). In a few areas all three rice crops are grown, but in most areas only one or two crops are included in the cropping system. The cultivation of azolla for these different crops is discussed below.

The spring rice crop

Most azolla cultivation occurs during spring when temperatures are optimum and insects rare. Azolla is occasionally grown as a monocrop and inoculated into the fields 20-30 days before the spring rice is transplanted. More commonly it is grown as an intercrop and inoculated into the fields a few days before the rice is transplanted, or a few days after transplanting when the rice seedlings have recovered from transplant shock. Superphosphate fertilizer (20% P_2O_5) is broadcast over the paddy at the rate of 3.75 g/m^2 every ten days. The total phosphorus applied usually ranges from 1.5 to 3.0 g/m^2. Azolla incorporation is done just before the stage of maximum rice tillering.

The summer rice crop

Summer rice is grown in the cooler areas of China where it is difficult or impossible to grow two rice crops each season. Since a winter cereal or a spring vegetable usually precedes the summer rice crop, the only azolla grown as a monocrop is that used as a green manure in seedling nurseries. In the main paddy fields it is usually grown only as an intercrop. As an intercrop, it must be incorporated as soon as the mat attains a biomass of 1.5-2.0 kg/m^2, because high summer temperatures, high humidity, and shading under the rice canopy are conducive to the development of azolla fungal rot.

Insect pests are much more prevalent in the summer season. The larva of *Nymphula* spp. *Pyralis* spp. *Chironomus* spp, and the azolla weevil are the most serious pests (Lumpkin & Plucknett, 1980). *Nymphula* and *Pyralis* larvae and the azolla weevil live on the azolla mat and feed on the young

Figure 4. Incorporation of azolla in intercropped plantings with rice.

a) The rotary azolla incorporator (above, minus handle) is a modified version of the common rotary rice weeder. This implement is used to soil incorporate azolla that is growing as an intercrop between rows of rice.

b) Intercropped azolla is often incorporated into soil by hand. Although this practice results in more complete incorporation of the azolla mat, it is being used less because of rising labor costs.

fronds. They can destroy the whole mat in a matter of days. Insect control is achieved by dusting or spraying the mat with organic phosphate or organic chloride insecticides. *Chironomus* larvae live under water and feed on young roots. They are difficult to detect though usually the adult midges can be seen flying away from an infected mat if the surface of the mat is fanned. *Chironomus* larvae are controlled by the application of lindane or carbofuran in a granular formulation.

The autumn, late rice crop

The cultivation of azolla for the late rice crop is limited to a few areas of China, the most prominent being southern Jiangsu province. After the spring or summer rice crop is harvested, the fields are plowed and fertilized with 150-200 kg/ha of superphosphate. Azolla is brought from the oversummering site (described in the following section) and inoculated into the fields at the rate of 300-450 g/m^2 for monocropping or at 600 g/m^2 as an intercropped green manure. A higher inoculum rate is used if algal blooms are expected. As typhoons are common in this season, the field may need to be drained to prevent the azolla from being blown into a pile. When the fronds begin to overlap, the azolla must be thinned to prevent fungal rot, by removing some for inoculation into other fields or by partial incorporation into the soil.

Since there is usually insufficient time or labor available to grow azolla as a monocrop, it is more commonly grown as an intercrop; incorporated into the paddy mud one or two times before the maximum tillering stage.

OVERSUMMERING *AZOLLA*

Oversummering techniques are necessary during the summer in most of central China, and before and after the monsoon in southern China, where field water temperatures are too high for *Azolla* cultivation and where azolla must be preserved through a hot season for later use. The best sites for oversummering azolla have good ventilation, partial shading and cool flowing water. Ponds, canals, and streams are favored oversummering sites. Weeds and algae are removed; then living fences are constructed by stringing floating aquatic plants such as *Alternanthera* and *Eichhornia* together (see Figure 5). These floating fences are anchored to the bottom or tied to stakes on the shore. Long anchor lines accommodate to changes in the water level. Azolla is then grown within these fenced-off areas.

If sites similar to those described above are not available, azolla may be oversummered in field plots. This requires careful monitoring of water temperature during the hottest part of the day. If the water temperature exceeds 40° C, the field is either irrigated with cool water or drained. Drainage lowers the temperature of the azolla because mud usually has a lower temperature than shallow stagnant water.

Figure 5. Slow-flowing streams and rivers are also used for oversummering and for autumn multiplication. The azolla mat is sectioned off by floating fences of larger aquatic weeds intertwined with rope.

Under field conditions where the water exceeds 40° C for long periods, the azolla is partially shaded to reduce the temperature. Shading is accomplished by placing frames over the azolla, covering these with loosely woven reed or straw mats, and spraying the mats with water during the hottest part of the day.

In some areas plants such as *Sesbania* are raised along the edges of rivers, ditches, and ponds to provide shade. *Alternanthera philoxeroides, Eichhornia crassipes* and *Pistia statiotes* may also be intercropped with azolla to provide shade.

Oversummered azolla is fertilized by spraying a 1-2% aqueous solution of superphosphate directly onto the plants. In addition, scientists in Guangdong province claim that the application of gibberellin improves the heat tolerance of azolla by reducing its respiration rate.

The control of diseases, insects and free-living algae is a most important aspect of oversummering azolla. Only healthy plants that have green growing points and are free of fungal rot and insects are selected for oversummering. The most prevalent disease of azolla is a fungal rot sometimes identified as *Rymanae* or *Rhizoctonia.*

The disease usually occurs when the azolla mats become overcrowded (>500 g/m^2), or when the water at the oversummering site is too shallow and dirty. Precautionary measures include keeping the sites free of weeds and algae, frequent thinning and dispersion of the azolla mat, and flushing with clear, cool water. When diseased plants are noticed, they are removed as soon as possible, and the remainder are sprayed with an ethylmercuric chloride solution containing 1 part chemical to 800-1000 parts water (w/v) or with 50% dinitrophenyl thiocyanate solution diluted 1:300 (w/v). Algae can be controlled by dispersing the azolla mat with a light rake so that the mat uniformly shades the whole water surface, or by manually removing the algae. Regular stirring of the water and spraying the sites with 1% aqueous solution of calcium carbonate also helps to control algae.

AUTUMN NURSERY PROPAGATION

Azolla is maintained in autumn nurseries from mid-September to mid-November. A certain amount is propagated for pig feed, and in some areas, extra azolla is used as a green manure for wheat and rape.

Autumn nurseries are inoculated with azolla from oversummering sites. Propagation techniques are the same as in spring propagation, except that insect pests such as *Nymphula* spp., *Pyralis* spp., *Chironomus* spp., and azolla weevils are more prevalent and must be carefully controlled. Superphosphate and a small amount of N fertilizer are applied at the beginning and near the end of the autumn propagation season. The autumn nursery season ends with the first frost. In late October or early November, healthy, vigorously growing azolla plants are selected for further propagation in preparation for overwintering. These plants are grown in uncrowded conditions with superphosphate and N fertilizer. During this season they are too fragile to be dispersed with the bamboo azolla rake. Pesticides are applied if necessary to insure that all insects are destroyed.

CONCLUSION

China is the country by far most advanced in the use of azolla as a green manure. A limited amount of *Azolla* research began during the 1950's and has intensified since the early 1960's. The tremendous effort at all levels, from the communes to the national academies, should keep China at the forefront of new discoveries. Present innovative efforts are being made to extend the range of conditions under which azolla can be cultivated through intraspecific crossbreeding, the testing of imported varieties, transfer of algal symbionts, and the use of plant growth substances. Efforts are also being made in such areas as the use of spores as seeding material, biological insect control, the relationship of actinomycetes to the decomposition of azolla, and the development of effective handtools for the soil incorporation of azolla when it is grown as an intercrop with rice.

REFERENCES

Anon. (1978) Red azolla cultivation experiences. Agricultural Publishing House, Beijing. P.R.C.

Anwei Academy of Agriculture and Forestry Sciences (1977) "Three water... one duckweed" cultivation techniques, (water lettuce hyacinth, water peanut, red azolla). Agricultural Publishing House, Beijing, P.R.C.

Beijing Agricultural University (1979) Fertilizer handbook. Agricultural Publishing House. Shanxi Province, P.R.C.

Compiling Committee (1975) Fertilizer knowledge. Shanghai People's Press, Shanghai. P.R.C.

Guangdong Academy of Agricultural Sciences (1980) *Azolla filiculoides*. Guangdong Scientific Publishing House, P.R.C.

Guangdong Department of Agriculture (1975) Cultivating azolla: Questions and answers. Guangdong People's Publishing House, P.R.C.

Hunan Agricultural College (1970) Farmer's fertilizer. Hunan People's Press, P.R.C.

Lumpkin, T.A., Li Zhuo-xin, Zu Shou-xian & Mao Mei-fei (1981) The effect of six azolla varieties under three management systems on the yield of paddy rice. *In:* Biological nitrogen fixation technology for tropical agriculture. P.H. Graham & S.C. Harris (Eds.). CIAT, Cali, Colombia. Pp. 549-553.

Lumpkin. T.A. & D.L. Plucknett (1980) Azolla: botany, physiology, and use as green manure. *Economic Bot.* 34(2), 111-153.

Prayoon. S. & S. Wittaya (1979) Azolla as a nitrogen source for rice in northeast Thailand. *Internat. Rice Res. Newsl.* 4 (5), 24.

Singh. P.K. (1970) Use of Azolla in rice production in India. *In: Nitrogen and Rice.* Internat. Rice Res. Inst., Los Baños, Philippines. Pp. 407-418.

Talley. S.N. & Rains D.W. (1980) *Azolla filiculoides* Lam. as a fallow-season green manure of rice in a temperate climate. *Agron. J.* 72, 11-18.

Zhejiang Academy of Agricultural Sciences. (1975) Azolla cultivation, propagation and utilization. Agricultural Publishing House, Beijing, P.R.C.

THE EFFECT OF SPECIES OF *AZOLLA* UNDER THREE MANAGEMENT PRACTICES ON THE YIELD OF PADDY RICE

T.A. Lumpkin, Li Zhuo-zing, Zu Shou-xian and Mao Mei-fei[1]

Summary

The experiment compared rice yields and nitrogen (N) accumulation when six different selections of *Azolla* were used as a green manure, under three different management practices. Rice yields varied significantly with management practice and, to some degree with selection of *Azolla* used. However, the highest rice yield was obtained using a species of *Azolla* relatively weak in N_2 accumulation. This is assumed to be due to differences between species in rate of decomposition in soil.

INTRODUCTION

The genus *Azolla* is comprised of seven species that demonstrate considerable morphological and physiological variation. *Azolla pinnata* has been used as a green manure crop for rice in China and Vietnam for centuries (Zhejiang Academy of Agricultural Science, 1975; Lumpkin & Plucknett, 1980) and *A. filiculoides*, *A. pinnata*, and *A. mexicana* have been studied in experiments in the USA (Watanabe *et al.*, 1977; Talley & Rains, 1980). However, the seven species have never been simultaneously compared as green manure crops for rice. In the present paper six *Azolla* selections, representing five different species, are compared as green manures for rice under three different management practices.

MATERIALS AND METHODS

Germplasm of *Azolla* was collected by the senior author in 1979, and representative accessions evaluated for cold tolerance in 1979-80 in China. As

[1] A cooperative experiment between the Dept. of Agronomy and Soil Science, Univ. of Hawaii, Honolulu, HI. 96822 USA. and the Zhejiang Province Academy of Agricultural Sciences, Zhejiang, People's Republic of China.

Figure 1. Differences in the response of rice to the treatments were visible within a few days after transplanting. This photo was taken from one corner of the experimental site at the time of panicle initiation. The response of rice to the high level of azolla nitrogen available under the M_3 management practice is clearly visible in the labeled M_3 plot.

There are, however, some anomalies in rice yield and N accumulation data for individual *Azolla* selections. Thus, the highest rice yield in the experiment was obtained in M_3 using *A. pinnata*, a species apparently weak in N accumulation, while the lowest average rice yields were obtained using *A. filiculoides* V_1, the selection which accumulated most N_2. It is assumed that these differences are due to variation in the rates of decomposition of *Azolla* spp. (Shi Su-lian *et al.*, 1980), but this will require further testing.

REFERENCES

Chandler, R.F. (1979) Rice in the tropics: A guide to the development of national programs. Westview Press, Boulder, CO, USA.

Lumpkin, T.A. & Plucknett, D.L. (1980) *Azolla:* Botany, physiology, and use as a green manure. *Econ. Bot.* 34, 111-153.

Su-Lian, Shi., Lin Xin-ziong, & Wen Qi-xiao (1980) Decomposition of plant materials in relation to their chemical compositions in paddy soil. Proc. Symp. on Paddy Soils, Nanjing, China, 19-24 Oct. (In press.)

Talley, S.N. & Rains, D.W. (1980) *Azolla filiculoides* Lam. as a fallow-season green manure for rice in temperate climates. *Agron. J.* 72, 11-18.

Watanabe, I., Espinas, C.R., Berja, N.S., & Alimango, B.V. (1977) Utilization of the *Azolla-Anabaena* complex as a nitrogen fertilizer for rice. IRRI Research Paper Series No. 11. 15 p.

Zheijiang Academy of Agricultural Sciences (1975) The cultivation, propagation and utilization of azolla. Agricultural Publishing House, Beijing, People's Republic of China.

THE NITROGEN BALANCE OF PADDY FIELDS CROPPED TWO TO THREE TIMES PER YEAR TO CEREAL GRAINS, INCLUDING RICE

Lee Shi Ye[1]

Summary

This paper discusses the N balance of multiple cropped paddy fields in southern China. High application rates of manure and fertilizer N permit overall yields of 12.0 to 20.0 tons/ha without material soil N depletion. Soil N losses vary from 6.4-28.7%, and are affected by soil type. The relative contribution of different N sources to N uptake varies with semester.

INTRODUCTION

In southern China more than 60% of the paddy fields are cropped at least twice each year, mainly with cereal grains such as rice, wheat, and barley. This intensive system of production requires careful management of soil fertility, particularly of the soil nitrogen (N) status. This paper examines some aspects of the developing patterns of N usage in this region.

THE NITROGEN BALANCE OF PADDY SOILS IN SOUTHERN CHINA

Table 1 summarizes N inputs to paddy fields in the Soochow, Shanghai, and Zhejiang regions of southern China (Hsueng, 1980; Xi Zhen-bang, 1980; T.L. Wu, unpublished data), where more than one cereal grain crop per year is normally taken. For this region of approximately 2.2 million ha, chemical fertilizers currently supply 43-72% of the N input; green manures or *Azolla*, 5-9%; and animal manures, 10-40%. While improved animal husbandry systems, especially for pigs, have made available increased organic N sources (with pig manure constituting 75.8-85.6% of these) the increase in the rate of N

[1] Institute of Soil & Fertilizer Zhejiang Academy of Agricultural Sciences, Zhejiang, People's Republic of China.

TABLE 1: The N balance of double and triple cropped paddy fields of some districts in China (1978-1979).

Location	Multiple cropped area (1000 ha)	Level of yield (t/ha·yr)	N input (kg/ha)					N output (kg/ha)			Balance of N (kg/ha)
			Chemical fertilizer	Green manure	Animal manure	Others	Total	Crop recovery	Loss	Total	
Soochow region	400	8- 9	246	16	50	26	338	204	131	335	+3
Shanghai suburb	360	11-12	324	15	89	33	461	243	178	421	+40
Zhejiang Province	1460	10-11	182	41	170	30	423	218	135	353	+70

fertilization recommended has demanded greater use of chemical N fertilizer (see Table 2). Thus, in Zhejiang Province the amount of N applied rose from 248 to 450 kg/ha between 1977 and 1979, with the proportion derived from chemical sources increased from 27 to 43%.

TABLE 2: Relative use of chemical and organic N in multiple-cropped paddy fields in Zhejiang Province[1]

Year	Amount of nitrogen applied (kg/ha)	Proportion of N from different sources			
		Organic manure		Chemical fertilizer	
		(kg/ha)	(%)	(kg/ha)	(%)
1977	248	181	73	67	27
1978	375	225	60	150	40
1979	450	275	57	193	43

[1]From the Provincial Bureau of Agriculture.

With winter cereal crops now grown in the paddy fields, the opportunities for winter green manure crops (such as milk vetch) and the propagation of *Azolla* have been reduced, and N_2 fixation now plays a lesser role in the agriculture of this region than in previous decades.

Table 1 also shows that the efficiency of N recovery varies from 61-69%, with a positive soil N balance of 3-70 kg N/ha per year. In a long-term experiment, from 1974-1979, with barley and two rice crops planted each year, and with pig manure supplied at 22.5 or 45 ton/ha and urea at 625 kg/ha, soil N was increased from 9.2-14.9%, even though 1784-1904 kg N was removed with the crops.

There is now considerable evidence that organic N is used more efficiently than fertilizer N. In an experiment where the same total amount of N was applied, but the proportion of organic to inorganic material varied, the loss of N increased with increasing chemical fertilizer, with yields reduced appreciably (see Table 3).

THE INFLUENCE OF SOIL TYPE ON THE N BALANCE OF TRIPLE-CROPPED PADDY FIELDS

Even where significant N inputs are made, an appreciable amount of the N in a rice crop is still derived from soil N (Koyama & App, 1978). Because of this, experiments with triple cropping (two rice crops and barley taken each

TABLE 3: The effects of the ratio of organic manure and chemical fertilizer on nitrogen balance of the multiple cropping system (1974-1979, Huangyan, China).

Symbol	Treatments (organic N: chemical N)	Total N applied (kg/ha)	N recovery				N losses		Annual yield[1]
			Soil accumulated (kg/ha)	Soil accumulated (%)	Crop uptake (kg/ha)	Crop uptake (%)	(kg/ha)	(%)	(t/ha)
N_H	6:4	2571	315	12.3	1865	72.5	391	15.2	14.9
N_M	4:6	2571	258	10.0	1859	72.3	454	17.7	15.8
N_L	2:8	2571	281	10.9	1785	68.4	532	20.7	14.0

[1]Average over six years.

TABLE 4: The effect of soil type on the N balance of various paddy fields multiple cropped during 1979-80.

Site	Topography	Soil type	Texture	Total N (%)	N applied[1] (kg/ha)	Soil accumulation		Crop uptake		Losses	
						(kg/ha)	(%)	(kg/ha)	(%)	(kg/ha)	(%)
Huangyan	Coastal plain	Rust mottled clayey soil	clay loam	0.20	1125	79	7	723	64.3	323	28.7
Jia Xing	River plain	Bluish gray clayey soil	loamy clay	0.15	1125	203	18	746	66.3	176	15.7
Qu Xian	Lowhill regions	Red grume soil	loamy clay	0.13	1125	169	15	690	61.3	266	23.7
Xian Ju	Valley plain	Gray clay loamy soil	sandy clay loam	0.13	1125	191	17	862	76.6	72	6.4

[1]Pig manure, 45 t/ha, and $(NH_4)_2SO_4$, 1687.5 kg/ha, were applied annually in each soil.

year) have been carried out on a range of soil types. Though annual yields reached 16.5 to 20.6 ton/ha, there was an N accumulation in soil of 79 to 203 kg/ha over the two years of the experiment. Losses of N were from only 6.4 to 28.7% (see Table 4). Lowest N losses were in a sandy clay loam, where yields were 1.7 tons/ha more than in the other soils.

RELATIVE UPTAKE OF N FROM SOIL, FERTILIZER, AND MANURE

In a cropping system with two rice and one barley or wheat crop each year, the two rice crops contribute over 75% to the final yield, and remove the most N.

Field trials with ^{15}N-labeled fertilizer have studied the relative contribution of soil, fertilizer and manure N to the early and late rice crops. When 562.2 kg/ha of $(NH_4)_2SO_4$ was applied to each crop, early rice derived 32.3% of its N from the fertilizer while late rice obtained only 23.7% of its N from this source. When $(NH_4)_2SO_4$ was applied in association with 15 ton/ha pig manure, the percentage of plant N derived from manure was greater in late than in early rice (19.6 vs 11.2%). For the early rice addition of pig manure reduced fertilizer N uptake more than the absorption of soil N, but in the late crop the use of manure appeared to have a sparing action on soil N.

REFERENCES

Hseung, Y. (1980) *Acta Pedologica Sinica* 17, 111.

Koyama, T. & App. A. (1978) *In:* Nitrogen and rice. IRRI, Los Baños, Philippines. Pp. 95-104.

Xi Zhen-Bang (1980) Proceedings of a symposium on paddy soils. *Academia Sinica* 72 (abstract).

PROPAGATION OF AN *AZOLLA* SP. AND ITS POTENTIAL AS A GREEN MANURE FOR CORN IN MEXICO.

R. Ferrera-Cerrato and A. Miranda Romero[1]

Summary

Cultures of *Azolla* were collected in Tabasco, Mexico, and maintained on synthetic medium devoid of nitrogen (N). Preliminary studies using inundated soil trays showed that fresh weight yields of 7.3 to 14.2 times that used as inoculum could be obtained in only 30 days, but that growth varied with N and phosphorus (P) source.

When *Azolla* was incorporated into soil as a green manure for maize at rates of 1, 3 and 5 t/ha, growth of the corn was enhanced, but the increase in dry matter production was not as great as that achieved with the application of 69 kg N/ha.

INTRODUCTION

Azolla, an aquatic fern of the Salvinaceae, is capable of a symbiotic relationship with the cyanobacterium *Anabaena azollae*, as a result of which appreciable quantities of nitrogen (N_2) can be fixed (Food and Agriculture Organization (FAO), 1977; Watanabe, 1977). *Azolla* has been used extensively as a green manure in Asia, especially in rice production, but has been little used or studied in other areas of the world. Problems in its wider adoption include (FAO, 1978):

Development of strains more tolerant of temperature extremes;
Preservation;
Diseases and pests;
Vegetative propagation; and
Production, management, and transport.

Since Mexico has large areas with seemingly appropriate conditions for the growth of *Azolla*, we have initiated research to determine methods of

[1] Sección de Microbiología y Bioquímica, Centro de Edafología, Colegio de Posgraduados, Chapingo, México.

propagation and use appropriate to Mexico. This paper gives some early results.

MATERIALS AND METHODS

Primary propagation

Samples of *Azolla* were collected from Tabasco State and cultured on Jensen or Norris medium, devoid of N. They were grown under continuous light at 30° C without additional aeration.

Secondary propagation

For fertilizer and growth studies, *Azolla* was inoculated into 950 cm^2 plastic trays containing 1 kg of a sandy clay loam soil and 3 l distilled water. An inoculum of 2.5 g/tray was used, and trays were maintained under controlled greenhouse conditions with temperatures from 10-12° C by night and 25-30° C by day.

Effect of nitrogen and phosphorus fertilization

Three sources of phosphorus (P) — simple superphosphate, triple superphosphate and rock phosphate — and two N sources — urea and ammonium sulfate — applied alone, or as mixed N and P sources, were tested for their effects on the growth of *Azolla*. A single rate equivalent to 40 kg/ha of N and/or P was applied, the trays inoculated with 2.5 g of *Azolla*; then incubated for 30 days in the glasshouse. The *Azolla* was then harvested, and its fresh and dry weight were determined.

When N application was shown to have little effect on growth of *Azolla*, a second series of experiments with the three P sources, but applied at rates equivalent to 20, 40, 80, 160, and 320 kg P/ha was undertaken. This experiment was terminated after 15 days, by which time trays receiving the heavier fertilizer dressings were completely covered with *Azolla*.

Productivity evaluation

A series of trays were inoculated with 2.5 g fresh weight of *Azolla* and fertilized with simple superphosphate at a rate equivalent to 120 kg P/ha. When *Azolla* covered the tray's surface, half the *Azolla* was harvested and weighed; the remainder was allowed to reproduce, and, in turn was harvested. Growth rates were determined as tons/ha per day.

Azolla for corn fertilization

Plastic pots containing 3 kg soil were fertilized with 40 kg/ha triple superphosphate; then 0, 1, 3, or 5 t/ha equivalent of *Azolla* were added and incorporated. Pots were maintained at field capacity for 12 days, at which time 4 corn seeds/pot were planted. These were thinned to 2 seeds/pot after germination. Three replicates of each treatment were used, and controls supplied 23 or 69 kg N/ha included. Sixty days after germination the corn was harvested, and its height, leaf number, plant dry weight and root weight were determined.

RESULTS AND DISCUSSION

Response to fertilization

Effect of different N and P sources on the growth of *Azolla* is shown in Figure 1. As stated earlier, N fertilization did not enhance the growth of *Azolla*, which obtained all the N it required through N_2 fixation by the microsymbiont. Responses were obtained to P application, but were somewhat variable (see Figures 1 & 2). Most consistent results were obtained with the application of simple superphosphate. With 120 kg P/ha as simple superphosphate, the rate of growth of the fern was linear and equivalent to 0.47 t/ha per day.

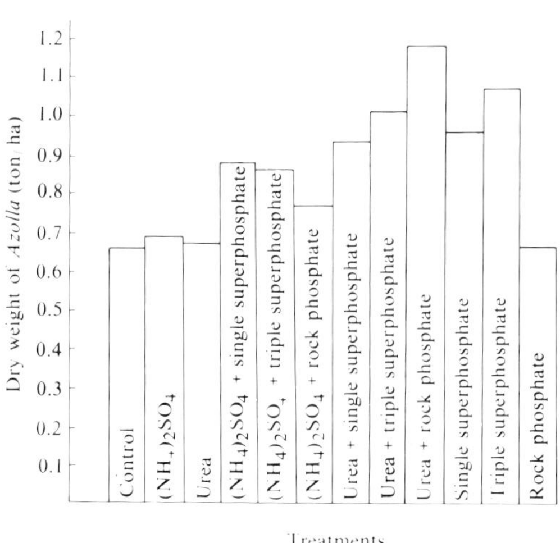

Figure 1.
Development of *Azolla* with different N and P sources (30 days growth).

Response of corn to fertilization with *Azolla*

Parameters of corn supplied with different rates of *Azolla* as a green manure are shown in Table 1. Corn responded to *Azolla* application, though the increased dry matter production with 5 t/ha *Azolla* incorporated was not as great as that achieved by applying 69 kg N/ha.

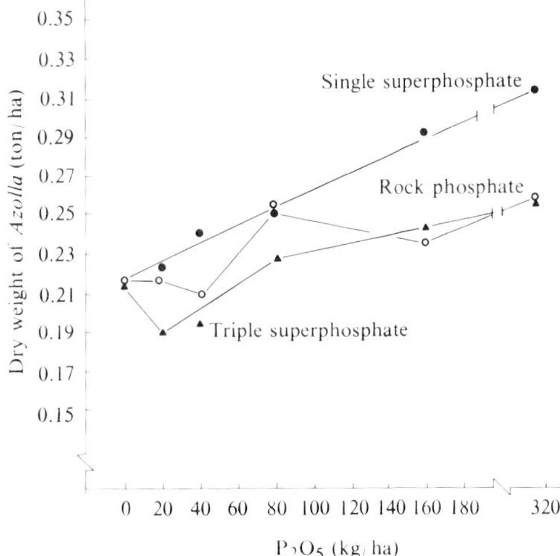

Figure 2.
Fertilizer effect of three phosphorus sources on *Azolla* development (harvested at 15 days).

TABLE 1: Effect of *Azolla* addition as fertilizer for corn.

Dose of *Azolla* (t/ha)	Corn growth parameters					
	No. of leaves	Height (cm)	Fresh weight (g)	Dry weight (g)	Root weight (g)	Root volume (ml)
0	7.3	63.3	5.9	0.90	0.70	6.6
1	7.5	68.8	8.6	1.25	0.58	8.3
3	7.7	75.0	10.0	1.46	0.71	9.9
5	7.9	78.0	11.7	1.71	0.72	9.3

REFERENCES

Food and Agriculture Organization (FAO) (1977) Organic scrap in agriculture. *In*: Biofertilization. FAO Soils Bulletin No. 40. FAO, Rome, Italy.

Food and Agriculture Organization (FAO) (1978) *Azolla* propagation and small-scale biogas technology. *In*: Propagation and agricultural use of *Azolla*. FAO Soils Bulletin No. 41. FAO, Rome, Italy.

Watanabe, I. (1977) The utilization of the *Azolla-Anabaena* complex as a nitrogen fertilizer for rice. IRRI Research Bulletin No. 11. IRRI, Los Baños, The Philippines.

THE USE OF *AZOLLA* IN WEST AFRICA

P.A. Reynaud[1]

The presence of *Azolla pinnata* var. *africana* has been reported in Benin, Ghana (Ada), Guinea Bissao, Guinea Conakry, Gambia, Ivory Coast (Dabou Bouaké), Mali (Bamako), Senegal (Casamance) and Sierra Leone. Until 1977, it was considered a curiosity, and sometimes treated as a weed. Its effective use as a green manure in Africa is currently limited to Guinea Conakry where the management procedures have been imported directly from China, and to remote valleys of the Sine Saloum in Senegal. The northern climatic limit of its potential use in West Africa would be the 15th parallel.

This note reports some observations on azolla in western Africa.

Light intensity: Near the 15th parallel, the high light intensity (100 klux at 1300 h) limits the growth of *Azolla.* In such situations it is essential to grow *Azolla* inocula under cover, and to add them to rice paddies only when the rice canopy can provide some protection

Temperature: In the Sahelian region of west Africa the temperature range from January to April is 15-23° C, and the growth of *Azolla* is very slow. The average doubling time is 20 days, when plants are protected from excessive light, but only 42 days without a canopy (see Figure 1). In April when the temperature increases the doubling time is markedly reduced.

Dryness: Desiccation reduces N_2 (C_2H_2) activity to zero within 24 h and stops growth. The changes are not reversible (Reynaud, 1980). Addition of alginate (0.05%) to the growth medium slows the effects of desiccation and can be used in shipping inoculants.

Biotic factors: Competition from aquatic weeds such as *Salvinia nymphellula* has been observed in Dabou (Ivory Coast) (V. Jacq, personal communication). The small fish *Lebistes reticulatus* damages *Azolla* fronds and roots, facilitating fungus attack (Reynaud & Paycheng, 1981). Insect damage to *Azolla* in Africa has not been evaluated.

Yield of azolla: Maximum azolla productivity obtained under our laboratory conditions has been 128 g fresh weight/m^2 in 15 days.

[1] ORSTOM, BP 1386 Dakar, Senegal.

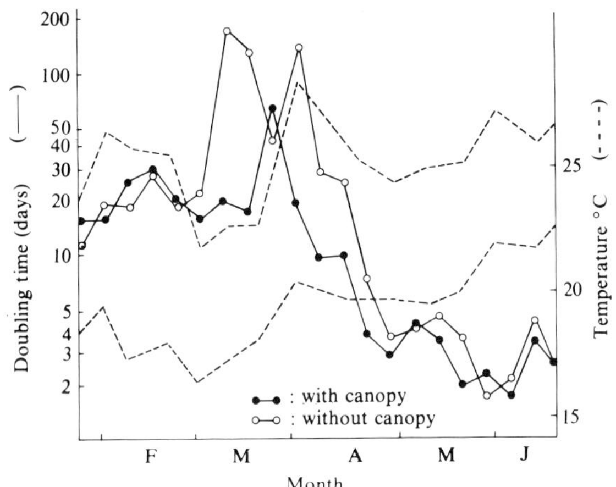

Figure 1. Variations in the doubling time (fresh weight) of *Azolla pinnata* var. *africana*, and maximum and minimum temperatures for Dakar (Senegal) from January-June, 1980.

Experimental results with azolla: Two experiments have been conducted at the ORSTOM Bel-Air station in Dakar. The first showed that dry azolla incorporated at a rate of 50 kg N/ha resulted in rice yields similar to those achieved by applying 15 kg N as urea. When fresh azolla was applied at 200 g/m^2, yields were equivalent to applying 50 kg N/ha as urea. In the second experiment application of azolla to rice without N fertilization increased grain yields 38-40%, similar to the application of 30 kg N/ha as urea, with best yields obtained with two azolla inoculations, one before and one after transplanting. The combination of azolla inoculation plus 30 kg N/ha as urea increased grain yield more than applying 60 kg N/ha as urea. Drying of azolla before incorporation reduced the benefit obtained.

Other uses for azolla: Irrigated sweet potatoes (*Ipomea batatas*) are economically important during the dry season. Sweet potatoes cultivated on ridges have been successfully inoculated with *A. africana* applied in the furrows, where fresh water at pH 5.7 to 6.3 flows continuously. In such conditions the doubling time of the azolla surface area is four days.

REFERENCES

Reynaud, P.A. (1980 Fixation d'azote chez les Cyanobactéries libres ou en symbiose (*Azolla*); *Possibilités d'utilisation agronomique en Afrique Tropicale. In*: Proc. Workshop on Agronomic Matters. FAO/SIDA, Rome, Italy. (In press.)

Reynaud, P.A. & Paycheng, C. (1981) *Cah. ORSTOM Ser. Biol.* 43, 61-66.

SOME EXPERIMENTS ON THE USE OF *AZOLLA* FOR RICE PRODUCTION IN INDONESIA

S. Brotonegoro,[1] M. Sudjadi,[2] S. Partohardjono,[3] H. Sukiman,[1] T. Prihatini,[2] and V. Hendriks[3]

Summary

Experiments have been carried out in the field to find the best method for propagating *Azolla in situ* and to determine the response of rice plants to the addition of *Azolla* as a green manure in wetland rice fields.

The results showed that an inoculum density of 400 g of fresh *Azolla*/m² was optimal for the propagation of *Azolla* in the open field in West Java, Indonesia. Application of P fertilizers, as either double or triple superphosphate invariably improved the growth of the water fern. At high rates of P application, splitting the application into three or four portions gave higher yield of *Azolla* than a single application. The application of Mo in the form of 0.25 kg Na_2MoO_4/ha. did not improve the growth of *Azolla*. Shading with covers made from palm leaves improved the appearance of the fern but reduced its biomass considerably.

Rice yields benefited significantly from the use of *Azolla* as a green manure.

INTRODUCTION

Green manure, in the form of young leaves of various plants, but mostly of Leguminosae (*Sesbania*, *Crotalaria*, *Tephrosia*, etc.), has been used by Indonesian farmers for many years to increase production in flooded rice fields. The leaves are added to soil after the land has been prepared for the next planting season, plowed in, and then irrigation water is run on to the land. A strong objection to green manuring is that to grow plants for this

[1] National Research Institute Bogor, Indonesia.
[2] Soil Research Institute. Bogor. Indonesia.
[3] Centre Research Institute. Bogor, Indonesia.

purpose involves considerable labor and occupies land required for other purposes. Because of this, green manuring has progressively been abandoned in favor of using nitrogen (N) fertilizers which are available now in Indonesia at a relatively inexpensive, subsidized price. However, in some areas, where the infrastructure for fertilizer sale and use has not yet developed, green manuring is the only means for soil amendment.

The choice of plants to be used as a green manure depends on local conditions, but it is suggested that the plant should have the following characteristics:

Easy propogation by either seed or cutting,
Fast growth,
Production of abundant leaves with a relatively high N content,
Easy and rapid decomposition in soil, and
Lack of disease or pest harmful to the subsequent crops.

Azolla satisfies these criteria, doubling in weight in three to four days, having a relatively high N content of 3-5% dry matter (0.15 - 0.25% of fresh weight), and being easily decomposed in wet soils. It is not surprising, therefore, that this plant has long been used by Vietnamese and Chinese farmers for manuring their rice fields.

In Indonesia, the possibility of using *Azolla* as a green manure in rice fields was explored by Saubert before and during the Second World War (Saubert, 1949), but this work was discontinued on his death. Since 1974, experiments on growth and N_2 fixation of *Azolla pinnata* have been conducted in the greenhouse at Bogor (Brotonegoro & Abdulkadir, 1976, 1978).

Two years ago this work was extended to include field investigations. On the one hand, these studies evaluated factors that could affect *Azolla* reproduction, such as inoculum density, mineral nutrition, and light intensity; on the other hand, they sought to confirm the value of *Azolla* as a green manure under Indonesian conditions.

FACTORS AFFECTING THE FIELD PROPAGATION OF *AZOLLA*

Inoculum density

The period usually allowed for the growth of *Azolla* is relatively short (approximately 12 days). If insufficient inoculum is used, space and sunlight are wasted, and insufficient green manure is available for the adequate development of the rice plant. With too heavy inoculants, both N_2 fixation and growth rate will be reduced (Ashton, 1974).

Studies at Cimanglit and Ciriung, West Java, compared the effect of inoculum density (in one trial 200 or 300 g fresh wt. of *Azolla*/ m^2; in a second trial 200, 400, or 600 g fresh wt. of inoculant/ m^2) on yields of *Azolla*. Results are shown in Table 1. In the first trial no significant difference was found

TABLE 1: Effect of inoculum density on the yield of *Azolla* grown in the field.

Inoculum density (g fresh wt/m^2)	*Azolla* yield[1] (t fresh wt/ha)
Cimanglit, West Java, wet season 1979	
200	15.03 a
300	17.23 a
Ciriung, West Java, dry season 1979	
200	17.15 a
400	23.50 b
600	22.00 b

[1]Harvested after 12 days. Any two numbers followed by the same letter are not significantly different at the 0.05 level.

between inoculation at 200 and 300 g *Azolla*/m^2. In the later trial, in the 1979 dry season, maximum yields were obtained using 400 g *Azolla*/m^2.

Mineral requirements

Deficiency of phosphorus (P) is observed frequently in Java and South Sulawesi. With P deficiency *Azolla* plants are reduced in size and reddish in color. Experiments were carried out to study the effect of rates and times of application of P fertilizer. In these experiments application of triple or double superphosphate invariably improved the growth and yield of *Azolla*. At high rates of P amendment, splitting the application into three or four applications gave higher yields of *Azolla* than did a single, big application (Table 2).

By contrast, and while molybdenum deficiency is rather common in Java (Newton & Anwar Said, 1957), application of Mo to *Azolla* did not improve the growth or yields of this water fern (Table 3).

Shading

During a survey conducted in South Sulawesi, it was noted that the growth of *Azolla* in shaded areas was better, greener, and denser than in the field. Tuan & Thuyet (1979) also report earlier studies in which shading with a gauze cloth proved beneficial to *Azolla*. Because of these observations an experiment was undertaken at Cicurug, West Java, to determine the effects of shading, produced by a cover of palm leaves, on the growth and appearance of

TABLE 2: Effect of P fertilizer on the growth of *Azolla* under field conditions.

Rate of P_2O_5 application (kg/ha)		Fresh wt (t/ha)
A. *Ciriung, West Java*		
0	Control	2.90
6	Single appl.	4.22
6	Three appl. of 2 kg/ha	5.16
B. *Cicurug, West Java*		
4	Two appl. of 2 kg/ha	8.43
8	Four appl. of 2 kg/ha	9.28
16	Four appl. of 4 kg/ha	11.00
C. *Cimanglit, West Java*		
30	Single appl.	8.20
30	Two appl. of 15 kg/ha	12.45
30	Four appl. of 7.5 kg/ha	27.73

TABLE 3: Response of *Azolla* to the addition of Mo to the soil; Cicurug, West Java, wet season 1980-1981.

Treatment	*Azolla* biomass (t fresh wt/ha)	% of control
Control	6.88	100
0.25 kg $Na_2MoO_4.2H_2O$/ha	6.38	93

Azolla grown with moderate amounts (9 kg P_2O_5/ ha) of phosphate. From Table 4, it is evident that shading improves the appearance of *Azolla*, but reduces its biomass appreciably.

CROP RESPONSE TO *AZOLLA*

Field trials were carried out to examine the benefit of *Azolla* as a supplement or substitute for N fertilizer in rice production under flooded conditions. In the first of these trials, carried out in a randomized complete block design having three replicates, rice plants received 60 kg N/ ha in the

TABLE 4: Effect of shading on the growth of *Azolla* in the open field; Cicurug, West Java, wet season 1980-1981.

Treatment	Biomass (t fresh wt/ha)	Color
Full sunlight; control	9.57	Reddish
Shaded	6.63	Dark green

form of *Azolla*, fertilizer N, or a mixture of the two. All plots received 30 kg/ha P_2O_5 as triple superphosphate, KC, and Furadan. One plot also received Mo in the form of $Na_2MoO_4.2H_2O$ at a rate of 4 kg/ha. The height of rice plants, and the number of tillers they had, was determined one month after transplanting, at the primordial stage, and at the beginning of flowering. At harvest yield determinations were made in all plots.

While fertilizer treatments did not affect the height of the rice or the degree of tillering, there was a significant difference between treatments in final yield (see Table 5). The application of *Azolla* alone, or of urea at a rate of 60 kg N/ha raised rice yields substantially. When both *Azolla* and urea were applied, in different proportions, but at a combined rate of N fertilization of 60 kg N/ha, yields were higher than, but not significantly different from, control plot yields.

TABLE 5: Duncan's Multiple Range Test for grain yield of rice variety IR 36 grown on different sources of N; Ciriung, West Java, dry season, 1979.

Treatment[1]	Grain yield (kg/ha)	Statistical significance[2]
Control	3008	a
Azolla 60 + Mo	4494	b
Azolla 60	4386	b
Urea 60	4079	b
Azolla 20 + Urea 40	3712	ab
Azolla 40 + Urea 20	3691	ab

[1]*Azolla* 60 = *Azolla* equivalent to 60 kg N/ha added.
Urea 60 = urea equivalent to 60 kg N/ha added.
[2]Any two numbers followed by the same letter are not significantly different at the .05 level.

In a second trial rice plants were fertilized with different sources (*Azolla*, urea, or a combination of both) and different levels (30, 60, 90 kg/ha) of N.

Azolla were seeded and incorporated into the soil at two different times, namely before and after transplanting rice seedlings. An inoculum density of 200 g fresh wt/m^2 was used in this trial with incorporation of *Azolla* carried out after the fern fully covered the plots. In one treatment, *Azolla* were not incorporated into the soil. Yield data obtained from this trial is shown in Table 6. In general plots fertilized with *Azolla*, either singly or in combination with urea, gave greater yields than those that received urea alone, while plots that received the inoculum after transplanting the rice seedlings gave higher yields than did plots which were inoculated before transplanting. There was a slight decline in yields when *Azolla* was not incorporated, but the difference was not significant. The highest grain yields in this trial, with a yield 40% higher than that of the control, was obtained when plots were inoculated both before and after transplanting. Yields in this plot were significantly better than those achieved when 90 k N/ha as urea was applied.

TABLE 6: Duncan's Multiple Range Test for grain yield of rice variety Cisadane grown with various sources and levels of N; Muara, West Java, dry season 1980.

No.	Treatment	Grain yield (kg/ha)	Statistical significance[2]
1	Control	4993	a
2	Urea 30[1]	5209	ab
3	Urea 60	5995	bcd
4	Urea 90	6064	cd
5	*Azolla;* inoculated before transplanting[3]	5375	abc
6	*Azolla;* inoculated after transplanting	6285	de
7	Treatment No. 6; not incorporated	6136	cde
8	Treatment No. 5 + Urea 30	6384	de
9	Treatment No. 6 + Urea 30	6565	de
10	Treatment No. 5 + No. 6	6975	e
11	Treatment No. 5 + Urea 60	6370	de

[1]Urea 30–urea equivalent to 30 kg N/ha added.

[2]Any two numbers followed by the same letter are not significantly different at the .05 level.

[3]*Azolla;* inoculated before transplanting–seeded with *Azolla* at an inoculum density of 200 g fresh wt/m^2 before transplanting; then incorporated into the soil when plots were fully covered.

From the results of the field trials reported above, it can be concluded that *Azolla* can be used as a green manure in wetland rice fields substituting for N fertilizer. In one of the locations used for the trials, *Azolla* could also be used as a supplement applied in combination with urea.

REFERENCES

Ashton, P.J. (1974) The effect of some environmental factors on the growth of *Azolla filiculoides* Lam. *In:* The Orange River progress report, E.M. van Zinderen-Bakker (Ed.). Bloemfontein, South Africa. Pp. 123-138.

Brotonegoro, S. & Adbulkadir, S. (1976) Growth and nitrogen-fixing activity of *Azolla pinnata*. *Ann. Bogorienses* 6 (2), 69-77.

CRITIQUE O

Brotonegoro, S. & Abdulkadir, S. (1978) The decomposition of *Azolla pinnata* in moist and flooded soils. *Ann. Bogorienses* 6 (4), 169-175.

Newton, J.D. & Said, A. (1957) Molybdenum deficiency in latosols of Java. *Nature* (Lond.) 180, 1485.

Saubert G.G.P. (1949) Provisional communication of the fixation of elementary nitrogen by a floating fern. *Ann. Roy. Gard.* (Buitenzorg) 51, 177-179.

Tuan, D.T. & Thuyet, T.Q. (1979) Use of *Azolla* in rice production in Vietnam. In: Nitrogen and rice. IRRI, Los Baños, Laguna, Philippines. Pp. 395-405.

^{15}N AS A TOOL IN BIOLOGICAL NITROGEN FIXATION RESEARCH

P.B. Vose, A.P. Ruschel, R.L. Victoria, S.M.T. Saito, and E. Matsui[1]

Summary

Nitrogen-15 provides a means of quantifying nitrogen (N_2) fixation in situations where estimates based on yield or total N determinations are insufficiently specific. Use of ^{15}N-enriched atmospheres is the standard by which other methods must be judged, and is the critical method for confirming any new N_2-fixing association. The use of ^{15}N-enriched culture solutions is briefly discussed. The extension of isotope dilution procedures to soil environments is a major step in quantifying N_2 fixation in the field, using ^{15}N-labeled fertilizer and the equation:

$$\%\ \text{N fixed} = 1 - \left[\frac{\%\ \text{atom excess}\ ^{15}\text{N (fixing crop)}}{\%\ \text{atom excess}\ ^{15}\text{N (non-fixing)}}\right] \times 100$$

A major advantage of the method is that one can isolate the effect of fertilizer and soil N on N_2 fixation, and separate the effects of agronomic practice that may affect yield in ways other than through N fixation. The A-level approach, though it has been valuable in developing thinking, is less suitable, as it is yield dependent and may be affected by losses of fertilizer N. The special problems of determining associative N_2 fixation, especially in long season and perennial crops are discussed. Problems inherent in the determination of N_2 fixation by means of natural ^{15}N abundance ratios ($\delta\ ^{15}N\ ^{0}/_{00}$) are considered, and it is concluded that it could become a useful and inexpensive technique, but that very careful attention to analytical detail and better knowledge of plant isotope discrimination factors are needed.

---

[1] UNDP/IAEA Project. Centro de Energía Nuclear na Agricultura, CP 96, 13400, Piracicaba, Sao Paulo, Brazil.

$$\%\ \text{N derived from nutrient solution} = \frac{\text{atom }\%\ ^{15}\text{N excess, plant part}}{\text{atom }\%\ ^{15}\text{N excess, nutrient solution}} \times 100$$

the remainder being the proportion of N derived from fixation.

An advantage of the method is that it is possible to calculate the percentage of N derived from the nutrient solution or from fixation and, by reference to N content data of the different plant parts, provide an estimate of the derivation and amount of nitrogen in every plant part, and the total, without reference to the N content of the nutrient solution. This removes a potential major source of error, and moreover, makes it possible to determine N_2 fixation by plants grown in continuous-flow nutrient solutions, which is otherwise almost impossible, except with non-nodulating comparison lines. Conversely, we have used the ^{15}N label in a continuous-flow nutrient solution to confirm the absence of N_2 fixation in an experiment to investigate the redistribution of leaf N in *Phaseolus* (Vose *et al.,* 1981). Even with a total loss system of continous-flow, the cost of labeling the solution with 1.5% atom excess ^{15}N for a ten-week period was rather small.

MEASUREMENT OF N_2 FIXATION IN SOILS USING ^{15}N ISOTOPE DILUTION

^{15}N-labeled fertilizers are now used routinely to obtain a sensitive and direct measure of the proportion of total N in the plant crop that has been derived from the applied fertilizer N and the proportion that has come from the soil:

$$\%\ \text{N due to fertilizer} = \frac{\%\ ^{15}\text{N excess in plant material}}{\%\ ^{15}\text{N excess in fertilizer}} \times 100$$

If the total amount of N in the plant or crop is known it is then very easy to calculate the actual amounts of N in the plant due to fertilizer and soil-derived N (Broeshart, 1974; IAEA, 1976; Vose, 1980). In the case of N_2-fixing plants, although a perfectly valid determination of fertilizer-derived N is obtained, the value obtained for "soil N" is in fact the sum of soil pool N and N_2 derived from fixation. The problem, therefore, is to separate these two components.

All methods using isotope dilution in soil situations depend on the comparison of $^{15}N/^{14}N$ ratios of N_2-fixing with nonfixing test plants. Vallis *et al.*, (1967) suggested the possibility of using the dilution of ^{15}N-enriched soil nitrogen by atmospheric N_2 as a means of quantifying N_2 fixation. However, development of the isotope dilution approach came through the A-level approach (Broeshart, 1974), and the work of Legg & Sloger (1975) and Rennie *et al.* (1976).

Use of A value for determining N_2 fixation

The A value refers to the amount of an available nutrient in the soil in terms of a standard (Fried & Dean, 1963). Broeshart (1974) and Fried & Broeshart (1975) noted that for an N_2-fixing plant there were, in effect, three A values corresponding to the three sources of N: A(soil), A(fertilizer), and A(symbiosis). A(soil) + A(symb) can readily be calculated for a N_2-fixing crop. If a nonfixing crop is confronted with the same source of soil N as the fixing crop, the A(soil) can be independently estimated. It follows that A(symb) is equivalent to the difference A(soil + symb) - A(soil). The actual amount of N fixed can be calculated as:

$$N_2 \text{ fixed (kg/ha)} = \text{A(symb)} \times \frac{\text{total N yield in crop}}{\text{total N supply to crop}}$$

which becomes in practice:

$$N_2 \text{ fixed (kg/ha)} = \begin{bmatrix} \text{A value} & & \text{A value} \\ \textit{fixing} & - & \textit{nonfixing} \\ \textit{system} & & \textit{system} \end{bmatrix} \times \frac{\text{\%N dff x total plant N (kg/ha)}}{\text{fertilizer N applied (kg/ha) fixing system}} \times 100$$

An advantage of the A-value method is that the fixing and nonfixing test crop can receive different rates of fertilizer N (Rennie *et al.*, 1978). However, an overwhelming disadvantage of the procedure is that it is yield dependent, and, thus, its precision can never be better than that of other yield dependent methods. As Rennie (1979) has pointed out, legume N_2 fixation experiments are carried out with low levels of applied fertilizer N, and it is under these circumstances that A-values can be least precisely estimated. Additionally, the A-value method includes a term for the rate of applied fertilizer N which means that any loss of fertilizer N by denitrification or volatilization will result in error. Such losses may be substantial (Gasser *et al.*, 1967). This seems to introduce a complication which is avoided by the yield-independent, direct isotope dilution procedure, which shows insignificant isotope discrimination in the gaseous loss process.

Therefore, while the use of A value to estimate N_2 fixation was a useful step towards developing the more direct isotope dilution equation (Fried & Mellado. 1977). it is doubtful if we should now put much emphasis on it. The concept is difficult for many nonspecialists, and can lead to arguments of interpretation that the more straightforward equation is able to avoid.

TABLE 1: The proportions of shoot N coming from fertilizer, soil, and biological fixation in soybean at 75 days. Calculations based on total N content, and also on ^{15}N content of the shoots (Ruschel *et al.*, 1979b).

Treatment	Calculations based on total N			Calculations based on ^{15}N data		
	N from fertilizer	N from soil	N_2 fixed	N from fertilizer	N from soil	N_2 fixed
0 kg N	0.0	46.46	53.54	0.0	56.00	44.00[1]
25 kg N	37.79	32.77	29.44	10.31	62.32	27.37
50 kg N	36.96	30.00	33.04	23.67	72.09	4.24
Sig. diff. (P = 0.05)	*4.15*	*8.23*	*10.06*	*3.29*	*7.67*	*11.03*

[1]By calculation from $\delta\,^0/_{00}$ values.

field, and of distinguishing differences between cultivars. When cultivars with the 20 kg N/ha treatment were compared, it was apparent that 'Carioca' showed the highest and 'Goiano Precoce' the lowest rates of N_2 fixation, whether judged by seed yield, total N yield or as calculated from ^{15}N isotope dilution. However, the yield and total-N data alone did not provide a direct measure of N_2 fixation nor estimate the proportion of fixed to total N in the crop or in plant parts. In this experiment the major potential source of error in determining N_2 fixation by the isotope dilution method was that % N fixed had to be calculated against a nonfixing crop of another species, having different root patterns and depth, and potentially exploiting different volumes of soil. In this experiment it seemed that the dwarf wheat and *Phaseolus* roots were of reasonably similar extent. A second potential source of error was that different species may vary in $^{15}N/^{14}N$ discrimination between roots and shoots. While the available data is limited, Moore & Croswell (1976) have reported slightly lower ^{15}N values in wheat roots than in the tops, and Shearer *et al.* (1980) found a similar situation in a non-nodulating soybean isoline. We, too, have found differences in 'Ticena-2' wheat, with the tops having higher ^{15}N values than the roots. While this could mean that the calculated N_2 fixation values for beans might be as much as 15% too high, such differences do not affect comparative evaluations. The efficiency of cultivars for N_2 fixation could be ranked (Ruschel *et al.*, 1981) from the natural ^{15}N data alone and this ranking was the same as that derived from seed yield, total N yield, or ^{15}N fertilizer dilution.

Some will see the parallel results achieved by the isotope dilution and classical methods as justification for the latter. This is a reasonable viewpoint for many practical situations. In the example given here we could rank *Phaseolus* cultivars on their ability to fix N_2 using only seed yield or total N yield. This, however, overlooks the major advantage of the isotope method. It makes possible the determination of N_2 fixation, irrespective of other experimental factors. Thus, one can isolate the effect of fertilizer or soil N on N_2 fixation and separate out the effects of particular agronomic practices that might affect yield in ways other than through N_2 fixation. The dilution method can also provide information on the partitioning of the N_2 fixed between different plant parts.

The latter point deserves additional comment. In the development of new grain legumes it is important to know to which plant part the fixed N_2 goes. If protein-rich grain legumes are sought, varieties that are capable of active symbiosis with *Rhizobium*, but that channel most of the N_2 fixed to leaves, rather than to increased seed yield or percent of protein, will have little value. There is a considerable difficulty in legumes in separating the factors concerned with N-use efficiency, from the capacity *per se* to fix N_2. Amaral (1975) using over 100 varieties of *Phaseolus* in solution culture has already shown differences in the efficiency of conversion of N into grain and leaves.

Combining ^{15}N isotope dilution with a comparison of nodulating and non-nodulating soybeans enabled us to demonstrate (Ruschel *et al.*, 1979b) that with 25 kg N/ha, 69% of the N in the pod was derived from fixation, while with 50 kg N/ha applied only 41% was. Roots of nodulated plants did not contain any detectable N derived from fixation, whereas about 80% of nodule N was derived from fixation. N from N_2 fixation only provided a significant proportion of the total N in the shoots at the last harvest. The data suggested that the roots develop, grow and elaborate their structural N from soil and fertilizer N, without any contribution from fixed N. Subsequently, the nodules develop and commence to fix N_2, which is initially translocated to the still developing shoots, but which later is preferentially translocated to the developing pods. This provides a good experimental basis for the common field practice of supplying a small quantity of N fertilizer as a "starter" for the crop to support initial growth before N_2 fixation can become significant (see Table 2).

There is a problem in using this technique to determine distribution differences in cases when we do not have a non-nodulating isoline or rhizobia-free soils. If one is making a comparison with a nonfixing test plant like wheat, it is obviously not possible to made direct comparisons of root with root, leaves with leaves, and pods with pods, as one can with nodulating and non-nodulating soybean isolines. The alternative is to take the single determinations for wheat top as a base figure, but there is of course a built-in error. The figures obtained for fixed N in the plant parts will, therefore, be relative, but nonetheless useful for comparison of fixed N distribution in different genotypes.

The long-term solution is to develop, by mutation techniques, non-nodulating isolines of *Phaseolus* and other major legumes. This would make truly quantitative studies of the assimilation and distribution of fixed N possible in other legumes, as is possible for soybean using nodulating and non-nodulating isolines.

Measurement of associative N_2 fixation

$^{15}N_2$ has been used to confirm associative N_2 fixation in grasses (De-Polli *et al.*, 1977), sugarcane seedlings (Ruschel *et al.*, 1975; 1978), and associated with sugarcane rhizosphere soil in the field (Matsui *et al.*, 1981). However, for any extensive work the isotope dilution technique is essential. With an annual crop such as wheat, there is no real problem. A nonfixing genotype of similar physiological growth pattern can be obtained quite easily, and the isotope dilution technique applied successfully, both in the field (Rennie & Larson, 1981) and in pots (Rennie *et al.*, 1981).

There are, however, some major problems with long-growing or perennial grasses. In many cases it is difficult to obtain an adequate nonfixing control genotype. Thus, we have been unable to do isotope dilution experiments with

TABLE 2: The origin and distribution of N in plant parts of soybean, as determined from ^{15}N data and comparisons with a non-nodulating isoline (Ruschel *et al.*, 1979b).

Treatments	Origin of N	Shoots		Roots		Pods		Nodules		Total
		N percent	N content/ plant (mg)	N percent	N content/ plant (mg)	N percent	N content/ plant (mg)	N percent	N content/ plant (mg)	N content/ plant (mg)
0 kg N	Fixation	44.00[1]	92.13	ND[2]	ND[2]	ND[2]	ND[2]	ND[2]	ND[2]	92.13
	Soil	56.00	117.26	100.00	36.90					154.16
	Fertilizer	0.00	0.00	0.00	0.00					0.00
	Total		209.39		36.90				30.15	276.44
25 kg N	Fixation	27.37	88.07	0.02	0.00	69.00	18.29	81.30	28.18	134.54
	Soil	62.32	200.55	87.23	32.55	26.13	6.94	16.29	5.65	245.69
	Fertilizer	10.31	33.17	12.75	4.76	4.87	1.29	2.41	0.83	40.05
	Total		321.79		37.31				34.66	420.28
50 kg N	Fixation	4.24	13.75	0.00	0.00	40.80	8.60	77.20	22.73	45.08
	Soil	72.09	233.76	76.73	40.13	44.95	9.48	17.50	5.16	288.53
	Fertilizer	23.67	76.75	23.27	12.16	14.25	3.00	5.30	1.56	93.47
	Total		324.26		52.29		21.08		29.45	427.08

[1]By calculation from $\delta\ ^0/_{00}$ values.
[2]Calculations not possible.

sugarcane in the field because we have not found a crop plant with a development that parallels the 14-month growing period of sugarcane in Brazil. A second problem in handling grasses, which have a long growing period, is that they normally have successive harvests over a whole growing season. Finding nonfixing tropical grass genotypes also seems very difficult.

In 1979 we carried out an experiment to determine whether Sudan grass *(Sorghum sudanense)* could support associative N_2 fixation under field conditions. We compared Sudan grass against 'Ticena-2' dwarf wheat, a crop that we have checked using both the acetylene reduction and ^{15}N techniques (Rennie *et al.*, 1981) and that we know is incapable of supporting associative N_2 fixation. The results summarized in Table 3 clearly show isotope dilution in Sudan grass, implying that there has been associative N_2 fixation. Data for ^{15}N excess show wheat > Sudan grass > beans. The same order is found for natural ^{15}N content of the N_0 treatments: wheat (0.386), Sudan grass (0.371), beans (0.366-0.370). Rates of N_2 fixation in Sudan grass would thus range from 14.6 to 19.2 kg N/ha; not an outstanding amount, but a significant proportion of plant N (about one-third). Although this work is possibly the first to evaluate N_2 fixation by grass in the field using the ^{15}N isotope dilution

TABLE 3: Putative N_2 fixation in Sudan grass (*Sorghum sudanense*), at the first harvest, as compared with *Phaseolus* under the same conditions.

	Treatment	Content of straw		N due to N_2 fixation	
		(% ^{15}N)	(% ^{15}N excess)	(kg/ha)	(%)
Phaseolus vulgaris	N_0	0.368	–		
cv. Carioca Precoce	N_{20}	0.666	0.305	41.6	57.0
	N_{100}	0.757	0.387	31.0	33.0
Sorghum sudanense	N_0	0.371	–		
	N_{20}	0.843	0.472	19.2	35.0
	N_{100}	0.814	0.460	14.6	24.0
Triticum aestivum	N_0	0.386	–		
(non N_2-fixing test	N_{20}	1.148	0.766		
plant)	N_{100}	0.969	0.588		
Sig. diff. (P = 0.05).		0.319	0.190		

technique, we have not hitherto published it because we could not be entirely certain that deep roots, common in tropical grasses, have not taken up a disproportionate amount of ^{15}N from lower in the soil. However, as the ^{15}N content of the N_0 treatment shows the same pattern as the ^{15}N fertilizer treatments, we are inclined to believe it to be a true representation of associative N_2 fixation.

The technical problem remains that grasses and clovers have indeterminate growth and will be cut (or grazed) several times during a season. Therefore, the amount of fixation as determined in the above experiment is probably only a part of the total for a year's growth. We need to develop methods appropriate to the problem of crops that have successive harvests during the season; and subsequent regrowth. Haystead and Lowe (1977) tried to determine the fixation capacity of white clover (*Trifolium repens*) in British hill pasture over a six-week period, giving 90% atom excess ^{15}N at the rate of 2 kg N/ha to microplots. They calculated N_2 fixation according to Vallis *et al.* (1967), and then estimated the annual rate of fixation by using the ^{15}N data in conjunction with seasonal data from intact-core acetylene reduction technique. It should be possible to develop a purely isotope dilution technique in which ^{15}N is given to fresh plots following each defoliation throughout the season, in order to obtain an integrated value for seasonal fixation.

USE OF NATURAL ISOTOPE ABUNDANCE RATIOS

Delwiche & Steyn (1970) noted that legumes that do not fix N_2 and nonlegumes have ^{15}N values similar to the soil, while legumes that have fixed N_2 have $^{15}N/^{14}N$ ratios modified by the N of the atmosphere. It followed that the application of isotope dilution principles to natural N isotope abundance determinations may provide an estimate of plant N_2 fixation under some circumstances (Rennie *et al.*, 1976; Bardin *et al.*, 1977). The method has now been tentatively applied to investigate N_2 fixation in *Lupinus luteus* (Amarger *et al.* 1977), sugarcane (Ruschel & Vose, 1978; Vose *et al.*, 1977), and soybean (Amarger *et al.*, 1979; Ruschel *et al.*, 1979; Kohl *et al.*, 1980).

The N of the atmosphere has a constant isotopic content over variations in location and altitude. In the case of soil, denitrification tends to produce N_2 gas depleted in ^{15}N with the residual nitrate slightly enriched, while nitrification leads to nitrite and nitrate depleted in ^{15}N with the residual ammonium enriched in ^{15}N (Delwiche & Steyn, 1970; Wellman *et al.*, 1968). However, it has now been generally established that the effect of the various soil microbiological reactions that affect the fractionation process of N isotopes in soils is to give an increase in the ^{15}N abundance of soil N compared with atmospheric N (Hauck & Bremner, 1976). Plant N coming from the soil should, therefore, have a higher abundance of ^{15}N than N_2 fixed directly from the atmosphere.

For expressing the level of natural ^{15}N levels it is now usual to use the more sensitive expression $\delta^{15}N\ ^0/_{00}$, where

$$\delta^{15}N\ ^0/_{00} = \left[\frac{^{15}N/^{14}N \text{ sample}}{^{15}N/^{14}N \text{ standard}} - 1 \right] \times 100$$

If plants actively fixing N_2 are grown on a medium which has a higher $\delta^{15}N$ value than the atmosphere, then it should be possible to calculate the N fraction in the plant derived from N_2 fixation. If this is N(fix), then following isotope dilution principles:

$$\%\ \text{N fixed} = \left[1 - \frac{^{15}N\ ^0/_{00} \text{ in plant leaves} - {^{15}N}\ ^0/_{00} \text{ atmosphere}}{\underset{\text{(test plant)}}{^{15}N\ ^0/_{00} \text{ available soil N}} - {^{15}N}\ ^0/_{00} \text{ atmosphere}} \right] \times 100$$

^{15}N values of available soil N should be determined on the N taken up by a nonfixing test crop.

At present this method is experimental, and due in some circumstances to low soil $\delta^{15}N\ ^0/_{00}$ values or to extreme variability of values in field situations, it is clear that it will not be universally applicable. Nevertheless, for some special problems such as determining associative N_2 fixation in sugarcane, which has a long growing season and is very large plant for experimentation, both from the point of view of dilution of ^{15}N in tracer experiments and of general handling and culture, it probably has a valuable role to play. Similarly it should be useful for integrated N_2 fixation estimates for natural vegetation, and pasture plants that are grown and harvested over a period. We have used it for determining N_2 fixation in the zero-N control of a soybean experiment that was otherwise given ^{15}N-enriched fertilizer (Ruschel *et al.*, 1979b). A deficiency of the method is that only a small variation in $\delta^{15}N\ ^0/_{00}$ corresponds to a comparatively large difference in N_2 fixation.

Some of the present difficulties concern our lack of knowledge of fractionation factors for the uptake of N isotopes by plants, and particularly the differences inherent in assimilation and transport between plant parts. This is despite the work of Amarger *et al.* (1977; 1979) and of Kohl & Shearer (1980). Further work along these lines is necessary, because a small difference in the fractionation factor of experimental and test plants could substantially affect the accuracy of estimates of N_2 fixation.

In field experimentation using this method, it is obviously essential that the experimental soil has a reasonably high initial $\delta^{15}N$ value, so that a value essentially obtained by dilution can be obtained. Secondly, in the field experiments there should be no gradient in $\delta^{15}N$ within the profile of the active rooting zone. Although $\delta^{15}N$ values tend to increase down the profile (Feign *et al.*, 1974; Rennie & Paul, 1974; Black & Waring, 1977), these variations are largely in the profile beyond the rooting zone and are not relevant. Relatively small differences due to depth seem likely to be encountered in the normal rooting zone (Kohl *et al.*, 1973; Black & Waring, 1977). Broadbent & Carlton (1978) found spatial variability in soil to be sufficiently low that calculations based on uptake of ^{15}N-depleted fertilizer were not affected.

Since we need to know the δ^{15}N values of the plant-available soil N, we must either grow a nonfixing test crop beside the experimental crop, or undertake very careful soil sampling for available N from the active rooting depth from soil which has received all the treatments of the planted area, but which itself is free from plants and crop roots. Such areas can be found at the side of the planted areas or from "blank" areas that can often be found in row crops. As regards the N_2-fixing plant, the extensive plant root system is an extremely effective averaging device for the small variations likely in substrate, though in pot experiments this problem hardly arises. Either the whole plant can be taken for analysis, or a generally accepted sampling portion (e.g., in sugarcane, the center of the lamina of the fourth last-emerged leaf).

Probably the analytical determination of δ^{15}N is the smallest of the problems inherent in the method, though discrimination effects can arise during sample processing, and very great attention to detail is required. However, we can agree with Turner & Bergersen's recent (1980) view that with attention to sources of error δ^{15}N methods may be a convenient method for field measurement of N_2 fixation.

REFERENCES

Amaral, F.A.L. (1975) Eficiencia de utilização de nitrogenio, fósforo e potássio de 104 variedades de feijoeiro (*Phaseolus vulgaris* L.). PhD thesis, ESALQ, Piracicaba, S.P., Brazil.

Amarger, N., Mariotti, A. & Mariotti, F. (1977) *R. Acad. Sci. Paris* 284 (D) 2179-2182.

Amarger, N., Mariotti, A., Mariotti, F., Durr, J.C., Bourguignon, C., & Lagacherie, B. (1979) *Plant Soil* 52, 269-280.

Bardin, R., Domenach, A.M. & Chalamet, A. (1977) *Rev. Ecol. Biol. Sol* 14, 394-402.

Black, A.S. & Waring, S.A. (1977) *Aust. J. Soil Res.* 15, 51-77.

Bond, G. & Scott, G.D. (1955) *Ann. Bot.* 19, 65.

Broadbent, F.E. & Carlton, A.B. (1978) Field trials with isotopically labelled nitrogen fertilizer. *In*: Nitrogen in the environment, Vol. I. D.R. Nielsen & J.G. MacDonald (Eds.). Academic Press, New York, NY, USA. Pp. 1-41.

Broeshart, H. (1974) *Neth. J. Agric. Sci.* 22, 245-254.

Burris, R.H. & Miller, E.C. (1941) *Science* 93, 114-115.

Burris, R.H. & Wilson, P.W. (1957) Methods for measurement of N_2 fixation. *In*: Methods in enzymology. Vol. 4. S.O. Colowick & N.O. Kaplan (Eds.). Academic Press, New York, NY, USA. Pp. 355-366.

Deibert, E.J., Bijeriego, M. & Olson, R.A. (1979) *Agron. J.* 31.

De-Polli H., Matsui, E., Döbereiner, J., & Salati, E. (1977) *Soil Biol. Biochem.* 9, 119-123.

Delwiche, C.C. & Steyn, P.L. (1970) *Environ. Sci. Tech.* 4. Pp. 929.

Feign, A. Shearer, G., Kohl, D.H., & Commoner, B. (1974) *Proc. Soil. Sci. Soc. Amer.* 38, 465-471.

Freid, M. & Broeshart, H. (1975) *Plant Soil* 43, 713-715.

Fried, M. & Dean, L.A. (1953) *Soil Sci.* 73, 263-271.

Fried, M. & Mellado, L. (1977) A method for determining the amount of nitrogen fixed in the field using ^{15}N. *In*: Internat. Symp. on Limitations and Potentials of Biological Nitrogen Fixation in the Tropics. Basic Life Sciences, Vol. 10. Plenum Press, New York, NY, USA. (1978). P. 362.

Fried, M. & Middleboe, J. (1977) *Plant Soil* 47, 713-715.

Gasser, J.K.R., Greenland, D.J. & Rawson, R.A.G. (1967) *J. Soil Sci.* 18, 289-300.

Hauck, R.D. & Bremner, J.M. (1976) *Adv. Agron.* 28, 219-266.

Haystead, A. & Lowe, A.G. (1977) *J. Brit. Grassl. Soc.* 32, 57 63.

International Atomic Energy Agency (IAEA) (1976) Tracer manual on plants and soils. Tech. Rept. Series, No. 171. IAEA, Vienna, Austria.

Kohl, D.H., Shearer, G. & Commoner, B. (1973) *Soil Sci. Soc. Amer. Proc.* 37, 888-892.

Kohl, D.H. & Shearer, G. (1980) *Plant Physiol.* 66, 51-56.

Kohl, D.H., Shearer, G. & Harper, J.E. (1980) *Plant Physiol.* 66, 61-65.

Legg, J.O. & Sloger, C. (1975) Proc. 2nd Intnat. Conf. Stable Isotopes, Oak Brook, IL, USA. Pp. 661-666.

Matsui, E., Vose, P.B., Rodrigues, N.S., & Ruschel, A.P. (1981) Use of ^{15}N enriched gas to determine N_2 fixation by undisturbed sugarcane plants in the field. *In*: Associative dinitrogen fixation, P.B. Vose, & A.P. Ruschel (Eds.). CRC Press, Boca Raton, Fla, USA.

Moore, A.N. & Croswell, E.T. (1976) *Commun. Soil Sci. Plant Analysis* 7(4), 335-344.

Rennie, R.J. (1979) *Rev. Ecol. Biol. Sol.* 16(4), 455-463.

Rennie, D.A. & Paul, E.A. (1974) *In*: Proc. Symp. Isotope Ratios as Pollutant Sources and Behaviour Indicators. IAEA, Vienna, Austria.

Rennie, D.A., Paul, E.A. & Johns, L.E. (1976) *Can. J. Soil Sci.* 56, 43-50.

Rennie, R.J., Rennie, D.A. & Fried, M. (1978) Concepts of ^{15}N usage in dinitrogen fixation studies. *In*: Isotopes in biological dinitrogen fixation. IAEA, Vienna, Austria. Pp. 107-133.

Rennie, R.J. & Larson, R.I. (1979) Dinitrogen fixation associated with disomic chromosome substitution lines of spring wheat in the phytotron and in the field. *In*: Associative dinitrogen fixation, P.B. Vose & A.P. Ruschel (Eds.). CRC Press, Boca Raton, Fla, USA.

Rennie, R.J. *et al.* (1981) CENA. (In preparation.)

Ruschel, A.P., Henis, Y. & Salati, E. (1975) *Soil Biol. Biochem.* 7, 181-182.

Ruschel, A.P. & Vose, P.B. (1977) Present situation concerning studies on associative nitrogen fixation in sugarcane. *Boletim Científico* BC-045. CENA, Piracicaba, Brazil.

Ruschel A.P., Victoria, R.L., Salati, E., & Henis, Y. (1978) *Ecol. Bull.* (Stockholm) 26, 297-303.

Ruschel, A.P., Salati, E. & Vose, P.B. (1979a) *Plant Soil* 51, 425-429.

Ruschel, A.P., Vose, P.B., Victoria, R.L., & Salati, E. (1979b) *Plant Soil* 53, 513-525.

Ruschel, A.P., Vose, P.B., Matsui, E., Victoria, R.L., & Saito, S.M.T. (1981) Field evaluation of N_2 fixation and nitrogen utilization by *Phaseolus* bean varieties determined by ^{15}N isotope dilution. (In press.).

Shearer, G., Kohl, D.H. & Harper, J.E. (1980) *Plant Physiol.* 66, 57-60.

Stewart, W.D.P. (1966) Nitrogen fixation in plants. Anthlone Press, Univ. of London, London, England. Pp. 1-128.

Turner, G.L. & Bergersen, F.J. (1980) Evaluating methods for the determination of ^{15}N in nitrogen fixation studies. Proc. IV Symp. N_2 Fixation, Canberra, ACT, Australia, Abstract 280.

Vallis, I., Haydock, K.P., Ross, P.J., & Henzell, E.F. (1967) *Aust. J. Agric. Res.* 18, 865-877.

Virtanen, A.I., Moisio, T., Allison, R.M., & Burris, R.H. (1954) *Acta Chem. Scand.* 8, 1730-1731.

Vose, P.B. (1980) Introduction to nuclear techniques in agronomy and plant biology. Pergamon Press. Oxford, England. 165. 391 pp.

Vose P.B., Ruschel, A.P. & Salati, E. (1978) Determination of N_2 fixation especially in relation to the employment of nitrogen-15 and of natural isotope variation. Proc. II Latin American Bot. Congr. Brasilia. Mimeo.

Vose, P.B., Ruschel, A.P., Freitas, R. de, Victoria, R.L., & Matsui, E. (1981) Redistribution of leaf nitrogen in *Phaseolus* as measured by ^{15}N pulse labelling. (In preparation.)

Wellman, R.P., Cook, F.D. & Krouse, H.R. (1968) *Science*, 161, 296-270.

Witty, J.F. & Day, J.M. (1978) Use of ^{15}N in evaluating asymbiotic N_2 fixation. *In*: Isotopes in biological dinitrogen fixation. IAEA, Vienna, Austria. Pp. 135-150.

Yoshida, T. & Yoneya.na, T. (1980) Atmospheric dinitrogen fixation in the flooded rice rhizosphere determined by N-15 isotope dilution technique. Proc. IV Symp. N_2 Fixation, Canberra, ACT, Australia. Abstract 278.

A WHOLE-SYSTEM APPROACH TO QUANTIFYING BIOLOGICAL NITROGEN FIXATION BY LEGUMES AND ASSOCIATED GAINS AND LOSSES OF NITROGEN IN AGRICULTURAL SYSTEMS

D.F. Herridge[1]

Summary

Although a lot of effort has gone into estimating nitrogen (N_2) fixation by legumes in agricultural systems during the past 30 years, little emphasis has been given to placing these estimates in perspective relative to the overall N economy of the system. Potential losses of N are of at least the same magnitude as gains. A whole-system approach to the study of legumes in agricultural systems is proposed, where measurements of a number of components are made and inefficiencies identified. These may include suppression of N_2 fixation by soil nitrate, losses of N through various pathways, inefficient conversion of total crop protein to harvested protein, and so on. Details of methods to measure the various components are presented and evaluated in terms of precision, ease of use, cost, and availability.

INTRODUCTION

The value of legumes is two-fold. They produce vegetation and grain of high protein content and quality. They also fix atmospheric nitrogen (N_2) in association with appropriate strains of *Rhizobium*. Fixation may not only provide N for the legume itself, but in some cases will also build up the soil N, permiting more vigorous growth of companion species and of succeeding crops and pastures. However, the high rates of N_2 fixation required to achieve these desired effects are produced with only varying degrees of success.

Agronomic studies where cropping systems involving legumes and non-legumes grown together or in sequence and evaluated purely in terms of

[1] New South Wales Dept. of Agriculture, Agricultural Research Centre, R.M.B. 944, Tamworth, NSW, Australia.

production have proved useful in extending the much-researched principles of biological N_2 fixation into agricultural production. The publications detailing research done during the 1950's and 1960's by scientists of the Commonwealth Scientific and Industrial Research Organization (CSIRO) at Katherine, Northern Territory, are an excellent example. In a four-year study, previous cropping had a significant effect on yield of peanut in one year out of three, when yield was highest after peanut and lowest after cotton; yield of sorghum was considerably lower following sorghum than following peanut or cotton in three of the four seasons, but there was no effect of previous crop on cotton yields (Phillips, 1959). In further studies (Phillips & Norman, 1961) grain yields of sorghum were 77% higher when grown after peanut than when preceded by sorghum.

When such empirical measurements are supported by additional data on the N economy of the cropping system under study, inefficiencies in the system can be identified. By estimating rates of N_2 fixation, the cost of production of legume protein and the possible benefits of a legume crop to succeeding crops can be predicted. Measurement of the losses of N from the system can also be critical. Losses of up to 500 kg N/ha have been reported in some tropical cropping systems (Bartholomew, 1977), and this could nullify potential gains from N_2 fixation. It would, obviously, be foolish to deploy all resources to improving rates of N_2 fixation when reducing the loss of N from the system could be achieved more readily.

If the various components of gains, transfers, and losses of N are compiled, a balance sheet, or budget of N, can be made (Henzell & Vallis, 1977; Heal, 1979). Briefly:

$$\Delta N = F_L + F_F + M + DR + A - C - L - V - E$$

where: N = change in the soil N over time.
F_L = the rate of symbiotic N_2 fixation.
F_F = the rate of nonsymbiotic N_2 fixation.
M = N added in fertilizers, seed, or manures.
DR = N added in dust and rainfall.
A = N added via ammonia (NH_3) fixation by plants.
C = harvested N (grain and vegetation).
L = N lost through leaching.
V = gaseous losses of N through denitrification, burning, ammonia volatilization.
E = N lost through erosion.

(from Greenland, 1977)

Not all these components will have equal importance in a particular agricultural system. The succeeding sections examine methodologies for the establishment of N balance sheets, and consider particularly their precision, ease of use, and cost. The emphasis will be toward the measurement of gains in soil N, and on cropping rather than grazing systems. An effort will be made, however, to put potential gains in perspective by discussing the fate of fixed, unharvested N and concomitant losses from the system.

MEASUREMENT OF GAINS, TRANSFERS, AND LOSSES OF N

N gains

N fixation accounts for a large percentage of the N gained in cropping systems that include legumes, with rates of up to 450 kg N/ha per year recorded (Williams & Cooke, 1972). Inputs associated with rain and dust are small and rarely exceed 15 kg N/ha per year (Jenkinson, 1971; Greenland, 1977). Inputs resulting from nonsymbiotic fixation are also likely to be small with values under most situations not exceeding 10 kg N/ha per year (Greenland, 1977). Upward mobility of subsoil N is a further source of N that may be significant in the short term. Bartholomew (1977) argued that deep rooted perennial plants will return substantial amounts of subsoil N to the surface of tropical agricultural systems previously leached during the cropping phase. Over an extended period of time, however, any net gain of N from the subsoil has to be negligible, since this N must be derived from the surface in the first instance. In dealing with N gains we shall only consider methods to quantify N_2 fixation in detail. For details of techniques associated with N gains via other pathways the reader should refer to Greenland (1977). The methods of measuring N_2 fixation reviewed here include N balance sheets, comparative uptake of N by the test legume and a nonlegume or non-nodulated legume of the same genotype, and the acetylene reduction assay. The recently published ureide technique and methods using ^{15}N are discussed elsewhere in this volume (McNeil, p. 609; Vose *et al.*, p. 575).

N balance sheets

This approach involves measuring increments of N in the soil/plant system over a period of time (usually a number of years) and estimating losses of N during the same period. N_2 fixation can then be estimated as the sum of both of these components (Greenland, 1977). Measurements of N in soil (as organic N and mineral N), rainwater, and plant material established that guar (*Cyamopsis tetragonoloba*) fixed 220 kg N/ha, peanut (*Arachis hypogaea*) 123 kg N/ha, cowpea (*Vigna unguiculata*) 269 kg N/ha, and Townsville stylo (*Stylosanthes humilis*) 220 kg/ha over a three-year period at Katherine, Northern Territory (Wetselaar, 1967). Associated work suggested that losses due to denitrification were negligible, as were gains associated with N dissolved in rainwater (Wetselaar & Hutton, 1963).

Fundamental to this method is the need to measure accurately the different components, especially soil organic N, which accounts for approximately

90% of total system N (Date, 1973). Errors arise from inadequate sampling techniques, faulty determination of N contents, and insufficient attention to sampling exactly the same mass (not volume) on each occasion (Greenland, 1977). Any errors associated with the organic component will be magnified when estimating amounts of N_2 fixed. For instance, an error of 5% in the Wetselaar study was equivalent to 80 kg N/ha or approximately two-thirds of the estimated N_2 fixed by peanut (see also Kohl, Shearer & Vithayanunil, 1978). In some soils, N in the organic soil fraction is much greater (up to 15,000 kg/ha (Heal, 1979) making the potential error astronomic.

It is also important to estimate losses of N from the system. In the Wetselaar study sodium nitrate was applied to bare soil and losses estimated over a five-year period. In this case virtually all of the fertilizer N was recorded, albeit deep in the soil profile. In tropical systems especially, sampling for mineral N should be to a depth of two to three meters to allow for leaching caused by heavy rains (Bartholomew, 1977).

In summary, estimates of N_2 fixation by the N balance method are as good as the estimates of N in all of the components.

Comparative uptake of N by legume and nonlegume or non-nodulated legume

The major assumption of this technique is that the test legume and reference crop (or legume) remove identical amounts of N from the soil. This in turn depends upon the success of the operator to match growth rates and to ensure that insects, diseases, and other factors known to affect plant growth are similar in both crops. This may be difficult to achieve.

Uptake of N by a legume and a nonlegume

Bell & Nutman (1971) estimated N_2 fixation by effectively nodulated lucerne by relating uptake of N by the lucerne to amounts assimilated by ryegrass at five sites over a four-year period. Estimates of fixation in fertilized (lime + P + K) plots ranged from 40-343 kg N/ha and in the unfertilized plots, 34-225 kg N/ha. The mean amounts of N_2 fixed over the five locations and four years of the trials were 152 and 103 kg/ha in the fertilized and unfertilized plots, respectively.

Uptake of N by a nodulated and a non-nodulated legume

Most reports of this technique refer to soybeans where non-nodulating isolines are used as the reference plant. Originally these isolines were used to examine various aspects of nodulation (Saers & Lynch, 1951; Williams & Lynch, 1954; Clark, 1957). In 1966, Weber compared the uptake of N by two isolines, one of which was non-nodulating, as a measure of N_2 fixation.

Subsequent reports (see Table 1) established that this technique gave reasonable estimates of fixation. The N contents of the non-nodulating isolines shown in Table 1 range from 70-197 kg N/ha, and are equivalent to the soil N available to the nodulating isoline. N_2fixation in these lines ranged from 14-320 kg N/ha and represented between 14% and 80% of total N in the nodulated crop. Unfortunately, widespread application of this extremely useful technique is limited to those species for which non-nodulating cultivars have been reported.

Uptake of N by a legume can also be compared with uptake by an uninoculated (and non-nodulated) legume of the same genotype (see Table 2, Ratner *et al.*, 1979). This is only possible in soils devoid of rhizobia able to nodulate the host legume, and care must be taken to ensure that cross-contamination does not occur.

Matching growth rates and total uptake of N remains the major disadvantage of this technique. The potential for N assimilation by most nonlegumes is not as high as for legumes (Date, 1973), resulting in an over-estimation of N_2 fixation. Even if non-nodulated legumes are used as the reference crop, there are three possibilities:

Identical amounts of N will be assimilated by host and reference crops;

There will be a synergistic effect (Ruschel *et al.*, 1979), where the nodulated crop will explore a greater volume of soil, taking up more mineral N with an overestimation of fixation; or

The non-nodulated crop will assimilate more soil N than the nodulated because of a competition advantage of the test plant's symbiotic system (Amarger *et al.*, 1979), resulting in an underestimation of fixation.

Acetylene (C_2H_2) reduction assay

The acetylene reduction assay arose from the observation that the enzyme, nitrogenase, reduced acetylene to ethylene (Dilworth, 1966; Shollhorn & Burris, 1966). Since that time the reliability of acetylene reduction as an indicator of nitrogenase (N_2-fixing) activity has been established for a wide range of biological systems, and the technique has assumed a vital role in studies of N_2 fixation (Hardy *et al.*, 1968; 1971; Hardy, Burns & Holsten, 1973). In this method, nodules, soil containing nodules, or whole plant/soil systems are enclosed in gas-tight containers and exposed to an atmosphere containing acetylene. The atmosphere is sampled after a suitable incubation period (0.5 to 24 hours, depending on the system) and analyzed for ethylene using gas-liquid chromatography with a flame ionization detector.

Techniques for field assays include excavating the nodulated root minus soil and incubating in a gas-tight vessel of the appropriate size (Sprent & Bradford, 1977; Nelson & Weaver, 1980), excavation of the nodulated root in a soil core and incubating (Hardy *et al.*, 1968) or assaying *in situ* (Sinclair,

TABLE 1: Use of comparative uptakes of N by nodulated and non-nodulated legumes to estimate seasonal N_2 fixation by field-grown legumes.

Crop	Soil NO_3-N status at sowing[1]	Total crop N (kg/ha)		N_2 fixed (kg/ha)[2]	% of total N_2 fixed	References
Soybean	Medium/high	nod	100	14	14	Weber (1966)
		non-nod	86			
		nod	187	75	40	
		non-nod	112			
Soybean		nod	255	130	51	Bhangoo & Albritton (1976)
		non-nod	125			
		nod	252	161	64	
		non-nod	91			
		nod	253	56	22	
		non-nod	197			
Soybean	Medium	nod	178	108	61	Deibert, Bijeriego & Olson (1979)
		non-nod	70			
Soybean		nod	260	185	71	Nelson & Weaver (1980)
		non-nod	75			
		nod	400	320	80	
		non-nod	71			
Peanut	High	nod	382	223	58	Ratner *et al.* (1979)
		uninoc	159			
		nod	236	93	38	
		uninoc	143			

[1]Designated low, medium or high based on reported levels of soil nitrate or soil descriptions.

[2]N_2 fixation calculated by difference. Assumes that nodulated and non-nodulated plants deplete the soil of equal amounts of N.

TABLE 2: Comparisons of different methods of estimating N_2 fixation by field-grown legumes.

Crop	Total crop N (kg/ha)	N_2 fixed (kg/ha) estimated by			References
		^{15}N[1]	nod/non-nod[2]	C_2H_2 redn	
Soybean	368		263	105	Bezdicek *et al.* (1978)
Soybean	202-245	4- 46	7- 55	10- 55	Ham (1977)
Soybean	199-335	27-155	21-140	15-114	Ham (1978)
Broad bean	286	197	181		Fried & Broeshart
Subterranean clover	25-208	21-183		38- 89	Phillips & Bennett (1978)

[1]Estimated using the A-value technique (Fried & Broeshart, 1975).
[2]Estimated by difference of total N uptakes by test (nodulated legume) and reference (non-nodulating legume or cereal) crops.

1973). An excellent review and comparison of the three methods is given by Hardy, Criswell & Havelka (1977).

The acetylene reduction assay has been used more for biochemical and physiological studies on N_2 fixation than as a quantitative assay, but procedures for the latter have been detailed in several reviews (Hardy *et al.*, 1968; Dart, Day & Harris, 1971). Where seasonal profiles of C_2H_2 reduction have been integrated to estimate N_2 fixation, rates of from 17 to 76 kg N/ha, representing 13-33% of total crop N (Criswell, Hume & Tanner, 1976; Hardy & Havelka, 1976; Mahler, Bezdicek & Witter, 1979), have been obtained. These values are lower than those presented in Table 1, perhaps reflecting the high N status of the soils in which the crops were grown. Seasonal profiles of C_2H_2 activity have also been published to detail agronomic treatments (Farrington *et al.*, 1977; Witty, Roughley & Day, 1980) and environmental effects (Farrington *et al.*, 1977; Ratner *et al.*, 1979).

Recovery of all nodular tissue for assay remains one of the major sources of error with the technique, and is the same whether the nodulated roots are excavated or contained in soil cores. In data from our laboratory the C_2H_2 assay underestimated fixation by soybeans compared with other techniques, e.g., 50 kg N/ha (C_2H_2) *vs.* 211 kg N/ha using the ureide technique (D.F. Herridge, unpublished; see Table 2). This problem is worse with species such as soybean and fababean, than with lupin, and would be exacerbated by delayed nodulation leading to location of nodules on lateral roots rather than in the crown region of the plant. Poor recovery of nodules during reproductive growth may explain the puzzling results reported by Sprent & Bradford (1977) where the C_2H_2 assay underestimated N accumulation during pod-fill. Rates of N_2 fixation estimated from other published profiles (Dean & Clark, 1977; Wahua & Miller, 1978) are also low compared to estimates based on other techniques (Nelson & Weaver, 1980).

A conversion ratio of 3:1 is used commonly to relate C_2H_2 reduction to N_2 fixation. This is based on the fact that two electrons are needed to reduce C_2H_2 to C_2H_4, while six are required to reduce N_2 to ammonia. Good agreement with the theoretical 3:1 value has been obtained in some studies (Hardy *et al.*, 1971), but in other studies with soybean the actual conversion ratios have ranged from 1.2-4.1:1 (Hardy *et al.*, 1973; Ham, 1978; D.F. Herridge, unpublished data). No doubt these differences for the same species reflect different assay conditions and perhaps different efficiencies of the strains of *Rhizobium* involved with regard to hydrogen evolution (Schubert & Evans, 1976). It is, therefore, of the utmost importance to establish a quantitative relationship between C_2H_2 reduced and N_2 fixed for the particular host/ *Rhizobium* association under study, using carefully standardized procedures. Unfortunately, this has been done in very few cases (Rennie, Rennie & Fried, 1978). Even so, stress conditions (e.g., moisture) have been shown to affect the ratio (Sinclair *et al.*, 1978). Rates of C_2H_2 reduction are also subject to diurnal variation, and such variation must be considered when extrapolating from short-term (0.5-1 hour) assays to a full 24-hour period. Our experiences with glasshouse and field-grown plants of soybean and lupin suggest larger diurnal fluctuations in activities of field-grown plants.

In summary, there are a number of techniques available for the measurement of N_2 fixation. Under carefully controlled conditions, each will give reasonable estimates of N_2 fixation (see Table 2; Ham 1977; 1978). The acetylene reduction assay is perhaps the most susceptible to error. Thus, Phillips & Bennet (1978) found a complete lack of precision in data derived from C_2H_2 reduction assays. Similarly, C_2H_2 reduction underestimated N_2 fixation when compared to estimates using nodulating and non-nodulating isolines of soybean in a study by Bezdicek *et al.* (1978) (see Table 2). Goh, Edmeades & Robinson (1978) also found this technique unsuitable in their long-term measurements of fixation by pasture legumes. In our laboratory the acetylene reduction assay has proved unsuitable for measuring N_2 fixation by soybeans but suitable to estimate fixation by lupins. Differences relate to nodule recovery. *In situ* C_2H_2 reduction measurements (Balandraeu & Ducerf, 1978) appear to be the most accurate, but though suitable for smaller pasture legumes such as white clover, may not be as manageable with larger crop legumes such as pigeonpea and soybean.

By contrast the A-value technique, while not reviewed in detail here, requires minimum sampling and appears to give accurate and consistent estimates of fixation. Analytical costs are the major drawback to this technique. Basically the methods used by different laboratories will be governed by the funds available, the species studied, and general facilities such as the availability of a gas-liquid chromatograph to measure ethylene. When possible at least two methods should be used and soil nitrate data collected. Estimates of fixation can then be compared for consistency and related to predicted rates of fixation.

N transfer (mineralization and subsequent uptake)

N is harvested from legume crops as seed and vegetative protein. The residual plant material is then subject to microbial degradation (mineralization). The degree to which an agricultural system really benefits from a legume crop depends upon the proportion of legume N remaining in residues and utilization of these residues by other crops, as well as on amounts of N_2 fixed.

During mineralization, organic N is first converted into amino compounds and ammonia, the latter acting as substrate for the final transformation to nitrate. The end product is the form of N most readily available and used for plant growth. Not all of the legume residues will be mineralized immediately following plant harvest. In a study of medic (*Medicago* spp.) decomposition in South Australian wheat soils, A.J. Ladd and co-workers (personal communication) found that only 11-17% of the ^{15}N-labeled medic residues added to the soil was utilized by a succeding wheat crop, while 72-78% remained in the soil organic pool. These values reflect a Mediterranean-type environment, and higher rates of mineralization would be expected in humid tropical soils with stimulation of microbial activity provided by higher moisture and temperature regimes. Henzell & Vallis (1977) reported that as much as 30% of tropical legume residues were mineralized and taken up by a tropical grass after 24 weeks. The rate of mineralization appeared to be directly affected by N content of the residue.

Although N in the nitrate form is most suitable for plant growth it is also the most labile form of N and can easily be lost from the system through leaching and volatilization. It is, therefore, of the utmost importance that rates of mineralization and plant uptake are matched, thereby regulating levels of nitrate in the soil. This is one advantage of no-till agriculture, in which nitrification is not stimulated by cultivation. Another way to reduce nitrate losses is to "tie up" nitrate with plant material containing a high C:N ratio. Fresh plant material mineralizes at a faster rate than dried material (van Schreven, 1968) and buried residues decay at a faster rate than do residues remaining on the soil surface (Moore, 1974).

Losses of N

Harvested plant material

The N harvested as vegetative or grain protein represents, in most cases, the largest single loss of N from the system (Henzell & Vallis, 1977). In a grain crop, the proportion of N removed in seeds will obviously depend on the efficiency of the legume crop as a grain producer. For instance, the harvest indices (seed N as a proportion of maximum crop N) of eight commercial soybean crops range from 0.30-0.76 with a mean of 0.57 (D.F. Herridge, unpublished data), while in lupins, harvest indices for N ranged from 0.33-0.44 with a mean of 0.40. Absolute amounts of N in the grain ranged from 136-254 kg N/ha in soybean and from 54-86 kg N/ha in lupin.

Leaching

Leaching and surface run-off of N (as nitrate) account for small losses in most systems — less than 20 kg N/ha per year (Greenland, 1977; Heal, 1979). The value may be higher in areas of extremely heavy rainfall and in some irrigation systems. Bilal, Henderson & Tanji (1979) recorded loss of up to 36 kg N/ha per year in irrigated rice. Lysimeters are used to measure both leaching and run-off; methods are detailed by Burford (1977).

Gaseous N

N is also lost in the gaseous phase as N_2 and N_2O (nitrous oxide) following denitrification; as volatile oxides of N due to burning; and as ammonia (NH_3) through ammonia volatilization. Small losses of N are also associated with aerobic nitrification (Denmead, Freney & Simpson, 1979). Denitrification is the most important of these pathways of loss and represents the anaerobic conversion of nitrate to N_2 and N_2O. Under field conditions rates of reaction are closely dependent upon the presence of nitrate, organic matter, and low redox potential. Estimates of losses vary considerably, mainly because of the problems of measurement. Allison (1955) showed that between 10 and 30% of the N in a large number of lysimeter studies could not be accounted for when mass balance sheets were constructed. He proposed that these losses were due to denitrification. Greenland (1962) reported losses of 50 kg N/ha in flooded soils in a few days, while Burns & Hardy (1975) estimated that the global flux of denitrified N was in excess of the flux of biologically fixed N. In other studies, losses due to denitrification were negligible (Wetselaar, Jakobsen & Chaplin, 1973).

An exhaustive review of techniques for estimating denitrification is provided by Focht (1978) and includes analyses (measurements of bacterial numbers, available substrate, redox potential), disappearance of nitrate, use of ^{15}N and ^{13}N tracers, and direct measurements of N_2 and N_2O. This latter technique has been greatly simplified by the observation of Federova, Milekhina & Il'yukhina (1973) that acetylene inhibits the reduction of N_2O to

N_2. Measurement of N_2O is a simple procedure using gas chromatography. Smith, Firestone & Tiedje (1978) and Ryden, Lund & Focht (1979a) later showed that low concentrations of acetylene had no effect on the rate of denitrification, but that the reduction of N_2O to N_2 was quantitatively inhibited by acetylene concentrations as low as 0.1% (v/v). Data of Ryden *et al.*, (1979a) suggested that a concentration of 1% provided the most suitable level for all soils and incubation conditions and could be easily maintained in the atmosphere on a field soil. Details of field assays using this method are given by Ryden *et al.* (1979b).

Various studies of denitrification have been made and the different methods compared (e.g., Smith *et al.*, 1978; Rolston, Broadbent & Goldhamer, 1979). The acetylene inhibition method and subsequent measurement of nitrous oxide looks very promising and has a considerable cost advantage over tracer N methods (Smith *et al.*, 1978; Ryden *et al.*, 1979a).

Losses of ammonia are not accurately quantified, and much of what is released from the soil surface may be re-absorbed by vegetation. Denmead, *et al.*, (1976) showed a closed ammonia cycle within an ungrazed pasture, which when grazed, released much larger amounts. Volatilization of ammonia from a unfertilized legume crop would be expected to be minor, although losses from the standing crop rather than soil may be significant (Henzell & Vallis, 1977). Stutte, Weiland & Blem (1979) estimated a loss of 45 kg N/ha in a soybean crop, with rates of loss being highly correlated with elevated temperatures and stress conditions.

Losses of N by burning of plant residues is easily estimated as approximately 90% of plant N will be lost if dry residues are burnt (Henzell & Vallis, 1979).

Erosion

Water and soil erosion can result in considerable losses of N, especially organic N. Barrows & Kilmer (1963) reported losses of approximately 100 kg N/ha per year, 94% of which was organic N. Losses of N through erosion will obviously be more of a problem on sloped, cultivated land.

N BUDGETING IN AN AGRICULTURAL SYSTEM: AN EXAMPLE

Kohl *et al.* (1978) suggested that the essence of N balance studies is a model often represented by a flow diagram containing pools and showing transfer. Values are assigned where possible and unknown values are estimated. If all components of the pool are measured or estimated, then decisions can be made regarding the functioning of the system. Research in our laboratory aims to promote the use of N_2-fixing grain legumes in the cereals-dominated agriculture on the region, and so we have sought quantitative data on the N economy of cropping systems incorporating legumes. A whole-system approach has been adopted and various legumes compared. Figure 1 shows

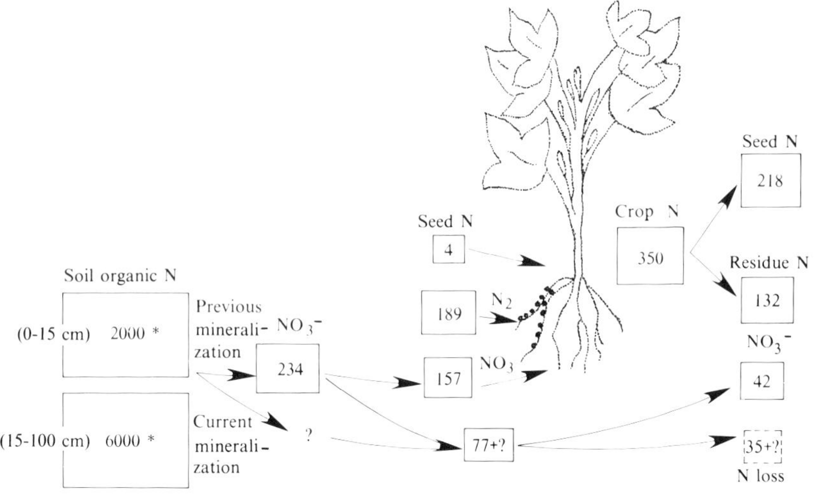

Figure 1. N budget of a single irrigated soybean crop (in kg N/ha) Data from D.F. Herridge, unpublished.

results with a single, irrigated soybean crop. Organic and inorganic levels of N in soil were measured at sowing and near plant maturity. Fixation of N was estimated throughout growth of the crop using the ureide technique for stem tissues (Herridge, 1981). N contents of sown seed, above and belowground plant parts, and harvested seed were also measured. Nitrate uptake by the crop was estimated by difference, as were crop residue N and nonaccountable N. There is a question mark next to current mineralization —this was not measured in this particular study, but data of Stanford *et al* (1977) suggest values well in excess of 100 kg N/ha per growing season for a similar cropping system. N losses are inflated accordingly if this component is included in the budget. Estimates of seasonal nitrification and denitrification would further add to the budget.

Two inefficiencies of our cropping system are obvious. First, a substantial amount of N is unaccounted for and probably lost from the system. We suspect denitrification, because the soil is a heavy clay and frequently irrigated. Second, only 54% of crop N came from N_2 fixation. Clearly, there is little point in enhancing fixation in this system if the saved nitrate will probably be lost through denitrification. In this case, better management could reduce N losses, and this coupled with N_2 fixation could substantially improve the productivity of the system.

REFERENCES

Allison, F.E. (1955) *Adv. Agron.* 7, 213-250.

Amarger, N., Marioti. A., Marioti, F., Durr, J.C., Bourguignon, C., & Lagacherie, B. (1979) *Plant Soil* 52, 269-280.

Balandreau, J. & Ducerf. P. (1978) Activite nitrogenasique (C_2H_2) *in situ*: Mesure, analyse des facteurs limitants, comparison de systemes fixateurs d'azote. *In*: Isotopes in biological dinitrogen fixation. IAEA, Vienna, Austria. Pp. 173-189.

Barrows, H.L. & Kilmer. V.J. (1963) *Adv. Agron.* 15, 303-316.

Bartholomew, W.V. (1977) Soil nitrogen changes in farming systems in the humid tropics. *In*: Biological nitrogen fixation in farming systems of the tropics, A.N. Ayanaba & P.J. Dart (Eds.). Wiley, New York, NY, USA. Pp. 27-42.

Bell, F. & Nutman. P.S. (1971) *Plant Soil* (Sp. Vol.), 231-264.

Bezdicek, D.F., Evans. D.W., Abede, B., & Witters, R.E. (1978) *Agron. J.* 70, 865-868.

Bhangoo, M.S. & Albritton, D.J. (1976) *Agron. J.* 68, 642-645.

Bilal, I.M., Henderson. D.W. & Tanji, K.K. (1979) *Agron. J.* 71, 279-284.

Burford, J.R. (1977) Determination of losses of nitrogen from soils in the humid tropics by lysimeter studies. *In*: Biological nitrogen fixation in farming systems of the tropics. A.N. Ayanaba & P.J. Dart (Eds.). Wiley, New York, NY, USA. Pp. 353-363.

Burns, R.C. & Hardy. R.W.F. (1975) Nitrogen fixation in bacteria and higher plants. Springer-Verlag. Berlin, Germany.

Clark, F.E. (1957) *Can. J. Microbiol.* 3, 113-123.

Criswell, J.G., Hume, D.J. & Tanner, J.W. (1976) *Crop Sci.* 16, 400-404.

Dart, P.J., Day. J.M. & Harris, D. (1971) IAEA Report 149. Pp. 85-100.

Date, R.A. (1973) *Soil Biol. Biochem.* 5, 5-18.

Dean, J.R. & Clark. K.W. (1977) *Can. J. Plant Sci.* 57, 1055-1061.

Deibert, E.J., Bijeriego. M. & Olson, R.A. (1979) *Agron. J.* 71, 717-723.

Denmead, O.T., Freney. J.R. & Simpson, J.R. (1976) *Soil Biol. Biochem.* 8, 161-164.

Denmead, O.T., Freney. J.R. & Simpson, J.R. (1979) *Soil Sci. Soc. Amer. J.* 43, 726-728.

Dilworth, M.J. (1966) *Biochim. Biophys. Acta* 127, 285-194.

Farrington, P., Greenwood, E.A.N., Titmanis, Z.V., Trinick, M.J., & Smith, D.W. (1977) *Aust. J. Agric. Res.* 28, 237-248.

Federova, R.I., Milekhina, E.I. & Il'yukhina, N.I. (1973) *Izv. Akad. Nauk. SSSR. Ser. Biol.* 6, 797-806.

Focht, D.D. (1978) Methods for analysis of denitrification in soils. *In*: Nitrogen in the environment. Vol. 2. D.R. Nielson & J.G. MacDonald (Eds.). Academic Press, New York, NY, USA. Pp. 433-490.

Fried, M. & Broeshart, H. (1975) *Plant Soil* 43, 707-711.

Goh, K.M., Edmeades, D.C. & Robinson, B.W. (1978) *Soil Biol. Biochem.* 10, 13-20.

Greenland, D.J. (1962) *J. Agric. Sci.* (Camb.) 58, 227-233.

Greenland, D.J. (1977) Contribution of microorganisms to the nitrogen status of tropical soils. *In*: Biological nitrogen fixation in farming systems of the tropics, A.N. Ayanaba & P.J. Dart (Eds.). Wiley, New York, NY, USA. Pp. 13-25.

Ham, G.E. (1977) The acetylene-ethylene assay and other measures of nitrogen fixation in field experiments. *In*: Biological nitrogen fixation in farming systems of the tropics. A.N. Ayanaba & P.J. Dart (Eds.). Wiley, New York, NY, USA. Pp. 325-334.

Ham, G.E. (1978) Use of ^{15}N in evaluating symbiotic N_2 fixation of field-grown soybeans. *In*: Isotopes in biological dinitrogen fixation. IAEA, Vienna, Austria. Pp. 151-161.

Hardy, R.W.F., Burns, R.C., Hebert, R.R., Holsten, R.D., & Jackson, E.K. (1971) *Plant Soil* (Sp. Vol.). 561-590.

Hardy, R.W.F., Burns, R.C. & Holsten, R.D. (1973) *Soil Biol. Biochem.* 5, 47-81.

Hardy, R.W.F., Criswell, J.G. & Havelka, U.D. (1977) Investigations of possible limitations of nitrogen fixation by legumes: (1) Methodology, (2) Identification, and (3) Assessment of significance. *In*: Recent developments in nitrogen fixation. W. Newton, J.R. Postgate & C. Rodríguez-Barrueco (Eds.). Academic Press, New York, NY, USA. Pp. 451-467.

Hardy, R.W.F. & Havelka, U.D. (1976) Photosynthate as a major factor limiting nitrogen fixation by field-grown legumes with emphasis on soybeans. *In*: Symbiotic nitrogen fixation in plants, P.S. Nutman (Ed.). Cambridge University Press, Cambridge, England. Pp. 421-439.

Hardy, R.W.F., Holsten, R.D., Jackson, E.K., & Burns, R.C. (1968) *Plant Physiol.* 43, 1185-1207.

Heal, O.W. (1979) Consequences of non-assimilation of nitrogen by plants. *In*: Nitrogen assimilation of plants, E.J. Hewitt & C.V. Cutting (Eds.). Academic Press, New York. NY, USA. Pp. 625-636.

Henzell, E.F. & Vallis. I. (1977) Transfer of nitrogen between legumes and other crops. *In*: Biological nitrogen fixation in farming systems of the tropics, A.N. Ayanaba & P.J. Dart (Eds.). Wiley, New York, NY, USA. Pp. 73-88.

Herridge, D.F. (1981) Estimating N_2 fixation in field-grown soybeans using ureide and nitrate analyses of plant parts and nodulation status of the plant throughout growth. *In*: Proc. IV Internat. Symp. N_2 Fixation. Canberra, ACT, Australia. (In press.)

Jenkinson, D.S. (1971) Report Rothamsted Expt. Stn. 1970. Part 2, Pp. 113-137.

Kohl, D.H., Shearer, G. & Harper, J.E. (1980) *Plant Physiol.* 66, 61-65.

Kohl, D.H. Shearer G. & Vithayanthil, F. (1978) Critique of nitrogen inputs and outputs: A valley basin study. *In*: Nitrogen in the environment. Vol 1. D.R. Nielson & J.G. MacDonald (Eds.). Academic Press. New York, NY, USA. Pp. 183-200.

Mahler, R.L., Bezdicek. D.F. & Witters, R.E. (1979) *Agron. J.* 71, 348-351.

Moore, A.W. (1974) *Soil Biol. Biochem.* 6, 249-255.

Nelson, A.N. & Weaver. R.W. (1980) *Agron. J.* 72, 613-616.

Phillips, D.A. & Bennett. J.P. (1978) *Agron. J.* 70, 671-674.

Phillips, J.L. (1959) CSIRO Aust. Div. Land Res. Reg. Surv. *Techn. Paper* No. 2.

Phillips, L.J. & Norman. M.J.T. (1961) *Aust. J. Expl. Agric. Anim. Husb.* 1, 144-149.

Ratner, E.I., Lobel R.. Feldhay, H., & Hartzook, A. (1979) *Plant Soil* 51, 373-386.

Rennie, R.J., Rennie. D.A. & Fried, M. (1978) Concepts of ^{15}N useage in dinitrogen fixation studies. *In*: Isotopes in biological dinitrogen fixation. IAEA, Vienna, Austria. Pp. 107-130.

Rolston, D.E., Broadbent. F.E. & Goldhamer, D.A. (1979) *Soil Sci.* Soc. *Amer. J.* 43, 703-708.

Ruschel, A.P., Vose. P.B., Victoria, R.L., & Salati, E. (1979) *Plant Soil* 53, 513-525.

Ryden, J.C., Lund. L.J. & Focht, D.D. (1979a) *Soil Sci. Soc. Amer. J.* 43, 104-110.

Ryden, J.C., Lund. L.J., Letey, J., & Focht, D.D. (1979b) *Soil Sci. Soc. Amer. J.* 43, 110-118.

Saers, D.H. & Lynch, D.L. (1951) *Soybean Digest* 11, 15-17.

Schollhorn, R. & Burris, R.H. (1966) *Fed. Proc.* 24, 710.

Schreven, D.A. van (1968) *Plant Soil* 28, 226-245.

Schubert, K.R. & Evans, H.J. (1976) *Proc. Nat. Acad. Sci.* (USA) 73, 1207-1211.

Sinclair, A.G. (1973) *N.Z. J. Agric. Res.* 16, 263-270.

Sinclair, A.G., Hannagan, R.B., Johnstone, P., & Hardacre, A.K. (1978) *N.Z.J. Expl. Agric.* 6, 65-68.

Smith, M.S., Firestone, M.K. & Tiedje, J.M. (1978) *Soil Sci. Soc. Amer. J.* 42, 611-615.

Sprent, J.I. & Bradford, A.M. (1977) *J. Agric. Sci.* (Camb.) 88, 303-310.

Stanford, G., Carter, J.N., Westermann, D.T., & Meisinger, J.J. (1977) *Agron. J.* 69, 303-308.

Stutte, C.A., Weiland, R.T. & Blem, A.R. (1979) *Agron. J.* 71, 95-97.

Wahua, T.A.T. & Miller, D.A. (1978) *Agron. J.* 70, 387-392.

Weber, C.R. (1966) *Agron. J.* 58, 46-49.

Wetselaar, R. (1967) *Aust. J. Expl. Agric. Anim. Husb.* 7, 518-522.

Wetselaar, R. & Hutton, J.T. (1963) *Aust. J. Agric. Res.* 14, 319-329.

Wetselaar, R., Jakobsen, P. & Chaplin, G.R. (1973) *Soil Biol. Biochem.* 5, 35-40.

Williams, L.F. & Lynch, D.L. (1954) *Agron. J.* 46, 28-29.

Williams, R.J.B. & Cooke, G.W. (1972) Report Rothamsted Expt. Stn., 1971. Part 2, Pp. 95-121.

Witty, J.F., Roughley, R.J. & Day, J.M. (1980) *J. Agric. Sci.* (Camb.) 94, 203-208.

QUANTIFICATION OF SYMBIOTIC NITROGEN FIXATION USING UREIDES: A REVIEW

D.L. McNeil[1]

Summary

This paper considers the genera of legumes known to produce ureides; the tissues on which ureide analysis can be made; and the advantages and disadvantages of ureide analysis as a means of estimating symbiotic nitrogen fixation.

INTRODUCTION

Ureide compounds in plants have been extensively studied, with numerous reviews on their biochemistry (Tracey, 1955; Bollard, 1959; Reinbothe & Mothes, 1962; Van der Drift, & Vogels, 1966) and production in legume nodules (Atkins, Rainbird & Pate, 1980; Woo, Atkins & Pate, 1980) already published.

In legumes, allantoin and allantoic acid are the principal ureides. These substances can be regarded as the ultimate product of nitrogen (N_2) fixation for a range of legume species (Matsumoto, Yatazawa & Yamamoto, 1977a) and are transported in the xylary sap to support plant growth (Israel & McClure, 1979). Both have a low C:N ratio, and so are conservative of carbon (C) relative to N when used in N storage or transport.

Measurement of the ureides found in nodulated legumes has attracted considerable interest in recent years, both as a means of estimating total N_2 fixation and for determination of the amount of N_2 fixed, relative to other sources of N. This approach assumes that the rate of xylary ureide output is a direct measure of N_2 fixation (McClure, Israel & Volk, 1980) whereas other sources of N for the plant are present as other compounds in the xylary sap (McClure & Israel, 1979). Measurement of ureide and non-ureide N would, thus, permit determination of the relative contribution of fixed and absorbed N to plant development.

[1] NifTAL Project, Dept. Agronomy & Soil Science, Univ. of Hawaii, P.O Box O, Paia, Hawaii, 96779, USA.

This is a great oversimplification. In this presentation I will consider technical problems associated with ureide measurement, as well as some strengths and limitations.

THE DISTRIBUTION OF UREIDE PRODUCTION AMONG SYMBIOTIC N_2-FIXING SPECIES

Ureides are not the sole form in which fixed N is exported from legume nodules. Many temperate legumes including *Lupinus albus* (Pate *et al.*, 1979a), *Pisum sativum* (Lewis & Pate, 1973), *Trifolium repens* (Copeland & Pate, 1970), and *Vicia faba* (Pate, Gunning & Briarty, 1969) export reduced N from the roots predominantly as amides (asparagine and glutamine). The reduced N in the xylary sap of these species is apparently independent of the form of N supplied (Pate, Sharkey & Lewis, 1975; Sharkey & Pate, 1975). Several nonlegume N_2-fixing systems including *Alnus* spp. (Leaf, Gardner & Bond, 1958) export citrulline, a compound also found in the xylary sap of the legume *Albizzia lophantha* (Bollard, 1957). There are, however, a range of legumes, including many tropical species, for which ureides are the dominant form of xylary N. These include *Glycine max* (Streeter, 1979), *Cajanus cajan* (Kumar Rao *et al.*, 1980), *Phaseolus vulgaris* (Cookson, Hughes & Coombs, 1980) and several species of *Vigna* (Pate *et al.*, 1980).

From the above comments it follows that absence of ureides in a legume does not necessarily mean that the legume is not fixing N_2. Conversely, it will be demonstrated in the following sections that the presence of ureides in nonlegumes (Mothes, 1961) and legumes is not necessarily indicative of N_2 fixation.

SAMPLING SITES FOR UREIDE DETERMINATIONS

The analysis of xylary sap composition is the most direct measure of N_2 fixation that can be performed on the aboveground portion of a plant; therefore, it has frequently been used for this purpose (Israel & McClure, 1979; McClure & Israel, 1979; McClure *et al.*, 1980; D.L. McNeil & T.A. LaRue, unpublished data). The linkage between xylary constituents and fixation is extremely tight. For *Lupinus albus* in both late vegetative and early flowering stages Pate, Layzell & McNeil (1979b) have shown that more than 80% of the N_2 fixed proceeds to the tops in the xylary stream, and less than 10% of the N in the stream arose elsewhere. Presumably values for other legumes are similar. Direct measurement of the sap at the nodule surface (Herridge *et al.*, 1978; Pate *et al.*, 1979b) gives higher concentrations of nitrogenous solutes; often with some specific enrichment of ureides or amides, but there are few other differences from measurements made using bleeding sap. A typical result for xylary sap from 40- to 75-day-old greenhouse-grown soybeans shows 87% of the N as ureides when the soybeans were dependent on fixation alone, as contrasted with 18% when they were grown on nitrate and 28% when the N source was ammonia (D.L. McNeil & T.A. LaRue, unpublished data).

Short-term changes in xylary sap composition have also been found to correlate well with rapid changes in N_2 fixation (McNeil, 1979; McClure *et al.*, 1980) and xylary sap collections have, therefore, been used to determine the early products of $^{15}N_2$ fixation (Herridge *et al.*, 1978).

Exudation rates can also fluctuate widely (McNeil, 1979; McClure *et al.*, 1980) decreasing at night or as a result of a variety of stresses. This reduced exudation can lead to compensatory increases in xylary N concentration, necessitating measurement of both xylary components and exudation rate to gain accurate information on N_2 fixation.

Collections are usually taken for periods of less than an hour, during which time soybeans show little variation in concentration of xylary sap (Israel & McClure, 1979), though concentrations are usually higher than for comparable tracheal sap (Pate *et al.*, 1979b). Passage through the stem may also alter xylary sap composition (McNeil, Atkins & Pate, 1979); thus collections are usually made at the base of the plant.

Some difficulties with xylary sap ureide measurement have led to attempts to measure tissue levels of ureides (Herridge, 1980) and to correlate them with N_2 fixation (Fujihara & Yamaguchi, 1978; Matsumoto, Yatazawa & Yamamoto, 1978); this is in spite of the fact that ureide storage is a step further removed from the site of fixation. For tissue analyses of ureides to be useful, the form of storage of N in the plant must be at least partially dependent on the transport form. This need not, however, be the case as the level in the tissues will also depend on the rates of export and metabolism and how these are affected by changes in the concentration of the ureides. In mature soybean leaflets, ureide levels remain quite low (Matsumoto, Yatazawa & Yamamoto, 1977b), often less than 10-15% of the total soluble N (D.L. McNeil & T.A. LaRue, unpublished data) irrespective of the amount of ureides in the xylary stream. This is not surprising, as virtually all (92%) of the ureides entering the shoots of cowpea (*Vigna unguiculata*) are metabolized there (Herridge *et al.*, 1978). Enzymatic determinations also suggest rapid metabolism of ureides in the leaflets due to high allantoicase levels (Tajima, Yatazawa & Yamamoto, 1977). Export of ureide N from leaflets must also be large. The C:N ratio (between 5:1 and 40:1) of soybean phloem sap (D.L. McNeil & T.A. LaRue, unpublished data) is lower than that of *Lupinus albus* petiole phloem sap, which cycles up to 99% of the incoming N back out of mature leaflets (McNeil, 1979; Pate *et al.*, 1979b). An additional factor hindering leaflet analyses is the high level of interfering background substances that are present (D.L. McNeil & T.A. LaRue, unpublished data).

Stem analysis, however, offers an alluring possibility. Enzyme levels for some of the steps involved in allantoin metabolism do not vary between fixing and nonfixing soybeans (Tajima *et al.*, 1977), but products of N_2 fixation are preferentially absorbed by stems. Thus, D.L. McNeil and T.A. La Rue (unpublished data) found that 64-day-old soybeans fed $^{15}N_2$ or $^{15}NO_3^-$ absorbed into the stem 54% and 15%, respectively, of the ^{15}N reaching the tops in the first 1½ hours after feeding. Streeter (1979) also reports high stem ureide levels. N_2-fixing and nonfixing soybeans, therefore, differ strikingly in stem ureide content (Matsumoto *et al.*, 1977b). Herridge (1980) also shows large differences in stem ureides between soybeans having different proportions of their N derived from N_2 fixation. Unfortunately, 15-fold differences in ureide levels at different sites in the stem (Kumar Rao *et al.*, 1980) and in stems of different ages (Streeter, 1979) necessitate that samples be chosen extremely carefully.

ADVANTAGES AND DISADVANTAGES OF USING UREIDES FOR THE ESTIMATION OF N_2 FIXATION

As an estimate of N_2 fixation the analysis of ureides has three principal advantages:

Ureides can be readily separated and analyzed (Young & Conway, 1942; Atkins & Canvin, 1971; Nirmala & Sastry, 1972; Herridge & Pate, 1977; Urbaski, Grujic-Injac & Gajic, 1978; Borders, 1979) using methods which are readily automated. Even for tissue analysis, where extraction of ureides would be an additional, restrictive step, personal observation has shown that leakage of ureides into buffered alcohol solutions extracts a high proportion of the ureides without the need to grind and separate.

Ureide analysis can be used to distinguish between N sources and so can distinguish improved N utilization and/or uptake from enhanced N_2 fixation.

One can measure an aboveground part of the plant and thereby gain information on the conditions below soil level. It is often assumed that a legume must be dug from the soil to give an accurate measure of N_2 fixation.

The advantages and disadvantages of the acetylene reduction technique are discussed on p. 597. Herridge (1980) has obtained better estimates of fixation in soybeans using ureide tissue analysis than with nodule mass. Problems in nodule recovery and differences in nodule activity at different stages of development are well documented. The use of xylary sap or tissue ureide levels greatly simplifies analysis (Kumar Rao *et al.*, 1980).

At the same time the method is not without problems — some of them serious. The use of ureide content for interspecific comparisons of N_2 fixation has already been ruled out. Even in known ureide-exporting legume species relying entirely on N_2 fixation, the percentage of ureides in the xylary sap may range from less than 25% (Pate, Walker & Wallace, 1965; Pate *et al.*, 1980) through 60-80% (Kumar Rao *et al.*, 1980) to more than 80% (McClure *et al.*, 1980). Intercultivar variations are also possible; Israel & McClure (1979) have shown a range of from 73-89% ureides in the xylary sap of three soybean cultivars when inoculated with two different *Rhizobium* strains. The less effective strain consistently gave the highest percentage of ureides in the sap. This incongruity disappeared if the total rate of ureide export, rather than the concentration relative to other nitrogenous solutes of the sap, was measured. For determination of stem ureides the variation reported above may mitigate against the comparison of stem ureides in varieties of different growth habits or maturity characteristics.

Problems can arise even in soybean, a crop in which consistently close relationships between ureides and N_2 fixation have been obtained. Thus D.L. McNeil & T.A. LaRue (unpublished data) have shown that under N stress non-nodulated soybeans can export more than 50% of the xylary N as ureides (see Table 1). Further, this percentage will vary according to whether nitrate or ammonia is the N source. Similar results have been obtained for *P. vulgaris* (Thomas *et al.*, 1979; Cookson *et al.*, 1980) and *Vigna* (Pate, *et al.*, 1980). Soybean seedlings also show anomolously high ureide concentrations long before N_2 fixation commences. This is due to the conversion and export of stored N from the cotyledons as ureides (Matsumoto *et al.*, 1977b). The presence of ureides in nonfixing plants should not be surprising. All the reactions for the incorporation of ammonium into ureides takes place in the tissue of the nodule (Woo *et al.*, 1980) without recourse to the *Rhizobium*. In fact, Pate *et al.* (1980) showed that each of the nine legumes they tested, which had significant xylary ureide levels when dependent on N_2 fixation, also produced some ureides when grown on nitrate and non-nodulated.

Other stress conditions have equally disturbing effects on the simple relationship between fixation and ureides. At high temperatures and under restricted carbon regimes *Phaseolus coccineus* has high levels of ureides in both tissues and xylary sap (Mothes, 1956; Mothes & Engelbrecht, 1956).

Finally, it is often difficult to make xylary sap measurements under field conditions. Problems include the failure of many plants to exude, or the need for soil wetting to encourage exudation. The method is also inapplicable to single plants because of the small quantities of material obtained, the possible failure to exude, and the need to destroy the plant.

CONCLUSIONS

The physiology, biochemistry and cytology of ureide production in legumes is becoming well documented. However, there is no obligate linkage between N_2 fixation and ureide production. Even in the "ureide exporters" measurements of tissue or xylary ureide levels are insufficient by themselves, to determine N_2 fixation. A thorough physiological study is an essential

TABLE 1: The relationship between N_2 fixation and xylary ureide level in nodulating and non-nodulating isolines of *Glycine max* cv. Harosoy at different levels of N application.[1]

Nodule status	Nitrate applied (kg/ha)		Xylary N as ureides[2] (% of total N)		Nitrogenase activity (µmol C_2H_4/plant·min)	
	Week 1	Week 8	Week 6	Week 11	Week 6	Week 11
Nodulating	0	0		79		0.34
			77		0.14	
	0	100		34		0.22
	100	0		69		0.43
			37		0.04	
	100	100		34		0.14
Non-nodulating	0	0		34		0
			35		0	
	0	100		16		0
	100	0		41		0
			7		0	
	100	100		13		0

[1]Data of D.L. McNeil & T.A. LaRue (unpublished).
[2]Mean standard errors were ± 6 % for ureides in the xylary sap. Standards errors for N_2-ase activity ranged from ± 0.01 to ± 0.11 µmol C_2H_4 produced/plant per min.

prerequisite to interpret the values obtained. If this is done (as it was for soybeans by Herridge, 1980) the standard curves produced under controlled conditions may be applied to the field to determine fixation by an entire crop. It must be remembered, however, that several stress situations can increase the prominence of the ureides without any relationship to fixation.

Evidence suggests that the amount of ureides in the xylary sap and tissues depends on species, cultivar, and bacterial strain; as a result some intercultivar comparisons have shown large discrepancies between methods of measuring N_2 fixation, whereas others have shown good agreement (Kumar Rao *et al.*, 1980).

Of most promise is the concept of combining ureide analyses with some other analysis of the nitrogenous components of a plant (e.g., amides or nitrate). This, however, greatly reduces the number of analyses possible and may eliminate the possibility of use on single plants in a breeding program. Looking at the nodules is a simpler method for determining presence or absence of N_2 fixation under these conditions (E.L. Pulver, personal communication), though this is difficult in some soil types where nodulation is deep. The domain of the method is, therefore, with physiological studies and intercultivar comparisons rather than with single plant selection.

In the field both xylary sap and tissue analyses are possible. Xylary sap determinations are probably more accurate, though more subject to the caprices of the environment and to short-term changes in fixation. Analyses of ureides in plant stems, or uppermost, but not mature, leaflets, though distant from the site of fixation are restricted only by the great changes that take place as the plant matures and between different regions of the same plant. If careful selection and matching of the areas to be analyzed is employed, this method has great promise.

REFERENCES

Atkins, C.A. & Canvin. D.T. (1977) *Photosynthetica* 5, 341, 351.

Atkins, C.A., Herridge. D.F. & Pate, J.S. (1977) The economy of carbon and nitrogen fixing annual legumes: Experimental observations and theoretical considerations. *In:* Isotopes in biological dinitrogen fixation, C.N. Welsh (Ed.). FAO/IAEA Advisory Group, Vienna, Austria. Pp. 211-247.

Atkins, C.A., Rainbird. R.M. & Pate, J.S. (1980) *Z. Pflanzenphysiol.* 97 (Suppl.). 249-260.

Borders, R. (1979) *Analyt. Biochem.* 79, 612-613.

Bollard, E.G. (1957) *Aust. J. Biol. Sci.* 10, 292-301.

Bollard, E.G. (1959) Urease, urea and ureides in plants: Utilization of nitrogen and its compounds by plants. Cambridge University Press, Cambridge, England. Pp. 304-329.

Cookson, C., Hughes. H., & Coombs, J. (1980) *Planta* 148, 338-345.

Copeland, R. & Pate. J.S. (1970) Nitrogen metabolism of nodulated white clover in the presence and absence of nitrate nitrogen. *In:* White clover research. British Grasslands Society. Pp. 71-77.

Fujihara, S. & Yamaguchi. M. (1978) *Phytochem.* 17, 1239-1243.

Herridge, D.F. (1982) Estimating N_2 fixation in field grown soybeans using ureide and nitrate analyses of plant parts and nodulation status of the plant throughout growth. *In:* Proceedings, IV Internat. Symp. N_2 Fixation, Canberra, Australia.

Herridge, D.F., Atkins, C.A., Pate, J.S., & Rainbird, R.M. (1978) *Plant Physiol.* 62, 495-499.

Herridge, D.F. & Pate, J.S. (1977) *Plant Physiol.* 60, 759-764.

Israel, D.W. & McClure, P.R. (1979) Nitrogen translocation in the xylem of soybeans. *In:* Proceedings, 2nd World Soybean Research Conference, F.T. Corbin (Ed.). Westview Press, Boulder, CO, USA. Pp. 111-127.

Kumar Rao, J.V.D.K., Dart, P.J., Day, J.M., & Matsumoto, T. (1980) Nitrogen fixation by pigeonpea. *In:* International workshop on pigeonpea, ICRISAT Hyderabad, India. (In press.)

Leaf, G., Gardner, I.C. & Bond, G. (1958) *J. Expl. Bot.* 9, 320-331.

Lewis, O.A.M. & Pate, J.S. (1973) *J. Expl. Bot.* 24, 596-606.

Matsumoto, T., Yatazawa, M. & Yamamoto, Y. (1977a) *Plant Cell Physiol.* 18, 459-462.

Matsumoto, T., Yatazawa, M. & Yamamoto, Y. (1977b) *Plant Cell Physiol.* 18, 353-359.

Matsumoto, T., Yatazawa, M. & Yamamoto, Y. (1978) *Plant Cell Physiol.* 19, 1161-1168.

McClure, P.R. & Israel, D.W. (1979) *Plant Physiol.* 64, 411-416.

McClure, P.R., Israel, D.W. & Volk, R.J. (1980) *Plant Physiol.* 66, 720-725.

McNeil, D.L. (1979) The interchange of minerals and nitrogenous solutes between the xylem and phloem and plant tissues of a grain legume. PhD thesis, University of Western Australia, Nedlands, WA, Australia. 176 pp.

McNeil, D.L., Atkins, C.A. & Pate, J.S. (1979) *Plant Physiol.* 63, 1076-1081.

Mothes, K. (1956) *Die Kulturpflanze Beith.* 1, p. 103.

Mothes, K. (1961) *Can. J. Botany* 39, 1785-1807.

Mothes, K. & Engelbrecht, L. (1956) *Flora* 143, 428-472.

Nirmala, J. & Sastry, K.S. (1972) *Analyt. Biochem.* 47, 218-227.

Pate, J.S., Atkins, C.A. Hamel, K., McNeil, D.L., & Layzell, D.B. (1979) *Plant Physiol.* 63, 1082-1088.

Pate, J.S., Atkins, C.A., White, S.T., Rainbird, R.M., & Woo, K.C. (1980) *Plant Physiol.* 65, 961-965.

Pate, J.S. Gunning, B.E.S. & Briarty, G. (1969) *Planta* 85, 11-34.

Pate, J.S., Layzell, D.B. & McNeil, D.L. (1979) *Plant Physiol.* 63, 730-737.

Pate, J.S., Sharkey, P.J. & Lewis, O.A.M. (1975) *Planta* 122, 11-26.

Pate, J.S., Walker, J. & Wallace, W. (1965) *Annals of Botany* 29, 475-493.

Rheinbothe, H. & Mothes, K. (1962) *Ann. Rev. Plant Physiol.* 19, 129-150.

Sharkey, P.J. & Pate, J.S. (1975) *Planta* 127, 251-262.

Streeter, J.G. (1979) *Plant Physiol.* 63, 478-480.

Tajima, S., Yatazawa, M. & Yamamoto, Y. (1977) *Soil Sci. Plant Nutr.* 23, 225-235.

Thomas, R.J., Feller, U. & Erismann, K.H. (1979) *New Phytol.* 82, 657-669.

Tracey, M.V. (1955) Urea & ureides: Modern methods of plant analysis. Springer Verlag, Berlin. Germany. Pp. 119-141.

Urbaski, M.M., Grujic-Injac, B. & Gajic, D. (1978) *Analyt. Biochem.* 91, 304-308.

Van der Drift, C. & Vogels, G.M.D. (1966) *Acta Bot. Nerrl.* 15, 209.

Woo, K.C., Atkins, C.A. & Pate, J.S. (1980) *Plant Physiol.* 66, 735-739.

Young, E.G. & Conway, C.F. (1942) *J. Biol. Chem.* 142, 839-853.

GENETIC FINGERPRINTING AS A TOOL IN RESEARCH ON BIOLOGICAL NITROGEN FIXATION

J.E. Beringer[1]

Summary

Genetic fingerprinting is a technique for characterizing strains of micro-organisms based on the behavior of the strains in a number of tests. The most common tests are those that determine the resistance of an organism to antibiotics or phages and those that use serology to determine antigenic differences.

Resistance can be tested with low levels of antibiotics to determine intrinsic resistance, or at higher levels when resistant mutants are used. The concentration of antibiotic used depends very much on the species and can vary many fold. Mutants resistant to high levels of antibiotics are convenient to handle and have been used quite extensively in ecological studies of *Rhizobium*. However, they have the disadvantage that the mutant has to be selected in the laboratory, and many drug-resistant mutants have been shown to have altered symbiotic properties.

Resistance to phages and low levels of antibiotics are properties of wild-type micro-organisms that can be tested without having previously isolated the organisms. Therefore, fingerprinting based on these properties is particularly useful for ecological studies where knowledge of existing organisms is at least as important as the ability to follow the fate of introduced ones.

The relative merits of fingerprinting strains on the basis of intrinsic properties or selected mutations is discussed in relation to the type of work for which strain recognition is required.

Strain recognition is an important prerequisite to studies of ecology, competition and the survival, success, and persistence of inoculated organisms. The aim of this brief report is to describe some of the techniques that are available and to comment on their use.

[1] Soil Microbiology Department, Rothamsted Experimental Station, Harpenden, Herts, AL5 2JQ, England.

GENETIC VARIATION

The differences observed between organisms are due to differences in the functioning of genes. The more closely interrelated organisms are, the fewer gene differences they will have. Thus, it is usually relatively simple to characterize genera, but more difficult to distinguish strains. The ultimate example is two strains that differ only in the functioning of a single gene. If that gene has an easily recognizable function, the two can be distinguished. However, if the function is not known they will be grouped together as the same strain. Therefore, the problem in finding techniques for strain recognition is in observing differences between micro-organisms that can be measured and tested without difficulty.

Because all differences are basically genetic, all systems of classification are "genetic fingerprinting." For the purposes of this report, genetic fingerprinting will be discussed in respect to differences in the resistance of strains to antibiotics, phages, and bacteriocins. Serology, which is very important as a method for characterizing strains, will not be considered because it will be discussed elsewhere. The ability of organisms to utilize different substances as carbon and nitrogen sources can also be used for strain characterization (Graham, 1964). However, a real problem with many soil micro-organisms is that they are very efficient at scavenging small amounts of nutrients and will grow on standard agar in petri dishes without added carbon or nitrogen sources.

THE USE OF MUTANT STRAINS

The simplest strains to handle for ecological studies are those that have been selected in the laboratory, either after mutagenesis or following spontaneous mutation. Usually these are strains that have been selected for their resistance to high levels of antibiotics; though mutants with specific requirements for amino acids or nucleotides (auxotrophic mutants) can be used. Especially when more than one characteristic is altered, these strains are very easy to recognize, and the chance of finding similar strains in the soil are remote. Drug-resistant mutants also have the advantage that they can be isolated from mixed populations of bacteria on the basis of their drug resistance. This is particularly useful when looking at mixed inoculations and assessing the competition that occurs between strains. The antibiotics most commonly used for this purpose are streptomycin, spectinomycin, and rifampicin (Schwinghamer & Dudman, 1973; Johnston & Beringer, 1976b; Bromfield & Gareth Jones, 1979).

The most important problem with the use of mutants is that the bacteria are different from the parent. Whether or not the mutation affects either the competitiveness or the nitrogen-fixing properties of the strain must be tested before mutant strains can be used in comparative studies. From the data available (Schwinghamer, 1967; Levin & Montgomery, 1974; Pankhurst, 1977; Pain, 1979; Bromfield & Gareth Jones, 1979), it would appear that there is no simple correlation between the type of drug used to obtain mutants and its effects on the agriculturally important properties of a strain. A further problem is that the same mutation may already exist in the field in which the marked strain is to be used. Unless more than one characteristic is available for recognition purposes it is not possible to confirm the identify of strains. This difficulty is compounded by the limited choice of drugs that can be used for some species. For example, with fast-growing strains of *Rhizobium* only three or four antibiotic resistances have been found to be suitable for ecological studies.

THE USE OF FINGERPRINTING BY INTRINSIC RESISTANCE

The main disadvantage of the use of mutants for ecological studies is that the mutant strains must be produced in the laboratory and then introduced into the soil. Therefore, it is not a technique that can be used for examining existing populations of micro-organisms. Intrinsic resistance to drugs, phages, or bacteriocins can be tested for any organism without previous knowledge of that organism's properties. All that is generally required is a knowledge of the species and data from tests with laboratory cultures of strains that belong to this species. These laboratory tests will have defined optimal concentrations of antibiotics for known strains, and those strains will have been used for the isolation of phages and suitable bacteriocinogenic strains. Thereafter, new isolates can be tested against the previously isolated phages.

How many different phages, bacteriocin producers or antibiotics are used for fingerprinting is determined by the degree of precision required and the physical and economic constraints of doing the tests. An advantage of using these characteristics is that the potential number of tests that can be carried out is enormous. Therefore, it should always be possible to differentiate strains. It should also be remembered that other characteristics such as enzyme activities, restriction enzyme digests of DNA, and growth on different nutrients can also be included in the range of tests used for a fingerprint (Graham, 1964; Graham & Parker, 1965).

The main disadvantage of fingerprinting is the property that makes it so valuable: the number of different tests required. The amount of work involved can be reduced by using a multiple inoculator such as described by Josey *et al.* (1979) that is capable of transferring 25 samples at a time to different test media. A further problem is that when intrinsic resistance to drugs is being determined, one is looking at very small differences in the concentration of that drug to distinguish sensitive and resistant strains (e.g., 2.5 and 5 mg/l). Media must, therefore, be prepared very carefully and used uniformly, but even then there will always be strains that give variable results. Until more data are available on the use of intrinsic drug resistance in ecological studies the significance of such variability cannot be determined.

Resistance to phages and bacteriocins is usually fairly simple to determine, and both are used routinely for characterizing hospital isolates of bacteria (Darrell & Wahba, 1964). It is most important that great care is taken to ensure that standard preparations of phages and bacteriocin producers are used. These are not chemical reagents, which can be purchased and are of guaranteed purity. If cultures become contaminated or mixed up, or the wrong host is used to propagate the typing phages, test results will be of little value. Phages used for typing have two levels of host specificity: one determined by phage genes and the other determined by the modification of the phage in its previous host. Modification is the enzymic alteration of bases in DNA so that enzymes recognizing specific DNA sequences, and cutting them at these points (i.e., restriction enzymes), cannot function. Because there is a range of different modification and restriction enzymes the host range of phages is influenced by the last host on which the phages were propagated. Different hosts can be used to propagate phages to provide a degree of "fine-tuning" of phage-resistance patterns. While there have been a number of reports of phages (Bruch & Allen, 1957; Jones & Sneath, 1970; Staniewski, 1970a; 1970b) and bacteriocins (Roslycky, 1967; Schwinghamer, 1971; Hirsch, 1979) active against N_2-fixing micro-organisms, they have not been widely used for ecological studies.

THE CHOICE OF FINGERPRINTING TECHNIQUE

The choice of technique must depend upon the type of experiment that is planned, the facilities available, and personal prejudice. For carefully controlled *in vitro* experiments, when accurate estimates of relative numbers of different strains are required, mutants are particularly useful. Indeed, studies of mixed infections with *Rhizobium* have become much easier to undertake because of the availability of suitable mutant strains (Johnston & Beringer, 1976a; Bromfield & Gareth Jones, 1980). Mutant strains should always be used when genetic studies are being conducted. Far too many reports of the "genetic effects" of a range of treatments on *Rhizobium* have appeared in which it was not possible to determine whether the "modified strains" were truly modified or were contaminants.

When the fate of an inoculant is to be studied, serology, fingerprinting, or the use of mutant strains can all be useful (Read, 1953; Schwinghamer & Dudman, 1973; Pinto, Yao & Vincent, 1974; Kishinevsky & Bar-Joseph, 1978; Beynon & Josey, 1980; Bromfield & Gareth Jones, 1980). Because it is relatively simple to screen for the high-level resistance of mutants, many more samples can be taken compared to the number that can be handled when fingerprinting is used. This may be a decisive factor in making a choice. However, if possible adverse effects on a strain's performance are to be avoided, fingerprinting or serology must be used.

When sampling of indigenous populations is being attempted in order to gain some insight into the range and relative importance of different strains, fingerprinting is essential. An example of the type of project with this requirement is the isolation of strains of *Rhizobium* for inoculation purposes. Selection of the most suitable strain is often based on the isolation of a limited number of rhizobia from nodules that were selected because of their size or other characteristics. A more rational approach is to isolate from many nodules, and determine how many strains are present, the relative proportions of each strain, and, thus, how competitive the rhizobia are. Thereafter, tests of symbiotic proficiency can be performed with strains that can be recognized and have known competitive abilities.

CONCLUSIONS

Micro-organisms can be characterized on the basis of "genetic" differences that are intrinsic or have resulted from directed mutation. Mutant strains are relatively easy to handle and can be used to obtain fairly accurate values for the proportions of different strains. They suffer from the disadvantage that they are different from the wild-type parent and that the difference may also affect their ecological characteristics. For example, Döbereiner & Baldani (1979) have shown that in a particular environment maize roots were selectively infected by streptomycin-resistant derivatives of *Azospirillum lipoferum*. The problem of altering a strain is avoided by using intrinsic differences for characterization purposes. Many different characteristics can be screened making this technique suitable for handling many strains. Probably the main drawback is the care that must be taken to ensure that test conditions are standardized.

With all procedures for strain recognition, a problem that has hardly been considered is the micro-organism's potential for mutation. Very large populations of micro-organisms can occur in soil or water, so that spontaneous mutants are going to be formed continually. Such mutants will be of no consequence if they are not better adapted than the wild-type parent. However, if the inoculant strain is not well adapted, for example auxotrophic and some rifampicin-resistant mutants of *Rhizobium,* mutants that are no longer auxotrophic or drug-resistant will be selected and become dominant (Pain, 1979; Beringer, Brewin & Johnston, 1980). Whether or not selection of this nature occurs in strains being used for inoculation purposes is not clear. A number of quite different methods for characterizing strains will need to be used and the results compared. If discrepancies in typing do occur, a reassessment of techniques and of what may be happening to strains in nature will be required.

REFERENCES

Beringer J.E., Brewin N.J. & Johnston, A.W.B. (1980) *Heredity* 45, 161-186.

Beynon, J.L. & Josey. D.P. (1980) *J. Gen. Microbiol.* 118, 437-442.

Bromfield, E.S.P. & Gareth Jones, D. (1979) *Ann. Appl. Biol.* 91, 211-219.

Bromfield, E.S.P. & Gareth Jones, D. (1980) *Ann. Appl. Biol.* 94, 51-59.

Bruch, C.W. & Allen. O.N. (1957) *Can. J. Microbiol.* 3, 181-189.

Darrell, J.H. & Wahba. A.H. (1964) *J. Clin. Path.* 17, 236-242.

Döbereiner. J. & Baldani. V.L.D. (1979) *Can. J. Microbiol.* 25, 1264-1269.

Graham, P.H. (1964) *Antonie van Leeuwenhoek J. Microbiol. Serol.* 30, 68-72.

Graham, P.H. & Parker. C.A. (1969) *Plant Soil* 20, 383-396.

Hirsch, P.R. (1979) *J. Gen. Microbiol.* 113, 219-228.

Johnston. A.W.B. & Beringer, J.E. (1976a) *Nature* (Lond.) 263, 502-504.

Johnston, A.W.B. & Beringer, J.E. (1976b) *J. Appl. Bacteriol.* 40, 375-380.

Jones, D. & Sneath. P.H.A. (1970) *Bact. Rev.* 34, 40-81.

Josey, D.P., Beynon. J.L., Johnston, A.W.B., & Beringer, J.E. (1979) *J. Appl. Bacteriol.* 46. 343-350.

Kishinevsky. B. & Bar-Joseph, M. (1978) *Can. J. Microbiol.* 24, 1537-1543.

Levin, R.A. & Montgomery. M.P. (1974) *Plant Soil* 41, 669-676.

Pain, A.N. (1979) *J. Appl. Bacteriol.* 47, 53-64.

Pankhurst, C.E. (1977) *Can. J. Microbiol.* 23, 1026-1033.

Pinto, C.M. Yao. P.Y. & Vincent, J.M. (1974) *Aust. J. Agric. Res.* 25, 317-329.

Read, M.P. (1953) *J. Gen. Microbiol.* 9, 1-14.

Roslycky, E.B. (1967) *Can. J. Microbiol.* 13, 431-432.

Schwinghamer, E.A. (1967) *Antonie van Leeuwenhoek J. Microbiol. Serol.* 33, 121-136.

Schwinghamer. E.A. (1971) *Soil Biol. Biochem.* 3, 353-363.

Schwinghamer. E.A. & Dudman, W.F. (1973) *J. Appl. Bacteriol.* 36, 263-272.

Staniewski, R. (1970a) *Acta Microbiol. Polon.* 19, 3-12.

Staniewski. R. (1970b) *Can. J. Microbiol.* 16, 1003-1009.

APPLICATION OF INHERENT ANTIBIOTIC RESISTANCE TO ECOLOGICAL STUDIES OF RHIZOBIA

O.P. Rupela,[1] D.P. Josey,[2] B. Toomsan,[1] S. Mittal,[1] P.J. Dart,[1] and J.A. Thompson[1]

Summary

The inherent antibiotic resistance technique shows promise for use in ecological studies. The technique involves the use of readily available chemicals for growing rhizobia, antibiotics and a simple, easily manufactured multi-inoculator. The main requirement of the method is precise maintenance of conditions throughout the experiment for all variables and laboratory processes. These precautions are discussed.

In a study of 473 field isolates from a trial inoculated with a streptomycin (str 200) marked mutant, the use of 30 characteristics (10 antibiotics x 2-4 concentrations) classified the strains into 203 groups when all characteristics had to match perfectly, and into 119 groups when one mismatching characteristic was allowed. The 22 isolates having str 200 resistance were placed in three groups with no mismatches, and into two groups with one mismatching character allowed.

INTRODUCTION

The success of introduced *Rhizobium* strains in field trials has been monitored using both serology and strains marked with antibiotic resistance (Read, 1953; Dudman & Brockwell, 1968; Schwinghamer & Dudman, 1973). Neither of these techniques, however, gives much information concerning the composition of the indigenous population of *Rhizobium*. Using the inherent antibiotic resistance technique described by Josey *et al.* (1979), the indigenous soil population of *Rhizobium* has been shown to be heterogeneous (Beynon & Josey, 1980). This technique could be used in examining some current

[1] CP No. 43, ICRISAT, Patancheru P.O., Andra Pradesh 502-324, India.
[2] John Innes Institute, Colney Lane. Norwich NR4 74H, England.

problems in field inoculation trials: the heterogeneity of indigenous populations, changes in the population over cropping season and with particular agricultural practices, and, in some cases, the reason for the success of particular inoculant strains. This paper discusses precautions to be observed in adapting the technique to local conditions, and reports on application of the technique to study rhizobia nodulating chickpea (*Cicer arietinum* L.) at ICRISAT.

SOURCES OF ERROR IN THE INHERENT ANTIBIOTIC RESISTANCE METHOD

Every effort must be made to maintain rigid control of the experimental conditions. If the test conditions are not completely standardized, it will be very difficult to draw any conclusions about the relationship between strains examined in different test series. Potential sources of error using this technique are:

Medium composition: The concentration of all constituents of the growth medium must be constant, and media should always be prepared using the same grade and brand of reagents. The number of ions available in one make of yeast extract may be widely different from those in another brand, and this can affect strain growth and antibiotic resistance differentially.

Medium sterilization and melting: Growth medium should always be sterilized and melted in the same way. If the medium is heated for different periods of time or at different temperatures, its composition may also vary, and hence affect growth.

Antibiotics: The same supplier should be used, as the strength and formulation of antibiotics can vary between manufacturers. The potency of nearly all antibiotics will decrease with age, particularly when made up into stock solution, so large amounts of stock solution should not be prepared. Repeated freezing and thawing of antibiotics should also be avoided as much as possible.

Mixing of antibiotics in media: When mixing the antibiotic with agar medium the temperature should be kept at 60° in a water bath. Once the plates are poured some antibiotics also will start to lose activity; thus, plates should be inoculated as soon as the whole set of plates is ready. If the agar is cool during mixing (c. 45° C), an even distribution of antibiotic throughout the medium may not be achieved, and strict comparisons between plates will not be possible. It is very important that the antibiotic concentrations in the medium are accurately reproduced on each occasion.

Inoculum condition: Sensitivity to some antibiotics (such as penicillin) may depend on cell growth phase, and it is very desirable to use inocula of a reasonably uniform stage of growth. Cells in the stationary phase may survive exposure to an antibiotic to which they are normally considered sensitive and then commence to grow again after concentration of antibiotic in the medium has decreased below the threshold value for activity against that particular strain.

Thickness of plate: If the thickness of medium in the plates varies, then the colony morphology will be influenced; e.g., slime may only be produced by large colonies making it difficult to assess the difference between control and antibiotic plates, if they are of different thickness. Plates with bubbles should also be discarded because of lack of homogeneity.

Drying of plates: As plates should be used immediately, drying may not be practical unless a laminar flow sterile hood is available. If plates are dried the same procedure must be used on every occasion.

Contamination: Contaminated plates should be discarded, as waste products from the contaminants may be synergistic with, or destroy, the antibiotics, and these effects may permeate the whole plate; not just the region where the contaminant is growing. For similar reasons, fast- and slow-growing strains of *Rhizobium* should not be tested on the same plate.

AN APPLICATION OF THE TECHNIQUE TO RHIZOBIA NODULATING CHICKPEA AT ICRISAT

In an experiment with chickpea at ICRISAT, in which the mutant strain 9036, resistant to 200 μg/ml streptomycin was used, 473 nodule isolates were obtained that lacked this resistance, and 22 were found with resistance to streptomycin. Inherent antibiotic resistance studies were undertaken to characterize these strains.

The technique used was as follows: Yeast extract mannitol agar (YMA), was made up accurately, sterilized, and kept at 60-65° C ready for use. Just before pouring the plates, the required volume of antibiotic stock solution (see Table 1) was added to the known volume of medium in the flask and swirl-mixed to ensure its proper distribution in the medium.

The same volume of medium was added to each petri dish, using either a sterile measuring cylinder or a sterile graduated beaker; for 9 cm diameter glass petri dishes, 30 ml was used. The plates were then poured on a flat surface to achieve uniform thickness.

Rhizobium strains used for strain typing were grown on YMA slopes in McCartney bottles, and as soon as growth was seen (usually four to five days with *Cicer* rhizobia) the cells were suspended in sterile, 20% (v/v) glycerol, dispensed in small quantities suitable for one day's testing, and stored in a deep freeze at -10° C.

The antibiotic test plates and controls were inoculated with a pronged, multiple inoculator (Josey *et al.*, 1979). Glycerol-stored cultures were diluted with sterile distilled water to give approximately 10^5 cells/ml and placed in the wells of the pin inoculator. At this concentration each prong of the inoculator transferred aproximately 10^3 rhizobia to the test plates. After incubation at about 28° C for 7 days the growth on antibiotic medium was compared with

TABLE 1: List of antibiotics and their concentrations.[1]

Antibiotics [2]	Concentrations (mg/1)
Carbenicillin	1.0, 2.5, 5.0
Erythromycin	1.25, 2.5, 10
Kanamycin	2.5, 10, 20
Nalidixic acid	2.5, 10, 15
Neomycin	2.5, 10, 15
Polymyxin	5, 10, 20
Rifampicin	0.25, 0.5, 2.5
Streptomycin	2.5, 10, 20, 200
Tetracycline	0.1, 0.5
Vancomycin	1.25, 2.5, 10

[1]All antibiotics are from Sigma except carbenicillin which is from 'Pyopen', Beecham.
[2]Antibiotic solutions were made in sterile deionized water, except erythromycin (in ethanol) and nalidixic acid (in 1 M NaOH).

that on control plates. Colony growth was scored numerically (1: no growth; 2: weak growth; 3: good growth) so that the results were amenable to computer analysis.

When the 473 isolates were scored on the basis of resistance to 10 antibiotics at 2-4 concentrations. 203 distinct groups were found. When one mismatch in the array of tests was permitted, 119 groups were distinguished. Samples of strain 9036 (reference culture) could be separated into two groups by inherent antibiotic resistance, while streptomycin-resistant field isolates fell into these two groups, plus one other.

When one mismatch was allowed, all reference cultures fell into one group as did 21 of the 22 streptomycin resistant field isolates.

The results demonstrated again the heterogeneity of soil populations. Characterization of the properties of the different groups of isolates, and of their frequency in soil, could help explain the basis for their competition with inoculant rhizobia.

REFERENCES

Beynon, J.L. & Josey. D.P. (1980) *J. Gen. Microbiol.* 118, 437-442.

Dudman, W.F. & Brockwell, J. (1968) *Aust. J. Agric. Res.* 19, 739-747.

Josey, D.P., Beynon, J.L., Johnston, A.W.B., & Beringer, J.E. (1979) *J. Appl. Bacteriol.* 46, 343-350.

Read, M.P. (1953) *J. Gen. Microbiol.* 9, 1-3.

Schwinghamer, E.A. & Dudman, W.F. (1973) *J. Appl. Bacteriol.* 36, 263-272.

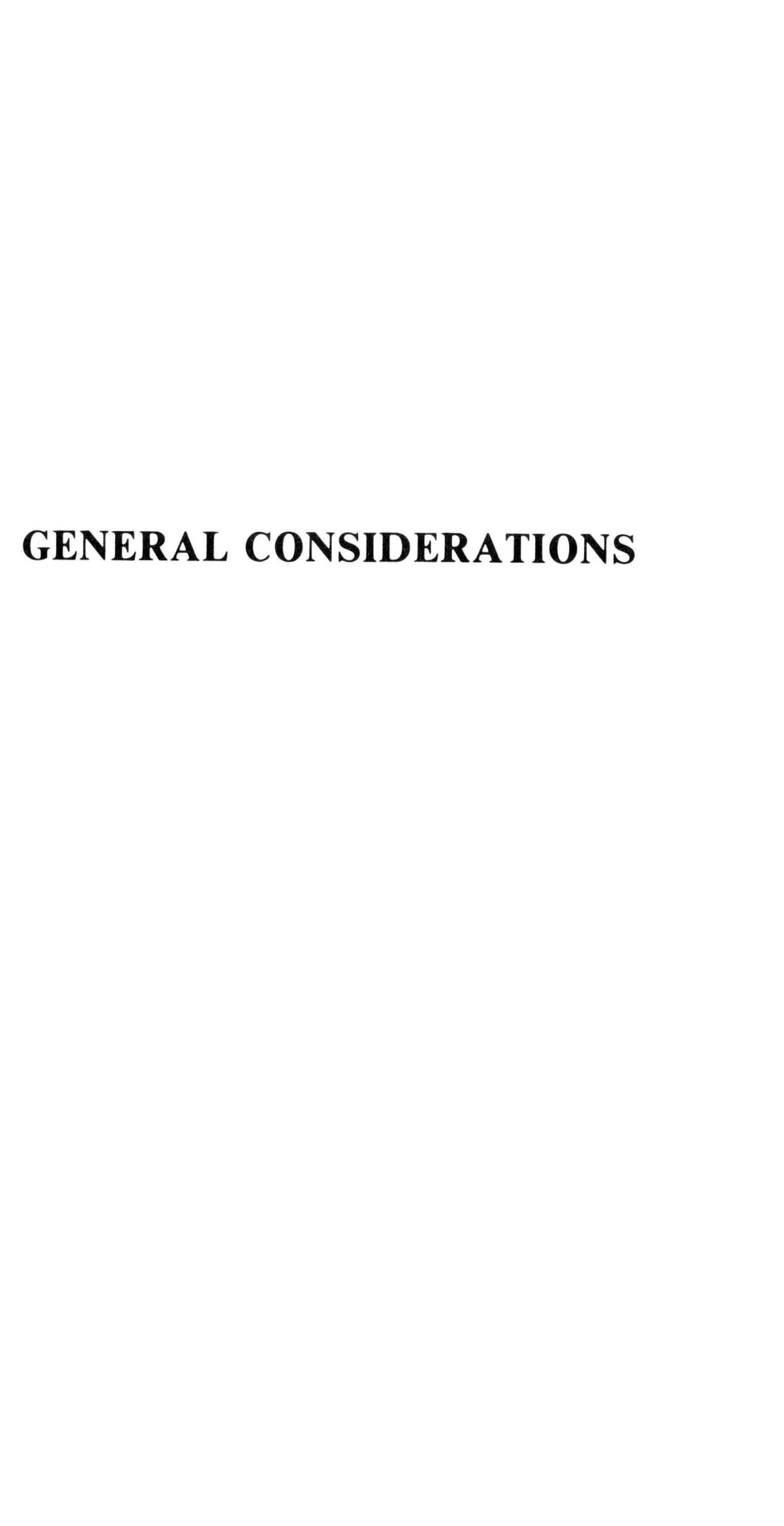

GENERAL CONSIDERATIONS

THE NITROGEN RELATIONSHIPS OF MAIZE/BEAN ASSOCIATIONS

S.M.T. Saito[1]

Summary

Intercropping of maize and beans is practiced widely throughout the tropical and subtropical regions of Latin America, particularly among small farmers with limited technical resources. This paper reviews how association affects the nitrogen (N) balance of legumes and nonlegumes, paying particular attention to N_2 fixation and N transfer.

INTRODUCTION

Hernández-Bravo (1973) reported that 75% of the beans produced in Latin America are grown associated with another crop, principally maize. Similar figures are provided by Scobie, Infante & Gutiérrez (1974) and Vieira (1978).

Despite the importance of this cropping system there have been relatively few studies on the biological consequences of association. Wahua & Miller (1978) report that benefits from association are: balanced nutrient supply of energy and protein, protein and resource maximization, efficient utilization of water, inexpensive weed control, risk minimization and improved soil fertility. Other reported benefits include modified pressure from pests (Altieri *et al.*, 1978), reduced maize lodging in association (Francis, 1978) and reduced erosion and water infiltration (Noia, 1977).

Some authors have criticized the associated system claiming that intercropping promotes the incidence of some diseases and pests and reduces yields of both components (Lepiz, 1971; Moreno, 1972). Certainly yield reductions of from 38-70% have been shown in beans associated with maize (Francis, 1978); maize yields may also be affected (Fisher, 1977).

---

[1] Centro de Energía Nuclear na Agricultura (CENA), C.P. 96, 13400 Piracicaba, São Paulo, Brasil.

A common assumption in discussing maize/bean intercrops is that nitrogen (N_2) fixed by the bean benefits the maize. The documentation for this is limited. In this review I examine the N economy of the maize/bean intercrop and some of the factors influencing it.

N RELATIONSHIPS IN MIXED PLANTINGS

Figure 1, simplified from that of Henzell & Vallis (1977), shows that the bean/maize intercrop has three major sources of nitrogen: N_2 fixed by the bean and possibly by the maize; fertilizer N applied routinely to the maize, but also sometimes to beans (Bazán, 1975); and soil N. Some N is also introduced in the seeds, but normally this would not contribute more than 3 kg N/ha. N in the legume may be removed as fruit or pods at harvest, may be grazed, may become available to the maize, or may simply be incorporated as residues and move into the soil pools of organic or mineralized N. The story for the maize is similar: it may even be that where the crops are intercalated, as in Central America, with the maize planted first, that the decomposition of fallen cereal leaves and roots provides some N to the beans! Under tropical conditions the high mobility and rate of mineralization of N can lead to appreciable losses by volatilization and leaching. Discussion in the present review will emphasize four areas: N fertilization, N_2 fixation, N excretion, and N residues for subsequent crops.

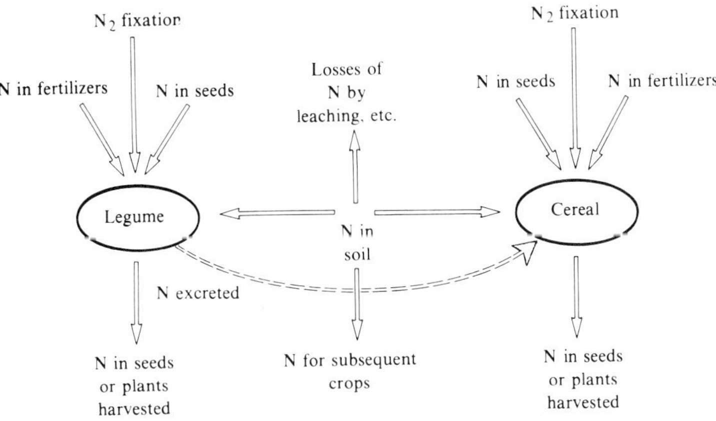

Figure 1: Movement of nitrogen in legume-cereal intercrops.

N FERTILIZATION

Maize has a higher requirement for N than beans, and produces an equivalently high amount of biomass. Mineral N absorbed by the maize plant under monoculture conditions can be as much as 141 kg N/ha per growth cycle (Andrade, 1975). Maximum requirement for N occurs around 80 days after germination when vegetative growth ceases and grain filling starts. As much as 3 kg N/ha per day can be absorbed (Malavolta & Dantas, 1978) with the maize plant highly efficient in recovering applied N (Reichardt *et al.*, 1979). While the N requirement of maize in the lower yielding, intercrop situation would probably be less, supply of this N presents a dilemma.

Thus, on the one hand, N deficiency is common throughout the production region (Díaz-Romeu, Balerdi & Fassbender, 1970; Malavolta, 1971; Bazan, 1975) with rates of N fertilization for maize of up to 120 kg N/ha per cycle recommended (Laird & Rodríguez, 1965; Laird et al., 1969; Arnon, 1975). On the other hand, and while small doses of N can sometimes be beneficial (Graham & Halliday, 1977), application of combined N to the maize is likely to reduce the nodule development and function of beans grown in association (Rigaud, 1976).

P.H. Graham & S.R. Viteri (unpublished data) found seasonal rates of $N_2(C_2H_2)$ fixation in some bean cultivars reduced almost 40% by the application of only 15 kg/ha of combined N. Cultivar (Franco & Döbereiner, 1968), strain of *Rhizobium* (Guss & Dobereiner, 1972; Saito, 1980) and rate and source of N (Ruschel & Saito, 1977; Santa Cecilia & Prado, 1977; Ruschel, Saito & Tulmann Neto, 1979) would all affect this interaction.

Compatible maize/bean, fertilizer N/N_2 fixation systems must be developed. The following points urgently need study:

Since legumes are generally poor competitors for applied N (Henzell & Vallis, 1975), will N fertilization disadvantage the legume in ways other than the expected effects on N_2 fixation?

Can deep placement of fertilizer N (Harper & Cooper, 1971; Crasswell & Vlek, 1979) provide N for the maize without damaging fixation?

Could the use of organic manures for the maize reduce the effects on the bean (Yoshida, 1979)?

N_2 FIXATION

Ruschel *et al.* (1981) found nodulated bean plants in a monocrop situation to fix up to 65 kg N/ha per cycle under field conditions. Other authors have reported values ranging from 9.12 to 73.7 kg N_2 fixed/ha per growth cycle (Table 1). Graham & Rosas (1978b) found $N_2(C_2H_2)$ fixation by a vigorous climbing cultivar essentially unaffected by association, but gave no N data. In this study both maize and bean development were affected by association but competition effects were not apparent during the period of active N_2 fixation.

TABLE 1: N_2 fixation in bean (*Phaseolus vulgaris*) and maize (*Zea mays*), estimated by different methods.

Crop	Amount fixed	Method	Reference
Bean	(kg N/ha)		
	9-12	Kjeldahl, C_2H_2 reduction	Janssen (1972)
	30-40	Kjeldahl, C_2H_2 reduction	Graham & Halliday (1977)
	12.2-73.7	C_2H_2 reduction	CIAT (1977)
	25-65	Isotopic dilution $^{15}N_2$	Ruschel *et al.* (1981)
Maize	(kg N/ha · day)		
	2.4	Kjeldahl, C_2H_2 reduction	von Bülow & Döbereiner (1975)
	(g N/ha · day)		
	2.8	Kjeldahl, C_2H_2 reduction	Tjepkema & van Berkum (1976)

In a later study (P.H. Graham & S.R. Viteri, unpublished data) N_2 fixation by a bush bean cultivar was severely reduced by association, though nodule development prior to flowering was enhanced. Delay in the planting date of beans relative to maize further reduced $N_2(C_2H_2)$ fixation, presumably as the result of increased competition for light.

It is possible that maize also has a potential for N_2 fixation and could contribute to the N economy of intercropped plants (see Table 1).

Effects of association on the light, water, and nutrients needed for N_2 fixation need to be further studied. Reference has already been made to the decreased $N_2(C_2H_2)$ fixation of bush bean/maize associations. Antoniw & Sprent (1978) also report overall capacity for N_2 fixation affected by sub-optimum light conditions with nodule size particularly reduced. Conversely shading can reduce soil temperatures and so enhance nodulation (Graham & Rosas, 1978a).

Competition for P was not a problem in cowpea/maize intercrops (Remison, 1978). As maize and beans show sowewhat different root profiles, with the bean roots located mainly in the top 10 cm of soil (Inforzato & Miyasaka, 1963; Malavolta & Dantas, 1978), it is possible that each exploits different soil volumes, thus reducing the likelihood of competition for nutrients. By the same logic, and while both beans and N_2 fixation are highly susceptible to water stress (Sprent, 1976; Bonnetti, Montanheiro & Saito, 1980; CIAT, 1980) the likelihood and severity of water stress might be little affected by association.

TABLE 2: ^{15}N enrichment of root, top parts, and soil rhizosphere of *Phaseolus* beans and soybean (both nodulated), and of maize, incubated under ^{15}N atmosphere[1] for 24 hours (Ruschel, Salati & Vose, 1979).

	^{15}N excess			Fixed N μg		
	Root	Tops	Soil	Root	Tops	Soil
Bean	0.210	0.281	0.005	18.74 ± 0.18	117.01 ± 0.84	28.19 ± 11.28
Soybean	0.047	0.096	0.001	2.55 ± 0.11	21.65 ± 0.45	5.27 ± 10.55
Maize	0	0.004	0	0 ± 0.65	1.46 ± 0.74	0 ± 11.32
Bean	1.345	—[2]	0.007	171.96 ± 0.26	—[2]	38.51 ± 11.01
Soybean	0.494	0.211	0.002	19.06 ± 0.07	63.78 ± 0.61	11.36 ± 11.36
Maize	0	0.002	0	0 ± 0.69	0 ± 0.81	0 ± 13.65

[1] $pN_2 = 0.66$; $pO_2 = 0.12$: pAr 0.20; pCO_2, 0.20; $^{15}N_2$ enrichment 43%.
[2] Lost sample.

N EXCRETION

The idea that legumes could excrete N during growth is not new (Nicol, 1935; Virtanen, von Hausen & Laine, 1937; Wilson & Burton, 1938). Recently Ruschel, Salati & Vose (1979) showed some soil enrichment of fixed $^{15}N_2$ from beans (see Table 2). Whether this phenomenon is a normal physiological process or occurs in response to a condition such as shading is not known. Willey (1979a; 1979b) has reviewed and discussed this subject to some extent. Apparently, excretions are more frequent where legumes are subject to shading, but this may only be important after good growth has already been made under reasonsable light conditions. Nodule breakdown and root decomposition during senescence could also transfer nitrogenous compounds to the nonlegume companion (Walker, Orchiston & Adams, 1954). Agboola & Fayemi (1972), however, found little contribution of the associated legumes *Vigna sinensis* and *Calopogonium mucunoides* to maize, but did show that *Phaseolus aureus* benefited intercropped maize early in the growing season. Unfortunately the majority of the excretion experiments have been conducted in pots, and little information is available from field situations.

N RESIDUES

The importance of legumes in crop rotations has been taken for granted for many years. Recently some authors have begun to question this, pointing out that if the N_2 fixed is equal to or less than that removed in the grain, then subsequent crops cannot benefit. Recent studies have also shown variation in the rate of mineralization of plant N, with the rate of decomposition of root and stem tissue in some species delayed. The residual effects of maize/bean associations can only be guessed at. At best, using the monoculture and high technology figures from Ruschel *et al.* (1981) and Okon (p. 459), the N_2 fixed by an association of maize and beans might reach 140 kg N_2 fixed/ha per growth cycle, with 130-150 kg N removed in the grain of both crops. Fixation rates in farmers' fields are more likely to sum less than 95 kg N/ha per cycle, a substantial loss of N to the soil.

REFERENCES

Agboola, A.A. & Fayemi, A.A. (1972) *Agron. J.*, 64, 409-412.

Altieri, M.A., Francis, C.A., Schoonhoven, A. van, & Doll, J.D. (1978) *Field Crops Res.* 1 (1), 33-49.

Andrade, A.G. (1975) Acumulação diferencial de nutrientes por cinco cultivares de milho (*Zea mays* L.). Mg. Sci. thesis, E.S.A. "Luiz de Queiroz," USP, Piracicaba, Brazil.

Antoniw, L.D. & Sprent, J.I. (1978) *Annals of Botany* 42, 399-140.

Arnon, I. (1975) Mineral nutrition of maize. International Potash Institute, Bern, Switzerland. 452 pp.

Bazán, R. (1975) Nitrogen fertilization and management of grain legumes in Central America. *In:* Soil management in tropical America, E. Bornemisza & A. Alvarado (Eds.). North Carolina State Univ. Raleigh, NC, USA. Pp. 228-245.

Bonetti, R., Montanheiro, M.N.S. & Saito, S.M.T. (1980) Influencia da umidade do solo na nodulação e utilização de fósforo (^{32}P) em *Phaseolus vulgaris*. I. Efeito na nodulação e no desenvolvimento da planta. X Reunión Latinoamericana do *Rhizobium,* Maracay, Venezuela.

Bülow, J.W.F. von & Döbereiner, J. (1975) *Proc. Natl. Acad. Sci.* (USA) 72, 2389-2393.

Centro Internacional de Agricultura Tropical (CIAT) (1977) Annual report of the bean production program. 85 pp.

Centro Internacional de Agricultura Tropical (CIAT) (1980) Annual report of the bean production program. 87 pp.

Crasswell, E.T. & Vlek, P.L.G. (1979) Fate of fertilizer nitrogen applied to wetland rice. *In*: Nitrogen and rice. IRRI, Los Baños, Philippines. Pp. 174-192.

Díaz-Romeu, R., Balerdi, F. & Fassbender, H.W. (1970) *Turrialba* 20, 185-192.

Fisher, N.M. (1977) *Expl. Agric.* 13, 177-184.

Francis, C.A. (1978) *Hortscience* 13, 12-17.

Franco, A.A. & Döbereiner, J. (1968) *Pesq. Agropec. Bras. Ser. Agron.* 3, 223-227.

Graham, P.H. & Halliday, J. (1977) Inoculation and nitrogen fixation in the genus *Phaseolus. In*: Exploiting the legume-*Rhizobium* symbiosis in tropical agriculture, J.M. Vincent, A.S. Whitney & J. Bose (Eds.). Univ. Hawaii College Trop. Agric. Misc. Publ. 145. Pp. 313-334.

Graham, P.H. & Rosas, J.C. (1978a) *J. Agric. Sci.* (Camb.) 90, 19-29.

Graham, P.H. & Rosas, J.C. (1978b) *J. Agric. Sci.* (Camb.) 90, 311-317.

Guss, A. & Döbereiner, J. (1972) *Pesq. Agropec. Bras. Ser. Agron.* 7, 87-92.

Harper, J.E. & Cooper, R.L. (1971) *Crop Sci.* 11, 438-440.

Henzell, E.F. & Vallis, I. (1977) Transfer of nitrogen between legumes and other crops. *In:* Biological nitrogen fixation in farming systems of the tropics, A.

Ayanaba & P.J. Dart (Eds.). Wiley Interscience, Chichester, England. Pp. 73-88.

Hernández-Bravo, G. (1973) Potentials and problems of production of dry beans in the lowland tropics. *In:* Potentials of field beans and other food legumes in Latin America. CIAT, Cali, Colombia. Pp. 144-150.

Inforzato, R. & Miyasaka, S. (1963) *Bragantia* 22, 477-481.

Janssen, K.A. (1972) Effect of physical and nutritional factors of the environment on nitrogen fixation, plant composition, and yield of dark red kidney beans (*Phaseolus vulgaris* L.). PhD thesis. Michigan State University, East Lansing, MI, USA. 72 p.

Laird, R.J. & Rodríguez, J.H. (1965) *Foll. Tecn. Inst. Nac. Invest. Agric.* 50, 1-71.

Laird, R.J., Ruiz, A., Rodríguez, J.H., & Cady, F.B. (1969) CIMMYT Research Bull. 12. Pp.

Lépiz, R.I. (1971) *Agr. Tecnica en México* 3, 98-101.

Malavolta, E. (1971) *Anais I Simp. Brasileiro de Feijao (Campinas)* 1, 211-242.

Malavolta, E. & Dantas, J.P. (1978) Nutrição e adubação do milho. *In:* Melhoramento e produção do milho no Brasil, E. Paterniani (Coord.). Marprint. Piracicaba/ESALQ/USP, Brasil. Pp. 429-479.

Moreno, R.O.H. (1972) Las asociaciones de maíz y fríjol, un uso alternativo de la tierra. Mag. Sci. thesis, Chapingo, Mexico, 80 pp.

Nicol, H. (1935) *Emp. J. Expl. Agric.,* 3 189-195.

Noia, R.J.A. (1977) Erosión de suelos de pendientes cultivadas con maíz y fríjol con diferentes grados de covertura viva dentro de una plantación forestal. Mag. Sc. thesis, Univ. de Costa Rica, Centro Agronómico Tropical de Investigación y Enseñanza, Turrialba, Costa Rica. 182 pp.

Reichardt, K., Libardi, P.L., Victória, R.L., & Viegas, G.P. (1979) *Rev. Bras. Ci. Solo* 3, 17-20.

Remison, S.U. (1978) *Expl. Agric.* 14, 205-212.

Rigaud, J. (1976) *Physiol. Végét.* 14, 298-308.

Ruschel, A.P. & Saito, S.M.T. (1977) *Rev. Bras. Ci. Solo* 1, 21-24.

Ruschel, A.P., Saito, S.M.T. & Tulmann Neto, A. (1979) *Rev. Bras. Ci. Solo* 3, 13-17.

Ruschel, A.P., Salati, E. & Vose, P.B. (1979) *Plant Soil* 51, 425-429.

Ruschel, A.P., Vose, P.B., Matsui, E., Victória, R.L., & Saito, S.M.T. (1981). Field evaluation of N_2-fixation and nitrogen utilization by *Phaseolus* bean varieties determined by ^{15}N isotope dilution. (In press.)

Saito, S.M.T. (1980) Avaliação em campo da capacidade de fixação simbiótica de estirpes de *Rhizobium phaseoli.* X Reunión Latinoamericana do *Rhizobium,* Maracay, Venezuela.

Santa Cecília, F.C. & Prado, E. de C. (1977) *Ciencia e Prática* 1, 17-21.

Scobie, G.M., Infante, M.A. & Gutiérrez, U. (1974) Production and consumption of dry beans and their role in protein nutrition: a review. CIAT, Cali, Colombia.

Sprent, J.I. (1976) Nitrogen fixation by legumes subjected to water and light stresses. *In*: Symbiotic nitrogen fixation in plants, P.S. Nutman (Ed.). Cambridge Univ. Press, Cambridge, England. Pp. 405-420.

Tjepkema, J.D. & Berkum, P. van (1977) *App. Environ. Microbiol.* 33, 626-629.

Vieira, C. (1978) Cultura do feijao. Univ. Federal de Vicosa. Vicosa, MG, Brasil. 146 pp.

Virtanen, A.I., Hausen, S. von & Laine, T. (1937) *J. Agric. Sci.* (Cambr.) 27, 610.

Wahua, T.A.T. & Miller, D.A. (1978) *Agron. J.* 70, 287-291.

Walker, T.W., Orchiston, H.D. & Adams, A.F.R. (1954) *J. Br. Grassl. Soc.* 9, 249-274.

Willey, R.W. (1979a) *Field Crop Abst.* 32, 1-10.

Willey, R.W. (1979b) *Field Crop Abst.* 32, 73-85.

Wilson, P.W. & Burton, J.C. (1938) *J. Agric. Sci.* (Cambr.) 28, 307-323.

Yoshida, S. (1979) *Jap. J. Crop. Sci.* 48, 17-24.

ASSESSING THE NITROGEN CONTRIBUTION OF COWPEA *(VIGNA UNGUICULATA)* IN MONOCULTURE AND INTERCROPPED

A.R.J. Eaglesham[1]

Summary

In a field trial with four cultivars of *Vigna unguiculata* (L.) Walp. N_2 fixation, estimated by the difference method with ^{15}N, ranged from 49 to 101 kg N_2 fixed/ha per cycle. With 25 kg fertilizer N applied/ha, the soil showed a positive N balance of 2-52 kg N/ha. In a trial with cowpea and maize intercropped, the N content of intercropped maize was significantly greater than that obtained in monoculture.

INTRODUCTION

Under shifting cultivation after land clearance, the initially high organic nitrogen (N) levels of tropical soils decline rapidly (Bartholomew, 1977), and fertilizer N must be added, or N_2 fixed to maintain productivity. While several species of grain legumes are important sources of dietary protein throughout the developing world, there are few reliable estimates of their ability to fix N_2 under field conditions in the tropics, and no data as to their contribution to soil N levels and to other species grown in association. In this paper I examine the N balance of monocropped cowpeas at different levels of fertilizer N usage and provide evidence of N transfer from cowpea to intercropped maize.

EXPERIMENTAL METHODS

The experiments detailed here were undertaken at the International Institute of Tropical Agriculture (IITA), Ibadan, Nigeria, on an Alfisol of pH 6.5, which contained only 0.073% N.

[1] Boyce Thompson Institute, Cornell University, Ithaca 14853, NY, USA.

In the first trial, four cowpea (*Vigna unguiculata* (L.) Walp.) cultivars (ER-1, TVu 1190, Ife Brown and TVu 4552) were used, and their N_2 fixation capacity determined by the difference and "A-value" methods described by Ham (1977). Nonfixing controls included maize *(Zea mays)*, celosia *(Celosia argentia)* and a non-nodulating soybean (*Glycine max* cv. N59-52-59).

Estimates of N_2 fixation were made at three N levels: 0, 25, 100 kg N applied per hectare, and nodule samples and N_2 (C_2H_2) fixation assays were made to show the seasonal effects of applied N on nodule development and N_2 fixation.

At maturity, total crop N and amount of N_2 fixed were calculated, and N uptake from soil was obtained by subtraction. Grain N harvested was obtained at maturity, and the N added back to the soil was calculated by subtraction. The net N gain or depletion from the soil was then calculated as:

N (CHANGE) = N (RESIDUES) — N (UPTAKE FROM SOIL)

or

N (CHANGE) = N FIXED — N IN GRAIN

In an intercropping component of the experiment described above, cowpeas (cv. TVu 1190) were alternate-row intercropped with maize and grown under the same N regimes as the sole crops: -N, 25 kg N, and 100 kg N.

RESULTS AND DISCUSSION

The mean fertilizer efficiencies were 12% at 25 kg N/ha applied and 27% at 100 kg N/ha applied. With only 3 kg N/ha taken up at the lower fertilizer level, no significant effect of this low level of N on nodulation or N_2 fixation was experienced. The application of 100 kg fertilizer N/ha did, however, influence both nodule development during the growth season (see Figure 1) and N_2 (C_2H_2) fixation, as shown early in pod-fill in Figure 2.

Both the difference method and A-value method gave similar estimates of N_2 fixation for the four cowpca cultivars, with the different nonfixing controls also not significantly different.

Cultivar TVu 1190 fixed 101 kg N_2/ha when only 25 kg fertilizer N was applied per ha. With only 49 kg N/ha removed in the grain, this represented a gain of 52 kg N/ha to the soil (see Table 1). By contrast, when 100 kg fertilizer N/ha was applied, the soil neither lost nor gained N. However, with the cultivar TVu 4552 at the higher level of fertilizer N, there was a net loss of 34 kg N/ha from the soil.

Table 2 shows a striking increase in N content, as mg N/plant and % N, in intercropped compared to monoculture maize, with low levels of N fertilization. Table 3 shows that fertilizer N uptake by the maize and cowpeas was similar and was not affected by intercropping. As the fertilizer N was well incorporated into the soil, with soil N uptake likely to parallel fertilizer N uptake, it seems unlikely that the increased N content of the intercropped

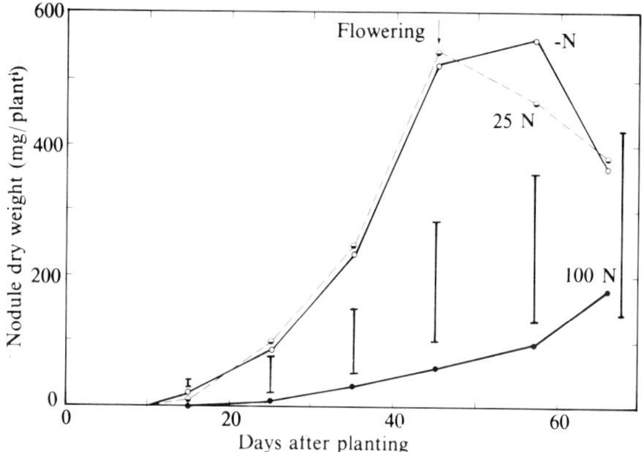

Figure 1. Patterns of seasonal accumulation of nodule dry weight in cowpea, cv. TVu 1190, grown at three levels of applied N: 0(-N), 25 kg N/ha (25N) and 100 kg N/ha (100N). Bars represent LSD values at P=0.05. (Data of A.R.J. Eaglesham, A. Ayanaba, D.L. Eskew & V. Ranga Rao, unpublished).

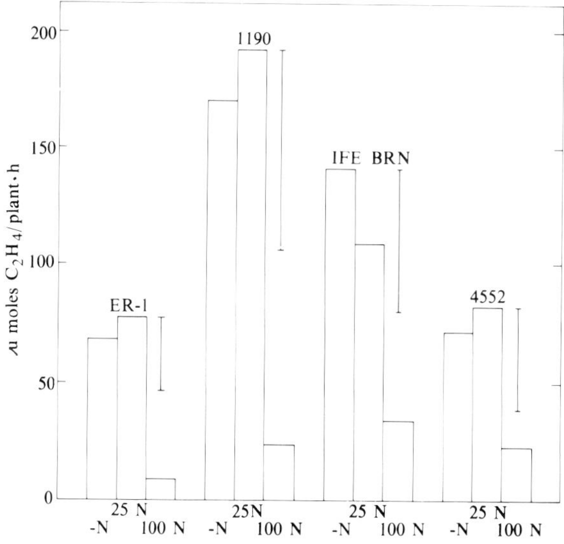

Figure 2. Acetylene reduction activities of cowpeas (cvs. ER-1, TVu 1190, Ife Brown, and TVu 4552) at 45 days after planting, at three levels of applied N (-N, 25 kg N/ha (25N) and 100 kg N/ha (100N)). Bars represent LSD values at P=0.05. (Data of A.R.J. Eaglesham, A. Ayanaba, D.L. Eskew & V. Ranga Rao, unpublished).

TABLE 1: The net N balances of cowpeas at two levels of mineral N availability. (Data of A.R.J. Eaglesham, A. Ayanaba, D.L. Eskew & V. Ranga Rao, unpublished).

N treatment	Cultivar	Mineral N uptake	Fixed N input	Grain N removed	Residue N returned	N balance
				(kg/ha)		
25N	ER-1	32	50	48	34	+ 2
	TVu 1190	33	101	49	85	+52
	Ife Brown	25	81	57	49	+24
	TVu 4552	27	49	46	30	+ 3
100N	ER-1	66	28	54	40	–26
	TVu 1190	69	49	49	69	0
	Ife Brown	64	44	52	56	– 8
	TVu 4552	54	19	53	20	–34

TABLE 2: N accumulated by sole cropped and intercropped maize (after Eaglesham *et al.*, 1981).

Treatment		N content (mg/plant)	% N	% atom excess ^{15}N
–N	Sole crop	469	0.70	–
	Intercrop	915*	0.92**	–
25N	Sole crop	426	0.58	0.7727
	Intercrop	782*	0.83***	0.3714*
100N	Sole crop	810	0.67	0.8867
	Intercrop	989ns	070ns	0.6225ns

Statistical comparison are within N treatments and columns.
ns = not significantly different.
* = significantly different at P= 0.05.
** = significantly different at P= 0.01.
*** = significantly different at P= 0.001.

maize plants can be explained on the basis of soil or fertilizer N. Clearly, intercropped maize had access to a source of N not available to monoculture maize. It is unlikely that this could be due to recovery of N low in the soil profile; to benefit from decaying cowpea leaves (since no significant leaf fall had occurred at harvest); or to sloughing off and decay of cowpea nodules, which is normally only 5-7% of the total plant N (Earles an *et al.*, 1977). The significant dilution of ^{15}N in the intercropped maize compared to maize in monoculture (see Table 2) is consistent with the additional N having been derived from cowpeas.

At 100 kg N, although the N nutrition of intercropped maize was improved over the sole crop, the differences were not statistically significant, possibly because of the inhibitory effect of the applied N on N_2 fixation.

The data presented here show that it is a misconception that legumes always contribute N. Moreover, it would be wrong to extrapolate freely from these data (e.g., that soybean having a high N_2-fixing potential will be likely to contribute N, by way of vegetative residues, to the soil). Two factors are important in addition to N_2-fixing potential: mineral N availability, and the harvest index for N. Field-grown soybeans in the USA fixed 76 kg N/ha and absorbed 219 kg N/ha from the soil (Hardy & Havelka, 1976). Assuming an N harvest index of 70% (a relatively low figure for soybean), 206 kg N/ha would be removed in the grain and 89 kg N/ha would be added back as vegetative residues, a net depletion of 130 kg N/ha.

TABLE 3: Comparison of fertilizer N uptake as mg N/m of row, of sole cropped and intercropped cowpeas and maize (after Eaglesham *et al.*, 1981).

Treatment	Crop	Fertilizer N content (mg/m)
Sole crop 25N	Cowpea	188 a
	Maize	187 a
Sole crop 100N	Cowpea	1265 b
	Maize	1491 b
Intercrop 25N	Cowpea	172 a
	Maize	190 a
Intercrop 100N	Cowpea	882 b
	Maize	1302 b

Statistical comparisons are within sole crop or within intercrop. Numbers followed by different letters are significantly different at $P = 0.05$.

The data presented here confirm those of others that N benefit may accrue to a cereal by intercropping with a grain legume. This phenomenon is significant to agricultural productivity only where levels of available N are low—a condition that often affects farmers in the tropics.

REFERENCES

Bartholomew, W.V. (1977) Soil nitrogen changes in farming systems in the humid tropics. *In*: Biological nitrogen fixation in farming systems of the tropics, A. Ayanaba & P.J. Dart (Eds.). Wiley, New York, NY, USA. Pp. 29-41.

Eaglesham, A.R.J., Minchin, F.R., Summerfield, R.J., Dart, P.J., Huxley, P.A., & Day, J.M. (1977) *Expl. Agric.* 13, 369-380.

Finlay, R.C. (1975) *INTSOY Series* 6, 77-85.

Ham, G.E. (1977) The acetylene-ethylene assay and other measures of nitrogen fixation in field experiments. *In*: Biological nitrogen fixation in farming systems of the tropics, A. Ayanaba & P.J. Dart (Eds.). Wiley, New York, NY, USA. Pp. 325-334.

Hardy, R. W. F. & Havelka, U.D. (1976) Photosynthate as a major factor limiting nitrogen fixation by field-grown legumes with emphasis on soybeans. *In*: Symbiotic nitrogen fixation in plants, P.S. Nutman (Ed.). Cambridge University Press, Cambridge, England. Pp. 421-439

NITROGEN FIXATION BY GROUNDNUT (*ARACHIS HYPOGAEA*) IN INTERCROPPED AND ROTATIONAL SYSTEMS

P.C.T. Nambiar, M.R. Rao, M.S. Reddy, C. Floyd, P.J. Dart, and R.W. Willey[1]

Summary

This paper examines the nodulation and nitrogen fixation of groundnut when grown in pure culture or in association with pearl millet, maize or sorghum. In all cases, association of groundnut with a cereal resulted in reduced nodulation and nitrogen fixation. This was ascribed to shading of the groundnut, leading to reduced photosynthesis. When grain millet was planted in rotation with groundnut or maize supplied 20 kg N/ha, yield following groundnut were 524 kg/ha greater than obtained in the millet/maize rotation.

INTRODUCTION

Legumes play a key role in many rotational and intercropping systems. In rotations part of the nitrogen (N_2) fixed by the legume can become available to subsequent crops; in intercropping systems, especially under small farm conditions, the ability of the legume to grow without N fertilization permits better allocation of limited resources, and lowers risk of total crop failure.

Surprisingly, there are few studies of the effects of intercropping on nodulation and N_2 fixation in legumes. Interplant competition has been shown to influence nodule function in *Phaseolus vulgaris* (Graham & Rosas, 1978a), *Trifolium subterraneum* (Phillips & Bennett, 1978) and *Vicia faba* (Sprent & Bradford, 1977). Interspecies competion between maize and beans did not affect the nodulation and N_2 fixation of a climbing cultivar of *Phaseolus vulgaris* (Graham & Rosas, 1978b), while in a soybean/sorghum intercrop, N_2 fixation by the soybean was markedly affected by association with tall, but not with dwarf, sorghum varieties (Wahua & Miller, 1978).

[1] CP No. 61, ICRISAT, Patancheru P.O., Andra Pradesh 502 324, India.

Groundnut (*Arachis hypogaea* L.) is grown in semiarid tropical regions, both as an intercrop and in rotations. In this paper we examine some effects of cropping pattern on N_2 fixation in groundnut and subsequent crop yield.

MATERIALS AND METHODS

In the three intercropping experiments reported here, we compare the nodulation and N_2 fixation of groundnut when grown in monoculture, and:

- When associated with maize at four different levels of applied N;
- When associated with sorghum partially defoliated to simulate different degrees of competition for light; and
- When associated with pearl millet.

In each case, the cereal and groundnut were grown in separate rows, with optimum sole crop plant-to-plant spacings, using ratios of 1 row millet:3 rows groundnut; 1 row sorghum:2 rows groundnut; and 1 row maize:2 rows groundnut. Both crops were sown at the same time, and received recommended fertilization, save for N. The sorghum/groundnut experiments were conducted during the post-rainy season; the others during the rainy season.

In the experiment with maize, 0, 50, 100, 150 kg N/ha was applied to the maize at planting, while in the experiment with sorghum, a range of groundnut cultivars were tested and in half the treatments alternate leaves of the sorghum were defoliated to enhance light penetration. In all experiments nodulation and N_2 fixation were measured throughout the growing season.

Two experiments to determine the benefit from groundnut to subsequent crops were also carried out. The first compared the yield of grain millet grown after groundnut, unfertilized maize, or maize supplied 20 kg N/ha; the second, also with grain millet, compared yield after groundnut, millet, or fallow.

RESULTS AND DISCUSSION

In all three crop combinations studied, intercropping reduced nodulation and N_2 fixation by the groundnut. With millet this inhibition occurred both with and without applied fertilizer N (see Figures 1 & 2). In the maize experiment N fertilization of the maize further reduced nodulation and N_2 fixation by the groundnut (see Table 1). However, nodule formation was less affected than nodule weight or nitrogenase activity, presumably because most nodules were formed before the cereal provided any substantial competition for light. The reduction in nitrogenase activity was most closely related to the reduction in nodule weight, with an 80% reduction in activity at the highest N fertilizer level (150 kg N/ha). Final yield per plant was also decreased at the high N levels. Our results suggest that N fertilizer effects are

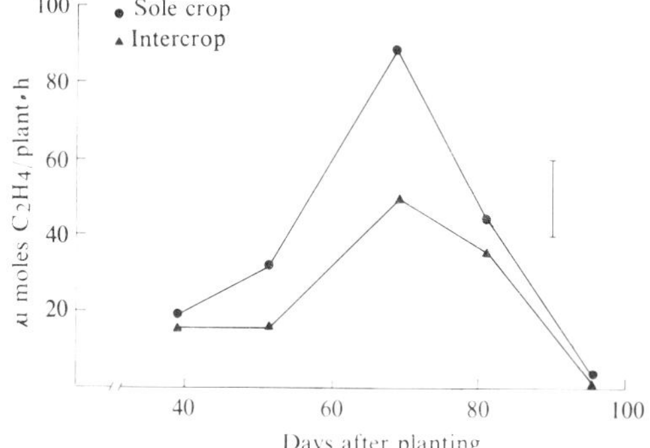

Figure 1.
Nitrogenase activity of groundnut in monoculture and intercropped with millet.

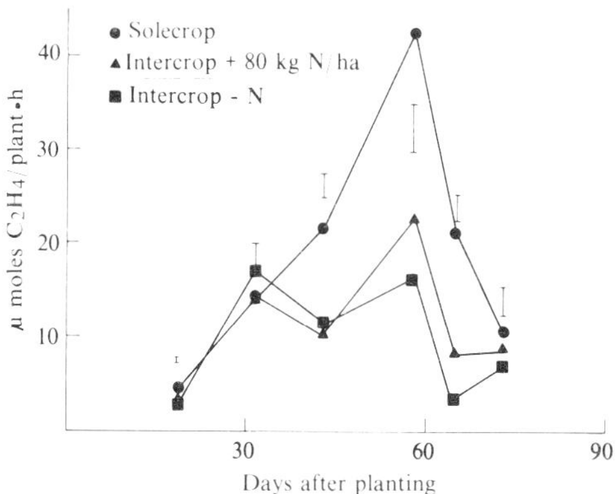

Figure 2.
Effect of intercropping with millet on nitrogenase activity of groundnut.

not directly on legume fixation, but rather due to the decrease in available light resulting from more vigorous growth of the cereal.

Decreasing the competition for light by the sorghum by removing alternate leaves increased the N_2 fixation by the intercropped groundnut (see Table 2). There was little difference between groundnut cultivars in this response. Even the sorghum with 50% of its leaves removed provided a substantial competition for the groundnut, and nodule number and nitrogenase activity per plant were both substantially less than for the sole crop. Top weight per plant was also decreased in the intercropped groundnut.

In the rotation experiments, grain millet grown in the irrigated post-rainy season yielded 45% more following the groundnut cultivar Robut 33-1 than when maize was the preceding crop (see Table 3). However, in a second experiment, where grain millet was grown following groundnut, millet, or fallow, there was no apparent yield benefit.

One of the earliest recognized advantages of a legume crop was the residual benefit for a subsequent crop. It has been suggested that some legumes excrete

TABLE 1: Nodulation and N_2 fixation of groundnut in sole culture and intercropped with maize.

Treatment	Nodule number/ plant	Nodule weight (mg/ plant)	Nitrogenase activity (μmoles C_2H_4/plant per h)	Light reaching groundnut canopy (%)
Sole groundnut	171	124	21.3	100
Intercropped groundnut N added to maize (kg/h)				
0	165	117	20.1	67
50	160	94	9.4	54
100	150	78	7.0	43
150	134	65	3.5	46
SEM ±	6.3	11.0	1.92	

some of the N_2 fixed into the soil during the growth of the crop, but present evidence suggests that the amounts involved under field conditions are small, and likely to be of little benefit to an intercrop (Henzell & Vallis, 1977). The main residual effect of a legume will depend on the proportion of N retained in nonharvested residues and their rate of mineralization. Clearly, the planting of groundnuts in association with cereals could limit the rate of N_2 fixation by the legume, and thus the benefits for subsequent crops. In an attempt to alleviate this, we are examining different groundnut and cereal genotypes for compatability and hope to find both groundnut cultivars more tolerant of low light intensities, and so able to maintain high levels of N_2 fixation in the intercropping situation, and cereal lines whose plant architecture permits light penetration. Adjusting season durations and sowing times of the two crops, relative to each other, also offers some scope for increasing fixation by the groundnut, since it changes the pattern of competion of the cereal in relation to the maximum period of nitrogenase activity of the groundnut.

TABLE 2: Nodulation and nitrogenase activity of five groundnut cultivars in sole culture and intercropped with sorghum.

Cultivar	Nodule number/plant			N_2ase activity (μ moles C_2H_4/plant·h)		
	Sole crop	Intercrop (partial sorghum canopy[1])	Intercrop (normal sorghum canopy)	Sole crop	Intercrop (partial sorghum canopy[1])	Intercrop (normal sorghum canopy)
Chico-17200	104	75	64	15.2	11.8	6.8
TMV-2	108	81	64	18.1	12.6	8.3
MK-374	190	137	100	25.8	23.6	12.2
Robut 33-1	118	86	75	21.5	15.9	12.2
MH 2	151	66	68	15.4	7.9	9.1
Gangapuri	137	84	62	15.7	10.6	6.5
SEM ±		11.38			1.36	

[1]70 days after planting, groundnut with a partial sorghum canopy received 57 % of the light, and that with a normal sorghum canopy received 42 % of the light intercepted by the sole crop.

TABLE 3: Residual effect of groundnut and maize on millet grain yield in an Alfisol.[1]

Preceding crop	Yield (kg/ha)
Groundnut	1980
Maize, unfertilized	1325
Maize, fertilized with 20 kg N/ha	1456
LSD (0.01)	360

[1]Groundnut and maize grown in rainy season 1977 at ICRISAT, followed by irrigated millet, in dry winter season 1977-78.

REFERENCES

Graham, P.H. & Rosas, J.C. (1978a) *J. Agric. Sci.* (Camb.) 90, 19-29.

Graham, P.H. & Rosas, J.C. (1978b) *J. Agric. Sci.* (Camb.) 90, 311-17.

Henzell, E.F. & Vallis, I. (1977) Transfer of nitrogen between legumes and other crops. *In:* Biological nitrogen fixation in farming systems of the tropics, A. Ayanab & P.J. Dart (Eds.). Wiley-Interscience, New York, NY, USA. Pp. 73-88.

Phillips, D.A. & Bennett, J.P. (1978) *Agron. J.* 70, 671-74.

Sprent, J.I. & Bradford, A.M. (1977) *J. Agric. Sci.* (Camb.) 88, 303-10.

Wahua, T.A.T. & Miller D.A. (1978) *Agron. J.* 70, 292-95.

EFFECT OF COWPEAS IN CEREAL ROTATIONS ON SUBSEQUENT CROP YIELDS UNDER SEMIARID CONDITIONS IN UPPER VOLTA

W.A. Stoop[1] and J.P. van Staveren[2]

Summary

In Upper Volta millet is grown on the relatively dry plateau and upper slope soils, whereas sorghum and maize are planted on the wetter lower slopes. Cowpeas are rotated and intercropped with each cereal. When sorghum without fertilization followed cowpea, yields were 225, 410, and 330 kg/ha more on upper, middle, and lower slopes, respectively, than when sorghum followed millet. Yields of millet were affected by both the cultivar of cowpea used in the rotation and its planting density. Time of plowing also affected the benefits from prior cropping with cowpea.

INTRODUCTION

Upper Volta can be divided into three broad ecological zones with rainfall increasing from 400 mm in the Sahelian zone to more than 1000 mm in the South Sudanian region (see Table 1). The crops grown in each region are linked closely with rainfall pattern, with millet predominant in the north, sorghum and millet in the center, and sorghum and maize in the south.

However, the major soil types commonly present in toposequences will also affect crop use, with millet grown on the relatively dry soils of the plateau and upper slopes and sorghum and maize planted more on the moist lower slopes. Cereal yields in these systems tend to be low (of the order of 500 kg/ha) and the use of fertilizer restricted; so the presence of a legume intercrop or sole crop in the rotation may be an important factor in maintaining soil productivity.

---

[1] Royal Tropical Institute, Mauritskade 63, Amsterdam, The Netherlands.
[2] ICRISAT/PNUD, BP 1165, Ouagadougou, Upper Volta.

TABLE 1: Characterization of the rainfall pattern in three major ecological zones in Upper Volta.

Ecological zone	Mean annual rainfall (mm)	Approx. start of rainy season	Duration of rainy season (months)	Approx. no. of rainy days	Peak rainfall months
South Sudanian zone	$>$1000	May	5 to 6	80 to 95	Jul., Aug. Sept.
North Sudanian zone	650-1000	June	4 to 5	60 to 70	Jul., Aug.
Sahelian zone	$<$ 650	July	2.5 to 4	40 to 50	Aug.

MATERIALS AND METHODS

The three experiments reported here are part of a larger study on legume/cereal rotations and management undertaken by ICRISAT in Upper Volta.

Management trial for a shallow gravelly soil

This trial combined three soil preparation treatments (no plowing; plowing in October after harvest; plowing in May before planting), with two crop residue treatments (with or without removal of residues after harvest) and with two crop rotations (cereal/cereal or cowpea/cereal). Thc cxperimental design was a 3 x 2 x 2 factorial with three replications laid out as a split plot with soil preparation treatments as major blocks.

Cowpea management trial in rotation with millet

The trial was part of a largc sorghum/cowpea intercropping trial at Kamboinse in 1979, which was planted to millet in 1980. The various intercropping treatments had no significant effect on the subsequent millet crop, but the pure cowpea treatments did, and therefore, they were analyzed as a separate experiment. In this trial three cowpea cultivars, varying in plant type and in days to flower were each sown at two different plant densities. In the following year millet was planted and its yield determined.

Nakomtenga toposequence - fertility and rotation trial

The trial was initiated on land of a local village in 1979 and linked crop responses (cowpea, millet, sorghum, and maize) to soil types present in a toposequence. In 1979, the area came out of a long-term fallow and no fertilizer was applied. In 1980, the cowpea and millet strip were again left unfertilized, and planted to sorghum; the other strips received 100 kg 14-24-15 compound fertilizer/ha before planting pure sorghum and a sorghum/cowpea intercrop. In an adjacent strip the farmer applied the same chemical fertilizer rate, but in addition added manure (~ 6, t/ha).

RESULTS AND DISCUSSION

While high coefficients of variation are a major obstacle to the interpretation of results, there can be little doubt that the inclusion of cowpea in the cereal rotation had beneficial effects. Figure 1 shows that enhanced yield of sorghum after cowpea occurred for all three methods of soil preparation, including the traditional hand cultivation. A possible criticism of this trial is that at least part of the apparent benefit of cowpea could be due to allelopathic effects in continuous sorghum rotations. For this reason millet was used as the test crop in the Nakomtenga trial. Results for this trial are summarized in Table 2. When sorghum without fertilization followed cowpea, yields were 225, 410 and 330 kg/ha more on the upper, middle and lower slopes, respectively, than after millet.

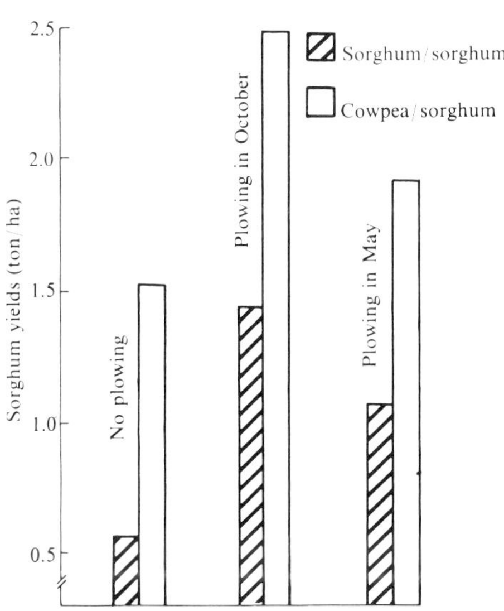

Figure 1.
Effects of plowing and time of plowing on sorghum grain yields for sorghum/sorghum and cowpea/sorghum rotations.

An important aspect of the data in Table 2 is that, by selecting suitable positions on a slope (mainly linked to the soil moisture situation), and by a correct rotation, relatively high yields can still be obtained, even without chemical fertilizers. The drop of sorghum yield on the upper slope can be compensated for by switching to millet, which under similar conditions in the same field yielded from 500 kg grain/ha (no fertilizer; previous crop millet) to 1000 kg grain/ha (100 kg cotton fertilizer; previous crop millet).

Benefits from cowpea in the rotation will obviously depend on management practices and varieties used. This is evident in Table 3, which compares the effect of three cultivars and two planting densities of cowpea, grown in one season, on subsequent millet yields. In this trial both cowpea planting density and the variety x density interaction had significant effects on the yield of the following millet crop. While the local cultivar with its spreading growth habit required less seed/unit area to achieve ground cover and enhance millet yields, one would require long-term data providing information on the

TABLE 2: Comparisons between grain yields for four crops obtained at different toposequence positions (1979) and sorghum grain yields from the same plots in 1980 as affected by rotation in absence of fertilizers (F_0) or with fertilizer treatments (F_1 = 100 kg 14:24:15 compound/ha; M ~ 6 tons manure/ha).

1979 treatments	1979 grain yields (kg/ha)		
	Upper slope (dry)	Mid-slope (moist)	Lower slope (wet)
Cowpea (F_0)	350	360	150
Millet (F_0)	400	380	80
Sorghum (F_0)	320	320	125
Maize (F_0)	0	0	0
Previous crop and soil treatment	**1980 sorghum yields (kg/ha)**		
	Upper slope	Mid-slope	Lower slope
Cowpea (F_0)	465	1115	925
Millet (F_0)	245	605	595
Sorghum (F_1)			
	1155	1010	1200
Maize (F_1)			
Sorghum (F_1 + M) (farmer's field)	1575	1635	2055

TABLE 3: Rotational effects of three cowpea varieties planted at two plant densities each on a subsequent millet crop.

Cowpea varieties	Plant type	Days to 50% flowering	1979 cowpea plant density (pl/ha)	1980 millet grain yields (kg/ha)
Kamboinse local	Spreading, photosensitive	70	11,250 22,500	620 1600
KN-1	"Semi-spreading," non-photosensitive	47	22,500 45,000	860 1040
TVx1193-9F	Erect, non-photosensitive	40	45,000 90,000	690 800

maintenance of soil fertility, economic returns, and the risk associated with using the later-maturing cultivar, before recommending a particular cropping system.

Given the response of subsequent crops to pure cowpea stands, the question arises as to the benefit to be derived by cereal crops following cereal/cowpea intercrops. Clearly this will be a more complex situation with important points being the extent of competition, time of planting, and fertilizer influences.

RESIDUAL EFFECTS OF PIGEONPEA (*CAJANUS CAJAN*)

J.V.D.K. Kumar Rao, P.J. Dart and P.V.S. Subrahmanya Sastry[1]

Summary

An experiment conducted on a Vertisol field at ICRISAT compared the residual effect of monocropped pigeonpea, intercropped pigeonpea/sorghum (1 row:2 rows) with 0 and 80 kg N/ha, monocropped sorghum with 0 and 80 kg N/ha, and fallow treatments on a subsequent maize crop. Monocropped pigeonpea had a large residual effect on maize, increasing the grain yield by 57% and total plant dry matter by 32% over fallow. Intercropped pigeonpea had little residual effect on maize. Benefits from a previous crop of monocropped pigeonpea were equivalent to about 40 kg N/ha applied to the maize crop grown in land kept fallow during the previous rainy season.

INTRODUCTION

While the role of legumes in maintaining agricultural productivity in temperate regions is well documented, there are few papers showing benefits from grain legumes in the tropics. In Nigeria a previous groundnut crop increased the yield of a subsequent maize crop (Jones, 1974). Giri & De (1979) reported that yields of pearl millet were significantly increased when grown after legume crops such as groundnut (22.6%), cowpea (24.2%), or pigeonpea (12.1%), instead of after pearl millet.

Pigeonpea (*Cajanus cajan*) is an important grain legume of the semiarid tropics. In India it is grown mostly as an intercrop with sorghum, millet or maize, but it is also planted in monoculture. There is little information on the residual effect of pigeonpea grown as either a sole or intercrop on the availability of soil N for subsequent cereal crops. Because of this we conducted an experiment to test the growth and yield of maize when grown after pigeonpea in monocrop or intercropped with sorghum.

[1] ICRISAT, Patancheru P.O., Andra Pradesh 502324, India.

MATERIALS AND METHODS

Six treatments were compared for residual effect:

Pigeonpea, monoculture.
Sorghum, monoculture, with 0 N applied.
Sorghum, monoculture, with 80 kg/ha N applied.
Sorghum/pigeonpea intercropped with 0 N.
Sorghum/pigeonpea intercropped with 80 N.
Fallow.

They were planted in 1979 in randomized plots 50 m x 6 m, replicated four times in a split plot design. The soil used was a Vertisol with 0.03% total N (0-30 cm depth), 40 ppm available N, and 4 ppm available P. Single superphosphate was broadcast before planting to supply 17 kg P/ha.

Sorghum cv. CSH-6 (3.5 months duration) and pigeonpea cv. ICP-1 (maturity about 6 months) were sown alone, or in a constant arrangement of two rows of sorghum to one row of pigeonpea, in rows 45 cm apart on broad beds of width 1.5 m. The pigeonpea seed was inoculated with peat inoculant containing a mixture of four effective *Rhizobium* strains. The crops were grown under rainfed conditions. At harvest, observations on grain yield and biological yield were taken, and all aboveground plant parts were removed, except for fallen plant parts of pigeonpea.

In 1980, the former main treatments were divided into subplots, each 9x5 m, and received 0, 20, 40, 60, or 80 kg N/ha, applied as urea. The 60 and 80 kg N/ha treatments were split, with 40 kg N/ha applied before planting and the remainder after two months. The whole area was then planted to 'Deccan hybrid 101' maize, at a spacing of 75 cm between rows and 20 cm between plants. At maturity, observations on grain yield and biological yield were made on plots 7x3 m.

RESULTS AND DISCUSSION

Seed and total top yields of pigeonpea and sorghum grown as sole or intercrops in the 1970 planting are given in Table 1. The yields were normal for the cultivars in this environment. Total land equivalent ratios (LER's) for the intercrops showed a yield advantage of 47% and 37% in grain and plant top dry matter yields, respectively, over monoculture pigeonpea and sorghum (see Table 1). However, at 80 kg N, the yield advantage of intercropping was less than at 0 kg N/ha, suggesting more effective utilization of available resources by intercropping under limitations of land, water and nutrients.

Grain yield of maize grown without N in the 1980 planting was significantly affected by the crop planted in 1979; the most beneficial effect being that from pigeonpea in monoculture (see Table 2). Maize after sole cropped pigeonpea significantly outyielded maize following fallow, sole cropped sorghum, and sorghum/pigeonpea intercrop, with or without N, in 1979. This superiority

TABLE 1: Seed and total top dry matter yield (kg/ha) of crops grown in the first year (rainy season, 1979).

Treatment		Seed yield		Total dry matter	
		Sole	LER[1]	Sole	LER
Pigeonpea		1630	1.0	6040	1.0
Sorghum at 0 kg N		3950	1.0	9870	1.0
Sorghum at 80 kg N		5000	1.0	12610	1.0
Sorghum/pigeonpea at 0 kg N	S	3800	0.96	9035	0.92
	P	840	0.51	2690	0.45
	S + P		1.47		1.37
Sorghum/pigeonpea at 80 kg N/ha	S	4730	0.95	11550	0.92
	P	680	0.42	2460	0.41
	S + P		137		1.33
Fallow		0	–	0	–

[1]LER – Land equivalent ratio: the relative land area required for sole crop(s) to produce the yield(s) achieved in intercropping. An LER of 0.5 for a given crop indicates that it has produced in intercropping the equivalent of 50 % of its sole crop yield.

TABLE 2: Effect of previous cropping and fertilizer treatments on grain yields of maize (kg/ha) (rainy season, 1980).

Previous crop	N fertilization in the 1980 planting (kg/ha)					Mean
	0	20	40	60	80	
Pigeonpea	1364	2095	2595	3153	4385	2720
Sorghum at 0 kg N	300	620	1450	1924	2963	1450
Sorghum at 80 kg N	508	954	1373	2105	3463	1680
Sorghum/pigeonpea at 0 kg N	768	861	1406	2236	2956	1650
Sorghum/pigeonpea at 80 kg N	629	1064	1893	2148	3411	1830
Fallow	530	898	1387	2765	3086	1730
Mean	680	1080	1680	2390	3380	

Comparison of Means	S.E. of means
Previous crops	± 119
Nitrogen rates	± 85
Previous crops x N rates	± 220

was maintained with the treatments receiving additional N, although the magnitude of the yield difference varied. In terms of total biological yield, pigeonpea as a sole crop again had the maximum beneficial effect (see Table 3). There were significant differences in response between the levels of N applied to maize but no significant interaction between the effects of previous crops and the rates of N applied to maize. In terms of both grain yield and total dry matter, yields of maize following pigeonpea in monoculture were similar to maize yields obtained with 40 kg N following sorghum or fallow. In the absence of applied N, intercropped pigeonpea only provided a small benefit — it is evident from Table 1 that its growth and yield were only half that of sole pigeonpea.

Although the mechanism has not been clarified, the present experiment shows the beneficial effect of pigeonpea as a sole crop on following maize, increasing grain yield by 57% and dry matter by 32% over fallow. A feature of pigeonpea growth in this environment is the considerable leaf fall, calculated to provide 30-40 kg N/ha (Sheldrake & Narayanan, 1979). There is clearly a need to further examine this and other potential sources of the N that has apparently been made available to the subsequent crop.

TABLE 3: Effect of previous cropping and fertilizer treatments on total top dry matter yield of maize (kg/ha) (rainy season, 1980).

Previous crop	N fertilization in the 1980 planting (kg/ha)					Mean
	0	20	40	60	80	
Pigeonpea	5925	7842	8856	8863	11016	8500
Sorghum at 0 kg N	2177	3945	6148	6651	8901	5560
Sorghum at 80 kg N	2249	4547	6292	6922	9175	5840
Sorghum/pigeonpea at 0 kg N	3267	4618	5979	7175	8574	5920
Sorghum/pigeonpea at 80 kg N	3049	5176	7177	6941	9150	6300
Fallow	3129	4931	6466	8550	9089	6430
Mean	3300	5180	6820	7520	9320	

Comparison of means	S.E. of means
Previous crops	± 295
Nitrogen rates	± 178
Previous crops x N rates	± 488

REFERENCES

Giri, G. & De, R. (1979) *Expl. Agric.* 15, 169-172.

Jones, M.J. (1974) *Expl. Agric.* 10, 273-279.

Sheldrake, A.R. & Narayanan, A. (1979) *J. Agric. Sci.* (Camb.) 92, 513-526.

A TECHNOLOGY ASSESSMENT OF BIOLOGICAL NITROGEN FIXATION

R.H. Randolph and B. Koppel[1]

Summary

The varied and rapidly developing technologies for biological nitrogen fixation (BNF) offer important possibilities for reducing mankind's dependence on fertilizers manufactured from fossil fuels. Many uncertainties exist, not only about the feasibility of certain new technologies (e.g., nitrogen-fixing cereals), but also about the many socio-economic factors which may affect, or be affected by, widespread application of technologies which would improve currently achievable rates of N_2 fixation or extend the range of species which benefit.

This paper describes a proposed "technology assessment" of BNF, aimed at clarifying these uncertainties through case-study examination of two crops (rice and corn) in two countries (the Philippines and the USA). The goal is not to determine whether BNF will "work" for these crops but to identify possible future developments in BNF technology relevant to these crops and to examine systematically: the societal factors which may influence the rate and scope of utilization for such new technologies; the broad range of effects that may ensue if and when such technologies are introduced on a large scale; and the policy options implied for both government and the private sector by all of the foregoing. This paper details initial issue and uncertainties, research objectives and foci and method and organization for this study.

INTRODUCTION

In thinking of the future of biological nitrogen fixation (BNF) technology and the policy issues raised by its present rapid development, the question is

[1] East-West Center, Resource Systems Institute, 1777 East-West Road, Honolulu, Hawaii 96848, USA.

definitely not, "Will it work?" Most BNF technologies already work, and produce N available for plant intake. The question rather is, "What if it works?"

Partial answers to this question have been offered from time to time, but they have tended to be mainly technical in focus (National Science Foundation, 1977; Döbereiner *et al.*, 1978). Technical evaluations of this kind are, of course, extremely important. We must not forget, however, that for most of the world, agriculture remains the *economic* activity on which most developed societies depend. Even in the most developed societies, agriculture is a major part of the economic system. It can be argued, then, that answers to the question, "What if it works?" should be couched at least partly in non-technological terms and should be arrived at through a process that explores the complex socio-economic consequences likely to follow from the use of different levels and patterns of a particular technology. Such a process can suggest and publicize the socio-economic benefits of the technology or provide advance warning about potential difficulties, facilitating their removal or circumvention. To have meaning such an assessment of BNF technology would need to be both multi-disciplinary and international in scope.

Recognizing these points the East-West Center Resource Systems Institute has instituted a plan for an international technology assessment of BNF. In the remainder of this paper we shall offer some initial ideas on the framework for such an assessment, touch on key issues, research objectives and methods.

ISSUES AND UNCERTAINTIES

The many specific issues that would need to be addressed in a technology assessment of BNF can be grouped into three overall questions:

What are the major societal factors which will influence the rate and scope of utilization?

Who will be affected by changes in BNF technologies, and in what ways?

What are the major policy issues that emerge from answering the above questions?

Societal factors affecting rate and scope of utilization

Several main types of variables can be identified which seem likely to affect the rate and scope of utilization of any given BNF technology. The large number and interrelated character of these variables clearly demonstrate the complexity of the technical assessment problem.

Anticipated physical effects, on N availability, soil condition, evolution of pest biotypes, etc., and, in the last analysis, on crop yield.

Anticipated economic effects, including savings through fertilizer substitution; costs for complementary fertilizers, land preparation, pest control, product transportation, etc.; and size and distribution of net farm income. Most of these costs and savings can also be measured in energy terms, for analyses in which this measurement is more useful.

Related technologies and technological conditions, such as cropping and crop management patterns; soil and hydrological regimes; risks and risk aversion propensities; energy availability, and hence fertilizer cost; national technological endowments; etc.

Agricultural organization, including farm size and ownership patterns, rural population structure, marketing systems, economic policies affecting agriculture, etc.

Regulatory constraints governing quality control, health hazards, hazards to non-host plants, etc.

Legal issues in such areas as technology ownership, licensing, and transfer; testing and liability, etc.

Import/export strategies and agreements, including trade policies regarding fertilizer, food, non-food agricultural commodities, etc., and links with international commodity markets.

Parties at interest

Here, too, the question is far from simple. There are a number of societal groups that are likely to be affected by changes in BNF technology, and that should, therefore, be considered in the technology assessment.

Farmers, with sub-groupings by farm size, tenure, ethnicity, market position, type of crop, type of land, etc.

Agribusiness firms, including producers, processors, export/import firms, etc.

Nitrogen fertilizer industry.

BNF-support industry, e.g., inoculant manufacturers.

Research and development community, with sub-groupings by field of activity.

Consumers, with sub-groupings by geographical location (domestic/foreign, urban/rural), socio-economic status.

Government agencies concerned with food and agriculture, energy, commerce, human settlements, environment protection, science and technology, etc.

Policy issues

Although many more policy issues would emerge from the technology assessment itself, several policy-relevant issues which are likely to arise regarding implementation of new BNF technologies are already obvious. Most of them lie outside the purview of technology assessment *per se* and must be left for eventual resolution by policy-making bodies, but the technology study should at least help to clarify options and implications.

What types of farmers and other stakeholders should benefit?

Can others be permitted to suffer loss?

What help will farmers need to ensure that they have access to the technology, use it properly, etc.?

What types of crops should get priority emphasis?

How can R&D be managed and supported over time to ensure that end?

How would associated technologies, such as minimum tillage, be evaluated in trade-off terms with BNF technologies?

What should be agriculture's role in national energy planning?

What is agriculture's role in economic development scenarios?

Where is the research done? Principally in the public or private sector? What if BNF techniques, for example inoculant preparations, are proprietary? If they are proprietary in the US, how is a country like the Philippines likely to respond?

RESEARCH OBJECTIVES AND FOCI

Coates (1976) defined technology assessment as:

> ". . . a class of policy studies which systematically examine the effects on society that may occur when a technology is introduced, extended, or modified. It emphasizes those consequences that are unintended, indirect, or delayed."

Technology assessments generally feature (Koppel, 1979):

A holistic and systemic rather than reductionist perspective.

An orientation toward the future.

A concern for higher-order impacts, i.e., the effects of effects

A concern for irreversibility, particularly in undesired effects.

A concern for sustainability, particularly in desired effects.

A concern for values and goals.

A concern for identification and evaluation of alternatives.

Practical objectives (Porter *et al.*, 1980) of technology assessments are:

To provide valid information on the likely consequences of certain courses of action.

To have this information prove useful to the policy making process.

For the technological assessment of BNF we are proposing to focus on rice and corn as the crops to be studied, and to consider their situation in the USA and Philippines.

For much of the world's population, rice is the mainstay of life. The United States, though not a leading rice consumer, is the world's largest rice exporter, a fact that has significant implications for the southeast US in particular. The Philippines is illustrative of many countries in the developing world that look to rice as their principal grain, that have been the basic setting for the playing out of the "green revolution," that have traditionally been major importers of rice, and that have rice economies that have been, and will continue to be, significantly impacted by rising costs of petrochemical products such as N fertilizers.

The US is the world's leading producer of corn, a commodity that plays numerous roles in the US food system and that also has a large and important international market. N fertilizer applied annually in the US to corn accounts for half the total N fertilizer applied in the US. The Philippines, like many developing countries, depends on corn as an animal feed as well as basic human food for the poorer sections of the population. Philippine production has been constrained by the planting of corn on poorer soils, usually by poorer farmers, with very low applications of fertilizer. Moreover, the economic status of the corn economy in the Philippines is significantly influenced by the large volume of US production.

Because considerable data are available on both crops in both countries, and because alternate BNF and fertilizer technologies can be identified, the choice of crops and countries is both significant in policy terms and operationally feasible.

Precise specification of alternate technologies will be an essential task in the first phase of this project. For rice in the Philippines alternate, or perhaps complementary, strategies would be: development of cropping systems that depend on legume grain or cover crops after rice; the utilization of *Azolla* and/or heterotrophic N_2 fixers to maintain soil N balance; and the genetic manipulation of rice plants to enhance their potential to fix N_2 in association. In the southern USA rice is often alternated with soybeans or cowpeas, but this practice is less common in California. Studies on *Azolla* have also been initiated in the USA, but as currently managed, green manuring with *Azolla* is a labor-intensive activity.

Corn in the Philippines is grown principally in upland areas unsuited to rice. It is already extensively intercropped with legumes, but often these are not inoculated. N_2 fixation can also suffer from N fertilizer applied to the maize. Use of *Azolla* for corn is still in the university research/extension phase. Multiple cropping has not been practiced extensively in the USA, but it is now being studied in more detail. Maize soybean rotations are an integral part of midwestern US agriculture.

METHODS AND ORGANIZATION

Various methodologies have been proposed for technological assessment projects (National Academy of Engineering, 1969; Mitre, 1971; OECD, 1975;

Coates, 1976; Armstrong & Harmsen, 1977). We have synthesized these approaches in Table 1.

Although numerous authors have recognized the potential importance of internationalizing technological assessment (TA) (Weisband & Franck, 1971; OECD, 1975; Chen & Zacher, 1978), the difficulties involved in this are considerable. Because TA is concerned largely with the acceptance of new technology by a given society, its "content and concept" will depend on the social and cultural background of that society (Oshima, 1975). Chen & Zacher (1978) offer a potentially promising approach to internationally oriented

TABLE 1: A possible sequence for the technology assessment of BNF technology.

Preparation Phase

1. Identification of need
2. Definition of problem
3. Definition of scope, methods, etc.

Descriptive Phase

4. Development of data base
5. Description of present
6. Projection of future changes in the technology
7. Specification of systems alternatives for assessment
8. Description of state-of-society assumptions
9. Description of decision apparatus
10. Identification of other parties at interest
11. Identification of exogenous and international variables or events

Assessment Phase

12. Identification of impact areas
13. Measurement (prediction) of impacts
14. Evaluation of impacts

Policy Analysis Phase

15. Elaboration of action options
16. Evaluation of action options
17. Identification of macrosystems alternatives
18. Preparation of conclusions and recommendations

Validation Phase

19. Validation and final report

---

technology assessment. Briefly, they suggest explicit joint examination of the differences and similarities between the two (or more) societies' premises and processes relevant to TA. Examples of premises are the degree of unity or convergence in social values and the presence or absence of socially managed technology. Processes include the roles of the private sector, the multinational corporations, and various social formations in the planning process. In the proposed study, it will be necessary to examine such variables for the two countries involved as part of the initial background research.

Our proposed assessment of BNF will be divided into the three phases.

Preparatory/descriptive phase: In this phase we will review existing knowledge about BNF and the rice and corn agricultural systems in the US and the Philippines; identify the most crucial technological and institutional uncertainties linked to probable policy-specific impacts; indicate those data and judgments that will be needed to examine those uncertainties, thus defining the scope of the TA; and develop a coherent framework for actually implementing the analysis, including both data and an appropriate set of analytic procedures.

Assessment/policy analysis phase: In this phase we will describe alternative futures, based on different assumptions about political, economic, social, and institutional changes, the rate at which BNF technology diffuses, the relative roles of government and the private sector, the distribution of socio-economic costs and benefits, and the values assigned to competing goals (e.g., equity and efficiency, long-term energy goals, short-term productivity goals); identify possible unplanned and higher-order institutional and policy effects of BNF; and compare alternative policy choices and actions, with emphasis on the potential benefits, costs, uncertainties, and risks likely to be involved.

Validation phase: During this phase we will evaluate and review our assessment, debate its implications, and plan to monitor real-world activities with implications for our assessment.

DESCRIPTION OF ACTIVITIES

A steering committee with persons chosen for pre-eminence in the issue areas likely to be important to the BNF technology assessment will be established. An assessment planning workshop with panels to consider socio-economic, policy institutional, and technological implications of BNF technologies will be convened to consider the broad range of questions involved in a technical assessment of BNF.

Data, identified in the workshop as crucial for implementation of the BNF assessment will be located and made available to an assessment team. This team of six people selected from different disciplinary perspectives, together with additional short-term consultants, will be responsible for most of the assessment work, including simulation modeling and other policy-oriented forms of data analysis. Evaluation panels will also be constituted to review the assessment made by the team. These will be composed of persons from the planning workshop, persons from relevant policy and use audiences, and representatives from countries where the assessment could have significant impact. They will be charged with evaluating the assessment in the light of questions asked at the planning meeting and its implications in their own areas of expertise. A final report having an outline such as shown in Table 2 will be prepared.

TABLE 2: Possible outline for final report. (Adapted from Lawless 1977).

1. Introduction.
2. Nitrogen use in agriculture: Needs, methods, and international comparisons.
3. Manufactured nitrogen fertilizers: History, industry and marketing, benefits, disbenefits and controversies.
4. Current status and trends in biological nitrogen fixation technologies.
5. Technological forecast: State-of-society factors, R&D trends, use of manufactured nitrogen fertilizers, diffusion of BNF.
6. Consequences of substituting BNF for manufactured nitrogen fertilizers: Agronomic, environmental, socio-economic, institutional-political.
7. Policy-making arenas: Parties at interest, goals and values, policy-making processes.
8. Policy issues and options: Incentives for R&D, incentives/controls on supply and use, other issues.
9. References.
10. Appendix: study methodology.

REFERENCES

Armstrong, J.E. & Harman, W.W. (1977) Strategies for conducting technology assessment. Stanford Univ., Department of Engineering—Economic Systems, Stanford, CA, USA.

Chen, K. & Zacher, L. (1978) Toward effective international technology assessment. *In*: Systems assessment of new technology: International perspectives, G.M.

Dobroy, R.H. Randolph, & W.D. Rauch (Eds.). CP-78-8. International Institute for Applied Systems Analysis, Loxenburg, Australia. Pp. 1-12.

Coates, J.F. (1976) Technology assessment — A tool kit. *Chemtech*. Pp. 372-383.

Döbereiner, J., *et al.* (Eds.) (1978) Limitations and potentials for biological nitrogen fixation in the tropics. Plenum, New York, NY, USA.

Koppel, B. (1979) The changing functions of research management: Technology assessment and the challenges to contemporary agricultural research organization. *Agric. Admin.* 6, 123-129.

Lawless, E.W. *et al.* (1977) A technology assessment of biological substitutes for chemical pesticides. (Final report.) Midwest Research Institute, Kansas City, MO, USA.

Mitre Corporation (1971) A technology assessment methodology. Vol. 1. Mitre Corp. Washington, D.C., USA.

National Academy of Engineering (NAE) (1969) A study of technology assessment. US House of Representatives, Committee on Science and Technology, Washington, D.C., USA.

National Science Foundation (NSF) (1977) Genetic engineering for nitrogen fixation. NSF, Washington, D.C., USA.

OECD (1975) Methodological guidelines for social assessment of technology. OECD, Paris, France.

Oshima, K. (1975) Practical use of technology assessment. *In*: Methodological guidelines for social assessment of technology. OECD, Paris, France.

Porter, A.L., *et al.* (1980) A guidebook for technology assessment and impact analysis. Elsevier, North-Holland, New York, NY, USA.

Weisband, E. & Franck, T.M. (1971) A rationale for international technology assessment. Towards an ethical science. New York Univ. Center for Internat. Studies, New York, NY, USA.

ECONOMIC ANALYSIS OF BIOLOGICAL NITROGEN FIXATION

D.E. Welsch[1]

Summary

The economic benefits from nitrogen (N_2) fixation are assumed to be substantial, but have rarely been documented, even for the more temperate regions. This paper considers briefly the economic tools that could be used in the economic evaluation of N_2 fixation by legumes and mentions the need for a parallel investigation of the social and private profitability of inoculation. A number of the constraints to a detailed economic analysis of inoculant usage are discussed.

INTRODUCTION

App, in the opening paper for this workshop, stressed that we have had ample time to establish our research programs, and that we must now demonstrate how biological nitrogen (N_2) fixation can profitably increase yields in farmers' fields. In this paper I want to discuss some of the problems associated with undertaking an economic analysis of inoculant technologies.

ECONOMICS OF FARM PRODUCTION AND MANAGEMENT

The economic analysis of agricultural production deals with the allocation of scarce resources among alternative and competing uses such that an objective function is maximized, subject to certain constraints. The constraints are resource availabilities, and the objective is usually profit maximization. The objectives, however, can contain other goals set by the unit doing the allocating. *Scarce* and *competing* are the key concepts.

Prices of resources are derived from their scarcity and the competing uses in which they can be employed productively. Increased scarcity, indicated by

[1] Dept. of Agricultural Economics, University of Minnesota, St. Paul, MN, 55108, USA.

rising prices, induces farmers both to moderate their uses of such resources and to use alternate resources. Such normal market behavior is currently even evident in the oil and natural gas cartel, in that consumption of these products has declined markedly, with enormous investments in alternate energy sources. The same applies to nitrogenous fertilizers.

We have heard repeatedly in this meeting of rising fertilizer prices, and of the difficulty that farmers in third world countries have in obtaining and paying for them. Legume inoculation provides a potential substitute; what is required is an evaluation of both its profitability and the likelihood of its adoption by farmers. In turn, profitability as an objective will probably be moderated by consideration of risk factors; not only of the risks involved in utilizing inoculants and legume-based cropping systems, but also of the risks involved in the use of fertilizer N, often under conditions of uncertain rainfall, limiting response to the fertilizer.

Moreover, a complete evaluation would include what economists call the "social profitability" of inoculant technology, i.e., a profitability assessment of the technology at the opportunity cost for pricing domestic factors of production rather than at often "distorted" market prices. The reason for doing this kind of analysis is that, if private profitability is so low that adoption is unlikely, but the social profitability is high, then government policy can be bought to bear to increase private profitability and enhance adoption. This might well apply in a number of third world situations where the cost of imported N fertilizer can be a real, and increasingly severe, drain on a country's balance of payments (i.e., the opportunity cost of foreign exchange to the economy is high), a strain that might well be reduced by the promotion of inoculant usage.

The focus in this paper, however, is on evaluating farmer adoption, particularly in terms of private profitability. We can evaluate profitability using the principle of equimarginal returns; that is that profit is maximized when the last unit of a resource applied raises production by a value equal to the cost of the resource input. In other words marginal cost equals marginal return (MC=MR). The MC=MR condition must apply for all competing uses of the input. This concept is expressed graphically in Figure 1a. In this figure X_1 and X_2 are the inputs needed to produce a product Y. The paired lines 1, 2, 3, 4, etc., represent different levels of production of Y. At each level of production the curved line—or isoproduct line—shows the possible combinations of inputs X_1 and X_2 that would give that level of production while the straight line—or isocost line—represents a fixed amount of expenditure all spent on X_1 or X_2, or on some combination of these in producing Y.

In this diagram, and at each level of production there is a point where the isocost line is tangential to the isoproduct line. This point represents the least-cost combination (LCC) of X_1 and X_2 to produce Y. If we join these points of tangency (LCC), then the line formed is called an expansion path, and

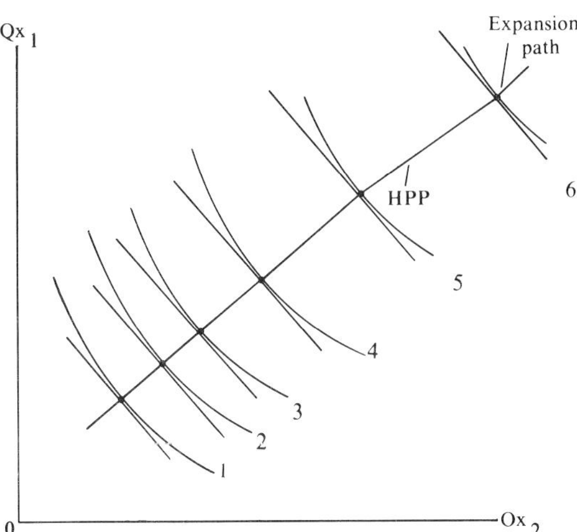

Figure 1a.
Factor x factor diagram.

represents the most profitable way to move up the response surface. At some point on that path, MC = MR, and profit will be maximized. Exactly the same principle can be used in studying a range of products within a farming system. In Figure 1b, Y_1 and Y_2 are different products; the curved line —or production possibilities frontier—represents the maximum amount of Y_1 and Y_2 that can be produced by the bundle of resources controlled by the farmer. The straight line, PP, is the ratio of the prices received for Y_1 and Y_2. The point of tangency in this case (C) is the point at which the profit-maximizing combination of Y_1 and Y_2 is realized.

Profit maximization criteria can be applied both to evaluation of past production activities and to planning future farm production. Normally the economist must collect data from a number of farms and treat each farm as an observation and a point on the response surface. The trouble with this approach is that in most farming areas, a majority of the farmers apply about the same level of input, and so we get a cluster of observations around the mean and our estimation of the surface is not stable. Because of this, it is usually difficult to establish whether or not farmers are maximizing profits. To do this we have to build a model in which profit is maximized, and then compare the actual farmers' enterprise with that model. If there is a divergence, we must explain why. This may lead us into areas of risk aversion and constraints on resources that were not recognized in the ideal model, and into household goals other than profit maximization.

Even building the ideal model can be difficult. The main problem is obtaining sufficient data for the determination of a response surface. When agronomic experiments are conducted on farmers' fields, and include enough input levels to estimate response surfaces, we can extrapolate such data to farmers' conditions and determine the profit-maximizing input combination.

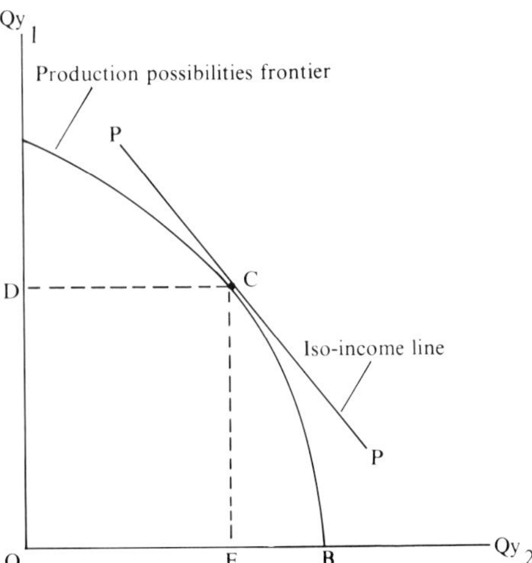

Figure 1b.
Product x product diagram.

Unfortunately such experiments are mostly conducted on experiment stations. Commonly then we must establish an enterprise budget, developed from response surface data, partial budgeting, and discussion with farmers, which details farm operations and costs, farm inputs, and product levels and prices on sale. These enterprise budgets can then be used in whole-farm budgeting or linear program studies.

FARMING SYSTEMS RESEARCH

There are numerous definitions of a farming system and of the research methods by which it is studied. Norman (1980) states that, "a specific farming system arises from the decision taken by a small farmer or a farming family with respect to allocating different quantities of land, labor, capital and management to crop, livestock, and off farm enterprises in a manner which, given the knowledge the household possess, will maximize the attainment of the family goals." Dillon (1976) notes, "farming system research recognizes and focuses on the interdependencies and interrelationships between the technical and human elements in the farming system. As such, it is more holistic in orientation than the reductionist approach traditionally used by technical agricultural scientists —an approach that requires studying one or two factors at a time while attempting to control all others."

"Downstream" farming system research — research applying new technology to improve existing farming systems — has four stages: description, design, testing, and extension (Norman, 1980). Description implies that particular areas be selected for study. Byerlee *et al.* (1980) suggest that a particular region under study be stratified into roughly homogenous target areas having similar agroclimatic characteristics and farmer circumstance, and that, within these zones, particular regions be selected appropriate to the farming system under study. Description also implies multi-disciplinary investigation teams able to assemble background information and exploratory or formal surveys (Byerlee *et al.*, 1980). In the design stage, improved technologies from "upstream" research stations or experimental centers are introduced into the farming system. Sanders & Lynam (1981) stress that such technology must "fit" into the whole farm system. Norman (1980) points out that introduced technologies must be economically feasible, dependable, socially acceptable, and compatible with the farming system in use. In the design stage farmers' perceptions of problems are particularly important. Development of theory and technique in analysis of farmer decision-making under risk and uncertainty is a rapidly moving field. Anderson, Dillon, and Hardaker (1977) and Roumasset (1976) offer examples of recently published major works in the field.

Methods for the testing of improved technologies under on-farm conditions in the tropics is also a rapidly moving field, stimulated in part by the international agricultural research centers. Reference is made to recent articles by Hildebrand (1979) and Sanders & Lynam (1981).

ECONOMIC ANALYSIS OF BIOLOGICAL NITROGEN FIXATION

How do these concepts of economic analysis and farming systems research apply to biological N_2 fixation in the tropics? How can we determine the profitability and potential adoption of inoculant technologies?

Following the models discussed above, such studies would need to be undertaken in a country or region where tropical legumes are part of the existing production system. Examples might include countries emphazising intercropped maize/beans production systems, as in Central America; the larger scale soybean regions of Brazil; or the pasture lands of the Colombian Llanos or Brazilian Cerrados. The selected country, or countries would need to have a domestic capacity for inoculant production and at least some people experienced in the use of inoculants, and in legume production. An interdisciplinary team would be necessary for the descriptive and design phases. Such a team might comprise a production agronomist, a production economist, and a microbiologist or inoculation specialist.

Selection of a particular region or regions within the country of choice will depend on the availability of inoculant technology thought by the team to be appropriate for that region. An obvious consideration is that existing fertilizer recommendations and/or experimental results stress the need for added N. Ideally the region selected would be one in which some farmers have already adopted the proposed BNF technology.

The descriptive stage would be a critical one. Clearly, a key task in the analysis would be to construct cost functions for fertilizer N. These would depend on the world price, transportation cost, and, in many cases, interest payments during the production season. In some multiple cropping systems, N is applied, not to the legume, but to the cereal grown in the association. We would need to have information of the interaction of this N with N_2 fixation by the legume. This could be a major point in the acceptance of new inoculant technologies. Details of other fertilizer needs for legume growth would also be required. Phosphorus, for example, is often deficient in tropical soils (see Munns & Franco, p. 133) and is critical for N_2 fixation. The need to apply P in place of N might alter the perception of risk held by the farmer. We would also need, of course, detailed information on the farming system. Would, for example, the farmer accept the need to inoculate and/or lime pellet seed, or would granular inoculants fit better into his hand planting system?

The question of whether inoculant usage is economically viable appears on the surface to be a somewhat trivial one. After all, the cost of the inoculant is very low. In the USA, it represents 10% or less of seed cost, and seed cost is 10% or less of variable costs per ha. In the tropics, we are hearing about prices of $1/ha for inoculant, which is probably no more than 5% of seed cost. If not trivial, then at least this question is not very interesting.

Problems of education, training, information, cultural or religious restrictions, etc., in getting peasant farmers to use inoculants loom very large compared to the small cost of the inoculants. For some countries, the cost of raising inoculant quality to an acceptable level will also be significant, though conceivably this cost could be subsidized by governments interested in reducing N imports.

In undertaking an analysis of the benefits of N_2 fixation, the economic tools mentioned in Section 1 of this paper would be essential. However, we would have to make some arbitrary decisions as to what represents the economic returns to BNF. Should we consider only the current crop, or the additional effects on subsequent crops and soil fertility. Should we also consider the availability of fertilizer N for other farm activities, or perhaps even speculate on the use of green manure cropsor legume trees to enhance the N available through more traditional legume usage?

Many other questions remain to be resolved before economic evaluations of N_2 fixation can realistically be carried through. For example, what should level of availability of an inoculant technology before its economies are studied? In this presentation I hope I have stimulated thought as to the complexity of the evaluation process.

REFERENCES

Anderson, J.R., Dillon J.L. & Hardaker, J.B. (1977) Agricultural decision-analysis. Iowa State Univ. Press, Ames, IO, USA.

Byerlee, D., Collinson, M., Perrin, R., Winkelmann, D., Biggs, S., Moscardi, E., Martinez, J.C., Martinez, J.E., Harrington, L.,& Benjamin, A. (1980) Planning technologies appropriate to farmers' concepts and procedures. CIMMYT, Mexico City, Mexico. 71pp.

Dillon, J.L. (1976) The economics of systems research. *Agricultural Systems*. 1(1), 5-22.

Hildebrand, P.E. (1979) Summary of the Sondeo methodology used by ICTA. Instituto de Ciencia y Tecnología Agrícolas, Guatemala City, Guatemala, C.A. 10 pp.

Norman, D.W. (1980) The farming systems approach: relevancy for the small farmer. Michigan State Univ. Rural Development Paper No. 5. East Lansing, MI, USA. 26 pp.

Roumasset, J.A. (1976) Rice and risk. North Holland Publ. Co. Amsterdam, Holland.

Sanders, J.H. & Lynam, J.K. (1981) Evaluation of new technology on farms: methodology and some results from two crop programs at CIAT. CIAT, Cali, Colombia. (Unpublished paper).

RESEARCH AND DEVELOPMENT FOR BIOLOGICAL NITROGEN FIXATION IN INDIA

G. Rangaswami[1]

Summary

Interest in BNF research and development in India has increased in recent years because of the gap in nitrogen fertilizer demand and supply. Currently some Rs 2 million is spent annually on BNF research, with Rs 12 million for development. Emphasis is toward a better understanding of the legume/*Rhizobium* symbiosis, but greater attention has been paid recently to the use of *Azolla*, N_2-fixing blue-green algae and associative symbioses. It is hoped that savings in N fertilizer use of as much as Rs 150 million can be achieved.

INTRODUCTION

Interest in biological nitrogen (N_2) fixation (BNF) in India was inspired by Rothamsted long before India attained independence. Indian scientists have undertaken research on soil micro-organisms in general, and N_2-fixing bacteria in particular since 1920. However, it is only during the past two decades that deeper interest in BNF has been generated. Today about one hundred microbiologists and biochemists in more than 20 laboratories throughout the country are experimenting with different basic and applied aspects of BNF. Research work on BNF may be listed under three categories:

Symbiotic N_2 fixation,
N_2 fixation by algae, and
N_2 fixation by nonsymbiotic bacteria.

Work in India on associative symbioses is still limited. This paper describes results obtained in BNF research to the present, and gives an outline of projected activities.

---

[1] Adviser (Agriculture) Planning Commission, Government of India, New Delhi 11-0001, India.

SYMBIOTIC N_2 FIXATION

Cajanus cajan, *Cicer arietinum*, *Vigna radiata*, *Vigna mungo*, *Lablab purpureus*, *L. biflorus*, *Lathyrus sativus*, *Vigna unguiculata* ssp. *cylindrica* (catjang), *Glycine max*, *Phaseolus vulgaris*, *P. lunatus*, *Pisum sativum*, and *Lens culinaris*, are cultivated for grains and pods in most parts of India. *Arachis hypogaea* is an important oilseed crop. The total area under pulses and leguminous vegetables is about 31 million ha and under groundnut (peanut) about 7 million ha; in total one-fourth of the cultivated land in the country. About 90% of legume production occurs under rainfed conditions and in association with cereals, such as wheat, sorghum, *Pennisetum, Setaria,* etc. Irrigated legumes are grown in rotation with rice, wheat, sugarcane, and cotton. More recently, short duration legumes such as *Phaseolus* spp. have begun to be used as intercrops in irrigated sugarcane and cotton fields and also in perennial orchards. Additionally, there is some area under forage legumes, including lucerne, clover, and berseem. Legumes such as sunnhemp (*Crotalaria juncea*), agati (*Sesbania grandiflora*), and daincha (*Sesbania aculeata*) are also grown as green manure crops in rotation with rice, sugarcane, and wheat. The area under pasture legumes is very limited and mostly found in the higher elevations and in hilly terrain where dairy and sheep husbandry is practiced. Land being limited, the scope for expanding the area under pasture legumes in the country is very restricted.

Rhizobia for each of these legumes have been isolated from a range of environments and assayed for N_2 fixation. For most of the legumes, inoculant strains have been selected and are now available commercially. Tolerance of the crop/*Rhizobium* symbiosis to constraints such as drought, salinity/alkalinity, and low soil phosphorus, has also been investigated.

Results obtained to date suggest that N_2 fixation by crop legumes is commonly from 0-40 kg/ha, though in pastures such as alfalfa, rates of fixation as high as 600 kg/ha per year have been recorded. Given the extremely variable rates of N_2 fixation, it is not surprising that yield increases following inoculation also vary, with 100% yield increases obtained in some trials, 0% in others. Starter doses of N from 10-20 kg/ha have enhanced crop development and yield in some areas, while doses of phosphatic fertilizer (30-40 kg/ha) have also proved essential for N_2 fixation in a number of locations.

AZOLLA AND BLUE-GREEN ALGAE

Use of *Azolla* as a biofertilizer in India is a relatively recent development. Under a collaborative program initiated by the Indian Council of Agricultural Research (ICAR), it has been shown that as much as 330 tons fresh weight of *Azolla* can be produced per ha each year. The fern matures in 20-30 days, and when incorporated into soil is the equivalent of 25-30 kg N/ha. Yield increases of up to 40% have been obtained in field trials in the coastal districts of India.

Blue-green algae have been utilized as biofertilizers in India for more than 10 years. Technology for the mass multiplication of algae in fields has been developed, with optimum production often dependent on adequate P fertilization. When the algae are inoculated into rice fields 3-4 weeks before the planting of rice, yield increases of 10-15% are often recorded, while fertilizer N application can be reduced by about 25 kg/ha without yield loss. Residual effects with subsequent crops and differences between strains and species of N_2-fixing blue-green algae in tolerance of soil acidity and alkalinity have also been demonstrated. A major problem is the competition between N_2-fixing and nonfixing algae. Multiplication of the algal inoculant is also difficult.

NONSYMBIOTIC N_2-FIXING BACTERIA

Yield increases of from 5-60% have been reported following inoculation experiments with nonsymbiotic N_2-fixing bacteria, with estimated fixation rates of 5-51 kg N_2 fixed/ha per crop season. Inconsistency in field response has limited the acceptance by farmers.

RESEARCH AND DEVELOPMENT IN BNF

The Indian Government has realized the need for research on BNF to reduce the growing gap between fertilizer demand and supply in India. Three All India Coordinated Research Projects with BNF components have been initiated in recent years.

The All India Coordinated Project on Forage Crops has been underway since 1974, with 14 centers involved. The main objective of the project is to develop high-yielding forage plants and to evolve improved production and management technologies. Since most of the forage plants are legumes, the field testing of crop varieties for root nodule formation and fixation is also included under the objectives. The total cost of the project is about Rs 6.5 million for a five-year period, and of this, about 5% is to be spent on BNF experiments.

The All India Coordinated Project on Pulses has been in operation since 1976. While the main objective of the project is to substantially increase productivity of the various species of grain legumes important in India, one of the means to achieve this objective is to improve symbiotic N_2 fixation by the crops. There are 25 research centers involved in the project, of which perhaps 15 are involved in work on *Rhizobium*. The total cost of the project is approximately Rs 35 million for a five year period, of which about 10% is allotted for microbiological research, mainly N_2 fixation by the legumes through better *Rhizobium* strain selection and by identification of better host/*Rhizobium* combinations for the various soil and environmental conditions.

The All India Project on Biological N_2 Fixation was initiated in 1979 with 10 centers involved and a five-year budget of about Rs 7 million. The main objectives of the project are to survey and isolate N_2-fixing organisms and test them for field use; to improve their quality through genetic means; and to better understand the basic aspects of physiology and biochemistry of N_2 fixation.

During the last five years the number of inoculant producing centers has increased substantially. There are now 29 centers, most of them in agricultural universities, and they have a joint capacity to produce *Rhizobium* inoculants for some 600.000 ha and *Azotobacter* inoculants for a further 250,000 ha. The facilities for blue-green algal production have grown from a capability for less than 1000 kg in 1975 to a capacity for 200,000 ha in 1980. During the coming five years, intensive BNF development programs are to be undertaken in the States of Uttar Pradesh, West Bengal, Tamil Nadu, Andhra Pradesh, Karnataka, Kerala, Assam. Nagaland and Tripura at a total cost of about Rs 5 million.

A national project for the development and use of biofertilizers has also been formulated recently and will be implemented soon. This project will popularize the use of biofertilizers (*Rhizobium*, *Azolla*, *Azospirillum*, and blue-green algae) in Indian agriculture. The development program will cost Rs 50 million for a four-year period and will affect some 200,000 ha. It will include creation of a National Fertilizer Development and Production Center; four regional centers to produce inoculants for state governments and other agencies; and field demonstrations and extension activities.

THE BRAZILIAN PROGRAM IN BIOLOGICAL NITROGEN FIXATION

J. Döbereiner[1]

Because of the large area involved, Brazilian agriculture has traditionally favored low-input production systems, with interest in biological nitrogen (N_2) fixation dating from the 1940's. In the 1950's research on N_2 fixation began at various centers, with the largest group in the South, and under the leadership of J.R. Jardim Freire. In the 1960's the legume inoculation experiments were extended to the study of soil and plant limiting factors and their effects on the legume symbiosis, with new centers such as the Instituto Agronomico in Campinas, the Centro de Energia Nuclear na Agriculture (CENA) in Piracicaba, and the Instituto de Pesquisas Agropecuarias do Centro-Sur (IPEACS) at Km 47, prominent. The Latin American *Rhizobium* meetings, in 1968 in Porto Alegre and in 1970 at Km 47, in addition to further stimulating research, showed that the Brazilian programs for the integrated study of soil, plant and bacterial involvement in N_2 fixation were among the strongest in Latin America and comparable with most others in the world.

Once locally selected legume inoculants had been developed to replace the frequently unsatisfactory imported ones, inoculation with *Rhizobium* began to replace N fertilization in both experimental and farm plantings. The change was particularly rapid with soybeans, and since 1963 all experimental work with this crop has been based on inoculation rather than N fertilization. Current cultivars, while producing up to 4 tons/ha, only respond to N fertilizer where inoculation procedures have been unsatisfactory, or other nutritional problems limiting to N_2 fixation. It has been estimated that the use of inoculants for soybeans currently saves more than 800 million dollars annually in fertilizer costs (Döbereiner & Duque, 1980).

Observation of nonsymbiotic N_2-fixing organisms in the rhizosphere of sugarcane (Döbereiner & Alvahydo, 1959) led to further studies on N_2 fixation in grasses at Km 47, and resulted in both Brazilian Research Council

1 EMBRAPA/SNLCS-CNPq, Km 47, 23460 Seropedica, Rio de Janeiro, Brazil.

and international support for this program. Associative N_2 fixation studies resulting from an agreement between CENA and the International Atomic Energy Agency (IAEA) further contributed to make Brazil the center for this type of research in the world.

A major factor in the development of Brazilian programs in N_2 fixation has been the opportunity for graduate student and thesis research. Four full-time and ten part-time fellowships, funded by CNPq and EMBRAPA, respectively, have been available at Km 47 for a number of years, and have permitted the best students to receive intensive training. More than 46 graduate students from Brazil have received training through this program, and most of these are still actively engaged in research. Further opportunity for training — this time in the area of legume inoculation technology — came with the formation of a UNESCO/UNEP/ICRO supported MIRCEN unit at the Universidad Federal do Rio Grande do Sul in Porto Alegre in 1976. This unit has organized several short courses (both for Brazilian students and others), serves as a source of *Rhizobium* cultures, and undertakes some documentation activities.

Because of this potential for training, there is now a network of researchers on N_2 fixation in Brazil, and a constant interchange of ideas, methodologies and results. Typical is the grouping together of the workers at Km 47, UFRGS, CENA, the national bean center in Goiania, and the Empresa Capixaba de Pesquisa Agropecuaria (EMCAPA) for a coordinated research project on N_2 fixation in *Phaseolus vulgaris*. Currently symbiotic N_2 fixation projects in Brazil range from studies on the importance of legumes in the Amazon to the factors limiting nodulation in the Cerrado. Studies in the associative fixation area span the specificity in N_2 fixation in C_4 tropical grasses to the range of N_2-fixing organisms in the rhizosphere of sugarcane. The quality of this work is evident from several papers in these proceedings.

REFERENCES

Döbereiner, J. & Alvahydo, R. (1959) *Rev. Bras. Biol.* 19, 401-412.

Döbereiner, J. & Duque, F.F. (1980) *R. Econ. Rural Brasilia* 18, 447-460.

INTERNATIONALLY SPONSORED DEVELOPMENT OF BIOLOGICAL NITROGEN FIXATION TECHNOLOGY

Compiled by S. C. Harris[1]

from data of E.J. Da Silva,[2] L.R. Frederick,[3] F. Maignon,[4] G. Persley,[5] and F. Riveros[4]

Summary

Efforts of international funding agencies interested in promoting biological nitrogen fixation technology are increasing. These efforts center on training inoculant production personnel, on increasing the availability of germplasm and inoculants, and on field experiments to demonstrate the viability of inoculation, particularly with regard to the legume/*Rhizobium* symbiosis.

INTRODUCTION

An increasing awareness of the potential for improving agricultural productivity in the tropics through intensified field research into biological nitrogen fixation (BNF) is evidenced in the programs of the major international agencies that fund agricultural research. Efforts are concentrated on training personnel for production, testing, and use of inoculants; on increasing the availability of germplasm and inoculants; and on field experiments to demonstrate the benefits of using effective inoculants. Institutions, in most cases universities (notable exceptions are the CGIAR-funded centers, see p. 695), serve as the medium for these activities, while the international agencies provide funds and technical assistance. Collaborative efforts that involve scientists from two or more institutions are seen as particularly beneficial.

[1] Formerly Univ. of Hawaii NifTAL Project; now CIAT, AA 67-13, Cali, Colombia.

[2] Division of Sci. Research & Higher Ed., UNESCO, 7 Place de Fontenoy, 75700, Paris, France.

[3] USAID, DS/AGR-420 SA-18, Washington, D.C. 20523, USA.

[4] FAO, Via delle Terme di Caracalla, 00100, Rome, Italy.

[5] Research for Development, ADAB, Box 887, Canberra, ACT, 2601, Australia.

Efforts to date have promoted legume/*Rhizobium* associations, especially in grain and forage legumes. Currently, however, there is an increasing amount of support being given to work with N_2-fixing trees, with *Azolla*, and with potential application of associative N_2 fixation to agricultural production.

TRAINING ACTIVITIES

FAO (1981) reports that trained personnel with the agronomic and microbiological skills to implement BNF technology are urgently needed. Between 1975 and 1979, about 80 persons from 35 countries were trained. However, there are still many countries with no trained personnel or with a single individual working in isolation. Thus, training is a key area in which the international agencies can have an impact.

Africa

Several French institutes have training programs in Africa. The Institut National de la Recherche Agronomique (INRA) and Institut de Recherches Agronomiques Tropicales (IRAT) have been collaborators in BNF research in Africa for over ten years, with IRAT concentrating on tropical crops. INRA organizes two kinds of training courses. In the first type, organized with the Universite Claude Bernard Lyon for agronomists, agricultural engineers, and advanced students, both theoretical and practical information is given. The second type, which exemplifies a recent trend in training activities, is based on the need to get BNF information out to the farm and provides practical work for agronomists and extentionists.

The African Microbial Resources Centres (MIRCENs) funded by UNESCO/UNEP/ICRO are located at the University of Nairobi in Kenya, and at Ain Shams University in Cairo, Egypt. The Nairobi MIRCEN and NifTAL, a University of Hawaii *Rhizobium* project sponsored by USAID, sponsored a six-week course on practical applications of BNF technology in 1980. The Cairo MIRCEN, again with assistance from NifTAL, also included a *Rhizobium* component in a broader based microbiology course in 1980.

Latin America and the Caribbean

The Brazil MIRCEN, located at the Universidade Federal do Rio Grande do Sul in Porto Alegre, offers courses mixing the theory and practice of BNF and aims mainly to train technicians and researchers. A course for extension workers is planned for 1981. Additionally, an advanced course on BNF is offered biennially by the Universidade Federal Rural do Río de Janeiro and EMBRAPA-CNPq with support from the Royal Society and the US National Academy of Science.

Other training activities scheduled for 1981 in Latin America include a USAID-sponsored course to be conducted by North Carolina State University (NCSU) in Lima, Peru, and one at Chapingo, Mexico. The NCSU course for research or extension personnel with little or no formal training in BNF technology will emphasize practical microbiology, plant physiology, and soil science. The Postgraduate College of the University will co-sponsor the Chapingo course with NifTAL. This course will be more technically advanced than that in Peru, but still be of practical orientation.

Asia and Pacific

The Malaysian Agricultural Research and Development Institute (MARDI) will co-sponsor with NifTAL, a six-week course similar to those held at Nairobi, Kenya, and Chapingo, Mexico. Key technicians from SE Asia, Indonesia, the Philippines, and other Pacific areas will be selected.

Non-regional training activities

The Australian Development Assitance Bureau (ADAB) sponsors postgraduate training in BNF at Australian universities. The Universities of New South Wales and Western Australia are particularly active in this field.

USAID, through the Consortium on Tropical Biological Nitrogen Fixation; through 17 US universities with cooperative research projects in N_2 fixation; and through NifTAL, sponsors postgraduate training at US universities. The World *Rhizobium* Collection and Study Center (Beltsville, MD, USA) and NifTAL also have "intern" training programs that offer work opportunities of a two to six month duration, but without university credit.

UNESCO has collaborated in supporting training programs at IITA and IRRI and also at several national centers within the framework of its network programs. This support has been directed mainly at Southeast Asia and the Caribbean.

GERMPLASM COLLECTION AND DISTRIBUTION

Full utilization of legumes in an N_2-fixing symbiosis is dependent on the availability of effective *Rhizobium* strains, appropriate hosts and a supply of high quality inoculant. Effective strains are maintained in the culture collections located at the MIRCENs (Nairobi, Kenya; Porto Alegre, Brazil; Cairo, Egypt; and Bangkok, Thailand) and at NifTAL in Hawaii and in the USDA *Rhizobium* collection at Beltsville, MD (both US groups are also soon to be named MIRCENs). IRAT and INRA also keep a *Rhizobium* culture collection and send inocula to several countries. The international research centers also maintain extensive collections of *Rhizobium* and in most cases will supply either freeze-dried cultures or high quality inoculant for field research. Additionally, UNESCO will be providing assistance in this area, sponsoring the second edition of the IBP *Rhizobium* Catalog that will list those strains recommended for use with various legumes.

RESEARCH AND NETWORKING

Research on legume inoculation can be grouped into three types. The most frequent type of research tests the ability of a plant species to respond to inoculation under particular environmental conditions. Specific host/strain interactions must also be tested under field conditions; at times even in farmers' fields. Multi-locational trials are conducted to test host/strain relationships and the recommendations developed during earlier tests across as many sites as possible. These last trials also serve as demonstrations of the feasilibity of inoculating to local farmers and extension workers and facilitate the gathering of data on soils, management, and farming systems.

Most past research funded by the international agencies has concentrated on site-specific inoculation trials. Now, however, multi-locational trials are being conducted to probe the across-systems viability of inoculation.

Africa

Once the importance of inoculation became established, INRA proposed to use inoculation whenever the benefit would be obviously visible to the farmer without weighing. This is the case with soybean research in Senegal and Upper Volta. With groundnut and cowpea, where inoculation has not increased yield, INRA, IRAT, and Institut de Recherches sur les Huiles ét Oléageneaux (IRHO) have collaborated to study other limiting factors of N_2 fixation. They also aim to find species with high capacity for N_2 fixation and adapted to high temperature soils, salinity, and drought, especially in Algeria.

The Office de la Recherche Scientifique et Technique Outre-Mer (ORSTOM), based in Senegal, is also involved in several types of BNF research. ORSTOM has funded work with N_2-fixing trees in Senegal (see p. 395) in addition to their work with cowpea. Additional research efforts deal with *Azolla* and *Sesbania* as green manures for rice in western Africa (see p. 441).

Multi-locational trials with soybean and others are conducted under the auspices of the Nairobi MIRCEN and the NifTAL-coordinated International Network of Legume Inoculation Trials (INLIT). The INLIT trials will have technical support including experimental design, seed, and inoculants supply; thus, the possibility of achieving meaningful across-site results, even under difficult conditions, is strengthened.

Latin America and Caribbean

Research funded by international agencies is scattered throughout Latin America and the Caribbean. Much is fairly site-specific. In Haiti, INRA's program is looking at limiting factors in cowpea and soybean. FAO's funds are behind research in Peru on soybean and pasture legumes. Forages are also under study at the FAO-supported livestock programs in Argentina. In Brazil, greenleaf desmodium, perennial soybean, and siratro are being evaluated for use as summer legumes in pastures by the Porto Alegre MIRCEN. Other crops of interest include soybean, common bean, and alfalfa. INLIT trials for a wide range of legumes have been planted in locations in Latin America and the Caribbean. Results from the First International Bean Inoculation Trial sponsored by CIAT are given on p. 223.

Asia and Pacific

ADAB provides indirect support for various bilateral projects in Southeast Asia and the South Pacific, where legumes are involved as part of an improved farming system. Substantial support has been provided for research and development of tropical pastures in Malaysia and the Solomon Islands.

NifTAL has also promoted INLIT trials in the Pacific (Fiji, Guam, Philippines, Indonesia), in SE Asia (Malaysia, Thailand), in Pakistan, and in India. Additionally, All-India Coordinated Pulse Improvement Program sponsored by the India Council for Agricultural Research (ICAR) has agreed to make the INLIT trials part of their own multi-locational research plan.

CONCLUSION

Current annual worldwide support for BNF programs probably exceeds 25 million dollars (L.R. Frederick, personal communication). Incorporating BNF technology into farming systems in a practical and beneficial way will require millions more. This sort of effort is obviously beyond the means of any one nation, and the benefits will accrue to more than national groups. Collaborative international programs will, thus, surely continue to be a key part of the BNF research effort.

REFERENCES

Food and Agriculture Organization (FAO) (1981) Biological nitrogen fixation (symbiotic): Report on FAO/UNEP meeting. FAO, Rome, Italy. 25 pp.

RESEARCH ON BIOLOGICAL NITROGEN FIXATION IN THE INTERNATIONAL AGRICULTURAL RESEARCH CENTERS

Compiled by P.H. Graham[1]

from data and publications of A.A. Ayanaba,[2] R.S. Bradley,[1] P.J. Dart,[3] P.H. Graham, R. Islam,[4] E.L. Pulver,[2] V. Ranga Rao,[2] J.A. Thompson,[3] and I. Watanabe[5]

Summary

Five of the international agricultural research centers (IARC's) currently have research programs in the area of biological nitrogen (N_2) fixation. This paper reviews the activities of the centers in this area and highlights common and distinctive features of the programs, as well as their links with BNF activities in national programs and developed country laboratories.

INTRODUCTION

Thurston (1977), Ruttan (1978) and the Consultative Group on International Agricultural Research (CGIAR, 1980) have described the evolution of the international agricultural research centers (IARC's) system and something of their operating philosophy. Currently there are 13 centers or institutions funded through the CGIAR system (CGIAR, 1980), and five of these have research programs on biological nitrogen (N_2) fixation. This paper will briefly review the activities of these centers in the area of N_2 fixation, and will show common and distinctive features of the programs and how they link with activities in national programs and other institutions.

---

[1] Centro Internacional de Agricultura Tropical (CIAT) Cali, Colombia.

[2] International Institute of Tropical Agriculture (IITA), Ibadan, Nigeria.

[3] International Crops Research Institute for the Semi-Arid Tropics (ICRISAT), Patancheru, India.

[4] International Center for Agricultural Research in the Dry Areas (ICARDA), Aleppo, Syria.

[5] International Rice Research Institute (IRRI), Los Baños, Philippines.

CROP AND AREA RESPONSIBILITIES OF IARC's WITH PROGRAMS ON BIOLOGICAL N_2 FIXATION

The five centers with programs on N_2 fixation have markedly different crop and area responsibilities (see Table 1). Thus IRRI, the first formed of the IARC's, has a worldwide mandate for research on rice but has, until recently, stressed production of irrigated rice grown under relatively favored conditions in Asia (Ruttan, 1978). The ICRISAT mandate, in contrast, is the semiarid regions with a dry season of five to ten months; where rainfall is unreliable and probably the major constraint to production. Because of this climatic emphasis, ICRISAT must work with a number of crops, including millet, sorghum, chickpea, pigeonpea, and groundnut (Dart & Krantz, 1977) and pay particular attention to the farming systems traditional for these crops. The role of CIAT lies somewhere between these extremes. On the one hand, it has worldwide responsibility within the IARC system for research on *Phaseolus vulgaris,* but it must also emphasize the development of pastures for the 800 million ha of under-utilized, acid, infertile soils found in Latin America (CIAT, 1981). Important in the CIAT philosophy is the emphasis on reduced-input technology, necessary in part because bean production occurs mainly on small holdings with farmers often unable to obtain or afford costly technical inputs, but also because of the extensive nature of cattle operations in the Cerrados of Brazil and in the Colombian Llanos.

Assumed in all the centers' research activities is the idea of comparative advantage: not to work on problems that are likely to be site specific (for example, fertilizer response), but to emphasize problems the resolution of which would permit widespread adoption of a new technology or introduction of higher yielding varieties. Because of this, the BNF programs at the five centers, have emphasized the collection and evaluation of germplasm and the selection or development of cultivars or strains of micro-organisms that are active in N_2 fixation. They have also sought to develop agronomic practices appropriate for plants at least partly dependent on fixed N_2. For IRRI the study of *Azolla* and the evaluation of traditional methods for its use have been important activities, while several of the legume centers have sought improved methods of inoculation.

CULTIVAR AND STRAIN VARIATION IN ABILITY TO FIX N_2

The plant germplasm and micro-organism holdings of the five IARC's with work on biological N_2 fixation are shown in Table 2.

Wide variation between representative grain legume cultivars in ability to fix N_2 in symbiosis has been shown for *Arachis* (Nambiar & Dart, 1980); *Cajanus* (ICRISAT, 1978-79), *Glycine* (Pulver *et al.,* 1978; Nangju, 1980), *Phaseolus vulgaris* (Graham & Halliday, 1977; Graham & Rosas, 1977; Graham, 1981) and *Vigna* (IITA, 1979). In this last study, 400 to 485 lines of

TABLE 1: International agricultural research centers undertaking research on biological N_2 fixation, and their mandates.

Center	Location	Year Founded	Mandate	Microbiologist(s)[1]
International Rice Research Institute (IRRI)	Los Baños, Philippines	1959	Rice research: Worldwide mandate	I. Watanabe
International Institute of Tropical Agriculture (IITA)	Ibadan, Nigeria	1965	Farming systems in lowland tropics: Worldwide mandate, but emphasizing Africa.	A.A. Ayanaba
			Grain legumes, especially cowpea and soybean: Worldwide mandate, but emphasizing Africa.	E. Pulver
Centro Internacional de Agricultura Tropical (CIAT)	Cali, Colombia	1968	*Phaseolus vulgaris*: Worldwide mandate, but emphasizing Latin America.	P.H. Graham
			Pasture systems for the acid infertile tropical regions: Worldwide mandate, but current work almost entirely in Latin America.	R.S. Bradley
International Crops Research Institute for the Semi-Arid Tropics (ICRISAT)	Hyderabad, India	1972	Sorghum and pearl millet: Worldwide mandate.	J.A. Thompson
			Grain legumes, especially pigeonpea, chickpea and groundnut: Worldwide mandate.	P.J. Dart
International Center for Agricultural Research in Dry Areas (ICARDA)	Aleppo, Syria	1976	Crop and mixed farming systems research with emphasis on broad beans and lentils: Semiarid regions.	R. Islam

[1]As of March 1, 1981

TABLE 2: The plant germplasm and micro-organism holdings of the IARC's with programs in biological N_2 fixation.

Center	Program	Plant species held (and number)		Micro-organisms maintained		References
IRRI	Rice	*Oryza sativa*	(47,743)	*Anabaena*		IRRI (1979)
		O. glaberrima	(2,278)	*Gloeotrichia*		
		Wild species	(961)	*Nostoc*		
		Azolla pinnata				
		A. filiculoides				
		A. mexicana				
		A. caroliana				
IITA	Grain Legume	*Vigna unguiculata*	(10,471)	*R. japonicum*	(82)	IITA (1979; 1980)
		Glycine max	(310)	*Rhizobium* spp.		
		Voandzeia subterranea	(2,271)	(cowpea)	(242)	
		Others	(2,484)			
CIAT	Bean	*Phaseolus vulgaris*	(27,404)	*R. phaseoli*	(300 +)	CIAT (1980)
		P. coccineus	(1,098)	*R. japonicum*	(36)	P.H. Graham (unpublished)
		P. acutifolius	(129)			
		P. lunatus	(1,900)			
		Phaseolus spp.	(161)			
	Tropical Pasture	*Stylosanthes* spp.	(1,723)	*Rhizobium* spp.	(2000 +)	R.S. Bradley (unpublished)
		Desmodium spp.	(865)			
		Zornia spp.	(561)			
		Aeschynomene spp.	(377)			
		Centrosema spp.	(605)			
		Miscellaneous	(2,276)			

(continued on page 699)

(continuation)

Center	Program	Plant species held (and number)		Micro-organisms maintained		References
ICRISAT	Sorghum	*Sorghum bicolor*	(17,986)	*Azospirillum, Derxia*		ICRISAT (1978 - 79; 1979 - 80)
	Millet	*Pennisetum americanum*	(14,074)			
	Pigeonpea	*Cajanus cajan*	(8,815)	*Rhizobium* spp. from *Cajanus*	(480)	
	Chickpea	*Cicer arietinum*	(12,195)	*R. leguminosarum*	(500 +)	
	Groundnut	*Arachis hypogaea*	(8,363)	*Rhizobium* spp. from *Arachis*		
ICARDA	Grain Legume	*Cicer arietinum*	(3,400)	*Rhizobium* strains for legume spp. listed in grain and pasture legume program	(400 +)	P.R. Goldsworthy & R. Islam (unpublished)
		Vicia faba	(2,000)			
		Lens culinaris	(4,800)			
	Pasture Legume	*Medicago* spp.	(2,810)			
		Pisum spp.	(2,200)			
		Vicia spp.	(2,550)			
		Astragalus spp.	(240)			
		Lathyrus spp.	(350)			
		Trifolium spp.	(725)			
		Onobrychis spp.	(675)			

cowpea were sown, with and without N, at three sites which differed in pH and background rhizobial population. Ability to symbiose with native soil rhizobia was evaluated according to relative vegetative development (RE growth - N/growth + N x 100). At each site roughly 16% of the lines tested were selected, with some at each site performing better without N than when N fertilizer was used. Four of the lines selected for high symbiotic efficiency performed well at each of the three test sites, but TVu 175 was uniformly weak in development when dependent on fixed N. Additional papers on this theme are included in this volume (see p 49, p 57).

Unexpected host/strain interations have been found in a number of these studies. Thus, when 250 lines of *Glycine max* were evaluated for compatibility with native, and presumably "cowpea-type" rhizobia, 90% proved incompatible, but eight (mainly of Asiatic origin) symbiosed effectively with these rhizobia (IITA, 1978; Nangju, 1980). In groundnut, non-nodulation has been observed in a number of lines (see p. 49; p. 57).

Because of this variation in N_2-fixing ability, programs to monitor the ability to fix N_2 of lines selected for disease resistance or agronomic merit have been established in most of the grain legume programs. Programs to breed for enhanced N_2 fixation in agronomically desirable materials are also under way. For *P. vulgaris,* these have been described by Graham (1981). At IITA, cultivars of *G. max* able to symbiose effectively with the indigenous soil rhizobia have been crossed with higher yielding and agronomically desirable soybean lines. Early generation progeny are being screened, both for effective nodulation in the absence of inoculation and for agronomic traits. Nodule scoring methods for chickpea are detailed on p. 57.

Active programs of strain selection parallel the work with host cultivars (ICRISAT, 1977-1978; 1978-1979; Islam, 1981; At ICRISAT yields of pigeonpea were increased from 1427 to 2059 kg/ha following inoculation, with dry matter production with the best strain raised from 5390 to 8275 kg/ha (ICRISAT 1978-79). In trials with numerous chickpea rhizobia, nodule number following inoculation ranged from 7-48/plant, and nodule dry weight from 13-74 mg/plant. Yield following inoculation rose from 1564 to 2006 kg/ha (ICRISAT, 1977-78). Results with peanut have been generally less satisfactory, though with the Robut 33-1 cultivar, yield increases of up to 291 kg/ha have been obtained. At CIAT, following numerous evaluations of strain performance in Leonard jars, and in the field, an international bean inoculation trial (IBIT) has been developed. First results are discussed on p. 223.

With excellent strains identified in the various programs, emphasis in strain selection is now turning to additional strain properties that could affect their competitive or survival capabilities in tropical or subtropical soils. Thus, Islam & Ghoulam (1981) evaluated strain performance with *Vicia faba* in the presence of 0.32% NaCI, while at IITA and CIAT the ability of strains to survive and form nodules under acid soil conditions has been considered in some detail (Date & Halliday, 1979; IITA, 1979; Graham *et al.*, 1982). With the soybean cultivars Mandarin and Bossier in Nigeria, inoculant strains produced 72.5-92.5% of nodules even in the third crop after inoculation. Further studies with strain survival over the fallow period are detailed on p. 309. Graham *et al.* (1982) with *R. phaseoli* demonstrated strain differences in tolerance to pH and showed these correlated with strain survival in acid soils and with response to inoculation.

In the CIAT pasture program, with many different genera and species of legumes being considered for adaptation to the acid, infertile soils of the tropics, host and *Rhizobium* selection must go hand in hand. Legume accessions under initial evaluation are not inoculated, but are supplied fertilizer N when N deficient. As agronomically promising forage species are identified, the ease and efficiency with which they nodulate naturally in the field is evaluated. For those accessions having relatively specific *Rhizobium* requirements, the isolation and screening of a wide range of strains is then initiated. Again because many different species and accessions are involved, much of the evaluation is done in the glasshouse, with only the very best strains for each legume field tested. A difficulty in this work is that many of the strains isolated do not grow well on routine laboratory medium and must be maintained on medium having pH values near 5.5.

The nonlegume programs on N_2 fixation in the international centers have benefited from the increased interest in associative fixation. At ICRISAT numerous accessions of sorghum and millet have been evaluated for N_2 (C_2H_2) fixation. Thus, Dart (1978) reported 59 of 200 sorghum accessions to have some N_2-fixing activity, but found only two accessions with rates of fixation in excess of 230 μg N/soil core per day. In the millets, plant to plant variation in N_2 fixation was marked, but approximately half of the accessions tested in rainy season plantings fixed some N_2. Activity was greatest after flowering and continued well into grain fill. In the summer season under irrigation only 8 of 89 accession showed N_2-fixing activity, and accessions of the minor millets were generally more active than was pearl millet. A review of this work is in preparation (P.J. Dart, personal communication).

Under traditional systems of agriculture, moderate rice yields can be maintained without N fertilization. At IRRI, 23 successive rice crops, each yielding more than 4 tons/ha, have been taken without N fertilization (Watanabe, Lee & Alimagno, 1978). The lack of suitable methods for estimating N_2 fixation under irrigation has hindered investigation of this phenomenon, but it is now probable that from 10-50 kg N is fixed/ha per crop (Koyama & App, 1979; Watanabe & Cholitkul, 1979). The major contribution is from free-living algae (Watanabe *et al.*, 1978). While fixation occurs in both phyllosphere and rhizosphere, with as many as 10^8 N_2-fixing organisms/g of root (Watanabe & Cholitkul, 1979), there is as yet little evidence of varietal differences in ability to fix N_2.

AGRONOMIC PRACTICES INFLUENCING N_2 FIXATION

N Fertilization

With N deficiency and grain legume/cereal intercrops common in the tropics, all centers have tried to develop practices of N fertilization that are compatible with legume inoculation. These have included studies on the use of starter N dressings (Graham & Halliday, 1977; IITA, 1979), evaluation of the effects of fertilizer N on seasonal profiles of N_2 fixation (P.H. Graham & S.R. Viteri, unpublished), and in rice the effect of fertilizer N placement on N_2 fixation by photosynthetic and heterotrophic organisms (Crasswell & Vlek, 1979; IRRI, 1979).

Some studies have also been undertaken at different levels of applied N. Nodulation and N_2 fixation in *P. vulgaris* has proved extremely susceptible to added fertilizer N, with seasonal rates of $N_2(C_2H_2)$ fixation reduced as much as 39.6% by the application of only 15 kg N/ha (CIAT, 1979).

Cereal/legume intercropping and rotations

The influence of grain or green-manure legumes on the N nutrition of associated or subsequent cereal crops has been extensively studied at the IARC's, with two papers on this theme in these proceedings (see p. 641; p. 647). Pulver *et al.*, (1978) also report on the variation in N harvest index among cowpea varieties. *Leucaena* alley cropped with maize yielded 95.7-111.2 kg foliage N/ha. When this material was cut and incorporated at rates equivalent to 10 tons of foliage/ha, maize yields were increased significantly, and were almost equivalent to those of plots receiving 100 kg N/ha (IITA, 1979).

Studies at CIAT have emphasized the effect of intercropping maize and beans on N_2 fixation by the legume. When a vigorous climbing bean was associated with maize, rates of N_2 fixation were not significantly different from those obtained in monoculture (Graham & Rosas, 1978), whereas $N_2(C_2H_2)$ fixation by bush bean cultivars was reduced substantially by association (P.H. Graham & S.R. Viteri, unpublished data).

Methods of inoculation

Methods of inoculation have been studied at both ICRISAT and CIAT. At ICRISAT, granular inoculants have not proved superior to those applied to the seed (see p. 241). At CIAT, however, and for soils of low pH, granular inoculants prepared using 40-mesh peat, have consistently proved as good as or better than seed application (Graham *et al.*, 1980; 1982).

Utilization of *Azolla*

Studies on *Azolla* at IRRI confirm the benefits from the use of this fern, and have examined some of the requirements for growth (Watanabe *et al.,* 1977; IRRI, 1978; 1979). Thus N_2 fixation by azolla of from 70-110 kg N/ha per rice crop has been demonstrated, with yields in rice significantly greater when azolla was used, than when 60 kg/ha of N was applied. In these studies incorporation of the azolla was a major factor. When azolla was not incorporated only 3.9% of fern N was taken up by rice during a 42-day period; when it was incorporated, 52% of the azolla N was absorbed by rice in the same period. In these studies emphasis has also been placed on the P requirement for growth of *Azolla* sp. and on their temperature tolerance.

COLLABORATIVE ACTIVITIES AND TRAINING

Opportunities exist for collaborative activities between the IARC's and other institutions. Perhaps the best example of this has been the project funded by the Overseas Development Administration for collaborative studies on cowpea physiology and N_2 fixation at IITA and the University of Reading (see for example, papers by Huxley *et al.,* 1976; Summerfield *et al.*, 1976; Eaglesham *et al.,* 1977; Summerfield *et al.,* 1977; 1978; Minchin *et al.,* 1978a; b) and now extended to work on chickpea (Minchin *et al.,* 1980) at ICRISAT. More recently both IITA and IRRI have received support for collaborative activities with the Boyce Thompson Institute, while at ICRISAT and CIAT less formal relationships have been established with North Carolina State University and the University of Wisconsin, respectively. These associations allow center scientists to remain practically oriented while receiving some in-depth support on the more basic areas.

Training is also a major function of institute staff and can involve short courses on inoculation technology or *Rhizobium* isolation and culture; assigment of national program scientists to specific programs for periods of up to six months, or even advanced degree training.

REFERENCES

Centro Internacional de Agricultura Tropical (CIAT) (1979) Annual report.

Centro Internacional de Agricultura Tropical (CIAT) (1980) Annual report.

Centro Internacional de Agricultura Tropical (CIAT) (1981) CIAT in the 1980's. Series 12E-S, 182 pp.

Consultative Group on International Agricultural Research (1980) United Nations Development Program, CGIAR office, New York. 67 pp.

Crasswell, E.T. & Vlek, P.L.G. (1979) Fate of fertilizer nitrogen applied to wetland rice. *In*: Nitrogen and rice. IRRI, Los Baños, Philippines. Pp. 175-192.

Dart, P.J. (1978) The ICRISAT microbiology program. *In*: Isotopes in biological dinitrogen fixation. IAEA, Vienna, Austria. Pp. 257-268.

Dart, P.J. & Krantz, B.A. (1977) Legumes in the semi-arid tropics. *In*: Exploiting the legume-*Rhizobium* symbiosis in tropical agriculture, J.M. Vincent, A.S. Whitney & J. Bose (Eds.). Univ. Hawaii Col. Trop. Agric. *Misc. Publ.* 145, 119-154.

Date, R.A. & Halliday, J. (1979) *Nature* 277, 62-64.

Eaglesham, A.R.J., Minchin, F.R., Summerfield, R.J., Dart, P.J., Huxley, P.A., & Day, J.M. (1977) *Expl. Agric.* 13, 369-380.

Graham, P.H. (1981) *Field Crops Res.* 4, 93-112.

Graham, P.H. & Halliday, J. (1977) Inoculation and nitrogen fixation in the genus *Phaseolus*. *In*: Exploiting the legume-*Rhizobium* symbiosis in tropical agriculture, J.M. Vincent, A.S. Whitney & J. Bose (Eds.). Univ. Hawaii Col. Trop. Agric. *Misc. Publ.* 145. Pp. 313-334.

Graham, P.H., Ocampo, G. & Ruiz, L.D. (1980) *Agron. J.* 72, 625-627.

Graham, P.H. & Rosas, J.C. (1977) *J. Agric. Sci.* (Camb.) 88, 503-508.

Graham, P.H. & Rosas, J.C. (1978) *J. Agric. Sci.* (Camb.) 90, 311-317.

Graham, P.H., Viteri, S.E., Mackie, F., Vargas, A.T., & Palacios, A. (1982) *Field Crops Res.* 5. (In press.)

Huxley, P.A., Summerfield, R.J., & Hughes, A.P. (1976) *Ann. Appl. Biol.* 82, 117-133.

International Crops Research Institute for the Semi-Arid Tropics (ICRISAT) (1977-1978) Annual report.

International Crops Research Institute for the Semi-Arid Tropics (ICRISAT) (1978-1979) Annual report.

International Crops Research Institute for the Semi-Arid Tropics (ICRISAT) (1979-1980) Annual report.

International Institute of Tropical Agriculture (IITA) (1978) Annual report.

International Institute of Tropical Agriculture (IITA) (1979) Annual report.

International Rice Research Institute (IRRI) (1978) Annual report.

International Rice Research Institute (IRRI) (1979) Annual report.

Islam, R. (1981) *FABIS* 3, 32-33.

Islam, R. & Ghoulam, W. (1981) *FABIS* 3, 34-35.

Koyama, T. & App, A. (1979) Nitrogen balance in flooded rice soils. *In*: Nitrogen and rice. IRRI, Los Baños, Philippines. Pp. 95-104.

Minchin, F.R., Summerfield, R.J. & Eaglesham, A.R.J. (1978) *Trop. Agric.* (Trin.). 55, 107-115.

Minchin, F.R., Summerfield, R.J., Eaglesham, A.R.J., & Stewart, K.A. (1978) *J. Agric. Sci.* (Camb.) 90, 355-366.

Minchin, F.R., Summerfield, R.J., Hadlee, P., & Roberts, E.H. (1980) *Expl. Agric.* 16, 241-261.

Nambiar, P.T.C. & Dart, P.J. (1980) Studies on nitrogen fixation by groundnut at ICRISAT. *In*: Proc. Internat. Workshop on Groundnuts, R.W. Gibbons (Ed.). ICRISAT, Patancheru, AP India. Pp. 125-132.

Nangju, D. (1980) *Agron. J.* 72, 403-406.

Pulver, E.L., Brockman, F., Nangju, D., & Wien, H.C. (1978) IITA's program on dinitrogen fixation. *In*: Isotopes in biological dinitrogen fixation. IAEA, Vienna, Austria. Pp. 269-283.

Ruttan, V.W. (1978) *Agric. Admin.* 5, 293-308.

Summerfield, R.J., Dart, P.J., Huxley, P.A., Eaglesham, A.R.J., Minchin, F.R. & Day, J.M. (1977) *Expl. Agric.* 13, 129-142.

Summerfield, R.J., Huxley, P.A., Dart, P.J., & Hughes, A.P. (1976) *Plant Soil* 44, 527-546.

Summerfield, R.J., Minchin, F.R., Stewart, K.A., & Ndunguru, B.J. (1978) *Ann. Appl. Biol.* 90, 277-291.

Thurston, H.D. (1977) *Ann. Rev. Phytopath.* 15, 223-247.

Watanabe, I., & Cholitkul, W. (1979) Field studies on nitrogen fixation in paddy soils. *In*: Nitrogen and rice. IRRI, Los Baños, Philippines. Pp. 223-239.

Watanabe, I., Lee, K.K. & Alimagno, B.V. (1978) *Soil Sci. Plant Nutr.* (Tokyo) 24, 1-13.

Watanabe, I., Lee, K.K., Alimagno, B.V., Sato, M., Del Rosario, D.C., & Guzman, M.R. de (1977) IRRI Research Paper Series. No. 3.

PARTICIPANTS

PARTICIPANTS

ABDEL GHAFFAR, S.A.M. — Dept. of Soil & Water Science
Faculty of Agriculture
Alexandria University
Chatby, Alexandria
EGYPT

ALAA EL-DIN, M.N. — Microbiology Dept.
Soil & Water Institute
Agriculture Research Center
Giza
EGYPT

APP, A. — Boyce Thompson Institute
Cornell University
Tower Road
Ithaca, NY 14853
USA

ARAUJO, S.C. DE — Turfal
Caixa Postal 7410
8000, Curitiba, Pr.
BRAZIL

BALATTI, A.P. — Cindefi
Calle 9, No. 126
Tolosa
ARGENTINA

BALEVICH, L. — Universidad del Oriente
Nucleo Monagas, Jusepin
VENEZUELA

BARKER, T.C. — 102 Curtis Hall, UMC
Columbia, MO 65211
USA

BATTHYANY, C. — Nitrasoil
Florida 622 4° Piso
Buenos Aires
ARGENTINA

BERINGER, J.E. — Dept. of Soil Microbiology
Rothamsted Exp. Station
Harpenden, Hertz AL52JQ
ENGLAND

BERKUM, P. VAN
Cell Culture & Nitrogen Fixation Lab
Agricultural Research Service
US Dept. of Agriculture
Beltsville, MD 20705
USA

BEZDICEK, D.F.
Dept. of Agronomy & Soils
Washington State University
Pullman, WA 99164
USA

BLISS, F.A.
Dept. of Horticulture
University of Wisconsin
Madison, WI 53706
USA

BOONKERD, N.
Dept. of Soil & Crop Sciences
Texas A & M University
College Station, TX 77843
USA

BRADLEY, R.S.
CIAT
Apartado Aéreo 6713, Cali
COLOMBIA

BREWBAKER, J.
Dept. of Horticulture
3190 Maile Way
University of Hawaii
Honolulu, HI 96822
USA

BROTONEGORO, S.
Treub Laboratory
National Biological Institute
Bogor
INDONESIA

BRYAN, W.
Division of Plant & Soil Sciences
College of Agriculture & Forestry
Morgantown, WV 26506
USA

BURTON, J.C.
4930 N Elkhart Avenue
Milwaukee, WI 53217
USA

CAKMAKCI, L.
Dept. of Agricultural Microbiology
Faculty of Agriculture
University of Ankara
Ankara
TURKEY

CASTILLEJA G., G.	Inst. Nacional de Investigación sobre Recursos Bióticos Apartado Postal 63 Xalapa, Veracruz MEXICO
CHEE, Y.K.	Rubber Research Institute Experiment Station Project Research Division Sugei Buloh, Selangor MALAYSIA
CHOWDHURY, M.S.	Dept. of Soil Science University of Dar Es Salaam P.O. Box 643 Morogoro TANZANIA
CUATLE FABIAN, M.E.	Colegio de Postgraduados Chapingo MEXICO
DART, P.J.	ICRISAT, 1-11-256 Begumpet Hyderabad, 500-016, AP INDIA
DA SILVA, E.	Div. of Scientific Research & Higher Education, UNESCO 7, Place de Fontenoy 75700 Paris FRANCE
DAVIS, R.	NifTAL Project P.O. Box O Paia, Maui, HI 96779 USA
DAZZO, F.B.	Dept. of Microbiology & Public Health Michigan State University East Lansing, MI 48814 USA
DÖBEREINER, J.	EMBRAPA, Km. 47 23460 Seropedica Rio de Janeiro BRAZIL
DOMMERGUES, Y.R.	ORSTOM Center Boite Postale No. 1386 Dakar SENEGAL

DONAWA, A.	Dept. of Soil Science Faculty of Agriculture University of the West Indies St. Augustine, Trinidad WEST INDIES
DUBE, J.N.	Microbiology Section Faculty of Agriculture Jawaharlal Nehru Krishi Vishwa Didyalaya Jabalpur, 482004 INDIA
DUQUE, F.	EMBRAPA, Km. 47 23460 Seropedica Rio de Janeiro BRAZIL
DUQUE, M.A.	CIAT Apartado Aéreo 6713 Cali COLOMBIA
EAGLESHAM, A.R.J.	Boyce Thompson Institute at Cornell University Tower Road Ithaca, NY 14853 USA
EL HALFAWI, M.	Dept. of Plant & Soil Science Montana State University Bozeman, MT 59717 USA
ELKAN, G.H.	Dept. of Microbiology North Carolina State University P.O. Box 5476 Raleigh, NC 27650 USA
ESPINOSA, M.F.J.	UNIDAD CREGIT Instituto Tecnológico Regional de Veracruz Apartado Postal 539 Veracruz MEXICO
FERRERA-CERRATO, R.	Rama de Suelos Colegio de Postgraduados Chapingo MEXICO

FOCHT, D.D.	Dept. of Soil & Environmental Science University of California Riverside, CA 92521 USA
FOSTER, K.	Dept. of Agronomy & Range Sciences University of California Davis, CA 95616 USA
FRANCO, A.A.	Dept. Land, Air & Water Resources Soils and Plant Nutrition Section University of California Davis, CA 95616 USA
FREDERICK, L.R.	US Agency for International Development DS/ AGR-420 SA-18 Washington, D.C. 20523 USA
GARG, O.P.	Dept. of Botany Punjab University Chandigarh, 160014 INDIA
GOMEZ, G.	Dept. of Química, Facultad de Ciencias Universidad Nacional de Colombia Bogotá, D.E. COLOMBIA
GOMEZ, C.J.	Universidad Nacional Mayor de San Marcos Avenida Arenales 1256, Apartado 1109 Lima PERU
GONZALEZ, N.M. DE	Depto. de Química, Facultad de Ciencias Universidad Nacional de Colombia Facultad de Ciencias Bogotá, D.E. COLOMBIA
GRAHAM, P.H.	CIAT Apartado Aéreo 6713 Cali COLOMBIA

GRITZNER, J.A.

Board on Science & Technology for International Development (BOSTID)
National Academy of Sciences
2101 Constitution Avenue, N.W.
Washington, D.C. 20418
USA

GROSS, H.D.

Dept. of Crop Science
North Carolina State University
P.O. Box 5155
Raleigh, NC 27650
USA

GUALDRON, R.

CIAT
Apartado Aéreo 6713
Cali
COLOMBIA

GUEYE, M.

Laboratorie de Microbiología des Sols
ORSTOM B. P. 1386
Dakar
SENEGAL

HADAD, M.

Dept. of Agronomy
Iowa State University
Ames, IO 50011
USA

HAGEDORN, C.

Dept. of Agronomy
Mississipi State University
P.O. Box 5248
Mississipi State, MS 39762
USA

HALLIDAY, J.

NifTAL Project
P.O. Box O
Paia, Maui, HI 96779
USA

HAMDI, Y.A.

Institute of Soil & Water Research
Dept. of Microbiology
Agricultural Research Center
Giza
EGYPT

HARRIS, S.C.

Dept. of Agronomy & Soil Sci.
3190 Maile Way
University of Hawaii
Honolulu, HI 96822
USA

HARTMAN, J.	Backstop 10, USAID Washington, D.C. 20523 USA
HEDGE, S.V.	Dept. of Microbiology University of Agricultural Sci. GKVK, Alalasandra P.O. Bangalore, 560065 INDIA
HERRIDGE, D.	NSW Dept. of Agriculture Agricultural Research Center Tamworth, NSW 2340 AUSTRALIA
HESS, D.	University of Höhenheim Dept. of Plant Physiology Postfach 106 D-7000 Stuttgart -70 WEST GERMANY
HU, T.S.	USDA Nitrogen Fixation Lab. Bldg. 001A, Rm. 116, BARC-W Beltsville, MD 20705 USA
HUBBELL, D.H.	Dept. of Soil Science, University of Florida, Gainesville, FL 32611 USA
HUTTON, E.M.	CIAT Apartado Aéreo 6713 Cali COLOMBIA
ISHAC, Y.Z.	Faculty of Agriculture Ain Shams University Shobra, Cairo EGYPT
ISLAM, R.	ICARDA, P.O. Box 5466 Aleppo SYRIA

JUANG, T.C. — National Chung Hsing University
250 Kuo Kuang Road
Tai Chung, Taiwan 400
REPUBLIC OF CHINA

KERREY, B. — NifTAL Project
P.O. Box O
Paia, Maui, HI 96779
USA

KEYA, S.O. — Dept. of Soil Science
University of Nairobi
P.O. Box 30197
Nairobi
KENYA

KEYSER, H. — USDA Nitrogen Fixation Lab
Bldg. 001A, Rm. 116, BARC- W
Beltsville, MD 20705
USA

KLUCAS, R. — Dept. of Agricultural Biochemistry
Institute of Agriculture and Natural Resources
University of Nebraska
Lincoln, NE 68683
USA

KUMAR RAO, J.V.D.K. — ICRISAT
1-11-256 Begumpet
Hyderabad, 500 016, A P
INDIA

KVIEN, C. — SPCRC
P.O. Box 555
Watkinsville, GA 30677
USA

LABANDERA, C. — Ministerio de Agricultura
Laboratorio de Microbiología de Suelos
Bulevar Artigas 3802
Montevideo
URUGUAY

LATHWELL, D.J. — Dept. of Soil Science
Cornell University
Ithaca, NY 14853
USA

LI FU DI	Huachung Agricultural College Wuhan - Hubei PEOPLE'S REPUBLIC OF CHINA
LINDEMANN, W.C.	Dept. of Agronomy New Mexico State University Las Cruces, NM 88001 USA
LOPES, E.S.	Instituto Agronómico Caixa Postal 28 13100 Campinas Estado do São Paulo BRAZIL
LOWENDORF, H.S.	Dept. of Agronomy Cornell University Ithaca, NY 14853 USA
LOYNACHAN, T.E.	Dept. of Agronomy Iowa State University Ames, IO 50011 USA
LOZANO DE YUNDA, A.	Depto. de Química, Facultad de Ciencias Universidad Nacional de Colombia Bogotá, D.E. COLOMBIA
LUMPKIN, T.A.	Dept. of Agronomy and Soil Science 3190 Maile Way University of Hawaii Honolulu, HI 96822 USA
MC NEIL, D.	NifTAL Project P.O. Box O Paia, Maui, HI 96779 USA
MAHMOUD SAADZUKI	Faculty of Agriculture Ain Shams University Shobra, Khaima, Cairo EGYPT

MAIGNAN, F.
Food and Agriculture Organization of the United Nations
Via delle Terme di Caracalla
00100 Rome
ITALY

MALIK, K.A.
Soil Microbiology Division
Nuclear Institute for Agriculture and Biology
Jhang Road, P.O. Box 128
Faisalabad
PAKISTAN

MARCARIAN, V.
Dept. of Plant Sciences
Building No. 36
University of Arizona
Tucson, AZ 85721
USA

MARTINEZ, R.
Universidad Autonoma de Santo Domingo
Santo Domingo
DOMINICAN REPUBLIC

MATERON, L.A.
Dept. of Agronomy
Mississipi State University
P.O. Box 5248
Mississipi State, MS 39762
USA

MENDOZA, H.
Apartado Postal 6337
Guayaquil
ECUADOR

MILLER, J.C. JR.
Dept. of Horticultural Sciences
Texas A&M University
College Station, TX 77843
USA

MOAWAD, H.
Dept. of Microbiology
University of Hawaii
Honolulu, HI 96822
USA

MUNEVAR, F.
Programa de Suelos
Instituto Colombiano Agropecuario
Apartado Aéreo 151123
Bogotá, D.E.
COLOMBIA

MUNNS, D.N.	Dept. of Land, Air and Water Resources Soils and Plant Nutrition Section University of California Davis, CA 95616 USA
MUÑOZ GONZALES, D.	Apartado 55-535 Mexico, 13 DF MEXICO
MURPHY, W.M.	Dept. of Plant & Soil Science University of Vermont Burlington, VT 05405 USA
NAMBIAR, P.T.C.	ICRISAT 1-11-256, Begumpet Hyderabad, 500 016, A P INDIA
NAVARRO DE NAVARRO, Y.	Depto. de Química, Facultad de Ciencias Universidad Nacional de Colombia Bogotá, D.E. COLOMBIA
NEVES, M.C.P.	UFRRJ Dept. de Solos Km. 47, Seropedica 23460, Rio de Janeiro BRAZIL
NORMAN, M.J.T.	Dept. of Agronomy & Horticultural Science University of Sydney Sydney, NSW 2030 AUSTRALIA
OBLISAMI, G.	Tamil Nadu Agricultural University Dept. of Agricultural Microbiology Coimbatore, 641003 INDIA
OCAMPO, G.	CIAT Apartado Aéreo 6713 Cali, COLOMBIA
ODU, C.T.I.	Dept. on Agronomy University of Ibadan Ibadan NIGERIA

OKON, Y.	Dept. of Plant Pathology & Microbiology Faculty of Agriculture Hebrew University of Jerusalem Rehovoth 76100 ISRAEL
OROZCO F., H.	Universidad Nacional Apartado Aéreo 3840 Medellín COLOMBIA
PAREEK, R.P.	Soil Microbiology & Biochemistry Lab Dept. of Soil Science B.G. Plant University of Agriculture & Technology Pantnagar, Distt. Nainital, U P INDIA
PEPPER, I.L.	Dept. of Soils, Water & Engineering University of Arizona Tucson, AZ 85721 USA
PEREIRA, J.	Universidad del Oriente Nucleo Monagas, Jusepin VENEZUELA
PEREZ, G.	Depto. de Química, Facultad de Ciencias Universidad Nacional de Colombia Bogotá, D.E. COLOMBIA
PERSLEY, G.	Research for Development Section Australian Development Assistance Bureau Box 887 Canberra City, ACT 2601 AUSTRALIA
PETERSON, H.L.	Dept. of Agronomy Mississipi State University P.O. Box 5248 Mississipi Statc, MS 39762, USA
PIMENTEL, E.	Secretaria de Estado de Agricultura CESDA Apartado 24 San Cristóbal DOMINICAN REPUBLIC

PLUCKNETT, D.	World Bank 1818 H Street NW Washington, D.C. 20500 USA
POOSTCHI, I.	Dept. of Agricultural Botany University of Reading Reading ENGLAND
POZZO ARDIZZI DE FIDEL, M.G.	Centro Universitario Regional Viedma Universidad Nacional del Comahue Casilla Correos 149-8500 Viedma, Rio Negro ARGENTINA
PULVER, E.	IITA P.M.B. 5320 Ibadan NIGERIA
QUESENBERRY, K.H.	Agronomy Dept. 2185 McCarty Hall University of Florida Gainesville, FL 32611 USA
RAMIREZ, C.	Facultad de Agronomía Escuela de Fitotecnía Universidad de Costa Rica COSTA RICA
RANDOLPH, R.	Resource Systems Institute East-West Center 1777 East-West Road Honolulu, HI 96848 USA
RANGA RAO, V.	IITA P.M.B. 5320 Ibadan NIGERIA
RANGASWAMI, G.	Planning Commission Government of India Parliament Street New Delhi 110001 INDIA

REWARI, R.B.	Dept. of Microbiology Indian Agric. Res. Institute New Delhi INDIA
RIVERA, G.	Colegio Superior de Agricultura Tropical Apartado Postal No. 24, H. Cárdenas Tabasco MEXICO
ROSKOSKI, J.	Inst. Nacional de Investigación Recursos Bióticos Apartado Postal 63 Xalapa, Veracruz MEXICO
ROSSWALL, T.	Royal Swedish Academy of Sciences Scope/UNEP International Nitrogen Unit S. 10405 Stockholm SWEDEN
ROUGHLEY, R.J.	NSW Dept. of Agriculture Biological & Chemical Research Inst. PMB 10, Rydalmere, NSW 2116 AUSTRALIA
RUPELA, O.P.	ICRISAT 1-11-256 Begumpet Hyderabad, 500 016, A P INDIA
RUSCHEL, A.P.	CENA, Caixa Postal 96 Piracicaba Estado de São Paulo BRAZIL
RYAN, S.A.	Dept. of Agronomy University of Illinois Urbana, IL 61801 USA
SAITO, S.M.T.	CENA, Caixa Postal 96 Piracicaba Estado de São Paulo BRAZIL

SALEMA, M.P.
Dept. of Soil Sci. & Plant Nutrition
University of Western Australia
Nedlands, WA 6009
AUSTRALIA

SANCHEZ, G.A.
CIAT
Apartado Aéreo 6713
Cali
COLOMBIA

SANOGHO, S.T.
Unite Physiologie Cellulaire
Institut Pasteur 28 - Rue Dr.
Roux 75015
FRANCE

SAONO, S.
Treub Laboratory
National Biological Institute
Bogor
INDONESIA

SARTAIN, J.
Dept. of Soil Science
University of Florida
Gainesville, FL 32611
USA

SCHMIDT, E.L.
Dept. of Soil Science
University of Minnesota
St. Paul, MN 55108
USA

SCHRODER, E.C.
Dept. of Agronomy & Soils
University of Puerto Rico
Mayaguez Campus
Mayaguez, PR 00708
PUERTO RICO

SCHWEITZER, L.
Dept. of Agronomy
Purdue University
West Lafayette, IN 47906
USA

SHUMAN, L.M.
University of Georgia
Dept. of Agronomy
Georgia Expt. Stn., GA 30212
USA

SICARDI DE MALLORCA, M.	Centro de Microbiología de Biología Celular IVIC Apartado 1827 Caracas VENEZUELA
SIMS, J.R.	Montana State University Agricultural Experiment Station Plant & Soil Science Dept. Bozeman, MT 59717 USA
SKWIERINSKI, R.	Universidad de Los Andes Facultad de Ciencias Biológicas Merida Edo. Merida VENEZUELA
SMITH, R.S.	The Nitragin Company 3101 West Custer Avenue Milwaukee, WI 53209 USA
SOERIANEGARA, I.	BIOTROP SEAMEO Regional Center for Tropical Biology JI. Raya Tajur Km. 6 P.O. Box 17, Bogor INDONESIA
SOUSA COSTA, N.M. DE	EPAMIG Caixa Postal 295 35700 Sete Lagoas, MG BRAZIL
SRIVASTAVA, J.S.	Benares Hindu University Varanarsi, UP INDIA
STEARN, C.	INTSOY University of Puerto Rico Mayaguez, PR 00708 PUERTO RICO
STOOP, W.A.	Royal Tropical Institute Mauritskade 63 Amsterdam - Oost THE NETHERLANDS

TALLEY, S.	Dept. of Agronomy University of California Davis, CA 95616 USA
TAURO, P.	Dept. of Microbiology Haryana Agriculture University Hissar, 125004 INDIA
THOMPSON, J.	ICRISAT 1-11-256 Begumpet Hyderabad 500 016, A P INDIA
TORREY, J.	Harvard Forest, Petersham, MA 01366 USA
TRUJILLO, G.	FERTIMEX Anaxágoras 250 Colonia Narvate Mexico, 12 D.F. MEXICO
VALENCIA, H.Z.	Dept. of Biología Universidad Nacional de Colombia Apartado Aéreo 23227 Bogotá, D.E. COLOMBIA
VARELA, R.	Instituto Colombiano Agropecuario Apartado Aéreo 223 Palmira COLOMBIA
VARGAS, M.A.T.	CPAC/EMBRAPA Caixa Postal 70/0023 Planaltina, 73300 Brasilia, D.F. BRAZIL
VASUVAT, Y.	Bacteriology & Soil Microbiology Branch Division of Plant Pathology Dept. of Agriculture Bangkhen, Bangkok 9 THAILAND

VELASCO, M.E.	CSAT Cárdenas, Tabasco MEXICO
VELASQUEZ, E.	Estación Experimental de Guara Tucupita VENEZUELA
VIDOR, C.	Faculdade de Agronomía & Veterinaria UFRGS Caixa Postal 776 90000 Porto Alegre, RS BRAZIL
VITERI, S.	CIAT Apartado Aéreo 6713 COLOMBIA
VOSE, P.	CENA Caixa Postal 96 Piracicaba, Sao Paulo BRAZIL
WACEK, T.	North American Plant Breeders P.O. Box 404 - RRI Princeton, IL 61356 USA
WEAVER, R.W.	Dept. of Soil & Crop Science Texas A&M University College Station, TX 77843 USA
WEBER, D.F.	Cell Culture & Nitrogen Fixation Lab Agricultural Research Service US Dept. of Agriculture Beltsville, MD 20705 USA
WELSCH, D.	Dept. of Agric. & Applied Economics 316 G Classroom Office Building 1994 Buford Ave. University of Minnesota St. Paul, MN 55108 USA

WHAB, F.
Rubber Research Institute
Smallholder Project Research Division
P.O. Box 150
Kuala Lumpur 01-02
MALAYSIA

WILLIAMS, P.M.
Centro de Microbiología & Biología Celular
IVIC
Apartado 1827
Caracas
VENEZUELA

WILSON, D.O.
University of Georgia
Georgia Experiment Station
GA 30212
USA

WOLLUM, A.G.
Dept. of Soil Science
North Carolina State University
P.O. Box 5907
Raleigh, NC 27650
USA

WHITNEY, S.
University of Hawaii
Kula Experiment Station
Kula, Maui, HI
USA

WRIGHT, S.
West Virginia University
Division of Plant and Soil Sciences
College of Agriculture & Forestry
Morgantown, WV 26505
USA

WYNNE, J.C.
Dept. of Crop Sciences
North Carolina State University
Raleigh, NC 27650
USA

ZACARIA, A.B.
Institut Penyelikikan Dan Kemajuan
Pertanian Malaysia
Beg Berkunci No. 202
Pejabat Pos University Pertanian
Serdang, Selangor
MALAYSIA

ZAPATER R., J.M.

Universidad Nacional Agraria
La Molina, Apartado 456
Lima
PERU

ZUKERAN, K.

NifTAL Project
P.O. Box O
Paia, Maui, HI 96779
USA